LSAT
Logical Reasoning Prep

T0290913

LSAT® is a registered trademark of the Law School Admission Council, Inc. (LSAC), which is not affiliated with Kaplan and was not involved in the production of, and does not endorse, this product.

Acknowledgements

A great number of people were involved in the creation of the book you are holding. Glen Stohr was the primary author, with contributions from Kaplan LSAT experts Katarina Kurtz, Peggy Lee, and Bruce Symaka. Jack Chase contributed invaluable research, and Bonnie Wang created the graphics.

Prakash Jagannathan managed the production work for this book, with the help of editor Arunsanthosh Kannan. Joanna Graham oversaw layout and design. Beatriz Cortabarria copyedited the book, ensuring clarity and precision throughout the manuscript. Once typesetting was done, Joan R. Summerfold proofread the entire volume. Jeffrey Batzli designed the cover.

LSAT® is a registered trademark of the Law School Admission Council, Inc. (LSAC), which is not affiliated with Kaplan and was not involved in the production of, and does not endorse, this product.

This publication is designed to provide accurate information in regard to the subject matter covered as of its publication date, with the understanding that knowledge and best practice constantly evolve. The publisher is not engaged in rendering medical, legal, accounting, or other professional service. If medical or legal advice or other expert assistance is required, the services of a competent professional should be sought. This publication is not intended for use in clinical practice or the delivery of medical care. To the fullest extent of the law, neither the Publisher nor the Editors assume any liability for any injury and/or damage to persons or property arising out of or related to any use of the material contained in this book.

© 2025 Kaplan North America, LLC

Kaplan North America, LLC dba Kaplan Publishing
1515 West Cypress Creek Road
Fort Lauderdale, Florida 33309

All rights reserved. The text of this publication, or any part thereof, may not be reproduced in any manner whatsoever without written permission from the publisher.

10 9 8 7 6 5 4 3 2 1

ISBN: 978-1-5062-9102-4

Kaplan Publishing print books are available at special quantity discounts to use for sales promotions, employee premiums, or educational purposes. For more information or to purchase books, please call the Simon & Schuster special sales department at 866-506-1949.

TABLE OF CONTENTS

Getting Started

Let's start with an assumption: You have this book because you want to raise your LSAT score. Now, as you use this book, you'll discover that assumptions are often complicated, sometimes flawed, yet often necessary to reach the conclusions of many arguments, especially on the LSAT. Still, the assumption that you're here to improve on the LSAT feels pretty safe, and if you've made the assumption that this book will help, you're right.

This book covers the questions that make up nearly two-thirds of your LSAT score, the questions from the test's two scored Logical Reasoning sections. Among these are many of the test's most challenging analytical tasks and its most challenging items. As you use Kaplan's proven strategies to master them, you'll learn a lot about how to dissect arguments, make valid deductions, and recognize subtle errors in logic. You'll become a more strategic reader and thinker, and in the end, a better law student and legal professional down the road.

Let's get started!

How to Use This Book

First—Get Acquainted with the LSAT

Start by reading the "About the LSAT" chapter. There, you'll find details about the LSAT's structure and scoring, how to register for the test, how it is administered, and how best to study.

Second—Start Becoming a Logical Reasoning Expert

The LSAT is a skills-based exam. Its purpose is to show law schools what you can *do* more than what you know. Thus, the foundation of this book's pedagogy is **learning by doing.** You can't cram for the LSAT; there is no subject matter to memorize. Because of that, mastering the LSAT may feel more like learning a musical instrument or improving at a sport. You need to practice, review your practice with an expert coach, make adjustments, and practice some more. This book provides the practice, and the expert review. Take a look at how you'll be doing this.

Work with real questions. As you complete the subsequent chapters of this book, you'll do more than 200 official LSAT questions, covering every question type found in the Logical Reasoning sections. The Law School Admission Council (LSAC), the organization that makes the test, has released dozens of official full-length LSATs from previous administrations. These are called PrepTests (more on these terrific practice resources in a few pages). Kaplan licenses these official items so that you have more realistic practice available. This book contains questions from PrepTests 110, 111, 112, 122, 129, 131, 132, 142, and 143, and every full LSAT question you'll do in the book is an official LSAC item. Whenever you see a question ID like this, you'll know the official PrepTest, section, and question numbers for the item.

> (E) When international trade is free, countries can specialize in what they export.
>
> *PrepTest129 Sec3 Q3*

Have a Learning Objective. In each chapter of the book, Kaplan breaks down the skills you'll need for LSAT Logical Reasoning success. Some chapters have several Learning Objectives, others, just one or two. For every Learning Objective, you'll see pages marked **Prepare** and **Practice** . Prepare has the information you *need* to know about the skill or question type so that you can get to work. We'll keep Prepare sections as short and to-the-point as possible because Practice is where you want to spend your time. At the end of most chapters, you'll also have a section marked **Perform** where you can assess all of the skills you acquired and get recommendations for further practice. For Chapters 3–15, take the Perform quizzes under timed conditions to get an accurate assessment of your skills on each question type.

Review with Expert Examples. To learn new skills, you always need to try them out yourself. But then, reviewing your performance with an expert, and being able to *see*, not just hear about, how the expert performs can help you make big improvements. At Kaplan, our learning science team has put together *worked examples* that show you how an LSAT expert worked through any question you are asked to try. They look like this.

Expert Analysis

Step 2: Conclusion: Other operatic stage directions (beyond just scene changes) can also be reflected in the music.

The argument opens with an opposing view, so anticipate that it will be refuted. The refutation comes in the final sentence. *Hence* actually signals a subsidiary conclusion, supporting the overall main point which follows *which means*.

Step 1: An unusual Main Point question stem that cites one piece of the evidence and asks for the claim it supports; nonetheless, that claim is simply the argument's conclusion.

> Analyze the question in the same order as the expert to train yourself in using proven methods on the LSAT.

18. Some critics argue that an opera's stage directions are never reflected in its music. Many comic scenes in Mozart's operas, however, open with violin phrases that sound like the squeaking of changing scenery. Clearly Mozart intended the music to echo the sounds occurring while stage directions are carried out. Hence, a change of scenery—the most basic and frequent stage direction—can be reflected in the music, which means that other operatic stage directions can be as well.

In the argument, the statement that many comic scenes in Mozart's operas open with violin phrases that sound like the squeaking of changing scenery is offered in support of the claim that

(A) a change of scenery is the stage direction most frequently reflected in an opera's music

(B) an opera's stage directions are never reflected in its music

(C) an opera's music can have an effect on the opera's stage directions

(D) a variety of stage directions can be reflected in an opera's music

(E) the most frequent relation between an opera's music and its stage directions is one of musical imitation of the sounds that occur when a direction is carried out

PrepTest111 Sec1 Q1

> When studying, the expert will always analyze all of the answer choices—correct and incorrect.

Step 3: The correct answer will communicate the idea that opera scores can reflect multiple types of stage directions.

Step 4: (D) matches the argument's overall conclusion and is correct.

Wrong answers: (A) cites an example used as evidence (not conclusion) in the argument, and distorts it by adding "most frequent," an idea the author does not include. (B) 180. The argument cites one such example and concludes that more are possible as well. (C) distorts the argument which says that stage directions can "be reflected" in the music, not that the music has an effect on them. (E) The author mentions in the evidence (not conclusion) that *many* Mozart scenes open with a musical imitation of changing scenery but stops short of claiming this to be the *most* frequent such imitation.

Good work. Ready to finish up strong? On the following pages you'll have a timed Perform quiz to assess your newly minted Main Point question skills. Do your best!

As you review, follow the expert's thinking step by step to see the patterns they spot and the strategies they deploy. When you practice full Logical Reasoning questions, Kaplan will help you reinforce the same method the experts use by providing spaces for you to record your own thinking.

Step 2:	**Step 1:**

18. Some critics argue that an opera's stage directions are never reflected in its music. Many comic scenes in Mozart's operas, however, open with violin phrases that sound like the squeaking of changing scenery. Clearly Mozart intended the music to echo the sounds occurring while stage directions are carried out. Hence, a change of scenery—the most basic and frequent stage direction—can be reflected in the music, which means that other operatic stage directions can be as well.

In the argument, the statement that many comic scenes in Mozart's operas open with violin phrases that sound like the squeaking of changing scenery is offered in support of the claim that

(A) a change of scenery is the stage direction most frequently reflected in an opera's music

(B) an opera's stage directions are never reflected in its music

(C) an opera's music can have an effect on the opera's stage directions

(D) a variety of stage directions can be reflected in an opera's music

(E) the most frequent relation between an opera's music and its stage directions is one of musical imitation of the sounds that occur when a direction is carried out

PrepTest111 Sec1 Q1

Step 3:	**Step 4:**

You won't be writing out these notes on test day, of course, because before then, you'll have absorbed and internalized these steps and strategies for yourself. In practice, however, consciously attending to each step will help you realize where you're going off-track or skipping an essential step.

Even in its skill-building exercises and drills, this book provides a space for you to record your own analysis, and then compare it to that of an expert.

Practice   Identify, characterize, and paraphrase the conclusion in each of the following arguments. When you're finished, review your work with the expert analysis on the next pages.

LSAT Argument	My Analysis
5. Pundit: The average salary for teachers in our society is lower than the average salary for athletes. Obviously, our society values sports more than it values education. *PrepTest132 Sec3 Q4*	Paraphrase: Type:

Expert Analysis

Here's how an LSAT expert analyzed the arguments you just saw.

LSAT Argument	Analysis
5. Pundit: The average salary for teachers in our society is lower than the average salary for athletes. Obviously, our society values sports more than it values education. *PrepTest132 Sec3 Q4*	Paraphrase: Our society values sports more than it does education. Type: Comparison

---

When it comes to Perform quizzes, however, you'll do things a little differently.

Assess Your Skills. Mastering new skills takes a little preparation and, sometimes, a lot of practice. To really know how you're doing, however, you need to **Perform**. You need to try your new skills under more test-like conditions, timed and without any hints. So, when you have Perform quizzes at the end of a chapter, you'll see the LSAT questions like this, more or less as they'll appear on-screen when you're taking the test.

20. Although free international trade allows countries to specialize, which in turn increases productivity, such specialization carries risks. After all, small countries often rely on one or two products for the bulk of their exports. If those products are raw materials, the supply is finite and can be used up. If they are foodstuffs, a natural disaster can wipe out a season's production overnight.

Which one of the following most accurately expresses the conclusion of the argument as a whole?

(A) Specialization within international trade comes with risks.

(B) A natural disaster can destroy a whole season's production overnight, devastating a small country's economy.

(C) A small country's supply of raw materials can be used up in a short period.

(D) Some countries rely on a small number of products for the export-based sectors of their economies.

(E) When international trade is free, countries can specialize in what they export.

PrepTest129 Sec3 Q3

Take Perform quizzes under the timing restrictions in the instructions; you need to know how you'd do on these questions in a real LSAT setting. When you're finished, assess yourself rigorously. Kaplan provides recommendations for additional practice after each Perform quiz. That practice will take place online where there are two vital resources: this book's online companion, and LSAC's LawHub.

How to Use Your Online Book Companion
First—Register Your Book to Access the Online Companion

The online book companion gives you access to even more prep, including the Spotlight video lessons from instructors on Kaplan's exclusive LSAT Channel, analysis and explanations for free PrepTests from LSAC, study planning guidance, video explanations, and more.

Register for your book by following these simple steps:

1. Go to kaptest.com/booksonline and use this book's ISBN, or scan the QR code on the card inside the cover, to go to the appropriate book listing. Click the "Register" button next to it.

2. Enter the password as directed and click on "Next."

3. The online Study Plan will appear in your shopping cart free of charge. Click "Proceed to checkout" and complete your registration.

4. Once registered, click on the "personalized Student Homepage" link to access your online materials.

Please have your book with you because you will need information from the book to access your account. Access to the online Study Plan is limited to the original owner of this book and is not transferable. Kaplan is not responsible for providing access to the online Study Plan for customers who purchase or borrow used copies of this book. Access to the online Study Plan expires one year after you register.

Second—Getting Started Video

Kaplan's lead instructional designer explains how to make the most of your prep with the *LSAT Logical Reasoning Prep* book and its associated resources. You should watch the "Getting Started" video as soon as possible, in conjunction with this section of the book.

Third—Use Your Exclusive LSAT Prep Resources

With Kaplan's *LSAT Logical Reasoning Prep*, you've purchased much more than just a book. Here are the highlights of what's inside:

- **Study Planning Guidance and Sample Schedules.** Preparing for the LSAT is a lot of work, and LSAT test takers are busy people. For you, Kaplan's learning experience team has assembled best practices for planning your study and practice along with sample schedules for working through this book and incorporating other LSAT study resources.

- **LSAT Channel Spotlight Video Lessons.** This book features six special Spotlight sections on special Logical Reasoning strategies and topics with accompanying video lessons from members of Kaplan's LSAT Channel faculty. In the online companion, you'll find the video lessons for the following Spotlight features:

  - *Secrets of Logical Reasoning Preparation*
  - *Great Moments in Formal Logic*
  - *The Denial Test*
  - *Flaw School*
  - *Unusual Question Stems*
  - *Logical Reasoning—Managing the Section*

  The LSAT Channel instructors are among Kaplan's highest-rated and most veteran teachers. The LSAT Channel has long been included in our comprehensive LSAT courses, where students benefit from live-instruction lessons five or six nights per week. Now, self-prep students can also subscribe to the LSAT Channel with full access to live lessons and a library of recorded sessions on nearly every LSAT topic imaginable. Learn more at **www.kaptest.com/lsat/courses/lsat-self-study.**

- **Logical Reasoning Section Practice with Video Explanations.** After you read the Spotlight called Logical Reasoning—Managing the Section, and watch its accompanying video lesson, you'll want to practice these new skills on a real LSAT LR section. There is one, from an officially released PrepTest, waiting for you in your online companion. After you've taken it under timed conditions, you can review your performance with either written explanations or video explanations from a Kaplan expert instructor for every question.

- **Additional Practice Recommendations and the LR Question Database.** In Kaplan's *LSAT Logical Reasoning Prep*, chapters 3–7 and 9–15 cover all of the distinct question types found in the LR sections. Each of those Chapters ends with a Perform quiz. Based on your performance, Kaplan provides recommendations for further practice using official questions from official PrepTests. You'll find them in the book companion under *Additional Practice Recommendations*. In this part of the online companion, you'll also find a comprehensive index for every released Logical Reasoning question found in PrepTests 101 through 158 (more than 2,900 of them) with Question Type, Subtype, and Difficulty Rating to help you analyze your practice and find additional examples for any question type.

- **Full-Length PrepTest Analysis and Explanations.** The best full-length LSAT test practice experience is available through the testmaker, LSAC, on its LawHub platform. This is another vital online resource mentioned earlier. In LawHub, you can take released tests in the official digital interface, with the same tools and timing you'll see on test day. Register for LawHub at **www.lsac.org/lawhub.** There is a free version, LawHub Free, with (at the time of this writing) four released exams, PrepTests 140, 141, 157, and 158. Kaplan recommends that every self-prep student should use at least these free practice tests. To help you make the most of them, you'll find complete analysis and explanations for every question on these tests in your online companion to this book.

  For test takers who choose to upgrade to LSAC's paid option, called LawHub Advantage, Kaplan offers LSAT Link and Link+. These options are described in detail in the next section of this Preface called "Next-Level Self-Prep." The paid subscription to LawHub and Kaplan's LSAT Link are essentials for the serious self-prepping test taker.

- **Additional Free LSAT Resources.** This section contains links to additional free LSAT study and practice resources created by Kaplan. Click to see our latest free trials and assets.

There's an enormous amount of additional learning and practice in your online book companion for Logical Reasoning Prep, so don't miss out. Register your book as soon as possible!

Next-Level Self-Prep

Integrate Your Prep with LSAC's LawHub

LSAT Logical Reasoning Prep and its online companion contains expert strategies and tactics for every question in the Logical Reasoning section along with ample practice, but you'll almost certainly want to take additional tests and do additional practice.

As we mentioned in the discussion of your online companion resources, the best way to get additional practice with officially released LSAT questions is by subscribing to LSAC's LawHub Advantage. At the time of this writing, LawHub Advantage provides access to 58 released tests—that's more than 5,800 questions!—at a cost of $115 for a one-year subscription. LawHub will show you your scaled score for each test and what you got right and wrong. What LawHub does not offer, however, is detailed analysis of all those tests or explanations for all of those questions.

That's where Kaplan's LSAT Link comes in. When you *link* your LawHub Advantage subscription to Kaplan's LSAT Link, your answers from tests taken in LawHub automatically export to Link, where you'll get the same in-depth analysis and explanations for all 58 PrepTests. With our premium version, LSAT Link+, you'll also get access to more than 150 uniquely curated Mastery quizzes to target each LSAT question type at different levels of difficulty (including more than 1,500 officially released LSAT questions not available on LSAC's LawHub). Find out more about LSAT Link and LSAT Link+ in the next part of this Getting Started chapter under the heading Next-Level Self-Prep or by visiting **www.kaptest.com/lsat/courses/lsat-self-study.**

LawHub Lessons and Drill Sets

While the full-length PrepTests are the essential feature of LawHub for the self-prep LSAT test taker, LawHub also features a small library of lessons and drill sets originally designed in conjunction with Khan Academy, but no longer hosted on that company's website. These are available even on the free version of LawHub, so they're something literally anyone who registers with LSAC has access to.

The lessons include short, written "articles" about the different question types and skills on the test. Video assets include short introductory "video lessons" and "worked examples," each of which goes over a single question. To use these resources in conjunction with your Kaplan book and other resources, you'll need to know how the names and terminology on LawHub line up with those in the Kaplan LSAT universe. Here's a chart that should come in handy.

LOGICAL REASONING TERMS		READING COMPREHENSION TERMS	
LawHub	**Kaplan**	**LawHub**	**Kaplan**
Identify the conclusion	Main Point	Reading Comprehension Passage Types (subject matter)	
Identify an entailment	Inference	Humanities	Humanities
Infer what is most strongly supported		Law	Law
Identify or infer an issue in dispute	Point at Issue	Science	Natural Science
Identify the technique	Method of Argument	Social Science	Social Science
Identify the role	Role of a Statement	Reading Comprehension Passage Structures	
Identify the principle	Principle	N/A	Theory/Perspective
Match the structure	Parallel Reasoning	N/A	Event/Phenomenon
Match principles	Parallel Principle	N/A	Biography
Identify a flaw	Flaw	N/A	Debate
Match flaws	Parallel Flaw	Comparative Reading	Comparative Reading
Necessary Assumption	Assumption (Necessary Assumption)	Reading Comprehension Question Types	
Sufficient Assumption	Assumption (Sufficient Assumption)	Main point	Global
Strengthen	Strengthen	Recognition	Detail
Weaken	Weaken	Clarifying meaning	[Kaplan treats these as a subtype of Inference Qs.]
Identify what is most/least helpful to know	[Kaplan treats these as a subtype of Strengthen/Weaken questions]	Purpose of reference	Logic Function

(Continued)

LOGICAL REASONING TERMS		READING COMPREHENSION TERMS	
LawHub	**Kaplan**	**LawHub**	**Kaplan**
Explain	Paradox	Organizing information	[Khan's category includes Q-types Kaplan would put under Global, Logic Function, and Inference.]
Resolve a Conflict		Inferences about views	Inference
		Inferences about information	
		Inferences about attitudes	
		Applying to new contexts	Logic Reasoning: Principle
		Discovering principles and analogies	Logic Reasoning: Parallel / Logic Reasoning: Principle
		Additional evidence	Logic Reasoning: Strengthen/Weaken
		Primary purpose	Global

Go Deeper in Your Areas of Greatest Opportunity for Score Improvement

The LSAT Channel

Effective LSAT prep cannot be one-size-fits-all. Even two test takers with an identical score will have distinct strengths and weaknesses. As you learn yours from taking and reviewing practice tests and learning strategies and tactics from this book, you'll discover areas in which you need more work on the fundamentals and others where you're ready to challenge yourself with harder and harder questions. Enter the LSAT Channel, Kaplan's nightly live instruction platform for lessons on almost every conceivable concept and skill rewarded by the exam.

For years, students in Kaplan's comprehensive courses have enjoyed the LSAT Channel with dozens of distinct, hour-long episodes taught by some of the highest-rated instructors in the Kaplan faculty. Now, the LSAT Channel is available to self-prep students as well. You can attend live lessons where you can ask questions and interact with the instructor and online TAs. If you can't attend a live lesson, every episode is available in an archive of recordings available to stream on demand. You can search the upcoming schedule and the archive by subject matter, by difficulty level (Foundations, For Everyone, and Advanced lessons are available), and even by instructor (so that you can find more teaching from your newly discovered favorites).

With the LSAT Channel, you can personalize your instruction with the same specificity and nuance that LSAT Link+ provides for your test analyses and practice. Find out more about the LSAT Channel here: **www.kaptest.com/lsat/courses/lsat-self-study.**

The Hardest Real LSAT Questions

Diligent work with Kaplan's *LSAT Logical Reasoning Prep* and the supplemental tools and programs just outlined will raise your LSAT score, but what do you work on when you've already established a strong score and you're ready to push into the stratosphere? That's exactly the practice, analysis, and strategy Kaplan's LSAT Hardest Questions program provides.

Informed by the empirical results of tens of thousands of LSAT test takers, Kaplan experts have selected the 100 most challenging Logical Reasoning questions along with the 20 hardest Reading Comprehension passages of all time. With Kaplan's LSAT Hardest Questions, you'll try these head scratchers on your own and then watch video analysis by elite instructors from Kaplan's LSAT faculty. They'll break down what makes each question or passage so challenging; reveal patterns found in the hardest LSAT items; and provide strategies you can use to crack the toughest questions with increased confidence and speed.

These are the kinds of questions that distinguish scores among the top percentile test takers. This means that LSAT Hardest Questions won't be for everyone, but if you're ready for the challenge, you can find more information at **www.kaptest.com/lsat/courses/lsat-self-study.**

Looking for Even More?

At Kaplan, we're thrilled you've chosen us to help you on your journey to law school. Beyond this book, there's a wealth of additional resources that we invite you to check out to aid you with your LSAT preparation and your law school application.

- *LSAT Premium Prep*—Kaplan's book *LSAT Premium Prep* is a comprehensive guide to the LSAT exam with expert methods and strategies for every section and question type. It contains hundreds of officially released LSAC questions, along with the drills, exercises, and practice sets on all of the skills you'll need for LSAT mastery.

- **Comprehensive LSAT Courses**—Of course, we'd be remiss if we did not mention the world's most popular LSAT preparation courses. Visit our website to learn about our comprehensive prep options. Choose from Live Online, and Self-Paced options, depending on your needs and learning style. View course options and upcoming class schedules at **www.kaptest.com/lsat/lsat-courses.**

- **Private Tutoring**—After beginning their LSAT prep, students often realize the benefits of having some undivided, individual attention from an expert private tutor. At Kaplan, it is always easy to add a few hours of tutoring to your LSAT prep course enrollment. You may also realize that one of our comprehensive 10-, 20-, 30-, or 40-hour private tutoring packages is right for you. To find out more, ask your instructor, visit **www.kaptest.com/lsat/courses/lsat-tutoring**, or call us at 1-800-KAPTEST to discuss the best option for you.

- **Admissions Consulting**—A strong LSAT score is the foundation of a great law school application, but don't miss the opportunity to make the rest of your application stand out. An expert Kaplan admissions consultant can utilize your unique experience, goals, and passions to help you make a convincing case for admission to the law school of your choice. Kaplan Admission Consulting packages include Personal Statement review, expert guidance, and unlimited email support, but consider adding premium features such as additional consulting hours, total application review (including the diversity statement, essay, and resume), and mock interview practice. Explore your options at **www.kaptest.com/lsat/practice/law-school-admissions-consulting** or call us at 1-800-KAPTEST.

You have a lot to do, so let's get to it. Up next: Take a closer look at the format, content, and scoring of the LSAT test.

About the LSAT

Why the LSAT?

Each year, Kaplan surveys law school admissions officials, and consistently, over 60 percent say that the LSAT is their number-one consideration as they evaluate applications. Why do they put so much emphasis on this test? A breakdown of the components in the application offers the best explanation.

- 5 components of the standard law school application: LSAT score, undergraduate GPA, personal statement, letters of recommendation, and "resume factors," such as work experience, extracurricular activities, and so on

- 2 quantitative measures: LSAT score and undergraduate GPA

- 1 quantitative measure comparable for all applicants: LSAT score

The LSAT doesn't care what you majored in or where you went to school. It's the one element of the law school application that measures all applicants on a level playing field.

What the LSAT Tests

While the LSAT offers a standard, quantitative measure of all applicants, law school admissions officers would not value it so highly if the LSAT did not test skills relevant to—indeed, central to—an applicant's law school potential. Studies have consistently shown that LSAT score is more strongly correlated with law school performance, especially in a student's first year, than any other factor in the application.

THE FOUR CORE LSAT SKILLS

Reading Strategically—understanding the structure of a piece of text and the author's purpose for writing it

Analyzing Arguments—distinguishing an argument's conclusion from its evidence and identifying the implicit assumptions the author has made

Making Deductions—determining what follows logically from a set of statements or rules

Understanding Formal Logic—determining what must, can, or cannot be true on the basis of conditional "If/then" statements

Law schools know that these skills are crucial to a student's success as a law student and in the practice of law later on. Because they are so fundamental to the test, these four core skills underlie all of the Learning Objectives found in this workbook.

Structure of the LSAT

The LSAT consists of four multiple-choice sections: two Logical Reasoning sections, one Reading Comprehension section, and one unscored "experimental" section that will look exactly like one of the other multiple-choice sections. These four multiple-choice sections can appear in any order on test day. A short break is offered between the second and third sections of the test. The unscored, 35-minute LSAT Writing essay section is proctored separately. It is also done from the test taker's own computer and taken on-demand.

Here's how the four core skills align with the sections of the LSAT.

FOUR CORE LSAT SKILLS BY SECTION

Core Skill	Primary Section Tested	Secondary Section Tested
Reading Strategically	Reading Comprehension	Logical Reasoning
Analyzing Arguments	Logical Reasoning	Reading Comprehension
Making Deductions	Logical Reasoning	Reading Comprehension
Understanding Formal Logic	Logical Reasoning	

Note that Logical Reasoning is the primary section for three of the core skills and the secondary section for the other one. Indeed, Logical Reasoning is more-or-less the exclusive home of Formal Logic on the LSAT.

Section	Number of Questions	Minutes
Logical Reasoning (2x)	24–26	35
Reading Comprehension	27	35
"Experimental"	24–27	35
LSAT Writing	One essay	35

LSAC administers the LSAT in two modalities: remotely proctored/take-at-home or live-proctored/testing center administrations. The test content and format is identical regardless of the testing venue.

LSAT Scored Sections

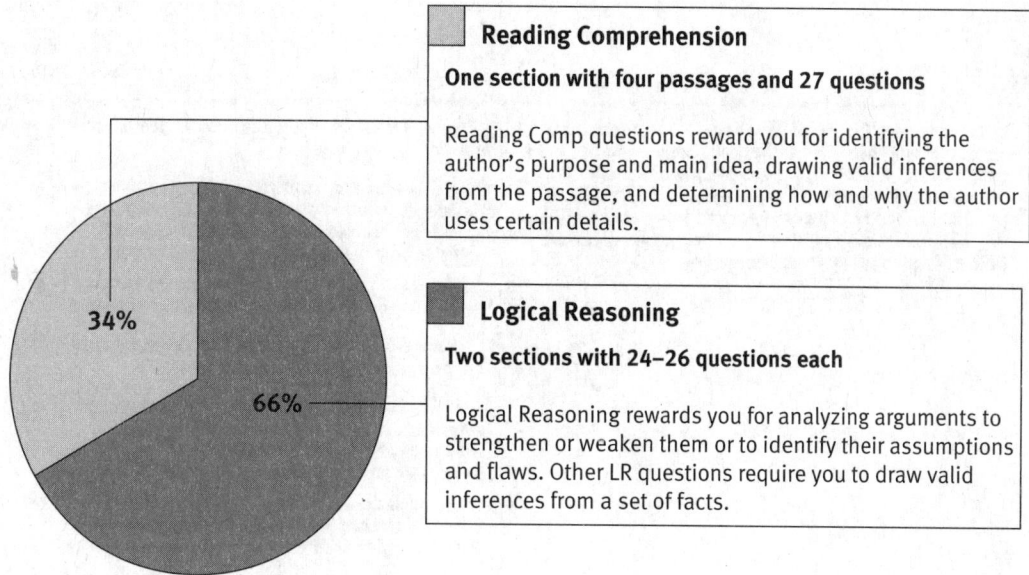

Reading Comprehension

One section with four passages and 27 questions

Reading Comp questions reward you for identifying the author's purpose and main idea, drawing valid inferences from the passage, and determining how and why the author uses certain details.

Logical Reasoning

Two sections with 24–26 questions each

Logical Reasoning rewards you for analyzing arguments to strengthen or weaken them or to identify their assumptions and flaws. Other LR questions require you to draw valid inferences from a set of facts.

LSAT Unscored Sections

Experimental

The Experimental section is an additional, unscored section of Logical Reasoning or Reading Comprehension. You will not know what type of section you will get, and it can show up anywhere, including after the break. You'll have to bring your A-game for the entire test, as there is no reliable way to determine which section is experimental while you're taking the test. The LSAT testmaker uses the unscored section to test questions for use as scored items on upcoming exams.

LSAT Argumentative Writing

Within one year after your official LSAT, you will write a short essay choosing between two possible courses of action. While unscored, your LSAT Argumentative Writing essay is submitted to all law schools to which you apply, and law schools use it as part of the evaluation process. Note: You need only one LSAT Argumentative Writing sample on record.

The Digital LSAT Interface

The official LSAT is administered digitally (taken on your personal device or at a testing center on the center's hardware), and getting practice with the interface and tools of the digital test is essential to your preparation. The most direct way to get familiar with the digital interface is to use the LSAC's officially released tests on LawHub: **lsac.org/lawhub.**

Make the most of those LSAC resources throughout your preparation. In the meantime, what follows is a quick introduction to the digital interface with some helpful strategy notes from Kaplan's expert instructors who have used it and have some best practices to pass on to test takers.

Here's a screenshot of a generic question, taken from the digital LSAT interface. The buttons are labeled to show you what each of them does.

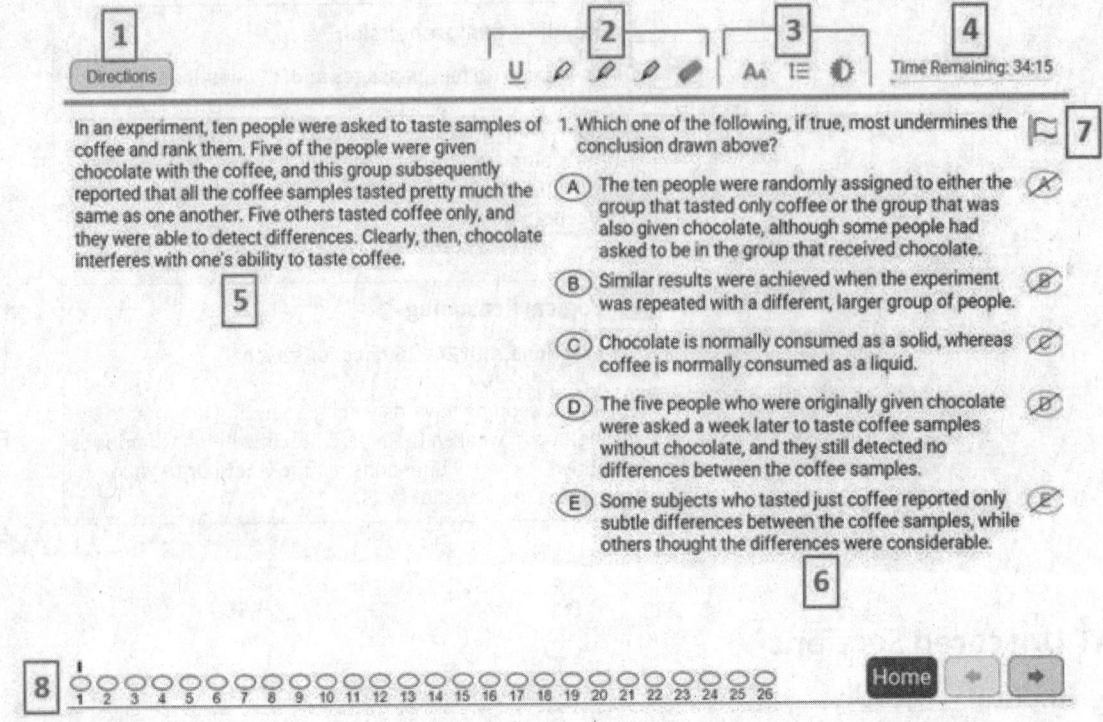

Digital LSAT screen layout LSAC.org

1. The "Directions" button will take you back to the Directions slide at the start of the test section. When you're on the Directions page, this button changes to say "Questions." If you click the button while you're on the Directions page, it will take you back to the last question at which you were looking.

2. These icons activate the underlining and highlighting tools (there are three highlighter colors), and an eraser tool to remove underlines or highlights you've made.

PRACTICE TIP

As you use the LSAC practice tests in the official interface, practice using your device. Do you prefer a mouse or touchpad? Or do you prefer to use your touchscreen or stylus? Make those decisions before test day.

3. These three tools allow you to adjust font size (four options), line spacing (three options), and brightness (a slider).

PRACTICE TIP

Practice using these tools until you're familiar and comfortable with them. That way, you'll know from the get-go how you want to adjust the view for each section of the test.

K

4. This is the section timer. It will start at 35:00 and count down to 00:00. For the first 30 minutes of the section, you can hide the timer by clicking on the numbers.

PRACTICE TIP

Some test takers like to see the timer. Others get anxious having the clock in their peripheral vision. There is no right or wrong way to use the timer. Try it out in practice to see what works best for you.

5. This is where the question's stimulus or prompt will be. For Logical Reasoning, that means the argument or paragraph on which the question is based, and for Reading Comprehension, it means the passage. For passages and paragraphs too long to fit on the screen, there will be a scroll bar that controls just the text in the left-hand column.

6. This column will always have the question stem and answer choices. Clicking a circle to the left of an answer choice selects that choice as the correct answer. Clicking a circle to the right of an answer choice will grey down that choice. Note: You must click a choice from the left-hand circles; greying down four answer choices does not automatically select the correct answer. This may look or sound confusing at first, but it's quite intuitive after just a few minutes of practice.

DIGITAL LSAT STRATEGY

Among the high-scoring LSAT experts we surveyed about their use of the digital interface, no feature gained as universally high praise as the "grey down" bubbles. Top scorers on the LSAT develop tremendous acumen and confidence that allows them to eliminate incorrect choices after one read-through. They all appreciated the added clarity of being able to visually eliminate the choice with one click.

6a. On questions in which the right-hand column text will not fit onscreen, you'll see upward arrows to the right of the answer choices. These allow you to collapse answer choices until the text no longer requires a scroll bar. Collapsing answers you've confidently eliminated will help you avoid rereading and confusion. See the image on the next page.

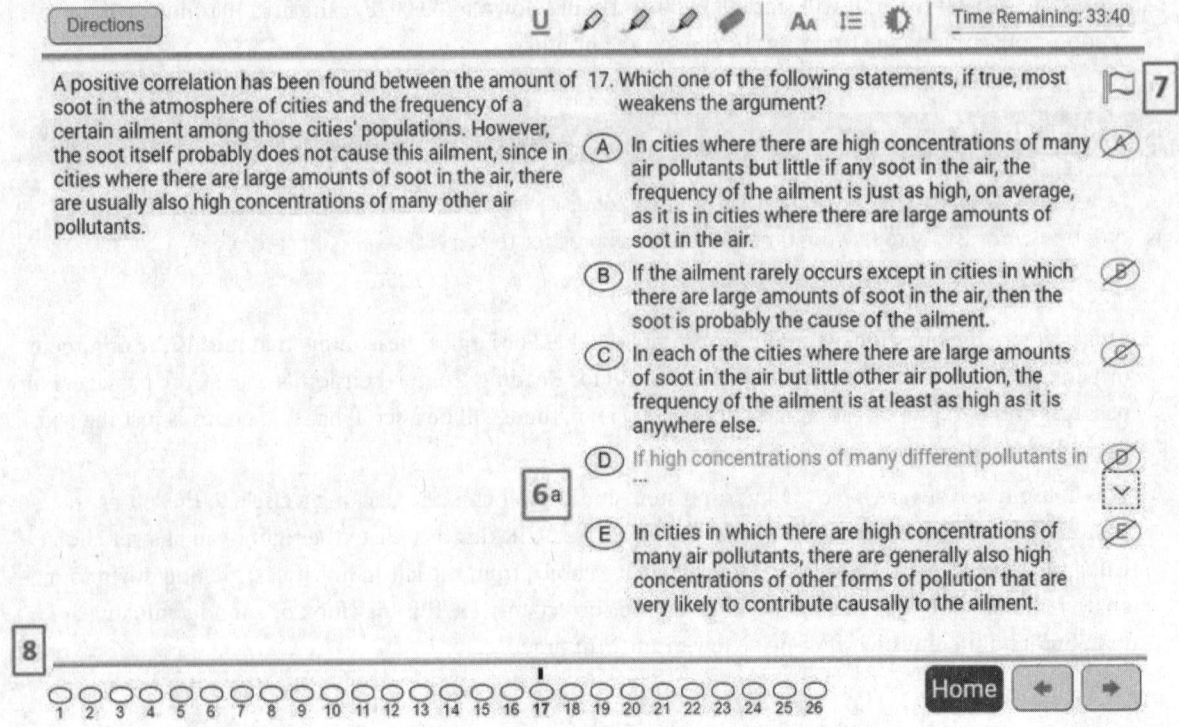

Collapsible answer choices LSAC.org

7. This flag allows you to mark questions. Our LSAT experts use it in two situations. Some flagged questions that they skipped or left unanswered. All of the experts, however, used the flag for questions to which they wanted to return, time permitting. In some cases, these were questions for which they had picked an answer, but had low confidence in their choice and wanted to give it one more look. In other cases, these were questions on which the expert had eliminated (greyed down) two or three of the answers and wanted to come back for a final decision on the remaining choices.

DIGITAL LSAT STRATEGY

Strategic skipping and guessing are important tactics for effective time management on the LSAT. Test experts know that all questions carry equal weight in calculating their final score, so they avoid wasting too much time on any single question. The flag tool provides an excellent way to keep track of skipped or incomplete questions.

8. The horizontal bar at the bottom of the screen is for navigation. This "bubble bar" indicates questions for which you've selected a correct answer, questions you've left blank, and any question you've flagged, answered or not. The current on-screen question is indicated by a small vertical bar above the bubble. Clicking on a bubble in the navigation bar will automatically advance you to that question. The forward and back buttons in the far bottom right will move you one question forward or back.

How the LSAT Is Scored

To understand how the LSAT is scored, and the implications of your score for your law school application, it is helpful to think about three different scales.

Raw Score

Your raw score on the LSAT refers to the number of questions you got correct. Each question on the LSAT has one correct answer and four demonstrably incorrect ones. The raw score is simply the sum of your correct answers. Moreover, there is no wrong answer penalty on the LSAT and no partial credit for any question, so you should answer every question, even if your answer is a pure guess.

Scaled Score

Scaled scores make the scores of test takers who took different administrations of the LSAT comparable. The score-conversion table for a given exam distributes raw scores on a standard bell curve. Raw-to-scaled conversions vary *very* slightly from test to test to account for slight differences in the difficulty of different administrations.

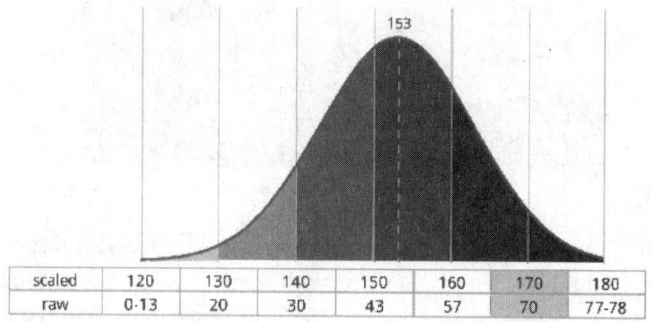

scaled	120	130	140	150	160	170	180
raw	0-13	20	30	43	57	70	77-78

Percentile Score

Percentile rankings allow schools to compare an applicant to their cohort. Your percentile score (or more accurately, your percentile *rank*) shows the percentage of test takers who had scaled scores below yours over the previous three testing years (July to June).

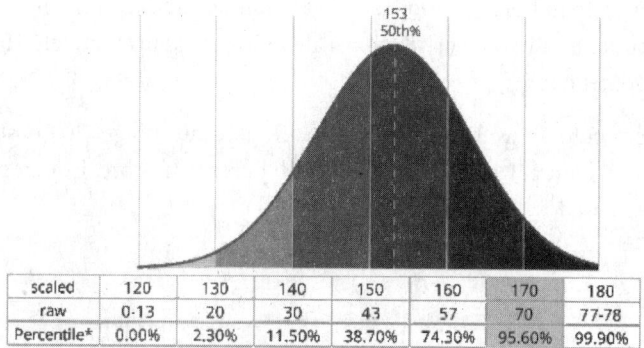

scaled	120	130	140	150	160	170	180
raw	0-13	20	30	43	57	70	77-78
Percentile*	0.00%	2.30%	11.50%	38.70%	74.30%	95.60%	99.90%

*for cumulative LSAT administrations 2020-2023

Note: 50th percentile is approximately 153 (~47 correct answers).
90th percentile is approximately 166 (~65 correct answers).

Adding percentile ranking to the chart illustrates the enormous power of even small improvements to your raw score, especially when you are scoring in the middle range of the bell curve.

Here's a table aligning typical percentile rankings with average scaled and raw scores. In the raw score column, you see also the number of additional correct answers needed on average to move up by approximately ten percentile points.

Percentile	Scaled	Raw
99.90%	180	77-78 (+11)
95%	**170**	**70**
90%	166-167	66 (+6)
80%	162	60 (+4)
70%	159	56 (+5)
60%	156	51 (+4)
50%	153	47 (+3)
40%	150-151	44 (+5)
30%	147	39 (+4)
20%	144	35 (+5)
10%	139	29 (+16)
0%	120	0-13

Let it sink in that, depending on where you're scoring, adding just seven correct responses can move you past approximately 15,000 other test takers. That makes a huge difference to any law school considering your application. Use this as motivation to keep studying and practicing even when your initial score gains feel modest.

What's a Good LSAT Score?

What you consider a good LSAT score depends on your own expectations and goals, but here are a few interesting statistics: Getting about half of all of the scored questions right (a raw score of roughly 39) will earn a scaled score of roughly 146 or 147, around the 30th percentile—not a great performance. However, getting only three additional questions right per section (that's less than one additional right answer every 10 minutes during the test) would produce a raw score of 48, or a scaled score of approximately 153, around the 50th percentile—a huge improvement.

So, you don't have to be perfect to do well. On a typical LSAT, you can still get 20 questions wrong and end up in the 160s, or about 11 wrong and get a 167, typically a 90th percentile score. Even a perfect score of 180 often allows for a question to be missed.

Here is a chart detailing some law schools and the scores of their admitted students:

RANK*	SCHOOL	25TH–75TH %ILE LSAT* (SCALED)	25TH–75TH %ILE UGPA*	25TH–75TH %ILE LSAT** (RAW)
1	Yale University	171–178	3.87–3.99	71–76
5 (tied)	New York University	169–174	3.72–3.94	69–73
5 (tied)	Duke University	168–171	3.73–3.94	68–71
10	University of California–Berkeley	167–172	3.74–3.9	67–71
16 (tied)	University of Texas–Austin	166–171	3.71–3.92	65–71
16 (tied)	University of Southern California	165–169	3.76–3.94	64–69
22	University of Florida	162–170	3.52–3.97	60–70
29	Boston College	162–167	3.55–3.81	60–67
32	Arizona State University	158–168	3.42–3.94	55–68
45	Pepperdine University	159–166	3.54–3.93	56–65
54	Temple University	160–165	3.38–3.74	57–64
56	University of Colorado—Boulder	159–166	3.45–3.83	56–65
71	Tulane University	157–163	3.42–3.76	53–62

U.S. News & World Report, 2023–2024 Best Law Schools
** Estimated score conversion

Registration for and Administration of the LSAT

The LSAT is administered nine times per testing cycle (July–June).

LSAT FACTS

The typical testing cycle features LSAT administrations in the following months:

- July or August
- September
- October
- November
- January
- February
- March or April
- June

Check **lsac.org/LSATdates** for complete, accurate, and up-to-date test administration information.

Test takers choose either to take the test on their own device or to appear at a testing center and use the center's hardware. For each administration, there are multiple days and time slots from which to schedule their individual test. Dates and times may be different for tests administered outside the United States, Canada, and the Caribbean.

How do I register for the LSAT? Register for the LSAT online at **lsac.org.** Check the LSAC website for details on the procedures, deadlines, and fee schedules.

When should I register? Register as soon as you have chosen your test date. Registration is typically due about five weeks before test day. As of 2018, there is no longer a "Late Registration" period.

Can I change my test date? You can change your test date (subject to an additional fee) via the LSAC website. Timely changes of test date are not reported to schools; "no-shows," however, are reported.

What is the CAS? Upon signing up for the LSAT, you also need to register with the Credential Assembly Service (CAS) as part of the application process required by every ABA-approved law school. CAS receives your undergraduate transcripts and distributes a summary of your undergraduate performance, along with your letters of recommendation, evaluations, and LSAT score report to each of the law schools to which you apply. **lsac.org/applying-law-school/jd-application-process/credential-assembly-service-cas** lists the fees and sign-up details for CAS.

When are law schools' application deadlines? All law schools provide their application deadlines on their websites. A small number of schools require the LSAT be taken by December for admission the following fall; most will accept a later LSAT score. Because most schools use a "rolling admissions" process, taking the test earlier is preferable; also, taking the test earlier gives the test taker a chance to repeat the LSAT prior to most application deadlines.

Can I repeat the LSAT? Yes. Test takers are limited to five administrations within any period of five testing years, and seven administrations in their lifetime. If you cancel your score (including cancellations under the Score Preview option) after taking the test, that test administration still counts toward your total allowed administrations, but absences and withdrawals prior to testing do not. Any test taker who achieves a score of 180 may not take another LSAT in her lifetime (but why would anyone want to?).

How do law schools view multiple LSAT scores? What is Score Preview? It is now standard practice for schools to evaluate candidates based on their highest LSAT score from the five-year period preceding the date of their application. Schools do, however, see all of your scores and cancellations, so you may wish to explain the circumstances of low scores or cancellations in an addendum. LSAC's Score Preview option allows you (for a fee) to cancel your score within five days of receiving your score report. No schools see that score, but they do see that you canceled (and the administration will count against your testing limit).

Can I receive accommodations? The LSAC grants accommodated testing for physical, learning, and cognitive impairments, and there are a wide variety of accommodations available. A test taker must be registered for a test date before requesting accommodations. Full information about accommodated testing is available at **lsac.org/lsat/register-lsat/accommodations/accommodations-may-be-available-lsat**.

LSAT Study Skills

The LSAT is a skills-based test. For this reason, improving your score is, in some ways, more like mastering a musical instrument or an athletic skill than it is like learning a subject in school. The LSAT is very practical, testing what you can do above what you know. As such, it is also practicable and coachable. Expect Kaplan to show you the best ways to practice. Expect us to show you the patterns of the test and how to tackle every question type. Expect us to show you how to manage every section. Expect us to show you how, when, and why to use your resources. In return, you're going to need to work—hard. Reaching your full potential on the LSAT takes lots of practice. We will show you precisely what you need to do, but ultimately it's up to you to do it.

LSAT Strategy and the Three Levels of Practice

On test day, you'll be asked to deal with stringent testing policies and procedures and answer approximately 104–105 multiple-choice questions (of which typically 77–78 will count toward your score). It's a grueling and intense two-and-one-half hours.

A strategic approach to the LSAT means increasing your speed only to the extent you can do so without sacrificing accuracy. Your goal is not to attempt as many questions as possible; your goal is to get as many questions right as possible. If you had unlimited time to take this test, you'd likely perform quite well. But you don't. You have a strict 35 minutes to complete each section, and many students are not able to tackle every question in the time allotted. For you, this means three things:

- It's important that you learn not only how to answer the questions effectively, but also how to answer them efficiently.

- It's important to approach each section strategically, knowing which questions to attack first and which questions to save for last.

- It's important that you prepare for the rigors of 2½ hours of testing. You'll want to maintain your focus in the final section as well as you did in the first.

To achieve your goals, you'll want to incorporate three levels of practice: Mastery, Timing, and Endurance.

Mastery is about learning the patterns of the exam and how to identify them in new questions. Kaplan provides a proven method for the questions in each section of the test. You will gain command of the method and master efficient, effective strategies and tactics through repeated practice on skill-based drills and individual questions. You'll study the answers and explanations to learn how the testmaker builds questions and answer choices. You'll identify why right answers are right, why wrong answers are wrong, what traps you consistently fall into, and how to avoid them. That's what **Mastery** practice is for.

Once you've learned the skills, you'll try section practice, or **Timing** practice. At about two-and-one-half hours of active testing, the LSAT can seem like a marathon, but it's really a series of sprints—four 35-minute tests. Learning section management—how to recognize and apply the patterns you've learned efficiently, maximizing the number of questions you get correct—is what Timing practice teaches you to do.

Finally, there's **Endurance** practice. Can you maintain your ability to identify and apply these patterns through the whole exam? Some test takers lose focus during the second hour of testing and struggle through the last two sections of the test. Others need warm-up time and underperform on the first section. Taking full-length practice tests will help you build your stamina and focus. As you'll learn in your course, practice tests are very important to your score improvement. Look for places in your schedule where you have an uninterrupted

2.5 hours and block them out for full-length practice. Then, the hours or days immediately following, look for at least two more hours (they do not need to be uninterrupted) and schedule them for test review. The process of reviewing the tests—especially with Kaplan's thorough and strategy-focused explanations—greatly enhances the benefits of testing.

By approaching your practice in this way—using Mastery practice to internalize the strategies for each new question type you learn, layering in Timing practice to build efficiency, and using consistent full-length Endurance practice throughout your preparation—you'll be fully and properly prepared by test day.

LSAT Attitude

In the main chapters, you'll learn, practice, and master the methods, strategies, and tactics that lead to test day success. Nevertheless, two students with equal LSAT proficiency still might not produce the same score. Of those two "equal" test takers, the one with greater confidence and less stress will likely outperform the other. You can develop these positive psychological characteristics just as you can your LSAT skill set.

Stay Positive

Those who approach the LSAT as an obstacle and rail against the necessity of taking it generally don't fare as well as those who see the LSAT as an opportunity, a chance to show law schools their proficiency with the four core skills. A great LSAT score will distinguish your application from those of your competition.

- Look at the LSAT as a challenge, but try not to obsess over it; you certainly don't want to psych yourself out of the game.
- Remember that the LSAT is important, but this one test will not single-handedly determine the outcome of your life.
- Try to have fun with the test. Learning how to unlock the patterns of the test and approach the content in the way the testmakers have crafted the exam can be very satisfying, and the skills you'll acquire will benefit you in law school and your career.

Confidence and Stress Management

Confidence in your ability leads to quick, sure answers and a sense of well-being that translates into more points. Confidence feeds on itself; unfortunately, so does self-doubt. If you lack confidence, you end up reading sentences and answer choices two, three, or four times, until you confuse yourself and get off-track. This leads to timing difficulties that perpetuate a downward spiral of anxiety, rushing, and poor performance. If you subscribe to the proper LSAT mind-set, however, you'll gear all of your practice toward taking control of the test. When you've achieved that goal—armed with the principles, techniques, strategies, and methods Kaplan has to offer—you'll be ready to face the LSAT with confidence. Your online resources have more good information, explanations, and other resources to help you minimize test anxiety, manage stress, and maximize your performance.

Secrets of LSAT Preparation

By Kaplan LSAT Channel Faculty

 Watch the video lesson for this Spotlight in your online Study Plan.

Students who come to *The LSAT Channel* get to hear from some of Kaplan's most experienced and highly rated LSAT faculty. The message they hear most clearly is: Kaplan knows the LSAT—inside out, forward and backward—and we've got the method and strategies that will (with practice) help you master it. Each of these coaches and mentors has their own special insights, as well. In the video that accompanies this Spotlight, you'll meet the LSAT Channel faculty, and hear what each of them tells students at the beginning of their logic games prep. Here are a few of the themes they hit upon:

You Use LSAT Skills All the Time

It is often remarked that the LSAT is like no other test you've ever taken. It is entirely skills-based and requires little to no outside knowledge. The skills tested here, however, are more familiar than you may realize. If you've ever pointed out an unwarranted assumption in a friend's argument, you've engaged in logical reasoning. Likewise, if you've ever combined two statements to reach a make a valid deduction. If you've ever questioned a pundit's point of view in an editorial, or analyzed an author's support for a position in an academic paper, you've tackled LSAT-style reading comprehension. So, while it may be true that you've never had to answer questions quite like these

on a test, you engage in LSAT-related tasks every day. LSAT questions and passages present you with small, real-world puzzles that may, at first, seem abstract or technical, but are really quite practical—and, you *can* do them.

There Is Always Enough Information to Answer Every Question

There are two criteria for a good game—even games we play with friends or against the computer: They need to be challenging, and they need to be fair. If we're honest, challenging games are more fun. We quickly lose interest in puzzles that are too easy to solve, or in games we always win. LSAT questions throughout the test are challenging, but always fair. Before a question appears on an official LSAT, it has been tested on thousands of test takers to ensure it has all the information needed to produce exactly one correct answer and four demonstrably incorrect ones. The experts on the LSAT Channel are fond of stating "One right, four rotten" as a principle of every LSAT question. As you gain experience and expertise with the test, you, too, will gain confidence that you can identify the correct answer and reject the incorrect ones, efficiently and effectively.

Patience Can Make You Faster

The scored sections of the LSAT are 35 minutes long, and they contain between 24 and 27 questions. In Logical Reasoning, you have approximately 1 minute 20 seconds per question. In the Reading Comprehension section, you have approximately 8½ minutes for each passage and its accompanying questions. The time pressure is real, but the best response to that pressure is counterintuitive. To increase your efficiency on the LSAT, you need patience. LSAT experts know that a methodical approach—untangling the stimulus of a Logical Reasoning question, for example or road-mapping a Reading Comprehension passage—reduces confusion, eliminates wasteful rereading, and makes you faster and more accurate overall. The other thing you must remember is that every LSAT test taker feels the clock ticking, but LSAT experts respond to that pressure with strategies for getting as many points as possible in 35 minutes instead of being frustrated that they don't have more time.

Small Improvements Produce Big Results

You saw this demonstrated earlier, in the section about LSAT scoring. There are only 77–78 scored questions on the typical LSAT test, and given that the LSAT is scored on a curve, adding just five more correct answers to your score can move you past 10 percent of test takers. Depending on your starting score, 10 additional correct answers could move your score past a quarter of all law school applicants (that's thousands of other test takers vying for admission). That means the improvements you make—even if it is "just" 2–3 more correct answers per section—can have an enormous impact on your law school application.

The LSAT Channel

Kaplan launched the LSAT Channel in 2015 to bring nightly live instruction from our most highly rated LSAT teachers to every student enrolled in a comprehensive LSAT prep course. Since then, students all over the country (and the world) have had access to over 100 unique hours of instruction for every testing cycle. The LSAT Channel faculty is constantly creating new lessons on special topics to provide their strategic insights to ambitious test takers.

Now, the LSAT Channel instructors have developed several Spotlight lessons exclusively for *LSAT Logical Reasoning Prep*. Whenever you see one of these Spotlight features in the book, you'll not only get the expertise provided on the page, but also have a chance to practice the strategies explained there, and to learn directly from the instructors through the videos in your online Study Plan.

Take a few minutes to meet the faculty, both on the following page and in the accompanying video. They'll motivate you and set you on the path to LSAT success. Let's get started …

JEFF BOUDREAU

BEST ADVICE FOR STUDENTS: If this is truly your dream, don't put an expiration date on it.

DESCRIBES TEACHING STYLE AS: Excited, fun-loving, caring

BOBBY GAUTAM

BEST ADVICE FOR STUDENTS: Work hard to get ready for the test, but when the test begins don't work harder than you have to.

DESCRIBES TEACHING STYLE AS: Clear, compassionate, lively, humorous, passionate

HANNAH GIST

BEST ADVICE FOR STUDENTS: So many students come to class and do the homework, but they keep using the same flawed methods they used on the Diag. If you want better results, have the courage to CHANGE.

DESCRIBES TEACHING STYLE AS: Patient, energetic, encouraging, accessible, proficient

GED HELM

BEST ADVICE FOR STUDENTS: The LSAT is not an IQ test, a test of character, or a test of worth. The LSAT tests a specific set of skills that are learned.

DESCRIBES TEACHING STYLE AS: Energetic, positive, strategic, honest

MELANIE TRIEBEL

BEST ADVICE FOR STUDENTS: It feels good to get everything right, but you learn more when you get things wrong. When you make a mistake, celebrate! Then learn. If you can figure out why you made the mistake, that's one fewer mistake on test day.

DESCRIBES TEACHING STYLE AS: Enthusiastic, simplified, geeky, detailed

Complete answers and explanations are provided in the LSAT Channel Spotlight video "Secrets of LSAT Preparation" in your online Study Plan.

Logical Reasoning Foundations

CHAPTER 1

The Logical Reasoning Method

Logical Reasoning by the Numbers

The Logical Reasoning sections of the LSAT test your ability to analyze and critique short arguments and to evaluate and apply factual statements. The skills associated with Logical Reasoning are the most important to your LSAT score. The reason is clear: Logical Reasoning accounts for roughly two-thirds of your LSAT score. Every administration of the LSAT contains exactly two scored Logical Reasoning sections of between 24 and 26 questions apiece. Among the 50 or so Logical Reasoning questions you'll see on test day, Kaplan identifies 14 distinct question types (some with important subtypes) which we group into three question families.

Percentage of All Questions per LSAT by Logical Reasoning Question Type

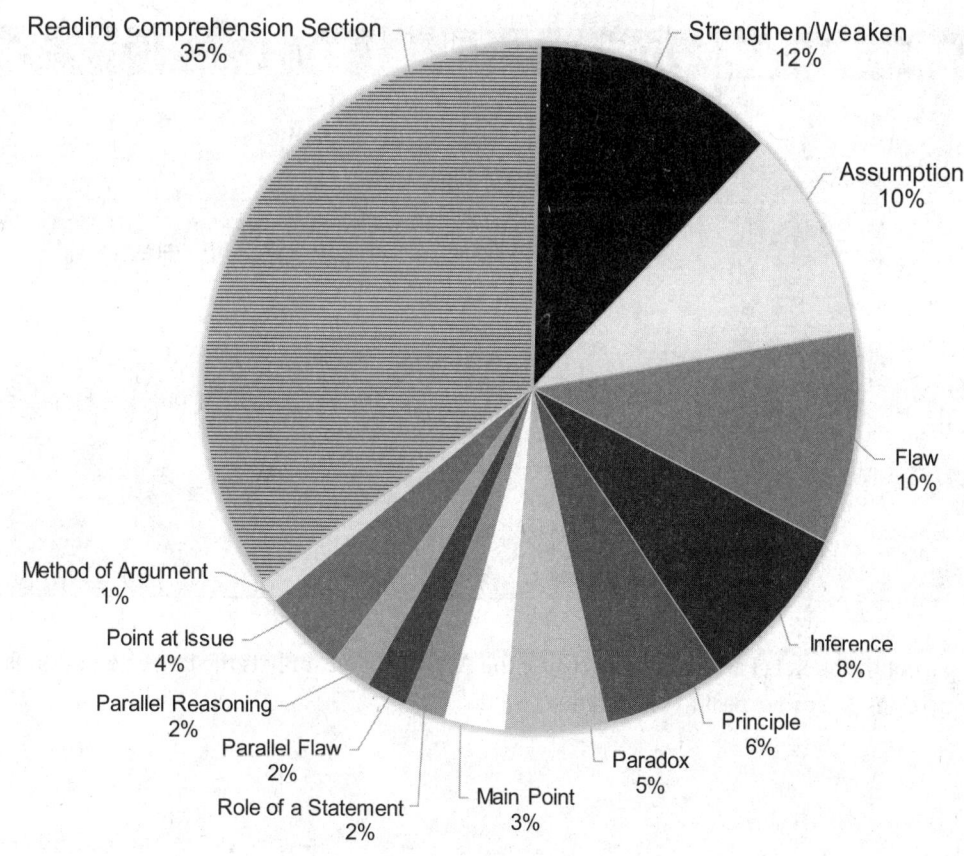

Reading Comprehension Section 35%
Strengthen/Weaken 12%
Assumption 10%
Flaw 10%
Inference 8%
Principle 6%
Paradox 5%
Main Point 3%
Role of a Statement 2%
Parallel Flaw 2%
Parallel Reasoning 2%
Point at Issue 4%
Method of Argument 1%

Source: All officially released LSAT exams, 2016-2020

Percentage of All Questions Per LSAT by Logical Reasoning Question Family

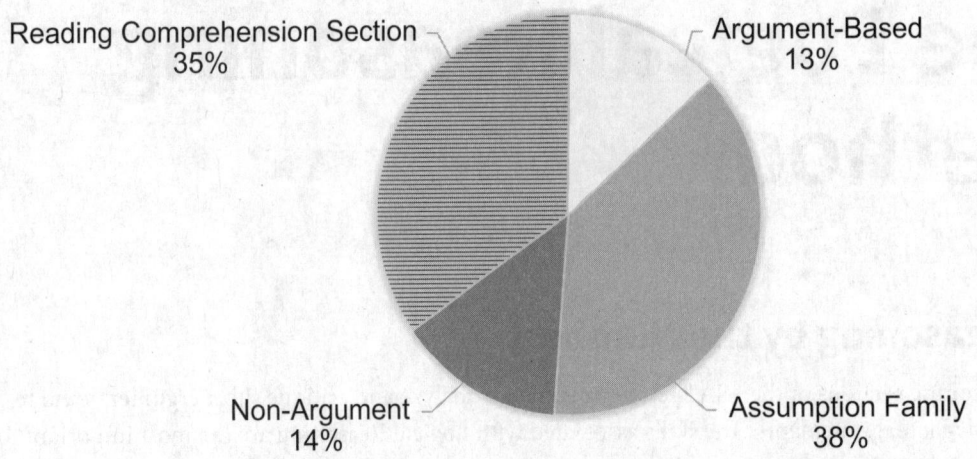

Source: All officially released LSAT exams, 2016-2020

As you work through this book, you'll learn to identify each of the question types, and you'll master the most important strategies and tactics LSAT experts apply to each one. After you finish this chapter and your introduction to formal logic on the LSAT in Chapter 2, you'll cover the question types in Parts II-IV.

LOGICAL REASONING QUESTION TYPES BY CHAPTER		
PART I - LOGICAL REASONING FOUNDATIONS Chapter 1 - The Logical Reasoning Method Chapter 2 - Formal Logic Basics		
PART II - ARGUMENT-BASED QUESTIONS	PART III - ASSUMPTION FAMILY QUESTIONS	PART IV - NON-ARGUMENT QUESTIONS
Chapter 3 - Main Point	Chapter 8 - Finding the Assumption	Chapter 14 - Inference and Inference-based Principle Questions
Chapter 4 - Role of a Statement	Chapter 9 - Assumption	Chapter 15 - Paradox
Chapter 5 - Point at Issue	Chapter 10 - Flaw	
Chapter 6 - Method of Argument	Chapter 11 - Strengthen/ Weaken	
Chapter 7 - Parallel Reasoning	Chapter 12 - Assumption-Family Principle Questions	
	Chapter 13 - Parallel Flaw	

The longest part of the book is Part III. That's because the Assumption Family is the largest question family by number of questions you can expect to see on your LSAT.

Approximate Number of Questions per LSAT by Logical Reasoning Question Type

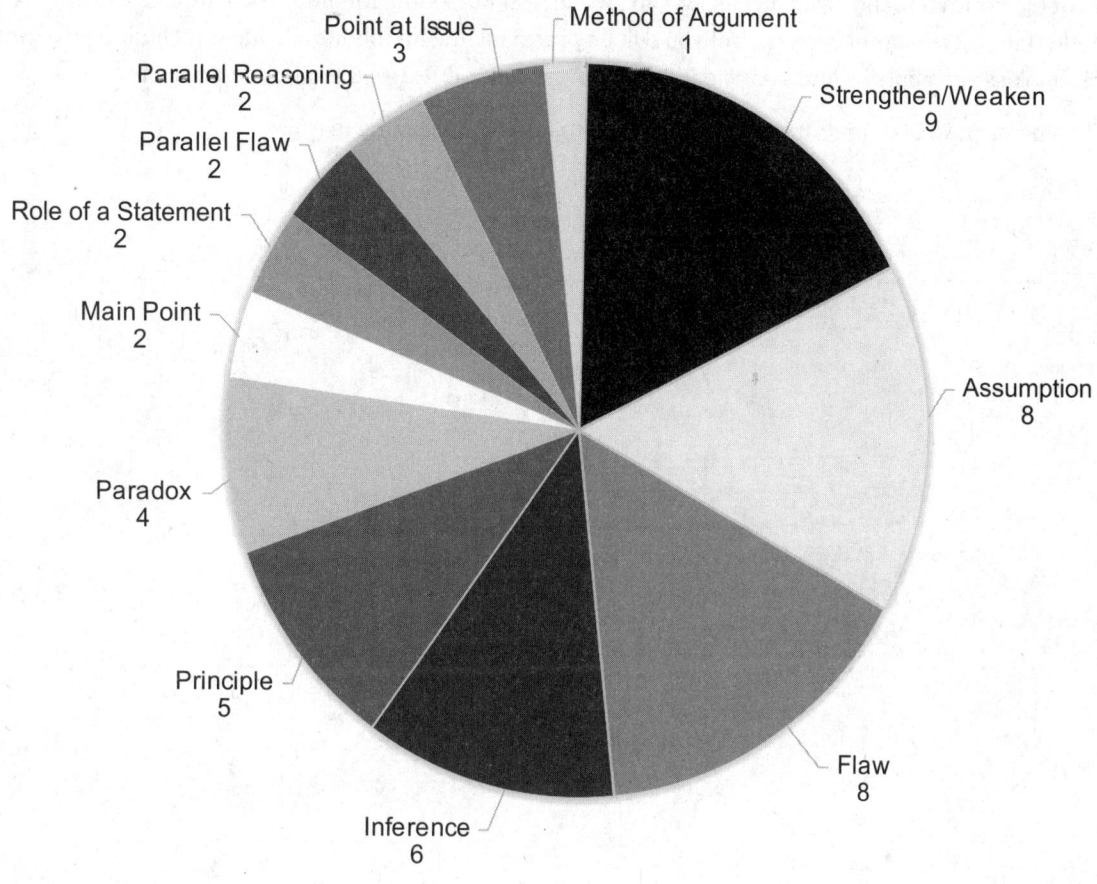

Source: All officially released LSAT exams, 2016-2020

The Assumption Family is so big that it will be worth more than a third of your LSAT score, larger in fact than the Reading Comprehension section. The Assumption Family contains the three most common Logical Reasoning question types: Assumption, Flaw, and Strengthen/Weaken. So, you know Part III of this book is essential to your LSAT score improvement. But, this also raises a good question: If the Assumption Family is so important, why don't you start there? The answer is that all of the skills you'll learn in Part II on Argument-Based questions create a foundation for the work you'll do in Part III. Without that foundation in place, improvement on the Assumption Family questions is a lot harder.

Really, all of the questions in Parts II and III are "argument based" because the stimulus in every Assumption Family question contains an argument. Kaplan distinguishes the two families as follows: Argument-Based questions can be answered entirely from the text of the argument, while in Assumption Family questions, you must consider the author's implicit (or "unstated") assumption in addition to the explicit parts of the argument. As the name suggests, the majority of Non-Argument questions covered in Part IV do not have arguments in their stimuli.

As you work through this book, you'll become intimately familiar with all of the question types featured on the LSAT, but first, you'll cover something that all of the questions have in common: All of them can be answered accurately and efficiently using Kaplan's Logical Reasoning Method. You'll be able to learn the Method in just a handful of pages, but you will be practicing the Method (quite literally) hundreds of times in this book as you apply its four consistent steps to every Logical Reasoning question on the test.

That's up next, so take your first steps on the road to Logical Reasoning mastery.

The Kaplan Logical Reasoning Method

LEARNING OBJECTIVES

In this chapter, you'll learn to:

- Apply each step of the Logical Reasoning Method to LSAT questions.
- Identify the most common wrong-answer types in LSAT Logical Reasoning questions.

The first and most important commonality among LSAT Logical Reasoning questions is their structure. Here's how all Logical Reasoning questions appear in the LSAC's digital testing interface.

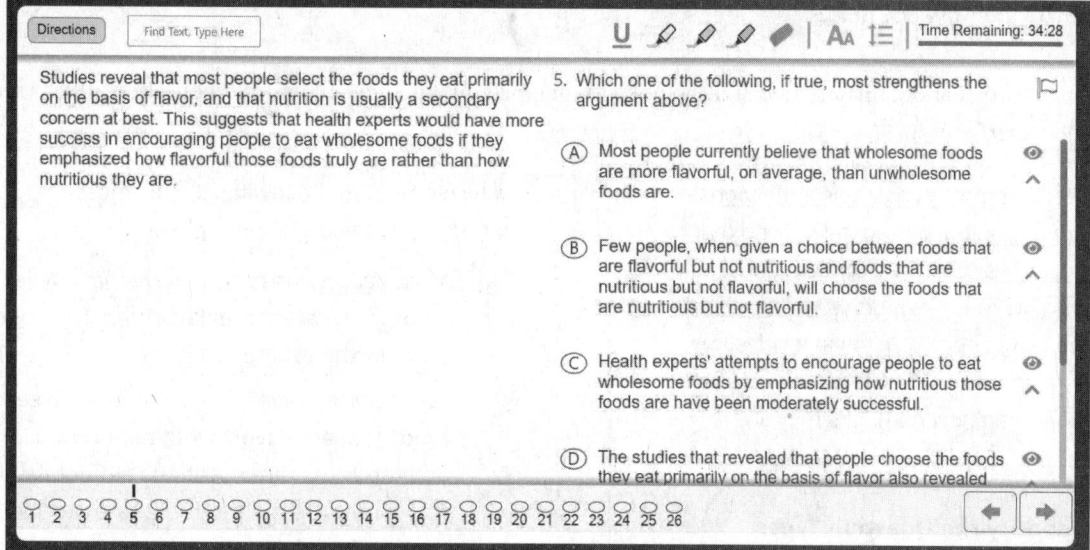

The first block of text in the upper left is the stimulus, a paragraph-length argument or set of assertions. The stimulus is the text you need to untangle or analyze to understand the author's argument or premises. To the right of the stimulus sits the question stem, a sentence that lays out the task the LSAT is asking you to perform in relation to the stimulus. Underneath the question stem, there are always five answer choices, of which exactly one is correct, while the other four are demonstrably incorrect.

On the next page, you'll see how Logical Reasoning questions are displayed in this book, and the strategic order in which LSAT experts tackle the parts of the question. It might not be immediately intuitive.

Logical Reasoning Question Format and the Kaplan Logical Reasoning Method

Although Logical Reasoning questions ask for several different kinds of analyses, the LSAT expert uses a consistent approach on all of the questions.

> **THE KAPLAN LOGICAL REASONING METHOD**
>
> **STEP 1** Identify the Question Type
>
> **STEP 2** Untangle the Stimulus
>
> **STEP 3** Predict the Correct Answer
>
> **STEP 4** Evaluate the Answer Choices

There is nothing abstract about this method. Take a look at it mapped onto a Logical Reasoning question. This is how the well-trained expert sees it.

Studies reveal that most people select the foods they eat primarily on the basis of flavor, and that nutrition is usually a secondary concern at best. This suggests that health experts would have more success in encouraging people to eat wholesome foods if they emphasized how flavorful those foods truly are rather than how nutritious they are.

Step 1: Identify the Question Type
Start here, so you know what to look for in the stimulus.

Step 2: Untangle the Stimulus
Zero in on what is relevant. Here, the underlined and highlighted text helps you to predict the correct answer.

Step 3: Predict the Correct Answer
In your own words, state what the correct answer must say.

Step 4: Evaluate the Answer Choices
Identify the answer that matches your prediction. Eliminate those that do not.

5. Which one of the following, if true, most strengthens the argument above?

(A) Most people currently believe that wholesome foods are more flavorful, on average, than unwholesome foods are.

(B) Few people, when given a choice between foods that are flavorful but not nutritious and foods that are nutritious but not flavorful, will choose the foods that are nutritious but not flavorful.

(C) Health experts' attempts to encourage people to eat wholesome foods by emphasizing how nutritious those foods are have been moderately successful.

(D) The studies that revealed that people choose the foods they eat primarily on the basis of flavor also revealed that people rated as most flavorful those foods that were least nutritious.

(E) In a study, subjects who were told that a given food was very flavorful were more willing to try the food and more likely to enjoy it than were subjects who were told that the food was nutritious.

PrepTest129 Sec2 Q5

Now, work through that question to get a feel for the Method in action.

The Logical Reasoning Method Step By Step

Try to apply the Logical Reasoning Method to that question one step at a time. Don't worry that you don't know all the names and terminology yet. You'll pick that up in subsequent chapters. For now, concentrate on what each step accomplishes and how it helps you anticipate what to look for next. When you're finished, compare your work to that of an LSAT expert with the worked example on the following page.

Step 2: *The question stem told you this text is an argument. How does that help you untangle it?*

Step 1: *Why do you start with the stem? How does it help you in Step 2?*

1. Studies reveal that most people select the foods they eat primarily on the basis of flavor, and that nutrition is usually a secondary concern at best. This suggests that health experts would have more success in encouraging people to eat wholesome foods if they emphasized how flavorful those foods truly are rather than how nutritious they are.

Which one of the following, if true, most strengthens the argument above?

(A) Most people currently believe that wholesome foods are more flavorful, on average, than unwholesome foods are.

(B) Few people, when given a choice between foods that are flavorful but not nutritious and foods that are nutritious but not flavorful, will choose the foods that are nutritious but not flavorful.

(C) Health experts' attempts to encourage people to eat wholesome foods by emphasizing how nutritious those foods are have been moderately successful.

(D) The studies that revealed that people choose the foods they eat primarily on the basis of flavor also revealed that people rated as most flavorful those foods that were least nutritious.

(E) In a study, subjects who were told that a given food was very flavorful were more willing to try the food and more likely to enjoy it than were subjects who were told that the food was nutritious.

PrepTest129 Sec2 Q5

Step 3: *Before evaluating the answer choices, can you predict (or at least get a good sense of) what the correct answer will say?*

Step 4: *Which is the correct choice? How do you know?*

Wrong answers: *Before turning to the expert analysis, can you explain clearly why each wrong answer is wrong? On test day, eliminating incorrect answers can be very helpful in finding the correct one.*

Expert Analysis

Here's how an LSAT expert worked through that question. Pay attention to what they noted in each step of the Logical Reasoning Method.

Step 2: *Conclusion:* Experts will have more success selling people on how good a healthy food tastes than on how good it is for them *because*

Evidence: Studies show people choose food based on taste more than on nutrition.

Step 1: This is a Strengthen question; the correct answer provides a fact that makes the argument's conclusion more likely to follow from the evidence.

1. Studies reveal that most people select the foods they eat primarily on the basis of flavor, and that nutrition is usually a secondary concern at best. This suggests that health experts would have more success in encouraging people to eat wholesome foods if they emphasized how flavorful those foods truly are rather than how nutritious they are.

Which one of the following, if true, most strengthens the argument above?

(A) Most people currently believe that wholesome foods are more flavorful, on average, than unwholesome foods are.

(B) Few people, when given a choice between foods that are flavorful but not nutritious and foods that are nutritious but not flavorful, will choose the foods that are nutritious but not flavorful.

(C) Health experts' attempts to encourage people to eat wholesome foods by emphasizing how nutritious those foods are have been moderately successful.

(D) The studies that revealed that people choose the foods they eat primarily on the basis of flavor also revealed that people rated as most flavorful those foods that were least nutritious.

(E) In a study, subjects who were told that a given food was very flavorful were more willing to try the food and more likely to enjoy it than were subjects who were told that the food was nutritious.

PrepTest129 Sec2 Q5

Step 3: The author assumes (takes for granted) that people will respond favorably to expert suggestions that are based on flavor rather than nutrition. The correct answer will supply a fact suggesting that assumption is correct.

Step 4: (E) is correct. This introduces a new study showing that people were more likely to try and to like foods they were told are flavorful, exactly what the argument concludes.

Wrong answers: (A) 180. This choice does the opposite of what it should, weakening rather than strengthening the argument. It offers a benefit of emphasizing a food's nutritiousness, not its flavor. (B) Irrelevant comparison. The argument predicts success from telling people how flavorful nutritious foods can be, not just giving them a choice between tasty junk and flavorless nutrition. (C) Irrelevant comparison. Knowing that people think junk food is the tastiest stuff around doesn't help or hurt an argument suggesting that people might be persuaded to try nutritious foods if they're told those foods taste good, too. (D) 180. This choice makes it less likely that people will be persuaded by the experts' suggestions.

Nice work. You'll get increasingly comfortable with the Logical Reasoning Method the more you use it. By test day, it should be second nature to work through the four steps without even thinking about it. Try it out on a couple more questions in the short Practice set that follows.

Practice   Use the Logical Reasoning Method to work through two more questions. Don't worry about your timing here. Go step by step, and be mindful of each step's goal. Do your best, and when you finish, compare your work with that of an LSAT expert in the analysis that follows.

Step 2:	Step 1:

2. Engineers are investigating the suitability of Wantastiquet Pass as the site of a new bridge. Because one concern is whether erosion could eventually weaken the bridge's foundations, they contracted for two reports on erosion in the region. Although both reports are accurate, one claims that the region suffers relatively little erosion, while the other claims that regional erosion is heavy and a cause for concern.

Which one of the following, if true, most helps to explain how both reports could be accurate?

(A) Neither report presents an extensive chemical analysis of the soil in the region.

(B) Both reports include computer-enhanced satellite photographs.

(C) One report was prepared by scientists from a university, while the other report was prepared by scientists from a private consulting firm.

(D) One report focuses on regional topsoil erosion, while the other report focuses on riverbank erosion resulting from seasonal floods.

(E) One report cost nearly twice as much to prepare as did the other report.

PrepTest132 Sec3 Q8

Step 3:	Step 4:

LSAT PREP STRATEGY

On test day, you won't actually take notes for each step, of course, but it can be helpful to do so in practice because it instills a consistent, disciplined approach to every question, and it provides a record of your thinking as you compare your work to that of an LSAT expert.

Step 2:

Step 1:

3. One of the advantages of Bacillus thuringiensis (B.t.) toxins over chemical insecticides results from their specificity for pest insects. The toxins have no known detrimental effects on mammals or birds. In addition, the limited range of activity of the toxins toward insects means that often a particular toxin will kill pest species but not affect insects that prey upon the species. This advantage makes B.t. toxins preferable to chemical insecticides for use as components of insect pest management programs.

Which one of the following statements, if true, most weakens the argument?

(A) Chemical insecticides cause harm to a greater number of insect species than do B.t. toxins.

(B) No particular B.t. toxin is effective against all insects.

(C) B.t. toxins do not harm weeds that do damage to farm crops.

(D) Insects build up resistance more readily to B.t. toxins than to chemical insecticides.

(E) Birds and rodents often do greater damage to farm crops than do insects.

PrepTest111 Sec4 Q5

Step 3:

Step 4:

Expert Analysis

Compare your analysis to that of an LSAT expert. Did you stick to the Logical Reasoning Method? Which steps are most or least intuitive? Did you select the correct answer? Was it clear to you why each wrong answer was wrong?

Step 2: Two studies looked at erosion near a bridge. Both are accurate.

Report 1—Relatively little erosion

Report 2—Heavy erosion

Step 1: The phrase "helps to explain" indicates a Paradox question; the correct answer provides a fact that explains how two (seemingly contradictory) reports can both be true.

2. Engineers are investigating the suitability of Wantastiquet Pass as the site of a new bridge. Because one concern is whether erosion could eventually weaken the bridge's foundations, they contracted for two reports on erosion in the region. Although both reports are accurate, one claims that the region suffers relatively little erosion, while the other claims that regional erosion is heavy and a cause for concern.

Which one of the following, if true, most helps to explain how both reports could be accurate?

(A) Neither report presents an extensive chemical analysis of the soil in the region.

(B) Both reports include computer-enhanced satellite photographs.

(C) One report was prepared by scientists from a university, while the other report was prepared by scientists from a private consulting firm.

(D) One report focuses on regional topsoil erosion, while the other report focuses on riverbank erosion resulting from seasonal floods.

(E) One report cost nearly twice as much to prepare as did the other report.

PrepTest132 Sec3 Q8

Step 3: For two reports to be accurate, and yet reach opposite conclusions, they must be studying (at least subtly) different things. The correct answer will explain this.

Step 4: (D) is correct. If the reports studied two different kinds of erosion, they may reach opposite conclusions without one being incorrect.

Wrong answers: (A) 180. This is yet another way in which the studies are similar. (B) 180. This is yet another way in which the studies are similar. (C) Irrelevant comparison. The fact that different people ran the two studies doesn't explain how both can be accurate. (E) Irrelevant comparison. The fact that the reports cost a different amount doesn't explain how both can be correct.

Step 2: *Conclusion*: B.t. toxins are preferable to chemical insecticides *because*

Evidence: (1) B.t. toxins don't harm mammals and birds and (2) B.t. toxins often kill pests but not insects that feed on pests.

Step 1: A standard Weaken question; the correct answer is a fact that makes it less likely that the argument's conclusion follows from its evidence.

3. One of the advantages of Bacillus thuringiensis (B.t.) toxins over chemical insecticides results from their specificity for pest insects. The toxins have no known detrimental effects on mammals or birds. In addition, the limited range of activity of the toxins toward insects means that often a particular toxin will kill pest species but not affect insects that prey upon the species. This advantage makes B.t. toxins preferable to chemical insecticides for use as components of insect pest management programs.

Which one of the following statements, if true, most weakens the argument?

(A) Chemical insecticides cause harm to a greater number of insect species than do B.t. toxins.

(B) No particular B.t. toxin is effective against all insects.

(C) B.t. toxins do not harm weeds that do damage to farm crops.

(D) Insects build up resistance more readily to B.t. toxins than to chemical insecticides.

(E) Birds and rodents often do greater damage to farm crops than do insects.

PrepTest111 Sec4 Q5

Step 3: The author concludes that B.t. toxins are preferable to chemical insecticides for two reasons. To weaken this argument, the correct answer will present an overlooked disadvantage of B.t. toxins or cite a comparative advantage of chemical pesticides.

Step 4: (D) presents a comparative disadvantage to B.t. toxins and thus weakens the argument.

Wrong answers: (A) 180. This supports the author's second piece of evidence and, thus, strengthens the argument. (B) This fact is too narrow to harm the argument, which is about B.t. toxins in general; the author would simply recommend finding the B.t. toxin effective against the pest species one is targeting. (C) Outside the Scope. The argument is about B.t. toxins as an insect pest control mechanism, not as an herbicide. (E) Outside the Scope. The argument focuses on insect pest control, not birds or rodents.

There is a lot going on in every LSAT Logical Reasoning question, but you'll see all of the strategies and tactics the LSAT experts have employed here as you work through the remaining chapters of this book. For the moment, pause to consider what you've learned about the steps of the Logical Reasoning Method. There will be a quiz!

Common Logical Reasoning Wrong Answer Types

As you reviewed the analysis of the previous questions, you probably noticed that certain wrong answer types appeared several times. While not every wrong answer fits neatly into one of the following types identified (and, arguably, some wrong answers fit into more than one category), an LSAT expert can use the common wrong answer types to quickly and confidently eliminate dozens of wrong answers on test day.

LOGICAL REASONING: WRONG ANSWER TYPES

- **Outside the Scope**—a choice containing a statement that is too broad, too narrow, or beyond the purview of the stimulus

- **Irrelevant Comparison**—a choice that compares two items or attributes in a way not germane to the author's argument or statements

- **Extreme**—a choice containing language too emphatic to be supported by the stimulus; Extreme choices are often (though not always) characterized by words such as all, never, every, or none

- **Distortion**—a choice that mentions details from the stimulus but mangles or misstates what the author says or implies about those details

- **180**—a choice that directly contradicts what the correct answer must say (for example, a choice that strengthens the argument in a Weaken question)

- **Faulty Use of Detail**—a choice that accurately states something from the stimulus but in a manner that answers the question incorrectly; this type is rarely used in Logical Reasoning but is more common in Reading Comprehension

---

The bottom line is that every wrong answer is wrong because it does not answer the question posed by the question stem. As you continue to study, practice, and review, make a point of explaining in your own words why each wrong answer is incorrect.

LSAT STRATEGY

Some wrong answers apply to specific question types. In Assumption and Main Point questions, for example, it is common to see wrong answers that simply repeat the author's evidence. You'll see more question-specific wrong answers as you move through the following chapters and learn why they are incorrect on the exam.

Chapter Perform Quiz

Perform   This Perform quiz is an unusual one. In Parts II, III, and IV, where you'll focus on mastering individual question types, the Perform quizzes at the end of each chapter will contain full LSAT questions. In this chapter, however, your focus should be on familiarity with the Logical Reasoning Method, and not yet on getting questions right or wrong. Thus, here you have an old-fashioned fill-in-the-blank quiz covering the steps of the Method and the common wrong answer types. Do your best. When you're finished, check your answers against the answer key. Review the Logical Reasoning Method before EVERY Logical Reasoning prep session until it is second nature and you are using it without even thinking about it.

Fill in the following blanks listing the steps and strategies associated with the Logical Reasoning Method.

Kaplan Logical Reasoning Method

Step 1: _____

What is the purpose of Step 1?

_____

Step 2: _____

What is the purpose of Step 2?

_____

Step 3: _____

What is the purpose of Step 3?

_____

Step 4: _____

What is the purpose of Step 4?

_____

Fill in the blanks listing the six common Logical Reasoning wrong answer traps, along with a brief description of each one.

Logical Reasoning Common Wrong Answer Traps

Wrong Answer Trap: _____

Description: _____

Wrong Answer Trap: _____

Description: _____

Wrong Answer Trap: _____

Description: _____

Wrong Answer Trap: _____

Description: _____

Wrong Answer Trap: _____

Description: _____

Wrong Answer Trap: _____

Description: _____

Perform—Answer Key
Kaplan Logical Reasoning Method

Step 1: *Identify the Question Type*

What is the purpose of Step 1?

> *By starting here, you know what to look for in the stimulus.*

Step 2: *Untangle the Stimulus*

What is the purpose of Step 2?

> *Zero in on what is relevant based on the question type.*

Step 3: *Predict the Correct Answer*

What is the purpose of Step 3?

> *A prediction allows you to stay focused on what to look for in the answer choices and will keep you from being tempted by wrong answers.*

Step 4: *Evaluate the Answer Choices*

What is the purpose of Step 4?

> *Identify the answer that matches your prediction. Eliminate those that do not. Do not try to gauge which answer is better than another. There is only one right answer.*

Logical Reasoning Common Wrong Answer Traps

Wrong Answer Trap: _**Outside the Scope**_

Description: *An answer that is beyond the purview of the stimulus, making it irrelevant to the question stem.*

Wrong Answer Trap: _**Irrelevant Comparison**_

Description: *A choice that compares two things in a way not relevant to the question stem.*

Wrong Answer Trap: _**Extreme**_

Description: *A choice that contains language too strong to be supported by the stimulus.*

Wrong Answer Trap: _**Distortion**_

Description: *An answer that mentions details from the stimulus but alters or misstates the relationship about those details.*

Wrong Answer Trap: _**180**_

Description: *A choice that directly contradicts what the correct answer should say.*

Wrong Answer Trap: _**Faulty Use of Detail**_

Description: *An answer that accurately states something from the stimulus, but in a manner that does not accurately answer the question stem.*

CHAPTER 2

Formal Logic Basics

Frequently on the LSAT, the premises from which you are able to make deductions can be written in conditional statements. These statements always have two parts—a sufficient term and a necessary result or requirement—and can always be translated into an "If-then" format. Once you've mastered that skill, some Logical Reasoning questions that seemed challenging and abstract will become much clearer. Conditional statements may appear in a Reading Comprehension passage (if they do, take note), but are far and away most important in Logical Reasoning.

For decades, test takers beginning their LSAT preparation would associate formal logic with the recently retired Analytical Reasoning (or Logic Games) section of the LSAT, but the truth is, formal logic was traditionally tested on more Logical Reasoning than Logic Games questions. The work you do in this chapter, and in the Formal Logic Workshops that appear in later parts of this book, will benefit you on Inference, Assumption, Flaw, Strengthen/Weaken, Parallel Reasoning, and Parallel Flaw questions.

LSAT STRATEGY

Although Formal Logic appears in a minority of LSAT questions, its importance is heightened by two considerations:

1. Most test takers have not refined the skill of understanding Formal Logic prior to preparing for the LSAT. Familiarity with Formal Logic will give you a competitive advantage.

2. Expertise in understanding and applying Formal Logic makes the correct answer to many LSAT questions unequivocal. There is little room for doubt or error if you have analyzed a question's conditional statements correctly.

Conditional Statements

LEARNING OBJECTIVE

In this section, you'll learn to:

- Identify what is and is not a conditional statement (that is, understand what it means for a statement to be a conditional statement).

Before you can work with conditional statements to make valid deductions and inferences (and answer LSAT questions), you must be able to identify such statements.

LSAT STRATEGY

Every conditional statement has two parts:

1. A sufficient term, also called the "trigger" or "if" term.

2. A necessary term, also called the "result/requirement" or "then" term.

Consider this conditional statement:

> If you are in the Empire State Building, then you are in New York City.

Knowing that you are in the Empire State Building is *sufficient* to establish that you are in New York City. That is because being in New York City is *necessary* for you to be in the Empire State Building. In this book, you'll get used to seeing that written in shorthand like this:

If in ESB → in NYC

But be careful, this statement is not correct:

~~If in NYC → in ESB~~

Knowing that you are in New York City is not sufficient to know that you are in the Empire State Building, and being in the Empire State Building is not necessary for you to be in New York City (after all, you might be in Grand Central Station or the Metropolitan Museum of Art, right?). You can't just flip conditional statements around.

There are a lot of sentences in English that can be used to communicate this relationship of sufficient and necessary terms. Each of the following is equivalent to the statement above.

> If you are not in New York City, then you cannot be in the Empire State Building. (This is called the *contrapositive* of the original statement, by the way.)

> Anybody in the Empire State Building is in New York City.

> You can't be in the Empire State Building unless you're in New York City.

> You're in the Empire State Building only if you're in New York City.

Learn to spot conditional statements whenever they appear in Logical Reasoning questions.

Take a look at how an LSAT expert identifies conditional statements that are expressed in ways other than the If-then sentence structure.

Statement/Premise	Analysis: Is this a conditional statement?
The State of Ohio requires a boat license for all kayaks that are used recreationally on the water.	Yes. Because a boat license is a *requirement* for all kayaks used recreationally on the water, it's a necessary condition.
Whenever Tom goes to the movie theater, he also eats popcorn.	Yes. The word *whenever* indicates that Tom will eat popcorn every time he goes to the movie theater. Going to the movie theater is the trigger, or the sufficient condition.
Emma likes visiting her grandma on the way home from work.	No. This is just a description of something an individual enjoys.
All of the students on this bus are either members of the school band or of the cheerleading squad.	Yes. Because this concerns *all* of the students on the bus, we know that each student on the bus must be either a member of the band or of the cheerleading squad.

Practice   In the following exercise, read each statement and decide whether it expresses a conditional relationship. If it does, identify which term is sufficient and which is necessary. When you're finished, compare your work to that of an LSAT expert on the next page.

Statement/Premise	My Analysis
1. Every dog in this animal shelter is a Golden Retriever.	
2. The gardener should consider planting another tree on the estate.	
3. It is impossible to complete this course unless you submit a final term paper.	
4. Paul is going to play the video game only if he can finish doing his laundry as well.	
5. To learn to play the piano, you need to practice your scales and arpeggios.	
6. Sometimes I want to walk in the park.	
7. Only employees of the company are allowed to enter the raffle.	
8. I can attend your birthday dinner only if my plane arrives on schedule.	

Expert Analysis for the Practice exercise may be found on the following page. ▶ ▶ ▶

Expert Analysis

Here's how an LSAT expert analyzed those statements.

	Statement/Premise	Analysis
1.	Every dog in this animal shelter is a Golden Retriever.	Yes. This could be written: If a dog is in this animal shelter, then it is a Golden Retriever. A dog being in this animal shelter is *sufficient* to establish that it is a Golden Retriever. It is *necessary* that a dog is a Golden Retriever for it to be in this animal shelter.
2.	The gardener should consider planting another tree on the estate.	No. This is a recommendation. The gardener has no obligation to plant another tree on the estate.
3.	It is impossible to complete this course unless you submit a final term paper.	Yes. This could be written: If the course is completed, then you have submitted a final term paper. The completion of the course is *sufficient* to know that you submitted a final term paper, and submitting a final term paper is *necessary* for you to complete the course.
4.	Paul is going to play the video game only if he can finish doing his laundry as well.	Yes. This could be written: If Paul plays the video game, then he will finish his laundry. Paul's playing the video game is *sufficient* to establish he finished his laundry, and Paul's finishing his laundry is *necessary* for him to play the video game.
5.	To learn to play the piano, you need to practice your scales and arpeggios.	Yes. This could be written: If you are to learn to play the piano, then you must practice your scales and arpeggios. According to this statement, one's learning to play the piano is *sufficient* to establish that they practice their scales and arpeggios, and one's practicing their scales and arpeggios is *necessary* to their ability to learn to play the piano.
6.	Sometimes I want to walk in the park.	No. This is an assertion of fact. There is neither a sufficient nor a necessary term in this statement.
7.	Only employees of the company are allowed to enter the raffle.	Yes. This could be written: If a person has entered the raffle, then they are a company employee. A person's entry into the raffle is *sufficient* to know they are an employee of the company, and the person's employment at the company is *necessary* for their entering the raffle.
8.	I can attend your birthday dinner only if my plane arrives on schedule.	Yes. This could be written: If I attend your birthday dinner, then my plane arrived on schedule. Knowing I can attend the birthday dinner is *sufficient* to know that my plane arrived on schedule. My plane's timely arrival is *necessary* for me to be able to attend your birthday dinner.

Understand Conditional Statements with *And* or *Or*

LEARNING OBJECTIVE

In this section, you'll learn to:

- Accurately interpret conditional statements that include *and* or *or* (i.e., conditional statements with two or more terms in either their sufficient or necessary clauses).

Some conditional statements have more than one term in either their sufficient or necessary clauses, with those terms connected by the words *and* or *or*. The two terms have quite different effects in conditional statements.

LSAT STRATEGY

In Formal Logic:

- *And* means both terms are needed for a sufficient condition to trigger a result or for a necessary condition to be fulfilled.

- *Or* means that at least one of the terms (the first or the second or both) is needed for a sufficient condition to trigger a result or for a necessary condition to be fulfilled.

Note how an LSAT expert analyzes conditional statements containing *and* or *or*.

Statement/Premise	Analysis
If Ariana and Junji join the circus, then Harry will also join.	Having both Ariana and Junji join the circus guarantees that Harry will join the circus, too. Having either Ariana or Junji join without the other does not guarantee that Harry will join, nor does it prevent him from joining.
If strawberries are in season, then so are blueberries and raspberries.	When strawberries are in season guarantees that both blueberries and raspberries are in season as well.
If Alex places first, second, or third in the marathon, then Juanita will be rewarded with a donation to her charity.	If Alex finishes in any of the top three positions in the marathon, then Juanita's charity will get a donation. (If Alex finishes lower than third, the charity *could* still get a donation.)
If the humane society does not have any rabbits for adoption, then it will have either kittens or puppies.	If the humane society does not have any rabbits for adoption, then it is guaranteed to have kittens or puppies available for adoption. (Note 1: If the humane society does not have rabbits for adoption, it could have both kittens *and* puppies available. Note 2: If the humane society *has* rabbits available, then nothing is known about whether there are also kittens or puppies available. The trigger here is *not having* rabbits for adoption.)

| Practice | Sharpen your understanding of conditional statements with *and* or *or* by analyzing the following conditional statements and answer three questions about each one. Remember that sometimes the correct answer is that nothing additional can be deduced. When you're finished, compare your work with that of an LSAT expert in the analysis on the pages following this exercise. |

Statement/Premise	My Analysis

If Paula or Briana passes the bar in February, then Diana will take the LSAT in July.

9. What do you know if we are told that Paula passes the bar in July?

10. What do you know if we are told that both Paula and Briana passed the bar in February?

11. What do you know if we are told that Diana took the LSAT in July?

If the store has bagels, then it has scones and croissants.

12. What do you know if the store has scones and croissants?

13. What do you know if the store doesn't have bagels?

14. What do you know if the store doesn't have scones?

Statement/Premise	My Analysis
When the CEO and CFO of the company cannot attend the board meeting, the COO sits in on their behalf.	

15. What can you deduce if we only know that the COO is in attendance?

16. What do you know if the COO is not in attendance?

17. What do you know if the CEO is not in attendance?

If one is happy, then one also feels more in control and interested in social activities.	

18. What do you know if one feels more in control or interested in social activities?

19. What do you know if one is happy?

20. What do you know if someone is feeling more energetic?

Expert Analysis

Here are an LSAT expert's answers to each of the questions in that exercise.

Statement/Premise	Analysis
If Paula or Briana passes the bar in February, then Diana will take the LSAT in July.	
9. What do you know if we are told that Paula passes the bar in July?	Nothing additional. Paula passing the bar in July triggers nothing.
10. What do you know if we are told that both Paula and Briana passed the bar in February?	Diana must take the LSAT in July.
11. What do you know if we are told that Diana took the LSAT in July?	Nothing additional. Though it's possible that Paula or Briana (or both) passed the bar, you do not know for sure.
If the store has bagels, then it has scones and croissants.	
12. What do you know if the store has scones and croissants?	Nothing additional. It might or might not also have bagels.
13. What do you know if the store doesn't have bagels?	Nothing additional. The store could still have scones or croissants (or both).
14. What do you know if the store doesn't have scones?	If the store does not have scones, then there's no way it could also have bagels, since bagels trigger scones being in the store.
When the CEO and CFO of the company cannot attend the board meeting, the COO sits in on their behalf.	
15. What can you deduce if we only know that the COO is in attendance?	Nothing additional. It is possible for the CEO or the CFO (or both) to be present or not present.
16. What do you know if the COO is not in attendance?	The CEO and the CFO are both present.
17. What do you know if the CEO is not in attendance?	Nothing additional. The absence of one is not sufficient to trigger the COO's attendance. It is possible the COO is present (or not present).
If one is happy, then one also feels more in control and interested in social activities.	
18. What do you know if one feels more in control or interested in social activities?	Nothing additional.
19. What do you know if one is happy?	One must also feel more in control or interested in social activities.
20. What do you know if someone is feeling more energetic?	Nothing additional. Feeling more energetic is outside the scope of this statement.

Great work so far with conditional statements. In the next section of this chapter, you'll learn to turn any conditional statement, regardless of how it is phrased in regular English, into an *If-then* shorthand that will be handy on several different Logical Reasoning question types.

Translate Conditional Statements into If-then Format

Prepare   It's helpful at this point to develop a simple system of notation for conditional statements. Having a uniform way of jotting down If-then statements on your scratch paper will make them easier to compare and combine during the test.

LEARNING OBJECTIVE

In this section, you'll learn to:

- Translate a sentence that expresses a conditional relationship into If-then format.

First, review a few examples of how an LSAT expert takes several conditional statements and turns them into If-then statements. Note the expert's use of a tilde (~) to represent "NOT" or negation of a term.

Statement/Premise	Analysis
If the shoes don't fit, I'll return them.	If don't fit → return
Jens can graduate if he gets an A in both Physics and Biology.	If As in Physics AND Biology → can graduate
All the Halloween candy will be eaten by the children.	If Halloween candy → eaten by children
No one gets a coupon unless they sign up for our newsletter.	If get coupon → sign up for newsletter
You can park in any spot only if it's not reserved for senior staff.	If parking in a spot → ~reserved for senior staff
Only completed forms will be processed by the Admissions Committee.	If processed → completed
Only classic rock or disco are played by this radio station.	If played → classic rock OR disco

Every test taker develops their own little variations on these shorthand notes. The important thing is that, by test day, your approach is quick, accurate, and consistent.

Formal Logic Shorthand Explained

If you found the expert's notes on the previous page to be more or less self-evident, you may choose to skim this section, but if formal logic gives you pause, take a little time to read it in some detail. Becoming confident and efficient with the interpretation of conditional statements and the relationship between sufficiency and necessity will be well worth the time you spend here.

Whenever you see a conditional statement on the LSAT, translate it into something that looks like this:

> If Trigger (sufficient) → Result (necessary)

Write the sufficient term on the left, the necessary term on the right, and an arrow in the middle pointing from left to right (to indicate which direction the logical trigger-and-result relationship flows). If the statement includes a negative (not or no), there are a couple of ways to handle this. Some people write out the word *not*, others use a tilde symbol to mean not, and still others strike through a negated term. So, you might write the statement "If A then not B," in shorthand in any of these ways:

> If A → NOT B
>
> If A → ~B
>
> If A → B̶

Symbolize negated terms however you like, but be consistent about it and make sure the entire term is legible. Kaplan materials tend to use the word NOT or the tilde depending on the statement and its context. Just remember that both indicate that the statement negates the term.

Armed with that simple notation, you're ready to learn how to distill conditional relationships from sometimes complicated prose into clear, brief shorthand notes. You've already learned that conditional statements can be phrased in lots of different ways; you'll see that some of those are more common than others on the LSAT, but they all appear from time to time. This section will give a library of ways that the testmaker phrases conditional statements so that you can quickly and easily translate them into If-then form.

Think of If-then statements as generalizations (or rules) that do not admit any exceptions. In the example we started with, every single time anybody is in the Empire State Building, that person has to be in New York City. The test could express this "rule" in a number of ways:

> All people in the Empire State Building are in New York City.
>
> Everyone who is in the Empire State Building is in New York City.
>
> Whenever someone is in the Empire State Building, that person is in New York City
>
> A person is in New York City every time that person is in the Empire State Building.

Sufficiency

In these sentences, the word that tells you that you're looking at a generalization (all, any, every, etc.) also serves to denote the sufficient term.

Here is a short catalog of words signaling a statement's sufficient clause:

LSAT STRATEGY

Words that denote that one thing is sufficient for another to happen:

- All
- Any (any time, any place, anybody, etc.)
- Every (every time, everybody, etc.)
- Whenever
- Each

Negatives

The same is true for the opposites of those words: Words such as *none*, *no one*, or *never* also signal a generalization without exceptions—that is, they also signal a sufficient-and-necessary relationship. These deserve special discussion, however, because sentences containing these negative words frequently employ a word order that can be confusing if you aren't familiar with how to parse it. Consider an example:

No one who is in the Empire State Building is in Europe.

It may be tempting, if you just glance at the word order, to start your If/Then translation with "If not in the Empire State Building . . ." But think about the statement's subject: The sentence isn't about people who are not in the Empire State Building. Rather, it's about people who are in the Empire State Building, and it's saying that those people are not in Europe.

If in ESB → NOT in Europe

Be very careful about the way sentences are worded. A good practice is to always ask yourself: Who or what is this sentence about? That will help point you to the sufficient term.

LSAT STRATEGY

Negative words that indicate a sufficient-necessary relationship include:

- None
- Never
- Not
- No one

Only

Just as there are words and phrases that signal a sufficient term, there are words and phrases that signal conditional relationships by denoting the necessary term, and a common one on the LSAT is the word *only*. To return to our original example:

Only people in New York City are in the Empire State Building.

Whom is this sentence about? It's about people in New York City. Thus, "[o]nly" signals the necessary term. You can translate *only* to *then* (or, in the shorthand used here, into the arrow symbol):

If in ESB → in NYC

Consider a similar example:

A person can be in the Empire State Building only if that person is in New York City.

Who is the subject of this sentence? The sentence is about a person who is in the Empire State Building. Don't let the word "if" throw you off there; when "if" follows "only" to make "only if," it always signals a necessary term:

If in ESB → in NYC

Treat this as another rule to memorize: *only if = only = then.*

There is one use of the word only, however, that produces a different interpretation. When *only* is preceded by a definite article, the ensuing phrase—*the only*—signals the sufficient term in a conditional relationship:

The only people who are in the Empire State Building are people who are in New York City.

Again, whom is this sentence about? People in the Empire State Building, so that's the sufficient term, and the translation should now look familiar:

If in ESB → in NYC

Note: The meaning of the statement remains the same throughout all three examples. (Of course it does, as it is a statement we know to be true from real life in this case.) The part of the conditional logic signaled by the word *only*, however, was different: *only* (by itself) and *only if* indicate necessity, whereas *the only* indicates sufficiency. While the sufficient term doesn't always appear first in the plain-language English sentence, it is always first in the Formal Logic "translation": If sufficient → necessary.

LSAT STRATEGY

The word *only* in formal logic

- *Only* signals the necessary term.
- *Only if* signals the necessary term.
- *The only* signals the sufficient term.

Unless/Without

Take a look at another way of expressing the same sufficient-necessary relationship we've been illustrating throughout this section:

No one is in the Empire State Building unless that person is in New York City.

Once again, this translates to our familiar If-then statement:

If in ESB → in NYC

This one needs some unpacking, but closer examination will show you that it conforms to the way you use *unless* all the time in day-to-day conversation. *Unless* signals a requirement—that is, it signals the necessary term—so you can think, "*unless = then*." But notice what *unless* does to the phraseology in the sufficient clause: it is now negated as *no one*. The original statement—If a person is in the Empire State Building, then that person is in New York City—didn't have a *no* in it. Do you see why? The word *unless* indicates the absence of the necessary condition, and if the necessary condition is absent, the sufficient condition has to be absent as well. That means that to fit the sufficient condition into a sentence containing *unless*, you must negate the sufficient term.

If this seems tricky, just put it into an easily understandable real-life situation. Most people don't want to eat dry cereal without milk. You may feel differently, but indulge their preferences for a moment. For those who don't care for dry cereal, "I will *not* eat cereal *unless* I have milk" is an easy rule to articulate. Now, just think through what that means in formal logic terms. Because the person won't eat cereal unless it has milk, "milk" is necessary for the person to eat cereal. Thus, the rule could just as easily be expressed in If-then terms:

If I eat cereal → I have milk

What does a sentence containing *unless* mean if the sufficient term is not negated? Again, apply a real-world example and work it out. Imagine you hear a friend say, "I will go to the mall unless it rains." (Notice that this time, the term at the beginning of the sentence is positive— "I *will* go to the mall"—as opposed to the "I will *not* eat cereal" in the example above.) Treat the statement as a rule: your friend means "I will go to the mall in every case except one: rain." So, your friend's rule translates as "If I do not go to the mall, then it is raining."

As the following Strategy Box illustrates, you can translate any Formal Logic statement with *unless* by negating the sufficient statement and substituting *then* for the word *unless*. Note: The word *without* functions exactly the same way as *unless* in conditional formal logic statements. For example, "I will not eat cereal without having milk" has the same meaning as "I will not eat cereal unless I have milk."

LSAT STRATEGY

Translate the word *unless* in formal logic as follows:

- "No X unless Y" translates to "If X then Y."
- "A unless B" translates to "If not A then B."

If, But Only If

One other conditional formal logic structure you'll occasionally see on the LSAT is *if, but only if* (or *if, and only if*, which means the same thing). Here's an example:

Piper goes to the beach if, but only if, Kinsley goes to the beach.

This means that Piper's going to the beach is both sufficient and necessary for Kinsley's going. (Note: The term "Kinsley goes to the beach" is preceded in the sentence by "if" [sufficient] and by "only if" [necessary].) It can be broken down into two statements:

If Piper goes to the beach → Kinsley goes to the beach

If Kinsley goes to the beach → Piper goes to the beach

Ultimately, the impact is this: Either they both go or neither of them does. That's what an Inference question containing an *if, but only if* sentence will reward you for understanding.

LSAT STRATEGY

The phrases "if, but only if" and "if, and only if" indicate a biconditional relationship. Each term in the relationship is both sufficient AND necessary for the other term. "X if, and only if Y" can be written:

If X → Y

If Y → X

or, alternatively

X ↔ Y

Formal Logic Statement Translation Chart

Here's a quick reference for all of the various conditional statement sentence structures you might encounter on the LSAT.

Formal Logic Statement		Analysis		
If A, then B	$\longrightarrow$	If A	$\longrightarrow$	B
All C are D	$\longrightarrow$	If C	$\longrightarrow$	D
Every E is F	$\longrightarrow$	If E	$\longrightarrow$	F
If G, then not H	$\longrightarrow$	If G	$\longrightarrow$	~H
No I are J	$\longrightarrow$	If I	$\longrightarrow$	~J
Only K are L	$\longrightarrow$	If L	$\longrightarrow$	K
M only if N	$\longrightarrow$	If M	$\longrightarrow$	N
The only O are P	$\longrightarrow$	If O	$\longrightarrow$	P
No Q unless R	$\longrightarrow$	If Q	$\longrightarrow$	R
S unless T	$\longrightarrow$	If ~S	$\longrightarrow$	T
No U without V	$\longrightarrow$	If U	$\longrightarrow$	V
Without W, no X	$\longrightarrow$	If X	$\longrightarrow$	W
Y if, but only if, Z	$\longrightarrow$	If Y If Z	$\longrightarrow$ $\longrightarrow$	Z Y
AA if, and only if, BB	$\longrightarrow$	If AA If BB	$\longrightarrow$ $\longrightarrow$	BB AA
If CC, then neither DD nor EE	$\longrightarrow$	If CC	$\longrightarrow$	~DD AND ~EE
FF if GG	$\longrightarrow$	If GG	$\longrightarrow$	FF
HH is always II	$\longrightarrow$	If HH	$\longrightarrow$	II

It's okay if your shorthand is different from what is shown here, but it must be consistent and accurate to ensure your success on the test.

Now, try your hand at translating conditional formal logic statements from plain English into If-then shorthand in the Practice exercises that follow.

Practice Accurate, efficient formal logic translation takes practice, and a lot of it. Here, you'll have two Practice sets to try out. After the first one, review your work with the expert analysis that follows. You may decide to proceed directly to Practice Set 2, or to review the preceding section on formal logic terms before trying that one.

Practice Set 1

Translate each of the following statements, each of which expresses a sufficient-and-necessary relationship, into simple If-then shorthand.

Statement/Premise	My Analysis
21. The novels Mina writes are always so sad.	
22. Aimee goes jogging only when the weather is beautiful.	
23. I'll order appetizers if no one objects.	
24. No one on the consulting panel objected to the new proposal.	
25. Every time I want to garden it rains.	
26. The only way to meet the performer after the concert is with a VIP ticket.	
27. Xavier won't play in the sandbox unless Amrita and Mitchell play with him.	
28. Italo will drive to Helsinki if, and only if, the train is not running.	
29. Whenever Tatiana goes sailing, she always brings lunch and a lifejacket.	
30. Unless I'm mistaken, this cheese is definitely Red Leicester.	

Expert Analysis for the Practice exercise may be found on the following page. ▶ ▶ ▶

LOGICAL REASONING FOUNDATIONS

Expert Analysis

Here's how an LSAT expert translated each of those statements into If-then shorthand.

Statement/Premise	Analysis
21. The novels Mina writes are always quite sad.	If novel by Mina → sad
22. Aimee goes jogging only when the weather is beautiful.	If Aimee jogging → weather beautiful
23. I'll order appetizers if no one objects.	If NO objections → order appetizers
24. No one on the consulting panel objected to the new proposal.	If on consulting panel → did NOT object
25. Every time I want to garden it rains.	If want to garden → rains
26. The only way to meet the performer after the concert is with a VIP ticket.	If meet performer → VIP ticket
27. Xavier won't play in the sandbox unless Amrita and Mitchell play with him.	If Xavier sandbox → Amrita AND Mitchell sandbox
28. Italo will drive to Helsinki if, and only if, the train is not running.	If drive to Helsinki → ~train running If ~train running → drive to Helsinki
29. Whenever Tatiana goes sailing, she always brings lunch and a lifejacket.	If Tatiana sailing → brings lunch and lifejacket
30. Unless I'm mistaken, this cheese is definitely Red Leicester.	If I'm NOT mistaken → Red Leicester or If NOT Red Leicester → I'm mistaken

Good job! Now, assess whether you are ready for more formal logic translation practice, or whether you'd prefer to review the notes and examples in the preceding section before moving on to Practice Set 2.

Practice Set 2

Translate each of the following statements, each of which expresses a sufficient-and-necessary relationship, into simple If-then shorthand.

Statement/Premise	My Analysis
31. Charles refuses to study without good lighting.	
32. Sandra will not be on time unless she gets up by 7 am.	
33. All fans attending the concert must purchase a ticket for entry.	
34. Any student that practices Formal Logic translation is building a key skill on the LSAT.	
35. All instances of rain were preceded by either lightning or thunder.	
36. If the meteorologist is not wrong, it will rain tomorrow.	
37. The school will be able to buy new equipment only if it can raise enough money from donations.	
38. Every toy purchased from the website was handmade.	
39. Only when the garments fitted correctly and were sewn accurately was the tailor satisfied.	
40. No meal is complete unless it has proteins or carbohydrates.	

Expert Analysis

Here's how an LSAT expert translated each of those statements into If-then shorthand.

Statement/Premise	Analysis
31. Charles refuses to study without good lighting.	If Charles study → good lighting or If NOT good lighting → Charles NOT study
32. Sandra will not be on time unless she gets up by 7 am.	If Sandra on time → gets up by 7 am or If NOT up by 7 am → Sandra NOT on time
33. All fans attending the concert must purchase a ticket for entry.	If fan attending concert → purchase ticket
34. Any student that practices Formal Logic translation is building a key skill on the LSAT.	If practices Formal Logic → building key LSAT skill
35. All instances of rain were preceded by either lightning or thunder.	If instance of rain → preceded by lightning or thunder
36. If the meteorologist is not wrong, it will rain tomorrow.	If NOT wrong → rain tomorrow
37. The school will be able to buy new equipment only if it can raise enough money from donations.	If buy new equipment → raise enough money
38. Every toy purchased from the website was handmade.	If toy purchased from website → handmade
39. Only when the garments fitted correctly and were sewn accurately was the tailor satisfied.	If tailor satisfied → garments fitted correctly and sewn accurately
40. No meal is complete unless it has proteins or carbohydrates.	If meal is complete → proteins OR carbohydrates

Congratulations! Completing these sets of formal logic translations marks a huge addition to your LSAT Logical Reasoning toolkit. It also sets you up for your next new skill: combining conditional statements to make valid deductions.

Make Valid Deductions from Conditional Statements

 **Prepare** Now that you understand conditional relationships and know how to spot them when you come across them in prose, you're ready to think about how to combine them to make deductions.

LEARNING OBJECTIVE

In this section, you'll learn to:

• Make deductions by combining conditional statements.

The idea is simple: You can combine conditional statements when the same term appears in more than one statement. Where the sufficient terms are the same, they can be combined like this:

If A, then B.

If A, then C.

Deduction: If A, then both B and C.

If the same term appears in the necessary parts of two conditional statements, you can combine them like this:

If T, then V.

If W, then V.

Deduction: If either T or W (or both), then V.

Finally, by far the most useful opportunity to combine conditional statements occurs when the same term appears in the necessary part of one conditional statement and in the sufficient part of another. In that case, those two statements allow you to deduce an altogether new idea:

If X, then Y.

If Y, then Z.

Deduction: If X, then Z.

(That pattern of three statements is called a syllogism, by the way. You certainly won't have to know that word on the LSAT, but the test will definitely reward your ability to accurately combine statements in this way.)

LSAT STRATEGY

Any time the necessary or "result" clause of one statement matches the sufficient (or "If") clause of another, the two statements can be combined. For example:

If N → ~P

If ~P → ~Q

Thus, **If N → ~P → ~Q**

Deduction: **If N → ~Q**

More than two premises with shared terms can produce multiple deductions:

If D, then E.

If E, then F.

If F, then G.

If G, then H.

Deductions:

If D, then E and F and G and H.

If E, then F and G and H.

If F, then G and H.

By the way, what can you deduce if you know that you have H? Answer: Not a thing. Remember, the necessary term of an If-then statement doesn't trigger any results.

Take a look at how an LSAT expert might draw deductions from a set of conditional statements:

Statements/Premises	Analysis
If Jyoti goes to the movies, she'll also go to the beach.	If movies → beach
If Jyoti goes to the beach, she won't go to the museum.	If beach → ~museum
If Jyoti goes to the beach, she'll go to the amusement park.	If beach → amusement park
If Jyoti goes to the amusement park, she will buy a funnel cake.	If amusement park → buy funnel cake
If you know Jyoti . . .	**then you can deduce that she . . .**
goes to the movies	— goes to the beach
	— does not go to the museum
	— goes to the amusement park
	— buys a funnel cake
goes to the beach	— does not go to the museum
	— goes to the amusement park
	— buys a funnel cake
	You do not know if Jyoti went to the movies.
doesn't go to the museum	No additional deductions
buys a funnel cake	No additional deductions

Practice Translate the given conditional statements and use them to create a chain of logic. Then, use the deductions in the chain to answer the questions. There are two Practice sets of statements and deductions to complete. After each, you may compare your work to that of an LSAT expert.

Practice Set 1

Statements/Premises	My Analysis
If Petra is the candidate for mayor, then Juan will run for city council.	
In the event that Juan runs for city council, Edward will also run.	
Edward will run for city council only if Gina runs for treasurer.	

Chain of Logic:

What do you know if...

41. Petra is the candidate for mayor?

What do you know if...

42. Juan is running for city council?

What do you know if...

43. Gina is running for treasurer?

Expert Analysis for the Practice exercise may be found on the following page. ▶ ▶ ▶

Expert Analysis

Here's how an LSAT expert translated the conditional statements, and then combined them to answer the questions in the exercise you just completed.

Statements/Premises	Analysis
If Petra is the candidate for mayor, then Juan will run for city council.	If P(M) → J(CC)
In the event that Juan runs for city council, Edward will also run.	If J(CC) → E(CC)
Edward will run for city council only if Gina runs for treasurer.	If E(CC) → G(T)
Chain of Logic:	If P(M) → J(CC) → E(CC) → G(T)
What do you know if... 41. Petra is the candidate for mayor?	If Petra is the candidate for mayor, then Juan and Edward run for city council and Gina will run for treasurer. If P(M) → J(CC) → E(CC) → G(T)
What do you know if... 42. Juan is running for city council?	If Juan is running for city council, then Edward is also running for city council and Gina is running for treasurer. If J(CC) → E(CC) → G(T)
What do you know if... 43. Gina is running for treasurer?	If Gina is selected, then it's not certain whether anyone else is running for any office. Gina running for treasurer does not trigger any other conditions.

Practice Set 2

Translate the given conditional statements and use them to create a chain of logic. Then, use the deductions in the chain to answer the questions. When you're finished, compare your work to that of an LSAT expert.

Statements/Premises	My Analysis
Franca will not plant basil in her herb garden unless she also plants sage.	
If Franca plants sage, she will also plant thyme and marjoram.	
Franca plants thyme only if she also plants dill.	
If Franca doesn't plant dill in her garden, then she won't plant cilantro.	

Chain of Logic:

What do you know if...

44. Franca plants sage?

What do you know if...

45. Franca plants thyme?

What do you know if...

46. Franca plants dill?

Expert Analysis

Here's how an LSAT expert translated the conditional statements, and then combined them to answer the questions in the exercise you just completed.

Statements/Premises	Analysis
Franca will not plant basil in her herb garden unless she also plants sage.	If B → S
If Franca plants sage, she will also plant thyme and marjoram.	If S → T AND M
Franca plants thyme only if she also plants dill.	If T → D
If Franca doesn't plant dill in her garden, then she won't plant cilantro.	If ~D → ~C
Chain of Logic:	↗D If B → S → T AND M
What do you know if. . . 44. Franca plants sage?	If Franca plants sage, she'll also plant thyme and marjoram. And if she plants thyme, she'll also plant dill. ↗D If S → T AND M
What do you know if. . . 45. Franca plants thyme?	If Franca plants thyme, she'll also plant dill. If T → D
What do you know if. . . 46. Franca plants dill?	Nothing else can be determined if all that is known is that Franca plants dill.

Whenever you encounter a Logical Reasoning stimulus that has multiple conditional statements, look for how the statements may combine to lead to additional deductions, and in Flaw, Parallel Flaw, and Weaken questions look for cases in which the author of the stimulus may have made a mistake when trying to combine the statements.

In the next section, you'll double the power of all the formal logic you've mastered so far by learning to form the contrapositive of a conditional statement.

Translate If-then Statements into Contrapositives

You've seen that, despite the many ways to express a conditional statement in prose, the logic underlying such statements is remarkably consistent. You're about to learn one more feature of these statements: the contrapositive. The contrapositive is simply another way to express any If/Then statement, but your ability to quickly and accurately form a statement's contrapositive is an incredibly important tool for you to have in your LSAT toolkit.

Prepare

LEARNING OBJECTIVE

In this section, you'll learn to:

- Translate a conditional statement into its contrapositive.

While a conditional statement and its contrapositive express exactly the same logical premise, forming contrapositives explicitly is valuable to the LSAT test taker because the contrapositive provides another logical trigger to work with. Here's what you need to know.

LSAT STRATEGY

To form the contrapositive:

- Reverse the sufficient and necessary terms.
- Negate each term.
- Change *and* to *or* and change *or* to *and* (whenever applicable).

Form the Contrapositive of an If-then statement

The contrapositive of a conditional statement is just another way of phrasing the sufficient/necessary relationship described in that statement. Take the following statement as an example:

> To board the ship, all travelers are required to present a valid passport.

> If board the ship → valid passport

Now, what happens if you do not present a valid passport? Well, then you can't board the ship.

> If NO valid passport → NOT board the ship

That's the contrapositive of the original statement. It simply spells what happens if the original statement's *necessary* clause is negated. And what happens if the necessary condition is negated, if it cannot happen? In that case, the sufficient condition cannot happen either. Every contrapositive is formed in exactly that way.

Form the Contrapositive of an If-then statement with *And* or *Or*

Now consider a conditional statement with two terms in the necessary condition:

> No artwork will be allowed in the competition unless the artist signs a certificate of originality, and an independent examiner verifies that artificial intelligence was not used in the artwork's creation.

Abbreviate that statement in Formal Logic shorthand:

> If artwork allowed → artist's certification AND independent verification

Now, what happens if *either one* of the two necessary conditions is not met?

> If NO artist's certification → artwork NOT allowed

> If NO independent verification → artwork NOT allowed

Thus, to form the contrapositive of the first statement, the *and* in the necessary condition must become *or* in the sufficient condition of the contrapositive:

> If NO artist's certification OR NO independent verification → artwork NOT allowed

Here is a chart of the most common Formal Logic statements and their contrapositives.

Formal Logic Statements		Analysis
All A are B	→	If A → B If ~B → ~A
No C are D	→	If C → ~D If D → ~C
E unless F	→	If ~E → F If ~F → E
If G then neither H nor I	→	If G → ~H AND ~I If H OR I → ~G
If J or K, then no L	→	If J OR K → ~L If L → ~J AND ~K

Why Getting the Contrapositive Right Is So Important

So, why is getting this peculiar formal logic skill right such a big deal? Put plainly, it is because a lot of LSAT questions reward the correct understanding of sufficiency and necessity, while others reward you for catching mistakes authors and speakers are making with sufficiency and necessity. Getting a contrapositive wrong means confusing necessity for sufficiency or vice versa, and a lot of LSAT points hinge on your ability to avoid that confusion.

So, one more time: To correctly form the contrapositive of an If-then statement, you must reverse *and* negate its terms. Take a real-life example:

> If this fan is running, then it is plugged in.

Here's the contrapositive:

> If this fan is NOT plugged in, then this fan is NOT running.

Being plugged in is necessary for this fan to run. Seeing that the fan is running is sufficient for you to know that it is plugged in.

What happens if you negate *without* reversing?

> If the fan is NOT running, then it is NOT plugged in.

Is that right? Not necessarily. The fan may be broken or just switched off. The fan's running is sufficient to know that it is plugged in, but it is not necessary for the fan to run for it to be plugged in. How about reversing without negating, is that bad, too? Yes, indeed.

> If the fan is plugged in, then the fan is running.

Again, with a real-world example, the mistake is easy to catch. Being plugged in is necessary, not sufficient, for the fan to run.

Really absorb the rule that you can never negate without reversing or reverse without negating. It's not too hard when you have a real-life example but it's easy to forget when you're in the heat of an Inference or Parallel Flaw question with a fictional scenario throwing around made-up names or plowing through an Assumption question with unfamiliar scientific terms. Wrap your head around this principle now so it doesn't trip you up later.

We said earlier that a conditional statement and its contrapositive express exactly the same relationship between sufficiency and necessity. As proof, notice that the contrapositive can be contraposed right back into the original statement:

> If you are not in New York City, then you are not in the Empire State Building.

Reverse and negate that, and it is our very first conditional statement of the chapter:

> If you are in the Empire State Building, then you are in New York City.

Practice You'll have two Practice sets for this important skill. After you complete and review the first one, decide if you're ready for the second, or whether you'd benefit from going over the Prepare materials again first.

Practice Set 1

Translate each of the following statements into simple shorthand, and form the correct contrapositive of each. When you're finished, review your work with the expert analysis on the following page.

Statement/Premise	My Analysis
47. All our senior faculty must have advanced degrees.	
48. The hiring committee will interview any applicant who has submitted an application.	
49. Every ingredient in this stew is delicious!	
50. Darian will agree to go hiking if Sam and Joon go as well.	
51. Glenn will only perform Bach at concerts.	
52. No cryptocurrencies were officially sanctioned locally this year.	
53. Reema never takes the bus to work on Fridays.	
54. Ruthie will not go to the movies unless Ellie and Bruce go with her.	
55. The product will do well in sales if, and only if, it tastes good to the general public.	

Expert Analysis for the Practice exercise may be found on the following page. ▶ ▶ ▶

Expert Analysis

Here's how an LSAT expert translated those statements and formed their contrapositives.

Statement/Premise	Analysis
47. All our senior faculty must have advanced degrees.	If senior faculty → advanced degree If ~advanced degree → ~senior faculty
48. The hiring committee will interview any applicant who has submitted an application.	If application submitted → committee interview If ~committee interview → ~application submitted
49. Every ingredient in this stew is delicious!	If in stew → delicious If ~delicious → ~stew
50. Darian will agree to go hiking if Sam and Joon go as well.	If S hiking AND J hiking → D hiking If ~D hiking → ~S hiking OR ~J hiking
51. Glenn will only perform Bach at concerts.	If G → perform Bach If ~perform Bach → ~G
52. No cryptocurrencies were officially sanctioned locally this year.	If cryptocurrencies → ~officially sanctioned locally this year If officially sanctioned locally this year → ~cryptocurrencies
53. Reema never takes the bus to work on Fridays.	If R takes the bus to work → ~Friday If Friday → ~R takes the bus to work
54. Ruthie will not go to the movies unless Ellie and Bruce go with her.	If R movies → E movies AND B movies If E ~movies OR B ~movies → R ~movies

Statement/Premise	Analysis
55. The product will do well in sales if, and only if, it tastes good to the general public.	If prod does well in sales → tastes good to public ~tastes good to public → prod ~do well in sales If tastes good to public → prod do well in sales If prod ~do well in sales → ~tastes good to public

Practice Set 2

Translate each of the following statements into simple shorthand, and form the correct contrapositive of each. When you're finished, review your work with the expert analysis on the following page.

Statement/Premise	My Analysis
56. Every car purchased comes with a 10-year warranty.	
57. Whenever Jack plays golf, Fran goes swimming.	
58. The record will play only if the needle is on the vinyl.	
59. The only students who got internships submitted compelling applications.	
60. The phone is not with the charger.	
61. None of today's specials are gluten-free.	
62. Margaret does not go anywhere without her cat.	
63. The LSAT is a condition precedent to law school.	
64. If Senator Zee votes yes or Senator Minsk votes no, then Senator Raison will advance the bill.	

Expert Analysis for the Practice exercise may be found on the following page. ▶ ▶ ▶

Expert Analysis

Here's how an LSAT expert translated those statements and formed their contrapositives.

Statement/Premise	Analysis
56. Every car purchased comes with a 10-year warranty.	If car purchased → 10-year warranty If ~10-year warranty → ~car purchased
57. Whenever Jack plays golf, Fran goes swimming.	If J golf → F swimming If ~F swimming → ~J golf
58. The record will play only if the needle is on the vinyl.	If record play → needle on vinyl If ~needle on vinyl → ~record play
59. The only students who got internships submitted compelling applications.	If student got internship → submitted compelling application If ~submitted compelling application → ~student got internship
60. The phone is not with the charger.	If phone → ~with charger If with charger → ~phone
61. None of today's specials are gluten-free.	If today's special → ~gluten-free If gluten-free → ~today's special
62. Margaret does not go anywhere without her cat.	If Margaret → cat If ~cat → ~Margaret
63. The LSAT is a condition precedent to law school.	If law school → LSAT If ~LSAT → ~law school

Statement/Premise	Analysis
64. If Senator Zee votes yes or Senator Minsk votes no, then Senator Raison will advance the bill.	If Zee votes yes OR → Raison will advance Minsk votes no the bill If ~Raison advance → ~Zee votes yes AND the bill ~Minsk votes no

Fantastic! Learning to form correct contrapositives quickly and confidently is a major accomplishment in your LSAT prep. Now, build on that by learning to use the contrapositives of multiple statements to make additional deductions with formal logic.

Make Valid Deductions from the Contrapositive of a Conditional Statement

You've learned how to form the contrapositive of a conditional statement by reversing and negating the statement's terms. Now, it's time to put contrapositives to work making the kinds of deductions that turn into points when applied to LSAT questions.

Prepare

LEARNING OBJECTIVE

In this section, you'll learn to:

* Make valid deductions from the contrapositive of a conditional statement.

Single Statements with Contrapositives

Just by forming the contrapositive, you double the number of triggers from any conditional statement. Here's an example:

> On game days, Mrs. Peterson always wears a Bulldogs sweater.

Translate the statement into If-then format and form its contrapositive.

> If game day → Bulldogs sweater

> If No Bulldogs sweater → NOT game day

The statement now triggers a necessary result if you know that it is game day or that Mrs. Peterson isn't wearing a Bulldogs sweater. (Remember, though, this statement doesn't tell you anything about what Mrs. Peterson wears when it is not a game day, or what day it is when she does wear a Bulldogs sweater.)

Sometimes all you need to spot a correct or incorrect answer to a Logical Reasoning question is an accurate formulation of a conditional statement's contrapositive.

Combining Statements Through Their Contrapositives

Even more important is the role that a contrapositive may play in helping you combine statements to make further deductions. Consider this pair of conditional statements:

> No one with an office on the third floor is a trained accountant, but all members of the Finance team are trained accountants.

Translating each of them into If-then format produces:

> Statement 1: If 3rd-floor office → NOT trained accountant
>
> Statement 2: If Finance team → trained accountant

If that's where you stop, you could miss a key deduction, but if you form the contrapositives for both statements, it becomes apparent that you can combine the statements.

> Contrapositive 1: If trained accountant → NOT 3rd-floor office
>
> Contrapositive 2: If NOT trained accountant → NOT Finance team

Now, the necessary clause of Statement 1 matches the sufficient clause of Contrapositive 2, so:

> If 3rd-floor office → NOT trained accountant → NOT Finance team

And, likewise, with the necessary clause of Statement 2 and the sufficient clause of Contrapositive 1; thus:

> If Finance team → trained accountant → NOT 3rd-floor office

You may be able to see the connection between the statements without jotting down the If-then shorthand, but once you've mastered formal logic, translating statements and forming their contrapositives will only take you a few seconds. Seeing the statements in a standard format and being confident that you've made the available deductions can help you manage Logical Reasoning tasks in Inference and Sufficient Assumption questions far more efficiently and accurately.

On the next page, try an exercise in which you will apply what you've learned about contrapositives to an exercise you tried earlier.

Practice Set 1

Practice Review the statements and the logic chain from this deduction exercise you tried earlier. Then, form the contrapositive of each statement and of the logic chain and add them to the My Analysis column. Use them to answer the questions. When you're finished, check your work against that of an LSAT expert with the analysis on the next page.

Statements/Premises	My Analysis
If Petra is the candidate for mayor, then Juan will run for city council.	If P(M) → J(CC)
In the event that Juan runs for city council, Edward will also run.	If J(CC) → E(CC)
Edward will run for city council only if Gina runs for treasurer.	If E(CC) → G(T)
Chain of Logic:	If P(M) → J(CC) → E(CC) → G(T)

What do you know if...

65. Gina is not selected?

What do you know if...

66. Edward is not selected?

What do you know if...

67. Juan is not selected?

What do you know if...

68. Petra is not selected?

Expert Analysis for the Practice exercise may be found on the following page. ▶ ▶ ▶

Expert Analysis

Here's how an LSAT expert analyzed the previous statements and answered the associated questions.

Statements/Premises	Analysis
If Petra is the candidate for mayor, then Juan will run for city council.	If P(M) → J(CC) If ~J(CC) → ~P(M)
In the event that Juan runs for city council, Edward will also run.	If J(CC) → E(CC) If ~E(CC) → ~J(CC)
Edward will run for city council only if Gina runs for treasurer.	If E(CC) → G(T) If ~G(T) → ~E(CC)
Chain of Logic:	If P(M) → J(CC) → E(CC) → G(T) If ~G(T) → ~E(CC) → ~J(CC) → ~P(M)
What do you know if. . . 65. Gina does not run for treasurer?	If Gina does *not* run for treasurer, then neither Edward nor Juan runs for city council, and Petra is not a candidate for mayor. If ~G(T) → ~E(CC) → ~J(CC) → ~P(M)
What do you know if. . . 66. Edward does not run for city council?	If Edward does *not* run for city council, then neither does Juan, and Petra is not a candidate for mayor. You know nothing, however, about Gina's potential candidacy. If ~E(CC) → ~J(CC) → ~P(M)
What do you know if. . . 67. Juan does not run for city council?	If Juan does *not* run for city council, then Petra is not a candidate for mayor. You know nothing, however, about Edward's or Gina's potential candidacies. If ~J(CC) → ~P(M)
What do you know if. . . 68. Petra is not a candidate for mayor?	If Petra is *not* a mayoral candidate, you know nothing about the potential candidacies of any of the other people mentioned in the rules.

On the next page, try a similar practice exercise, but one with statements you have not yet seen.

Practice Set 2

Translate each of the following statements into If-then shorthand, form the contrapositives, determine any chains of logic, and use that to answer the questions below. When you're finished, check your translations and deductions against those of an LSAT expert with analysis on the following page.

Statements/Premises	My Analysis
If Daphne goes to the park, then she will not go shopping for groceries.	
Daphne will go grocery shopping only if she buys ice cream.	
Daphne will not buy ice cream unless she buys butterscotch sauce.	

Chain of Logic:

What do we know if...

69. Daphne does not purchase ice cream?

What do we know if...

70. Daphne does not go grocery shopping?

What do we know if...

71. Daphne does not buy butterscotch sauce?

What do we know if...

72. Daphne does not go to the park?

What do we know if...

73. Daphne goes grocery shopping?

Expert Analysis

Here's how an LSAT expert analyzed the previous statements and answered the associated questions.

Statements/Premises	Analysis
If Daphne goes to the park, then she will not go shopping for groceries.*	If park → ~groceries If groceries → ~park
Daphne will go grocery shopping only if she buys ice cream.	If groceries → ice cream If ~ice cream → ~groceries
Daphne will not buy ice cream unless she buys butterscotch sauce.	If ice cream → butterscotch sauce If ~butterscotch sauce → ~ice cream
Chain of Logic:	If groceries → ice cream → butterscotch sauce If ~butterscotch sauce → ~ice cream → ~groceries
What do we know if. . . 69. Daphne does not purchase ice cream?	She did not go grocery shopping.
What do we know if. . . 70. Daphne does not go grocery shopping?	Nothing additional.
What do we know if. . . 71. Daphne does not buy butterscotch sauce?	She did not buy ice cream, and she did not go grocery shopping.
What do we know if. . . 72. Daphne does not go to the park?	Nothing additional.
What do we know if. . . 73. Daphne goes grocery shopping?	She does not go to the park, she purchases ice cream, and she purchases butterscotch sauce.

*Note: The first statement does not link to any of the others; neither the necessary clause of the original statement nor the necessary clause of its contrapositive matches the sufficient clause of any other statement or contrapositive in this exercise. Sometimes, the LSAT rewards you for knowing that you cannot make any additional deductions from a given statement. Keep that in mind especially when you get to Inference questions in Part III of this book.

Good work so far. In the next section, you'll finish up your introduction to formal logic on the LSAT by making deductions from the contrapositives of conditional statements with more than one term in one of their clauses.

Make Valid Deductions from Conditional Statements Containing *And* and *Or*

Prepare

LEARNING OBJECTIVE

In this section, you'll learn to:

* Make valid deductions from conditional statements containing *and* and *or*.

Earlier in the chapter, you learned that when a conditional statement includes an AND or an OR in one of its conditions, you must swap *and* for *or* (and vice versa) when forming the contrapositive. Here's another example to refresh your memory.

Whenever his family has a karaoke night, Ty always sings either "We Are Family" or "A Song for Mama."

In If-then shorthand, that statement becomes:

If family karaoke → Ty sings WAF *OR* ASFM

To form the contrapositive, reverse and negate the terms and swap the *or* for *and*.

If Ty does NOT sing WAF *AND* does NOT sing ASFM → NOT family karaoke

Now, consider what you know in each of the following cases:

a. If it is a family karaoke night …

b. If it is not a family karaoke night …

c. If Ty sings "We Are Family" but does not sing "A Song for Mama" …

d. If Ty sings "A Song for Mama" but does not sing "We Are Family" …

e. If Ty sings both "We Are Family" and "A Song for Mama" …

f. If Ty sings neither "We Are Family" nor "A Song for Mama" …

Think over the implications of each trigger and then check your answers on the next page.

Here is the original statement and its contrapositive:

If family karaoke → Ty sings WAF *OR* ASFM

If Ty does NOT sing WAF *AND* does NOT sing ASFM → NOT family karaoke

How did you do in evaluating the various triggers?

a. If it is a family karaoke night ... then Ty sings either WAF or ASFM (maybe both)

b. If it is not a family karaoke night ... then you don't know what Ty sings (he might still sing WAF or ASFM).

c. If Ty sings "We Are Family" but does not sing "A Song for Mama" ... then you don't know whether it is family karaoke night or not (it could be).

d. If Ty sings "A Song for Mama" but does not sing "We Are Family" ... then you don't know whether it is family karaoke night or not (it could be).

e. If Ty sings both "We Are Family" and "A Song for Mama" ... then you don't know whether it is family karaoke night or not (it could be).

f. If Ty sings neither "We Are Family" nor "A Song for Mama" ... then it is *not* family karaoke night.

Here's a chart showing all of the common conditional statements with *and* or *or* along with their contrapositives. You can refer to it as you complete the Practice set for this chapter and any time during your LSAT preparation when you need a refresher or a hint on how to translate and analyze complex conditionals.

Formal Logic Statement					**Contrapositive**		
If A	→	B OR C	→	If ~B AND ~C	→	~A
If D	→	E AND F	→	If ~E OR ~F	→	~D
If G OR H	→	J	→	If ~J	→	~G AND ~H
If K AND L	→	M	→	If ~M	→	~K OR ~L
If N AND O	→	P AND R	→	If ~P OR ~R	→	~N OR ~O
If S OR T	→	U AND V	→	If ~U OR ~V	→	~S AND ~T
If W AND X	→	Y OR Z	→	If ~Y AND ~Z	→	~W OR ~X
If AA OR BB	→	CC OR DD	→	If ~CC AND ~DD	→	~AA AND ~BB

Now, try your hand at translating and forming the contrapositives of a few more conditional statements with *and* or *or* in this chapter's Practice sets.

Practice In this exercise, translate the conditional statements into If-then shorthand and form their correct contrapositive. Use your work to answer the questions beneath each of the statements.

Statement/Premise	My Analysis
The agriculture bill will not pass without the support of both Senator Bowman and Senator Martinez.	
74. If both Senator Bowman and Senator Martinez support the agriculture bill, will it pass?	
75. If Senator Bowman supports the agriculture bill, but Senator Martinez opposes it, will the bill pass?	
76. If the agriculture bill passes, what do you know?	

Statement/Premise	My Analysis
If the IT manager hires both a new developer and a new tester, then the IT manager will also hire a new architect.	
77. If the IT manager hires a new developer but does not hire a new tester, can she hire a new architect?	
78. If the IT manager does not hire a new architect, what do you know?	
79. If the IT manager hires a new architect, what do you know?	

Expert Analysis

Here's how an LSAT expert analyzed the statements and answered the questions.

Statement/Premise	Analysis
The agriculture bill will not pass without the support of both Senator Bowman and Senator Martinez.	If bill passes → Bowman supports AND Martinez supports If Bowman ~support OR Martinez ~support → bill ~pass
74. If both Senator Bowman and Senator Martinez support the agriculture bill, will it pass?	You don't know. Their mutual support is necessary, but not sufficient, to ensure passage.
75. If Senator Bowman supports the agriculture bill, but Senator Martinez opposes it, will the bill pass?	No. The support of both Senators is necessary to passage.
76. If the agriculture bill passes, what do you know?	Both Senators supported it. The support of both is necessary to passage.

Statement/Premise	Analysis
If the IT manager hires both a new developer and a new tester, then the IT manager will also hire a new architect.	If D hired AND T hired → A hired If A ~hired → D ~hired OR T ~hired
77. If the IT manager hires a new developer but does not hire a new tester, can she hire a new architect?	Yes. The manager must hire a new architect when BOTH a new developer and new tester are hired, but the manager may also hire a new architect without hiring the other positions.
78. If the IT manager does not hire a new architect, what do you know?	Either the IT manager did not hire a new developer OR the IT manager did not hire a new tester.
79. If the IT manager hires a new architect, what do you know?	Nothing additional. The IT manager might hire a new architect in any case; the IT manager is required to when they hire a new developer AND a new tester.

Great Moments in Formal Logic

By Kaplan LSAT Channel Faculty

 Watch the video lesson for this Spotlight in your online Study Plan.

Let's tell it like it is: Formal Logic is abstract. Indeed, that is its strength. The goal of Formal Logic is to provide a precise, systematic, almost mathematical way to analyze the inferences derived from formal rules and conditions. In its pure form, Formal Logic has no "real world" content at all; it's just "If A → B" and "If ~B → ~A." On the LSAT, however, you can apply Formal Logic to statements and rules written in natural language by reducing those statements to their formal content. A rule such as "If Aloysius is selected for the committee, then Benjamin is also selected for the committee," for example, can be reduced to the more manageable "If A → B."

That abstract expression of the rule is valuable on the LSAT because after you memorize a few rules about how inferences work, you know confidently that if Benjamin is *not selected* for the committee, then neither is Aloysius. Perhaps more importantly, based on that one statement alone, the fact that Benjamin is selected for the committee implies nothing about whether Aloysius is selected, and the fact that Aloysius is rejected implies nothing about whether Benjamin is selected. On many Logical Reasoning questions, the correct answer amounts to nothing more than

the correct application of basic Formal Logic rules, and one or more of the wrong answers contain flawed applications of those same rules.

Depending on your experience and comfort level with Formal Logic, it can take some time to embrace the power of its abstract appearance. As you learn and practice the basics of Formal Logic in the course of your LSAT preparation, however, you will realize that conditional statements and rules are everywhere in your day-to-day life. "No admittance without proper ID" is simply "If ~I → ~A," and "Only club members may vote in the election for next year's officers" amounts to "If V → M."

In this Spotlight's video, an LSAT expert will take you on a journey through time that reveals some noteworthy (and humorous) examples of conditional statements made in history, politics, and culture. You may be surprised to realize that some of these familiar statements can be expressed in abstract terms, and that some of their contrapositives sound pretty bizarre. But, hey, that's going to be your life now. As an LSAT student, you'll start to realize that Formal Logic is with us all the time, and you'll be practicing whenever you spot an "If-then" statement. Embrace the abstract, my friend.

 **Complete answers and explanations are provided in the LSAT Channel Spotlight video "Great Moments in Formal Logic" in your online Study Plan.**

Congratulations on completing this chapter on the foundations of formal logic in LSAT Logical Reasoning questions. Keep your eyes peeled for conditional statements and questions that reward the accurate interpretation of sufficient-and-necessary relationships. You'll be using this work time and again during your LSAT preparation, and of course, on test day itself.

In Part II of this book, you'll cover the first of three "question families." First up are the Argument-Based questions. The work you do there will add several question types to your LSAT toolkit, and even more importantly, will set the stage for the all-important Assumption Family questions in Part III. Keep up the good work!

Argument-Based Questions

CHAPTER 3

Conclusions and Main Point Questions

Argument-Based Questions

On the LSAT, the word argument does not refer to a dispute between two people. An LSAT argument is one person's attempt to convince the reader that some assertion is true, some action is advisable, or some prediction is accurate. LSAT arguments are defined by two explicit components: the *conclusion* and the *evidence*.

LSAT STRATEGY

Every LSAT argument contains:

- A conclusion—the assertion, evaluation, or recommendation about which the author is trying to convince his readers

- Evidence—the facts, studies, or contentions the author believes support or establish the conclusion

---

The question types covered in Part II, the so-called Argument-Based questions—Main Point, Role of a Statement, Method of Argument, Point at Issue, and Parallel Reasoning questions—directly reward your ability to identify, paraphrase, and describe the explicit parts of the argument. Together, they account for around 10 questions per test or 13% of all LSAT points.

But the work you'll do in this part of the book also lays the foundation for success for the all-important Assumption Family questions covered in Part III of the book. Those questions are also argument-based, but they add the skill ability to determine the implicit part of an argument—the assumption—to the list of requisite skills. Because of their frequency—around 30 questions per test or 38% of available LSAT points—the Assumption Family questions are the most important group of Logical Reasoning question types.

Approximate Number of Questions per LSAT by Logical Reasoning Question Family

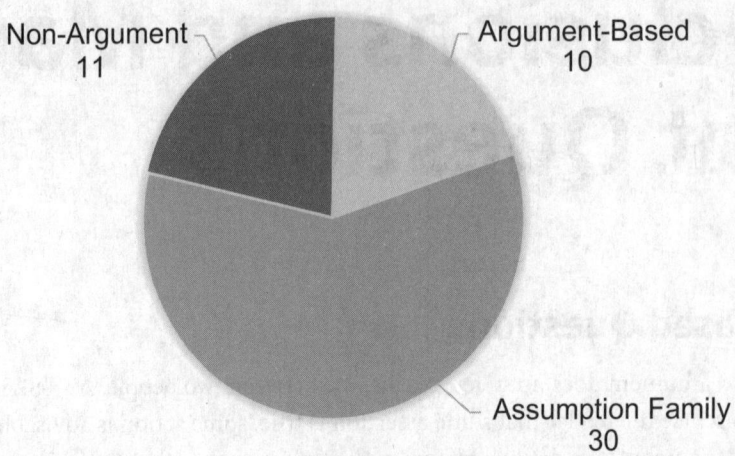

Source: All officially released LSAT exams, 2016-2020

Percentage of All Questions Per LSAT by Logical Reasoning Question Family

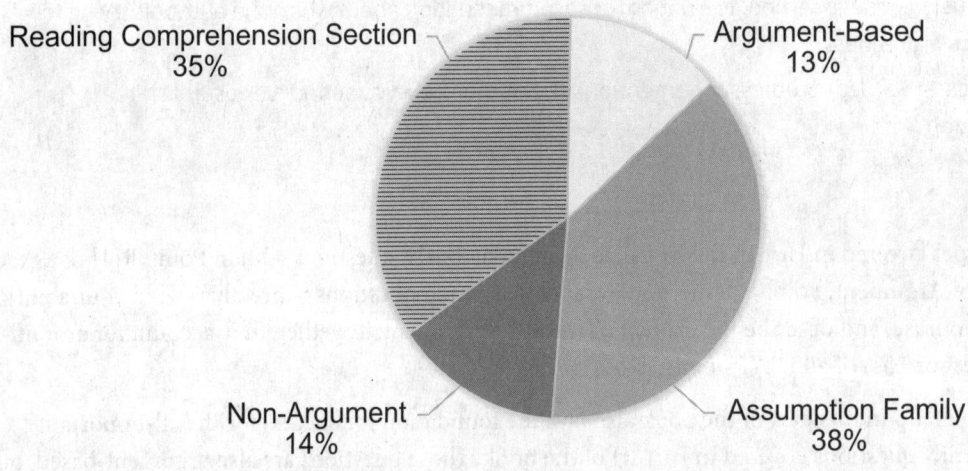

Source: All officially released LSAT exams, 2016-2020

When you see those figures, it may be tempting to jump ahead to Part III, but hit the brakes. Without the skills you'll develop with the explicit aspects of LSAT arguments here in Part II, the Assumption Family questions will be much more difficult to master.

Conclusions

Identify the Conclusion

Prepare Think of the conclusion as the author's point, the statement they are trying to convince you is true. In our day-to-day lives, we identify conclusions all the time, though we're seldom aware that we're doing so. When your spouse or roommate says, "I don't feel like cooking; we should order something for delivery," the second part of that sentence is a conclusion. This is because the second part of the sentence is what they're trying to convince you to do, and they offer the first part of the sentence (the evidence) as a reason why you should accept their point. Indeed, conclusions are statements that call out for a reason; they always elicit the question "Why?"

LEARNING OBJECTIVE

In this section, you'll learn to:

- Identify the conclusion in an LSAT argument.

LSAT arguments are usually (though not always) a good deal more complex than the example about ordering food, but they feature multiple ways in which to identify the conclusion.

Conclusion Keywords

Many LSAT arguments include Keywords that highlight the conclusion.

LSAT Argument	Analysis
Vanwilligan: Some have argued that professional athletes receive unfairly high salaries. But in an unrestricted free market, such as the market these athletes compete in, salaries are determined by what someone else is willing to pay for their services. These athletes make enormous profits for their teams' owners, and that is why owners are willing to pay them extraordinary salaries. Thus <u>the salaries they receive are fair</u>. *PrepTest122 Sec2 Q19*	"Thus" signals the author's conclusion here: *Professional athletes' salaries are fair*. Everything else is either background or evidence.

LSAT STRATEGY

Conclusion Keywords include:

- Thus
- Therefore
- As a result
- It follows that

- Consequently
- So
- [Evidence] is evidence that [conclusion]

Now, you try it. Circle the conclusion Keyword and mark the conclusion in the following argument.

LSAT Argument	My Analysis
Editorial: Clearly, during the past two years, the unemployment situation in our city has been improving. Studies show that the number of unemployed people who are actively looking for jobs has steadily decreased during that period. *PrepTest122 Sec4 Q1*	

Here's how an LSAT expert looks at that argument's conclusion.

LSAT Argument	Analysis
Editorial: Clearly, during the past two years, the unemployment situation in our city has been improving. Studies show that the number of unemployed people who are actively looking for jobs has steadily decreased during that period. *PrepTest122 Sec4 Q1*	Conclusions may be found at the beginning or in the middle of LSAT arguments, not only at the end.

TEST DAY TIP

Identify and annotate the conclusion of an argument. Get in the habit of doing this on all Argument-Based and Assumption Family questions.

Subsidiary Conclusions

Not every conclusion Keyword signals the author's main point or final conclusion. Some arguments on the LSAT contain subsidiary or intermediate conclusions.

LSAT Argument	Analysis
Economist: As should be obvious, raising the minimum wage significantly would make it more expensive for businesses to pay workers for minimum-wage jobs. Therefore, businesses could not afford to continue to employ as many workers for such jobs. So raising the minimum wage significantly will cause an increase in unemployment. *PrepTest129 Sec3 Q6*	Conclusion: "So" signals the author's main point: *Significantly increasing the minimum wage will increase unemployment.* "Therefore" signals a subsidiary conclusion that serves as evidence for the main point.

Subsidiary conclusions are premises derived from one piece of evidence that are, in turn, used as evidence for a further conclusion. That may sound complicated, but quite common in everyday life. There's a subsidiary conclusion in the middle of this argument, for example: "It's likely to rain this afternoon, *so fishing is out of the question*. Therefore, let's take the kids bowling instead." If you see two conclusion keywords in an argument, one of the conclusions is there to support the other, and sometimes, the testmaker will even give the subsidiary conclusion a keyword, but not give one to the final conclusion. Analyze all arguments thoroughly before turning to the answer choices.

Evidence Keywords

In other LSAT arguments, evidence Keywords signal the support for the author's conclusion.

LSAT Argument	Analysis
In a poll of a representative sample of a province's residents, the provincial capital was the city most often selected as the best place to live in that province. Since the capital is also the largest of that province's many cities, <u>the poll shows that most residents of that province generally prefer life in large cities to life in small cities.</u> *PrepTest131 Sec1 Q18*	The Keyword *[s]ince* signals the evidence in the argument. The conclusion begins after the comma in that sentence: *[T]he poll shows that most in the province prefer life in big cities to life in small cities.*

LSAT STRATEGY

Evidence Keywords include:

- Because
- Since
- [Evidence] is evidence of [conclusion]
- After all
- For

Now, you try it. Circle the evidence Keyword(s) and mark the conclusion in the following argument.

LSAT Argument	My Analysis
There is a difference between beauty and truth. After all, if there were no difference, then the most realistic pieces of art would be the best as well, since the most realistic pieces are the most truthful. But many of the most realistic artworks are not among the best. *PrepTest122 Sec4 Q16*	

Here's how an LSAT expert analyzes that argument.

LSAT Argument	Analysis
There is a difference between beauty and truth. After all, if there were no difference, then the most realistic pieces of art would be the best as well, since the most realistic pieces are the most truthful. But many of the most realistic artworks are not among the best.	*After all* and *since* both indicate evidence, and *[b]ut*, in this case, offers a contrasting point of evidence.
	The conclusion is the argument's first sentence: *There is a difference between beauty and truth.*
PrepTest122 Sec4 Q16	

Remember this earlier statement about conclusions: conclusions are statements that call out for a reason; they always elicit the question "Why?" Note that evidence keywords always signal an answer to that question.

Conclusion from Context

Still other LSAT arguments contain neither conclusion nor evidence Keywords.

LSAT Argument	Analysis
It is due to a misunderstanding that most modern sculpture is monochromatic. When ancient sculptures were exhumed years ago, they were discovered to be uncolored. No one at the time had reason to believe, as we now do, that the sculptures had originally been colorfully painted, but that centuries of exposure to moisture washed away the paint.	Conclusion: *Modern sculpture is monochromatic due to a mistaken understanding.*
	The facts in the rest of the argument are offered to support the first sentence.
PrepTest122 Sec4 Q13	

These arguments with neither conclusion nor evidence Keywords may be the toughest in which to locate the conclusion. Follow the logical flow of the argument by asking, "What is the author's point, and what are they offering to support that point?" Find the one sentence the author wants to convince the reader about: that's the argument's conclusion or main point.

Conclusion as a Negation of Opponent's Point

Be on the lookout for when an author asserts that another person's position is incorrect. This relatively common argument pattern on the LSAT will signal the author's conclusion.

LSAT Argument	Analysis
Musicologist: Many critics complain of the disproportion between text and music in Handel's *da capo* arias. These texts are generally quite short and often repeated well beyond what is needed for literal understanding. Yet such criticism is refuted by noting that repetition serves a vital function: it frees the audience to focus on the music itself, which can speak to audiences whatever their language.	Conclusion: *The disproportion between text and music is not a weakness in Handel's da capo arias.*
	The author's conclusion says that "such criticism is refuted," referring to those who criticize the disproportion between text and music in Handel's *da capo* arias.
PrepTest143 Sec4 Q6	

To paraphrase the author's main point in arguments like this, negate the point the author's opponent makes. This may sound tricky, but we do this in the "real world" all the time without even thinking about it. Take this argument, for example: "My mom thinks I look great in this blue shirt, but boy is she wrong. It doesn't go with my eyes or hair at all." What's the one-sentence version of the conclusion here? Simply, "I don't look great in this blue shirt."

Now, try your hand at identifying the conclusion in a handful of LSAT arguments.

Practice   Circle conclusion and evidence Keywords and mark the conclusion in each of the following arguments. When you're finished, review your work with the expert analysis on the next page.

LSAT Argument	My Analysis
1. 1990 editorial: Local pay phone calls have cost a quarter apiece ever since the 1970s, when a soft drink from a vending machine cost about the same. The price of a soft drink has more than doubled since, so phone companies should be allowed to raise the price of pay phone calls too. *PrepTest122 Sec2 Q8*	
2. Eating garlic reduces the levels of cholesterol and triglycerides in the blood and so helps reduce the risk of cardiovascular disease. Evidence that eating garlic reduces these levels is that a group of patients taking a garlic tablet each day for four months showed a 12 percent reduction in cholesterol and a 17 percent reduction in triglycerides; over the same period, a group of similar patients taking a medically inert tablet showed only a 2 percent reduction in triglycerides and a 3 percent reduction in cholesterol. *PrepTest122 Sec4 Q2*	

LSAT Argument	**My Analysis**
3. Scientist: A controversy in paleontology centers on the question of whether prehistoric human ancestors began to develop sophisticated tools before or after they came to stand upright. I argue that they stood upright first, simply because advanced toolmaking requires free use of the hands, and standing upright makes this possible. *PrepTest122 Sec2 Q14*	
4. Letter to the editor: Middle-class families in wealthy nations are often criticized for the ecological damage resulting from their lifestyles. This criticism should not be taken too seriously, however, since its source is often a movie star or celebrity whose own lifestyle would, if widely adopted, destroy the environment and deplete our resources in a short time. *PrepTest122 Sec2 Q5*	

Expert Analysis

Here's how an LSAT expert analyzed those arguments to identify the conclusion.

LSAT Argument	Analysis
1. 1990 editorial: Local pay phone calls have cost a quarter apiece ever since the 1970s, when a soft drink from a vending machine cost about the same. The price of a soft drink has more than doubled since, so phone companies should be allowed to raise the price of pay phone calls too. *PrepTest122 Sec2 Q8*	[S]o identifies the conclusion: *Phone companies should be allowed to raise the price of pay phone calls.*
2. Eating garlic reduces the levels of cholesterol and triglycerides in the blood and so helps reduce the risk of cardiovascular disease. Evidence that eating garlic reduces these levels is that a group of patients taking a garlic tablet each day for four months showed a 12 percent reduction in cholesterol and a 17 percent reduction in triglycerides; over the same period, a group of similar patients taking a medically inert tablet showed only a 2 percent reduction in triglycerides and a 3 percent reduction in cholesterol. *PrepTest122 Sec4 Q2*	[A]nd so signals the author's main point: *Eating garlic helps reduce the risk of cardiovascular disease.* The first part of the sentence indicates a direct result of eating garlic, and the word [e]vidence at the start of the second sentence indicates that the rest of the argument supports that direct result.

LSAT Argument	Analysis
3. Scientist: A controversy in paleontology centers on the question of whether prehistoric human ancestors began to develop sophisticated tools before or after they came to stand upright. I argue that they stood upright first, simply because advanced toolmaking requires free use of the hands, and standing upright makes this possible. *PrepTest122 Sec2 Q14*	*I argue that* signals the conclusion: *Human ancestors stood upright before developing sophisticated tools.*
4. Letter to the editor: Middle-class families in wealthy nations are often criticized for the ecological damage resulting from their lifestyles. This criticism should not be taken too seriously, however, since its source is often a movie star or celebrity whose own lifestyle would, if widely adopted, destroy the environment and deplete our resources in a short time. *PrepTest122 Sec2 Q5*	The letter writer negates a common criticism. The idea that middle-class lifestyles damage the environment, the author says, "should not be taken too seriously." So, the author's main point is: *Middle-class lifestyles result in ecological damage.*

Paraphrase and Characterize the Conclusion

Prepare Once you can spot conclusions, the next skill is understanding what they mean. LSAT arguments don't always use the simplest or most succinct language. Paraphrasing the conclusion is important because, in some questions, the LSAT will paraphrase the author's conclusion in the answer choices. Moreover, paraphrasing simplifies the argument and makes it easier to zero in on the author's main point.

LEARNING OBJECTIVE

In this section, you'll learn to:

- Paraphrase and characterize the conclusion in an LSAT argument.

Here's how an LSAT expert might simplify a fairly complex conclusion.

LSAT Argument	Analysis
From the fact that people who studied music as children frequently are quite proficient at mathematics, it cannot be concluded that the skills required for mathematics are acquired by studying music: it is equally likely that proficiency in mathematics and studying music are both the result of growing up in a family that encourages its children to excel at all intellectual and artistic endeavors.	Because it leads to further explanation or examples, a colon usually signals evidence. So, the author's conclusion is the first sentence. *Being good at music is correlated with being good at math, but that doesn't mean that the person's math skills were caused by studying music.*

PrepTest122 Sec4 Q17

Paraphrasing is made easier by knowing that nearly all LSAT conclusions fall into one of six categories.

CONCLUSION TYPES

In an LSAT argument, the conclusion almost always matches one or more of these six types:

- Value Judgment (an evaluative statement; e.g., Action X is unethical, or Y's recital was poorly sung)
- If/Then (a conditional prediction, recommendation, or assertion; e.g., If X is true, then so is Y or If you are an M, you should do N)
- Prediction (X *will* or *will not* happen in the future)
- Comparison (X is taller/shorter/more common/less common/etc. than Y)
- Assertion of Fact (X is true or X is false)
- Recommendation (we *should* or *should not* do X)

In this drill, identify the conclusion type in each of the following examples taken from official LSAT questions.

	LSAT Conclusion	**My Analysis**
a.	Therefore, these fat-free brownies are healthier than those cookies are. *PrepTest132 Sec3 Q22*	*[H]ealthier than* makes this conclusion a[n]
b.	This fact helps make large-animal species more vulnerable to extinction than small-animal species . . . *PrepTest122 Sec2 Q9*	*[M]ore . . . than* makes this conclusion a[n]
c.	It is time to put a halt to this trivial journalism. *PrepTest122 Sec4 Q4*	*It is time to* makes this conclusion a[n]
d.	I maintain, however, that to save lives, automobile manufacturers ought to stop equipping cars with them. *PrepTest122 Sec4 Q11*	*[O]ught* makes this conclusion a[n]
e.	Thus, it is unlikely that the airport will be built. *PrepTest143 Sec4 Q11*	*[W]ill* makes this conclusion a[n]
f.	This shows that a decrease in humidity can make people ill. *PrepTest131 Sec3 Q12*	*[A] . . . can* makes this conclusion a[n]
g.	Thus the salaries they receive are fair. *PrepTest122 Sec2 Q19*	*[F]air* makes this conclusion a[n]
h.	So if the screen is to be a hedge, it will be a hemlock hedge. *PrepTest131 Sec1 Q5*	*[I]f . . . will* makes this conclusion a[n]

Answers

a. Comparison; b. Comparison; c. Recommendation; d. Recommendation; e. Prediction; f. Assertion of Fact; g. Value Judgment; h. If/then + Prediction

Practice Identify, characterize, and paraphrase the conclusion in each of the following arguments. When you're finished, review your work with the expert analysis on the next pages.

LSAT Argument	My Analysis
5. Pundit: The average salary for teachers in our society is lower than the average salary for athletes. Obviously, our society values sports more than it values education. *PrepTest132 Sec3 Q4*	Paraphrase: Type:
6. Engineer: Thermophotovoltaic generators are devices that convert heat into electricity. The process of manufacturing steel produces huge amounts of heat that currently go to waste. So if steel-manufacturing plants could feed the heat they produce into thermophotovoltaic generators, they would greatly reduce their electric bills, thereby saving money. *PrepTest142 Sec2 Q16*	Paraphrase: Type:
7. Essayist: Lessing contended that an art form's medium dictates the kind of representation the art form must employ in order to be legitimate; painting, for example, must represent simultaneous arrays of colored shapes, while literature, consisting of words read in succession, must represent events or actions occurring in sequence. The claim about literature must be rejected, however, if one regards as legitimate the imagists' poems, which consist solely of amalgams of disparate images. *PrepTest129 Sec2 Q7*	Paraphrase: Type:

LSAT Argument	My Analysis
8. Bethany: Psychologists have discovered a technique for replacing one's nightmares with pleasant dreams and have successfully taught it to adults suffering from chronic nightmares. Studies have found that nightmare-prone children are especially likely to suffer from nightmares as adults. Thus, psychologists should direct efforts toward identifying nightmare-prone children so that these children can be taught the technique for replacing their nightmares with pleasant dreams. *PrepTest131 Sec2 Q13*	Paraphrase: Type:
9. Sometimes one reads a poem and believes that the poem expresses contradictory ideas, even if it is a great poem. So it is wrong to think that the meaning of a poem is whatever the author intends to communicate to the reader by means of the poem. No one who is writing a great poem intends it to communicate contradictory ideas. *PrepTest129 Sec2 Q24*	Paraphrase: Type:
10. In a poll of a representative sample of a province's residents, the provincial capital was the city most often selected as the best place to live in that province. Since the capital is also the largest of that province's many cities, the poll shows that most residents of that province generally prefer life in large cities to life in small cities. *PrepTest131 Sec1 Q18*	Paraphrase: Type:

LSAT Argument	My Analysis
11. Ecologists predict that the incidence of malaria will increase if global warming continues or if the use of pesticides is not expanded. But the use of pesticides is known to contribute to global warming, so it is inevitable that we will see an increase in malaria in the years to come. *PrepTest132 Sec3 Q24*	Paraphrase: Type:
12. Team captain: Winning requires the willingness to cooperate, which in turn requires motivation. So you will not win if you are not motivated. *PrepTest129 Sec2 Q19*	Paraphrase: Type:
13. Scientist: A controversy in paleontology centers on the question of whether prehistoric human ancestors began to develop sophisticated tools before or after they came to stand upright. I argue that they stood upright first, simply because advanced toolmaking requires free use of the hands, and standing upright makes this possible. *PrepTest122 Sec2 Q14*	Paraphrase: Type:

LSAT Argument	**My Analysis**
14. The typological theory of species classification, which has few adherents today, distinguishes species solely on the basis of observable physical characteristics, such as plumage color, adult size, or dental structure. However, there are many so-called "sibling species," which are indistinguishable on the basis of their appearance but cannot interbreed and thus, according to the mainstream biological theory of species classification, are separate species. Since the typological theory does not count sibling species as separate species, it is unacceptable. *PrepTest131 Sec1 Q15*	Paraphrase: Type:

Expert Analysis

Here's how an LSAT expert analyzed the arguments you just saw.

LSAT Argument	Analysis
5. Pundit: The average salary for teachers in our society is lower than the average salary for athletes. Obviously, our society values sports more than it values education. *PrepTest132 Sec3 Q4*	Paraphrase: Our society values sports more than it does education. Type: Comparison
6. Engineer: Thermophotovoltaic generators are devices that convert heat into electricity. The process of manufacturing steel produces huge amounts of heat that currently go to waste. So if steel-manufacturing plants could feed the heat they produce into thermophotovoltaic generators, they would greatly reduce their electric bills, thereby saving money. *PrepTest142 Sec2 Q16*	Paraphrase: If steel plants could cycle heat into TP generators, then they would save money. Type: If/Then, Prediction
7. Essayist: Lessing contended that an art form's medium dictates the kind of representation the art form must employ in order to be legitimate; painting, for example, must represent simultaneous arrays of colored shapes, while literature, consisting of words read in succession, must represent events or actions occurring in sequence. The claim about literature must be rejected, however, if one regards as legitimate the imagists' poems, which consist solely of amalgams of disparate images. *PrepTest129 Sec2 Q7*	Paraphrase: If imagist poems are literature, then literature does not have to depict events in sequence. Type: If/Then, Assertion of Fact

LSAT Argument	Analysis
8. Bethany: Psychologists have discovered a technique for replacing one's nightmares with pleasant dreams, and have successfully taught it to adults suffering from chronic nightmares. Studies have found that nightmare-prone children are especially likely to suffer from nightmares as adults. Thus, psychologists should direct efforts toward identifying nightmare-prone children so that these children can be taught the technique for replacing their nightmares with pleasant dreams. *PrepTest131 Sec2 Q13*	Paraphrase: Psychologists should focus on identifying nightmare-prone children (so that the kids can benefit from the new technique). Type: Recommendation
9. Sometimes one reads a poem and believes that the poem expresses contradictory ideas, even if it is a great poem. So it is wrong to think that the meaning of a poem is whatever the author intends to communicate to the reader by means of the poem. No one who is writing a great poem intends it to communicate contradictory ideas. *PrepTest129 Sec2 Q24*	Paraphrase: A poem's meaning is not determined by the author's intent. Type: Assertion of Fact
10. In a poll of a representative sample of a province's residents, the provincial capital was the city most often selected as the best place to live in that province. Since the capital is also the largest of that province's many cities, the poll shows that most residents of that province generally prefer life in large cities to life in small cities. *PrepTest131 Sec1 Q18*	Paraphrase: Most residents of the province prefer big-city life to life in small cities. Type: Comparison

LSAT Argument	Analysis
11. Ecologists predict that the incidence of malaria will increase if global warming continues or if the use of pesticides is not expanded. But the use of pesticides is known to contribute to global warming, so it is inevitable that we will see an increase in malaria in the years to come. *PrepTest132 Sec3 Q24*	Paraphrase: A rise in malaria is inevitable. Type: Prediction
12. Team captain: Winning requires the willingness to cooperate, which in turn requires motivation. So you will not win if you are not motivated. *PrepTest129 Sec2 Q19*	Paraphrase: Motivation is necessary for winning. *If win → motivated* *If not motivated → not win* Type: If/Then
13. Scientist: A controversy in paleontology centers on the question of whether prehistoric human ancestors began to develop sophisticated tools before or after they came to stand upright. I argue that they stood upright first, simply because advanced toolmaking requires free use of the hands, and standing upright makes this possible. *PrepTest122 Sec2 Q14*	Paraphrase: Human ancestors stood upright before they developed sophisticated tools. Type: Assertion of Fact

LSAT Argument	Analysis
14. The typological theory of species classification, which has few adherents today, distinguishes species solely on the basis of observable physical characteristics, such as plumage color, adult size, or dental structure. However, there are many so-called "sibling species," which are indistinguishable on the basis of their appearance but cannot interbreed and thus, according to the mainstream biological theory of species classification, are separate species. Since the typological theory does not count sibling species as separate species, it is unacceptable.	Paraphrase: The typological theory is unacceptable. Type: Value Judgment

PrepTest131 Sec1 Q15

Main Point Questions

Prepare Separating an author's main conclusion from the evidence is so critical on the LSAT that there is even a question type—Main Point questions—that asks you to do only that.

LEARNING OBJECTIVE

In this section, you'll learn to:

• Identify and answer Main Point questions.

There is an average of two Main Point questions per test, but three is not uncommon.

You can recognize Main Point questions from stems like these:

> Which one of the following most accurately expresses the main conclusion of the argument?
>
> *PrepTest131 Sec2 Q10*

> Which one of the following sentences best expresses the main point of the musicologist's reasoning?
>
> *PrepTest143 Sec4 Q6*

> Which one of the following most accurately expresses the conclusion of the argument as a whole?
>
> *PrepTest129 Sec3 Q3*

Approximate Number of Main Point Questions per LSAT

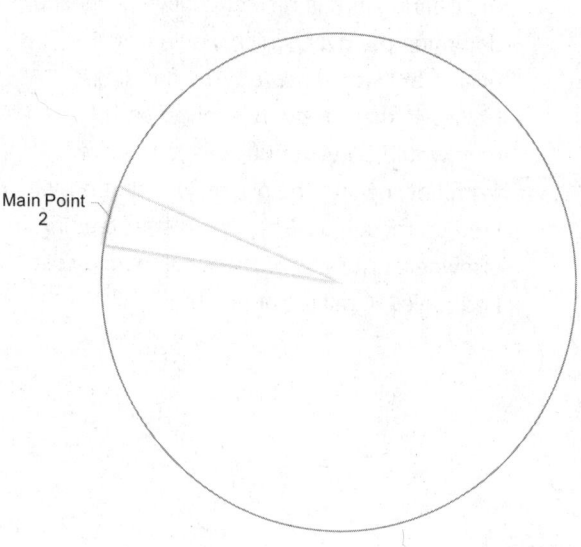

Main Point 2

Source: All officially released LSAT exams, 2016-2020

MAIN POINT QUESTIONS AT A GLANCE

Task: Identify the argument's main conclusion.

Strategies: Use conclusion Keywords, evidence Keywords, subsidiary conclusions, and/or the argument's structure to distinguish the author's main point from her supporting evidence.

Frequency: Main Point questions are not prevalent; on released LSAT tests administered from 2016 through 2020, there were an average of 1.2 Main Point questions per Logical Reasoning section, but keep in mind that identifying an argument's conclusion is a skill involved in more than 75% of Logical Reasoning questions.

Now, complete a Main Point question on your own. Jot down your analysis for each step so that when you're done, you can compare your work to that of an LSAT expert in the worked example on the next page.

Step 2:	**Step 1:**

Editorial: Almost every year the Smithfield River floods the coastal fishing community of Redhook, which annually spends $3 million on the cleanup. Some residents have proposed damming the river, which would cost $5 million but would prevent the flooding. However, their position is misguided. A dam would prevent nutrients in the river from flowing into the ocean. Fish that now feed on those nutrients would start feeding elsewhere. The loss of these fish would cost Redhook $10 million annually.

Which one of the following most accurately expresses the main conclusion of the editorial's argument?

(A) The Smithfield River should be dammed to prevent flooding.

(B) Nutrients from the Smithfield River are essential to the local fish population.

(C) Damming the Smithfield River is not worth the high construction costs for such a project.

(D) For Redhook to build a dam on the Smithfield River would be a mistake.

(E) The Smithfield River floods cost Redhook $3 million every year.

PrepTest131 Sec1 Q1

Step 3:	**Step 4:**

Expert Analysis

Here's how an LSAT expert evaluated and answered that question.

Step 2: *Conclusion*: Their [some residents'] position [damming the river] is misguided. *[M]isguided* signals the editorial's opinion and demands support. The rest of the facts are offered to support the author's rebuttal of those who advocate for a dam or as background context to the debate.	**Step 1:** A Main Point question: The correct answer will paraphrase the argument's final conclusion.

Editorial: Almost every year the Smithfield River floods the coastal fishing community of Redhook, which annually spends $3 million on the cleanup. Some residents have proposed damming the river, which would cost $5 million but would prevent the flooding. However, their position is misguided. A dam would prevent nutrients in the river from flowing into the ocean. Fish that now feed on those nutrients would start feeding elsewhere. The loss of these fish would cost Redhook $10 million annually.

Which one of the following most accurately expresses the main conclusion of the editorial's argument?

(A) The Smithfield River should be dammed to prevent flooding.

(B) Nutrients from the Smithfield River are essential to the local fish population.

(C) Damming the Smithfield River is not worth the high construction costs for such a project.

(D) For Redhook to build a dam on the Smithfield River would be a mistake.

(E) The Smithfield River floods cost Redhook $3 million every year.

PrepTest131 Sec1 Q1

Step 3: The correct answer will paraphrase the main point: Damming the river is a bad idea.	**Step 4:** (D) is correct. This matches the conclusion of the stimulus argument.

Wrong answers: (A) is a 180. The author's conclusion rejects this view. (B) This is part of the author's evidence for why building a dam would be a bad idea. (C) The author mentions the cost of construction when describing the argument of "some residents," but his discussion of costs is in the evidence. (E) This is background to the debate over damming the river.

Now, practice some more Main Point questions in the following pages.

Practice Try each of the following Main Point questions. Some may contain arguments you analyzed in the preceding chapter. Don't worry too much about your timing here. Complete all four steps of the Logical Reasoning Method for each question, jotting down your notes whenever it is helpful to do so. After each question, review your work with the expert analysis that follows.

Step 2:	Step 1:

15. Musicologist: Classification of a musical instrument depends on the mechanical action through which it produces music. So the piano is properly called a percussion instrument, not a stringed instrument. Even though the vibration of the piano's strings is what makes its sound, the strings are caused to vibrate by the impact of hammers.

Which one of the following most accurately expresses the main conclusion of the musicologist's argument?

(A) Musical instruments should be classified according to the mechanical actions through which they produce sound.

(B) Musical instruments should not be classified based on the way musicians interact with them.

(C) Some people classify the piano as a stringed instrument because of the way the piano produces sound.

(D) The piano should be classified as a stringed instrument rather than as a percussion instrument.

(E) It is correct to classify the piano as a percussion instrument rather than as a stringed instrument.

PrepTest142 Sec2 Q9

Step 3:	Step 4:

Expert Analysis

Review an example of an LSAT expert's work on the question you just tried.

Step 2: *So* signals the *conclusion*: The piano is properly categorized as a percussion instrument, not a string instrument. The rest of the argument explains why the author agrees with this categorization.	**Step 1:** A Main Point question: the correct answer will paraphrase the argument's final conclusion.

15. Musicologist: Classification of a musical instrument depends on the mechanical action through which it produces music. So the piano is properly called a percussion instrument, not a stringed instrument. Even though the vibration of the piano's strings is what makes its sound, the strings are caused to vibrate by the impact of hammers.

Which one of the following most accurately expresses the main conclusion of the musicologist's argument?

(A) Musical instruments should be classified according to the mechanical actions through which they produce sound.

(B) Musical instruments should not be classified based on the way musicians interact with them.

(C) Some people classify the piano as a stringed instrument because of the way the piano produces sound.

(D) The piano should be classified as a stringed instrument rather than as a percussion instrument.

(E) It is correct to classify the piano as a percussion instrument rather than as a stringed instrument.

PrepTest142 Sec2 Q9

Step 3: The piano is properly categorized as a percussion instrument, not a string instrument.	**Step 4:** (E) is correct. This paraphrases the author's main point.

Wrong answers: (A) This is the rule about how to categorize instruments. The author applies the rule to reach the conclusion. (B) is Outside the Scope. Not only is this not the author's conclusion, it actually disagrees with the rule stated in the evidence. (C) is Outside the Scope. How others classify the piano is not relevant to the author's conclusion, which expresses how it *should* be categorized. (D) is a 180. The author concludes the opposite.

Step 2:	Step 1:

16. Chemical fertilizers not only create potential health hazards, they also destroy earthworms, which are highly beneficial to soil. For this reason alone the use of chemical fertilizers should be avoided. The castings earthworms leave behind are much richer than the soil they ingest, thus making a garden rich in earthworms much more fertile than a garden without them.

Which one of the following most accurately expresses the main conclusion of the argument?

(A) Earthworms are highly beneficial to soil.

(B) Chemical fertilizers destroy earthworms.

(C) The castings that earthworms leave behind are much richer than the soil they ingest.

(D) The use of chemical fertilizers should be avoided.

(E) A garden rich in earthworms is much more fertile than a garden that is devoid of earthworms.

PrepTest131 Sec2 Q10

Step 3:	Step 4:

Expert Analysis

Review an example of an LSAT expert's work on the question you just tried.

Step 2: [T]*his reason* refers to the first sentence, so the first sentence must be evidence, and not the main point. Then, what follows [f]*or this reason* is a recommendation: Avoid chemical fertilizers. That calls for support.

The final sentence contains another reason to avoid chemical fertilizers, so it must be a subsidiary conclusion.

Step 1: A Main Point question: The correct answer will paraphrase the argument's final conclusion.

16. Chemical fertilizers not only create potential health hazards, they also destroy earthworms, which are highly beneficial to soil. For this reason alone the use of chemical fertilizers should be avoided. The castings earthworms leave behind are much richer than the soil they ingest, thus making a garden rich in earthworms much more fertile than a garden without them.

Which one of the following most accurately expresses the main conclusion of the argument?

(A) Earthworms are highly beneficial to soil.

(B) Chemical fertilizers destroy earthworms.

(C) The castings that earthworms leave behind are much richer than the soil they ingest.

(D) The use of chemical fertilizers should be avoided.

(E) A garden rich in earthworms is much more fertile than a garden that is devoid of earthworms.

PrepTest131 Sec2 Q10

Step 3: The correct answer will state or paraphrase the main recommendation: chemical fertilizers should not be used.

Step 4: (D) is correct. This states the argument's conclusion word for word.

Wrong answers: (A) This is part of the first sentence, which is evidence. (B) This is evidence used to support the conclusion. (C) This is evidence to support the conclusion. (E) This is a subsidiary conclusion that supports the author's recommendation. This choice is attractive to someone who jumps at the word *thus* without considering the author's main idea.

Step 2:

Step 1:

17. Moralist: Humans have a natural disposition to altruism—that is, to behavior that serves the needs of others regardless of one's own needs—but that very disposition prevents some acts of altruism from counting as moral. Reason plays an essential role in any moral behavior. Only behavior that is intended to be in accordance with a formal set of rules, or moral code, can be considered moral behavior.

Which one of the following most accurately states the main conclusion of the moralist's argument?

(A) All moral codes prohibit selfishness.

(B) All moral behavior is motivated by altruism.

(C) Behavior must serve the needs of others in order to be moral behavior.

(D) Not all altruistic acts are moral behavior.

(E) Altruism develops through the use of reason.

PrepTest111 Sec4 Q9

Step 3:

Step 4:

Expert Analysis

Review an example of an LSAT expert's work on the question you just tried.

Step 2: *Conclusion*: Human nature prevents some altruistic acts from being considered moral acts. The contrast word "but" in the middle of the first sentence signals the author's point of view, and the remaining sentences serve as evidence.	**Step 1:** A straightforward Main Point question; the correct answer will paraphrase the argument's conclusion.

17. Moralist: Humans have a natural disposition to altruism—that is, to behavior that serves the needs of others regardless of one's own needs—but that very disposition prevents some acts of altruism from counting as moral. Reason plays an essential role in any moral behavior. Only behavior that is intended to be in accordance with a formal set of rules, or moral code, can be considered moral behavior.

Which one of the following most accurately states the main conclusion of the moralist's argument?

(A) All moral codes prohibit selfishness.

(B) All moral behavior is motivated by altruism.

(C) Behavior must serve the needs of others in order to be moral behavior.

(D) Not all altruistic acts are moral behavior.

(E) Altruism develops through the use of reason.

PrepTest111 Sec4 Q9

Step 3: The correct answer will paraphrase the main point: some altruistic actions are not moral actions.	**Step 4:** (D) matches the conclusion and is correct.

Wrong answers: (A) Outside the Scope. The author never conveys the content of moral codes. (B) distorts the argument, which associates moral actions with reason, not with altruism (which sometimes, the author believes, arises from a "natural disposition"). (C) distorts the argument, which holds that altruism is "behavior that serves the needs of others," while moral behavior must be "intended to be in accordance with a formal set of rules." (E) 180. The author believes that at least some altruistic behavior does *not* come from reason; that's the altruistic behavior the author thinks does *not count* as moral.

PART TWO
ARGUMENT-BASED QUESTIONS

Step 2:	Step 1:

18. Some critics argue that an opera's stage directions are never reflected in its music. Many comic scenes in Mozart's operas, however, open with violin phrases that sound like the squeaking of changing scenery. Clearly Mozart intended the music to echo the sounds occurring while stage directions are carried out. Hence, a change of scenery—the most basic and frequent stage direction—can be reflected in the music, which means that other operatic stage directions can be as well.

In the argument, the statement that many comic scenes in Mozart's operas open with violin phrases that sound like the squeaking of changing scenery is offered in support of the claim that

(A) a change of scenery is the stage direction most frequently reflected in an opera's music

(B) an opera's stage directions are never reflected in its music

(C) an opera's music can have an effect on the opera's stage directions

(D) a variety of stage directions can be reflected in an opera's music

(E) the most frequent relation between an opera's music and its stage directions is one of musical imitation of the sounds that occur when a direction is carried out

PrepTest111 Sec1 Q1

Step 3:	Step 4:

Expert Analysis

Review an example of an LSAT expert's work on the question you just tried.

Step 2: *Conclusion:* Other operatic stage directions (beyond just scene changes) can also be reflected in the music. The argument opens with an opposing view, so anticipate that it will be refuted. The refutation comes in the final sentence. *Hence* actually signals a subsidiary conclusion, supporting the overall main point which follows *which means.*	**Step 1:** An unusual Main Point question stem that cites one piece of the evidence and asks for the claim it supports; nonetheless, that claim is simply the argument's conclusion.

18. Some critics argue that an opera's stage directions are never reflected in its music. Many comic scenes in Mozart's operas, however, open with violin phrases that sound like the squeaking of changing scenery. Clearly Mozart intended the music to echo the sounds occurring while stage directions are carried out. Hence, a change of scenery—the most basic and frequent stage direction—can be reflected in the music, which means that other operatic stage directions can be as well.

In the argument, the statement that many comic scenes in Mozart's operas open with violin phrases that sound like the squeaking of changing scenery is offered in support of the claim that

(A) a change of scenery is the stage direction most frequently reflected in an opera's music

(B) an opera's stage directions are never reflected in its music

(C) an opera's music can have an effect on the opera's stage directions

(D) a variety of stage directions can be reflected in an opera's music

(E) the most frequent relation between an opera's music and its stage directions is one of musical imitation of the sounds that occur when a direction is carried out

PrepTest111 Sec1 Q1

Step 3: The correct answer will communicate the idea that opera scores can reflect multiple types of stage directions.	**Step 4:** (D) matches the argument's overall conclusion and is correct.

Wrong answers: (A) cites an example used as evidence (not conclusion) in the argument, and distorts it by adding "most frequent," an idea the author does not include. (B) 180. The argument cites one such example and concludes that more are possible as well. (C) distorts the argument which says that stage directions can "be reflected" in the music, not that the music has an effect on them. (E) The author mentions in the evidence (not conclusion) that *many* Mozart scenes open with a musical imitation of changing scenery but stops short of claiming this to be the *most* frequent such imitation.

Good work. Ready to finish up strong? On the following pages you'll have a timed Perform quiz to assess your newly minted Main Point question skills. Do your best!

Chapter Perform Quiz

Perform This Perform quiz has 4 Main Point questions. They are presented without any notes, hints, or prompts for a more test-like experience while you work. Try to get as many correct answers as possible in 6 minutes. When you finish, check your performance against the Answer Key and Evaluate Your Performance for tips on how best to improve. Then, come back to complete any questions you skipped or guessed on and finish up by reviewing all the questions with the expert analyses in your online companion.

19. It is widely believed that eating chocolate can cause acne. Indeed, many people who are susceptible to acne report that, in their own experience, eating large amounts of chocolate is invariably followed by an outbreak of that skin condition. However, it is likely that common wisdom has mistaken an effect for a cause. Several recent scientific studies indicate that hormonal changes associated with stress can cause acne and there is good evidence that people who are fond of chocolate tend to eat more chocolate when they are under stress.

Of the following, which one most accurately expresses the main point of the argument?

(A) People are mistaken who insist that whenever they eat large amounts of chocolate they invariably suffer from an outbreak of acne.

(B) The more chocolate a person eats, the more likely that person is to experience the hormonal changes associated with stress.

(C) Eating large amounts of chocolate is more likely to cause stress than it is to cause outbreaks of acne.

(D) It is less likely that eating large amounts of chocolate causes acne than that both the chocolate eating and the acne are caused by stress.

(E) The more stress a person experiences, the more likely that person is to crave chocolate.

PrepTest112 Sec1 Q6

20. Although free international trade allows countries to specialize, which in turn increases productivity, such specialization carries risks. After all, small countries often rely on one or two products for the bulk of their exports. If those products are raw materials, the supply is finite and can be used up. If they are foodstuffs, a natural disaster can wipe out a season's production overnight.

Which one of the following most accurately expresses the conclusion of the argument as a whole?

(A) Specialization within international trade comes with risks.

(B) A natural disaster can destroy a whole season's production overnight, devastating a small country's economy.

(C) A small country's supply of raw materials can be used up in a short period.

(D) Some countries rely on a small number of products for the export-based sectors of their economies.

(E) When international trade is free, countries can specialize in what they export.

PrepTest129 Sec3 Q3

21. More women than men suffer from Alzheimer's disease—a disease that is most commonly contracted by elderly persons. This discrepancy has often been attributed to women's longer life span, but this theory may be wrong. A recent study has shown that prescribing estrogen to women after menopause, when estrogen production in the body decreases, may prevent them from developing the disease. Men's supply of testosterone may help safeguard them against Alzheimer's disease because much of it is converted by the body to estrogen, and testosterone levels stay relatively stable into old age.

Which one of the following most accurately expresses the main conclusion of the argument?

(A) A decrease in estrogen, rather than longer life span, may explain the higher occurrence of Alzheimer's disease in women relative to men.

(B) As one gets older, one's chances of developing Alzheimer's disease increase.

(C) Women who go through menopause earlier in life than do most other women have an increased risk of contracting Alzheimer's disease.

(D) The conversion of testosterone into estrogen may help safeguard men from Alzheimer's disease.

(E) Testosterone is necessary for preventing Alzheimer's disease in older men.

PrepTest111 Sec1 Q3

22. Musicologist: Many critics complain of the disproportion between text and music in Handel's *da capo* arias. These texts are generally quite short and often repeated well beyond what is needed for literal understanding. Yet such criticism is refuted by noting that repetition serves a vital function: it frees the audience to focus on the music itself, which can speak to audiences whatever their language.

Which one of the following sentences best expresses the main point of the musicologist's reasoning?

(A) Handel's *da capo* arias contain a disproportionate amount of music.

(B) Handel's *da capo* arias are superior to most in their accessibility to diverse audiences.

(C) At least one frequent criticism of Handel's *da capo* arias is undeserved.

(D) At least some of Handel's *da capo* arias contain unnecessary repetitions.

(E) Most criticism of Handel's *da capo* arias is unwarranted.

PrepTest143 Sec4 Q6

Answer Key

19. D; 20. A; 21. A; 22. C

Evaluate Your Performance

To assess your strengths and opportunities from this Perform quiz, go to the corresponding chapter in your online companion. There you'll find recommendations based on your performance along with complete worked-example explanations (written by a Kaplan LSAT expert) for each of the questions in this Perform quiz.

CHAPTER 4

Evidence and Role of a Statement Questions

Now that you've learned to spot the conclusion in an LSAT argument, the next step is learning to analyze the argument as a whole. In this chapter, you'll learn to spot the argument's evidence, and then to separate the relevant evidence from mere background information and from other people's views to which the argument may be responding. Mastering this will put you in a position to tackle Role of a Statement (covered in this chapter), Point at Issue (covered in Chapter 5), Method of Argument questions (covered in Chapter 6), and the entire Assumption Family (covered in Part III). Taken together, that's more than half of the questions on the LSAT.

Identify the Evidence

Prepare Once you've learned to identify the conclusion, the next step in analyzing an argument is to distinguish the relevant evidence from the conclusion and from any general background information. Then, you can see how the author intends the evidence to logically lead to the conclusion.

LEARNING OBJECTIVE

In this section, you'll learn to:

- Distinguish evidence from background information.

As a strategic reader, you should be able to describe the way each statement serves the argument. Take a look at how an LSAT expert might distinguish among the roles of various statements in an argument you've already seen.

LSAT Argument	Analysis
Editorial: Almost every year the Şmithfield River floods the coastal fishing community of Redhook, which annually spends $3 million on the cleanup. Some residents have proposed damming the river, which would cost $5 million but would prevent the flooding. However, their position is misguided. A dam would prevent nutrients in the river from flowing into the ocean. Fish that now feed on those nutrients would start feeding elsewhere. The loss of these fish would cost Redhook $10 million annually.	**Step 2:** Sentence 1—Background—the impetus for a debate: Flood cleanup costs $3 million per year. Sentence 2—Some residents' (not the author's) recommendation: Build a dam for $5 million. Sentence 3—The author's *conclusion*: some residents' recommendation is a mistake. Sentences 4, 5, and 6—The author's evidence: • A dam would stop nutrients. • Fish that need the nutrients would leave the area. • Losing the fish costs $10 million per year.

PrepTest51 Sec1 Q1

On test day, you won't write out a full analysis of every sentence. That would be too time consuming. But, don't hesitate to take notes now while you're learning to dissect the lengthy arguments used by the LSAT testmaker. Being conscious of the steps you're taking will train your brain to spot the parts of the argument and arrange them clearly for your analysis.

LSAT STRATEGY

One sentence does not always contain one "statement." A single sentence might contain two pieces of evidence or an evidentiary premise and the conclusion.

| **Practice** | Identify how each statement functions in the following LSAT arguments. Identify the conclusion first, and then describe the roles played by the other statements. |

LSAT Argument	**My Analysis**
1. Most of the employees of the Compujack Corporation are computer programmers. Since most computer programmers receive excellent salaries from their employers, at least one Compujack employee must receive an excellent salary from Compujack. *PrepTest122 Sec4 Q24*	**Conclusion:** **Roles of Other Statements:**
2. An art critic, by ridiculing an artwork, can undermine the pleasure one takes in it; conversely, by lavishing praise upon an artwork, an art critic can render the experience of viewing the artwork more pleasurable. So an artwork's artistic merit can depend not only on the person who creates it but also on those who critically evaluate it. *PrepTest143 Sec4 Q13*	**Conclusion:** **Roles of Other Statements:**
3. Vanwilligan: Some have argued that professional athletes receive unfairly high salaries. But in an unrestricted free market, such as the market these athletes compete in, salaries are determined by what someone else is willing to pay for their services. These athletes make enormous profits for their teams' owners, and that is why owners are willing to pay them extraordinary salaries. Thus the salaries they receive are fair. *PrepTest122 Sec2 Q19*	**Conclusion:** **Roles of Other Statements:**

LSAT Argument	My Analysis
4. Columnist: It has been noted that attending a live musical performance is a richer experience than is listening to recorded music. Some say that this is merely because we do not see the performers when we listen to recorded music. However, there must be some other reason, for there is relatively little difference between listening to someone read a story over the radio and listening to someone in the same room read a story. *PrepTest131 Sec2 Q7*	**Conclusion:** **Roles of Other Statements:**
5. Chiu: The belief that a person is always morally blameworthy for feeling certain emotions, such as unjustifiable anger, jealousy, or resentment, is misguided. Individuals are responsible for only what is under their control, and whether one feels such an emotion is not always under one's control. *PrepTest131 Sec1 Q16*	**Conclusion:** **Roles of Other Statements:**
6. Scientist: A controversy in paleontology centers on the question of whether prehistoric human ancestors began to develop sophisticated tools before or after they came to stand upright. I argue that they stood upright first, simply because advanced toolmaking requires free use of the hands, and standing upright makes this possible. *PrepTest122 Sec2 Q14*	**Conclusion:** **Roles of Other Statements:**

LSAT Argument	My Analysis
7. Bethany: Psychologists have discovered a technique for replacing one's nightmares with pleasant dreams, and have successfully taught it to adults suffering from chronic nightmares. Studies have found that nightmare-prone children are especially likely to suffer from nightmares as adults. Thus, psychologists should direct efforts toward identifying nightmare-prone children so that these children can be taught the technique for replacing their nightmares with pleasant dreams. *PrepTest131 Sec2 Q13*	**Conclusion:** **Roles of Other Statements:**
8. It is primarily by raising interest rates that central bankers curb inflation, but an increase in interest rates takes up to two years to affect inflation. Accordingly, central bankers usually try to raise interest rates before inflation becomes excessive, at which time inflation is not yet readily apparent either. But unless inflation is readily apparent, interest rate hikes generally will be perceived as needlessly restraining a growing economy. Thus, central bankers' success in temporarily restraining inflation may make it harder for them to ward off future inflation without incurring the public's wrath. *PrepTest122 Sec2 Q12*	**Conclusion:** **Roles of Other Statements:**

Expert Analysis

Now take a look at how an LSAT expert approached the arguments you just saw. Compare your work to that of the expert looking for places in which you could have more effectively expressed the purpose of sentences or statements in the arguments.

LSAT Argument	Analysis
1. Most of the employees of the Compujack Corporation are computer programmers. Since most computer programmers receive excellent salaries from their employers, at least one Compujack employee must receive an excellent salary from Compujack. *PrepTest122 Sec4 Q24*	**Conclusion:** [last part of Sentence 2] At least one CJ employee receives an excellent salary from CJ. Sentence 1 and first part of Sentence 2—**Two separate pieces of evidence:** • Most employees of CJ are programmers. • Most programmers have great salaries.
2. An art critic, by ridiculing an artwork, can undermine the pleasure one takes in it; conversely, by lavishing praise upon an artwork, an art critic can render the experience of viewing the artwork more pleasurable. So an artwork's artistic merit can depend not only on the person who creates it but also on those who critically evaluate it. *PrepTest143 Sec4 Q13*	**Conclusion:** [second sentence] A work's artistic merit can depend on both the artist and the critics. Sentence 1—**Two contrasting pieces of evidence:** • Critics can decrease pleasure in art. • But critics can increase pleasure, too.
3. Vanwilligan: Some have argued that professional athletes receive unfairly high salaries. But in an unrestricted free market, such as the market these athletes compete in, salaries are determined by what someone else is willing to pay for their services. These athletes make enormous profits for their teams' owners, and that is why owners are willing to pay them extraordinary salaries. Thus the salaries they receive are fair. *PrepTest122 Sec2 Q19*	**Conclusion:** [fourth sentence] Professional athletes' salaries are fair. Sentence 1—**Author's opponents' position:** Pro athletes' salaries are unfair. Sentence 2—**Author's evidence:** Free markets set fair salaries at what employers are willing to pay. Sentence 3—**Author's evidence:** Owners are willing to pay pro athletes' salaries.

LSAT Argument	Analysis
4. Columnist: It has been noted that attending a live musical performance is a richer experience than is listening to recorded music. Some say that this is merely because we do not see the performers when we listen to recorded music. However, there must be some other reason, for there is relatively little difference between listening to someone read a story over the radio and listening to someone in the same room read a story. *PrepTest131 Sec2 Q7*	**Conclusion:** [first part of Sentence 3] Seeing the musicians is not the reason live music is richer (my opponents' explanation is wrong). Sentence 1—**Background observation**: Live music is a richer experience than recorded music. Sentence 2—**The author's opponents' explanation for the observation**: Live music is richer because we see the musicians. Second part of Sentence 3—**Author's evidence**: An analogy showing why the opponents' explanation must be wrong.
5. Chiu: The belief that a person is always morally blameworthy for feeling certain emotions, such as unjustifiable anger, jealousy, or resentment, is misguided. Individuals are responsible for only what is under their control, and whether one feels such an emotion is not always under one's control. *PrepTest131 Sec1 Q16*	**Conclusion:** [first sentence] People are not always blameworthy for feeling negative emotions. Sentence 2—**Two related pieces of evidence**: • People are responsible only for things under their control. • Feeling emotions is not always under a person's control.
6. Scientist: A controversy in paleontology centers on the question of whether prehistoric human ancestors began to develop sophisticated tools before or after they came to stand upright. I argue that they stood upright first, simply because advanced toolmaking requires free use of the hands, and standing upright makes this possible. *PrepTest122 Sec2 Q14*	**Conclusion:** [first part of Sentence 2] Humans stood upright before making advanced tools. Sentence 1—**Background description of a scientific debate**: Which came first—standing upright or making advanced tools? Second part of Sentence 2—**Author's evidence**: • Free hands are needed to make advanced tools. • Standing up frees up the hands.

LSAT Argument	Analysis
7. Bethany: Psychologists have discovered a technique for replacing one's nightmares with pleasant dreams, and have successfully taught it to adults suffering from chronic nightmares. Studies have found that nightmare-prone children are especially likely to suffer from nightmares as adults. Thus, psychologists should direct efforts toward identifying nightmare-prone children so that these children can be taught the technique for replacing their nightmares with pleasant dreams. *PrepTest131 Sec2 Q13*	**Conclusion:** [first part of Sentence 3] Psychologists should focus on nightmare-prone kids. Sentence 1—**A scientific discovery that gives rise to the author's argument:** successful nightmare treatments Sentence 2—**A second discovery that makes the first important for one group:** nightmare-prone kids likely to become nightmare-prone adults Second part of Sentence 3—**The reason for the recommendation in the author's conclusion**
8. It is primarily by raising interest rates that central bankers curb inflation, but an increase in interest rates takes up to two years to affect inflation. Accordingly, central bankers usually try to raise interest rates before inflation becomes excessive, at which time inflation is not yet readily apparent either. But unless inflation is readily apparent, interest rate hikes generally will be perceived as needlessly restraining a growing economy. Thus, central bankers' success in temporarily restraining inflation may make it harder for them to ward off future inflation without incurring the public's wrath. *PrepTest122 Sec2 Q12*	**Conclusion:** [fourth sentence] Temporary success in halting inflation makes it harder to prevent future inflation without causing public anger. Sentences 1, 2, and 3 are **three related pieces of the author's evidence:** • The main way bankers try to halt inflation is by raising interest rates. • Bankers usually raise interest rates early before it becomes apparent. • If inflation isn't apparent, the public gets angry at steps that slow the economy.

Great work! Now that you're getting the hang of analyzing LSAT arguments into the purposes of their various statements, you've got a solid foundation for Role of a Statement questions.

Role of a Statement Questions

 Role of a Statement questions, which ask how a statement functions in an argument, reward your ability to identify the argument's conclusion, evidence, and other components.

LEARNING OBJECTIVE

In this section, you'll learn to:

- Identify and answer Role of a Statement questions.

On the typical LSAT, you'll see around two Role of a Statement questions. That's roughly 2.5% of your LSAT score.

You can identify Role of a Statement questions from question stems like these:

The statement that the educational use of computers enables schools to teach far more courses with far fewer teachers figures in the argument in which one of the following ways?

PrepTest129 Sec2 Q13

Which one of the following most accurately describes the role played in the argument by the claim that it is primarily by raising interest rates that central bankers curb inflation?

PrepTest122 Sec2 Q12

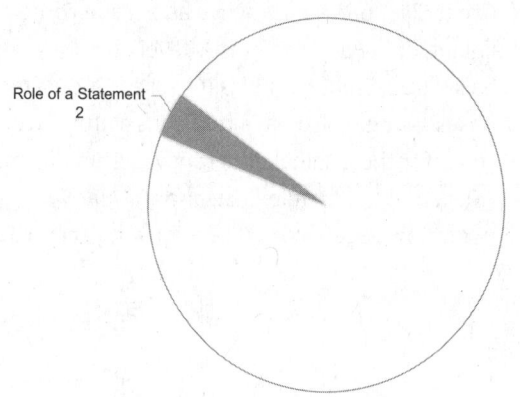

Approximate Number of Role of a Statement Questions per LSAT

Role of a Statement 2

Source: All officially released LSAT exams, 2016-2020

ROLE OF A STATEMENT QUESTIONS AT A GLANCE

Task: Identify how a specified statement or idea functions within the argument.

Strategy: Note the statement cited in the question stem; then, analyze the argument to characterize the role played by the statement.

Frequency: Released LSATs between 2016 and 2020 featured an average of 1.0 Role of a Statement question per section.

Now, get familiar with this question type by trying a Role of a Statement question on your own. When you're finished, explore how an LSAT expert tackled the same question in the worked example on the next page.

Step 2:	Step 1:

9. It would not be surprising to discover that the trade routes between China and the West were opened many centuries, even millennia, earlier than 200 b.c., contrary to what is currently believed. After all, what made the Great Silk Road so attractive as a trade route linking China and the West—level terrain, easily traversable mountain passes, and desert oases—would also have made it an attractive route for the original emigrants to China from Africa and the Middle East, and this early migration began at least one million years ago.

That a migration from Africa and the Middle East to China occurred at least one million years ago figures in the above reasoning in which one of the following ways?

(A) It is cited as conclusive evidence for the claim that trade links between China and the Middle East were established long before 200 b.c.

(B) It is an intermediate conclusion made plausible by the description of the terrain along which the migration supposedly took place.

(C) It is offered as evidence in support of the claim that trade routes between China and the West could easily have been established much earlier than is currently believed.

(D) It is offered as evidence against the claim that trade routes between China and Africa preceded those eventually established between China and the Middle East.

(E) It is the main conclusion that the argument attempts to establish about intercourse between China and the West.

PrepTest131 Sec1 Q14

Step 3:	Step 4:

Expert Analysis

Here's how an LSAT expert approached the Role of a Statement question you just tried.

Step 2: *Conclusion*: Trade routes between China and the West may very well have opened long before 200 b.c. *Evidence*: *After all* is the evidence signal. • What made the GSR a desirable route would've made it desirable for the original emigrants to China. • The original migration began a million years ago or more. [This is the statement in the question stem.]	**Step 1:** "Figures … in which one of the following ways" indicates a Role of a Statement question; the correct answer will accurately describe the statement's function in the argument.

9. It would not be surprising to discover that the trade routes between China and the West were opened many centuries, even millennia, earlier than 200 b.c., contrary to what is currently believed. After all, what made the Great Silk Road so attractive as a trade route linking China and the West—level terrain, easily traversable mountain passes, and desert oases—would also have made it an attractive route for the original emigrants to China from Africa and the Middle East, and this early migration began at least one million years ago.

That a migration from Africa and the Middle East to China occurred at least one million years ago figures in the above reasoning in which one of the following ways?

(A) It is cited as conclusive evidence for the claim that trade links between China and the Middle East were established long before 200 b.c.

(B) It is an intermediate conclusion made plausible by the description of the terrain along which the migration supposedly took place.

(C) It is offered as evidence in support of the claim that trade routes between China and the West could easily have been established much earlier than is currently believed.

(D) It is offered as evidence against the claim that trade routes between China and Africa preceded those eventually established between China and the Middle East.

(E) It is the main conclusion that the argument attempts to establish about intercourse between China and the West.

PrepTest131 Sec1 Q14

Step 3: The correct answer will describe the statement as one of two pieces of evidence included to support the conclusion.	**Step 4:** (C) is correct. The choice has the right role—"offered as evidence"—and the correct conclusion.

Wrong answers: (A) The statement is one of two parts of evidence, so by itself it cannot be "conclusive evidence." (B) The *and* before the statement means that it is another evidentiary fact, not an intermediate conclusion. (D) The author does not claim that routes between China and Africa came before those between China and the Middle East. (E) The main conclusion is the argument's first sentence, not the statement in question.

Nice work. Now build your skills with a Practice set of Role of a Statement questions.

Practice Try each of the following Role of a Statement questions. Some may contain arguments you analyzed earlier in this part of the book. Don't worry too much about your timing here. Complete all four steps of the Logical Reasoning Method for each question, jotting down your notes whenever it is helpful to do so. After each question, review your work with the expert Analysis that follows.

Hint: What do the author and their opponents agree about? What do they disagree about?

Step 2:	Step 1:

10. Columnist: It has been noted that attending a live musical performance is a richer experience than is listening to recorded music. Some say that this is merely because we do not see the performers when we listen to recorded music. However, there must be some other reason, for there is relatively little difference between listening to someone read a story over the radio and listening to someone in the same room read a story.

Which one of the following most accurately expresses the role played in the argument by the observation that attending a live musical performance is a richer experience than is listening to recorded music?

(A) It is what the columnist's argument purports to show.

(B) It is the reason given for the claim that the columnist's argument is attempting to undermine.

(C) It is what the columnist's argument purports to explain.

(D) It is what the columnist's argument purports to refute.

(E) It is what the position that the columnist tries to undermine is purported to explain.

PrepTest131 Sec2 Q7

Step 3:	Step 4:

Expert Analysis

Here's how an LSAT expert approached the Role of a Statement question you just saw.

Step 2: *Conclusion*: [first part of Sentence 3] Seeing the musicians is not the reason live music is richer (my opponents' explanation is wrong). Sentence 1—Background: Live music is a richer experience than recorded music. [This is the statement in the question stem.] Sentence 2—The opponents' explanation: Live music is richer because we see the musicians. Second part of Sentence 3—*Evidence*: an analogy showing why the opponents' explanation must be wrong.	**Step 1:** A standard Role of a Statement question stem: the correct answer describes how the statement fits into the argument

10. Columnist: It has been noted that attending a live musical performance is a richer experience than is listening to recorded music. Some say that this is merely because we do not see the performers when we listen to recorded music. However, there must be some other reason, for there is relatively little difference between listening to someone read a story over the radio and listening to someone in the same room read a story.

Which one of the following most accurately expresses the role played in the argument by the observation that attending a live musical performance is a richer experience than is listening to recorded music?

(A) It is what the columnist's argument purports to show.

(B) It is the reason given for the claim that the columnist's argument is attempting to undermine.

(C) It is what the columnist's argument purports to explain.

(D) It is what the columnist's argument purports to refute.

(E) It is what the position that the columnist tries to undermine is purported to explain.

PrepTest131 Sec2 Q7

Step 3: The statement in question stipulates a fact. The author and their opponents argue about the reason it is true.	**Step 4:** (E) is correct. The author and their opponents agree that live music is a richer experience. The opponents try to explain this by saying, "It is true because you see the musicians." The author rejects this explanation.

Wrong answers: (A) Distortion. The author wants to show that someone else's explanation for the statement is wrong. (B) Distortion. The statement in question is not the reason for the claim; it is the claim. Moreover, the author is not trying to undermine the claim, but rather, an opposing explanation of it. (C) Distortion. The author never offers an explanation for why live music is richer; rather, they argue that an opposing explanation is wrong. (D) The author does not want to refute the claim that live music is richer, a view both the author and the opponents at least implicitly accept. The argument's point is that *seeing* the musicians is not the reason it is richer.

Hint: Where is the conclusion of this argument? What do the other sentences do?

Step 2:	Step 1:

11. It is primarily by raising interest rates that central bankers curb inflation, but an increase in interest rates takes up to two years to affect inflation. Accordingly, central bankers usually try to raise interest rates before inflation becomes excessive, at which time inflation is not yet readily apparent either. But unless inflation is readily apparent, interest rate hikes generally will be perceived as needlessly restraining a growing economy. Thus, central bankers' success in temporarily restraining inflation may make it harder for them to ward off future inflation without incurring the public's wrath.

Which one of the following most accurately describes the role played in the argument by the claim that it is primarily by raising interest rates that central bankers curb inflation?

(A) It is presented as a complete explanation of the fact that central bankers' success in temporarily restraining inflation may make it harder for them to ward off future inflation without incurring the public's wrath.

(B) It is a description of a phenomenon for which the claim that an increase in interest rates takes up to two years to affect inflation is offered as an explanation.

(C) It is a premise offered in support of the conclusion that central bankers' success in temporarily restraining inflation may make it harder for them to ward off future inflation without incurring the public's wrath.

(D) It is a conclusion for which the statement that an increase in interest rates takes up to two years to affect inflation is offered as support.

(E) It is a premise offered in support of the conclusion that unless inflation is readily apparent, interest rate hikes generally will be perceived as needlessly restraining a growing economy.

PrepTest122 Sec2 Q12

Step 3:	Step 4:

Expert Analysis

Here's how an LSAT expert approached the Role of a Statement question you just saw.

Step 2: *Conclusion*: [fourth sentence] Temporary success in halting inflation makes it harder to prevent future inflation without causing public anger. Sentences 1, 2, and 3 are three related pieces of the *evidence*: • The main way bankers try to halt inflation is by raising interest rates. [This is the statement in the question stem.] • Bankers usually raise interest rates early, before it becomes apparent. • If inflation isn't apparent, the public gets angry at steps that slow the economy.	**Step 1:** This is a typical Role of a Statement question stem; the correct answer describes how the statement fits into the argument.

11. It is primarily by raising interest rates that central bankers curb inflation, but an increase in interest rates takes up to two years to affect inflation. Accordingly, central bankers usually try to raise interest rates before inflation becomes excessive, at which time inflation is not yet readily apparent either. But unless inflation is readily apparent, interest rate hikes generally will be perceived as needlessly restraining a growing economy. Thus, central bankers' success in temporarily restraining inflation may make it harder for them to ward off future inflation without incurring the public's wrath.

Which one of the following most accurately describes the role played in the argument by the claim that it is primarily by raising interest rates that central bankers curb inflation?

(A) It is presented as a complete explanation of the fact that central bankers' success in temporarily restraining inflation may make it harder for them to ward off future inflation without incurring the public's wrath.

(B) It is a description of a phenomenon for which the claim that an increase in interest rates takes up to two years to affect inflation is offered as an explanation.

(C) It is a premise offered in support of the conclusion that central bankers' success in temporarily restraining inflation may make it harder for them to ward off future inflation without incurring the public's wrath.

(D) It is a conclusion for which the statement that an increase in interest rates takes up to two years to affect inflation is offered as support.

(E) It is a premise offered in support of the conclusion that unless inflation is readily apparent, interest rate hikes generally will be perceived as needlessly restraining a growing economy.

PrepTest122 Sec2 Q12

Step 3: The correct answer will identify the statement as one piece of the evidence.	**Step 4:** (C) is correct. *Premise* means evidence, and the paraphrase of the author's conclusion here is accurate. The statement in question was just evidence for the conclusion.

Wrong answers: (A) is Extreme. The statement in question is one of three pieces of evidence offered for the conclusion. *Complete explanation* is too strong. (B) is a Distortion. The claim referred to in this choice is just a detail about the statement in question, not an explanation of it. (D) is a Distortion. The statement in question was actually the first piece in a string of evidence. (E) is a Distortion. What this answer identifies as the conclusion is actually another piece of evidence for the main point.

Hint: There's no opposing view here, so all statements represent the author's view. Does that help you describe the role played by the statement cited in the question stem?

Step 2:	Step 1:

12. People's political behavior frequently does not match their rhetoric. Although many complain about government intervention in their lives, they tend not to reelect inactive politicians. But a politician's activity consists largely in the passage of laws whose enforcement affects voters' lives. Thus, voters often reelect politicians whose behavior they resent.

Which one of the following most accurately describes the role played in the argument by the claim that people tend not to reelect inactive politicians?

(A) It describes a phenomenon for which the argument's conclusion is offered as an explanation.

(B) It is a premise offered in support of the conclusion that voters often reelect politicians whose behavior they resent.

(C) It is offered as an example of how a politician's activity consists largely in the passage of laws whose enforcement interferes with voters' lives.

(D) It is a generalization based on the claim that people complain about government intervention in their lives.

(E) It is cited as evidence that people's behavior never matches their political beliefs.

PrepTest110 Sec3 Q14

Step 3:	Step 4:

Expert Analysis

Here's how an LSAT expert approached the Role of a Statement question you just saw.

Step 1: The stem cites a claim and asks for its purpose in the argument; this is a Role of a Statement question.

Step 2: *Conclusion*: Sentence 4—Voters often reelect politicians they resent (a paradoxical result).

Sentence 1—States a principle: people's political actions often don't match their words.

Sentences 2 and 3—Describes the principle in action: Voters complain about interference, but don't reelect inactive politicians (i.e., those who don't interfere). [That's the claim from the stem.] Instead, voters elect politicians who actively make laws that interfere (thus, the paradox in the conclusion).

12. People's political behavior frequently does not match their rhetoric. Although many complain about government intervention in their lives, they tend not to reelect inactive politicians. But a politician's activity consists largely in the passage of laws whose enforcement affects voters' lives. Thus, voters often reelect politicians whose behavior they resent.

Which one of the following most accurately describes the role played in the argument by the claim that people tend not to reelect inactive politicians?

(A) It describes a phenomenon for which the argument's conclusion is offered as an explanation.

(B) It is a premise offered in support of the conclusion that voters often reelect politicians whose behavior they resent.

(C) It is offered as an example of how a politician's activity consists largely in the passage of laws whose enforcement interferes with voters' lives.

(D) It is a generalization based on the claim that people complain about government intervention in their lives.

(E) It is cited as evidence that people's behavior never matches their political beliefs.

PrepTest110 Sec3 Q14

Step 3: Don't overthink it. Sentences 2 and 3, where the cited claim comes from, provide the evidence to explain the paradoxical conclusion.

Step 4: (B) is simple, but accurate; the cited claim is part of the evidence for the argument's conclusion.

Wrong answers: (A) gets it backwards; the cited claim is part of an explanation for the conclusion, not the other way around. (C) Distortion. The cited claim is part of the evidence for a paradoxical result, not an example of political activity. (D) Distortion. The claim cited in the stem *conflicts* with the fact that people complain about governmental interference. (E) Extreme. The author says people's behavior *frequently* does not match their words, not that it *never* matches their beliefs.

Hint: How many points of view are cited in the stimulus? Who does the author side with?

Step 2:	Step 1:

13. Sociologist: Some people argue that capital punishment for theft was an essential part of the labor discipline of British capitalism. Critics of such a view argue that more people were executed for theft in pre-industrial England than were executed in England after industrialization. But such a criticism overlooks the fact that industrialization and capitalism are two very different social phenomena, and that the latter predated the former by several centuries.

Which one of the following most accurately describes the role played in the passage by the point that capitalism and industrialization are distinct?

(A) It is cited as some evidence against the claim that capital punishment for theft was an essential part of the labor discipline of British capitalism.

(B) It is cited as a direct contradiction of the claim that capital punishment for theft was an essential part of the labor discipline of British capitalism.

(C) It is an attempt to conclusively prove the claim that capital punishment for theft was an essential part of the labor discipline of British capitalism.

(D) It is cited as a fact supporting the critics of the view that capital punishment for theft was an essential part of the labor discipline of British capitalism.

(E) It is an attempt to undermine the criticism cited against the claim that capital punishment for theft was an essential part of the labor discipline of British capitalism.

PrepTest110 Sec2 Q22

Step 3:	Step 4:

Expert Analysis

Here's how an LSAT expert approached the Role of a Statement question you just saw.

Step 2: *Conclusion*: [first part of Sentence 3] The critics' point is flawed.

Sentence 1—States some peoples' view: capital punishment was central to British capitalism.

Sentence 2—The view of those who criticize the first view: there was more capital punishment before industrialization.

2nd part of Sentence 3 [the point in the question stem]—The reason the critics' view is flawed: capitalism started before industrialization.

Step 1: You're asked for the author's purpose in making a certain point in the argument; this is a Role of a Statement question.

13. Sociologist: Some people argue that capital punishment for theft was an essential part of the labor discipline of British capitalism. Critics of such a view argue that more people were executed for theft in pre-industrial England than were executed in England after industrialization. But such a criticism overlooks the fact that industrialization and capitalism are two very different social phenomena, and that the latter predated the former by several centuries.

Which one of the following most accurately describes the role played in the passage by the point that capitalism and industrialization are distinct?

(A) It is cited as some evidence against the claim that capital punishment for theft was an essential part of the labor discipline of British capitalism.

(B) It is cited as a direct contradiction of the claim that capital punishment for theft was an essential part of the labor discipline of British capitalism.

(C) It is an attempt to conclusively prove the claim that capital punishment for theft was an essential part of the labor discipline of British capitalism.

(D) It is cited as a fact supporting the critics of the view that capital punishment for theft was an essential part of the labor discipline of British capitalism.

(E) It is an attempt to undermine the criticism cited against the claim that capital punishment for theft was an essential part of the labor discipline of British capitalism.

PrepTest110 Sec2 Q22

Step 3: The point cited in the question stem serves to point out something the critics overlook. It is evidence for the author's conclusion.	**Step 4:** (E) accurately describes the role played by the point cited in the stem: It is evidence that critics of the first claim described in the passage overlook a key distinction.

Wrong answers: (A) 180. The author defends the view that capital punishment was an essential part of British capitalism. (B) 180. The author defends the view that capital punishment was an essential part of British capitalism. (C) Extreme. The author is defending the claim against its critics, not offering evidence to prove the claim. (D) 180. The author is attempting to weaken the critics' argument, not support it.

Good work. Now, assess your Role of a Statement skill level with the following Perform quiz.

Chapter Perform Quiz

Perform This Perform quiz has 4 Role of a Statement questions. They are presented without any notes, hints, or prompts for a more test-like experience while you work. Try to get as many correct answers as possible in 6 minutes. When you finish, check your performance against the Answer Key and Evaluate Your Performance for tips on how best to improve. Then, come back to complete any questions you skipped or guessed on and finish up by reviewing all the questions with the expert analyses in your online companion.

14. Legal theorist: It is unreasonable to incarcerate anyone for any other reason than that he or she is a serious threat to the property or lives of other people. The breaking of a law does not justify incarceration, for lawbreaking proceeds either from ignorance of the law or of the effects of one's actions, or from the free choice on the part of the lawbreaker. Obviously mere ignorance cannot justify incarcerating a lawbreaker, and even free choice on the part of the lawbreaker fails to justify incarceration, for free choice proceeds from the desires of an agent, and the desires of an agent are products of genetics and environmental conditioning, neither of which is controlled by the agent.

The claim in the first sentence of the passage plays which one of the following roles in the argument?

(A) It is offered as a premise that helps to show that no actions are under the control of the agent.

(B) It is offered as background information necessary to understand the argument.

(C) It is offered as the main conclusion that the argument is designed to establish.

(D) It is offered as evidence for the stated claim that protection of life and property is more important than retribution for past illegal acts.

(E) It is offered as evidence for the stated claim that lawbreaking proceeds from either ignorance of the law, or ignorance of the effects of one's actions, or free choice.

PrepTest112 Sec4 Q3

15. Administrators of educational institutions are enthusiastic about the educational use of computers because they believe that it will enable schools to teach far more courses with far fewer teachers than traditional methods allow. Many teachers fear computers for the same reason. But this reason is mistaken. Computerized instruction requires more, not less, time of instructors, which indicates that any reduction in the number of teachers would require an accompanying reduction in courses offered.

The statement that the educational use of computers enables schools to teach far more courses with far fewer teachers figures in the argument in which one of the following ways?

(A) It is presented as a possible explanation for an observation that follows it.

(B) It is a statement of the problem the argument sets out to solve.

(C) It is a statement that the argument is designed to refute.

(D) It is a statement offered in support of the argument's main conclusion.

(E) It is the argument's main conclusion.

PrepTest129 Sec2 Q13

PART TWO
ARGUMENT-BASED QUESTIONS

16. Geneticist: Ethicists have fears, many of them reasonable, about the prospect of cloning human beings, that is, producing exact genetic duplicates. But the horror-movie image of a wealthy person creating an army of exact duplicates is completely unrealistic. Clones must be raised and educated, a long-term process that could never produce adults identical to the original in terms of outlook, personality, or goals. More realistic is the possibility that wealthy individuals might use clones as living "organ banks."

The claim that cloning will not produce adults with identical personalities plays which one of the following roles in the geneticist's argument?

(A) It is a reason for dismissing the various fears raised by ethicists regarding the cloning of human beings.

(B) It is evidence that genetic clones will never be produced successfully.

(C) It illustrates the claim that only wealthy people would be able to have genetic duplicates made of themselves.

(D) It is evidence for the claim that wealthy people might use genetic duplicates of themselves as sources of compatible organs for transplantation.

(E) It is a reason for discounting one possible fear concerning the cloning of human beings.

PrepTest111 Sec4 Q15

17. Software reviewer: Dictation software allows a computer to produce a written version of sentences that are spoken to it. Although dictation software has been promoted as a labor-saving invention, it fails to live up to its billing. The laborious part of writing is in the thinking and the editing, not in the typing. And proofreading the software's error-filled output generally squanders any time saved in typing.

Which one of the following most accurately describes the role played in the software reviewer's argument by the claim that dictation software fails to live up to its billing?

(A) It is the argument's main conclusion but not its only conclusion.

(B) It is the argument's only conclusion.

(C) It is an intermediate conclusion that is offered as direct support for the argument's main conclusion.

(D) It is a premise offered in support of the argument's conclusion.

(E) It is a premise offered as direct support for an intermediate conclusion of the argument.

PrepTest129 Sec2 Q16

Answer Key

14. C; 15. C; 16. E; 17. B

Evaluate Your Performance

To assess your strengths and opportunities from this Perform quiz, go to the corresponding chapter in your online companion. There you'll find recommendations based on your performance along with complete worked-example explanations (written by a Kaplan LSAT expert) for each of the questions in this Perform quiz.

CHAPTER 5

Argument Outlines and Point at Issue Questions

All LSAT arguments—even those written in the most complicated prose—can be reduced to the pattern of "Conclusion *because* Evidence."

LEARNING OBJECTIVES

In this chapter, you'll learn to:

- Outline complete arguments.
- Identify and answer Point at Issue questions.

Learning to analyze arguments in this way makes them easier to compare, easier to describe, and thus easier to use in getting to the right answer in a wide variety of LSAT question types. Later in this chapter, you'll learn the best strategies for Point at Issue questions, but first, get some practice boiling down arguments to their essential parts.

Outline Complete Arguments

Prepare

LEARNING OBJECTIVE

In this section, you'll learn to:

- Outline complete arguments.

When you distill an LSAT argument down to its essence, accept the background information as given, and focus on the conclusion and the evidence the author offers in direct support of the main point.

Here's how an LSAT expert might outline one of the complete arguments you saw earlier.

LSAT Argument	Analysis
The typological theory of species classification, which has few adherents today, distinguishes species solely on the basis of observable physical characteristics, such as plumage color, adult size, or dental structure. However, there are many so-called "sibling species," which are indistinguishable on the basis of their appearance but cannot interbreed and thus, according to the mainstream biological theory of species classification, are separate species. Since the typological theory does not count sibling species as separate species, it is unacceptable.	*Conclusion*: The typological theory of species classification is unacceptable *because* *Evidence*: the typological theory of species classification does not count sibling species as separate species (while the mainstream theory does).

PrepTest131 Sec1 Q15

Expert readers use the background information—such as the definition of sibling species—to get the context they need, but their analysis of the argument zeroes in on the author's conclusion and evidence.

LSAT STRATEGY

When a Logical Reasoning question includes two arguments, or when a single argument involves the author's response to someone else's position, paraphrase both arguments and be sure you understand how they relate to one another.

Practice Outline the following LSAT arguments, simplifying each into its core "Conclusion *because* Evidence" structure. When you're finished, compare your work to that of an LSAT expert with the explanations that follow.

LSAT Argument	My Analysis
1. A survey of clerical workers' attitudes toward their work identified a group of secretaries with very positive attitudes. They responded "Strongly agree" to such statements as "I enjoy word processing" and "I like learning new secretarial skills." These secretaries had been rated by their supervisors as excellent workers—far better than secretaries whose attitudes were identified as less positive. Clearly these secretaries' positive attitudes toward their work produced excellent job performance. *PrepTest122 Sec2 Q13*	*Conclusion:* *because* *Evidence:*
2. There can be no individual freedom without the rule of law, for there is no individual freedom without social integrity, and pursuing the good life is not possible without social integrity. *PrepTest143 Sec4 Q25*	*Conclusion:* *because* *Evidence:*
3. Ilana: Carver's stories are somber and pessimistic, which is a sure sign of inferior writing. I have never read a single story of his that ends happily. Gustav: Carver was one of the finest writers of the past 30 years. Granted, his stories are characterized by somberness and pessimism, but they are also wryly humorous, compassionate, and beautifully structured. *PrepTest122 Sec2 Q1*	[**Ilana**] *Conclusion:* *because* *Evidence:* [**Gustav**] *Conclusion:* *because* *Evidence:*

LSAT Argument	My Analysis
4. Politician: The huge amounts of money earned by oil companies elicit the suspicion that the regulations designed to prevent collusion need to be tightened. But just the opposite is true. If the regulations designed to prevent collusion are not excessively burdensome, then oil companies will make profits sufficient to motivate the very risky investments associated with exploration that must be made if society is to have adequate oil supplies. But recent data show that the oil industry's profits are not the highest among all industries. Clearly, the regulatory burden on oil companies has become excessive. *PrepTest122 Sec4 Q12*	*Conclusion*: *because* *Evidence*:
5. Letter to the editor: Middle-class families in wealthy nations are often criticized for the ecological damage resulting from their lifestyles. This criticism should not be taken too seriously, however, since its source is often a movie star or celebrity whose own lifestyle would, if widely adopted, destroy the environment and deplete our resources in a short time. *PrepTest122 Sec2 Q5*	*Conclusion*: *because* *Evidence*:
6. Vanwilligan: Some have argued that professional athletes receive unfairly high salaries. But in an unrestricted free market, such as the market these athletes compete in, salaries are determined by what someone else is willing to pay for their services. These athletes make enormous profits for their teams' owners, and that is why owners are willing to pay them extraordinary salaries. Thus, the salaries they receive are fair. *PrepTest122 Sec2 Q19*	*Conclusion*: *because* *Evidence*:

LSAT Argument	My Analysis
7. Talbert: Chess is beneficial for school-age children. It is enjoyable, encourages foresight and logical thinking, and discourages carelessness, inattention, and impulsiveness. In short, it promotes mental maturity. Sklar: My objection to teaching chess to children is that it diverts mental activity from something with societal value, such as science, into something that has no societal value. *PrepTest142 Sec2 Q7*	[**Talbert**] *Conclusion:* *because* *Evidence:* [**Sklar**] *Conclusion:* *because* *Evidence:*
8. A development company has proposed building an airport near the city of Dalton. If the majority of Dalton's residents favor the proposal, the airport will be built. However, it is unlikely that a majority of Dalton's residents would favor the proposal, for most of them believe that the airport would create noise problems. Thus, it is unlikely that the airport will be built. *PrepTest143 Sec4 Q11*	*Conclusion:* *because* *Evidence:*

Expert Analysis

Here's how an LSAT expert broke down the arguments you just analyzed. Compare your work to theirs looking for patterns and clues you may have missed.

LSAT Argument	My Analysis
1. A survey of clerical workers' attitudes toward their work identified a group of secretaries with very positive attitudes. They responded "Strongly agree" to such statements as "I enjoy word processing" and "I like learning new secretarial skills." These secretaries had been rated by their supervisors as excellent workers—far better than secretaries whose attitudes were identified as less positive. Clearly these secretaries' positive attitudes toward their work produced excellent job performance. *PrepTest122 Sec2 Q13*	*Conclusion*: The positive attitudes of secretaries in the positive group caused their excellent job performance *because* *Evidence*: secretaries in the positive group were rated excellent workers by their supervisors. Secretaries not in the positive group were rated lower.
2. There can be no individual freedom without the rule of law, for there is no individual freedom without social integrity, and pursuing the good life is not possible without social integrity. *PrepTest143 Sec4 Q25*	*Conclusion*: Individual freedom requires the rule of law *because* *Evidence*: individual freedom requires social integrity.
3. Ilana: Carver's stories are somber and pessimistic, which is a sure sign of inferior writing. I have never read a single story of his that ends happily. Gustav: Carver was one of the finest writers of the past 30 years. Granted, his stories are characterized by somberness and pessimism, but they are also wryly humorous, compassionate, and beautifully structured. *PrepTest122 Sec2 Q1*	**[Ilana]** *Conclusion*: Carver's writing is inferior *because* *Evidence*: (1) somberness and pessimism are sure signs of inferior writing, and (2) I've never read a happy Carver story. **[Gustav]** *Conclusion*: Carver was one of the best writers of the last three decades *because* *Evidence*: while somber and pessimistic, Carver's stories are nevertheless funny, compassionate, and well-structured.

LSAT Argument	My Analysis
4. Politician: The huge amounts of money earned by oil companies elicit the suspicion that the regulations designed to prevent collusion need to be tightened. But just the opposite is true. If the regulations designed to prevent collusion are not excessively burdensome, then oil companies will make profits sufficient to motivate the very risky investments associated with exploration that must be made if society is to have adequate oil supplies. But recent data show that the oil industry's profits are not the highest among all industries. Clearly, the regulatory burden on oil companies has become excessive. *PrepTest122 Sec4 Q12*	*Conclusion*: Oil companies are excessively burdened by regulation *because* *Evidence*: oil companies' profits are not the highest among all industries.
5. Letter to the editor: Middle-class families in wealthy nations are often criticized for the ecological damage resulting from their lifestyles. This criticism should not be taken too seriously, however, since its source is often a movie star or celebrity whose own lifestyle would, if widely adopted, destroy the environment and deplete our resources in a short time. *PrepTest122 Sec2 Q5*	*Conclusion*: The criticism that middle-class lifestyles cause ecological damage should not be taken seriously *because* *Evidence*: those making the criticism are often celebrities who live worse lifestyles.
6. Vanwilligan: Some have argued that professional athletes receive unfairly high salaries. But in an unrestricted free market, such as the market these athletes compete in, salaries are determined by what someone else is willing to pay for their services. These athletes make enormous profits for their teams' owners, and that is why owners are willing to pay them extraordinary salaries. Thus the salaries they receive are fair. *PrepTest122 Sec2 Q19*	*Conclusion*: Professional athletes' salaries are fair *because* *Evidence*: (1) the free market sets salaries at what employers are willing to pay, and (2) team owners are willing to pay professional athletes' salaries.

LSAT Argument	**My Analysis**
7. Talbert: Chess is beneficial for school-age children. It is enjoyable, encourages foresight and logical thinking, and discourages carelessness, inattention, and impulsiveness. In short, it promotes mental maturity.	[**Talbert**] *Conclusion*: Chess is good for school kids *because* *Evidence*: chess promotes mental maturity (in three specific ways).
Sklar: My objection to teaching chess to children is that it diverts mental activity from something with societal value, such as science, into something that has no societal value. *PrepTest142 Sec2 Q7*	[**Sklar**] *Conclusion*: Teaching chess to school kids is objectionable *because* *Evidence*: chess diverts mental activity away from things with social value.
8. A development company has proposed building an airport near the city of Dalton. If the majority of Dalton's residents favor the proposal, the airport will be built. However, it is unlikely that a majority of Dalton's residents would favor the proposal, for most of them believe that the airport would create noise problems. Thus, it is unlikely that the airport will be built. *PrepTest143 Sec4 Q11*	*Conclusion*: The proposed Dalton airport probably will not be built *because* *Evidence*: if a majority of Dalton's residents favor building the proposed airport, it will be built, but a majority probably won't support building it.

Well done! You'll put that approach to argument analysis to work on literally dozens of questions on test day, so continue to practice it on upcoming questions. Next up, take a look at the fundamentals of Point at Issue questions.

Point at Issue Questions

Once you are able to summarize complete arguments, you have the skill necessary to answer Point at Issue questions. These questions require you to pinpoint the specific issue about which two speakers disagree. In rare cases, they will ask for a point of agreement between the speakers.

Prepare

LEARNING OBJECTIVE

In this section, you'll learn to:

- Identify and answer Point at Issue questions.

Expect to see around three Point at Issue statements per LSAT test, approximately 4% of available points.

Point at Issue questions always have a dialog stimulus, but not every dialog stimulus belongs to a Point at Issue question. You can identify Point at Issue questions from question stems like these:

Talbert's and Sklar's statements provide the strongest support for holding that they disagree with each other over whether

PrepTest142 Sec2 Q7

Megan and Channen disagree over whether

PrepTest122 Sec2 Q10

On the basis of their statements, Ilana and Gustav are committed to disagreeing over whether

PrepTest122 Sec2 Q1

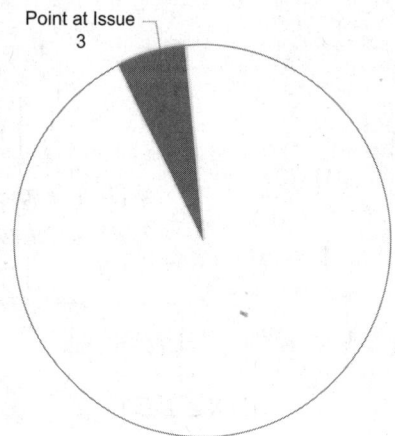

Approximate Number of Point At Issue Questions per LSAT

Point at Issue — 3

Source: All officially released LSAT exams, 2016-2020

POINT AT ISSUE QUESTIONS AT A GLANCE

Task: Identify the specific claim, statement, or recommendation about which two speakers disagree (or *very* rarely, about which they agree).

Strategy: Analyze both speakers' arguments and determine the point at issue between them, or use the Point at Issue Tree approach to identify the correct answer.

Frequency: On LSAT tests released from 2016 through 2020, there were an average of 1.4 Point at Issue questions per section.

Point at Issue Tree

In Point at Issue questions, one (and only one) answer choice will contain a statement about which the two speakers disagree. This provides a built-in way to evaluate the answer choices efficiently and effectively. It is depicted in the "decision tree" model that follows.

> **TEST DAY TIP**
>
> A great way to evaluate the answer choices in Point at Issue questions is to apply the questions from the Point at Issue Tree.

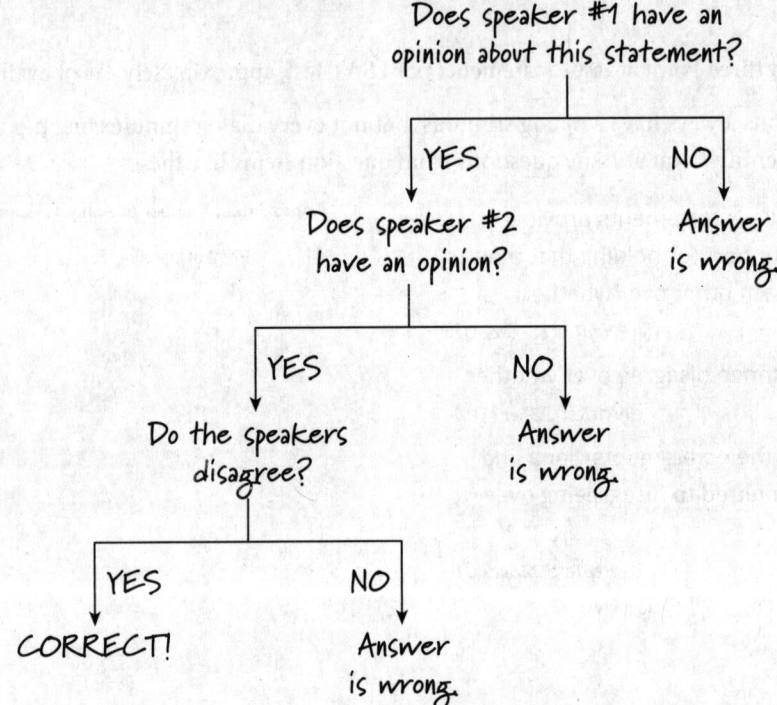

Because the correct answer must be the one statement over which the two speakers are committed to disagreeing, it will be the only choice that produces a "yes" to all three questions in the Decision Tree. In other words, if even one speaker doesn't express an opinion about an answer choice, you can immediately eliminate it.

Now, try a Point at Issue question on your own. When you're finished, compare your work to that of an LSAT expert in the worked example on the next page.

Step 2:	Step 1:

9. Talbert: Chess is beneficial for school-age children. It is enjoyable, encourages foresight and logical thinking, and discourages carelessness, inattention, and impulsiveness. In short, it promotes mental maturity.

    Sklar: My objection to teaching chess to children is that it diverts mental activity from something with societal value, such as science, into something that has no societal value.

Talbert's and Sklar's statements provide the strongest support for holding that they disagree with each other over whether

(A) chess promotes mental maturity

(B) many activities promote mental maturity just as well as chess does

(C) chess is socially valuable and science is not

(D) children should be taught to play chess

(E) children who neither play chess nor study science are mentally immature

PrepTest61 Sec2 Q7

Step 3:	Step 4:

Expert Analysis

Review an LSAT expert's work on the question you just saw. What strategies and tactics did they employ?

Step 2: [**Talbert**] *Conclusion*: Chess is good for school kids *because* *Evidence*: chess promotes mental maturity (in three specific ways). [**Sklar**] *Conclusion*: Teaching chess to school kids is objectionable *because* *Evidence*: Chess diverts mental activity away from things with social value.	**Step 1:** This is a standard Point at Issue question stem; the correct answer contains a point over which the two speakers explicitly express disagreement.

9. Talbert: Chess is beneficial for school-age children. It is enjoyable, encourages foresight and logical thinking, and discourages carelessness, inattention, and impulsiveness. In short, it promotes mental maturity.

    Sklar: My objection to teaching chess to children is that it diverts mental activity from something with societal value, such as science, into something that has no societal value.

Talbert's and Sklar's statements provide the strongest support for holding that they disagree with each other over whether

(A) chess promotes mental maturity

(B) many activities promote mental maturity just as well as chess does

(C) chess is socially valuable and science is not

(D) children should be taught to play chess

(E) children who neither play chess nor study science are mentally immature

PrepTest61 Sec2 Q7

Step 3: T and S disagree about whether chess is good for school children. The Point at Issue Tree can help evaluate each answer choice.	**Step 4:** (D) is correct. Does Talbert express an opinion? *Yes. They agree.* Does Sklar express an opinion? *Yes. They disagree.* Do Talbert and Sklar disagree? *Yes.*

Wrong answers: (A) Does Talbert express an opinion? *Yes.* Does Sklar express an opinion? *No.* (B) Does Talbert express an opinion? *No.* (C) Does Talbert express an opinion? *No.* (E) Does Talbert express an opinion? *No.*

Nice work. Continue to hone your skills at analyzing dialog stimuli and applying the Point at Issue Tree as you work through the following Practice set.

Practice Try each of the following Main Point questions. Some may contain arguments you analyzed in the preceding chapter. Don't worry too much about your timing here. Complete all four steps of the Logical Reasoning Method for each question, jotting down your notes whenever it is helpful to do so. After each question, review your work with the expert analysis that follows.

Hint: In LSAT Point at Issue questions, it's not usually enough to note that one person likes something and the other dislikes it; the answer choices will get a *why* and *how* each person justifies their opinion.

Step 2:	Step 1:

10. Ilana: Carver's stories are somber and pessimistic, which is a sure sign of inferior writing. I have never read a single story of his that ends happily.

 Gustav: Carver was one of the finest writers of the past 30 years. Granted, his stories are characterized by somberness and pessimism, but they are also wryly humorous, compassionate, and beautifully structured.

On the basis of their statements, Ilana and Gustav are committed to disagreeing over whether

(A) Carver's stories are truly compassionate

(B) Carver's stories are pessimistic in their vision

(C) stories that are characterized by somberness and pessimism can appropriately be called humorous

(D) stories that are well written can be somber and pessimistic

(E) there are some characteristics of a story that are decisive in determining its aesthetic value

PrepTest122 Sec2 Q1

Step 3:	Step 4:

Expert Analysis

Here's how an LSAT expert approached the question you just tried.

Step 2: [**Ilana**] *Conclusion*: Carver's writing is inferior *because*

Evidence: (1) somberness and pessimism are sure signs of inferior writing, and (2) I've never read a happy Carver story.

[**Gustav**] *Conclusion*: Carver was one of the best writers of the last three decades *because*

Evidence: while somber and pessimistic, Carver's stories are nevertheless funny, compassionate, and well structured.

Step 1: The phrase "committed to disagreeing" signals a Point at Issue question; the correct answer is the one over which both parties express disagreement.

10. Ilana: Carver's stories are somber and pessimistic, which is a sure sign of inferior writing. I have never read a single story of his that ends happily.

Gustav: Carver was one of the finest writers of the past 30 years. Granted, his stories are characterized by somberness and pessimism, but they are also wryly humorous, compassionate, and beautifully structured.

On the basis of their statements, Ilana and Gustav are committed to disagreeing over whether

(A) Carver's stories are truly compassionate

(B) Carver's stories are pessimistic in their vision

(C) stories that are characterized by somberness and pessimism can appropriately be called humorous

(D) stories that are well written can be somber and pessimistic

(E) there are some characteristics of a story that are decisive in determining its aesthetic value

PrepTest122 Sec2 Q1

Step 3: Ilana and Gustav disagree about whether Carver's somberness and pessimism make him a bad writer. The Point at Issue Tree can help you evaluate each answer choice.

Step 4: (D) is correct. Ilana has an opinion (she disagrees). Gustav has an opinion (he agrees). The two speakers disagree over this point.

Wrong answers: (A) Ilana expresses no opinion on this. (B) is a 180. Ilana and Gustav agree that Carver's stories are pessimistic. (C) Ilana expresses no opinion about this. (E) Ilana expresses agreement with this statement; for her, somberness and pessimism are *sure signs* of inferiority. From the quote in the stimulus, you cannot tell if there are any such characteristics for Gustav. It is possible, for example, that he thinks *any* story with wry humor or compassion is excellent, but he's not on record with that opinion.

Hint: Paying close attention to words like majority and average will help you answer Flaw and Weaken questions, too.

Step 2:	Step 1:

11. Goswami: I support the striking workers at Ergon Foods. They are underpaid. The majority of them make less than $20,000 per year.

    Nordecki: If pay is the issue, I must disagree. The average annual salary of the striking workers at Ergon Foods is over $29,000.

Goswami and Nordecki disagree over the truth of which one of the following statements?

(A) The average annual salary at Ergon Foods is over $29,000.

(B) Pay is the primary issue over which the workers are striking at Ergon Foods.

(C) It is reasonable to support striking workers who are underpaid.

(D) The striking workers at Ergon Foods are underpaid.

(E) It was unreasonable for the workers at Ergon Foods to go on strike.

PrepTest111 Sec3 Q10

Step 3:	Step 4:

Expert Analysis

Here's how an LSAT expert approached the Point at Issue question you just tried.

Step 2: [**Goswami**] *Conclusion*: Workers at Ergon Foods are underpaid *because* *Evidence*: the majority make under $20K/year. [**Nordecki**] *Conclusion*: Ergon Foods workers are not underpaid *because* *Evidence*: on average, their salaries are over $29K/year.	**Step 1:** In this Point at Issue question, the correct answer is the one about which one speaker would say, "That's true," and the other would say, "That's false."

11. Goswami: I support the striking workers at Ergon Foods. They are underpaid. The majority of them make less than $20,000 per year.

Nordecki: If pay is the issue, I must disagree. The average annual salary of the striking workers at Ergon Foods is over $29,000.

Goswami and Nordecki disagree over the truth of which one of the following statements?

(A) The average annual salary at Ergon Foods is over $29,000.

(B) Pay is the primary issue over which the workers are striking at Ergon Foods.

(C) It is reasonable to support striking workers who are underpaid.

(D) The striking workers at Ergon Foods are underpaid.

(E) It was unreasonable for the workers at Ergon Foods to go on strike.

PrepTest111 Sec3 Q10

Step 3: It is clear that the two speakers disagree on the question of whether Ergon Foods' workers are underpaid. That's what the correct answer will say. Take a moment to understand that the two speakers' evidence is *not* in conflict. Most workers could make less than $20K while having an average salary over $29K if there are a handful of employees with disproportionately high salaries.	**Step 4:** (D) is correct. Goswami explicitly agrees with this statement while Nordecki explicitly disagrees.

Wrong answers: (A) Goswami does not state an opinion on average salaries at Ergon Foods. (B) Neither speaker expresses an opinion on this point. Goswami may implicitly agree, but Nordecki simply conditions his reply with "*[i]f* pay is the issue," implying they don't know if that's the case or not. (C) Goswami at least implicitly agrees with this statement, and Nordecki might agree with it, too. Nordecki just doesn't think Ergon's workers are underpaid. (E) Goswami explicitly disagrees with this statement. Nordecki would agree with it *if* pay is the issue. If there are other issues—e.g., safety, health insurance, abusive treatment—prompting the strike, however, Nordecki might be supportive.

Hint: How does Sergio's use of superlatives such as "always" and "invariably" relate to Tina's position?

Step 2:	Step 1:

12. Tina: For centuries oceans and human eccentricity have been linked in the literary and artistic imagination. Such linkage is probably due to the European Renaissance practice of using ships as asylums for the socially undesirable.

Sergio: No. Oceans have always been viewed as mysterious and unpredictable— qualities that people have invariably associated with eccentricity.

Tina's and Sergio's statements lend the most support to the claim that they disagree about which one of the following statements?

(A) Eccentric humans were considered socially undesirable during the European Renaissance.

(B) Oceans have always been viewed as mysterious and unpredictable.

(C) The linkage between oceans and eccentricity explains the European Renaissance custom of using ships as asylums.

(D) People have never attributed the same qualities to oceans and eccentrics.

(E) The linkage between oceans and eccentricity predates the European Renaissance.

PrepTest112 Sec4 Q21

Step 3:	Step 4:

Expert Analysis

Here's how an LSAT expert approached the Point at Issue question you just tried.

Step 2: Tina: The linkage between the ocean and eccentric behavior is likely due to *ships of fools* (floating asylums) common in the European Renaissance.	**Step 1:** The correct answer will paraphrase the two speakers' disagreement making this a Point at Issue question.
Sergio: The linkage between the ocean and eccentric behavior is due to the age-old view of the ocean as mysterious and unpredictable.	

12. Tina: For centuries oceans and human eccentricity have been linked in the literary and artistic imagination. Such linkage is probably due to the European Renaissance practice of using ships as asylums for the socially undesirable.

Sergio: No. Oceans have always been viewed as mysterious and unpredictable—qualities that people have invariably associated with eccentricity.

Tina's and Sergio's statements lend the most support to the claim that they disagree about which one of the following statements?

(A) Eccentric humans were considered socially undesirable during the European Renaissance.

(B) Oceans have always been viewed as mysterious and unpredictable.

(C) The linkage between oceans and eccentricity explains the European Renaissance custom of using ships as asylums.

(D) People have never attributed the same qualities to oceans and eccentrics.

(E) The linkage between oceans and eccentricity predates the European Renaissance.

PrepTest112 Sec4 Q21

Step 3: Evaluate the choices asking, first, do both speakers have an opinion on the statement here, and second, are those opinions diametrically opposed?	**Step 4:** (E) identifies the point at issue: Tina would disagree with this statement, while Sergio would agree with it.

Wrong answers: (A) Neither speaker states an opinion on this statement. Even if we think Tina's statement might imply agreement here, Sergio's says nothing about the Renaissance view. (B) Tina offers no opinion on this statement. (C) Neither speaker offers an opinion on why floating asylums were created during the Renaissance. (D) 180. The statement here identifies a point of *agreement* as both Tina and Sergio would reject it.

Congratulations on adding another question type to your list. Now, assess your new-found Point at Issue skills with the following Perform quiz.

Chapter Perform Quiz

Perform This Perform quiz has 4 Point at Issue questions. They are presented without any notes, hints, or prompts for a more test-like experience while you work. Try to get as many correct answers as possible in 6 minutes. When you finish, check your performance against the Answer Key and Evaluate Your Performance for tips on how best to improve. Then, come back to complete any questions you skipped or guessed on and finish up by reviewing all of the questions with the expert analyses in your online companion.

13. Dr. Jones: The new technology dubbed "telemedicine" will provide sustained improvement in at least rural patient care since it allows rural physicians to televise medical examinations to specialists who live at great distances— specialists who will thus be able to provide advice the rural patient would otherwise not receive.

    Dr. Carabella: Not so. Telemedicine might help rural patient care initially. However, small hospitals will soon realize that they can minimize expenses by replacing physicians with technicians who can use telemedicine to transmit examinations to large medical centers, resulting in fewer patients being able to receive traditional, direct medical examinations. Eventually, it will be the rare individual who ever gets truly personal attention. Hence, rural as well as urban patient care will suffer.

Which one of the following is a point at issue between Dr. Jones and Dr. Carabella?

(A) whether medical specialists in general offer better advice than rural physicians

(B) whether telemedicine technology will be installed only in rural hospitals and rural medical centers

(C) whether telemedicine is likely to be widely adopted in rural areas in future years

(D) whether the patients who most need the advice of medical specialists are likely to receive it through telemedicine

(E) whether the technology of telemedicine will benefit rural patients in the long run

PrepTest110 Sec3 Q7

14. Megan: People pursue wealth beyond what their basic needs require only if they see it as a way of achieving high status or prestige.

    Channen: Not everybody thinks that way. After all, money is the universal medium of exchange. So, if you have enough of it, you can exchange it for whatever other material goods you may need or want even if you are indifferent to what others think of you.

Megan and Channen disagree over whether

(A) people ever pursue wealth beyond what is required for their basic needs

(B) it is irrational to try to achieve high status or prestige in the eyes of one's society

(C) the pursuit of monetary wealth is irrational only when it has no further purpose

(D) it is rational to maximize one's ability to purchase whatever one wants only when the motive for doing so is something other than the desire for prestige

(E) the motive for pursuing wealth beyond what one's basic needs require is ever anything other than the desire for prestige or high status

PrepTest122 Sec2 Q10

15. Lea: Contemporary art has become big business. Nowadays art has less to do with self-expression than with making money. The work of contemporary artists is utterly bereft of spontaneity and creativity, as a visit to any art gallery demonstrates.

    Susan: I disagree. One can still find spontaneous, innovative new artwork in most of the smaller, independent galleries.

Lea's and Susan's remarks provide the most support for holding that they disagree about whether

(A) large galleries contain creative artwork

(B) most galleries contain some artwork that lacks spontaneity and creativity

(C) contemporary art has become big business

(D) some smaller art galleries still exhibit creative new artwork

(E) contemporary art, in general, is much less concerned with self-expression than older art is

PrepTest110 Sec3 Q15

16. Kim: The rapidly growing world population is increasing demands of food producers in ways that threaten our natural resources. With more land needed for both food production and urban areas, less land will be available for forests and wildlife habitats.

    Hampton: You are overlooking the promise of technology. I am confident that improvements in agriculture will allow us to feed the world population of ten billion predicted for 2050 without significantly increasing the percentage of the world's land now devoted to agriculture.

Kim's and Hampton's statements most strongly support the claim that both of them would agree with which one of the following?

(A) Efforts should be taken to slow the rate of human population growth and to increase the amount of land committed to agriculture.

(B) Continued research into more-efficient agricultural practices and innovative bio-technology aimed at producing more food on less land would be beneficial.

(C) Agricultural and wilderness areas need to be protected from urban encroachment by preparing urban areas for greater population density.

(D) In the next half century, human population growth will continue to erode wildlife habitats and diminish forests.

(E) The human diet needs to be modified in the next half century because of the depletion of our natural resources due to overpopulation.

PrepTest111 Sec1 Q26

Answer Key

13. E; 14. E; 15. D; 16. B

Evaluate Your Performance

To assess your strengths and opportunities from this Perform quiz, go to the corresponding chapter in your online companion. There you'll find recommendations based on your performance along with complete worked-example explanations (written by a Kaplan LSAT expert) for each of the questions in this Perform quiz.

CHAPTER 6

Argumentative Strategies and Method of Argument Questions

The work you'll do in this chapter will feel different than the argument analysis you've learned so far. To this point, you've been focused on *what* arguments say—their conclusions and evidence—and the purposes of statements in them. In this chapter, you'll take a turn toward the abstract by learning to describe *how* authors are making their arguments. Here, the argument's subject matter takes a back seat to the strategy the author is using to try to convince the reader that the conclusion is correct.

LEARNING OBJECTIVES

In this chapter, you'll learn to:

- Describe an author's argumentative strategy.
- Identify and answer Method of Argument questions.

Mastering the skill of abstract description takes practice. In day-to-day conversations, we're a lot more likely to explain an argument by saying something like, "The author is saying the brain is like a computer" than "The argument proceeds by employing an analogy to support its main conclusion." In this chapter, pay attention to how LSAT experts predict correct answers and how they evaluate answer choices containing abstract descriptions. This is a skill set you'll use again on many Flaw questions on the LSAT.

Describe Argumentative Strategies

Prepare In the preceding chapter, you practiced outlining argument structures. Now, you're ready to learn how to describe an author's argumentative strategy. In other words, you're ready to summarize *how* an author uses evidence to try to convince a reader that the conclusion is sound.

LEARNING OBJECTIVE

In this section, you'll learn to:

* Describe an author's argumentative strategy.

You saw as you were working with different kinds of evidence in the previous section that authors make choices about how to support their conclusions. One might think that citing studies is compelling, while another tries to persuade the reader by applying commonsense principles. Others might make a generalization and back it up with an example, might claim that a statement must be true because an expert said so, or might simply attack an opponent's character (a flawed approach, by the way). All those choices can be thought of as argumentative strategies, or as the question type associated with this skill calls them: methods of argument.

Describing an author's method of argument may, at first, seem somewhat generic and abstract. Instead of focusing on the content of the argument, you have to summarize the author's technique. Keywords help keep your focus on what the author does rather than what she says. Here's how an LSAT expert might describe the argumentative strategy in an argument you saw in an earlier chapter.

LSAT Question	Analysis
Columnist: It has been noted that attending a live musical performance is a richer experience than is listening to recorded music. Some say that this is merely because we do not see the performers when we listen to recorded music. However, there must be some other reason, for there is relatively little difference between listening to someone read a story over the radio and listening to someone in the same room read a story.	*Conclusion*: The reason live music is a richer experience than recorded music is not because we see the musicians *because* *Evidence*: hearing a story read live isn't much different than hearing it on the radio. *Method of Argument*: The author offers an analogy (stories on the radio are like recorded music) as a counterexample to a claim (live music is richer because you see the musicians).

PrepTest131 Sec2 Q7

Notice that the expert still starts by identifying and paraphrasing the argument's conclusion and evidence. Now, though, when the task includes describing the argumentative strategy, the expert also considers *how* the author has chosen to try to support the conclusion.

It is impossible to anticipate exactly the argumentative strategies you'll see on test day, but a few methods of argument appear regularly on the LSAT.

LSAT STRATEGY

Methods of argument common on the LSAT include:

- Analogy, in which an author draws parallels between two unrelated (but purportedly similar) situations

- Example, in which an author cites specific cases to justify a generalization

- Counterexample, in which an author seeks to discredit an opponent's argument by citing a specific case in which the opponent's conclusion appears to be invalid

- Appeal to authority, in which an author cites an expert or another figure as support for the conclusion

- Elimination of alternatives, in which an author lists possibilities and discredits all but one

- *Ad hominem*, in which an author attacks an opponent's personal credibility rather than the substance of the opponent's argument

- Means/Requirements, in which an author argues that something is needed to achieve a desired result

- Definition, in which an author defines a term in a way that helps to justify the argument or undermine/point out a contradiction in an opponent's argument

Practice   Describe the method of argument used in each of the following stimuli. When you're finished, compare your descriptions with those of an LSAT expert in the expert analysis on the pages following this exercise.

LSAT Argument	My Analysis
1. The more modern archaeologists learn about Mayan civilization, the better they understand its intellectual achievements. Not only were numerous scientific observations and predictions made by Mayan astronomers, but the people in general seem to have had a strong grasp of sophisticated mathematical concepts. We know this from the fact that the writings of the Mayan religious scribes exhibit a high degree of mathematical competence. *PrepTest131 Sec3 Q8*	*Method of Argument:*
2. Archaeologist: After the last ice age, groups of paleohumans left Siberia and crossed the Bering land bridge, which no longer exists, into North America. Archaeologists have discovered in Siberia a cache of Clovis points—the distinctive stone spear points made by paleohumans. This shows that, contrary to previous belief, the Clovis point was not invented in North America. *PrepTest129 Sec2 Q22*	*Method of Argument:*
3. To predict that a device will be invented, one must develop a conception of the device that includes some details at least about how it will function and the consequences of its use. But clearly, then, the notion of predicting an invention is self-contradictory, for inventing means developing a detailed conception, and one cannot predict what has already taken place. *PrepTest131 Sec3 Q23*	*Method of Argument:*

LSAT Argument	My Analysis
4. Letter to the editor: Middle-class families in wealthy nations are often criticized for the ecological damage resulting from their lifestyles. This criticism should not be taken too seriously, however, since its source is often a movie star or celebrity whose own lifestyle would, if widely adopted, destroy the environment and deplete our resources in a short time. *PrepTest49 Sec2 Q5*	*Method of Argument:*
5. Gilbert: This food label is mistaken. It says that these cookies contain only natural ingredients, but they contain alphahydroxy acids that are chemically synthesized by the cookie company at their plant. Sabina: The label is not mistaken. After all, alphahydroxy acids also are found occurring naturally in sugarcane. *PrepTest59 Sec2 Q5*	*Method of Argument:*
6. In modern deep-diving marine mammals, such as whales, the outer shell of the bones is porous. This has the effect of making the bones light enough so that it is easy for the animals to swim back to the surface after a deep dive. The outer shell of the bones was also porous in the ichthyosaur, an extinct prehistoric marine reptile. We can conclude from this that ichthyosaurs were deep divers. *PrepTest61 Sec4 Q21*	*Method of Argument:*

Expert Analysis

Here's how an LSAT expert analyzed the arguments you just saw.

LSAT Argument	Analysis
1. The more modern archaeologists learn about Mayan civilization, the better they understand its intellectual achievements. Not only were numerous scientific observations and predictions made by Mayan astronomers, but the people in general seem to have had a strong grasp of sophisticated mathematical concepts. We know this from the fact that the writings of the Mayan religious scribes exhibit a high degree of mathematical competence. *PrepTest131 Sec3 Q8*	*Method of Argument*: Examples. The author cites the knowledge of Mayan religious scribes to reach a conclusion about the Mayan people in general.
2. Archaeologist: After the last ice age, groups of paleohumans left Siberia and crossed the Bering land bridge, which no longer exists, into North America. Archaeologists have discovered in Siberia a cache of Clovis points—the distinctive stone spear points made by paleohumans. This shows that, contrary to previous belief, the Clovis point was not invented in North America. *PrepTest129 Sec2 Q22*	*Method of Argument*: Counterexample. The author offers a supposed counterexample that purportedly undermines a previous belief.
3. To predict that a device will be invented, one must develop a conception of the device that includes some details at least about how it will function and the consequences of its use. But clearly, then, the notion of predicting an invention is self-contradictory, for inventing means developing a detailed conception, and one cannot predict what has already taken place. *PrepTest131 Sec3 Q23*	*Method of Argument*: Definition. The author uses two definitions to show that a certain type of prediction is a contradiction in terms.

LSAT Argument	Analysis
4. Letter to the editor: Middle-class families in wealthy nations are often criticized for the ecological damage resulting from their lifestyles. This criticism should not be taken too seriously, however, since its source is often a movie star or celebrity whose own lifestyle would, if widely adopted, destroy the environment and deplete our resources in a short time. *PrepTest122 Sec2 Q5*	*Method of Argument*: *Ad hominem* attack. The author concludes that a social critique need not be taken seriously because many who make the critique act hypocritically.
5. Gilbert: This food label is mistaken. It says that these cookies contain only natural ingredients, but they contain alphahydroxy acids that are chemically synthesized by the cookie company at their plant. Sabina: The label is not mistaken. After all, alphahydroxy acids also are found occurring naturally in sugarcane. *PrepTest131 Sec2 Q5*	*Method of Argument*: [**Gilbert**] Means/Requirement. Argues that an ingredient does not fit a definition. [**Sabina**] Means/Requirement. Argues that the ingredient does fit the definition.
6. In modern deep-diving marine mammals, such as whales, the outer shell of the bones is porous. This has the effect of making the bones light enough so that it is easy for the animals to swim back to the surface after a deep dive. The outer shell of the bones was also porous in the ichthyosaur, an extinct prehistoric marine reptile. We can conclude from this that ichthyosaurs were deep divers. *PrepTest143 Sec4 Q21*	*Method of Argument*: Analogy. From the fact that a modern animal displays a characteristic, the author concludes that ancient animals with the same characteristic must have behaved in the same way.

Nice work. Now, learn how to apply the skill of describing argumentative strategies to get points from Method of Argument questions.

Method of Argument Questions

Prepare Method of Argument questions ask you to focus on an argument's structure more than its content. In this way, these questions are similar to many Reading Comprehension questions. In a Method of Argument question, the correct answer will describe the author's argumentative strategy, usually in generic, abstract terms.

LEARNING OBJECTIVE

In this section, you'll learn to:

- Identify and answer Method of Argument questions.

On a typical recent LSAT, you can expect to see just one Method of Argument question, although they were more common previously (and may become a bit more common again). For now, however, expect just over 1% of your LSAT score to come from this question type.

Method of Argument questions regularly feature both standard single-argument stimuli and dialog stimulus. In questions with the latter, you will usually be asked to describe *how* the second speaker responds to the first. You can identify Method of Argument questions from question stems like these:

Which one of the following most accurately describes the technique of reasoning employed by the argument?

PrepTest59 Sec3 Q23

In the conversation, Hernandez responds to Green's objection in which one of the following ways?

PrepTest57 Sec3 Q5

The columnist's argument proceeds by

PrepTest45 Sec4 Q12

Approximate Number of Method of Argument Questions per LSAT

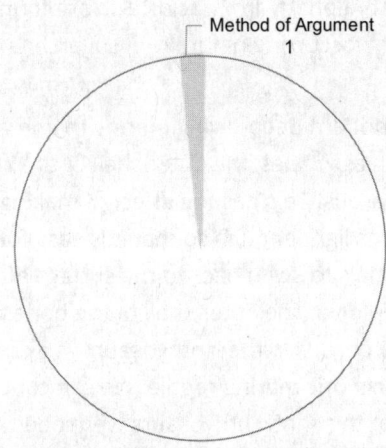

Method of Argument
1

Source: All officially released LSAT exams, 2016-2020

METHOD OF ARGUMENT QUESTIONS AT A GLANCE

Task: Describe the author's argumentative strategy, *how* they argue (not necessarily what they say).

Strategy: Identify the author's conclusion and evidence; take note of Keywords indicating the author's purpose; and summarize the author's strategy in generic, descriptive terms.

Frequency: Method of Argument questions are relatively rare in the Logical Reasoning sections of the test. LSAT tests released from 2016 through 2020 had an average of 0.6 Method of Argument questions.

To get familiar with Method of Argument questions, try the following example on your own. When you're finished, take a look at how an LSAT expert approached it.

Step 2:	Step 1:

7. It is widely believed that eating chocolate can cause acne. Indeed, many people who are susceptible to acne report that, in their own experience, eating large amounts of chocolate is invariably followed by an outbreak of that skin condition. However, it is likely that common wisdom has mistaken an effect for a cause. Several recent scientific studies indicate that hormonal changes associated with stress can cause acne and there is good evidence that people who are fond of chocolate tend to eat more chocolate when they are under stress.

The argument employs which one of the following argumentative strategies?

(A) It cites counterevidence that calls into question the accuracy of the evidence advanced in support of the position being challenged.

(B) It provides additional evidence that points to an alternative interpretation of the evidence offered in support of the position being challenged.

(C) It invokes the superior authority of science over common opinion in order to dismiss out of hand the relevance of evidence based on everyday experience.

(D) It demonstrates that the position being challenged is inconsistent with certain well established facts.

(E) It provides counterexamples to show that, contrary to the assumption on which the commonly held position rests, causes do not always precede their effects.

PrepTest112 Sec1 Q7

Step 3:	Step 4:

Expert Analysis

Compare your work to that of an LSAT expert on the question you just tried. There are several common patterns of LSAT argumentation on display here.

Step 2: *Conclusion*: The common belief that eating chocolate causes acne is probably wrong *because* *Evidence*: even though eating more chocolate is correlated with acne, both of them likely result from hormonal changes caused by stress.	**Step 1:** The phrase "argumentative strategies" indicates a Method of Argument question; the correct answer describes *how* the argument proceeds.

7. It is widely believed that eating chocolate can cause acne. Indeed, many people who are susceptible to acne report that, in their own experience, eating large amounts of chocolate is invariably followed by an outbreak of that skin condition. However, it is likely that common wisdom has mistaken an effect for a cause. Several recent scientific studies indicate that hormonal changes associated with stress can cause acne and there is good evidence that people who are fond of chocolate tend to eat more chocolate when they are under stress.

The argument employs which one of the following argumentative strategies?

(A) It cites counterevidence that calls into question the accuracy of the evidence advanced in support of the position being challenged.

(B) It provides additional evidence that points to an alternative interpretation of the evidence offered in support of the position being challenged.

(C) It invokes the superior authority of science over common opinion in order to dismiss out of hand the relevance of evidence based on everyday experience.

(D) It demonstrates that the position being challenged is inconsistent with certain well established facts.

(E) It provides counterexamples to show that, contrary to the assumption on which the commonly held position rests, causes do not always precede their effects.

PrepTest112 Sec1 Q7

K

Step 3: Here, a commonly held belief that one thing causes another is based on an observed correlation between those things. The author calls that belief into question by citing an unobserved third factor that likely causes both of the correlated things. The correct answer will describe this strategy of offering evidence to make the reader reconsider an earlier belief.

Step 4: (B) gets it right by describing how the author offered new facts to see the supposed relationship between chocolate and acne in a new way.

Wrong answers: (A) Distortion. The author does not question the evidence on which the common belief is based. Indeed, says the author, chocolate intake and acne *are* correlated, but chocolate isn't causing the acne. (C) Extreme. The author does not denigrate common opinion or dismiss anything "out of hand." (D) 180. The author says the position being challenged (chocolate causes acne) *is* consistent with established facts, but then offers additional evidence to show why those facts don't tell the whole story. (E) Distortion. Additional facts are not counterexamples, and the author certainly isn't arguing that effects come before causes.

Now, for good measure, try out a Method of Argument question with a dialog stimulus. Take your time and work through all four steps of the Logical Reasoning Method. When you're finished, review your work with the expert analysis on the following page.

Step 2:	Step 1:

8. Hernandez: I recommend that staff cars be replaced every four years instead of every three years. Three-year-old cars are still in good condition and this would result in big savings.

   Green: I disagree. Some of our salespeople with big territories wear out their cars in three years.

   Hernandez: I meant three-year-old cars subjected to normal use.

In the conversation, Hernandez responds to Green's objection in which one of the following ways?

(A) by explicitly qualifying a premise used earlier

(B) by criticizing salespeople who wear out their cars in three years

(C) by disputing the accuracy of Green's evidence

(D) by changing the subject to the size of sales territories

(E) by indicating that Green used a phrase ambiguously

PrepTest129 Sec3 Q5

Step 3:	Step 4:

Expert Analysis

Use this worked example to compare your work to the approach of an LSAT expert on the question you just tried out.

Step 2: Hernandez's response begins with "I meant," which suggests that they have to clarify something that they've said.

Examining the original statement, we see that Hernandez is adding a detail to clarify the comment regarding three-year-old cars.

Step 1: The structure "responds . . . in which . . . way" means the right answer will describe *how* Hernandez responds (not *what* they say in response). This is a Method of Argument question.

8. Hernandez: I recommend that staff cars be replaced every four years instead of every three years. Three-year-old cars are still in good condition and this would result in big savings.

   Green: I disagree. Some of our salespeople with big territories wear out their cars in three years.

   Hernandez: I meant three-year-old cars subjected to normal use.

In the conversation, Hernandez responds to Green's objection in which one of the following ways?

(A) by explicitly qualifying a premise used earlier

(B) by criticizing salespeople who wear out their cars in three years

(C) by disputing the accuracy of Green's evidence

(D) by changing the subject to the size of sales territories

(E) by indicating that Green used a phrase ambiguously

PrepTest129 Sec3 Q5

Step 3: The correct answer will describe how Hernandez responded *by* adding context to clarify an earlier statement.

Step 4: (A) is correct. Hernandez clarifies their own original evidence, so "explicitly qualifying a premise" is a perfect description of *how* Hernandez responds.

Wrong answers: (B) Hernandez doesn't criticize anyone. Moreover, the added qualification clarifies the statement to exclude the salespeople with big territories. (C) Hernandez seems to agree with Green's evidence; that's why Hernandez adds the qualification to exclude cars driven by people with big territories. (D) Hernandez does not change the subject; Green is the one who mentions territory size. (E) Hernandez says nothing about how Green used a phrase (although the qualification implies something about how Green may have understood the phrase Hernandez used).

Great work. Continue working with Method of Argument questions in the following Practice set.

Practice Try each of the following Method of Argument questions. Some may contain arguments you've analyzed earlier. Don't worry too much about your timing here. Complete all four steps of the Logical Reasoning Method for each question, jotting down your notes whenever it is helpful to do so. After each question, review your work with the expert analysis that follows.

Hint: The first speaker here claims that there is only one way to accomplish something. What is your instinctive response to such a claim?

Step 2:	Step 1:

9. Joanna: The only way for a company to be successful, after emerging from bankruptcy, is to produce the same goods or services that it did before going bankrupt. It is futile for such a company to try to learn a whole new business.

    Ruth: Wrong. The Kelton Company was a major mining operation that went into bankruptcy. On emerging from bankruptcy, Kelton turned its mines into landfills and is presently a highly successful waste management concern.

Ruth uses which one of the following argumentative techniques in countering Joanna's argument?

(A) She presents a counterexample to a claim.

(B) She offers an alternative explanation for a phenomenon.

(C) She supports a claim by offering a developed and relevant analogy.

(D) She undermines a claim by showing that it rests on an ambiguity.

(E) She establishes a conclusion by excluding the only plausible alternative to that conclusion.

PrepTest112 Sec1 Q1

Step 3:	Step 4:

Expert Analysis

Here's how an LSAT expert worked through the question you just saw.

Step 2: [**Joanna**] *Conclusion*: The only way for a company to come back after bankruptcy is to do the same kind of business it did before bankruptcy *because* *Evidence*: it cannot learn a new business.* [**Ruth**] *Conclusion*: That's not the only way for a business to rebound after bankruptcy *because* *Evidence*: after bankruptcy, the Kelton Co. successfully transitioned from mining to landfills.	**Step 1:** A classic Method of Argument question stem for a stimulus with a dialog: the correct answer describes *how* the second speaker responds to the first.

9. Joanna: The only way for a company to be successful, after emerging from bankruptcy, is to produce the same goods or services that it did before going bankrupt. It is futile for such a company to try to learn a whole new business.

   Ruth: Wrong. The Kelton Company was a major mining operation that went into bankruptcy. On emerging from bankruptcy, Kelton turned its mines into landfills and is presently a highly successful waste management concern.

Ruth uses which one of the following argumentative techniques in countering Joanna's argument?

(A) She presents a counterexample to a claim.

(B) She offers an alternative explanation for a phenomenon.

(C) She supports a claim by offering a developed and relevant analogy.

(D) She undermines a claim by showing that it rests on an ambiguity.

(E) She establishes a conclusion by excluding the only plausible alternative to that conclusion.

PrepTest112 Sec1 Q1

Step 3: This is a classic counterexample. When one side says there is only one way to do something, you can attack their conclusion with any example of another way.	**Step 4:** (A) correctly identifies Ruth's strategy as a counterexample.

Wrong answers: (B) Distortion. Ruth's example directly counters Joanna's claim; it doesn't reinterpret a case offered by Joanna. (C) Outside the Scope. Neither speaker uses an analogy or parallel here. (D) Outside the Scope. There's no debate over definitions or linguistic clarity here. (E) 180. It is Joanna who has preemptively ruled out all alternatives ("the only way"); Ruth's response offers an alternative, thereby attacking Joanna's conclusion.

*Joanna's argument is an example of circular reasoning: the evidence here is equivalent to the conclusion.

Hint: This question may feel rather abstract. Take control of the argument by identifying the conclusion and evidence before trying to describe its method.

Step 2:	Step 1:

10. To predict that a device will be invented, one must develop a conception of the device that includes some details at least about how it will function and the consequences of its use. But clearly, then, the notion of predicting an invention is self-contradictory, for inventing means developing a detailed conception, and one cannot predict what has already taken place.

Which one of the following most accurately describes the technique of reasoning employed by the argument?

(A) constructing a counterexample to a general hypothesis about the future

(B) appealing to definitions to infer the impossibility of a kind of occurrence

(C) countering a hypothesis by indicating the falsehood of the implications of that hypothesis

(D) pointing out how a problem is widely thought to be scientific yet is really conceptual

(E) attempting to show that predicting any event implies that it has in fact already taken place

PrepTest131 Sec3 Q23

Step 3:	Step 4:

Expert Analysis

Here's how an LSAT expert worked through the question you just saw.

Step 2: *Conclusion*: The idea of predicting an invention is self-contradictory *because*

Evidence: (1) predicting an invention has to include details about the device's function and use, and (2) detailing a device's function and use is inventing.

In short: If you have predicted an invention, then you have invented it, so you cannot predict what's already happened.

Step 1: The language "describes the technique of reasoning" signals a Method of Argument question; the correct answer accurately describes *how* the author makes their case.

10. To predict that a device will be invented, one must develop a conception of the device that includes some details at least about how it will function and the consequences of its use. But clearly, then, the notion of predicting an invention is self-contradictory, for inventing means developing a detailed conception, and one cannot predict what has already taken place.

Which one of the following most accurately describes the technique of reasoning employed by the argument?

(A) constructing a counterexample to a general hypothesis about the future

(B) appealing to definitions to infer the impossibility of a kind of occurrence

(C) countering a hypothesis by indicating the falsehood of the implications of that hypothesis

(D) pointing out how a problem is widely thought to be scientific yet is really conceptual

(E) attempting to show that predicting any event implies that it has in fact already taken place

PrepTest131 Sec3 Q23

Step 3: The author shows how two definitions make it a contradiction to say you've done something.

Step 4: (B) is correct. The author infers that one cannot predict an invention, because by the time one has sufficiently predicted it, then it is, by definition, invented.

Wrong answers: (A) Outside the Scope. No general hypothesis about the future is discussed, and the author presents no counterexamples to anything. (C) Distortion. Nothing indicates that to "predict a device will be invented" is anyone's hypothesis, and the author appeals to the definitions of terms (not the implications of a hypothesis) to make their case. (D) Outside the Scope. The author does not say that most people treat the idea of predicting an invention as scientific. (E) Extreme. The author's argument is about predicting inventions, not about predicting any event.

Chapter Perform Quiz

Perform This Perform quiz has 4 Method of Argument questions. They are presented without any notes, hints, or prompts for a more test-like experience while you work. Try to get as many correct answers as possible in 6 minutes. When you finish, check your performance against the Answer Key and Evaluate Your Performance for tips on how best to improve. Then, come back to complete any questions you skipped or guessed on and finish up by reviewing all of the questions with the expert analyses in your online companion.

11. Conservationist: The risk to airplane passengers from collisions between airplanes using the airport and birds from the wildlife refuge is negligible. In the 10 years since the refuge was established, only 20 planes have been damaged in collisions with birds, and no passenger has been injured as a result of such a collision. The wildlife refuge therefore poses no safety risk.

    Pilot: You neglect to mention that 17 of those 20 collisions occurred within the past 2 years, and that the number of birds in the refuge is rapidly increasing. As the number of collisions between birds and airplanes increases, so does the likelihood that at least one such collision will result in passenger injuries.

The pilot counters the conservationist by

(A) attempting to show that the conservationist's description of the facts is misleading

(B) questioning the conservationist's motives for reaching a certain conclusion

(C) asserting that dangerous situations inevitably become more dangerous with the passage of time

(D) discrediting the moral principle on which the conservationist's argument is based

(E) disputing the accuracy of the figures cited by the conservationist

PrepTest110 Sec2 Q8

12. Linguist: Some people have understood certain studies as showing that bilingual children have a reduced "conceptual map" because bilingualism overstresses the child's linguistic capacities. Vocabulary tests taken by bilingual children appear to show that these children tend to have a smaller vocabulary than do most children of the same age group. But these studies are deeply flawed, since the tests were given in only one language. Dual-language tests revealed that the children often expressed a given concept with a word from only one of their two languages.

The linguist's argument proceeds by

(A) offering evidence for the advantages of bilingualism over monolingualism

(B) pointing out an inconsistency in the view that bilingualism overstresses a child's linguistic capabilities

(C) offering evidence that undermines the use of any vocabulary test to provide information about a child's conceptual map

(D) providing a different explanation for the apparent advantages of bilingualism from the explanation suggested by the results of certain studies

(E) pointing out a methodological error in the technique used to obtain the purported evidence of a problem with bilingualism

PrepTest111 Sec1 Q11

13. Economist: A country's trade deficit may indicate weakness in its economy, but it does not in itself weaken that economy. So restricting imports to reduce a trade deficit would be like sticking a thermometer into a glass of cold water in the hope of bringing down a patient's feverish temperature.

The economist's argument employs which one of the following techniques?

(A) claiming that a crucial assumption entails a falsehood

(B) demonstrating that an analogy explicitly used to establish a certain conclusion is faulty

(C) appealing to an analogy in order to indicate the futility of a course of action

(D) calling into question the authority on the basis of which a claim is made

(E) showing that a recommended course of action would have disastrous consequences

PrepTest131 Sec3 Q14

14. Sales manager: The highest priority should be given to the needs of the sales department, because without successful sales the company as a whole would fail.

Shipping manager: There are several departments other than sales that also must function successfully for the company to succeed. It is impossible to give the highest priority to all of them.

The shipping manager criticizes the sales manager's argument by pointing out

(A) that the sales department taken by itself is not critical to the company's success as a whole

(B) the ambiguity of the term "highest priority"

(C) that departments other than sales are more vital to the company's success

(D) an absurd consequence of its apparent assumption that a department's necessity earns it the highest priority

(E) that the sales manager makes a generalization from an atypical case

PrepTest112 Sec4 Q16

Answer Key

11. A; 12. E; 13. C; 14. C

Evaluate Your Performance

To assess your strengths and opportunities from this Perform quiz, go to the corresponding chapter in your online companion. There you'll find recommendations based on your performance along with complete worked-example explanations (written by a Kaplan LSAT expert) for each of the questions in this Perform quiz.

CHAPTER 7

Parallel Reasoning Questions

Parallel Reasoning Question Basics

One more way in which the LSAT tests your ability to recognize argument structures is through Parallel Reasoning questions. These questions ask you to identify two arguments—on different subjects—that use the same *kind* of evidence to reach the same *kind* of conclusion.

Prepare

LEARNING OBJECTIVE

In this chapter, you'll learn to:

- Identify and answer Parallel Reasoning questions.

On a typical LSAT you're most likely to see two Parallel Reasoning questions, one per section. That's worth right around 2.5% of the points available on the LSAT. Occasionally, you'll see just one Parallel Reasoning question.

You are also likely to see two Parallel Flaw questions per test, and the strategies you'll learn in this chapter will help you tackle those questions as well. This book covers Parallel Flaw questions near the end of Part III.

You can recognize Parallel Reasoning questions from question stems such as these:

The pattern of reasoning in which one of the following arguments is most parallel to that in the argument above?

PrepTest122 Sec4 Q17

In which one of the following is the pattern of reasoning most similar to that in the landscape architect's argument?

PrepTest131 Sec1 Q5

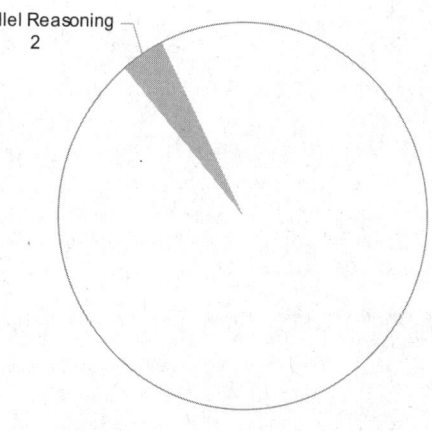

Approximate Number of Parallel Reasoning Questions per LSAT

Parallel Reasoning
2

Source: All officially released LSAT exams, 2016-2020

PARALLEL REASONING QUESTIONS AT A GLANCE

Task: Identify the answer choice in which the argument has the same structure and reaches the same type of conclusion as the argument in the stimulus.

Strategy: Use your knowledge of conclusion types, patterns of argument, Formal Logic, and/or principles to identify the answer containing an argument parallel to the one in the stimulus.

Frequency: On LSAT tests released from 2016 through 2020, there were an average of 0.8 Parallel Reasoning questions per section.

Parallel Reasoning Question Strategies

Parallel Reasoning questions are often very long; some, when you include their answer choices, have nearly as much text as a Reading Comprehension passage. Fortunately, there are a variety of tools and tactics to help you manage them efficiently and confidently. Here are four of them illustrated for you.

Compare Conclusions. For two arguments to have parallel structures, they must reach the same kind of conclusion. For example, consider this conclusion:

> The restaurant should decline the expansion plan.

Here are the conclusions of two other arguments. Which one comes from an argument that could be parallel to the argument from which the sample conclusion was drawn?

(1) The company's expanded delivery area will greatly increase costs.

(2) The athlete should not take on additional training.

The first conclusion, about the restaurant, is a negative recommendation. That makes choice (2) the parallel conclusion. Choice (1) is a prediction, not a recommendation. Thus, even though it is about a business, and cites a disadvantage to expansion, it cannot be the conclusion of an argument parallel to an argument that concludes with a recommendation.

Compare Formal Logic. When a Parallel Reasoning argument features a clear application of Formal Logic, the best approach is often to abstract the argument into an "A, B, C" shorthand, and evaluate the answer choices by doing the same to them. Consider the following argument:

> Armando is a talented social psychologist. All talented social psychologists are good statisticians. So, Armando must be a good statistician.

Here are two other arguments. Which is parallel to the argument in the example?

> (1) Ozzy is a full-blood boxer. All full-blood boxers enjoy human companionship. So, Ozzy will be a good dog for a large family.

> (2) Ernestine must have good balance. After all, excellent snowboarders always have good balance, and Ernestine is an excellent snowboarder.

First, outline the initial argument; it goes like this: [Evidence 1] If A → B and [Evidence 2] if B → C, therefore [Conclusion] If A → C. Choice (2) is presented in a different order, with the conclusion at the start of the argument, but when you rearrange it, you'll see that the pieces match up perfectly to the original argument. Choice (2) is parallel. Choice (1), on the other hand, introduces a different term in its conclusion, positing that Ozzy will be a "good dog for a large family" instead of determining that Ozzy "enjoys human companionship" (which would have been parallel to the original argument).

TEST DAY TIP

Parallel arguments will have the same argument structure, but the pieces of the argument need NOT appear in the same order. It's a Parallel *Reasoning* question, *not* a Parallel *Writing* question.

Compare Evidence. Evidence is not categorized as easily as conclusions, but you can still compare features in the evidence of the stimulus argument to features of the evidence in each answer choice and eliminate answers in which the evidence is clearly not parallel. For example, imagine that you see a stimulus argument with the following evidence:

> The more transportation alternatives a city provides, the more likely it is to attract younger families and individuals.

Here are pieces of evidence from two arguments. Which could be parallel to the argument from which the sample evidence came?

> (1) Chicago has more transportation alternatives than Nashville does.

> (2) In general, greater species diversity is likely to be found in areas with more annual precipitation.

The initial piece of evidence is an assertion of a direct proportional relationship between two phenomena. Choice (2) is parallel. Choice (1), a simple comparison of one criterion between two places, is not the same.

Compare Principles. Rarely, a Parallel Reasoning argument illustrates an easily identifiable principle. Consider an argument like this one:

> Policy X will strengthen national defense. Policy Y will not. One goal of good government is to strengthen national security. Therefore, our nation's legislature should vote for Policy X.

Here are two other arguments. Which is parallel to that in the example?

> (1) Destination P will be educational, but not relaxing. Destination Q will be relaxing. Since the goal of a good family vacation is relaxation, the Martinez family should choose Destination Q.

> (2) A Nursing degree offers many in-state employment opportunities. A Finance degree offers far fewer. Therefore, any student wishing to remain in the state after graduation should pursue a Nursing degree.

The original argument applies a principle—act in accordance with the goals of good government—to reach its conclusion. Of the two choices, only choice (1) has a parallel structure, applying the goal of a good family vacation. Choice (2) uses personal preference as its criteria, so it isn't a solid match.

Look for opportunities to use these strategies in the Practice set and Perform quiz later in the chapter.

TEST DAY TIP

Parallel Reasoning questions sometimes feature complete, unflawed arguments.

Before moving to full-question practice, take some time to refresh your memory on two important Parallel Reasoning skills: characterizing conclusions and translating Formal Logic statements.

Activate Prior Knowledge: Characterizing Conclusions

Before practicing on full Parallel Reasoning questions, refresh your conclusion types. You first learned the standard conclusion types in Chapter 3. Take that work a step further here, by accounting for the strength (strong/weak) and "charge" (positive/negative) of conclusions, as well.

Exercise: Characterizing Conclusions

For each of the following, identify the conclusion type: Assertion of Fact, Prediction, Comparison, Recommendation, Value Judgment, or If-then. Where applicable, characterize it as positive or negative; and designate each as "strong" or "weak." Compare your characterizations to those of the LSAT expert on the pages following this exercise. Make sure you accurately determined not only the conclusion type, but also the strength and "charge" of each conclusion.

Conclusion	My Analysis
1. The city's public services advisory council will neither delay construction of the new library nor increase its operating budget.	Type: +/−: Strength:
2. Ferdinand's experiment did not succeed because he did not follow the procedure exactly.	Type: +/−: Strength:
3. I'll probably prepare a vegetarian lasagna for tonight's dinner.	Type: +/−: Strength:
4. Columnist: In any work environment, whether in a large or small firm, there are few, if indeed any, reasons not to get along with your co-workers.	Type: +/−: Strength:
5. Ethicist: The appropriateness of participating in public protest, regardless of the popularity of the proposed point of view, depends on the strength of one's beliefs.	Type: +/−: Strength:
6. Whenever my dog sees a squirrel in my neighbor's tree, she barks.	Type: +/−: Strength:

Conclusion	My Analysis
7. As the newest recruit, Lucy was not chosen as team leader. However, she will likely still run for the position next year.	Type: +/−: Strength:
8. The proposal should be accepted because it had the most popularity.	Type: +/−: Strength:
9. Pursuing the unlawful denial of housing with the state enforcement agency is the better choice than a federal lawsuit because there is no risk of setting bad precedent.	Type: +/−: Strength:
10. If there are no additional breaks in the weather along the route, our cycling team will not be in the running for first place.	Type: +/−: Strength:
11. Adding a dedicated customer service telephone number could increase the efficiency of the department by 50%.	Type: +/−: Strength:
12. All high school seniors should be required to take a skills assessment or participate in a job shadowing program to help them determine their post-graduation plans.	Type: +/−: Strength:

Expert Analysis

Here's how an LSAT expert would characterize the conclusions in the preceding exercise.

	Conclusion	Analysis
1.	The city's public services advisory council will neither delay construction of the new library nor increase its operating budget.	Type: Prediction +/−: Negative (will not) Strength: Strong
2.	Ferdinand's experiment did not succeed because he did not follow the procedure exactly.	Type: Assertion of Fact +/−: Negative Strength: Strong
3.	I'll probably prepare a vegetarian lasagna for tonight's dinner.	Type: Assertion of Fact +/−: Positive Strength: Weak (probably)
4.	Columnist: In any work environment, whether in a large or small firm, there are few, if indeed any, reasons not to get along with your co-workers.	Type: Comparison +/−: Negative (few, if indeed any, reasons) Strength: Strong
5.	Ethicist: The appropriateness of participating in public protest, regardless of the popularity of the proposed point of view, depends on the strength of one's beliefs.	Type: Value Judgment (appropriateness) +/−: Positive Strength: Weak (dependent upon strength of beliefs)
6.	Whenever my dog sees a squirrel in my neighbor's tree, she barks.	Type: Conditional, Assertion of Fact (whenever x, then y) +/−: Positive Strength: Strong

Conclusion	Analysis
7. As the newest recruit, Lucy was not chosen as team leader. However, she will likely still run for the position next year.	Type: Prediction (will likely) +/−: Positive Strength: Weak (likely)
8. The proposal should be accepted because it had the most popularity.	Type: Recommendation (should be accepted) +/−: Positive Strength: Strong
9. Pursuing the unlawful denial of housing with the state enforcement agency is the better choice than a federal lawsuit because there is no risk of setting bad precedent.	Type: Comparison (better...than) +/−: Positive Strength: Strong (no risk)
10. If there are no additional breaks in the weather along the route, our cycling team will not be in the running for first place.	Type: Prediction, Conditional +/−: Negative (if not x, then will not y) Strength: Strong
11. Adding a dedicated customer service telephone number could increase the efficiency of the department by 50%.	Type: Assertion of Fact +/−: Positive Strength: Weak (could increase)
12. All high school seniors should be required to take a skills assessment or participate in a job shadowing program to help them determine their post-graduation plans.	Type: Recommendation (should be required) +/−: Positive Strength: Strong

Formal Logic Workshop 1

In Chapter 2, you learned how to translate conditional statements into an If-then format from a number of different sentence structures. Being able to quickly and accurately tell when conditional statements are equivalent is helpful in many Parallel Reasoning (and, later, Parallel Flaw) questions.

Activate Prior Knowledge: Formal Logic

Exercise: Recognize Equivalent Statements

In this exercise, enter the appropriate terms or phrases from the bolded conditional statement into the blanks in the statements beneath such that all of the statements are equivalent in meaning.

If Anthony goes to the movies, then Juliet goes to the movies.

13. Every time _____ goes to the movies, _____ must also go to the movies.

14. _____ does not go to the movies unless _____ also goes to the movies.

15. _____ goes to the movies only if _____ also goes to the movies.

16. _____ going to the movies is necessary for _____ to go to the movies.

Hector plays hockey if Sandi goes to the movies.

17. _____ goes to the movies only if _____ plays hockey.

18. If _____ goes to the movies, then _____ plays hockey.

19. _____ will not go to the movies unless _____ plays hockey.

20. Knowing that _____ goes to the movies is sufficient to know that _____ plays hockey.

All hamsters are mammals.

21. If a creature is a _____, then it is a _____.

22. A creature is a _____ only if it is a _____.

23. Only _____ are _____.

24. A creature is not a _____ unless it is a _____.

Only patrons at least 18 years of age are allowed to dine in the lounge.

25. _____ is necessary for a patron to _____.

26. If a patron is _____, then the patron is _____.

27. A patron _____ only if the patron is _____.

28. A patron is not _____ unless the patron is _____.

Being a good project manager requires strong organizational skills.

29. If a person _____, then the person _____.

30. _____ is/are necessary for a person to _____.

31. A person cannot _____ unless the person _____.

32. Only a person _____ can _____.

Construction of the company's new office building depends upon receiving tax breaks from the city.

33. Only if _____ will _____.

34. _____ will _____ unless _____.

35. If _____ is/are not _____, then _____ will not _____.

36. _____ necessitates _____.

Only if it is warm will Peter go to the beach.

37. _____ only if _____.

38. _____ not _____ unless _____.

39. If _____, then _____.

40. _____ requires _____.

Unless she plays the oboe, Ingrid cannot join the band.

41. If _____, then _____.

42. _____ only if _____.

43. If _____ cannot/does not _____, then _____ cannot/does not _____.

44. _____ depends on _____.

Every tournament game included the team's veteran outfielder.

45. If _____, then _____.

46. _____ needed _____.

47. Only _____ did _____.

48. _____ did not _____ unless _____.

Whenever April eats a sweet snack, she eats cookies.

49. _____ only if _____.

50. _____ not _____ unless _____.

51. If _____, then _____.

52. Every time _____, _____.

Expert Analysis

Check your work against that of an LSAT expert.

If Anthony goes to the movies, then Juliet goes to the movies.

13. Every time Anthony goes to the movies, Juliet must also go to the movies.

14. Anthony does not go to the movies unless Juliet also goes to the movies.

15. Anthony goes to the movies only if Juliet also goes to the movies.

16. Juliet's going to the movies is necessary for Anthony to go to the movies.

Hector plays hockey if Sandi goes to the movies.

17. Sandi goes to the movies only if Hector plays hockey.

18. If Sandi goes to the movies, then Hector plays hockey.

19. Sandi will not go to the movies unless Hector plays hockey.

20. Knowing that Sandi goes to the movies is sufficient to know that Hector plays hockey.

All hamsters are mammals.

21. If a creature is a hamster, then it is a mammal.

22. A creature is a hamster only if it is a mammal.

23. Only mammals are hamsters.

24. A creature is not a hamster unless it is a mammal.

Only patrons at least 18 years of age will be allowed to dine in the lounge.

25. Being at least 18 is necessary for a patron to be allowed to dine in the lounge.

26. If a patron is allowed to dine in the lounge, then the patron is at least 18.

27. A patron will be allowed to dine in the lounge only if the patron is at least 18.

28. A patron is not allowed to dine in the lounge unless the patron is at least 18.

Being a good project manager requires strong organizational skills.

29. If a person is a good project manager, then the person has strong organizational skills.

30. Strong organizational skills are necessary for a person to be a good project manager.

31. A person cannot be a good project manager unless the person has strong organizational skills.

32. Only a person who has strong organizational skills can be a good project manager.

Construction of the company's new office building depends upon receiving tax breaks from the city.

33. Only if the company receives tax breaks from the city will the new office building be constructed.

34. The company's new office building will not be constructed unless the company receives tax breaks from the city.

35. If tax breaks are not provided by the city, then the company will not construct a new office building.

36. Constructing the company's new office building necessitates receiving tax breaks from the city.

Only if it is warm will Peter go to the beach.

37. Peter goes to the beach only if it is warm.

38. Peter does not go to the beach unless it is warm.

39. If Peter goes to the beach, then it is warm.

40. Peter's going to the beach requires it to be warm.

Unless she plays the oboe, Ingrid cannot join the band.

41. If Ingrid joins the band, then she plays the oboe.

42. Ingrid joins the band only if she plays the oboe.

43. If Ingrid does not play the oboe, then she does not join the band.

44. Ingrid's joining the band depends upon her playing the oboe.

Every tournament game included the team's veteran outfielder.

45. If the team played a tournament game, then it included the team's veteran outfielder.

46. A tournament game needed the team's veteran outfielder.

47. Only when the team included the veteran outfielder did it play a tournament game.

48. The team did not play a tournament game unless it included the team's veteran outfielder.

Whenever April eats a sweet snack, she eats cookies.

49. April eats a sweet snack only if she eats cookies.

50. April does not eat a sweet snack unless she eats cookies.

51. If April eats a sweet snack, then she eats cookies.

52. Every time April eats a sweet snack, she eats cookies.

Now, get familiar with the Parallel Reasoning question type by trying one on your own. When you're finished, compare your work to that of an LSAT expert in the worked example that follows.

Step 2:	**Step 1:**

53. Ecologists predict that the incidence of malaria will increase if global warming continues or if the use of pesticides is not expanded. But the use of pesticides is known to contribute to global warming, so it is inevitable that we will see an increase in malaria in the years to come.

The pattern of reasoning in which one of the following is most similar to that in the argument above?

(A) The crime rate will increase if the economy does not improve or if we do not increase the number of police officers. But we will be able to hire more police officers if the economy does improve. Therefore, the crime rate will not increase.

(B) If educational funds remain at their current level or if we fail to recruit qualified teachers, student performance will worsen. But we will fail to recruit qualified teachers. Therefore, student performance will worsen.

(C) If interest rates increase or demand for consumer goods does not decline, inflation will rise. But if there is a decline in the demand for consumer goods that will lead to higher interest rates. Therefore, inflation will rise.

(D) If global warming continues or if the rate of ozone depletion is not reduced, there will be an increase in the incidence of skin cancer. But reduced use of aerosols ensures both that global warming will not continue and that ozone depletion will be reduced. Thus, the incidence of skin cancer will not increase.

(E) If deforestation continues at the current rate and the use of chemicals is not curtailed, wildlife species will continue to become extinct. But because of increasing population worldwide, it is inevitable that the current rate of deforestation will continue and that the use of chemicals will not be curtailed. Thus, wildlife species will continue to become extinct.

PrepTest133 Sec3 Q24

Step 3:	Step 4:

Expert Analysis

Here's how an LSAT expert approached the question you just completed.

Step 2: *Conclusion*: It is inevitable (a strong positive prediction) that there will be an increase in malaria incidence *because* *Evidence*: (1) if global warming continues or if pesticide use is not expanded, then malaria incidence will increase, and (2) pesticide use contributes to global warming.	**Step 1:** The phrase "most similar to" indicates a Parallel Reasoning question; the correct answer contains an argument with the same logical structure as the argument in the stimulus.

53. Ecologists predict that the incidence of malaria will increase if global warming continues or if the use of pesticides is not expanded. But the use of pesticides is known to contribute to global warming, so it is inevitable that we will see an increase in malaria in the years to come.

The pattern of reasoning in which one of the following is most similar to that in the argument above?

(A) The crime rate will increase if the economy does not improve or if we do not increase the number of police officers. But we will be able to hire more police officers if the economy does improve. Therefore, the crime rate will not increase.

(B) If educational funds remain at their current level or if we fail to recruit qualified teachers, student performance will worsen. But we will fail to recruit qualified teachers. Therefore, student performance will worsen.

(C) If interest rates increase or demand for consumer goods does not decline, inflation will rise. But if there is a decline in the demand for consumer goods that will lead to higher interest rates. Therefore, inflation will rise.

(D) If global warming continues or if the rate of ozone depletion is not reduced, there will be an increase in the incidence of skin cancer. But reduced use of aerosols ensures both that global warming will not continue and that ozone depletion will be reduced. Thus, the incidence of skin cancer will not increase.

(E) If deforestation continues at the current rate and the use of chemicals is not curtailed, wildlife species will continue to become extinct. But because of increasing population worldwide, it is inevitable that the current rate of deforestation will continue and that the use of chemicals will not be curtailed. Thus, wildlife species will continue to become extinct.

PrepTest133 Sec3 Q24

Step 3: Rule out choices in which the conclusion is *not* a strong positive prediction that something will get worse and/or compare the overall argument structure: *If A or not B, then C; but if B, then A. Therefore, C.*

Step 4: (C) is correct. The conclusion is a strong prediction that inflation will get worse. Structure: *If A or not B, then C; but if B, then A. Therefore, C.*

Wrong answers: (A) The conclusion is a *negative* prediction: the crime rate will *not* go up. That is enough to eliminate this choice. Structure: If not A or not B, then C; but if A, then D. Therefore, not C. (B) The conclusion is parallel, a strong positive prediction that student performance will get worse. Structure: If A or not B, then C; but B *will not* happen. Therefore, C. The second part of the evidence does not match. (D) The conclusion is a *negative* prediction: Skin cancer will *not* get worse. That is enough to eliminate this choice. Structure: If A or not B, then C; but if B, then not A and not D. Therefore, not C. (E) The conclusion is a prediction that extinction will continue, *not* that it will get worse. That is enough to eliminate this choice. Structure: If A and not B, then C; but A and not B will happen. Therefore, C.

Note how the expert had multiple strategies at the ready. On test day, it's quite likely that you will handle a Parallel Reasoning question—especially a long one like this—just this way, quickly eliminating as many wrong answer choices as possible, then turning to your secondary approach to eliminate the others or to confirm the correct answer. Continue employing multiple strategies and tactics as you work through the Parallel Reasoning Practice set.

Practice   Try each of the following Parallel Reasoning questions. Some may contain arguments you analyzed in the earlier chapters. Don't worry too much about your timing here. Complete all four steps of the Logical Reasoning Method for each question, jotting down your notes whenever it is helpful to do so. After each question, review your work with the expert analysis that follows.

Hint: In Parallel Reasoning questions with relatively short arguments, you can usually summarize the full argument (Conclusion-because-Evidence) and use it to evaluate the answer choices.

Step 2:	Step 1:

54. The notion that one might be justified in behaving irrationally in the service of a sufficiently worthy end is incoherent. For if such an action is justified, then one would be behaving rationally, not irrationally.

Which one of the following arguments is most similar in its reasoning to the argument above?

(A) A representative of the law, such as a judge or a police officer, ought not to commit crimes. For if representatives of the law commit crimes, they will be ineffective in preventing crime.

(B) One cannot intend to spill a glass of water accidentally. Spilling it accidentally means that the act will not have been done intentionally.

(C) One cannot live the good life and be unhappy. If one's own neighbors see that one is unhappy, then they will see that one is not living the good life.

(D) Doctors cannot perform self-diagnosis, for they cannot objectively evaluate their own symptoms, and thus will be practicing poor medicine.

(E) One ought not to have both a cat and a goldfish. The goldfish is the natural prey of the cat, so it is unethical to place it at the cat's disposal.

PrepTest110 Sec2 Q6

Step 3:	Step 4:

Expert Analysis

Here's how an LSAT expert approached the question you just completed.

Step 2: *Conclusion*: An irrational action serving a worthy end is a contradiction in terms (a strong assertion of self-contradiction) *because* *Evidence*: If the end is worthy of justifying the action, then the action is not irrational.	**Step 1:** This is a standard Parallel Reasoning question stem; the correct answer's argument matches the logical structure of the argument in the stimulus.

54. The notion that one might be justified in behaving irrationally in the service of a sufficiently worthy end is incoherent. For if such an action is justified, then one would be behaving rationally, not irrationally.

Which one of the following arguments is most similar in its reasoning to the argument above?

(A) A representative of the law, such as a judge or a police officer, ought not to commit crimes. For if representatives of the law commit crimes, they will be ineffective in preventing crime.

(B) One cannot intend to spill a glass of water accidentally. Spilling it accidentally means that the act will not have been done intentionally.

(C) One cannot live the good life and be unhappy. If one's own neighbors see that one is unhappy, then they will see that one is not living the good life.

(D) Doctors cannot perform self-diagnosis, for they cannot objectively evaluate their own symptoms, and thus will be practicing poor medicine.

(E) One ought not to have both a cat and a goldfish. The goldfish is the natural prey of the cat, so it is unethical to place it at the cat's disposal.

PrepTest110 Sec2 Q6

Step 3: The correct answer will match the structure of the stimulus argument: Saying you do A because of B is self-contradictory, because the definition of B makes A impossible.	**Step 4:** (B) is correct; this argument matches the structure of the stimulus argument: Saying you do A (intentionally spill) because of B (an accident) is self-contradictory, because the definition of B (an accident) makes A (intention) impossible.

Wrong answers: (A) The conclusion is a negative recommendation ("ought not to") not a strong assertion of self-contradiction. (C) starts out well, with a strong assertion of the incompatibility of two terms, but the introduction of outside observers means the evidence here is not parallel to that in the stimulus. (D) is a complete mismatch: the conclusion is just an assertion that something is impossible, not that it is a contradiction in terms, the evidence does not rely on the definition of one term to contradict the other, and the use of "poor medicine" introduces a value judgment not found in the stimulus. (E) The use of "it is unethical" introduces a value judgment not found in any part of the stimulus argument.

Hint: Pay attention to the strength of rules stated as evidence and of the conclusions drawn from them.

Step 2:	Step 1:

55. Manuscripts written by first-time authors generally do not get serious attention by publishers except when these authors happen to be celebrities. My manuscript is unlikely to be taken seriously by publishers for I am a first-time author who is not a celebrity.

The structure of which one of the following arguments is most similar to the structure of the argument above?

(A) Challengers generally do not win elections unless the incumbent has become very unpopular. The incumbent in this election has become very unpopular. Therefore, the challenger may win.

(B) Fruit salad that contains bananas is ordinarily a boring dish unless it contains two or more exotic fruits. This fruit salad has bananas in it, and the only exotic fruit it has is guava. Thus, it will probably be boring.

(C) Thursday's city council meeting is likely to be poorly attended. Traditionally, council meetings are sparsely attended if zoning issues are the only ones on the agenda. The agenda for Thursday is exclusively devoted to zoning.

(D) The bulk of an estate generally goes to the spouse, if surviving, and otherwise goes to the surviving children. In this case there is no surviving spouse; hence the bulk of the estate is likely to go to the surviving children.

(E) Normally about 40 percent of the deer population will die over the winter unless it is extremely mild. The percentage of the deer population that died over the recent winter was the normal 40 percent. I conclude that the recent winter was not unusually mild.

PrepTest112 Sec4 Q9

Step 3:	Step 4:

Expert Analysis

Here's how an LSAT expert approached the question you just completed.

Step 2: Conclusion: Publishers are not likely to take my manuscript seriously (*a weak negative prediction*) because *Evidence*: (1) Unless written by a celebrity, manuscripts from first-time authors don't usually get taken seriously, and (2) I am a first-time author and not a celebrity.	**Step 1:** A rather descriptive Parallel Reasoning question stem: the correct answer contains an argument with the same structure as that in the stimulus.

55. Manuscripts written by first-time authors generally do not get serious attention by publishers except when these authors happen to be celebrities. My manuscript is unlikely to be taken seriously by publishers for I am a first-time author who is not a celebrity.

The structure of which one of the following arguments is most similar to the structure of the argument above?

(A) Challengers generally do not win elections unless the incumbent has become very unpopular. The incumbent in this election has become very unpopular. Therefore, the challenger may win.

(B) Fruit salad that contains bananas is ordinarily a boring dish unless it contains two or more exotic fruits. This fruit salad has bananas in it, and the only exotic fruit it has is guava. Thus, it will probably be boring.

(C) Thursday's city council meeting is likely to be poorly attended. Traditionally, council meetings are sparsely attended if zoning issues are the only ones on the agenda. The agenda for Thursday is exclusively devoted to zoning.

(D) The bulk of an estate generally goes to the spouse, if surviving, and otherwise goes to the surviving children. In this case there is no surviving spouse; hence the bulk of the estate is likely to go to the surviving children.

(E) Normally about 40 percent of the deer population will die over the winter unless it is extremely mild. The percentage of the deer population that died over the recent winter was the normal 40 percent. I conclude that the recent winter was not unusually mild.

PrepTest112 Sec4 Q9

Step 3: Both the evidence and conclusion are probabilistic ("generally" and "unlikely"). The author lays out a rule with a condition and a possible exception, notes that he meets the condition, and that the exception does not apply, and draws the reasonable conclusion. The correct answer will do the same.	**Step 4:** (B) is correct; the argument lays out a rule with a condition and a possible exception, notes that the condition has been met and that the exception does not apply, and draws the reasonable conclusion. The strength of the statements is probabilistic throughout ("ordinarily" and "probably").

Wrong answers: (A) 180. Here, the author lays out a rule with a condition and a possible exception, notes that the exception *does* apply, and concludes that this time the unlikely result is possible. (C) Here, the rule has only one condition and no possible exception. (D) Here, the rule has a primary outcome and a secondary one, rather than a condition and a possible exception; the argument says the primary outcome does not apply, so the secondary one does. (E) The conclusion of this argument is a strong affirmative assertion of fact, not a weak negative prediction.

Hint: In very long Parallel Reasoning questions be sure to formulate a detailed, accurate characterization of the conclusion in the stimulus, so that you can use it to eliminate wrong answers.

Step 2:	Step 1:

56. From the fact that people who studied music as children frequently are quite proficient at mathematics, it cannot be concluded that the skills required for mathematics are acquired by studying music: it is equally likely that proficiency in mathematics and studying music are both the result of growing up in a family that encourages its children to excel at all intellectual and artistic endeavors.

The pattern of reasoning in which one of the following arguments is most parallel to that in the argument above?

(A) Although children who fail to pay attention tend to perform poorly in school, it should not necessarily be thought that their poor performance is caused by their failure to pay attention, for it is always possible that their failure to pay attention is due to un-diagnosed hearing problems that can also lead to poor performance in school.

(B) People who attend a university in a foreign country are usually among the top students from their native country. It would therefore be wrong to conclude from the fact that many foreign students perform better academically than others in this country that secondary schools in other countries are superior to those in this country; it may be that evaluation standards are different.

(C) People whose diet includes relatively large quantities of certain fruits and vegeta-bles have a slightly lower than average incidence of heart disease. But it would be premature to conclude that consuming these fruits and vegetables prevents heart disease, for this correlation may be merely coincidental.

(D) Those who apply to medical school are required to study biology and chemistry. It would be a mistake, however, to conclude that those who have mastered chemistry and biology will succeed as physicians, for the practical application of knowledge is different from its acquisition.

(E) Those who engage in vigorous exercise tend to be very healthy. But it would be silly to conclude that vigorous exercise is healthful simply because people who are healthy exercise vigorously, since it is possible that exercise that is less vigorous also has beneficial results.

PrepTest122 Sec4 Q17

Step 3:	Step 4:

Expert Analysis

Here's how an LSAT expert approached the question you just completed.

Step 2: *Conclusion*: Math skills are not necessarily acquired by studying music (*a qualified negative assertion that correlation does* not *prove causation*) *because* *Evidence*: proficiency in math and music may both be the result of growing up in a certain type of family.	**Step 1:** The phrase "most parallel to" identifies this as a Parallel Reasoning question; the argument in the correct answer will have the same structure as that in the stimulus.

56. From the fact that people who studied music as children frequently are quite proficient at mathematics, it cannot be concluded that the skills required for mathematics are acquired by studying music: it is equally likely that proficiency in mathematics and studying music are both the result of growing up in a family that encourages its children to excel at all intellectual and artistic endeavors.

The pattern of reasoning in which one of the following arguments is most parallel to that in the argument above?

(A) Although children who fail to pay attention tend to perform poorly in school, it should not necessarily be thought that their poor performance is caused by their failure to pay attention, for it is always possible that their failure to pay attention is due to undiagnosed hearing problems that can also lead to poor performance in school.

(B) People who attend a university in a foreign country are usually among the top students from their native country. It would therefore be wrong to conclude from the fact that many foreign students perform better academically than others in this country that secondary schools in other countries are superior to those in this country; it may be that evaluation standards are different.

(C) People whose diet includes relatively large quantities of certain fruits and vegetables have a slightly lower than average incidence of heart disease. But it would be premature to conclude that consuming these fruits and vegetables prevents heart disease, for this correlation may be merely coincidental.

(D) Those who apply to medical school are required to study biology and chemistry. It would be a mistake, however, to conclude that those who have mastered chemistry and biology will succeed as physicians, for the practical application of knowledge is different from its acquisition.

(E) Those who engage in vigorous exercise tend to be very healthy. But it would be silly to conclude that vigorous exercise is healthful simply because people who are healthy exercise vigorously, since it is possible that exercise that is less vigorous also has beneficial results.

PrepTest122 Sec4 Q17

Step 3: The argument's structure is easily summarized: A (musical ability) and B (math skills) are correlated, but both A and B may be the result of C (family encouragement). Therefore, A cannot be said to cause B. Compare the argument structures in the answer choices.	**Step 4:** (A) is correct. This argument has a structure identical to that in the stimulus. A (poor attention) and B (poor performance) are correlated, but A and B may be the result of C (hearing problems). Therefore, A cannot be said to cause B.

Wrong answers: (B) This argument includes too many terms. A (attend a foreign university) and B (top scholar in home country) are correlated, but C (foreign evaluation standards may be different). Therefore, D (the fact that foreign students outperform some domestic students) does not imply E (superiority of foreign high schools). (C) This argument is parallel but for one problem: instead of introducing a possible third factor, it says the correlation may be mere coincidence. (D) This argument does not attempt to refute a correlation-versus-causation argument. Rather, it says that the fact that A (apply to med school) requires B (study chem and bio) does not mean that B is sufficient for C (being a doctor). (E) The conclusion is a strong assertion that correlation does not prove causation, but the evidence is all wrong: instead of proposing a third factor that might cause both A (vigorous exercise) and B (health), the author states that another type of A (less vigorous exercise) might be generally beneficial.

Chapter Perform Quiz

Perform This Perform quiz has 4 Parallel Reasoning questions. They are presented without any notes, hints, or prompts for a more test-like experience while you work. Try to get as many correct answers as possible in 6 minutes. When you finish, check your performance against the Answer Key and Evaluate Your Performance for tips on how best to improve. Then, come back to complete any questions you skipped or guessed on and finish up by reviewing all of the questions with the expert analyses in your online companion.

57. Landscape architect: If the screen between these two areas is to be a hedge, that hedge must be of either hemlocks or Leyland cypress trees. However, Leyland cypress trees cannot be grown this far north. So if the screen is to be a hedge, it will be a hemlock hedge.

In which one of the following is the pattern of reasoning most similar to that in the landscape architect's argument?

(A) If there is to be an entrance on the north side of the building, it will have to be approached by a ramp. However, a ramp would become impossibly slippery in winter, so there will be no entrance on the north side.

(B) If visitors are to travel to this part of the site by automobile, there will be a need for parking spaces. However, no parking spaces are allowed for in the design. So if visitors are likely to come by automobile, the design will be changed.

(C) The subsoil in these five acres either consists entirely of clay or consists entirely of shale. Therefore, if one test hole in the area reveals shale, it will be clear that the entire five acres has a shale subsoil.

(D) Any path along this embankment must be either concrete or stone. But a concrete path cannot be built in this location. So if there is to be a path on the embankment, it will be a stone path.

(E) A space the size of this meadow would be suitable for a playground or a picnic area. However, a playground would be noisy and a picnic area would create litter. So it will be best for the area to remain a meadow.

PrepTest131 Sec1 Q5

58. It is inaccurate to say that a diet high in refined sugar cannot cause adult-onset diabetes, since a diet high in refined sugar can make a person overweight, and being overweight can predispose a person to adult-onset diabetes.

The argument is most parallel, in its logical structure, to which one of the following?

(A) It is inaccurate to say that being in cold air can cause a person to catch a cold, since colds are caused by viruses, and viruses flourish in warm, crowded places.

(B) It is accurate to say that no airline flies from Halifax to Washington. No airline offers a direct flight, although some airlines have flights from Halifax to Boston and others have flights from Boston to Washington.

(C) It is correct to say that overfertilization is the primary cause of lawn disease, since fertilizer causes lawn grass to grow rapidly and rapidly growing grass has little resistance to disease.

(D) It is incorrect to say that inferior motor oil cannot cause a car to get poorer gasoline mileage, since inferior motor oil can cause engine valve deteriora- tion, and engine valve deterioration can lead to poorer gasoline mileage.

(E) It is inaccurate to say that Alexander the Great was a student of Plato; Alex- ander was a student of Aristotle and Aristotle was a student of Plato.

PrepTest111 Sec3 Q14

59. Team captain: Winning requires the willingness to cooperate, which in turn requires motivation. So you will not win if you are not motivated.

The pattern of reasoning in which one of the following arguments is most similar to the pattern of reasoning in the argument above?

(A) Being healthy requires exercise. But exercising involves risk of injury. So, paradoxically, anyone who wants to be healthy will not exercise.

(B) Learning requires making some mistakes. And you must learn if you are to improve. So you will not make mistakes without there being a noticeable improvement.

(C) Our political party will retain its status only if it raises more money. But raising more money requires increased campaigning. So our party will not retain its status unless it increases its campaigning.

(D) You can repair your own bicycle only if you are enthusiastic. And if you are enthusiastic, you will also have mechanical aptitude. So if you are not able to repair your own bicycle, you lack mechanical aptitude.

(E) Getting a ticket requires waiting in line. Waiting in line requires patience. So if you do not wait in line, you lack patience.

PrepTest129 Sec2 Q19

60. The higher the altitude, the thinner the air. Since Mexico City's altitude is higher than that of Panama City, the air must be thinner in Mexico City than in Panama City.

Which one of the following arguments is most similar in its reasoning to the argument above?

(A) As one gets older one gets wiser. Since Henrietta is older than her daughter, Henrietta must be wiser than her daughter.

(B) The more egg whites used and the longer they are beaten, the fluffier the meringue. Since Lydia used more egg whites in her meringue than Joseph used in his, Lydia's meringue must be fluffier than Joseph's.

(C) The people who run the fastest marathons these days are faster than the people who ran the fastest marathons ten years ago. Charles is a marathon runner. So Charles must run faster marathons these days than he did ten years ago.

(D) The older a tree, the more rings it has. The tree in Lou's yard is older than the tree in Theresa's yard. Therefore, the tree in Lou's yard must have more rings than does the tree in Theresa's yard.

(E) The bigger the vocabulary a language has, the harder it is to learn. English is harder to learn than Italian. Therefore, English must have a bigger vocabulary than Italian.

PrepTest111 Sec4 Q23

Answer Key

57. D; 58. D; 59. C; 60. D

Evaluate Your Performance

To assess your strengths and opportunities from this Perform quiz, go to the corresponding chapter in your online companion. There you'll find recommendations based on your performance along with complete worked-example explanations (written by a Kaplan LSAT expert) for each of the questions in this Perform quiz.

PART THREE

Assumption Family Questions

CHAPTER 8

Finding the Assumption in LSAT Arguments

The Assumption Family

Part III of this book builds on Part II by adding another layer to your skills in the analysis of arguments: determining the author's assumption, or unstated premise. More practically speaking, in this part of the book, you'll learn the essential strategies and tactics for approximately 30 of the questions on your LSAT; that's nearly 40% of the available points. To put that in perspective: on most administrations of the LSAT, Assumption Family questions are a bigger part of your score than the entire Reading Comprehension section.

Approximate Number of Questions per LSAT by Logical Reasoning Question Family

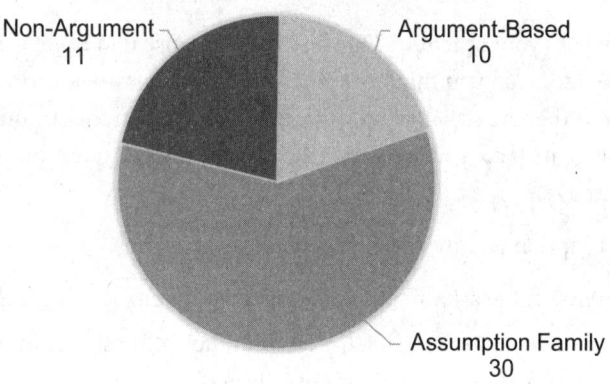

Source: All officially released LSAT exams, 2016-2020

Percentage of All Questions Per LSAT by Logical Reasoning Question Family

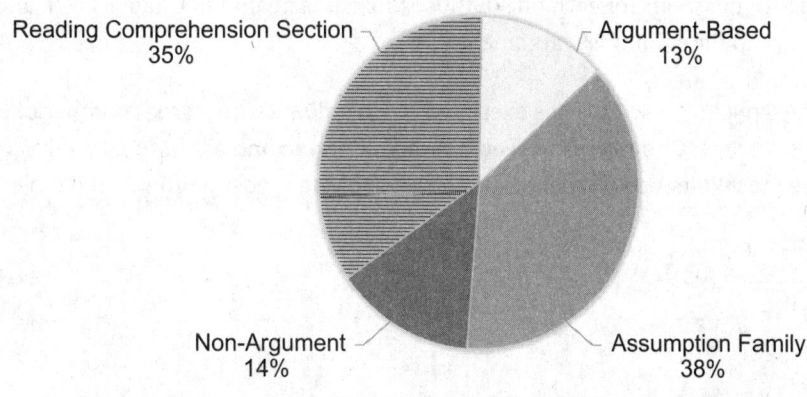

Source: All officially released LSAT exams, 2016-2020

Every argument you'll encounter in this part of the book is incomplete as written. There is an essential premise that the author has left unsaid. Developing an ability to quickly, calmly, and accurately put your finger on an author's key assumption is the foundational skill tested by more than half of all Logical Reasoning questions, and thus accounts for more than one-quarter of your LSAT score.

LSAT STRATEGY

Every argument in an Assumption Family question contains:

- **A conclusion**—the author's main point: an assertion, evaluation, or recommendation

- **Evidence**—the facts or premises the author presents to support the conclusion

- **An assumption**—the unstated premise that logically connects the evidence to the conclusion

---

As you analyzed the explicit parts of arguments in Chapter 7, it's likely that you felt that most of these arguments were not entirely convincing. Here's a good example:

24. Columnist: George Orwell's book *1984* has exercised much influence on a great number of this
    newspaper's readers. One thousand readers were surveyed and asked to name the one book that
    had the most influence on their lives. The book chosen most often was the Bible; *1984* was second.

PrepTest112 Sec1 Q24

As you see it again now, what's your reaction? Do you have the sense that there is more to this argument than what the author has presented? Can you think of things the author may be overlooking or failing to take into account? Can you think of other facts that would strengthen or weaken this argument, or that you would at least like to know to evaluate it? If so, you are anticipating all of the key question types in the Assumption Family of Logical Reasoning questions.

There are three main Assumption Family question types:

- **Assumption Questions**: These ask directly for an unstated premise in the argument.
- **Flaw Questions**: These ask you to describe the error in the author's reasoning; the error is most often related to what the author has overlooked, or how the evidence fails to establish the conclusion.
- **Strengthen/Weaken Questions**: These ask for facts that, if true, would make the argument more or less likely to be valid; you'll need to understand what the author is assuming to answer most of these questions accurately and efficiently.

You'll see full, official LSAT questions for each one of those (dozens, actually) in Chapters 8, 9, and 10, but here, try to apply the skills to the columnist's argument:

24. Columnist: George Orwell's book *1984* has exercised much influence on a great number of this
    newspaper's readers. One thousand readers were surveyed and asked to name the one book
    that had the most influence on their lives. The book chosen most often was the Bible; *1984* was
    second.

PrepTest112 Sec1 Q24

Take a moment and jot down your answers to each of these questions.

What is the difference between the terms of the conclusion and the terms of the evidence in this argument?

_____

How could the author logically bridge that gap between conclusion and evidence? _____

_____

Can you describe the reasoning error the author commits here? _____

_____

What fact, if added to the argument, would make it stronger? _____

_____

In this argument, the conclusion holds that 1984 influenced "a great number" of the paper's readers, but the evidence tells you only that *1984* came in second on the survey. [**Assumption**] So, to bridge that gap, the columnist must assume that the book coming in second place got a large number of votes. [**Flaw**] But, is that necessarily true? If hundreds of readers all picked different books, second place might have gotten only a few votes. So, the columnist's error in reasoning here is *taking for granted* (an unwarranted assumption) that second place means a high number. [**Strengthen/Weaken**] Even though the columnist's argument is vulnerable to criticism, it could still be right, and any fact that suggests that second place 1984 got a large chunk of votes will make the argument more likely to be true. Of course, a fact suggesting the opposite would further weaken it.

You'll see the full question that accompanies this stimulus in Chapter 11; it is a Strengthen/Weaken question. What's important to take away from this initial exercise is that you've just done exactly the types of reasoning rewarded in the all-important Assumption Family. As you move through this part of the book, you'll learn patterns and strategies that will improve your speed and accuracy, and tactics that will greatly boost your speed, but head in knowing that your instincts here are already strong.

TEST DAY TIP

Do not confuse the truth of a conclusion with the logical validity of an argument. Remember:

- A conclusion can be true even if the evidence for it is incomplete or the argument's reasoning is flawed.
- A logically valid argument can produce a false conclusion.

Assumption Basics

As you learned in Part II of this book, the ability to analyze arguments is a valuable skill for LSAT mastery. A test taker able to identify an LSAT argument's conclusion and evidence, and then logically outline the argument, can handle Main Point, Role of a Statement, and Method of Argument questions with confidence. Those skills are also the foundation of the even more important question types you'll encounter in this part of the book: Assumption, Flaw, Strengthen, Weaken, and select Principle questions—together known as the Assumption Family questions—also reward quick, effective analysis of arguments into their constituent parts.

The big difference between the types of questions you saw in Part II and those you'll learn now in Part III: Here, untangling arguments into their explicit parts (conclusion and evidence) is necessary but not sufficient for answering the questions. Assumption Family questions also depend on your ability to identify the implicit assumption, or if you like, the unstated premise. Assumption Family questions reward test takers who are constantly skeptical of the arguments presented and, more precisely, skeptical of shifts and gaps between evidence and conclusion.

Part III focuses on two big ideas: In this chapter, you'll learn to identify common argument patterns in LSAT Assumption Family arguments, patterns that help you see the kind of gap the author has left between the conclusion and evidence. You'll be anxious to get to the full questions, but stick with the pattern analysis; it will make you faster and more confident in the questions. In Chapter 8, you'll apply the patterns as you tackle Assumption questions. After that, there is a short Formal Logic Workshop, and then you'll learn the remaining question types in the Assumption family, starting with Flaw questions in Chapter 9 and Strengthen/Weaken questions in Chapter 10.

Here are your learning objectives for Chapter 8.

LEARNING OBJECTIVES

In this chapter, you'll learn to:

- Identify and articulate the assumption in a Mismatched Concepts argument.
- Identify and articulate the assumption in an Overlooked Possibilities argument.

These learning objectives set you up for success throughout this part of the book. You'll see that, broadly speaking, in Assumption Family arguments, the evidence and conclusion are different *in kind* or *in degree*. Where the evidence and conclusion are different in kind—Mismatched Concepts arguments—the author moves from facts or assertions about particular items, terms, concepts, or people to a conclusion about different items, terms, concepts, or people. Where the difference is one of degree—Overlooked Possibilities arguments—the author uses relevant, but limited, evidence to jump to a broad conclusion without explicitly addressing potential objections or alternatives to that conclusion.

Mismatched Concepts

Consider this argument:

> The product CleanPow is harmful because corrosives are harmful.

Are you fully convinced by this argument as it stands? Probably not. Can you intuit the information—the unstated evidence—you'd need to be fully convinced? This is a pretty simple argument, so simple, in fact, that you likely filled in the argument's assumption as you read it.

Now, though, look at that argument from a different angle. Imagine a game in which someone is given a piece of evidence, and their task is to predict a conclusion based on that evidence. If they guess correctly, there's a million-dollar prize. Imagine the contestant is given this piece of evidence: "Corrosives are harmful." How likely is it that their guess would be: "Therefore, the product CleanPow is harmful"? Frankly, that contestant is probably never going to see any prize money. The reason is simple: The term *corrosive* is related to many concepts but, without additional evidence, may or may not be related to the term *CleanPow*.

That's the dilemma for LSAT arguments that fit the Mismatched Concepts pattern. On the one hand, you may unconsciously make the same leap from evidence to conclusion that the author makes. On the other hand, you may find it difficult to see how the different terms in the evidence and conclusion relate to each other. In the lesson that follows, you'll learn to identify and accurately state the central assumptions in Mismatched Concepts arguments.

Mismatched Concepts: Foundations
Prepare

LEARNING OBJECTIVE

In this lesson, you'll learn to:

- Identify and articulate the assumption in a Mismatched Concepts argument.

In Assumption Family questions, the LSAT consistently tests your ability to determine when an author is using evidence that is not explicitly connected to the conclusion. Think of these as Apples-and-Oranges arguments: the author is concluding something about apples, while the evidence deals with oranges. Remember, that doesn't mean the argument is wrong, just that the connection the author assumes hasn't been made explicit. Your job is to spot the different terms and then build a bridge between them that matches the logical connection the author has taken for granted. How does the author assume the terms are connected?

LSAT STRATEGY

How can you spot an argument containing Mismatched Concepts?

- Without additional evidence, a key term or concept in the evidence appears unrelated to one in the conclusion.
- A term or concept not stated in the evidence appears in the conclusion.

Most arguments containing Mismatched Concepts fall into one of two patterns. In the first, the evidence and conclusion make different claims about the same subject.

Plato is a philosopher. Therefore, Plato is wise.

Here, the assumption is what is claimed in the conclusion is entailed by what is claimed in the evidence: "Philosophers are wise."

In the second pattern, the same claim is made about two different subjects.

Philosophers are wise. Therefore, Plato is wise.

In this type of Mismatched Concepts argument, the author assumes that the subject of the conclusion is logically related to the subject of the evidence: "Socrates is human." Although LSAT arguments are longer, wordier, and more complex than those examples, you may be surprised (and happy) to find that many of them boil down to one of those two patterns.

By the way, which pattern does the argument about CleanPow follow? If we rewrite it in the same form as the arguments about Plato, it says

Corrosives are harmful. Therefore, the product CleanPow is harmful.

It matches the second Plato example. The author is assuming that subjects of the evidence (corrosives) and of the conclusion (CleanPow) are identical in some relevant way.

You make and hear arguments in these patterns all the time.

John likes horseradish, so he'll like wasabi, too.

Elaine must follow a strict strength-training program. All members of the volleyball team follow a strict strength-training program.

Mismatched Concepts arguments won't always use such straightforward terminology. In fact, many arguments on the LSAT contain academic, legal, or philosophical jargon that might make it difficult to understand the argument in full. Don't get flustered. Sometimes, the abstract nature of the concepts presented in arguments makes it easier for you to spot the mismatched concepts in the evidence and conclusion. Take this argument as an example:

At the upcoming scientific conference, Dr. Dinglehorn will support the incrementalists' theory. After all, the incrementalists' theory rejects the Trombuloid doctrine.

These are all made-up people and terms, of course—there's no way you could know anything about them. But you can quickly and confidently identify the author's central assumption. Start by looking for different terms in the evidence and conclusion. The evidence and conclusion share "the incrementalists' theory" (whatever that is) but they differ in the terms "Dr. Dinglehorn" and "the Trombuloid doctrine" (whoever and whatever those are). Now, the only question is how the author believes those two terms are related. If the author concludes that Dr. D will support a theory because of a doctrine that theory rejects, the author must assume that Dr. D also rejects that doctrine.

Assumption: Dr. Dinglehorn will support theories that reject the Trombuloid doctrine.

You didn't need (indeed, you couldn't possibly have) real-world information about the subject matter of this argument to accurately analyze it and identify its central assumption. Remember that when you get caught up in dense scientific or philosophical language.

A word of caution, though, Mismatched Concepts arguments don't always involve the abstract or unfamiliar terms, and the more realistic or understandable an argument is, the more cognizant you need to be of your own assumptions. There are times on the LSAT when it can be all too easy to fill in an argument's assumption without even realizing it— you read the argument and think, "Oh, right, that makes sense." Take this argument as an example:

Kim is a nice person. Therefore, it's easy for Kim to make friends.

A quick look at the conclusion shows us that it's about making friends, while the evidence is about being a nice person. At that point, it's easy to think, "Okay, sure. Kim is nice. People like nice people. Makes sense to me!" and then start overthinking the issue. "How are they defining 'nice'? What other things might still make it hard for her to make friends?" etc. As you move into questions that ask you to strengthen or weaken an argument or to identify an author's reasoning error, you may need to engage in that higher-level, more abstract thinking, but your first job in all of the Assumption Family questions is to accurately state the author's assumption. Here, that is

Assumption: It is easy for nice people to make friends.

In the argument, the relevance of being nice to the ease of making friends is not explicitly stated; it has not, within this argument, been established. Indeed, if this assumption were not true, then the evidence would not support the conclusion.

So, even when an argument seems to make all the sense in the world, evaluate the evidence and conclusion with an eye toward spotting mismatched concepts. Are the terms and concepts presented in the evidence inherently relevant to those in the conclusion? When you are a lawyer, part of your job will be to expose the weaknesses in the other side's arguments. Looking at every argument and saying, "Sure, that argument makes all the sense in the world to me!" is, to put it mildly, an ineffective legal skill. Finding the gap in an argument, on the other hand, will expose its weakness. Starting today, train yourself to become a skeptical thinker.

LSAT STRATEGY

When tackling an argument containing Mismatched Concepts:

- Separate concepts, items, people, or items in the evidence from those in the conclusion.
- Identify the mismatched concepts that the author assumes are somehow related.
- Find the assumption by making a sentence that logically relates the mismatched concepts—this sentence serves as a bridge to make the evidence relevant to the conclusion.

Mismatched Concepts: Sample Arguments

Here are some brief Mismatched Concepts arguments and the assumption of each. After reviewing these examples, you'll have a chance to try some others on your own.

Argument	Analysis
Bobby is a chess champion. Hence, he trains every day.	*Conclusion*: Bobby trains every day *because* *Evidence*: Bobby is a chess champion. *Assumption*: Chess champions train every day.
Dogs are more affectionate animals than cats. Therefore, dogs make better pets than cats.	*Conclusion*: Dogs are better pets than cats *because* *Evidence*: Dogs are more affectionate than cats. *Assumption*: More affectionate animals make better pets.
Every kid loves graham crackers, so Joyti must love graham crackers.	*Conclusion*: Joyti must love graham crackers *because* *Evidence*: Every kid loves graham crackers. *Assumption*: Joyti is a kid.
Susan will not be able to go on the expedition because she is not a member of the hiking club.	*Conclusion*: Susan will not be able to go on the expedition *because* *Evidence*: Susan is not a member of the hiking club. *Assumption*: Only hiking club members may go on the expedition.
This piece of luggage weighs more than 50 pounds. Therefore, I will not be able to take it on my flight.	*Conclusion*: I will not be allowed to take this piece of luggage on the flight *because* *Evidence*: This piece of luggage weighs more than 50 lbs. *Assumption*: No luggage weighing over 50 lbs. is allowed on the flight.

Practice Practice your ability to spot the gap between concepts in the evidence and the conclusion and stating the author's central assumption. After each argument, feel free to look at the expert analysis on the following page, or if you're feeling confident, try all of the questions then review.

Argument	My Analysis
1. Brand D computers have state-of-the-art graphics cards; therefore, gamers love Brand D computers.	*Conclusion:* *because* *Evidence:* *Assumption:*
2. Because Arthur likes thrill rides, he will enjoy the new amusement park.	*Conclusion:* *because* *Evidence:* *Assumption:*
3. This fern grows only in the shade of conifers. Thus, the fern cannot be found in Thompson State Park.	*Conclusion:* *because* *Evidence:* *Assumption:*
4. Personnel who listen to podcasts while working in the lab are unsafe because one needs to be attentive to the measurements of the chemicals they are mixing in order to be a safe lab worker.	*Conclusion:* *because* *Evidence:* *Assumption:*
5. In a survey conducted outside City Hall, 75% of respondents said they supported Mayor Onwurah's education plan. Thus, the mayor's education plan is supported by three-quarters of the city's residents.	*Conclusion:* *because* *Evidence:* *Assumption:*

Expert Analysis

Take a look at how an LSAT expert might analyze the arguments you just saw.

Argument	Analysis
1. Brand D computers have state-of-the-art graphics cards; therefore, gamers love Brand D computers.	*Conclusion*: Gamers love Brand D computers *because* *Evidence*: Brand D computers have state-of-the-art graphics cards. *Assumption*: Gamers love computers with state-of-the-art graphics cards.
2. Because Arthur likes thrill rides, he will enjoy the new amusement park.	*Conclusion*: Arthur will enjoy the new amusement park *because* *Evidence*: Arthur likes thrill rides. *Assumption*: The new amusement park has thrill rides.
3. This fern grows only in the shade of conifers. Thus, the fern cannot be found in Thompson State Park.	*Conclusion*: The fern cannot be found in Thompson State Park *because* *Evidence*: The fern grows in the shade of conifers. *Assumption*: No part of Thompson State Park is in the shade of conifers.
4. Personnel who listen to podcasts while working in the lab are unsafe because one needs to pay close attention to the measurements of the chemicals they are mixing in order to be a safe lab worker.	*Conclusion*: Workers who listen to podcasts in the lab are unsafe *because* *Evidence*: Workers need to pay close attention to chemical measurements to be safe in the lab. *Assumption*: One cannot pay close attention to chemical measurements while listening to podcasts.
5. In a survey conducted outside City Hall, 75% of respondents said they supported Mayor Onwurah's education plan. Thus, the mayor's education plan is supported by right around three-quarters of the city's residents.	*Conclusion*: Three-quarters of city residents support the mayor's education plan *because* *Evidence*: Three-quarters of those surveyed outside City Hall support the mayor's education plan. *Assumption*: Those surveyed outside City Hall are representative of all city residents.

The LSAT, of course, will present longer, more difficult arguments than the ones you just saw, but the fundamental structure of arguments with mismatched concepts will remain the same. Regardless of the topic being discussed in the argument, your approach remains the same: (1) identify the conclusion and the evidence, (2) note any terms that appear in one but not the other, and (3) make a sentence that logically connects the terms to "bridge the gap" in the argument.

Try that now with an actual LSAT argument.

LSAT Argument	My Analysis
6. Publicity campaigns for endangered species are unlikely to have much impact on the most important environmental problems, for while the ease of attributing feelings to large mammals facilitates evoking sympathy for them, it is more difficult to elicit sympathy for other kinds of organisms, such as the soil microorganisms on which large ecosystems and agriculture depend. *PrepTest111 Sec4 Q16*	*Conclusion*: *because* *Evidence*: *Assumption*: Argument type:

Did you see a term or concept in the conclusion that is not in the evidence? Did the evidence contain terms that are not inherently or obviously related to those in the conclusion drawn by the author? How does the author assume they are related?

Expert Analysis

Take a look at how an LSAT expert would break down this argument.

LSAT Argument	Analysis
6. Publicity campaigns for endangered species are unlikely to have much impact on the most important environmental problems, for while the ease of attributing feelings to large mammals facilitates evoking sympathy for them, it is more difficult to elicit sympathy for other kinds of organisms, such as the soil microorganisms on which large ecosystems and agriculture depend. *PrepTest111 Sec4 Q16*	*Conclusion*: Publicity for endangered species probably won't solve the most important environmental problems *because* *Evidence*: It is difficult to elicit sympathy for organisms other than large mammals. *Assumption*: The most important environmental problems involve organisms other than large mammals. Argument type: Mismatched Concepts—Alike/Equivalent

Even though this argument comes from an actual LSAT question, it is really no more complicated than the examples you saw earlier in this chapter. Once you identify the evidence and conclusion, simplify the argument: "Okay, so endangered species' publicity won't solve the most important environmental problems because it's hard to get people to sympathize with animals that aren't big and furry." Phrased that way—that simply—the gap in the argument becomes much easier to spot. The author equates "won't solve the *most important problems*" with "animals *other than* large mammals," and once you've paraphrased that assumption, you're ready to answer an Assumption Family question about this argument.

Now that you're getting the hang of evaluating arguments that have distinct terms in their evidence and conclusion, dive in a little deeper to see some of the most common relationships between mismatched concepts in LSAT arguments.

Going Deeper: Common Relationships between Mismatched Concepts

Prepare A few relationships between the mismatched concepts will make up the bulk of the arguments you will see. Knowing how to spot them will make you faster and more efficient at tackling Assumption Family questions.

LSAT STRATEGY

The most common assumptions about the relationship between mismatched concepts:

- The terms or concepts are alike/equivalent.
- The terms or concepts are mutually exclusive.
- One term or concept is needed for the other.
- One term or concept represents another.

Alike/Equivalent is the assumption that two terms/concepts are similar enough to justify the conclusion.

Example: "This diner is decorated with photographs of famous actors and memorabilia like playbills and costumes. This diner will, therefore, appeal to any fan of Broadway musicals." The assumption here is that actors' photos and stage memorabilia appeal to Broadway fans.

Mutually Exclusive or Opposed To is the assumption that two terms/concepts are incompatible.

Example: "These blankets have beautiful examples of the geometric patterns used by the people of this region. They are, however, woven from cotton, and thus cannot be authentic products of this region's native inhabitants." The assumption here is that the native weavers did not weave cotton blankets.

One Term/Concept Needed for the Other is the assumption that A cannot happen without B. In other words, B is necessary for A.

Example: "Although similar in flavor, this cheese cannot be labeled "Roquefort Cheese" because it was not cultured in the caves of Roquefort-sur-Soulzon." The assumption here is that the label "Roquefort cheese" requires being cultured in the caves of Roquefort-sur-Soulzon.

LSAT arguments sometimes present a closely related argument with this structure: Something is necessary for something else; therefore, something else won't happen.

Example: "To label a cheese 'Roquefort' it is required to be cultured in the caves of Roquefort-sur-Soulzon. Therefore, our new cheese cannot be labeled 'Roquefort.'" The assumption here is that a necessary condition (aging in the caves of Roquefort-sur-Soulzon) was not met.

One Sample Representative of the Other is the assumption that the group or sample in the evidence is representative of the group or sample in the conclusion.

Example: "The band X-Patriot's concert is not likely to sell out. We know this from a survey of more than 200 students at the nearby university in which 90% said they would not attend an X-Patriot concert." The assumption here is that university students are representative of X-Patriot fans.

Take a look at the following LSAT argument and try to match it up with one of the four relationships you just learned about.

Practice   Now try some LSAT Mismatched Concepts arguments on your own. Analyze each of the following arguments to determine which of the four common patterns it fits:

- Alike/Equivalent
- Mutually exclusive/Opposed To
- One term/concept needed for the other
- One sample/person/term representative of the other

LSAT Argument	My Analysis
7. Novelists cannot become great as long as they remain in academia. Powers of observation and analysis, which schools successfully hone, are useful to the novelist, but an intuitive grasp of the emotions of everyday life can be obtained only by the kind of immersion in everyday life that is precluded by being an academic. *PrepTest111 Sec1 Q14*	*Conclusion*: *because* *Evidence*: *Assumption*: *Argument type*:
8. Columnist: A democratic society cannot exist unless its citizens have established strong bonds of mutual trust. Such bonds are formed and strengthened only by a participation in civic organizations, political parties, and other groups outside the family. It is obvious then that widespread reliance on movies and electronic media for entertainment has an inherently corrosive effect on democracy. *PrepTest110 Sec3 Q5*	*Conclusion*: *because* *Evidence*: *Assumption*: *Argument type*:

LSAT Argument	**My Analysis**
9. A group of 1,000 students was randomly selected from three high schools in a medium-sized city and asked the question, "Do you plan to finish your high school education?" More than 89 percent answered "Yes." This shows that the overwhelming majority of students want to finish high school, and that if the national dropout rate among high school students is high, it cannot be due to a lack of desire on the part of the students. *PrepTest110 Sec3 Q4*	*Conclusion:* *because* *Evidence:* *Assumption:* *Argument type:*
10. Lines can be parallel in a Euclidean system of geometry. But the non-Euclidean system of geometry that has the most empirical verification is regarded by several prominent physicists as correctly describing the universe we inhabit. If these physicists are right, in our universe there are no parallel lines. *PrepTest110 Sec3 Q9*	*Conclusion:* *because* *Evidence:* *Assumption:* *Argument type:*

Expert Analysis

Having an understanding of the specific relationship between mismatched terms will help you form the correct assumption. Do the terms have a positive relationship? Are they mutually exclusive? Check out how an LSAT expert evaluated the same arguments.

LSAT Argument	Analysis
7. Novelists cannot become great as long as they remain in academia. Powers of observation and analysis, which schools successfully hone, are useful to the novelist, but an intuitive grasp of the emotions of everyday life can be obtained only by the kind of immersion in everyday life that is precluded by being an academic. *PrepTest111 Sec1 Q14*	*Conclusion*: Novelists cannot become great if they stay in academia *because* *Evidence*: Academics cannot have the kind of immersion in everyday life required to have an intuitive understanding of everyday emotions. *Assumption*: An intuitive understanding of everyday emotions is *required* to become a great novelist. (If great novelist → intuitive understanding of everyday emotions) Argument type: Mismatched Concepts—One thing needed for the other
8. Columnist: A democratic society cannot exist unless its citizens have established strong bonds of mutual trust. Such bonds are formed and strengthened only by a participation in civic organizations, political parties, and other groups outside the family. It is obvious then that widespread reliance on movies and electronic media for entertainment has an inherently corrosive effect on democracy. *PrepTest110 Sec3 Q5*	*Conclusion*: Relying on movies and electronic media for entertainment corrodes democracy *because* *Evidence*: (1) Democracy requires mutual trust among citizens, and (2) mutual trust requires participation in civic and political groups. *Assumption*: Relying on movies and electronic media for entertainment undermines participation in civic and political groups. Argument type: Mismatched Concepts—Mutually Exclusive or Opposed To
9. A group of 1,000 students was randomly selected from three high schools in a medium-sized city and asked the question, "Do you plan to finish your high school education?" More than 89 percent answered "Yes." This shows that the overwhelming majority of students want to finish high school, and that if the national dropout rate among high school students is high, it cannot be due to a lack of desire on the part of the students. *PrepTest110 Sec3 Q4*	*Conclusion*: Students want to finish high school; a high national dropout rate cannot be blamed on a lack of desire among students *because* *Evidence*: In a survey of 1,000 high school students from one mid-sized city, 89% said they plan to finish high school. *Assumption*: The students from one mid-sized city are representative of high schoolers nationwide. Argument type: Mismatched Concepts—One sample representative of the other group

LSAT Argument	Analysis
10. Lines can be parallel in a Euclidean system of geometry. But the non-Euclidean system of geometry that has the most empirical verification is regarded by several prominent physicists as correctly describing the universe we inhabit. If these physicists are right, in our universe there are no parallel lines. *PrepTest110 Sec3 Q9*	*Conclusion*: If the prominent physicists are right, our universe has no parallel lines *because* *Evidence*: Some prominent physicists think the non-Euclidian system with the most empirical support accurately describes our universe. *Assumption*: The non-Euclidian system with the most empirical support has no parallel lines. Argument type: Mismatched Concepts—Alike/Equivalent

You now have a more solid understanding of the common relationships and patterns you'll see in Mismatched Concepts arguments. Later in this chapter, you'll get much more practice identifying and analyzing these types of arguments in Assumption Family questions. Now, though, let's turn our attention to the other type of argument structure you'll see in Assumption Family arguments: Overlooked Possibilities.

Overlooked Possibilities

The other common pattern in LSAT arguments involves those in which the author assumes a difference in scale, degree, or level of certainty, rather than a difference of kind; we'll refer to these assumptions as containing Overlooked Possibilities.

Consider this argument

> Why are you looking at all of the brands? WipeUps are the least expensive paper towels. You should just get those.

We've all heard arguments like this one, maybe from a roommate or family member. One reason or advantage is cited for a particular option, and from that, the conclusion recommends that option. The speaker is assuming—an assumption is simply an unstated premise of the argument—that the reason in their evidence is the most important or decisive factor in making the choice recommended in the conclusion. Now, it may be that WipeUps are the best paper towel choice for the person hearing this argument; maybe price is the decisive factor. But don't be too hasty. The argument overlooks—fails to address—several factors that might be worth considering. Maybe another brand is more absorbent, or has the option to tear off smaller sheets, or even comes in a color that goes with the kitchen. If, for the person buying paper towels, any one (or any combination) of those factors trumps price, then the conclusion "You should just get those" is weakened, isn't it?

Overlooked Possibilities: Foundations

Prepare

> **LEARNING OBJECTIVE**
>
> In this lesson, you'll learn to:
>
> - Identify and articulate the assumption in a Mismatched Concepts argument.

In Mismatched Concepts arguments, your concern is relevance: how does the evidence relate to the conclusion. With Overlooked Possibilities arguments, on the other hand, is degree or scale: price is *a* factor in the purchase decision, but is it *the* factor? Throughout the Assumption Family—and especially in Strengthen/Weaken questions—authors overlook not only possible reasons for a decision, but also possible explanations for an occurrence, causes for a result, or circumstances for a prediction. This is important on the test not only because the pattern is quite common, but also because once you recognize this kind of argument, you can weaken it by pointing out one of the overlooked alternatives, or strengthen it by showing that one or more of the alternatives are impossible.

LSAT STRATEGY

How can you identify an argument containing Overlooked Possibilities?

- The terms or concepts in the evidence are related to the conclusion.

- The conclusion reached is too strong or overbroad based on the evidence.

- The author has failed to consider possible objections to the conclusion.

What sort of overlooked possibilities do you spot in this argument?

> The state's budget surplus is large enough to upgrade the main east-west highway in the state or to build a new airport near the capital city. A recent study shows that the current airport is large enough to handle anticipated air traffic for at least the next five years, so the only viable project on which to spend the surplus is upgrading the state's main east-west highway.

Here, the author has given a false dichotomy. There may be any number of other projects that are viable and perhaps even preferable to his recommendation.

TEST DAY TIP

When tackling an argument containing Overlooked Possibilities:

- Focus on the conclusion.

- Determine the possible objections to that conclusion.

- Understand the assumption in negative terms: The author assumes that the possible objections are not present or did not happen.

Overlooked Possibilities: Sample Arguments

Here are some brief Overlooked Possibilities arguments and the assumption of each. After reviewing these examples, you'll have a chance to try some others on your own.

Argument	Analysis
The population of our city's Lower Downtown district has grown rapidly over the past three years. During that same time, several well-known chefs have opened restaurants in Lower Downtown. The boom in fine dining options must be attracting new residents to Lower Downtown.	*Conclusion*: The boom in new restaurants is causing the population surge *because* *Evidence*: The boom in new restaurants is correlated with the population surge. *Assumption*: The correlation between the two phenomena means that the restaurants are causing the growth; it is *not* the population growth that is spurring the new restaurants, and the correlation is *not* mere coincidence.
That man is not wearing a company ID badge, so he must be in the building illicitly.	*Conclusion*: That man is in the building illicitly *because* *Evidence*: That man is not wearing a company ID badge. *Assumption*: No person is authorized to be in the building without wearing a company ID badge; *only* persons wearing company ID badges are authorized to be in the building.
Edwina has better endurance than Jo. Clearly, Edwina will beat Jo in the upcoming bicycle race.	*Conclusion*: Edwina will beat Jo in the bicycle race *because* *Evidence*: Edwina has better endurance than Jo. *Assumption*: There is no other factor that could cause Edwina to lose; endurance is the *only* relevant factor to who will win.
Sundar's reorganization plan will decrease the time it takes for the company's technology team to complete its projects. Therefore, the company should adopt Sundar's plan.	*Conclusion*: The company should adopt Sundar's plan *because* *Evidence*: Sundar's plan has one advantage: It speeds up tech project completion. *Assumption*: There are no overlooked disadvantages to Sundar's plan; speeding up tech projects is the *only* (or at least primary) factor relevant to the company's decision.
Cereal A has lower fiber per serving than cereal B. Clearly, cereal B is the healthier option.	*Conclusion*: Cereal B is healthier than cereal A *because* *Evidence*: Cereal B has more fiber than cereal A. *Assumption*: No other factor other than fiber determines which cereal is healthier; fiber is the *only* factor in comparing health value.

Practice Practice your ability to evaluate Overlooked Possibilities arguments. Paraphrase the conclusion and evidence, and state the argument's central assumption. After each argument, feel free to look at the expert analysis on the following page, or if you're feeling confident, try all of the questions then review.

Argument	My Analysis
11. My cordless vacuum cleaner refuses to start this morning, so I must have forgotten to charge the battery.	Conclusion: because Evidence: Assumption:
12. Taking the subway ensures that Jason gets to school on time. Jason missed the subway this morning, so he will definitely be late to work.	Conclusion: because Evidence: Assumption:
13. This agency was created during the Cold War for the purposes of monitoring our adversaries at the time. That era is past, so the agency is clearly obsolete now.	Conclusion: because Evidence: Assumption:
14. I know Roger has a free period right now, but he's not at the coffee shop. Therefore, he must be at the soup-and-sandwich place.	Conclusion: because Evidence: Assumption:
15. The rate of deaths per 10,000 residents from heart attack are far lower in our state than in the state immediately north of ours. Our state must have a better medical system and better doctors than our neighbors to the north.	Conclusion: because Evidence: Assumption:

Expert Analysis

Now take a look at how an LSAT expert might analyze the arguments you've just evaluated.

Argument	Analysis
11. My cordless vacuum cleaner refuses to start this morning, so I must have forgotten to charge the battery.	*Conclusion*: I must have forgotten to charge my vacuum cleaner battery *because* *Evidence*: The vacuum cleaner won't start. *Assumption*: There is no other reason my vacuum cleaner won't start; an uncharged battery is the *only* reason my vacuum won't start.
12. Taking the subway ensures that Jason gets to school on time. Jason missed the subway this morning, so he will definitely be late to work.	*Conclusion*: Jason will be late to work today *because* *Evidence*: Jason missed the subway. *Assumption*: There is no other way Jason can make it to work on time; taking the subway is the *only* way for Jason to make it to work on time.
13. This agency was created during the Cold War for the purposes of monitoring our adversaries at the time. That era is past, so the agency is clearly obsolete now.	*Conclusion*: The agency is now obsolete *because* *Evidence*: It was created for a specific purpose during a past era. *Assumption*: The agency has no other currently relevant purpose; the agency's original purpose is the only thing it can do.
14. I know Roger has a free period right now, but he's not at the coffee shop. Therefore, he must be at the soup-and-sandwich place.	*Conclusion*: Roger must be at the soup-and-sandwich shop *because* *Evidence*: Roger has a free period and is not at the coffee shop. *Assumption*: During free period, there is no place Roger might be except the coffee shop or the soup-and-sandwich place; those two hangouts are the *only* places Roger might be during free period.
15. The rate of deaths per 10,000 residents from heart attack are far lower in our state than in the state immediately north of ours. Our state must have a better medical system and better doctors than our neighbors to the north.	*Conclusion*: Our state's medical system and doctors are better than those of our northern neighbor *because* *Evidence*: Our state's death rate from heart attack is much lower than that of our northern neighbor. *Assumption*: There is no other reason for our state's lower death rate; better healthcare and doctors are the *only* reasons for our state's superior numbers.

The LSAT, of course, will present more difficult arguments than the ones just shown, but the fundamental structure of Overlooked Possibilities arguments will remain the same. Regardless of the topic being discussed in the argument—whether it be on matters philosophical, legal, or scientific—your method and objective will always remain the same. First, separate evidence from conclusion. Then, evaluate the concepts discussed in both—if the author uses relevant information to draw a conclusion that is too strong or extreme, find the assumption by identifying the factors the author is not considering.

Try that now with an actual LSAT argument.

LSAT Argument	My Analysis
16. Archaeologist: The fact that the ancient Egyptians and the Maya both built pyramids is often taken as evidence of a historical link between Old- and New-World civilizations that is earlier than any yet documented. But while these buildings are similar to each other, there are important differences in both design and function. The Egyptian pyramids were exclusively tombs for rulers, whereas the Mayan pyramids were used as temples. This shows conclusively that there was no such link between Old- and New-World civilizations.	*Conclusion:* *because* *Evidence:* *Assumption:* *Argument type:*

PrepTest112 Sec4 Q8

Did the terms and concepts in the evidence relate to the conclusion drawn? Did the author then overlook potential objections to the conclusion?

Expert Analysis

Take a look at how an LSAT expert would break down this argument.

LSAT Argument	Analysis
16. Archaeologist: The fact that the ancient Egyptians and the Maya both built pyramids is often taken as evidence of a historical link between Old- and New-World civilizations that is earlier than any yet documented. But while these buildings are similar to each other, there are important differences in both design and function. The Egyptian pyramids were exclusively tombs for rulers, whereas the Mayan pyramids were used as temples. This shows conclusively that there was no such link between Old- and New-World civilizations.	*Conclusion*: There was no historical link between Old- and New-World civilizations *because* *Evidence*: Old-World civilizations used their pyramids for different things than New-World civilizations used theirs for. *Assumption*: There are no other possible historical links between the pyramids (i.e., having the same use is the only possible link). Argument type: Overlooked Possibilities—No other reason or explanation
PrepTest112 Sec4 Q8	

Hopefully you're starting to get the hang of evaluating these types of arguments. Let's dive in even deeper and discuss some of the most common types of Overlooked Possibilities arguments you'll see on the LSAT.

Going Deeper: Common Patterns and Relationships in Arguments with Overlooked Possibilities

Prepare   By now, you've seen the benefit of skeptically looking at an argument in which the author uses relevant evidence to support a conclusion that goes too far. In doing so, the author chooses to overlook alternative possibilities that would hurt his conclusion. Indeed, the author's assumption is that no potential objections to the conclusion exist. Now we'll take a look at several of the most common patterns that show up in Overlooked Possibilities arguments.

Assuming There Is No Other Explanation, Reason, or Outcome

Example: "The Smith Avenue location of our supermarket chain is running much more profitably this year than it did last year. Sales must have increased year over year." The assumption here is that increased sales is the only way the Smith Avenue location could be more profitable. The author has overlooked other possible reasons such as lower overhead, less loss from spoilage or theft, among others. Noting other ways the store could improve profitability will weaken this argument.

Assuming That What Is Sufficient Is Actually Necessary or Vice Versa

Example: "Paying for your ticket with SuperCard guarantees VIP seating at the show. Nathan paid for his ticket with CashFriend, so he won't be able to get VIP seating." The author mistakes a condition sufficient to secure VIP seating with one necessary to get VIP seating. The author (perhaps mistakenly) assumes that VIP seating is exclusive to tickets purchased with SuperCard.

Assuming That a Correlation Proves Causation

Example: "I notice that whenever the store has a poor sales month, employee tardiness is higher. It must be that employee tardiness causes the store to lose sales." The author assumes no factor other than tardiness causes the store's lost sales.

There are three ways in which an argument conflating correlation with causation could be wrong. Think of a correlation versus causation argument like this: X and Y are correlated, so X must cause Y.

1. It could be that a third factor is responsible for both the author's purported cause and effect. Maybe Z causes both X and Y. (In the previous example, maybe the manager goes on vacation or is out of the store during months when sales decrease and employees are tardy.)

2. It could be that the author confuses an effect for a cause. Maybe Y causes X. (In the previous example, maybe employees are showing up late because sales are so poor.)

3. It could be that the correlation is simply a coincidence. Maybe X and Y are unrelated. (In the previous example, maybe it is just by chance that poor sales and tardiness have happened to occur at the same time.)

Assuming Changed or Unchanged Circumstances to Make a Prediction

Example: "For the past nine elections, when the local economy has grown during election year, this district has reelected the incumbent. Any time the economy has contracted during election year, the district has elected the challenger. This year, the economy has grown, so Cavanaugh, the incumbent, is a shoo-in to keep her seat." The author assumes that the past trend will continue, thus overlooking any possibility that the district breaks from it. You can weaken this argument by finding potential differences about this year or this election's candidates that might cause voters to change their habits.

Assuming That There Are No Overlooked Advantages or Disadvantages to a Recommendation

Example: "You really ought to get the SG239 when you upgrade your phone. After all, it has the highest resolution camera on any phone currently produced." The author assumes that there are no factors that could trump camera resolution in the listener's buying decision. The argument overlooks any number of considerations: price, appearance, storage capacity, and so on. Pointing out any one of those as a possible concern of the listener would weaken this argument.

Assuming That Something That Can Occur, Will (or Should) Occur

Example: "A popular proposal before the university president would attract out-of-state students. Thus, for the first time in nearly a decade, out-of-state enrollments will increase next year." Not only does the author assume that the popular proposal will be enacted, but also assumes that nothing else will happen that could cause the university to lose out on potential out-of-state students.

As it was with the patterns in Mismatched Concepts arguments, the better you can become at spotting these various Overlooked Possibilities argument patterns, the more efficient you will become at analyzing arguments. You'll be ahead of the game when you encounter Assumption, Strengthen, Weaken, and Flaw questions—which, taken together, constitute nearly 40% of the points available on the LSAT.

On the next page, you get a chance to put all of this knowledge into practice and analyze some arguments from officially released LSAT questions.

Practice   Now try some Overlooked Possibilities arguments from official LSAT questions on your own. Analyze each of the following arguments to determine which of the four common patterns it fits:

- No other reason, explanation, or outcome
- Sufficient versus necessary
- Correlation versus causation
- No changed circumstances or changed circumstances (prediction)
- No additional advantages or disadvantages (recommendation)
- Possible versus certain

LSAT Argument	My Analysis
17. High school students who feel that they are not succeeding in school often drop out before graduating and go to work. Last year, however, the city's high school dropout rate was significantly lower than the previous year's rate. This is encouraging evidence that the program instituted two years ago to improve the morale of high school students has begun to take effect to reduce dropouts. *PrepTest112 Sec4 Q11*	*Conclusion:* *because* *Evidence:* *Assumption:* *Argument type:*
18. Nutritionist: Recently a craze has developed for home juicers, $300 machines that separate the pulp of fruits and vegetables from the juice they contain. Outrageous claims are being made about the benefits of these devices: drinking the juice they produce is said to help one lose weight or acquire a clear complexion, to aid digestion, and even to prevent cancer. But there is no indication that juice separated from the pulp of the fruit or vegetable has any properties that it does not have when unseparated. Save your money. If you want carrot juice, eat a carrot. *PrepTest112 Sec1 Q2*	*Conclusion:* *because* *Evidence:* *Assumption:* *Argument type:*

LSAT Argument	**My Analysis**
19. Mayor: The law prohibiting pedestrians from crossing against red lights serves no useful purpose. After all, in order to serve a useful purpose, a law must deter the kind of behavior it prohibits. But pedestrians who invariably violate this law are clearly not dissuaded by it; and those who comply with the law do not need it, since they would never cross against red lights even if there were no law prohibiting pedestrians from crossing against red lights. *PrepTest111 Sec4 Q13*	*Conclusion:* *because* *Evidence:* *Assumption:* *Argument type:*
20. On the basis of the available evidence, Antarctica has generally been thought to have been covered by ice for at least the past 14 million years. Recently, however, three-million-year-old fossils of a kind previously found only in ocean-floor sediments were discovered under the ice sheet covering central Antarctica. About three million years ago, therefore, the Antarctic ice sheet must temporarily have melted. After all, either severe climatic warming or volcanic activity in Antarctica's mountains could have melted the ice sheet, thus raising sea levels and submerging the continent. *PrepTest111 Sec1 Q17*	*Conclusion:* *because* *Evidence:* *Assumption:* *Argument type:*

Expert Analysis

Recognizing the patterns in arguments with overlooked possibilities will help you form the correct assumption. Is the author ignoring alternative explanations? Does the argument confuse correlation and causation? Check out how an LSAT expert evaluated the same arguments.

LSAT Argument	Analysis
17. High school students who feel that they are not succeeding in school often drop out before graduating and go to work. Last year, however, the city's high school dropout rate was significantly lower than the previous year's rate. This is encouraging evidence that the program instituted two years ago to improve the morale of high school students has begun to take effect to reduce dropouts. *PrepTest112 Sec4 Q11*	*Conclusion*: The high school dropout reduction program is working *because* *Evidence*: The dropout rate (students leaving high school to go to work) was significantly lower last year. *Assumption*: There was no other cause or factor that lowered the dropout rate. Argument type: Overlooked Possibilities—Correlation versus causation
18. Nutritionist: Recently a craze has developed for home juicers, $300 machines that separate the pulp of fruits and vegetables from the juice they contain. Outrageous claims are being made about the benefits of these devices: drinking the juice they produce is said to help one lose weight or acquire a clear complexion, to aid digestion, and even to prevent cancer. But there is no indication that juice separated from the pulp of the fruit or vegetable has any properties that it does not have when unseparated. Save your money. If you want carrot juice, eat a carrot. *PrepTest112 Sec1 Q2*	*Conclusion*: Juicers are a waste of money *because* *Evidence*: Juice has no special health properties you wouldn't get from just eating the fruit or vegetable it comes from. *Assumption*: There is no other advantage to juice versus whole fruits or vegetables. Argument type: Overlooked Possibilities—No other advantage or disadvantage (recommendation)

LSAT Argument	Analysis
19. Mayor: The law prohibiting pedestrians from crossing against red lights serves no useful purpose. After all, in order to serve a useful purpose, a law must deter the kind of behavior it prohibits. But pedestrians who invariably violate this law are clearly not dissuaded by it; and those who comply with the law do not need it, since they would never cross against red lights even if there were no law prohibiting pedestrians from crossing against red lights. *PrepTest111 Sec4 Q13*	*Conclusion*: Outlawing pedestrians from crossing against red is pointless *because* *Evidence*: (Principle) To be useful, laws must deter the behaviors they target, but (facts) these laws don't deter those who always cross anyway and those who never cross against red don't need it. *Assumption*: There are no types of pedestrians who would be deterred from crossing against the red light; those who always cross and those who never cross are the only categories. Note the false dichotomy. Argument type: Overlooked Possibilities—No other reason or explanation
20. On the basis of the available evidence, Antarctica has generally been thought to have been covered by ice for at least the past 14 million years. Recently, however, three-million-year-old fossils of a kind previously found only in ocean-floor sediments were discovered under the ice sheet covering central Antarctica. About three million years ago, therefore, the Antarctic ice sheet must temporarily have melted. After all, either severe climatic warming or volcanic activity in Antarctica's mountains could have melted the ice sheet, thus raising sea levels and submerging the continent. *PrepTest111 Sec1 Q17*	*Conclusion*: Around three million years ago, the Antarctic ice sheet melted temporarily *because* *Evidence*: Three-million-year-old fossils, previously found only on the ocean floor, were found under the ice sheet (thought to have been solid for 14 million years), and there are ways that could have happened (like climate change and volcanoes). *Assumption*: The only way the fossils could have been found under the ice sheet is if the ice sheet had melted (which it could have). Argument type: Overlooked Possibilities—Possible versus certain

Congratulations on working through examples of both key LSAT argument patterns: Mismatched Concepts and Overlooked Possibilities. In the next portion of this chapter, you'll have practice with arguments of both types mixed together in a drill. Then, you'll assess your argument pattern recognition skills with a set of official LSAT stimuli containing arguments fitting the various types you've seen so far.

Untangling and Analyzing LSAT Arguments

Prepare   Now that you have more confidence in your ability to identify the assumption in LSAT arguments, it's time to assess your new skills. First, you'll warm up with a mixed set of simple arguments; some fit the Mismatched Concepts pattern while others contain Overlooked Possibilities. Then, you'll see a similarly mixed set of arguments taken from official, released LSAT questions. In both cases, your job will be to analyze the arguments into their constituent parts—conclusion and evidence. If an argument contains a new concept in the conclusion that is not inherently relevant or related to the concept in the evidence, the author's assumption is that a logical relationship exists between mismatched concepts in the evidence and conclusion. On the other hand, if an argument uses clearly applicable or relevant evidence, but jumps to a conclusion that overlooks other potentially relevant factors, explanations, or criteria, then the author's assumption is that there are no possible objections to the conclusion. Understanding the common ways an LSAT argument moves from its evidence to its conclusion will help you tackle Assumption Family questions. Use this new knowledge to analyze a few LSAT arguments.

Practice   In each of the following arguments, separate the evidence from the conclusion. Paraphrase and then compare them. Is the author assuming that two different concepts are somehow related? Or is the author using relevant evidence to jump to a broad conclusion without considering other possibilities?

Argument	My Analysis
21. This natural cola has a strong caramel flavor. Thus, it will not pair well with the fish entrée.	*Conclusion:* *because* *Evidence:* *Assumption:* Argument type:
22. The house on Placer Place has a much more efficient heating-and-cooling system than the one on Lanier Lane. Clearly, the Placer Place place will have lower monthly expenses.	*Conclusion:* *because* *Evidence:* *Assumption:* Argument type:
23. Sam will not use at least 16 ounces of coffee beans per month. Therefore, a CoffeePal subscription will not be worth it for Sam.	*Conclusion:* *because* *Evidence:* *Assumption:* Argument type:
24. The school district should promote extracurricular activities. Extracurricular activities build interpersonal skills and social awareness, and students with interpersonal skills and social awareness are more likely to engage in community service.	*Conclusion:* *because* *Evidence:* *Assumption:* Argument type:

Argument	My Analysis
25. Our opponent's starting pitcher, Smith, has a devastating curveball, so our manager won't start any player who can't hit curveballs well in today's game. Rasmussen isn't starting, so he must not be able to hit curveballs well.	*Conclusion:* *because* *Evidence:* *Assumption:* *Argument type:*
26. In September, natural gas prices skyrocketed, which in turn drove up heating prices compared to last year. Shortly thereafter, the nursing home where my great uncle stays announced sharp cost increases. The natural gas price spike must be to blame for the increased price of my great uncle's care.	*Conclusion:* *because* *Evidence:* *Assumption:* *Argument type:*
27. Although never finished to the author's satisfaction, Robert Musil's novel *A Man Without Qualities* should be counted among the greatest literature of the interwar era. After all, its portrayal of the complexity of experience is on par with that in *Ulysses* or *To the Lighthouse*.	*Conclusion:* *because* *Evidence:* *Assumption:* *Argument type:*
28. South High School has won its first five games of the season. Clearly, they will play for the state championship this season.	*Conclusion:* *because* *Evidence:* *Assumption:* *Argument type:*
29. I requested a document through our government's information transparency act that I believe will prove the government's awareness of UFOs, but my request was denied because the document is classified. This proves the government knows about UFOs because if it didn't, why would the document be classified?	*Conclusion:* *because* *Evidence:* *Assumption:* *Argument type:*
30. Early polls taken in two of the state's large suburban counties indicate strong support for the proposed ballot measure. Therefore, the ballot measure is likely to receive strong support throughout the state.	*Conclusion:* *because* *Evidence:* *Assumption:* *Argument type:*

Expert Analysis

Now, take a look at how an LSAT expert would untangle and evaluate the arguments you've just examined.

Argument	Analysis
21. This natural cola has a strong caramel flavor. Thus, it will not pair well with the fish entrée.	*Conclusion*: The cola will not pair well with the fish dish *because* *Evidence*: The cola is quite sweet and has strong notes of caramel. *Assumption*: Sweet, caramel-flavored drink will not go with the fish entrée. Argument type: Mismatched Concepts—Mutually Exclusive/Opposed To
22. The house on Placer Place has a much more efficient heating-and-cooling system than the one on Lanier Lane. Clearly, the Placer Place place will have lower monthly expenses.	*Conclusion*: The house on Placer will have lower monthly expenses than the one on Lanier *because* *Evidence*: The house on Placer has more efficient climate control. *Assumption*: No factor aside from heating/cooling is needed to compare monthly expenses for the houses; heating/cooling is the *only* factor to consider. Argument type: Overlooked Possibilities—No other reason or explanation
23. Sam will not use at least 16 ounces of coffee beans per month. Therefore, a CoffeePal subscription will not be worth it for Sam.	*Conclusion*: A CoffeePal subscription is not a good deal for Sam *because* *Evidence*: Sam will not use at least 16 ounces of coffee beans per month. *Assumption*: The CoffeePal subscription is only a good deal for those who use 16 ounces or more of coffee beans each month. Argument type: Mismatched Concepts—One term needed for the other (Using 16 oz of beans is necessary for the subscription to be worth it.)

Argument	Analysis
24. The school district should promote extracurricular activities. Extracurricular activities build interpersonal skills and social awareness, and students with interpersonal skills and social awareness are more likely to engage in community service.	*Conclusion*: The school district should promote extracurricular activities *because* *Evidence*: Extracurricular activities make students more likely to engage in community service. *Assumption*: The school board should promote activities that build engagement in community service. Argument type: Mismatched Concepts—Alike/Equivalent
25. Our opponent's starting pitcher, Smith, has a devastating curveball, so our manager won't start any player who can't hit curveballs well in today's game. Rasmussen isn't starting, so he must not be able to hit curveballs well.	*Conclusion*: Rasmussen must not be able to hit curveballs well *because* *Evidence*: (1) The manager won't start any player who doesn't hit curveballs well, and (2) Rasmussen isn't starting. *Assumption*: There is no other reason Rasmussen might not start today; poor hitting against curveballs is the only reason Rasmussen isn't starting today. Argument type: Overlooked Possibilities—Necessary versus sufficient
26. In September, natural gas prices skyrocketed, which in turn drove up heating prices compared to last year. Shortly thereafter, the nursing home where my great uncle stays announced sharp cost increases. The natural gas price spike must be to blame for the increased price of my great uncle's care.	*Conclusion:* The natural gas price increase caused my uncle's nursing home price increase *because* *Evidence*: The natural gas price increase caused a rise in heating costs just before the nursing home price increase. *Assumption*: No other factor is responsible for the nursing home price increase; the natural gas price increase is the *only* reason for the nursing price increase. Argument type: Overlooked Possibilities—Correlation versus causation

Argument	Analysis
27. Although never finished to the author's satisfaction, Robert Musil's novel *A Man Without Qualities* should be counted among the greatest literature of the interwar era. After all, its portrayal of the complexity of experience is on par with that in *Ulysses* or *To the Lighthouse*.	*Conclusion*: AMWQ deserved to be considered with the greatest books of the interwar era *because* *Evidence*: Its complexity of experience equals that in *Ulysses* or *TTL*. *Assumption*: A novel portraying a depth of experience on par with that of *Ulysses* or *TTL* is among the greatest literature of the interwar era. *Argument type*: Mismatched Concepts—Alike/Equivalent
28. South High School has won its first five games of the season. Clearly, they will play for the state championship this season.	*Conclusion*: South High will play for the state championship *because* *Evidence*: South High has won its first five games this season. *Assumption*: South High's first five games are predictive of the rest of its season. *Argument type*: Overlooked Possibilities—Changed Circumstances
29. I requested a document through our government's information transparency act that I believe will prove the government's awareness of UFOs, but my request was denied because the document is classified. This proves the government knows about UFOs because if it didn't, why would the document be classified?	*Conclusion*: The government is aware of UFOs *because* *Evidence*: A document that might prove government awareness of UFOs is classified. *Assumption*: The document would not be classified *unless* it proves the government's awareness of UFOs. *Argument type*: Overlooked Possibilities—No other reason or explanation
30. Early polls taken in two of the state's large suburban counties indicate strong support for the proposed ballot measure. Therefore, the ballot measure is likely to receive strong support throughout the state.	*Conclusion*: The proposed ballot measure is likely to receive strong support statewide *because* *Evidence*: It appears to have strong support in two large suburban counties. *Assumption*: The suburban counties polled have voters representative of the state as a whole. *Argument type*: Mismatched Concepts—One group represents the other

Now, apply those same skills to a set of arguments from officially released LSAT questions. Then, you'll be ready to move into the chapters with full Assumption Family LSAT questions.

Chapter Perform Quiz

Perform In each of the following arguments, separate the evidence from the conclusion. Paraphrase and then compare them. Is the author assuming that two different concepts are somehow related? Or is the author using relevant evidence to jump to a broad conclusion without considering other possibilities?

LSAT Argument	My Analysis
31. One of the advantages of Bacillus thuringiensis (B.t.) toxins over chemical insecticides results from their specificity for pest insects. The toxins have no known detrimental effects on mammals or birds. In addition, the limited range of activity of the toxins toward insects means that often a particular toxin will kill pest species but not affect insects that prey upon the species. This advantage makes B.t. toxins preferable to chemical insecticides for use as components of insect pest management programs. *PrepTest111 Sec4 Q5*	*Conclusion:* *because* *Evidence:* *Assumption:* Argument type:
32. Sigatoka disease drastically reduces the yield of banana trees and is epidemic throughout the areas of the world where bananas are grown. The fungus that causes the disease can be controlled with fungicides, but the fungicides can pose a health hazard to people living nearby. The fungicides are thus unsuitable for small banana groves in populated areas. Fortunately, most large banana plantations are in locations so isolated that fungicides can be used safely there. Therefore, most of the world's banana crop is not seriously threatened by Sigatoka disease. *PrepTest110 Sec3 Q3*	*Conclusion:* *because* *Evidence:* *Assumption:* Argument type:

Argument	My Analysis
33. Restaurant manager: In response to requests from our patrons for vegetarian main dishes, we recently introduced three: an eggplant and zucchini casserole with tomatoes, brown rice with mushrooms, and potatoes baked with cheese. The first two are frequently ordered, but no one orders the potato dish, although it costs less than the other two. Clearly, then, our patrons prefer not to eat potatoes. *PrepTest110 Sec2 Q3*	*Conclusion:* *because* *Evidence:* *Assumption:* *Argument type:*
34. Marian Anderson, the famous contralto, did not take success for granted. We know this because Anderson had to struggle early in life, and anyone who has to struggle early in life is able to keep a good perspective on the world. *PrepTest111 Sec4 Q14*	*Conclusion:* *because* *Evidence:* *Assumption:* *Argument type:*
35. Zoologist: Animals can certainly signal each other with sounds and gestures. However, this does not confirm the thesis that animals possess language, for it does not prove that animals possess the ability to use sounds or gestures to refer to concrete objects or abstract ideas. *PrepTest110 Sec3 Q17*	*Conclusion:* *because* *Evidence:* *Assumption:* *Argument type:*
36. Camera manufacturers typically advertise their products by citing the resolution of their cameras' lenses, the resolution of a lens being the degree of detail the lens is capable of reproducing in the image it projects onto the film. Differences between cameras in this respect are irrelevant for practical photography, however, since all modern lenses are so excellent that they project far more detail onto the film than any photographic film is capable of reproducing in a developed image. *PrepTest110 Sec2 Q16*	*Conclusion:* *because* *Evidence:* *Assumption:* *Argument type:*

Argument	My Analysis
37. Physician: Heart disease generally affects men at an earlier age than it does women, who tend to experience heart disease after menopause. Both sexes have the hormones estrogen and testosterone, but when they are relatively young, men have ten times as much testosterone as women, and women abruptly lose estrogen after menopause. We can conclude, then, that testosterone tends to promote, and estrogen tends to inhibit, heart disease. *PrepTest111 Sec3 Q25*	*Conclusion:* *because* *Evidence:* *Assumption:* Argument type:
38. Having an efficient, attractive subway system makes good economic sense. So, the city needs to purchase new subway cars, since the city should always do what makes good economic sense. *PrepTest110 Sec2 Q2*	*Conclusion:* *because* *Evidence:* *Assumption:* Argument type:

Expert Analysis

Now, take a look at how an LSAT expert would untangle and evaluate the arguments you've just examined.

LSAT Argument	Analysis
31. One of the advantages of Bacillus thuringiensis (B.t.) toxins over chemical insecticides results from their specificity for pest insects. The toxins have no known detrimental effects on mammals or birds. In addition, the limited range of activity of the toxins toward insects means that often a particular toxin will kill pest species but not affect insects that prey upon the species. This advantage makes B.t. toxins preferable to chemical insecticides for use as components of insect pest management programs. *PrepTest111 Sec4 Q5*	*Conclusion*: B.t. toxins are preferable to chemical insecticides *because* *Evidence*: (1) B.t. toxins don't harm mammals and birds, and (2) B.t. toxins often kill pests but not insects that feed on pests. *Assumption*: B.t. toxins are preferable to chemical insecticides for the two reasons in the evidence; i.e., there are no overlooked disadvantages that would change the evaluation. Argument type: Overlooked Possibilities—No other advantage or disadvantage (recommendation)
32. Sigatoka disease drastically reduces the yield of banana trees and is epidemic throughout the areas of the world where bananas are grown. The fungus that causes the disease can be controlled with fungicides, but the fungicides can pose a health hazard to people living nearby. The fungicides are thus unsuitable for small banana groves in populated areas. Fortunately, most large banana plantations are in locations so isolated that fungicides can be used safely there. Therefore, most of the world's banana crop is not seriously threatened by Sigatoka disease. *PrepTest110 Sec3 Q3*	*Conclusion*: Sigatoka disease does not seriously threaten the world's banana crop *because* *Evidence*: Fungicides can control Sigatoka disease and although they can't be used on small groves near populated areas, they can be safely used on large, isolated banana plantations. *Assumption*: The world's banana crop is largely produced on large, isolated plantations. Argument type: Mismatched Concepts—Alike/Equivalent

LSAT Argument	Analysis
33. Restaurant manager: In response to requests from our patrons for vegetarian main dishes, we recently introduced three: an eggplant and zucchini casserole with tomatoes, brown rice with mushrooms, and potatoes baked with cheese. The first two are frequently ordered, but no one orders the potato dish, although it costs less than the other two. Clearly, then, our patrons prefer not to eat potatoes. *PrepTest110 Sec2 Q3*	*Conclusion*: Our customers don't want to eat potatoes *because* *Evidence*: Of our three new vegetarian entrees—eggplant and zucchini casserole, mushrooms and rice, and baked potatoes with cheese—people hardly ever order the third. *Assumption*: Customers don't order the baked potato and cheese because they don't want to eat potatoes (and not for some other reason . . . like the cheese). *Argument type*: Overlooked Possibilities—No other reason or explanation
34. Marian Anderson, the famous contralto, did not take success for granted. We know this because Anderson had to struggle early in life, and anyone who has to struggle early in life is able to keep a good perspective on the world. *PrepTest111 Sec4 Q14*	*Conclusion*: Marian Anderson did not take success for granted *because* *Evidence*: (1) Marian Anderson struggled early in life, and (2) those who struggle early in life have a good perspective on the world. *Assumption*: Anyone who has a good perspective on the world *does not* take success for granted. *Argument type*: Mismatched Concepts—Mutually exclusive
35. Zoologist: Animals can certainly signal each other with sounds and gestures. However, this does not confirm the thesis that animals possess language, for it does not prove that animals possess the ability to use sounds or gestures to refer to concrete objects or abstract ideas. *PrepTest110 Sec3 Q17*	*Conclusion*: Animal gestures do not confirm animal language *because* *Evidence*: Animal gestures do not prove the ability to refer to concrete objects or abstract ideas. *Assumption*: Without the ability to reference concrete objects or abstract ideas, there is no language; i.e., the ability to reference concrete objects and abstract ideas is necessary for language. *Argument type*: Mismatched Concepts—One term requires the other

LSAT Argument	Analysis
36. Camera manufacturers typically advertise their products by citing the resolution of their cameras' lenses, the resolution of a lens being the degree of detail the lens is capable of reproducing in the image it projects onto the film. Differences between cameras in this respect are irrelevant for practical photography, however, since all modern lenses are so excellent that they project far more detail onto the film than any photographic film is capable of reproducing in a developed image. *PrepTest110 Sec2 Q16*	*Conclusion*: From a practical standpoint, lens resolution is a meaningless distinction among modern cameras *because* *Evidence*: All modern lenses project more detail onto the film than can be reproduced in the developed image. *Assumption*: Because all modern lenses project more detail than can be reproduced, there is no meaningful distinction between modern cameras based on lens resolution; i.e., no other aspect of lens resolution is meaningful. *Argument type*: Overlooked Possibilities—No other reason or explanation
37. Physician: Heart disease generally affects men at an earlier age than it does women, who tend to experience heart disease after menopause. Both sexes have the hormones estrogen and testosterone, but when they are relatively young, men have ten times as much testosterone as women, and women abruptly lose estrogen after menopause. We can conclude, then, that testosterone tends to promote, and estrogen tends to inhibit, heart disease. *PrepTest111 Sec3 Q25*	*Conclusion*: Testosterone promotes heart disease; estrogen prevents heart disease *because* *Evidence*: (1) On average, men experience heart disease earlier than women, who tend to get it after menopause, (2) young men have 10x the testosterone of women, and (3) women lose estrogen after menopause. *Assumption*: The correlation of risk to age in men and women is causal (and not mere coincidence or evidence of a third factor). *Argument type*: Overlooked Possibilities—Correlation versus Causation
38. Having an efficient, attractive subway system makes good economic sense. So, the city needs to purchase new subway cars, since the city should always do what makes good economic sense. *PrepTest110 Sec2 Q2*	*Conclusion*: The city needs to purchase new subway cars *because* *Evidence*: (1) The city should do what makes good economic sense, and (2) having an efficient, attractive subway makes good economic sense. *Assumption*: New subway cars are needed for an efficient, attractive subway system. *Argument type*: Mismatched Concepts—One term needed for the other

You've now had a lot of practice breaking down LSAT arguments and identifying the author's central assumption. But just evaluating and analyzing arguments alone won't get you to your target score; to do that, you'll have to correctly answer the Assumption Family questions you'll face on test day. The good news is that the fundamental understanding you now have of the common ways LSAT arguments move from their evidence to their conclusion puts you light-years ahead of your competition. You'll soon see that Assumption, Strengthen, Weaken, and Flaw questions—which together constitute nearly 40% percent of the LSAT—will seem much easier to analyze, evaluate, and answer correctly.

Take a look at the first of these question types in the next chapter.

CHAPTER 9

Assumption Questions

Assumption Question Basics

The most direct application of the work you've been doing on finding the assumption in LSAT arguments is the Assumption question type. These questions reward you for being able to determine an author's unstated premise, i.e., the argument's central assumption. While that task is relatively straightforward, Assumption questions are consistently among the hardest on the test.

> **LEARNING OBJECTIVES**
>
> In this section, you'll learn to:
>
> - Identify and answer Necessary Assumption questions.
> - Use the Denial Test to confirm or eliminate answer choices in Necessary Assumption questions.
> - Identify and answer Sufficient Assumption questions.
> - Spot formal logic patterns in Sufficient Assumption questions.

On test day, you will be asked to correctly answer roughly eight Assumption questions. That's approximately 15% of all Logical Reasoning questions, or roughly 10% of all the questions on a given LSAT. This is a high-yield question type, and is even more important because finding the argument's assumption is central to your performance on Flaw and Strengthen/Weaken questions, too.

You can identify Assumption questions from stems like these.

Which one of the following is an assumption required by the argument?

PrepTest111 Sec1 Q18

The argument depends on assuming which one of the following?

PrepTest110 Sec2 Q16

The conclusion above follows logically if which one of the following is assumed?

PrepTest111 Sec1 Q22

The conclusion can be properly inferred if which one of the following is assumed?

PrepTest112 Sec1 Q22

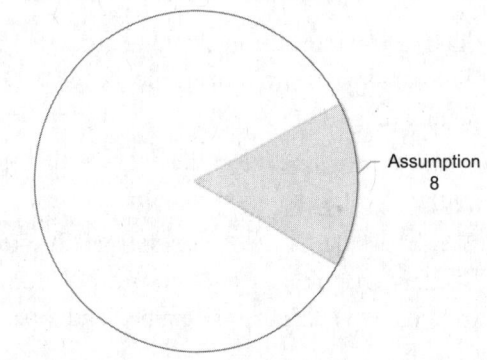

Approximate Number of Assumption Questions per LSAT

Assumption
8

Source: All officially released LSAT exams, 2016-2020

All four of those questions use the word "assume" in some form—assumption, assuming, assumed—the first two present you with a task distinct from that posed by the third and fourth. The first two ask you for the assumption "required by" the argument, or on which the argument "depends." These are Necessary Assumption questions. Of the eight or so Assumptions on a given LSAT, expect five to be of this variety (although it could vary by a question or two on a given test). The third and fourth question stems, on the other hand, prompt you to find the assumption that, if added to the argument, would ensure that the conclusion "follows logically" or "can be properly inferred" from the evidence. These are Sufficient Assumption questions. On the typical LSAT, expect three of the eight Assumption questions to be of this kind.

You'll tackle the two subtypes one at a time in this chapter, and each section will go into detail about what you need to know to master Necessary Assumption and Sufficient Assumption questions, respectively. But, to get the high-level distinction, consider the following simple argument:

> Plovers are short-billed wading birds. Therefore, plovers hunt by sight, rather than by feel.

Now, examine two assumptions. Which one is necessary (but not sufficient) for the conclusion to follow from the evidence, and which is sufficient (but not necessary) to guarantee the conclusion in that argument?

(1) All short-billed wading birds hunt by sight.

(2) At least some short-billed wading birds hunt by sight.

Choice (1) is *sufficient* to establish the conclusion. If every short-billed wading bird hunts by sight, the argument is a slam dunk. For the argument to be valid, it is not necessary that every short-billed wading bird hunts in this manner, but it is *necessary* (though not sufficient) that statement (2) is true, that at least some birds in this category hunt by sight. After all, if none do, the argument falls apart.

How This Chapter Is Organized

That example may help you see why the two subtypes are covered separately. You'll tackle the slightly more common Necessary Assumption questions first, followed by a Spotlight on a useful Necessary Assumption strategy called the Denial Test. When you turn to Sufficient Assumptions, you'll have a second Formal Logic Workshop, because conditional statements are found in many Sufficient Assumption arguments. Finally, you'll see a couple examples of a very rare variety, the generic Assumption question, that does not specify between necessary and sufficient. Once you've practiced the other two, these questions will feel routine. Finally, at the very end of the chapter, there is a comprehensive Perform quiz covering all Assumption questions.

ASSUMPTION QUESTIONS AT A GLANCE

Task: Determine the unstated premise that is either (1) sufficient to guarantee that the conclusion follows logically from the evidence or (2) necessary for the conclusion to follow logically from the evidence.

Strategy: Analyze the argument, identifying the author's conclusion and evidence. Consider what the author has taken for granted in making the argument.

Frequency: LSAT tests released from 2016 to 2020 had an average of 3.9 Assumption questions per section. Over that 2016–2020 stretch, Assumption questions were split about 63%–37% between those calling for a necessary assumption and those asking for a sufficient assumption.

Necessary Assumption Questions

LEARNING OBJECTIVES

In this section, you'll learn to:

- Identify and answer Necessary Assumption questions.
- Use the Denial Test to confirm or eliminate answer choices in Necessary Assumption questions.

Look again at the question stems indicating Necessary Assumption questions.

> Which one of the following is an assumption
> required by the argument?
>
> *PrepTest111 Sec1 Q18*

> The argument depends on assuming which
> one of the following?
>
> *PrepTest110 Sec2 Q16*

In these questions, the correct answer will be an unstated premise without which the conclusion cannot follow logically from the evidence. The author needs the correct answer to be true, although it might not, even when combined with the evidence, be sufficient to unequivocally establish the conclusion. You can identify these questions because they will use the terms "depends," "required," or "necessary" in their stems.

LSAT STRATEGY

Some facts to remember about Necessary Assumption questions:

- Recognize these questions by the phrasing "an assumption required by the argument" or "the argument depends on the assumption that."
- The correct answer doesn't have to be sufficient for the conclusion to be drawn, just necessary.
- Both Mismatched Concepts and Overlooked Possibilities arguments will be tested.
- Use the Denial Test to distinguish the correct answer or eliminate wrong ones.

In all Assumption questions—where the focus is directly on the "gap" between the conclusion and evidence—the argument pattern is more likely to be Mismatched Concepts than Overlooked Possibilities. As you'll see, the argument pattern in Sufficient Assumption questions is almost exclusively Mismatched Concepts. In Necessary Assumption questions, however, you will see both patterns, so take a few minutes to get a sense of how the patterns are tested in this question type.

If it's an Overlooked Possibilities argument, look for an assumption that removes at least one possible objection to the conclusion that the author has not considered. In both argument types, look for an assumption that is required or essential to the argument. Additionally, because you are looking for an assumption that is necessary for the argument, you can test the validity of answer choices by "denying" them. We'll talk about that strategy more later. Now, though, let's discuss Mismatched Concepts arguments in Necessary Assumption questions.

Mismatched Concepts in Necessary Assumption Questions

When a Necessary Assumption question has a Mismatched Concepts argument in its stimulus, look for an assumption that establishes a relationship between the mismatched concepts tailored to the argument.

Consider the following argument and the pair of answer choices that follow:

> Musicologist: A jazz musician will never become a true master through academic study and formal practice alone. While study and practice facilitate technical skill, the confidence to improvise daring solos in a variety of musical settings can only be obtained through live performance for an audience.

The argument depends on the assumption that

(1) Every musician who confidently improvises in a variety of settings is a master jazz musician.

(2) A jazz musician cannot be great without the confidence to improvise daring solos in a variety of musical settings.

The musicologist concludes that jazz musicians will never be great if all they do is study and practice in school. Why? Because, while school helps with the technical aspects of playing, live performance is required for learning the confidence to solo in different kinds of music. The author must assume that such confidence is necessary for a jazz musician to become great. If that confidence is not necessary for true mastery, the argument falls apart. So, choice (2) is correct. Notice that choice (1) is overbroad for the purposes of this question, and it fails to link the evidence ("only . . . obtained through live performance") to the conclusion.

Now, try completing a Necessary Assumption question that contains a Mismatched Concepts argument that you analyzed in the preceding chapter. Take your time and work through all four steps of the Logical Reasoning Method, even if you remember the argument. When you're finished, review an LSAT expert's work on the next page.

Step 2: *Conclusion*:	**Step 1:**
because	
Evidence:	

1. Publicity campaigns for endangered species are unlikely to have much impact on the most important environmental problems, for while the ease of attributing feelings to large mammals facilitates evoking sympathy for them, it is more difficult to elicit sympathy for other kinds of organisms, such as the soil microorganisms on which large ecosystems and agriculture depend.

Which one of the following is an assumption on which the argument depends?

(A) The most important environmental problems involve endangered species other than large mammals.

(B) Microorganisms cannot experience pain or have other feelings.

(C) Publicity campaigns for the environment are the most effective when they elicit sympathy for some organism.

(D) People ignore environmental problems unless they believe the problems will affect creatures with which they sympathize.

(E) An organism can be environmentally significant only if it affects large ecosystems or agriculture.

PrepTest111 Sec4 Q16

Step 3:	**Step 4:**

Expert Analysis

Step 2: *Conclusion*: Publicity for endangered species probably won't solve the most important environmental problems *because* *Evidence*: It is difficult to elicit sympathy for organisms other than large mammals.	**Step 1:** "[D]epends" indicates a Necessary Assumption question; the correct answer is an unstated premise required for the conclusion to follow from the evidence.

1. Publicity campaigns for endangered species are unlikely to have much impact on the most important environmental problems, for while the ease of attributing feelings to large mammals facilitates evoking sympathy for them, it is more difficult to elicit sympathy for other kinds of organisms, such as the soil microorganisms on which large ecosystems and agriculture depend.

Which one of the following is an assumption on which the argument depends?

(A) The most important environmental problems involve endangered species other than large mammals.

(B) Microorganisms cannot experience pain or have other feelings.

(C) Publicity campaigns for the environment are the most effective when they elicit sympathy for some organism.

(D) People ignore environmental problems unless they believe the problems will affect creatures with which they sympathize.

(E) An organism can be environmentally significant only if it affects large ecosystems or agriculture.

PrepTest111 Sec4 Q16

Step 3: The argument draws a conclusion about the most important environmental problems from evidence about species other than large mammals. It must be assumed that these other organisms are related to the most important environmental problems.	**Step 4:** (A) bridges the gap, appropriately linking the concept in the conclusion to that in the evidence. Using the Denial Test confirms that (A) is correct. If *no species* other than large mammals were involved in the most important environmental problems, then publicity campaigns likely would work, and the argument would fall apart.

Wrong answers: (B) Outside the Scope. The argument doesn't hinge on whether microorganisms actually have emotions, but on how they are perceived and their relationship to the most important environmental issues. (C) Outside the Scope. This choice fails the Denial Test. If something other than soliciting sympathy is effective, perhaps publicity campaigns could impact the most important environmental problems. (D) Extreme. The argument doesn't require that people *ignore* environmental problems unless they feel sympathy for an impacted creature. (E) Extreme. The author may consider many types of organisms significant even if they aren't involved in the most important environmental problems.

You'll get more practice with Mismatched Concepts arguments in Necessary Assumption questions later in this section, as well as at the end of the chapter. Now, though, let's take a look at how Overlooked Possibilities arguments show up in Necessary Assumption questions.

Overlooked Possibilities in Necessary Assumption Questions

For an Overlooked Possibilities argument to be valid, its author must assume that any and all of the potential objections to it are not true. That means that it is necessary that each individual objection is not true. To see how that plays out in a Necessary Assumption question with an Overlooked Possibilities argument, consider the following argument and two sample answer choices:

> Since ServCo instituted its green energy program last quarter, the company's costs are down 8 percent. Clearly, the green energy program is saving ServCo money.

> Which one of the following is an assumption required by the argument?

> (1) ServCo's reduction in expenses was not the result of reducing payroll.

> (2) Every company instituting the green energy program used at ServCo has seen a cost reduction of at least 8 percent as a result.

The author here concludes that ServCo's adoption of a green energy program is responsible for the company's cost savings. That could be true, but what's the evidence? It's a classic correlation: the company's costs are down during the period that the green energy program has been in place. To know for sure, you'd have to rule out all the other things that might have saved the company money. Choice (1) rules out one overlooked possibility, and is thus necessary for this argument to be valid. There's nothing special about payroll; the choice could have said ServCo saved by cutting shipping costs, rent, insurance, you name it. The correct answer to a Necessary Assumption question will typically pick one of the overlooked possibilities and rule it out.

Notice that choice (2) here sort of generally strengthens the argument—it is a little more likely that ServCo's savings came from the program if that's been the experience of several other companies who adopted it—but this choice is *not necessary* for the conclusion to follow. Even if ServCo is the only company that has ever seen cost savings from the green energy program, or even the only company to ever have tried it, it could be true that the program is responsible for the cost savings.

Try completing a Necessary Assumption question that contains an Overlooked Possibilities argument that you analyzed in the preceding chapter. Take your time and work through all four steps of the Logical Reasoning Method, even if you remember the argument. When you're finished, review an LSAT expert's work on the next page.

Step 2: *Conclusion*:	**Step 1:**
because	
Evidence:	

2. Camera manufacturers typically advertise their products by citing the resolution of their cameras' lenses, the resolution of a lens being the degree of detail the lens is capable of reproducing in the image it projects onto the film. Differences between cameras in this respect are irrelevant for practical photography, however, since all modern lenses are so excellent that they project far more detail onto the film than any photographic film is capable of reproducing in a developed image.

The argument depends on assuming which one of the following?

(A) The definition of the term "resolution" does not capture an important determinant of the quality of photographic instruments and materials.

(B) In determining the amount of detail reproduced in the developed photographic image, differences in the resolutions of available lenses do not compound the deficiencies of available film.

(C) Variations in the method used to process the film do not have any significant effect on the film's resolution.

(D) Flawless photographic technique is needed to achieve the maximum image resolution possible with the materials and equipment being used.

(E) The only factors important in determining the degree of detail reproduced in the final photographic print are the resolution of the camera's lens and the resolution of the film.

PrepTest110 Sec2 Q16

Step 3:	**Step 4:**

Expert Analysis

Step 2: *Conclusion*: From a practical standpoint, lens resolution is a meaningless distinction among modern cameras *because* *Evidence*: All modern lenses project more detail onto the film than can be reproduced in the developed image.	**Step 1:** The correct answer states a premise required for the argument to be valid; this is a Necessary Assumption question.

2. Camera manufacturers typically advertise their products by citing the resolution of their cameras' lenses, the resolution of a lens being the degree of detail the lens is capable of reproducing in the image it projects onto the film. Differences between cameras in this respect are irrelevant for practical photography, however, since all modern lenses are so excellent that they project far more detail onto the film than any photographic film is capable of reproducing in a developed image.

The argument depends on assuming which one of the following?

(A) The definition of the term "resolution" does not capture an important determinant of the quality of photographic instruments and materials.

(B) In determining the amount of detail reproduced in the developed photographic image, differences in the resolutions of available lenses do not compound the deficiencies of available film.

(C) Variations in the method used to process the film do not have any significant effect on the film's resolution.

(D) Flawless photographic technique is needed to achieve the maximum image resolution possible with the materials and equipment being used.

(E) The only factors important in determining the degree of detail reproduced in the final photographic print are the resolution of the camera's lens and the resolution of the film.

PrepTest110 Sec2 Q16

Step 3: The author concludes that lens resolution is of no practical use for distinguishing among modern cameras. This is based on evidence that all modern lenses project detail beyond that which any film can reproduce when developed. The author must assume that there is no other reason to care about lens resolution. The correct answer will paraphrase this assumption or rule out one or more other reasons to care about lens resolution.	**Step 4:** (B) rules out an additional reason to distinguish among cameras by their lens resolution. You can confirm this choice using the Denial Test: If differences in lens resolution *do* compound the deficiencies of the film, photographers still have a reason to care about different cameras' lens resolutions.

Wrong answers: (A) The argument clearly defines the term "resolution," and does not conclude or imply that the definition is inadequate. (C) Outside the Scope. Whether development methods affect film resolution is irrelevant to this argument about distinctions among cameras' lens resolutions. (D) Outside the Scope. The argument does not opine on all that goes into making high-resolution photographs; it argues only that lens resolution is no longer a practical concern because all lenses are so good these days. (E) Extreme. The existence of other factors in the outcome of photographs does not affect the argument's conclusion that lens resolutions no longer provide any practical distinctions among cameras.

The Denial Test

The expert analysis in both of the preceding worked examples mentioned the Denial Test. On those questions, the expert used the Denial Test in step 4 to confirm their choice for the correct answer, but you can use the Denial Test to eliminate wrong answers as well. Here's how.

Because the correct answer to a Necessary Assumption question must be true for the argument to be valid, it can be useful to evaluate the answer choices by negating them. When you deny or negate the correct answer to a Necessary Assumption question, the argument falls apart. Denying an incorrect answer does not destroy the argument.

See what happens when you deny the two statements from two pages ago associated with the jazz education argument.

> Musicologist: A jazz musician will never become a true master through academic study and formal practice alone. While study and practice facilitate technical skill, the confidence to improvise daring solos in a variety of musical settings can only be obtained through live performance for an audience.

> The argument depends on the assumption that

> (1) **Not every** musician who confidently improvises in a variety of settings is a master jazz musician.

> (2) A jazz musician **CAN** ~~cannot~~ be great without the confidence to improvise daring solos in a variety of musical settings.

Try it again on the two statements you just evaluated in light of the ServCo argument.

> Since ServCo instituted its green energy program last quarter, the company's costs are down 8 percent. Clearly, the green energy program is saving ServCo money.

> Which one of the following is an assumption required by the argument?

> (1) ServCo's reduction in expenses **WAS** ~~not~~ the result of reducing payroll.

> (2) **Not every** company instituting the green energy program used at ServCo has seen a cost reduction of at least 8 percent as a result.

When you read the negated sentences into the argument, it becomes clear that the correct answer, if negated, makes the conclusion impossible to derive from the evidence. The incorrect choices when negated don't have that effect.

The Denial Test works only in Necessary Assumption questions and is not meant to be your initial approach to these questions—tackling every Necessary Assumption question by denying each answer choice would be time-consuming—but the strategy is quite useful for confirming the correct answer or eliminating a pesky wrong one. It's so useful, in fact, that there is a Spotlight lesson dedicated to the Denial Test. It follows the Necessary Assumption Practice questions up next in this chapter.

Now, it's time to practice what you've learned about Necessary Assumption questions.

Practice Try each of the following Necessary Assumption questions. A handful contain arguments you analyzed in the preceding chapter. Don't worry too much about your timing here. Complete all four steps of the Logical Reasoning Method for each question, jotting down your notes whenever it is helpful to do so. After each question, review your work with the expert analysis that follows.

Hint: Are there different terms in the conclusion and the evidence? If so, how does the author believe they are related?

Step 2: *Conclusion*:	**Step 1:**
because	
Evidence:	

3. Columnist: A democratic society cannot exist unless its citizens have established strong bonds of mutual trust. Such bonds are formed and strengthened only by a participation in civic organizations, political parties, and other groups outside the family. It is obvious then that widespread reliance on movies and electronic media for entertainment has an inherently corrosive effect on democracy.

Which one of the following is an assumption on which the columnist's argument depends?

(A) Anyone who relies on movies and electronic media for entertainment is unable to form a strong bond of mutual trust with a citizen.

(B) Civic organizations cannot usefully advance their goals by using electronic media.

(C) Newspapers and other forms of print media strengthen, rather than weaken, democratic institutions.

(D) Relying on movies and electronic media for entertainment generally makes people less likely to participate in groups outside their families.

(E) People who rely on movies and electronic media for entertainment are generally closer to their families than are those who do not.

PrepTest110 Sec3 Q5

Step 3:	**Step 4:**

Expert Analysis

Here's how an LSAT expert approached the question you just tried.

Step 2: *Conclusion*: Relying on movies and electronic media for entertainment corrodes democracy *because* *Evidence*: (1) Democracy requires mutual trust among citizens, and (2) mutual trust requires participation in civic organizations, political parties, and other public groups.	Step 1: This is a Necessary Assumption question; the correct answer supplies a premise without which the columnist's argument falls apart.

3. Columnist: A democratic society cannot exist unless its citizens have established strong bonds of mutual trust. Such bonds are formed and strengthened only by a participation in civic organizations, political parties, and other groups outside the family. It is obvious then that widespread reliance on movies and electronic media for entertainment has an inherently corrosive effect on democracy.

Which one of the following is an assumption on which the columnist's argument depends?

(A) Anyone who relies on movies and electronic media for entertainment is unable to form a strong bond of mutual trust with a citizen.

(B) Civic organizations cannot usefully advance their goals by using electronic media.

(C) Newspapers and other forms of print media strengthen, rather than weaken, democratic institutions.

(D) Relying on movies and electronic media for entertainment generally makes people less likely to participate in groups outside their families.

(E) People who rely on movies and electronic media for entertainment are generally closer to their families than are those who do not.

PrepTest110 Sec3 Q5

Step 3: This is a classic Mismatched Concepts argument. A conclusion about movies and electronic media is drawn from evidence about participation in public groups and organizations. The author must assume that relying on movies and electronic media for entertainment is at odds with participation in the kinds of public groups that build bonds of trust. The two concepts are assumed to be opposed.	Step 4: (D) matches the prediction and accurately paraphrases the author's assumption.

Wrong answers: (A) Extreme. This would be sufficient to establish the conclusion of the argument, but it is not necessary that every individual using movies and electronics for entertainment be prevented from forming social bonds. (B) distorts the argument, which talks about a reliance on electronic media for entertainment, not its other potential uses. (C) The effect of newspapers and print media on society is Outside the Scope of this argument. (E) Outside the Scope. Family bonds play no role in the argument.

Hint: Two different cases are contrasted in the evidence. How does that play into the argument?

Step 2: *Conclusion:*	**Step 1:**
because	
Evidence:	

4. Sigatoka disease drastically reduces the yield of banana trees and is epidemic throughout the areas of the world where bananas are grown. The fungus that causes the disease can be controlled with fungicides, but the fungicides can pose a health hazard to people living nearby. The fungicides are thus unsuitable for small banana groves in populated areas. Fortunately, most large banana plantations are in locations so isolated that fungicides can be used safely there. Therefore, most of the world's banana crop is not seriously threatened by Sigatoka disease.

Which one of the following is an assumption on which the argument depends?

(A) It will eventually be possible to breed strains of bananas that are resistant to Sigatoka disease.

(B) Large plantations produce most or all of the world's bananas.

(C) Sigatoka disease spreads more slowly on large plantations than in small banana groves.

(D) Sigatoka disease is the only disease that threatens bananas on a worldwide scale.

(E) Most of the banana trees that have not been exposed to the Sigatoka fungus grow in small banana groves.

PrepTest110 Sec3 Q3

Step 3:	**Step 4:**

Expert Analysis

Here's how an LSAT expert approached the question you just tried.

Step 2: *Conclusion*: Sigatoka disease does not seriously threaten the world's banana crop *because* *Evidence*: Fungicides can control Sigatoka disease and can be safely used on large, isolated banana plantations (but not on small groves near populated areas).	**Step 1:** This is a classic Necessary Assumption question stem; the correct answer will state a premise without which the conclusion cannot follow from the evidence.

4. Sigatoka disease drastically reduces the yield of banana trees and is epidemic throughout the areas of the world where bananas are grown. The fungus that causes the disease can be controlled with fungicides, but the fungicides can pose a health hazard to people living nearby. The fungicides are thus unsuitable for small banana groves in populated areas. Fortunately, most large banana plantations are in locations so isolated that fungicides can be used safely there. Therefore, most of the world's banana crop is not seriously threatened by Sigatoka disease.

Which one of the following is an assumption on which the argument depends?

(A) It will eventually be possible to breed strains of bananas that are resistant to Sigatoka disease.

(B) Large plantations produce most or all of the world's bananas.

(C) Sigatoka disease spreads more slowly on large plantations than in small banana groves.

(D) Sigatoka disease is the only disease that threatens bananas on a worldwide scale.

(E) Most of the banana trees that have not been exposed to the Sigatoka fungus grow in small banana groves.

PrepTest110 Sec3 Q3

Step 3: The author reaches the conclusion that Sigatoka does not threaten the world's banana crop from evidence that fungicides can control the disease on large, isolated plantations. So, the author must assume that the world's banana crop is largely from large, isolated plantations. If that's not true, the argument would fall apart.	**Step 4:** (B) matches the prediction, accurately paraphrasing the author's assumption. You can confirm this choice using the Denial Test: If large plantations do *not* produce most of the world's bananas, the argument's conclusion would be in doubt.

Wrong answers: (A) Outside the Scope. This argument is about the threat of the disease in the present day. (C) The argument relies on the control of the disease through fungicide use; the rate of spread is irrelevant. Use the Denial Test to eliminate this choice: If Sigatoka spread no more slowly on large plantations, would it change the author's conclusion? No. (D) The existence of other diseases does not affect this argument, which is only about whether Sigatoka threatens the global banana crop. (E) cites a fact fortunate for small groves but irrelevant to the argument which hinges on being able to control the fungus on large plantations.

Hint: Obscure science and mathematics terminology can make an argument appear more complex than it really is. Focus on the difference between the conclusion and the evidence.

Step 2: *Conclusion:*	**Step 1:**
because	
Evidence:	

5. Lines can be parallel in a Euclidean system of geometry. But the non-Euclidean system of geometry that has the most empirical verification is regarded by several prominent physicists as correctly describing the universe we inhabit. If these physicists are right, in our universe there are no parallel lines.

Which one of the following is an assumption that is required by the argument?

(A) There are no parallel lines in the non-Euclidean system of geometry that has the most empirical verification.

(B) Most physicists have not doubted the view that the universe is correctly described by the non-Euclidean system of geometry that has the most empirical verification.

(C) There are no parallel lines in every non-Euclidean system of geometry that has any empirical verification.

(D) The universe is correctly described by the non-Euclidean system of geometry that has the most empirical verification if prominent physicists maintain that it is.

(E) Only physicists who are not prominent doubt the view that the universe is correctly described by the non-Euclidean system of geometry that has the most empirical verification.

PrepTest110 Sec3 Q9

Step 3:	**Step 4:**

Expert Analysis

Here's how an LSAT expert approached the question you just tried.

Step 2: *Conclusion*: If the prominent physicists are right, our universe has no parallel lines *because* *Evidence*: Some prominent physicists think the non-Euclidian system with the most empirical support accurately describes our universe.	**Step 1:** "[R]equired" indicates a Necessary Assumption question; the correct answer is an unstated premise without which the argument falls apart.

5. Lines can be parallel in a Euclidean system of geometry. But the non-Euclidean system of geometry that has the most empirical verification is regarded by several prominent physicists as correctly describing the universe we inhabit. If these physicists are right, in our universe there are no parallel lines.

Which one of the following is an assumption that is required by the argument?

(A) There are no parallel lines in the non-Euclidean system of geometry that has the most empirical verification.

(B) Most physicists have not doubted the view that the universe is correctly described by the non-Euclidean system of geometry that has the most empirical verification.

(C) There are no parallel lines in every non-Euclidean system of geometry that has any empirical verification.

(D) The universe is correctly described by the non-Euclidean system of geometry that has the most empirical verification if prominent physicists maintain that it is.

(E) Only physicists who are not prominent doubt the view that the universe is correctly described by the non-Euclidean system of geometry that has the most empirical verification.

PrepTest110 Sec3 Q9

Step 3: A classic Mismatched Concepts argument: the author reaches a conclusion about an absence of parallel lines from evidence about the non-Euclidian system of geometry with the most empirical support. The author must assume those concepts to be equivalent.	**Step 4:** (A) is correct. The Denial Test demonstrates this statement's necessity to the argument: If the non-Euclidian system with the greatest empirical support DOES contain parallel lines, the argument falls apart.

Wrong answers: (B) Outside the Scope. The argument does not care what *most* physicists believe, but whether "these physicists" (the ones convinced by the non-Euclidean system with the most empirical evidence) are right. (C) Extreme. This answer would be sufficient to establish the conclusion, but it is not necessary that *every* non-Euclidean system supported by *any* empirical data lacks parallel lines. (D) fails to bridge the gap between the stated geometric system and a lack of parallel lines, making this answer Outside the Scope. (E) Outside the Scope. The status of physicists who doubt the argument is irrelevant.

Hint: Make sure to characterize the relationship the author assumes exists between the terms of the conclusion and those in the evidence.

Step 2: *Conclusion:*	**Step 1:**
because	
Evidence:	

6. Novelists cannot become great as long as they remain in academia. Powers of observation and analysis, which schools successfully hone, are useful to the novelist, but an intuitive grasp of the emotions of everyday life can be obtained only by the kind of immersion in everyday life that is precluded by being an academic.

Which one of the following is an assumption on which the argument depends?

(A) Novelists require some impartiality to get an intuitive grasp of the emotions of everyday life.

(B) No great novelist lacks powers of observation and analysis.

(C) Participation in life, interspersed with impartial observation of life, makes novelists great.

(D) Novelists cannot be great without an intuitive grasp of the emotions of everyday life.

(E) Knowledge of the emotions of everyday life cannot be acquired by merely observing and analyzing life.

PrepTest111 Sec1 Q14

Step 3:	**Step 4:**

Expert Analysis

Here's how an LSAT expert approached the question you just tried.

Step 2: *Conclusion*: Novelists cannot become great if they stay in academia *because* *Evidence*: Academics cannot have the kind of immersion in everyday life required to have an intuitive understanding of everyday emotions.	**Step 1:** This is a Necessary Assumption question; the correct answer is a premise without which the argument will fall apart.

6. Novelists cannot become great as long as they remain in academia. Powers of observation and analysis, which schools successfully hone, are useful to the novelist, but an intuitive grasp of the emotions of everyday life can be obtained only by the kind of immersion in everyday life that is precluded by being an academic.

Which one of the following is an assumption on which the argument depends?

(A) Novelists require some impartiality to get an intuitive grasp of the emotions of everyday life.

(B) No great novelist lacks powers of observation and analysis.

(C) Participation in life, interspersed with impartial observation of life, makes novelists great.

(D) Novelists cannot be great without an intuitive grasp of the emotions of everyday life.

(E) Knowledge of the emotions of everyday life cannot be acquired by merely observing and analyzing life.

PrepTest111 Sec1 Q14

Step 3: This is a classic Mismatched Concepts argument. The author assumes that an intuitive grasp on everyday emotions is necessary for one to become a great novelist.	**Step 4:** (D) matches the prediction in Step 3 and is correct. Confirm it with the Denial Test: If novelists *can* become great without an intuitive grasp of everyday emotions, the whole argument about academia precluding this falls apart.

Wrong answers: (A) A requirement of impartiality is Outside the Scope of this argument. (B) This may be true, but these are things novelists *can* get as academics. There has to be another requirement of greatness unattainable in the Ivory Tower. (C) This choice outlines criteria sufficient for greatness, but these aren't required for the argument's validity. (E) more or less repeats the evidence (*immersion* in everyday life is required) but this choice doesn't link that evidence to novelists' greatness, so it cannot be the argument's assumption.

Hint: This argument's conclusion comes from combining parts of two sentences.

Step 2: *Conclusion*:	**Step 1:**
because	
Evidence:	

7. Zoologist: Animals can certainly signal each other with sounds and gestures. However, this does not confirm the thesis that animals possess language, for it does not prove that animals possess the ability to use sounds or gestures to refer to concrete objects or abstract ideas.

Which one of the following is an assumption on which the zoologist's argument depends?

(A) Animals do not have the cognitive capabilities to entertain abstract ideas.

(B) If an animal's system of sounds or gestures is not a language, then that animal is unable to entertain abstract ideas.

(C) When signaling each other with sounds or gestures, animals refer neither to concrete objects nor abstract ideas.

(D) If a system of sounds or gestures contains no expressions referring to concrete objects or abstract ideas, then that system is not a language.

(E) Some animals that possess a language can refer to both concrete objects and abstract ideas.

PrepTest110 Sec3 Q17

Step 3:	**Step 4:**

Expert Analysis

Here's how an LSAT expert approached the question you just tried.

Step 2: *Conclusion*: Animal gestures do not confirm animal language *because* *Evidence*: Animal gestures do not prove the ability to refer to concrete objects or abstract ideas.	**Step 1:** "[D]epends" signals a Necessary Assumption question; you can use the Denial Test to confirm the correct answer or eliminate wrong ones.

7. Zoologist: Animals can certainly signal each other with sounds and gestures. However, this does not confirm the thesis that animals possess language, for it does not prove that animals possess the ability to use sounds or gestures to refer to concrete objects or abstract ideas.

Which one of the following is an assumption on which the zoologist's argument depends?

(A) Animals do not have the cognitive capabilities to entertain abstract ideas.

(B) If an animal's system of sounds or gestures is not a language, then that animal is unable to entertain abstract ideas.

(C) When signaling each other with sounds or gestures, animals refer neither to concrete objects nor abstract ideas.

(D) If a system of sounds or gestures contains no expressions referring to concrete objects or abstract ideas, then that system is not a language.

(E) Some animals that possess a language can refer to both concrete objects and abstract ideas.

PrepTest110 Sec3 Q17

Step 3: The argument concludes that animal gestures do not prove animals have language from evidence that animal gestures do not prove reference to concrete objects or abstract ideas. This is a classic Mismatched Concepts argument. The author assumes that something that cannot prove reference to concrete objects or abstract ideas cannot prove the possession of language. Stated affirmatively, the author assumes reference to concrete objects or abstract ideas is *necessary* for the possession of language.	**Step 4:** (D) states the argument's assumption in negative terms. Writing it as formal logic, the choice says: *If no reference to concrete objects or abstract ideas → not a language.* The contrapositive would also have been correct: *If a language → reference to concrete objects or abstract ideas.*

Wrong answers: (A) Extreme. The zoologist doesn't rule out that animals might be capable of language, just that their gestures don't prove it. (B) This choice mistakes sufficiency for necessity; it reverses the clauses in the argument's assumption without negating them. (C) Extreme. The zoologist doesn't go quite this far, saying that the animals' gestures don't *prove* the ability to refer to concrete objects or abstract ideas, not that the animals definitely aren't doing so. (E) Extreme. This argument stops short of declaring that any animals have language; it focuses on whether gestures are proof of animal language and surmises that they are not.

Hint: This is not an argument you've seen before in this book, and it is quite dense, and rewards careful reading. Use what you've learned about argument patterns to spot the gap between the conclusion and evidence.

Step 2: *Conclusion:*	**Step 1:**
because	
Evidence:	

8. Editorialist: To ensure justice in the legal system, citizens must be capable of criticizing anyone involved in determining the punishment of criminals. But when the legal system's purpose is seen as deterrence, the system falls into the hands of experts whose specialty is to assess how potential lawbreakers are affected by the system's punishments. Because most citizens lack knowledge about such matters, justice is not then ensured in the legal system.

The editorialist's argument requires assuming which one of the following?

(A) Most citizens view justice as primarily concerned with the assignment of punishment to those who deserve it.

(B) In order to be just, a legal system must consider the effect that punishment will have on individual criminals.

(C) The primary concern in a legal system is to administer punishments that are just.

(D) In a legal system, a concern for punishment is incompatible with an emphasis on deterrence.

(E) Citizens without knowledge about how the legal system's punishments affect potential lawbreakers are incapable of criticizing experts in that area.

PrepTest112 Sec1 Q20

Step 3:	**Step 4:**

K

Expert Analysis

Here's how an LSAT expert approached the question you just tried.

Step 2: *Conclusion*: Justice is not ensured when the legal system's purpose is deterrence *because* *Evidence*: (1) [principle] Ensuring justice in the legal system requires that citizens be able to criticize those who determine punishments, but [application] (2) when the purpose is deterrence, the system is controlled by experts who calculate how punishments affect potential lawbreakers, and (3) most citizens lack this knowledge.	**Step 1:** The correct answer is a premise the argument "requires"; this is a Necessary Assumption question.

8. Editorialist: To ensure justice in the legal system, citizens must be capable of criticizing anyone involved in determining the punishment of criminals. But when the legal system's purpose is seen as deterrence, the system falls into the hands of experts whose specialty is to assess how potential lawbreakers are affected by the system's punishments. Because most citizens lack knowledge about such matters, justice is not then ensured in the legal system.

The editorialist's argument requires assuming which one of the following?

(A) Most citizens view justice as primarily concerned with the assignment of punishment to those who deserve it.

(B) In order to be just, a legal system must consider the effect that punishment will have on individual criminals.

(C) The primary concern in a legal system is to administer punishments that are just.

(D) In a legal system, a concern for punishment is incompatible with an emphasis on deterrence.

(E) Citizens without knowledge about how the legal system's punishments affect potential lawbreakers are incapable of criticizing experts in that area.

PrepTest112 Sec1 Q20

Step 3: Focus on the Mismatched Concepts to simplify this dense argument. The conclusion is that justice is not ensured in a legal system based on deterrence, so the author must assume that the principle and its application in the evidence explain why. Justice has a requirement—citizen criticism—but in deterrence-based systems, it is experts who determine punishments, and citizens don't know about such things. Thus, the author must assume that citizens without that knowledge cannot criticize the experts. Look for that in the correct answer.	**Step 4:** (E) cites the missing premise required by the argument: If, in a deterrence-based system, citizens cannot criticize the experts who determine punishments, then the requirement for justice in the principle is not met, and the conclusion can follow. Confirm the choice with the Denial Test: If citizens *can* criticize the experts in a deterrence-based system, the requirement for ensuring justice *is* met, and the conclusion has no support from the evidence.

Wrong answers: (A) This might explain why citizens lack expert knowledge about how punishment influences deterrence, but it is not a necessary premise in the argument. (B) offers yet another principle establishing a requirement for justice, but this is irrelevant to the argument in this question. (C) gives a meta-principle, if you will, for the legal system but is Outside the Scope of the argument here. (D) Extreme. The argument does not assume deterrence and punishment are mutually exclusive, but argues that seeing deterrence as the goal puts experts in the role of determining punishments.

Well done! Now, take a few minutes to learn more about the Denial Test in the following Spotlight.

The Denial Test

By Kaplan LSAT Channel Faculty

 Watch the video lesson for this Spotlight in your online Study Plan.

When evaluating the answer choices in Necessary Assumption questions, LSAT experts often use a tactic we refer to as the Denial Test. It is easy to explain how the Denial Test works, but making efficient, effective use of it takes some practice. Let's start with the definition: When you deny, or negate, each of the answer choices in a Necessary Assumption question, only the negation of the correct answer will make the conclusion impossible based on the evidence. Now consider an example:

> My roommate promised that he was going to buy milk for the house today because we are entirely out of milk. However, when I left this morning, he was asleep on the couch, and when I got home, I found him asleep on the couch. Thus, I'm sure we are still entirely out of milk.

Consider whether any of the following statements constitutes an assumption *necessary* to the argument.

- My roommate was wearing the same clothes when I got home that he was wearing when I went out.
- It is not uncommon for the house to be out of milk for days at a time.
- My roommate always takes very long naps.
- No one else got any milk for the house today.

What happens when you deny (and, again, in this context, that means to negate) each of those assumptions? Here's what that would look like:

- My roommate was *not* wearing the same clothes when I got home that he was wearing when I went out.
- It is ~~not~~ uncommon for the house to be out of milk for days at a time.
- My roommate ~~always~~ *sometimes* takes ~~very long~~ *shorter* naps.
- ~~No one~~ *Someone* else got ~~any~~ *some* milk for the house today.

The negations of the first three statements weaken the author's conclusion, but they do not disprove it. If the roommate has different clothes on, you at least know that he got up at some point. You do not, however, know that he even left the house, let alone that he went and bought milk. If it is rare that the house is out of milk for days, it is less likely that the roommate would have ignored his promise, but not impossible that he would have done so. Similarly, if the roommate sometimes takes short naps, there is at least the chance that he got up and went to the store, but no guarantee that he did so.

When you negate the fourth statement, however, the argument falls apart. Notice that the conclusion was not that the roommate did not get milk, but that the house still had no milk. If someone else supplied the house with milk, then the author's conclusion just falls apart. What the alternate source was in this case doesn't matter; maybe there is a responsible third roommate, or maybe someone's mom stopped by with milk after going to the store. Who knows?!? The point of this example is a universal truth about Necessary Assumption questions: Denying the correct answer will simply obliterate the conclusion. The question stem tells you, after all, that the assumption is *required* by the conclusion.

In the video that accompanies this Spotlight, an LSAT Channel expert will explain why the Denial Test works only in Necessary Assumption questions, why it is not meant to be your initial approach to these questions, and how you can effectively use it as a final strategy to "prove" the correct answer. Here are two official LSAT questions that you'll go over in the video lesson.

8. Economist: In the interaction between producers and consumers, the only obligation that all parties have is to act in the best interests of their own side. And distribution of information about product defects is in the best interests of the consumer. So consumers are always obligated to report product defects they discover, while producers are never obligated to reveal them.

Which one of the following is an assumption required by the economist's argument?

(A) It is never in the best interests of producers for a producer to reveal a product defect.

(B) No one expects producers to act in a manner counter to their own best interests.

(C) Any product defect is likely to be discovered by consumers.

(D) A product defect is more likely to be discovered by a consumer than by a producer.

(E) The best interests of consumers never coincide with the best interests of producers.

PrepTestB Sec1 Q8

17. When exercising the muscles in one's back, it is important, in order to maintain a healthy back, to exercise the muscles on opposite sides of the spine equally. After all, balanced muscle development is needed to maintain a healthy back, since the muscles on opposite sides of the spine must pull equally in opposing directions to keep the back in proper alignment and protect the spine.

Which one of the following is an assumption required by the argument?

(A) Muscles on opposite sides of the spine that are equally well developed will be enough to keep the back in proper alignment.

(B) Exercising the muscles on opposite sides of the spine unequally tends to lead to unbalanced muscle development.

(C) Provided that one exercises the muscles on opposite sides of the spine equally, one will have a generally healthy back.

(D) If the muscles on opposite sides of the spine are exercised unequally, one's back will be irreparably damaged.

(E) One should exercise daily to ensure that the muscles on opposite sides of the spine keep the back in proper alignment.

PrepTestJun07 Sec3 Q17

 **Complete answers and explanations are provided in the LSAT Channel Spotlight video "The Denial Test" in your online Study Plan.**

Sufficient Assumption Questions

Take another look at these Sufficient Assumption question stems:

> The conclusion above follows logically if
> which one of the following is assumed?
>
> *PrepTest111 Sec1 Q22*

> The conclusion can be properly inferred if
> which one of the following is assumed?
>
> *PrepTest112 Sec1 Q22*

Sufficient Assumption questions call for an assumption that, "if assumed," allows the conclusion to be drawn logically: i.e., Evidence + Assumption = Conclusion, guaranteed. You can identify these questions, which make up about 40 percent of all Assumption questions, from stems featuring phrases like "if assumed," "conclusion follows logically," or "allows the conclusion to be drawn." You can also distinguish Sufficient Assumption questions by the terms they don't include; unlike Necessary Assumption questions, Sufficient Assumption questions won't use words like "needs," "requires," or "depends."

In Sufficient Assumption questions, the argument pattern is overwhelmingly Mismatched Concepts, quite often with Formal Logic. Your goal for most of these questions, then, is to find the mismatched terms between the evidence and the conclusion and to seal that gap up tight. Remember, when you add the correct answer to a Sufficient Assumption's argument, the conclusion is guaranteed. If you should stumble across the rare Sufficient Assumption question that has an Overlooked Possibilities argument, be sure to find an answer choice providing a blanket statement that rules out any potential objection to the conclusion. Because the correct answer choice to a Sufficient Assumption question will, when added to the argument's evidence, definitely lead to the author's conclusion, it is acceptable for these assumptions to be broader than the argument itself.

LSAT STRATEGY

Some facts to remember about Sufficient Assumption questions:

- Recognize these questions by the phrasing "if assumed" or "conclusion follows logically."
- The correct answer, when combined with the evidence, will guarantee the conclusion.
- Mismatched Concepts arguments with Formal Logic dominate Sufficient Assumption questions.

To demonstrate how Sufficient Assumption questions operate, review an LSAT expert's work on the following LSAT question.

Now, try completing a Sufficient Assumption question that contains a Mismatched Concepts argument that you analyzed in the preceding chapter. Take your time and work through all four steps of the Logical Reasoning Method, even if you remember the argument. When you're finished, review an LSAT expert's work on the next page.

Step 2: *Conclusion*: *because* *Evidence*:	**Step 1:**

9. Having an efficient, attractive subway system makes good economic sense. So, the city needs to purchase new subway cars, since the city should always do what makes good economic sense.

The conclusion drawn above follows logically if which one of the following is assumed?

(A) The city should invest in an efficient, attractive subway system.

(B) Cost-effective subway cars are an integral part of an efficient subway system.

(C) Investment in new subway cars makes better economic sense than many of the other investment options open to the city.

(D) New subway cars are financially affordable.

(E) New subway cars are required in order for the city to have a subway system that is efficient and attractive.

PrepTest110 Sec2 Q2

Step 3:	**Step 4:**

Expert Analysis

Here's how an LSAT expert approached the question you just tried.

Step 2: *Conclusion*: The city needs to purchase new subway cars *because* *Evidence*: (1) The city should do what makes good economic sense, and (2) having an efficient, attractive subway makes good economic sense.	**Step 1:** Because the conclusion will be established by the correct answer, this is a Sufficient Assumption question.

9. Having an efficient, attractive subway system makes good economic sense. So, the city needs to purchase new subway cars, since the city should always do what makes good economic sense.

The conclusion drawn above follows logically if which one of the following is assumed?

(A) The city should invest in an efficient, attractive subway system.

(B) Cost-effective subway cars are an integral part of an efficient subway system.

(C) Investment in new subway cars makes better economic sense than many of the other investment options open to the city.

(D) New subway cars are financially affordable.

(E) New subway cars are required in order for the city to have a subway system that is efficient and attractive.

PrepTest110 Sec2 Q2

Step 3: This is a classic Mismatched Concepts argument. The conclusion is that the city needs to buy new subway cars. The evidence is about having an efficient, attractive subway system. The author assumes that new subway cars are needed to have an efficient, attractive subway. If that's correct, the evidence establishes the conclusion.	**Step 4:** (E) correctly states the assumption: New subway cars are *needed* for the city to have an efficient, attractive subway.

Wrong answers: (A) This is a repeat of the evidence, but not the unstated assumption sufficient to establish the conclusion. (B) "Cost-effective" subway cars are Outside the Scope. (C) Irrelevant Comparison. The evidence establishes that an efficient, attractive subway makes good economic sense; where it ranks among all such projects is neither here nor there. (D) Knowing that new cars are affordable isn't enough to establish the conclusion here. The correct answer links the evidence "an efficient, attractive subway system" to the purchase of new subway cars, and thus completes the argument.

In the Practice problems later in this section and in the Perform quiz at the end of the chapter, you'll have ample opportunity to try more Sufficient Assumption questions. First, though, take a look at how Formal Logic appears in Sufficient Assumption questions and others in the Assumption Family. The following Formal Logic Workshop will help you spot patterns that will make you more confident and efficient on test day.

Formal Logic Workshop 2: Formal Logic in Mismatched Assumptions

A firm understanding of Formal Logic fundamentals can be an enormously useful skill in mastering Logical Reasoning. Confidence with the translation of conditional statements will help you make short work of some dense LR stimuli. Nowhere is this truer than in Sufficient Assumption questions, which nearly always feature Mismatched Concepts arguments, and often turn on the accurate analysis of Formal Logic. While that makes this the perfect time to revisit Formal Logic, you may wind up using the skills covered in this short workshop on Flaw, Strengthen/Weaken, and Parallel Flaw questions, too.

LEARNING OBJECTIVES

In this section, you'll learn to:

- Recognize common Formal Logic patterns in Mismatched Concepts arguments.
- Use knowledge of Formal Logic and contrapositives to determine an argument's assumption.
- Understand when the "direction" of link between terms is important.

When Mismatched Concepts arguments on the LSAT contain Formal Logic, the most basic structural pattern is as follows: "If A then B. Therefore, if A then C," where the letters A, B, and C represent unique terms.

Structure	Sample Argument	My Analysis
Evidence	If A $\to$ B	
Assumption		
Conclusion	If A $\to$ C	

Do you see this argument's mismatched concepts? The evidence discusses A and B, while the conclusion cites A and C. This is about as straightforward as a Mismatched Concepts argument gets. The author must assume that B and C are in some way connected. Give it a shot: How would you fill in the assumption in this argument?

If you said that the assumption must be "If B then C" (or drew If B $\to$ C), then good work.

Structure	Sample Argument	Analysis
Evidence	If A $\to$ B	If A $\to$ **B**
Assumption		**If B $\to$ C**
Conclusion	If A $\to$ C	If A $\to$ **C**

This assumption, combined with the evidence, produces a chain of logic: If A $\to$ B $\to$ C. It is then clear that the author can conclude: If A $\to$ C.

To see how this would play out in an argument using less abstract terms, consider this argument:

Demosthenes was a gifted orator. Therefore, Demosthenes was politically persuasive.

Both the evidence and the conclusion have the subject "Demosthenes," but only the evidence mentions him as a "gifted orator," while the conclusion ascribes the characteristic "politically persuasive." Therefore, it's easy to see that this is a Mismatched Concepts argument. Here's the argument written as Formal Logic:

Structure	Sample Argument	My Analysis
Evidence	If Demos → gifted orator	
Assumption		
Conclusion	If Demos → politically persuasive	

To make this argument work, you'll need to make a connection between "gifted orator" and "politically persuasive." But in which direction? Is it that all gifted orators are politically persuasive? Or is it that politically persuasive people are all gifted orators? The missing piece, the assumption, will not just connect the mismatched terms but connect them in the right direction:

Structure	Sample Argument	Analysis
Evidence	If Demos → gifted orator	If Demos → **gifted orator**
		If **gifted orator** → **politically persuasive**
Conclusion	If Demos → politically persuasive	If Demos → **politically persuasive**

This argument fits the original pattern of "If A → B; therefore, If A → C." The mismatched terms are the *necessary* terms in each statement. That means the assumption must be If B → C for the conclusion to be logically inferred. Now, based on the previous example, which of these would be an assumption that would allow the conclusion to be logically drawn?

(1) All gifted orators are politically persuasive.

(2) Any person who is politically persuasive is a gifted orator.

In this case—and in all cases that fit this pattern—the correct choice is (1), not (2). The assumption is that gifted orators are all politically persuasive, and not that all politically persuasive people are gifted orators (they might be persuasive in other ways, right?). The testmaker won't always include answer choices with the same terms relating to each other in different ways, but it does happen. For the unprepared test taker, seeing two answer choices that appear so similar—both have the same terms, and indeed, both assert that the relationship between the terms alike/equivalent—increases the difficulty of a question. This shows up most often in Sufficient Assumption questions, so remember: When you analyze an argument that contains Formal Logic, pay attention to which terms are sufficient and which are necessary.

To see why distinguishing mismatched concepts in the necessary terms from those in the sufficient terms is so valuable, consider another Formal Logic pattern often found in Mismatched Concepts arguments: "If A, then B. Therefore, if C, then B."

Structure	Sample Argument	My Analysis
Evidence	If A → B	
Assumption		
Conclusion	If C → B	

This time, the mismatched terms or concepts are in the *sufficient* terms of the evidence and of the conclusion. Identify them.

Structure	Sample Argument	Analysis
Evidence	If A → B	If **A** → B
Assumption		
Conclusion	If C → B	If **C** → B

What is the assumption here? Think of a real-world example that fits this pattern if you can.

Structure	Sample Argument	Analysis
Evidence	If A → B	If **A** → B
Assumption		If **C** → **A**
Conclusion	If C → B	If **C** → B

In this case, the author assumes that if something is a C (or has the characteristic C), then that thing is an A (or has the characteristic A).

If you had trouble thinking of a real-world case, here's one:

> Talented sculptors were in high demand in 5th century (B.C.) Athens. Therefore, Phidias was in high demand in 5th century (B.C.) Athens.

Lay out the argument about Phidias to match the diagrams above and determine the author's unstated assumption.

Structure	Sample Argument	My Analysis
Evidence	If talented sculptor → in high demand	
Assumption		
Conclusion	If Phidias → in high demand	

Here, the mismatched concepts are in the *sufficient* terms of both the evidence and the conclusion.

Structure	Sample Argument	Analysis
Evidence	If talented sculptor → in high demand	If **talented sculptor** → in high demand
Assumption		
Conclusion	If Phidias → in high demand	If **Phidias** → in high demand

What is the author's assumption?

Structure	Sample Argument	Analysis
Evidence	If talented sculptor → in high demand	If **talented sculptor** → in high demand
Assumption		If **Phidias** → **talented sculptor**
Conclusion	If Phidias → in high demand	If **Phidias** → in high demand

For the argument to be valid, the author must assume that Phidias was a talented sculptor (which, indeed, he was).

A quick note about the "direction" of the connection between the mismatched terms in these diagrams. If the mismatched concepts are on the right side of the arrow (i.e., they are the *necessary* terms in the formal logic statements), then the connection goes "down" from evidence to conclusion. If the mismatched concepts are on the left side of the arrow (i.e., they are the *sufficient* terms in the formal logic statements), then the connection goes "up" from conclusion to evidence. This could also be visualized and remembered by using clockwise arrows going around the diagram connecting the four terms (note: the clockwise illustration only works when evidence is placed above the conclusion). This always shows you the proper direction of connection. Here are the two arguments you just analyzed with arrows to illustrate this approach:

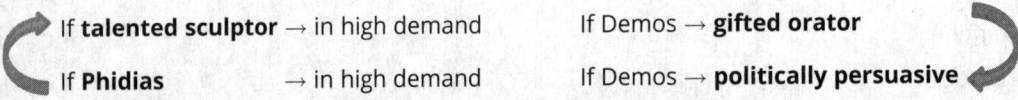

Making It More Difficult: Adding an Extra Concept in the Evidence

While the standard Formal Logic Mismatched Concepts argument structures you've just covered include three terms (two terms in the evidence and two terms in the conclusion, with one of the terms shared between the evidence and conclusion), many LSAT arguments contain more than three concepts. A common pattern used by the testmaker has one or more additional terms in the evidence. If the terms are necessary for each other, combine them and remove the redundant term. This makes the evidence simpler and, in turn, easier to compare to the conclusion. Here is the most common pattern for this type of argument on the LSAT:

Structure	Sample Argument	My Analysis
Evidence	Ev1: If A → B Ev2: If B → C	
Assumption		
Conclusion	If A → D	

Since the two evidentiary statements in the evidence share term B—and note that B is the necessary term in one statement and the sufficient term in the other—they can be combined to simplify the evidence. Doing this reveals the terms that are unique to the evidence and to the conclusion.

Structure	Sample Argument	Analysis
Evidence	Ev1: If A → ~~B~~ Ev2: ~~If B~~ → C	If A → **C**
Assumption		
Conclusion	If A → D	If A → **D**

That step reveals that we are back to the simple pattern illustrated by the argument about Demosthenes you saw above. The author assumes that all Cs (or things with the attribute C) are Ds (or things with the attribute D).

Structure	Sample Argument	Analysis
Evidence	Ev1: If A → ~~B~~ Ev2: ~~If B~~ → C	If A → **C**
Assumption		If **C** → **D**
Conclusion	If A → D	If A → **D**

Here's another "real world" argument to illustrate this pattern as you will analyze it on the LSAT:

> All student editors on the law journal passed first year Legal Writing. One requirement of first-year Legal Writing is completion of a legal memorandum. Thus, all student editors on the law journal are familiar with the Bluebook rules for case citations.

Start by laying out the argument in the diagram we've been using.

Structure	Sample Argument	My Analysis
Evidence	If student editor → 1L Writing If 1L Writing → legal memo	
Assumption		
Conclusion	If student editor → Bluebook citation	

Make sure that the two statements in the evidence can be combined. Once again, because the necessary term in one statement is equivalent to the sufficient term in the other, they can. (Note that the order of the statements in the argument does not matter, but you may choose to jot them down in the most helpful order when analyzing an argument.) Now, combine the statements and identify the mismatched concepts.

Structure	Sample Argument	Analysis
Evidence	If student editor → ~~1L Writing~~ ~~If 1L Writing~~ → legal memo	If student editor → **legal memo**
Assumption		
Conclusion	If student editor → Bluebook citation	If student editor → **Bluebook citation**

Once again, you're on familiar formal logic ground, so formulate the statement that logically links the author's evidence to his conclusion (i.e., the main assumption).

Structure	Sample Argument	Analysis
Evidence	If student editor → ~~1L Writing~~ ~~If 1L Writing~~ → legal memo	If student editor → **legal memo**
Assumption		If **legal memo** → **Bluebook citation**
Conclusion	If student editor → Bluebook citation	If student editor → **Bluebook citation**

Now, when you read through the argument, you can see that it is complete. If (1) all the student editors passed Legal Writing, (2) anyone who passed Legal Writing wrote a legal memorandum, and (3) writing a legal memorandum will make you familiar with the Bluebook rules for citing cases, then it is certain that all the student editors are familiar with those Bluebook rules. (By the way, you will be, too, by the end of your 1L year.)

That pattern, with two pieces of evidence that can be combined, is very common in LSAT arguments. Familiarity with this pattern will help you efficiently tackle one or more Assumption Family questions (most likely a Sufficient Assumption question) on test day.

Mismatched Concepts in the Evidence

Mismatched Concepts arguments typically involve an assumption concerning the connection between one concept in the evidence and a distinct concept in the conclusion, but it's also possible for an argument to have both its mismatched concepts in the evidence. Though rare, this pattern shows up occasionally on the LSAT, so it's best to be ready in case you see an argument like this on your exam. Here's the algebraic diagram for an argument of this type:

Structure	Sample Argument	My Analysis
Evidence	Ev1: If A → B Ev2: If C → D	
Assumption		
Conclusion	If A → D	

Notice two things. First, both terms in the conclusion are also present in the evidence; there is no mismatch there. Second, there is no way to link up the two evidentiary terms; they share no common terms. In such a case, the author's assumption (her missing, unstated "bridge") lies between the two pieces of evidence. Rewriting the diagram like this makes this clear.

Structure	Sample Argument	Analysis
Evidence 1	If A → B	
Assumption		
Evidence 2	If C → D	
Conclusion	If A → D	

Use that to determine what's missing from the argument.

Structure	Sample Argument	Analysis
Evidence 1	If A → B	If A → **B**
Assumption		If **B** → **C**
Evidence 2	If C → D	If **C** → D
Conclusion	If A → D	If A → D

Reading through this argument, you can see that it is complete and logical. If As are Bs, and Bs are Cs, and Cs are Ds, then it is valid to conclude that As are Ds.

That may be well and good in the abstract, but you want to be sure you can recognize an argument like this on the test, so for good measure, here's a final "real world" example.

> If forecasts are correct and this region sees excessive rain this summer, then local vignerons could see their businesses fail. That's because excessive rain will waterlog the soil, and vignerons depend on a strong late summer grape harvest to remain solvent.

Plug that argument into the diagram. Can you untangle the pieces of the argument?

Structure	Sample Argument	My Analysis
Evidence 1		
Assumption		
Evidence 2		
Conclusion		

How did you do? Here's the LSAT expert's outline.

Structure	Sample Argument	Analysis
Evidence 1	If excess rain → waterlogged soil	
Assumption		
Evidence 2	If poor harvest → grape growers fail	
Conclusion	If excess rain → grape growers fail	

Once again, both terms in the conclusion are found in the evidence, and there is no term shared between the two pieces of evidence. The author needs to logically bridge the two pieces of evidence to complete the argument. Give it a shot.

Structure	Sample Argument	Analysis
Evidence 1	If excess rain → waterlogged soil	If excess rain → **waterlogged soil**
Assumption		
Evidence 2	If poor harvest → grape growers fail	If **poor harvest** → grape growers fail
Conclusion	If excess rain → grape growers fail	If excess rain → grape growers fail

And what does that make the author's assumption?

Structure	Sample Argument	Analysis
Evidence 1	If excess rain → waterlogged soil	If excess rain → **waterlogged soil**
Assumption		If **waterlogged soil** → **poor harvest**
Evidence 2	If poor harvest → grape growers fail	If **poor harvest** → grape growers fail
Conclusion	If excess rain → grape growers fail	If excess rain → grape growers fail

Voila! A complete, valid argument has emerged.

Again, an argument with mismatched concepts in the evidence is rare—in fact, you might not even see it on the LSAT you take. Just know that the testmaker can present an argument this way; to find the assumption, find the mismatched concepts in the evidence and logically connect them.

Strict Formal Logic statements tend to show up most often in Sufficient Assumption questions, and you'll see several more examples as you work through the remainder of this chapter.

TEST DAY TIPS

Formal Logic in arguments containing Mismatched Concepts:

- The most common structure is: "If A → B; therefore, If A → C." It often emerges after you translate conditional statements and combine statements sharing a common term.

- Whenever possible, connect multiple terms in the evidence and simplify.

- Difficult wrong answer choices may confuse necessary and sufficient terms.

Now, try completing a Sufficient Assumption question that contains a Mismatched Concepts argument featuring Formal Logic. You analyzed this argument in the preceding chapter, but do it again here, now that you've completed the latest Formal Logic Workshop. Take your time and work through all four steps of the Logical Reasoning Method, even if you remember the argument. When you're finished, review an LSAT expert's work on the next page.

Step 2: *Conclusion*:	**Step 1:**
because	
Evidence:	

10. Marian Anderson, the famous contralto, did not take success for granted. We know this because Anderson had to struggle early in life, and anyone who has to struggle early in life is able to keep a good perspective on the world.

The conclusion of the argument follows logically if which one of the following is assumed?

(A) Anyone who succeeds takes success for granted.

(B) Anyone who is able to keep a good perspective on the world does not take success for granted.

(C) Anyone who is able to keep a good perspective on the world has to struggle early in life.

(D) Anyone who does not take success for granted has to struggle early in life.

(E) Anyone who does not take success for granted is able to keep a good perspective on the world.

PrepTest111 Sec4 Q14

Step 3:	**Step 4:**

Expert Analysis

Here's how an LSAT expert approached the question you just tried.

Step 2: *Conclusion*: Marian Anderson did not take success for granted *because* *Evidence*: (1) Marian Anderson struggled early in life, and (2) those who struggle early in life have a good perspective on the world.	**Step 1:** The correct answer will establish the conclusion from the evidence; thus, this is a Sufficient Assumption question.

10. Marian Anderson, the famous contralto, did not take success for granted. We know this because Anderson had to struggle early in life, and anyone who has to struggle early in life is able to keep a good perspective on the world.

The conclusion of the argument follows logically if which one of the following is assumed?

(A) Anyone who succeeds takes success for granted.

(B) Anyone who is able to keep a good perspective on the world does not take success for granted.

(C) Anyone who is able to keep a good perspective on the world has to struggle early in life.

(D) Anyone who does not take success for granted has to struggle early in life.

(E) Anyone who does not take success for granted is able to keep a good perspective on the world.

PrepTest111 Sec4 Q14

Step 3: Outlining the argument's formal logic reveals the Mismatched Concepts clearly: (Ev1) *MA → struggle early* (Ev2) *Struggle early → good perspective on the world* (Concl) *MA → not take success for granted* To reach this conclusion from the evidence, the author assumes that anyone with a good perspective on the world does not take success for granted. (Assump) *Good perspective → not take success for granted*	**Step 4:** (B) gets the logic right and completely establishes the conclusion from the evidence.

Wrong answers: (A) doesn't connect to the evidence about those who have a good perspective on the world. (C) distorts the second piece of evidence (it reverses without negating) and fails to connect it to the conclusion about not taking success for granted. (D) confuses necessity and sufficiency by reversing without negating; this choice would be sufficient to establish the conclusion if it read "Anyone who has to struggle early in life does not take success for granted." (E) confuses necessity and sufficiency; it reverses but does not negate the terms in the prediction from Step 3.

Did you recognize the most common Formal Logic pattern in this question's argument? Once you've combined the two pieces of evidence, it's the standard "If A → B; therefore, If A → C" pattern. Now, try your hand at some Sufficient Assumption practice questions.

Practice   Try each of the following Sufficient Assumption questions. You may see arguments you analyzed in the preceding chapter. Don't worry too much about your timing here. Complete all four steps of the Logical Reasoning Method for each question, jotting down your notes whenever it is helpful to do so. After each question, review your work with the expert analysis that follows.

Hint: Don't let the glib tone of the argument distract you; focus on the shift from evidence to conclusion.

Step 2: *Conclusion*:	**Step 1:**
because	
Evidence:	

11. Columnist: Almost anyone can be an expert, for there are no official guidelines determining what an expert must know. Anybody who manages to convince some people of his or her qualifications in an area—whatever those may be—is an expert.

The columnist's conclusion follows logically if which one of the following is assumed?

(A) Almost anyone can convince some people of his or her qualifications in some area.

(B) Some experts convince everyone of their qualifications in almost every area.

(C) Convincing certain people that one is qualified in an area requires that one actually be qualified in that area.

(D) Every expert has convinced some people of his or her qualifications in some area.

(E) Some people manage to convince almost everyone of their qualifications in one or more areas.

PrepTest111 Sec1 Q20

Step 3:	**Step 4:**

Expert Analysis

Here's how an LSAT expert approached the question you just tried.

Step 2: *Conclusion*: Almost anyone can be an expert *because* *Evidence*: (1) there are no guidelines for establishing qualifications, and (2) if you can convince some people of your qualifications, you're an expert.	**Step 1:** The correct answer ensures that the conclusion follows from the evidence, so this is a Sufficient Assumption question.

11. Columnist: Almost anyone can be an expert, for there are no official guidelines determining what an expert must know. Anybody who manages to convince some people of his or her qualifications in an area—whatever those may be—is an expert.

The columnist's conclusion follows logically if which one of the following is assumed?

(A) Almost anyone can convince some people of his or her qualifications in some area.

(B) Some experts convince everyone of their qualifications in almost every area.

(C) Convincing certain people that one is qualified in an area requires that one actually be qualified in that area.

(D) Every expert has convinced some people of his or her qualifications in some area.

(E) Some people manage to convince almost everyone of their qualifications in one or more areas.

PrepTest111 Sec1 Q20

Step 3: To paraphrase this bizarre little argument: Don't worry about qualifications (there are no guidelines, anyway). If you can convince somebody of your qualifications, then you're an expert. *So*, almost anyone can be an expert. However glib, there is still a gap in this argument, one the author fills with this assumption: *Almost anyone can convince somebody of their qualifications.* If that's true, the conclusion follows from the evidence.	**Step 4:** (A) offers the premise that guarantees the conclusion follows from the evidence: Almost anyone can convince another of their qualifications. By the columnist's logic, that means almost anyone can be an expert.

Wrong answers: (B) The correct answer needs to lead to the conclusion that *almost anyone* can be an expert; this choice leads to *some* people being super experts. (C) Outside the Scope. The sufficient assumption will say almost anyone can convince *someone* they're qualified; it doesn't have to be one of these sticklers for actual qualifications. (D) For the columnist, being able to convince someone of your qualifications is *sufficient* to make you an expert; this choice treats that ability as *necessary* for being an expert. Thus, this choice doesn't fit the argument. (E) Like choice (B), this answer suggests that *some* people can be super experts, but does not say that *almost anyone* can be an expert, which is what the sufficient assumption says.

Hint: Which of the standard Mismatched Concepts relationships does the author assume here?

Step 2: *Conclusion*:	**Step 1:**
because *Evidence*:	

12. Several critics have claimed that any contemporary poet who writes formal poetry—poetry that is rhymed and metered—is performing a politically conservative act. This is plainly false. Consider Molly Peacock and Marilyn Hacker, two contemporary poets whose poetry is almost exclusively formal and yet who are themselves politically progressive feminists.

The conclusion drawn above follows logically if which one of the following is assumed?

(A) No one who is a feminist is also politically conservative.

(B) No poet who writes unrhymed or unmetered poetry is politically conservative.

(C) No one who is politically progressive is capable of performing a politically conservative act.

(D) Anyone who sometimes writes poetry that is not politically conservative never writes poetry that is politically conservative.

(E) The content of a poet's work, not the work's form, is the most decisive factor in determining what political consequences, if any, the work will have.

PrepTest111 Sec4 Q19

Step 3:	**Step 4:**

Expert Analysis

Here's how an LSAT expert approached the question you just tried.

Step 2: *Conclusion*: Writing formal poetry is not necessarily a politically conservative act *because* *Evidence*: Peacock and Hackler are liberal feminists and they write formal poetry.	**Step 1:** "[F]ollows logically if . . . assumed" pegs this as a Sufficient Assumption question; the correct answer will ensure that the conclusion follows from the evidence.

12. Several critics have claimed that any contemporary poet who writes formal poetry—poetry that is rhymed and metered—is performing a politically conservative act. This is plainly false. Consider Molly Peacock and Marilyn Hacker, two contemporary poets whose poetry is almost exclusively formal and yet who are themselves politically progressive feminists.

The conclusion drawn above follows logically if which one of the following is assumed?

(A) No one who is a feminist is also politically conservative.

(B) No poet who writes unrhymed or unmetered poetry is politically conservative.

(C) No one who is politically progressive is capable of performing a politically conservative act.

(D) Anyone who sometimes writes poetry that is not politically conservative never writes poetry that is politically conservative.

(E) The content of a poet's work, not the work's form, is the most decisive factor in determining what political consequences, if any, the work will have.

PrepTest111 Sec4 Q19

Step 3: For the argument's conclusion to follow unequivocally from its evidence, the author must assume that politically progressive people can never act in a politically conservative way.	**Step 4:** (C) captures the author's broad assumption that one's political identity can never be at odds with their actions.

Wrong answers: (A) distorts the argument by assuming the incompatibility of two broad political identities, while the author assumes the incompatibility of one's identity and certain actions. (B) Outside the Scope. The author focuses solely on what it means to write formal verse. (D) distorts the argument by assuming the incompatibility of two different actions, while the author assumes the incompatibility of one's political identity and certain actions. (E) Outside the Scope/Irrelevant Comparison. The argument doesn't touch on the *consequences* of any works of poetry, and does not compare form and content.

Hint: Translate and rearrange the statements to see the relationship assumed by the author.

Step 2: *Conclusion:*	**Step 1:**
because	
Evidence:	

13. No chordates are tracheophytes, and all members of Pteropsida are tracheophytes. So no members of Pteropsida belong to the family Hominidae.

The conclusion above follows logically if which one of the following is assumed?

(A) All members of the family Hominidae are tracheophytes.

(B) All members of the family Hominidae are chordates.

(C) All tracheophytes are members of Pteropsida.

(D) No members of the family Hominidae are chordates.

(E) No chordates are members of Pteropsida.

PrepTest111 Sec1 Q22

Step 3:	**Step 4:**

Expert Analysis

Here's how an LSAT expert approached the question you just tried.

Step 2: *Conclusion*: No P's belong to family H *because* *Evidence*: (1) No c's are t's, and (2) all P's are t's.	**Step 1:** The conclusion is completely established if the correct answer is added to the argument; thus, this is a Sufficient Assumption question.

13. No chordates are tracheophytes, and all members of Pteropsida are tracheophytes. So no members of Pteropsida belong to the family Hominidae.

The conclusion above follows logically if which one of the following is assumed?

(A) All members of the family Hominidae are tracheophytes.

(B) All members of the family Hominidae are chordates.

(C) All tracheophytes are members of Pteropsida.

(D) No members of the family Hominidae are chordates.

(E) No chordates are members of Pteropsida.

PrepTest111 Sec1 Q22

Step 3: Translate the formal logic into if-then statements first:

(Ev1) *If c → NOT t*
(Ev2) *If P → t*
(Concl) *If P → NOT H*

Next, take the contrapositive of the first evidence statement so it will link up with the second.

(Ev1)(contrapositive): *If t → NOT c*
(Ev2) *If P → t*

Combine the two evidence statements to get:

(Ev)(combined): *If P → NOT c*

Now the argument looks like this:

(Ev) *If P → NOT c*
(Concl) *If P → NOT H*

That makes the assumption clear:

(Assump) *If NOT c → NOT H*

The correct answer will probably be written in the contrapositive of that:

If H → c

Look for the choice that says, "All members of family H are c's."

Step 4: (B) [*If H → c*] matches the prediction, gets the formal logic right, and ensures the validity of the conclusion. Huzzah!

Wrong answers: (A) The sufficient assumption needs to match H (Hominidae) to c (chordate), not t (tracheophytes). (C) This choice distorts the second piece of evidence by reversing without negating. (D) 180. This says exactly the opposite of what the sufficient assumption holds. (E) This choice repeats the combined evidence statement but does not tie it to the conclusion.

Hint: This is a densely written argument; use Formal Logic to simplify and reveal the gap between the evidence and conclusion.

Step 2: *Conclusion:*	**Step 1:**
because	
Evidence:	

14. Any writer whose purpose is personal expression sometimes uses words ambiguously. Every poet's purpose is personal expression. Thus no poetry reader's enjoyment depends on attaining a precise understanding of what the poet means.

The conclusion can be properly inferred if which one of the following is assumed?

(A) Writers who sometimes use words ambiguously have no readers who try to attain a precise understanding of what the writer means.

(B) Writers whose purpose is personal expression are unconcerned with whether anyone enjoys reading their works.

(C) No writer who ever uses words ambiguously has any reader whose enjoyment depends on attaining a precise understanding of what the writer means.

(D) Most writers whose readers' enjoyment does not depend on attaining a precise understanding of the writers' words are poets.

(E) Readers who have a precise understanding of what a writer has written derive their enjoyment from that understanding.

PrepTest112 Sec1 Q22

Step 3:	**Step 4:**

Expert Analysis

Here's how an LSAT expert approached the question you just tried.

Step 2: *Conclusion*: A poetry reader's enjoyment does not require precise understanding of the poet's meaning *because*

Evidence: (1) If a writer's purpose is personal expression, then they sometimes use words ambiguously, and (2) the purpose of poets is always personal expression.

Step 1: The correct answer allows the conclusion to be "properly inferred"; this is a Sufficient Assumption question.

14. Any writer whose purpose is personal expression sometimes uses words ambiguously. Every poet's purpose is personal expression. Thus no poetry reader's enjoyment depends on attaining a precise understanding of what the poet means.

The conclusion can be properly inferred if which one of the following is assumed?

(A) Writers who sometimes use words ambiguously have no readers who try to attain a precise understanding of what the writer means.

(B) Writers whose purpose is personal expression are unconcerned with whether anyone enjoys reading their works.

(C) No writer who ever uses words ambiguously has any reader whose enjoyment depends on attaining a precise understanding of what the writer means.

(D) Most writers whose readers' enjoyment does not depend on attaining a precise understanding of the writers' words are poets.

(E) Readers who have a precise understanding of what a writer has written derive their enjoyment from that understanding.

PrepTest112 Sec1 Q22

Step 3: Organize this abstract argument into a logical series of if-then statements:

If poet → ~~purpose is personal expression~~

~~If purpose is personal expression~~ → use words ambiguously

Thus: If poetry reader → enjoyment does NOT depend on precise understanding of poet's meaning

Now, it's a little easier to see the central assumption: If you're a writer who uses words ambiguously, your reader's enjoyment does not depend on getting your meaning exactly right. If that's true, the conclusion is established.

Step 4: (C) builds a bridge between the argument's mismatched concepts that is sufficient to guarantee that the conclusion follows from the evidence. With arguments this abstract, formal logic can often help you spot the mismatched concepts, and spot the author's assumed relationship between them.

Wrong answers: (A) Some poetry readers may try to determine the meaning, but if the argument is correct, their enjoyment does not depend on succeeding. (B) This seems unlikely, but it is Outside the Scope of the argument in any case. (D) Outside the Scope. The argument does not opine on the source of enjoyment for other readers. (E) This may be true, but according to the argument, if they are poetry readers, their enjoyment does not depend on such an understanding.

Generic Assumption Questions

From time to time, an Assumption question will emerge with a stem that doesn't use any of the language that identifies other questions as Necessary Assumption or Sufficient Assumption questions. Here are a couple of examples.

> The argument assumes that
>
> *PrepTest111 Sec3 Q15*

> The argument above is based on which one of the following assumptions?
>
> *PrepTest110 Sec3 Q11*

Should you encounter one of these rare creatures, don't be alarmed. Since you don't know whether the correct answer will be necessary for the conclusion or sufficient to establish it, simply look for the argument's central assumption as it is revealed by the argument. The good news is that the argument will still fit one of the common LSAT patterns. If it's an Overlooked Possibilities argument, the author will assume that one or more of those possibilities does not exist or will not occur. If it's a Mismatched Concepts argument, the author will assume that the distinct terms in the conclusion and evidence are related in one of the typical patterns.

In short, use what you know about both common Assumption question subtypes and about LSAT arguments in general to guide you effectively through the four steps of the Logical Reasoning Method.

Try that now with a generic Assumption question on the next page.

Now, try completing a generic Assumption question. Take your time and work through all four steps of the Logical Reasoning Method. Pause to consider if the Argument type helps you determine whether this question more resembles a Necessary Assumption or a Sufficient Assumption question. When you're finished, review an LSAT expert's work on the next page.

Step 2: *Conclusion*:	**Step 1:**
because	
Evidence:	

15. During the recent economic downturn, banks contributed to the decline by loaning less money. Prior to the downturn, regulatory standards for loanmaking by banks were tightened. Clearly, therefore, banks will lend more money if those standards are relaxed.

The argument assumes that

(A) the downturn did not cause a significant decrease in the total amount of money on deposit with banks which is the source of funds for banks to lend

(B) the imposition of the tighter regulatory standards was not a cause of the economic downturn

(C) the reason for tightening the regulatory standards was not arbitrary

(D) no economic downturn is accompanied by a significant decrease in the amount of money loaned out by banks to individual borrowers and to businesses

(E) no relaxation of standards for loanmaking by banks would compensate for the effects of the downturn

PrepTest111 Sec3 Q15

Step 3:	**Step 4:**

Expert Analysis

This example turned out to be similar to a Necessary Assumption question. That's no surprise given the Overlooked Possibilities argument in its stimulus.

Step 2: *Conclusion*: If loan regulations are relaxed, banks will loan more money *because*

Evidence: (1) Banks have loaned less money during the downturn, and (2) prior to the downturn, loan regulations were tightened.

Step 1: This is a rare Assumption question stem that does not define whether the correct answer will be necessary or sufficient for the argument to be valid. Analyze the argument to determine the clearest central assumption, and use that as a prediction to evaluate the answer choice.

15. During the recent economic downturn, banks contributed to the decline by loaning less money. Prior to the downturn, regulatory standards for loanmaking by banks were tightened. Clearly, therefore, banks will lend more money if those standards are relaxed.

The argument assumes that

(A) the downturn did not cause a significant decrease in the total amount of money on deposit with banks which is the source of funds for banks to lend

(B) the imposition of the tighter regulatory standards was not a cause of the economic downturn

(C) the reason for tightening the regulatory standards was not arbitrary

(D) no economic downturn is accompanied by a significant decrease in the amount of money loaned out by banks to individual borrowers and to businesses

(E) no relaxation of standards for loanmaking by banks would compensate for the effects of the downturn

PrepTest111 Sec3 Q15

Step 3: This is a classic Overlooked Possibilities argument. The author provides one reason banks might be loaning less and assumes that it is the only thing preventing them from loaning more. For this generic Assumption question, the correct answer will, in essence, say that argument assumes there is no other reason for the bank's tight lending practices.

Step 4: (A) rules out one alternate possibility, that the downturn itself has tightened the banks' purse-strings. The author, who concludes that relaxing regulations is all that's needed, would have to assume this alternate reason for reduced lending is not true.

Wrong answers: (B) Outside the Scope. This argument is about the reasons banks are lending more, not the causes of the recession. (C) is irrelevant to the author's reasoning, which holds that the tight regulations—whatever the good or bad reasons for them—have caused the banks to lend less money. (D) contradicts the facts of this argument; it cannot be an assumption of the argument. (E) suggests that relaxed lending regulations won't spur enough new loans to offset the effects of the downturn, but the argument's prediction is not that specific. It just says the banks will lend *more* if regulations are relaxed.

Now, practice one more generic Assumption question, just for good measure.

Practice Try each of the following Sufficient Assumption questions. You may see arguments you analyzed in the preceding chapter. Don't worry too much about your timing here. Complete all four steps of the Logical Reasoning Method for each question, jotting down your notes whenever it is helpful to do so. After each question, review your work with the expert analysis that follows.

Hint: What relationship does the author assume between brain transplants and the curing of degenerative brain disorders?

Step 2: *Conclusion:*	**Step 1:**
because	
Evidence:	

16. The present goal of the field of medicine seems to be to extend life indefinitely. Increasingly, the ability to transplant such organs as hearts, lungs, livers, and kidneys will allow us to live longer. But we can never achieve brain transplants. There are, for a start, ten million nerves running from the brain down the neck, not to mention the millions joining the brain to the sensing organs. Clearly, then, as the transplantation of organs allows more and more people to live longer, those with degenerative brain disorders will form an ever-increasing proportion of the population.

The argument above is based on which one of the following assumptions?

(A) Degenerative brain disorders will increasingly strike younger and younger patients.

(B) It is still quite rare for people to live long enough to need more than one transplant of any given organ.

(C) There are degenerative brain disorders that will not be curable without brain transplants.

(D) Degenerative brain disorders account for a very small proportion of deaths in the population at large.

(E) More is being spent on research into degenerative brain disorders than on research into transplantation.

PrepTest110 Sec3 Q11

Step 3:	**Step 4:**

Expert Analysis

Here's how an LSAT expert approached the question you just tried.

Step 2: *Conclusion*: As the population gets older, there will be a greater percentage of people with degenerative brain disorders *because*

Evidence: Brain transplants will remain impossible.

Step 1: The correct answer states the argument's central assumption.

16. The present goal of the field of medicine seems to be to extend life indefinitely. Increasingly, the ability to transplant such organs as hearts, lungs, livers, and kidneys will allow us to live longer. But we can never achieve brain transplants. There are, for a start, ten million nerves running from the brain down the neck, not to mention the millions joining the brain to the sensing organs. Clearly, then, as the transplantation of organs allows more and more people to live longer, those with degenerative brain disorders will form an ever-increasing proportion of the population.

The argument above is based on which one of the following assumptions?

(A) Degenerative brain disorders will increasingly strike younger and younger patients.

(B) It is still quite rare for people to live long enough to need more than one transplant of any given organ.

(C) There are degenerative brain disorders that will not be curable without brain transplants.

(D) Degenerative brain disorders account for a very small proportion of deaths in the population at large.

(E) More is being spent on research into degenerative brain disorders than on research into transplantation.

PrepTest110 Sec3 Q11

Step 3: There is a lot of background information here, but zeroing in on the conclusion and evidence makes the argument clearer. The author concludes that as medical advances extend people's lives, a higher percentage of the population will have degenerative brain disorders. The evidence is that brain transplants will remain impossible. So, the author assumes brain transplants are necessary to cure at least some degenerative brain disorders. If transplants aren't necessary (if we find another way), then the argument falls apart.

Step 4: (C) accurately expresses the argument's core assumption: brain transplants are necessary to cure (at least some) degenerative brain disorders.

Wrong answers: (A) gets the author's point backwards; the author thinks the percentage of people with degenerative brain disorders will grow because the population is aging, not because the condition will hit younger people. (B) Outside the Scope. The argument is about the future, but this choice just states the situation today. (D) The number of deaths from degenerative brain disorders is Outside the Scope of this argument, which predicts that a growing percentage of the population will have the condition. (E) The comparison in current research funding is irrelevant to this argument's assumption.

There's a good chance you will not see a generic Assumption question stem on your official test, but if you do, remember these examples, and use your overall LSAT argument expertise to approach the question with confidence. Now, it's time for some skills assessment on the following Assumption question Perform quiz. You'll encounter both Necessary Assumption and Sufficient Assumption questions here, just as you will on test day.

Chapter Perform Quiz

Perform This Perform quiz has 10 questions, a mix of Necessary Assumption and Sufficient Assumption questions. They are presented without any notes, hints, or prompts for a more test-like experience while you work. Try to get as many correct answers as possible in 15 minutes. When you finish, check your performance against the Answer Key and Evaluate Your Performance for tips on how best to improve. Then, come back to complete any questions you skipped or guessed on and review all of the questions with the expert analyses in your online companion.

17. Finnish author Jaakko Mikkeli was accused by Norwegian author Kirsten Halden of plagiarizing a book that she had written and that had been published 20 years before Mikkeli's. The two books, although set in different periods and regions, contain enough plot similarities to make coincidental resemblance unlikely. Mikkeli's defense rests on his argument that plagiarism was impossible in this case because Halden's book has been published only in Norwegian, a language Mikkeli does not understand, and because no reviews of Halden's book have ever been published.

The argument in Mikkeli's defense depends on the assumption that

(A) Mikkeli has never met Halden

(B) Halden's book did not become popular in Norway

(C) nobody related the plot of Halden's book in detail to Mikkeli before Mikkeli wrote his book

(D) there is a common European myth to which both authors referred subconsciously in the books in question

(E) Mikkeli is not familiar with Old Icelandic, an extinct language related to an earlier form of Norwegian

PrepTest112 Sec1 Q3

18. Teacher to a student: You agree that it is bad to break promises. But when we speak to each other we all make an implicit promise to tell the truth, and lying is the breaking of that promise. So even if you promised Jeanne that you would tell me she is home sick, you should not tell me that, if you know that she is well.

Which one of the following is an assumption on which the teacher's argument depends?

(A) Most people always tell the truth.

(B) It is sometimes better to act in a friend's best interests than to keep a promise to that friend.

(C) Breaking a promise leads to worse consequences than does telling a lie.

(D) Some implicit promises are worse to break than some explicit ones.

(E) One should never break a promise.

PrepTest111 Sec3 Q11

19. A government ought to protect and encourage free speech, because free speech is an activity that is conducive to a healthy nation and thus is in the best interest of its people.

The main conclusion above follows logically if which one of the following is assumed?

(A) An activity that is in the best interest of the people ought to be protected and encouraged by a nation's government.

(B) Basic, inalienable rights of the people ought to be protected and encouraged by government.

(C) An activity that helps a government to govern ought to be protected and encouraged by it.

(D) A government ought to protect and encourage an activity that is conducive to the interests of that government.

(E) Universal human rights that are in the best interest of the people ought to be protected and encouraged by a nation's government.

PrepTest112 Sec4 Q1

20. In the paintings by seventeenth-century Dutch artist Vermeer, we find several recurrent items: a satin jacket, a certain Turkish carpet, and wooden chairs with lion's head finials. These reappearing objects might seem to evince a dearth of props. Yet we know that many of the props Vermeer used were expensive. Thus, while we might speculate about exactly why Vermeer worked with a small number of familiar objects, it was clearly not for lack of props that the recurrent items were used.

The conclusion follows logically if which one of the following is assumed?

(A) Vermeer often borrowed the expensive props he represented in his paintings.

(B) The props that recur in Vermeer's paintings were always available to him.

(C) The satin jacket and wooden chairs that recur in the paintings were owned by Vermeer's sister.

(D) The several recurrent items that appeared in Vermeer's paintings had special sentimental importance for him.

(E) If a dearth of props accounted for the recurrent objects in Vermeer's paintings, we would not see expensive props in any of them.

PrepTest112 Sec1 Q26

21. The current pattern of human consumption of resources, in which we rely on nonrenewable resources, for example metal ore, must eventually change. Since there is only so much metal ore available, ultimately we must either do without or turn to renewable resources to take its place.

Which one of the following is an assumption required by the argument?

(A) There are renewable resource replacements for all of the nonrenewable resources currently being consumed.

(B) We cannot indefinitely replace exhausted nonrenewable resources with other nonrenewable resources.

(C) A renewable resource cannot be exhausted by human consumption.

(D) Consumption of nonrenewable resources will not continue to increase in the near future.

(E) Ultimately we cannot do without nonrenewable resources.

PrepTest111 Sec1 Q18

22. Essayist: One of the claims of laissez-faire economics is that increasing the minimum wage reduces the total number of minimum-wage jobs available. In a recent study, however, it was found that after an increase in the minimum wage, fast-food restaurants kept on roughly the same number of minimum-wage employees as before the increase. Therefore, laissez-faire economics is not entirely accurate.

The essayist's argument depends on assuming which one of the following?

(A) If laissez-faire economics makes an incorrect prediction about the minimum wage, then all the doctrines of laissez-faire economics are inaccurate.

(B) Minimum-wage job availability at fast-food restaurants included in the study was representative of minimum-wage job availability in general.

(C) No study has ever found that a business has decreased the number of its minimum-wage employees after an increase in the minimum wage.

(D) The fast-food restaurants included in the study did not increase the average wage paid to employees.

(E) The national unemployment rate did not increase following the increase in the minimum wage.

PrepTest110 Sec2 Q13

23. Although the charter of Westside School states that the student body must include some students with special educational needs, no students with learning disabilities have yet enrolled in the school. Therefore, the school is currently in violation of its charter.

The conclusion of the argument follows logically if which one of the following is assumed?

(A) All students with learning disabilities have special educational needs.

(B) The school currently has no student with learning disabilities.

(C) The school should enroll students with special educational needs.

(D) The only students with special educational needs are students with learning disabilities.

(E) The school's charter cannot be modified in order to avoid its being violated.

PrepTest110 Sec2 Q10

24. Moderate exercise lowers the risk of blockage of the arteries due to blood clots, since anything that lowers blood cholesterol levels also lowers the risk of hardening of the arteries, which in turn lowers the risk of arterial blockage due to blood clots; and, if the data reported in a recent study are correct, moderate exercise lowers blood cholesterol levels.

The conclusion drawn above follows logically if which one of the following is assumed?

(A) The recent study investigated the relationship between exercise and blood cholesterol levels.

(B) Blockage of the arteries due to blood clots can be prevented.

(C) Lowering blood cholesterol levels lowers the risk of blockage of the arteries.

(D) The data reported in the recent study are correct.

(E) Hardening of the arteries increases the risk of blockage of the arteries due to blood clots.

PrepTest112 Sec1 Q18

25. The folktale that claims that a rattlesnake's age can be determined from the number of sections in its rattle is false, but only because the rattles are brittle and sometimes partially or completely break off. So if they were not so brittle, one could reliably determine a rattlesnake's age simply from the number of sections in its rattle, because one new section is formed each time a rattlesnake molts.

Which one of the following is an assumption the argument requires in order for its conclusion to be properly drawn?

(A) Rattlesnakes molt exactly once a year.

(B) The rattles of rattlesnakes of different species are identical in appearance.

(C) Rattlesnakes molt more frequently when young than when old.

(D) The brittleness of a rattlesnake's rattle is not correlated with the length of the rattlesnake's life.

(E) Rattlesnakes molt as often when food is scarce as they do when food is plentiful.

PrepTest111 Sec3 Q22

26. Professor Chan: The literature department's undergraduate courses should cover only true literary works, and not such frivolous material as advertisements.

Professor Wigmore: Advertisements might or might not be true literary works but they do have a powerfully detrimental effect on society—largely because people cannot discern their real messages. The literature department's courses give students the critical skills to analyze and understand texts. Therefore, it is the literature department's responsibility to include the study of advertisements in its undergraduate courses.

Which one of the following is an assumption on which Professor Wigmore's argument depends?

(A) Texts that are true literary works never have a detrimental effect on society.

(B) Courses offered by the literature department cannot include both true literary works and material such as advertisements.

(C) Students who take courses in the literature department do not get from those courses other skills besides those needed to analyze and understand texts.

(D) Forms of advertising that convey their message entirely through visual images do not have a detrimental effect on society.

(E) The literature department's responsibility is not limited to teaching students how to analyze true literary works.

PrepTest110 Sec2 Q21

Answer Key

17. C; 18. D; 19. A; 20. E; 21. B; 22. B; 23. D; 24. D; 25. E; 26. E

Evaluate Your Performance

To assess your strengths and opportunities from this Perform quiz, go to the corresponding chapter in your online companion. There you'll find recommendations based on your performance along with complete worked-example explanations (written by a Kaplan LSAT expert) for each of the questions in this Perform quiz.

CHAPTER 10

Flaw Questions

Flaw Question Basics

Prepare The second major Assumption Family question type is the Flaw question. These will directly reward your skills in understanding and summarizing the kinds of reasoning errors you've learned to identify in LSAT arguments.

> ### LEARNING OBJECTIVES
>
> In this section, you'll learn to:
>
> - Recognize and characterize common patterns of flawed reasoning.
> - Identify and answer Flaw questions.

On a typical LSAT test, you'll see seven or eight Flaw questions. That's approximately 10% of your overall LSAT score, so this is a high-yield question type. Flaw questions warrant continued attention throughout your LSAT prep.

You can recognize Flaw questions from question stems like these.

Which one of the following most accurately describes a flaw in the archaeologist's argument?

PrepTest112 Sec4 Q8

The reasoning of the argument above is questionable because the argument

PrepTest110 Sec3 Q4

The reasoning in the philosopher's argument is flawed because the argument takes for granted that

PrepTest110 Sec3 Q10

The reasoning above is most vulnerable to criticism on the grounds that it fails to consider the possibility that

PrepTest111 Sec4 Q8

Approximate Number of Flaw Questions per LSAT

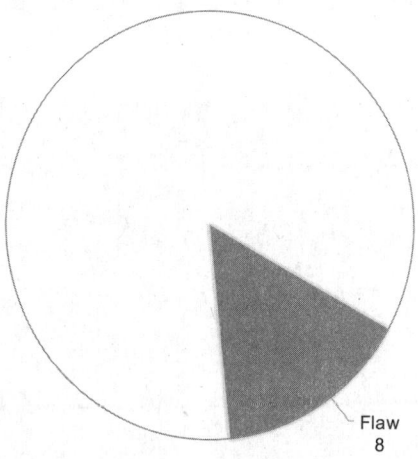

Flaw
8

Source: All officially released LSAT exams, 2016-2020

FLAW QUESTIONS AT A GLANCE

Task: Describe the author's reasoning error.

Strategy: Analyze the argument to identify the conclusion and evidence; determine the assumption and use it to help you describe the argument's logical fallacy or reasoning error.

Frequency: LSAT tests released from 2016 to 2020 had an average of 3.7 Flaw questions per section.

To get familiar with this question type, try a Flaw question on your own. Take your time and work through all four steps of the Logical Reasoning Method. When you're finished, compare your work to that of an LSAT expert by reviewing the worked example on the next page.

Step 2:	Step 1:

1. Archaeologist: The fact that the ancient Egyptians and the Maya both built pyramids is often taken as evidence of a historical link between Old- and New-World civilizations that is earlier than any yet documented. But while these buildings are similar to each other, there are important differences in both design and function. The Egyptian pyramids were exclusively tombs for rulers, whereas the Mayan pyramids were used as temples. This shows conclusively that there was no such link between Old- and New-World civilizations.

Which one of the following most accurately describes a flaw in the archaeologist's argument?

(A) The argument equivocates with respect to the term "evidence."

(B) The argument appeals to emotion rather than to reason.

(C) The argument assumes the conclusion it is trying to prove.

(D) The argument incorrectly relies on words whose meanings are vague or imprecise.

(E) The argument presumes that no other evidence is relevant to the issue at hand.

PrepTest112 Sec4 Q8

Step 3:	Step 4:

Expert Analysis

Study this worked example to see how an LSAT expert applies the Logical Reasoning Method to a Flaw question.

Step 2: *Conclusion*: There was no historical link between Old- and New-World civilizations *because* *Evidence*: Old-world civilizations used their pyramids for different things than New-world civilizations used theirs for.	**Step 1:** This is a straightforward Flaw question stem; the correct answer describes the archaeologist's error in reasoning.

1. Archaeologist: The fact that the ancient Egyptians and the Maya both built pyramids is often taken as evidence of a historical link between Old- and New-World civilizations that is earlier than any yet documented. But while these buildings are similar to each other, there are important differences in both design and function. The Egyptian pyramids were exclusively tombs for rulers, whereas the Mayan pyramids were used as temples. This shows conclusively that there was no such link between Old- and New-World civilizations.

Which one of the following most accurately describes a flaw in the archaeologist's argument?

(A) The argument equivocates with respect to the term "evidence."

(B) The argument appeals to emotion rather than to reason.

(C) The argument assumes the conclusion it is trying to prove.

(D) The argument incorrectly relies on words whose meanings are vague or imprecise.

(E) The argument presumes that no other evidence is relevant to the issue at hand.

PrepTest112 Sec4 Q8

Step 3: This is an archetypal Overlooked Possibilities argument. The archaeologist uses one reason to doubt a link (pyramids of different design and function) to conclude "conclusively" that there is no link at all. The correct answer will point out that the archaeologist hasn't ruled out all possibilities or might cite one or more of the overlooked possibilities.	**Step 4:** (E) gives a generalized description of the classic overlooked possibilities flaw and is correct.

Wrong answers: (A) The archaeologist uses the word "evidence" only once, and the rest of the argument is consistent with that usage. (B) There is no language in the archaeologist's argument suggesting an emotional appeal to the listener. (C) describes the circular reasoning flaw, but the archaeologist here doesn't commit this error, which would sound something like "We know there's no link between Old- and New-world civilizations, for if there were, those civilizations would have had to be in contact, and we know they weren't." (D) All terms are used clearly in the archaeologist's argument; it is just incomplete.

Recognizing Common Flaws

| Prepare | Before you take a deep dive into the patterns of flawed reasoning most often tested on the LSAT, pause for a second and remind yourself of two things: first, Flaw questions are |

Assumption Family questions, and second, you already know the two overarching patterns of argumentation featured on the LSAT, mismatched concepts and overlooked possibilities. As you read that sentence, it might seem obvious, but sometimes patterns on the LSAT are so obvious that you overlook them.

Go back to the question stems you saw earlier in the chapter.

> The reasoning in the philosopher's argument
> is flawed because the argument takes for
> granted that
>
> *PrepTest110 Sec3 Q10*

> The reasoning above is most vulnerable
> to criticism on the grounds that it fails to
> consider the possibility that
>
> *PrepTest111 Sec4 Q8*

Do you see how they are already guiding you toward mismatched concepts and, especially in the second example, overlooked possibilities? Take advantage of these kinds of clues from Flaw question stems as you're completing Step 1 of the Logical Reasoning Method. It will make your argument analysis that much more efficient in Step 2.

Even when the question stem just gives you a generic Flaw description, you will get help as you're evaluating the answer choices in Step 4. The wording in this Flaw question stem is very common.

> The argument's reasoning is flawed because
> the argument
>
> *PrepTest111 Sec4 Q24*

And the answer choices that follow will begin with phrases such as

> presumes, without providing justification . . .
> presumes, without warrant . . .

indicating a mismatched concepts flaw, or like these

> overlooks the possibility that . . .
> ignores the possibility that . . .

signaling overlooked possibilities. Don't approach each argument as if it is a mystery. Instead look for patterns, and use them to increase your efficiency and confidence.

The Most Common Flaws on the LSAT

Flaw questions are dominated by these common argument types:

- **Overlooked Possibilities (no other reason or explanation)**—A failure to consider alternative explanations or possible objections

- **Overlooked Possibilities (correlation versus causation)**—A conclusion of causation based on evidence of correlation

- **Overlooked Possibilities (necessity versus sufficiency)**—A conclusion treating a sufficient term in the evidence as if it were necessary, or vice versa
- **Mismatched Concepts (including alike/equivalent, mutually exclusive, and representativeness)**—A conclusion the scope or terms of which are unwarranted given the evidence

These are the patterns most likely to appear in the stimulus and to be represented by the correct answer, but they aren't the only ones you need to know. There are a few more flaws you should recognize, and you should recognize them for two reasons: first, they will be the flaw in the stimulus and thus the correct answer from time to time, and second, they will very often be described in wrong answer choices. To eliminate such choices quickly and confidently, you need to know when answer choices do not match the argument you're analyzing as well as when they do.

Less Common Flaws on the LSAT

While the majority of arguments in Flaw questions fit into the categories above, you should be prepared to see examples and descriptions of these slightly less common flaws as well.

- **Mismatched Concepts (equivocation)**—An argument in which the same word or term is used inconsistently in the conclusion and evidence
- **Mismatched Concepts (part versus whole)**—An argument in which a conclusion is drawn about a group based on evidence about individual members, or vice versa
- **Circular Reasoning**—An argument in which the evidence provided simply assumes the truth of the conclusion (Note: Circular reasoning is quite often described in wrong answers on questions where the real flaw is quite different.)
- **Evidence Contradicts Conclusion**—An argument that blatantly draws a conclusion in conflict with what its evidence implies; e.g., "Management's position in the negotiations is strong. You can see this from the numerous concessions they've made to labor."

Rare Flaws on the LSAT

Finally, here's a list of flaws that are rarely seen as correct answers on the LSAT. While there's a good chance you won't run into any given example, it's worth it to be aware of them as all have appeared in past Flaw questions and are used from time to time in wrong answers as well.

- Conflating numerical values with percent values
- Using evidence of belief to draw a conclusion of fact
- Attacking the person making the argument instead of the argument (ad hominem)
- Stating that absence of evidence is evidence of absence
- Making an inappropriate appeal to authority ("Professor Y says it's true, so it must be true.")
- Concluding that something does or will happen simply because it is possible for it to happen
- Indicating that what is true of a group is also true of its members (essentially the reverse of Part versus Whole)

LSAT STRATEGY

Some facts to remember about Flaw questions:

- The correct answer will describe the error in the author's reasoning.
- You will be tested on your ability to identify flaws in both Mismatched Concepts and Overlooked Possibilities arguments.
- Correct answer choices are often written in abstract terms; form a prediction and match it to the most appropriate answer choice.

Practice   Now, try your hand at identifying some errors of reasoning in LSAT Flaw question stimuli. Don't hesitate to refer back to the lists of most common, less common, and rare flaws as you complete this exercise. When you're finished, compare your work to that of an LSAT expert on the pages that follow. You will see all of these stimuli again in the full-question practice later in this chapter.

LSAT Stimulus	My Analysis
2. A group of 1,000 students was randomly selected from three high schools in a medium-sized city and asked the question, "Do you plan to finish your high school education?" More than 89 percent answered "Yes." This shows that the overwhelming majority of students want to finish high school, and that if the national dropout rate among high school students is high, it cannot be due to a lack of desire on the part of the students. *PrepTest110 Sec3 Q4*	**Analyze the Argument:** **Describe the Flaw:**
3. Philosopher: People are not intellectually well suited to live in large bureaucratic societies. Therefore, people can find happiness, if at all, only in smaller political units such as villages. *PrepTest110 Sec3 Q10*	**Analyze the Argument:** **Describe the Flaw:**

LSAT Stimulus	My Analysis
4. Joseph: My encyclopedia says that the mathematician Pierre de Fermat died in 1665 without leaving behind any written proof for a theorem that he claimed nonetheless to have proved. Probably this alleged theorem simply cannot be proved, since—as the article points out—no one else has been able to prove it. Therefore it is likely that Fermat was either lying or else mistaken when he made his claim.	**Analyze BOTH Arguments:**
Laura: Your encyclopedia is out of date. Recently someone has in fact proved Fermat's theorem. And since the theorem is provable, your claim—that Fermat was lying or mistaken—clearly is wrong. *PrepTest112 Sec4 Q14*	**Describe the Flaw in Laura's argument:**
5. Only a very small percentage of people from the service professions ever become board members of the 600 largest North American corporations. This shows that people from the service professions are underrepresented in the most important corporate boardrooms in North America. *PrepTest111 Sec3 Q17*	**Analyze the Argument:**
	Describe the Flaw:

LSAT Stimulus	**My Analysis**
6. Birds need so much food energy to maintain their body temperatures that some of them spend most of their time eating. But a comparison of a bird of a seed-eating species to a bird of a nectar-eating species that has the same overall energy requirement would surely show that the seed-eating bird spends more time eating than does the nectar-eating bird, since a given amount of nectar provides more energy than does the same amount of seeds. *PrepTest112 Sec4 Q19*	**Analyze the Argument:** **Describe the Flaw:**
7. Cotrell is, at best, able to write magazine articles of average quality. The most compelling pieces of evidence for this are those few of the numerous articles submitted by Cotrell that are superior, since Cotrell, who is incapable of writing an article that is better than average, must obviously have plagiarized superior ones. *PrepTest112 Sec1 Q10*	**Analyze the Argument:** **Describe the Flaw:**

Expert Analysis

Here's how an LSAT expert untangled the Flaw question stimuli you've been working on.

LSAT Stimulus	Analysis
2. A group of 1,000 students was randomly selected from three high schools in a medium-sized city and asked the question, "Do you plan to finish your high school education?" More than 89 percent answered "Yes." This shows that the overwhelming majority of students want to finish high school, and that if the national dropout rate among high school students is high, it cannot be due to a lack of desire on the part of the students. *PrepTest110 Sec3 Q4*	**Analyze the Argument**: *Conclusion*: Students want to finish high school and a high national dropout rate cannot be blamed on a lack of desire among students *because* *Evidence*: In a survey of 1,000 high school students from one mid-sized city, 89% said they plan to finish high school. **Describe the Flaw**: The argument draws a conclusion about the reasons for national dropout rates from a survey conducted in one city. The author assumes those surveyed are **representative** of all high school students nationwide.
3. Philosopher: People are not intellectually well suited to live in large bureaucratic societies. Therefore, people can find happiness, if at all, only in smaller political units such as villages. *PrepTest110 Sec3 Q10*	**Analyze the Argument**: *Conclusion*: People can be happy only in smaller political units *because* *Evidence*: People are not intellectually suited to large bureaucratic societies. **Describe the Flaw**: The author takes quite a leap, assuming that intellect suitedness is necessary for happiness. The correct answer will paraphrase this unsupported **mismatched concepts** assumption.

LSAT Stimulus	Analysis
4. Joseph: My encyclopedia says that the mathematician Pierre de Fermat died in 1665 without leaving behind any written proof for a theorem that he claimed nonetheless to have proved. Probably this alleged theorem simply cannot be proved, since—as the article points out—no one else has been able to prove it. Therefore it is likely that Fermat was either lying or else mistaken when he made his claim. Laura: Your encyclopedia is out of date. Recently someone has in fact proved Fermat's theorem. And since the theorem is provable, your claim—that Fermat was lying or mistaken—clearly is wrong. *PrepTest112 Sec4 Q14*	**Analyze BOTH Arguments:** Joseph—*Conclusion*: Fermat was probably lying or mistaken in claiming to have proved his theorem *because* *Evidence*: An encyclopedia article states that Fermat left no written proof and no one else has proven the theorem. Laura—*Conclusion*: Your conclusion is wrong *because* *Evidence*: Someone proved Fermat's theorem after your encyclopedia was printed. **Describe the Flaw in Laura's argument**: Laura's evidence demonstrates that Fermat's theorem *can* be proved, but it does not rule out the possibility that Fermat was lying or mistaken when claiming that he had proved the theorem. Thus, Laura has **confused** a fact **necessary** to disprove Joseph's conclusion for one **sufficient** to disprove it.
5. Only a very small percentage of people from the service professions ever become board members of the 600 largest North American corporations. This shows that people from the service professions are underrepresented in the most important corporate boardrooms in North America. *PrepTest111 Sec3 Q17*	**Analyze the Argument**: *Conclusion*: People from service professions are underrepresented in top corporate boardrooms *because* *Evidence*: Only a small percentage of people from service professions ever become board members of the 600 top corporations. **Describe the Flaw**: There is a huge **mismatched concepts** gap between the evidence (only a small percentage of those in the service professions will sit on the boards of large corporations) and the conclusion (the service professions are poorly represented on those boards). Service professions might be well represented on the boards—imagine ten service professionals on every one of the top 600 corporate boards—and that would still be only a few thousand people, a very small percentage of the millions of people who work in the service professions.

LSAT Stimulus	Analysis
6. Birds need so much food energy to maintain their body temperatures that some of them spend most of their time eating. But a comparison of a bird of a seed-eating species to a bird of a nectar-eating species that has the same overall energy requirement would surely show that the seed-eating bird spends more time eating than does the nectar-eating bird, since a given amount of nectar provides more energy than does the same amount of seeds. *PrepTest112 Sec4 Q19*	**Analyze the Argument**: *Conclusion*: Between birds with equal energy requirements, seed-eaters spend more time eating than nectar-eaters *because* *Evidence*: A given amount of seeds provides less energy than the same amount of nectar. **Describe the Flaw**: The author draws a conclusion about *time spent* eating from evidence about the *amount* eaten (**mismatched concepts**), so the assumption is that it takes the same amount of time to eat equal portions of seeds and nectar. There is no evidence to suggest that's the case, and if it isn't true, this argument falls apart.
7. Cotrell is, at best, able to write magazine articles of average quality. The most compelling pieces of evidence for this are those few of the numerous articles submitted by Cotrell that are superior, since Cotrell, who is incapable of writing an article that is better than average, must obviously have plagiarized superior ones. *PrepTest112 Sec1 Q10*	**Analyze the Argument**: *Conclusion*: Cotrell's writing is average at best *because* *Evidence*: Cotrell must have plagiarized the superior articles he submitted because he's not capable of superior writing. **Describe the Flaw**: This argument employs **circular reasoning**. The author concludes that, at best, Cotrell is capable of writing average quality articles, and the evidence for this is Cotrell "is incapable of writing an article that is better than average." The evidence is dressed up a bit with the author's accusations of plagiarism on any above-average article submitted by Cotrell, but at its heart, this argument simply assumes what it sets out to prove.

CHANNEL SPOTLIGHT

Flaw School

By Kaplan LSAT Channel Faculty

 Watch the video lesson for this Spotlight in your online Study Plan.

This isn't talked about very much, but it's time for you to know. There's something a bit unpleasant that happens to a lot of students when they study for the LSAT. It may happen to you, too. In fact, it's something that gets even worse when you get to law school. It will annoy your friends, and maybe even your loved ones. Lively conversations may grind to a halt when you approach, and there will likely be a measurable uptick in eye rolling in your immediate vicinity. You, dear test taker, are going to start picking apart every argument you hear.

You see, as we mature, our argumentative skills develop. Childhood staples—like "No. You are!"—give way to more subtle approaches—such as the evergreen "She started it." Later, we learn to dispute the factual basis of an opponent's position, and with higher education comes the art of supporting contentions with citations and evidence.

What lies beyond that is reserved to a select group, and as someone bound for law school, you are definitely a member. These are the people able to attack an argument's reasoning. These are the people who actually know what they are talking about when they say things like, "You're mistaking necessity for sufficiency," "That conclusion is based on an unrepresentative sample," or "C'mon, man, you can infer the contrapositive, but not the converse." You'll use terms such as "ad hominem," "equivocation," and "circular reasoning" the way sportscasters use catchphrases. Yes, that's going to be you if it isn't already. Try not to be too hard on your friends' arguments . . . if you can help it.

In this Spotlight's video, an LSAT Channel expert (and some friends who make a lot of errors in their reasoning) will give you an introduction to the logical reasoning flaws most frequently tested on the LSAT. It's a fun way to start building some very important LSAT skills, skills that you will use throughout law school, and even in law practice. Welcome to Flaw School.

 **Complete answers and explanations are provided in the LSAT Channel Spotlight video "Flaw School" in your online Study Plan.**

Understanding Flaw Question Answer Choices

For many test takers, finding the assumption or determining the pattern of an argument in a Flaw question is not hugely challenging. Instead, the difficult part of correctly answering a Flaw question is matching a prediction to the correct answer choice. This is because the LSAT words the correct answers to Flaw questions differently than it does the correct answers to other Assumption Family questions. Consider, for example, the following argument:

> Joe started feeling sick a short while after eating at the restaurant around the corner. Clearly, he got food poisoning from the food he ate there!

This is a classic causal argument. The author takes two things that happened around the same time, eating at the restaurant and getting sick, and concludes that one of them must have caused the other. "Causation versus Correlation" is, of course, a type of overlooked possibilities argument. The author assumes, without providing evidence, that Joe did not get sick in any other way.

The correct answer to a Necessary Assumption question based on this scenario would rule out an alternative:

> Joe did not catch a stomach virus from his neighbor.

That's straightforward. It rules out an alternative cause. Now, a Flaw question's answer might say the argument is flawed because it

> overlooks the possibility that Joe caught a stomach virus from his neighbor

but, and here's where it gets tricky, it could instead say that the argument is flawed because it

> interprets the temporal proximity of two events as evidence of a causal relationship

The difference between the first two of these answer choices is not very great. The only distinction is that the Flaw answer choice is descriptive—it tells us that the author is overlooking something rather than ruling out a specific possibility. The difference between the Necessary Assumption answer and the second Flaw answer, however, is much bigger. The second Flaw answer is also describing the problem, but it is doing so in much more abstract terms.

One key to success in Flaw questions is learning how to spot your prediction when it is stated in abstract, generic language. Take a few minutes to study the list on the following page (and refer back to it whenever you are practicing or reviewing Flaw questions). It gives examples of the kinds of verbiage the test uses to describe common reasoning errors.

COMMON FLAW QUESTION ANSWER-CHOICE LANGUAGE

Overlooked Possibilities—No Other Reason or Explanation

"overlooks the possibility that" / "ignores the possibility that" / "fails to consider"

"assumes only one possibility when more exist"

"treats one explanation of many as though it were the only one"

Overlooked Possibilities—Causation

"mistakes a correlation for causation"

"presumes that because one event was followed by another, the first event caused the second"

"ignores the possibility that two things that occur together may be only coincidentally related"

Overlooked Possibilities—Necessary versus Sufficient

"confuses a result with a condition that is required to bring about that result"

"mistakes something that is necessary for a particular outcome for something that is merely sufficient for that outcome"

"ignores the possibility that a particular outcome may be sufficient but not necessary for another"

Mismatched Concepts—General

"relies on irrelevant evidence"

"facts that are not directly related to the case are used to support a conclusion about it"

"draws an analogy between two things that are not alike enough in the ways they would need to be in order for the conclusion to be properly drawn"

Mismatched Concepts—Representativeness

"draws a general conclusion from a few isolated instances"

"generalizes from an unrepresentative sample"

"treats the children living in County X as though they were representative of all children that age living in State Y"

Mismatched Concepts—Equivocation

"relies on an ambiguity in the term plant"

"allows a key phrase to shift in meaning from one use to the next"

Circular Reasoning

"the conclusion is no more than a restatement of the evidence used to support it"

"restates its conclusion without providing sufficient justification for accepting it"

"presupposes the truth of what it seeks to establish"

Evidence Contradicts the Conclusion

"the evidence given actually undermines the argument's conclusion"

"some of the evidence given is inconsistent with other evidence presented"

"draws a recommendation that is inconsistent with the evidence given to support it"

Now, get some practice identifying flaws as they are described in LSAT Flaw question answer choices with the following drill.

Practice **Drill: Identifying Argument Types in Flaw Question Answer Choices**

For each of the following, name the flaw described in the answer choice.

Answer Choice	My Analysis
8. presumes, without justification, that increased civic revenue will be spent for the public good	
9. treats a characteristic known to be true of one class of things as if that characteristic were unique to that class	
10. mistakes a condition sufficient for bringing about a result for a condition necessary for doing so	
11. takes the failure of evidence to establish the truth of a statement as evidence that that statement is false	
12. concludes that two things that occur at the same time have a common cause	
13. overlooks the possibility that most customers don't order decaf	

Answer Choice	My Analysis
14. treats as similar two cases that are different in a critical respect	
15. confuses the two cities' rates of infection with the number of residents of each infected	
16. assumes the truth of what it attempts to demonstrate	
17. bases its conclusion about a group on survey results that may not be representative of the group	
18. assumes that because something is true of each of an object's parts, it is true of the object	
19. improperly exploits an ambiguity in the phrase "pedestrian"	

Expert Analysis

Here's how an LSAT expert identifies the flaw described by each of the answer choices you just saw.

Answer Choice	Analysis
8. presumes, without justification, that increased civic revenue will be spent for the public good	**Mismatched Concepts.** "*Presumes*, without justi-fication" signals an unwarranted assumption.
9. treats a characteristic known to be true of one class of things as if that characteristic were unique to that class	**Overlooked Possibilities: Necessary versus Sufficient.** The author treats a characteristic necessary to a group as if it were sufficient to designate things as being in that group.
10. mistakes a condition sufficient for bringing about a result for a condition necessary for doing so	**Overlooked Possibilities: Necessary versus Sufficient.** The author has treated a sufficient condition as though it were a necessary one.
11. takes the failure of evidence to establish the truth of a statement as evidence that that statement is false	**Overlooked Possibilities.** The specific flaw here is often stated as "absence of evidence is not evidence of absence." For example, absence of evidence for the existence of aliens is NOT evidence for the absence of aliens.
12. concludes that two things that occur at the same time have a common cause	**Overlooked Possibilities: Correlation versus Causation**
13. overlooks the possibility that most customers don't order decaf	**Overlooked Possibilities.** Arguments in which the author assumes only one possibility with-out giving a reason to rule out others are inher-ently flawed.
14. treats as similar two cases that are different in a critical respect	**Mismatched Concepts: Alike/Equivalent.** The author assumes an equivalence between two different things. The argument might contain a faulty analogy.
15. confuses the two cities' rates of infection with the number of residents of each infected	**Mismatched Concepts: Number versus Percent**
16. assumes the truth of what it attempts to demonstrate	**Circular Reasoning**
17. bases its conclusion about a group on a sample that may not be representative of the group	**Mismatched Concepts: Representativeness.** The author relies on a sample that may be too small, non-random, or biased in some way.
18. assumes that because something is true of each of an object's parts, it is true of the object	**Mismatched Concept: Part/Whole.** The part or whole can have properties that are lacking in the other.
19. improperly exploits an ambiguity in the phrase "pedestrian"	**Mismatched Concepts: Equivocation.** This flaw occurs when one word or term is used in two incompatible ways in the argument.

Practice Try each of the following Main Point questions. Some of them contain arguments you analyzed in the preceding chapter. Don't worry too much about your timing here. Complete all four steps of the Logical Reasoning Method for each question, jotting down your notes whenever it is helpful to do so. After each question, review your work with the expert analysis that follows.

Hint: Is the author of the argument actually critiquing R's book?

Step 2:

Step 1:

20. In his new book on his complex scientific research, R frequently imputes bad faith to researchers disagreeing with him. A troubling aspect of R's book is his stated conviction that other investigators' funding sources often determine what "findings" those investigators report. Add to this that R has often shown himself to be arrogant, overly ambitious, and sometimes plain nasty, and it becomes clear that R's book does not merit attention from serious professionals.

The author of the book review commits which one of the following reasoning errors?

(A) using an attack on the character of the writer of the book as evidence that his person is not competent on matters of scientific substance

(B) taking it for granted that an investigator is unlikely to report findings that are contrary to the interests of those funding the investigation

(C) dismissing a scientific theory by giving a biased account of it

(D) presenting as facts several assertions about the book under review that are based only on strong conviction and would be impossible for others to verify

(E) failing to distinguish between the criteria of being true and of being sufficiently interesting to merit attention

PrepTest110 Sec2 Q1

Step 3:

Step 4:

Expert Analysis

Here's how an LSAT expert approached the question you just completed.

Step 2: *Conclusion*: R's book does not deserve serious consideration *because* *Evidence*: (1) In the book, R accuses opposing scientists of bad faith and of tailoring their findings in the interest of their funders. (2) R is just arrogant, ambitious, and nasty.	**Step 1:** A Flaw question: the correct answer describes a reasoning error committed by the author.

20. In his new book on his complex scientific research, R frequently imputes bad faith to researchers disagreeing with him. A troubling aspect of R's book is his stated conviction that other investigators' funding sources often determine what "findings" those investigators report. Add to this that R has often shown himself to be arrogant, overly ambitious, and sometimes plain nasty, and it becomes clear that R's book does not merit attention from serious professionals.

The author of the book review commits which one of the following reasoning errors?

(A) using an attack on the character of the writer of the book as evidence that his person is not competent on matters of scientific substance

(B) taking it for granted that an investigator is unlikely to report findings that are contrary to the interests of those funding the investigation

(C) dismissing a scientific theory by giving a biased account of it

(D) presenting as facts several assertions about the book under review that are based only on strong conviction and would be impossible for others to verify

(E) failing to distinguish between the criteria of being true and of being sufficiently interesting to merit attention

PrepTest110 Sec2 Q1

Step 3: The author of the stimulus is a book reviewer who concludes that a book does not deserve the attention of serious scientists because of its author's accusations toward others and his generally unpleasant character. Unfortunately, using a person's character to attack the substance of what they say (the book they wrote in this case) is called the *ad hominem* flaw. It will be described in the correct answer.	**Step 4:** (A) describes the ad hominem flaw committed by the book review author and is correct.

Wrong answers: (B) The reviewer calls R's accusations troubling (because of R's "conviction" on the matter) but does not indicate that such behavior is to be expected or taken for granted. (C) The reviewer does not directly attack any theories; the reviewer trashes the book, but we don't have enough information to know where they stand on R's theories (or whether R even articulates theories in the book). (D) The statements about the book's contents would be easy enough to verify; the other statements are about R's character, not about the book. (E) Irrelevant Comparison. The reviewer doesn't accuse the book of being uninteresting.

K

Hint: What key language does the author of the stimulus argument miss?

Step 2:	Step 1:

21. Raymond Burr played the role of Perry Mason on television. Burr's death in 1993 prompted a prominent lawyer to say, "Although not a lawyer, Mr. Burr strove for such authenticity that we feel as if we lost one of our own." This comment from a prestigious attorney provides appalling evidence that, in the face of television, even some legal professionals are losing their ability to distinguish fiction from reality.

The reasoning in the argument is flawed because the argument

(A) takes the views of one lawyer to represent the views of all lawyers

(B) criticizes the lawyer rather than the lawyer's statement

(C) presumes that the lawyer is qualified to evaluate the performance of an actor

(D) focuses on a famous actor's portrayal of a lawyer rather than on the usual way in which lawyers are portrayed on television

(E) ignores the part of the lawyer's remark that indicates an awareness of the difference between reality and fiction

PrepTest111 Sec3 Q2

Step 3:	Step 4:

Expert Analysis

Here's how an LSAT expert approached the question you just completed.

Step 2: *Conclusion*: Some lawyers have lost the ability to distinguish between fact and fiction *because*

Evidence: A lawyer said the passing of an actor who had played a lawyer on TV felt like losing a professional colleague even though the actor wasn't actually a lawyer.

Step 1: A straightforward Flaw question stem; the correct answer will describe the author's error in reasoning.

21. Raymond Burr played the role of Perry Mason on television. Burr's death in 1993 prompted a prominent lawyer to say, "Although not a lawyer, Mr. Burr strove for such authenticity that we feel as if we lost one of our own." This comment from a prestigious attorney provides appalling evidence that, in the face of television, even some legal professionals are losing their ability to distinguish fiction from reality.

The reasoning in the argument is flawed because the argument

(A) takes the views of one lawyer to represent the views of all lawyers

(B) criticizes the lawyer rather than the lawyer's statement

(C) presumes that the lawyer is qualified to evaluate the performance of an actor

(D) focuses on a famous actor's portrayal of a lawyer rather than on the usual way in which lawyers are portrayed on television

(E) ignores the part of the lawyer's remark that indicates an awareness of the difference between reality and fiction

PrepTest111 Sec3 Q2

Step 3: The author treats a quote that plainly acknowledges that the deceased actor wasn't a lawyer to draw the conclusion that its speaker can't distinguish between reality and fiction. The flaw here is an obvious misinterpretation of the lawyer's quote.

Step 4: (E) uses an appropriate verb—"ignores"—to describe the author's treatment of the part of the lawyer's quote that proves they could, in fact, tell fact from fiction. It is the correct answer.

Wrong answers: (A) distorts the argument; the author clearly limits the conclusion to "some legal professionals," not all. (B) accuses the author of an *ad hominem* attack, and while the author calls the quote "appalling evidence," there is no attack on the lawyer's character. (C) Outside the Scope. Nothing about this argument hinges on the lawyer's qualifications as a TV critic. (D) Outside the Scope. The argument was spurred by a lawyer's comment on the passing of Raymond Burr. Other TV lawyers are irrelevant.

Hint: What is the scope of the conclusion? How about that of the evidence?

Step 2:	**Step 1:**

22. A group of 1,000 students was randomly selected from three high schools in a medium-sized city and asked the question, "Do you plan to finish your high school education?" More than 89 percent answered "Yes." This shows that the overwhelming majority of students want to finish high school, and that if the national dropout rate among high school students is high, it cannot be due to a lack of desire on the part of the students.

The reasoning of the argument above is questionable because the argument

(A) fails to justify its presumption that 89 percent is an overwhelming majority

(B) attempts to draw two conflicting conclusions from the results of one survey

(C) overlooks the possibility that there may in fact not be a high dropout rate among high school students

(D) contradicts itself by admitting that there may be a high dropout rate among students while claiming that most students want to finish high school

(E) treats high school students from a particular medium-sized city as if they are representative of high school students nationwide

PrepTest110 Sec3 Q4

Step 3:	**Step 4:**

Expert Analysis

Here's how an LSAT expert approached the question you just completed.

Step 2: *Conclusion*: Students want to finish high school and a high national dropout rate cannot be blamed on a lack of desire among students *because*

Evidence: In a survey of 1,000 high school students from one mid-sized city, 89% said they plan to finish high school.

Step 1: This is a standard Flaw question stem; the correct answer will describe the reasoning error in the argument.

22. A group of 1,000 students was randomly selected from three high schools in a medium-sized city and asked the question, "Do you plan to finish your high school education?" More than 89 percent answered "Yes." This shows that the overwhelming majority of students want to finish high school, and that if the national dropout rate among high school students is high, it cannot be due to a lack of desire on the part of the students.

The reasoning of the argument above is questionable because the argument

(A) fails to justify its presumption that 89 percent is an overwhelming majority

(B) attempts to draw two conflicting conclusions from the results of one survey

(C) overlooks the possibility that there may in fact not be a high dropout rate among high school students

(D) contradicts itself by admitting that there may be a high dropout rate among students while claiming that most students want to finish high school

(E) treats high school students from a particular medium-sized city as if they are representative of high school students nationwide

PrepTest110 Sec3 Q4

Step 3: The argument draws a conclusion about the reasons for national dropout rates from a survey conducted in one city. The author assumes those surveyed are representative of all high school students nationwide. This is a classic representativeness flaw; without a reason to think these students are typical of high schoolers across the country, there is reason to doubt the author's conclusion here.

Step 4: (E) describes the unrepresentative sample flaw to explain why this argument is questionable.

Wrong answers: (A) Few people would dispute that 89% constitutes an overwhelming majority. (B) The two parts of the conclusion—that high schoolers want to finish school and that high dropout rates are not due to a lack of desire—are consistent with one another, and not conflicting. (C) A quick check confirms that the author makes this part of the conclusion conditional: "*if* the national dropout rate . . . is high," so the actual dropout rate is irrelevant. (D) The part of the conclusion about dropout rates is conditional—"*if* the national dropout rate . . . is high"—so there's no contradiction. Moreover, the conclusion's assertion isn't that the rate is high, but that low student motivation is not the reason.

Hint: When answer choices are written to paraphrase the content of the argument, be careful of 180 wrong answer choices.

Step 2:	Step 1:

23. Attorney: I ask you to find Mr. Smith guilty of assaulting Mr. Jackson. Regrettably, there were no eyewitnesses to the crime, but Mr. Smith has a violent character: Ms. Lopez testified earlier that Mr. Smith, shouting loudly, had threatened her. Smith never refuted this testimony.

The attorney's argument is fallacious because it reasons that

(A) aggressive behavior is not a sure indicator of a violent character

(B) Smith's testimony is unreliable since he is loud and aggressive

(C) since Smith never disproved the claim that he threatened Lopez, he did in fact threaten her

(D) Lopez's testimony is reliable since she is neither loud nor aggressive

(E) having a violent character is not necessarily associated with the commission of violent crimes

PrepTest111 Sec4 Q7

Step 3:	Step 4:

Expert Analysis

Here's how an LSAT expert approached the question you just completed.

Step 2: *Conclusion*: Smith should be found guilty of assaulting Jackson *because* *Evidence*: Lopez says Smith threatened her and Smith did not refute Lopez's claim.	**Step 1:** "[F]allacious" indicates a Flaw question; the correct answer will describe the attorney's reasoning error.

23. Attorney: I ask you to find Mr. Smith guilty of assaulting Mr. Jackson. Regrettably, there were no eyewitnesses to the crime, but Mr. Smith has a violent character: Ms. Lopez testified earlier that Mr. Smith, shouting loudly, had threatened her. Smith never refuted this testimony.

The attorney's argument is fallacious because it reasons that

(A) aggressive behavior is not a sure indicator of a violent character

(B) Smith's testimony is unreliable since he is loud and aggressive

(C) since Smith never disproved the claim that he threatened Lopez, he did in fact threaten her

(D) Lopez's testimony is reliable since she is neither loud nor aggressive

(E) having a violent character is not necessarily associated with the commission of violent crimes

PrepTest111 Sec4 Q7

Step 3: There are several problems with the attorney's argument: (1) it calls for a guilty verdict in an assault case on the basis of the defendant's character, (2) it uses Lopez's claim that Smith threatened her as evidence of Smith's violent character, and (3) it rests on the unwarranted assumption that Smith's lack of rebuttal means that Lopez's claim is accurate.	**Step 4:** (C) correctly cites one of the attorney's mistakes in reasoning, the unwarranted assumption that Smith's lack of rebuttal means that Lopez's claim is true.

Wrong answers: (A) 180. The attorney's argument is flawed because it reasons that aggressive behavior (in this case, loud threats) *does* indicate a violent character. (B) Outside the Scope. There is no suggestion that Smith has testified. (D) Outside the Scope. The argument does not touch on Lopez's character or behavior. (E) 180. The attorney's argument is flawed because it argues the opposite, calling for a guilty verdict in this assault case on the basis of the defendant's violent character.

Hint: How does the phrase "takes for granted" in the question stem help you zero in on the author's flaw?

Step 2:	Step 1:

24. Philosopher: People are not intellectually well suited to live in large bureaucratic societies. Therefore, people can find happiness, if at all, only in smaller political units such as villages.

The reasoning in the philosopher's argument is flawed because the argument takes for granted that

(A) no one can ever be happy living in a society in which she or he is not intellectually well suited to live

(B) the primary purpose of small political units such as villages is to make people happy

(C) all societies that are plagued by excessive bureaucracy are large

(D) anyone who lives in a village or other small political unit that is not excessively bureaucratic can find happiness

(E) everyone is willing to live in villages or other small political units

PrepTest110 Sec3 Q10

Step 3:	Step 4:

Expert Analysis

Here's how an LSAT expert approached the question you just completed.

Step 2: *Conclusion:* People can be happy only in smaller political units *because* *Evidence:* People are not intellectually suited to large bureaucratic societies.	**Step 1:** The correct answer to this Flaw question will state what the author "takes for granted," i.e., the author's *unwarranted* assumption.

24. Philosopher: People are not intellectually well suited to live in large bureaucratic societies. Therefore, people can find happiness, if at all, only in smaller political units such as villages.

The reasoning in the philosopher's argument is flawed because the argument takes for granted that

(A) no one can ever be happy living in a society in which she or he is not intellectually well suited to live

(B) the primary purpose of small political units such as villages is to make people happy

(C) all societies that are plagued by excessive bureaucracy are large

(D) anyone who lives in a village or other small political unit that is not excessively bureaucratic can find happiness

(E) everyone is willing to live in villages or other small political units

PrepTest110 Sec3 Q10

Step 3: The author takes quite a leap, assuming that intellectual suitedness is necessary for happiness. The correct answer will paraphrase this unsupported assumption.	**Step 4:** (A) accurately states the author's unwarranted assumption that intellectual suitedness is necessary for happiness.

Wrong answers: (B) Outside the Scope. The argument makes no assumptions about the primary purposes of different societies. (C) distorts the author's evidence—the author doesn't blame "excessive" bureaucracy—while missing the argument's flawed assumption (what the author "takes for granted"). (D) doesn't match the argument by implying that it treats village life as *sufficient* for happiness, but the author actually assumes it is *necessary*. (E) is irrelevant; the author does not assume that everyone will be able to live in smaller societies, just that those who do not won't find happiness.

Hint: Occasionally, a rare flaw will be the correct answer.

Step 2:	**Step 1:**

25. Cotrell is, at best, able to write magazine articles of average quality. The most compelling pieces of evidence for this are those few of the numerous articles submitted by Cotrell that are superior, since Cotrell, who is incapable of writing an article that is better than average, must obviously have plagiarized superior ones.

The argument is most vulnerable to criticism on which one of the following grounds?

(A) It simply ignores the existence of potential counterevidence.

(B) It generalizes from atypical occurrences.

(C) It presupposes what it seeks to establish.

(D) It relies on the judgment of experts in a matter to which their expertise is irrelevant.

(E) It infers limits on ability from a few isolated lapses in performance.

PrepTest112 Sec1 Q10

Step 3:	**Step 4:**

Expert Analysis

Here's how an LSAT expert approached the question you just completed.

Step 2: *Conclusion*: Cotrell's writing is average at best *because*

Evidence: Cotrell must have plagiarized the superior articles he submitted because he's not capable of superior writing.

Step 1: "[V]ulnerable to criticism . . ." indicates a Flaw question; the correct answer describes the argument's faulty reasoning.

25. Cotrell is, at best, able to write magazine articles of average quality. The most compelling pieces of evidence for this are those few of the numerous articles submitted by Cotrell that are superior, since Cotrell, who is incapable of writing an article that is better than average, must obviously have plagiarized superior ones.

The argument is most vulnerable to criticism on which one of the following grounds?

(A) It simply ignores the existence of potential counterevidence.

(B) It generalizes from atypical occurrences.

(C) It presupposes what it seeks to establish.

(D) It relies on the judgment of experts in a matter to which their expertise is irrelevant.

(E) It infers limits on ability from a few isolated lapses in performance.

PrepTest112 Sec1 Q10

Step 3: This argument is circular. The author concludes that, at best, Cotrell is capable of writing average quality articles, and the evidence for this is Cotrell "is incapable of writing an article that is better than average." The evidence is dressed up a bit with the author's accusations of plagiarism on any above-average article submitted by Cotrell, but at its heart, this argument simply assumes what it sets out to prove.

Step 4: (C) is the answer choice that describes circular reasoning, and is correct.

Wrong answers: (A) The argument does not ignore counterevidence; rather, it assumes that the counterevidence is fraudulent (plagiarized). (B) The argument appears to judge Cotrell's full body of work but presupposes that the bad stuff is really Cotrell's writing and the good stuff is plagiarized. (D) Outside the Scope. The author does not appeal to any outside authority here. (E) This distorts the argument, which states that the good submissions are "few" among Cotrell's numerous submissions, so this choice doesn't describe the author's faulty reasoning.

Hint: Dialog stimuli are rare in Flaw questions, but the mistake the second speaker makes here is a very common LSAT flaw.

Step 2:	Step 1:

26. Joseph: My encyclopedia says that the mathematician Pierre de Fermat died in 1665 without leaving behind any written proof for a theorem that he claimed nonetheless to have proved. Probably this alleged theorem simply cannot be proved, since—as the article points out—no one else has been able to prove it. Therefore it is likely that Fermat was either lying or else mistaken when he made his claim.

   Laura: Your encyclopedia is out of date. Recently someone has in fact proved Fermat's theorem. And since the theorem is provable, your claim—that Fermat was lying or mistaken—clearly is wrong.

Which one of the following most accurately describes a reasoning error in Laura's argument?

(A) It purports to establish its conclusion by making a claim that, if true, would actually contradict that conclusion.

(B) It mistakenly assumes that the quality of a person's character can legitimately be taken to guarantee the accuracy of the claims that person has made.

(C) It mistakes something that is necessary for its conclusion to follow for something that ensures that the conclusion follows.

(D) It uses the term "provable" without defining it.

(E) It fails to distinguish between a true claim that has mistakenly been believed to be false and a false claim that has mistakenly been believed to be true.

PrepTest112 Sec4 Q14

Step 3:	Step 4:

Expert Analysis

Here's how an LSAT expert approached the question you just completed.

Step 2: Joseph—*Conclusion*: Fermat was probably lying or mistaken in claiming to have proved his theorem *because*

Evidence: An encyclopedia article states that Fermat left no written proof and no one else has proven the theorem.

Laura—*Conclusion*: Your conclusion is wrong *because*

Evidence: Someone proved Fermat's theorem after your encyclopedia was printed.

Step 1: A somewhat rare Flaw question with a dialog stimulus; the correct answer describes the reasoning error in the second speaker's argument.

26. Joseph: My encyclopedia says that the mathematician Pierre de Fermat died in 1665 without leaving behind any written proof for a theorem that he claimed nonetheless to have proved. Probably this alleged theorem simply cannot be proved, since—as the article points out—no one else has been able to prove it. Therefore it is likely that Fermat was either lying or else mistaken when he made his claim.

    Laura: Your encyclopedia is out of date. Recently someone has in fact proved Fermat's theorem. And since the theorem is provable, your claim—that Fermat was lying or mistaken—clearly is wrong.

Which one of the following most accurately describes a reasoning error in Laura's argument?

(A) It purports to establish its conclusion by making a claim that, if true, would actually contradict that conclusion.

(B) It mistakenly assumes that the quality of a person's character can legitimately be taken to guarantee the accuracy of the claims that person has made.

(C) It mistakes something that is necessary for its conclusion to follow for something that ensures that the conclusion follows.

(D) It uses the term "provable" without defining it.

(E) It fails to distinguish between a true claim that has mistakenly been believed to be false and a false claim that has mistakenly been believed to be true.

PrepTest112 Sec4 Q14

Step 3: Laura's evidence demonstrates that Fermat's theorem can be proved, but it does not rule out the possibility that Fermat was lying or mistaken when claiming that he had proved the theorem. Thus, Laura has confused a fact necessary to disprove Joseph's conclusion for one sufficient to disprove it.

Step 4: (C) accurately describes Laura's necessity-versus-sufficiency error and is correct.

Wrong answers: (A) This choice misstates Laura's error; her evidence is insufficient to disprove Joseph's claim, but it does not strengthen his claim. (B) Outside the Scope. Neither Joseph nor Laura is attacking Fermat's character; the argument allows that he may have been lying or merely mistaken about his purported proof. (D) Laura used "proved" in line with its everyday definition and in the same way Joseph uses it in his argument. (E) There is a lot of proving and disproving going on in this pair of arguments, but both speakers are clear and consistent about Fermat's claim that he proved the theorem before his death; they just disagree about whether it was true.

Hint: Don't let subtle differences in the language of the conclusion and evidence hide huge shifts in their meanings.

Step 2:	Step 1:

27. Only a very small percentage of people from the service professions ever become board members of the 600 largest North American corporations. This shows that people from the service professions are underrepresented in the most important corporate boardrooms in North America.

Which one of the following points out a flaw committed in the argument?

(A) Six hundred is too small a sample on which to base so sweeping a conclusion about the representation of people from the service professions.

(B) The percentage of people from the service professions who serve on the boards of the 600 largest North American corporations reveals little about the percentage of the members of these boards who are from the service professions.

(C) It is a mistake to take the 600 largest North American corporations to be typical of corporate boardrooms generally.

(D) It is irrelevant to smaller corporations whether the largest corporations in North America would agree to have significant numbers of workers from the service professions on the boards of the largest corporations.

(E) The presence of people from the service professions on a corporate board does not necessarily imply that that corporation will be more socially responsible than it has been in the past.

PrepTest111 Sec3 Q17

Step 3:	Step 4:

Expert Analysis

Here's how an LSAT expert approached the question you just completed.

Step 2: *Conclusion*: People from service professions are underrepresented in top corporate boardrooms *because* *Evidence*: Only a small percentage of people from service professions ever become board members of the 600 top corporations.	**Step 1:** A clear Flaw question stem; the correct answer will describe the author's error in reasoning.

27. Only a very small percentage of people from the service professions ever become board members of the 600 largest North American corporations. This shows that people from the service professions are underrepresented in the most important corporate boardrooms in North America.

Which one of the following points out a flaw committed in the argument?

(A) Six hundred is too small a sample on which to base so sweeping a conclusion about the representation of people from the service professions.

(B) The percentage of people from the service professions who serve on the boards of the 600 largest North American corporations reveals little about the percentage of the members of these boards who are from the service professions.

(C) It is a mistake to take the 600 largest North American corporations to be typical of corporate boardrooms generally.

(D) It is irrelevant to smaller corporations whether the largest corporations in North America would agree to have significant numbers of workers from the service professions on the boards of the largest corporations.

(E) The presence of people from the service professions on a corporate board does not necessarily imply that that corporation will be more socially responsible than it has been in the past.

PrepTest111 Sec3 Q17

Step 3: There is a huge mismatch between the evidence (only a small percentage of those in the service professions will sit on the boards of large corporations) and the conclusion (the service professions are poorly represented on those boards). Even if every one of those 600 boards had two or ten or twenty people from the service professions (which might be good representation on the boards), the total would be a few thousand at most, a very small percentage of the millions of people who work in the service professions.

Step 4: (B) explains why the shift in scope between evidence and conclusion is so damaging to the conclusion of this argument. Evidence and conclusion here are measuring two different things.

Wrong answers: (A) The conclusion is limited to "the most important" corporations; if anything, 600 seems generous. (C) The argument does not reach a conclusion about corporations generally. (D) Smaller corporations are Outside the Scope of this argument. (E) Outside the Scope. The argument makes no claims about how the presence of those from service professions influence boards to behave.

Hint: Scientific and medical subject matter can make a stimulus sound complicated, but the underlying flaw may be a simple reasoning error.

Step 2:	Step 1:

28. On the basis of the available evidence, Antarctica has generally been thought to have been covered by ice for at least the past 14 million years. Recently, however, three-million-year-old fossils of a kind previously found only in ocean-floor sediments were discovered under the ice sheet covering central Antarctica. About three million years ago, therefore, the Antarctic ice sheet must temporarily have melted. After all, either severe climatic warming or volcanic activity in Antarctica's mountains could have melted the ice sheet, thus raising sea levels and submerging the continent.

The reasoning in the argument is most vulnerable to which one of the following criticisms?

(A) That a given position is widely believed to be true is taken to show that the position in question must, in fact, be true.

(B) That either of two things could independently have produced a given effect is taken to show that those two things could not have operated in conjunction to produce that effect.

(C) Establishing that a certain event occurred is confused with having established the cause of that event.

(D) A claim that has a very general application is based entirely on evidence from a narrowly restricted range of cases.

(E) An inconsistency that, as presented, has more than one possible resolution is treated as though only one resolution is possible.

PrepTest111 Sec1 Q17

Step 3:	Step 4:

Expert Analysis

Here's how an LSAT expert approached the question you just completed.

Step 2: *Conclusion*: Around three million years ago, the Antarctic ice sheet melted temporarily *because* *Evidence*: Three-million-year-old fossils, previously found only on the ocean floor, were found under the ice sheet (thought to have been solid for 14 million years), and there are ways that it could have melted (like climate change and volcanoes).	**Step 1:** "[V]ulnerable to" signals a Flaw question; the correct answer will describe the argument's faulty logic.

28. On the basis of the available evidence, Antarctica has generally been thought to have been covered by ice for at least the past 14 million years. Recently, however, three-million-year-old fossils of a kind previously found only in ocean-floor sediments were discovered under the ice sheet covering central Antarctica. About three million years ago, therefore, the Antarctic ice sheet must temporarily have melted. After all, either severe climatic warming or volcanic activity in Antarctica's mountains could have melted the ice sheet, thus raising sea levels and submerging the continent.

The reasoning in the argument is most vulnerable to which one of the following criticisms?

(A) That a given position is widely believed to be true is taken to show that the position in question must, in fact, be true.

(B) That either of two things could independently have produced a given effect is taken to show that those two things could not have operated in conjunction to produce that effect.

(C) Establishing that a certain event occurred is confused with having established the cause of that event.

(D) A claim that has a very general application is based entirely on evidence from a narrowly restricted range of cases.

(E) An inconsistency that, as presented, has more than one possible resolution is treated as though only one resolution is possible.

PrepTest111 Sec1 Q17

Step 3: This is an argument that concludes something happened one way because it could have happened that way, but without ruling out any of the other ways it could have happened. Notice, for example, that the evidence says the fossils had only been found in ocean sediments, but doesn't rule out that they had washed there from the land. Alternatively, maybe the fossils under the ice sheet were animals that fell down a deep crevasse. Don't waste time trying to think of more, just find the choice that says the author has overlooked one or more alternatives to ice-melt.

Step 4: (E) gets at the heart of this argument's possible-versus-certain flaw and is correct.

Wrong answers: (A) Here, the author opposes the widely held view that the ice sheet has been frozen for 14 million years straight. (B) The author doesn't rule out climatic warming and volcanic activity acting together. (C) The author concludes that the melting happened, but only speculates about its cause. (D) The problem with the author's conclusion isn't the narrow range of cases; it is that the cases allow for so many other conclusions.

Hint: When you can see that an author is making an unsupported assumption about something or someone, you don't have to know what the truth is (and, indeed, in a fictional scenario, you can't) to know that the argument's reasoning is flawed.

Step 2:	Step 1:

29. Although it has been suggested that Arton's plays have a strong patriotic flavor, we must recall that, at the time of their composition, her country was in anything but a patriotic mood. Unemployment was high, food was costly, and crime rates were soaring. As a result, the general morale of her nation was at an especially low point. Realizing this, we see clearly that any apparent patriotism in Arton's work must have been intended ironically.

The reasoning above is questionable because it

(A) posits an unstated relationship between unemployment and crime

(B) takes for granted that straightforward patriotism is not possible for a serious writer

(C) takes for granted that Arton was attuned to the predominant national attitude of her time

(D) overlooks the fact that some citizens prosper in times of high unemployment

(E) confuses irony with a general decline in public morale

PrepTest112 Sec1 Q19

Step 3:	Step 4:

Expert Analysis

Here's how an LSAT expert approached the question you just completed.

Step 2: *Conclusion*: "Patriotism" in Arton's plays must have been ironic *because* *Evidence*: At the time Arton wrote her plays, her country's morale was very low because of unemployment, costly food, and high crime.	**Step 1:** This is a Flaw question; the correct answer will describe the author's error in reasoning.

29.   Although it has been suggested that Arton's plays have a strong patriotic flavor, we must recall that, at the time of their composition, her country was in anything but a patriotic mood. Unemployment was high, food was costly, and crime rates were soaring. As a result, the general morale of her nation was at an especially low point. Realizing this, we see clearly that any apparent patriotism in Arton's work must have been intended ironically.

The reasoning above is questionable because it

(A) posits an unstated relationship between unemployment and crime

(B) takes for granted that straightforward patriotism is not possible for a serious writer

(C) takes for granted that Arton was attuned to the predominant national attitude of her time

(D) overlooks the fact that some citizens prosper in times of high unemployment

(E) confuses irony with a general decline in public morale

PrepTest112 Sec1 Q19

Step 3: The author concludes that Arton could not have intended her plays to be sincerely patriotic at a time when her country was suffering and "in anything but a patriotic mood." So, the author assumes that Arton was writing in a way that matched that mood, but does not provide any evidence to back that up. Maybe she thought the country needed a change of mood or a boost of pride, or maybe she just didn't go along with the prevailing attitudes. Without evidence, we can't "clearly see" her intentions.	**Step 4:** (C) points out the author simply assumes Arton was trying to write in a way that matched the popular mood, but without providing any support for that position.

Wrong answers: (A) The author states that both unemployment and crime were happening at the same time in Arton's country, but does not posit any further relationship. (B) The author thinks straightforward patriotism is unlikely in Arton's play because of the poor state of her nation, not because she is serious. (D) This is a real reach. Are we to think "maybe Arton was prospering"? Even so, would she have written patriotic plays for a downcast population? It's all just speculation unrelated to the argument's flaw. (E) Perhaps the author thinks that ironic patriotism plays better at a time of low public morale, but there is no indication that the author confuses the two concepts.

Hint: The question stem reminds you to focus on the argument's assumption.

Step 2:	Step 1:

30. Birds need so much food energy to maintain their body temperatures that some of them spend most of their time eating. But a comparison of a bird of a seed-eating species to a bird of a nectar-eating species that has the same overall energy requirement would surely show that the seed-eating bird spends more time eating than does the nectar-eating bird, since a given amount of nectar provides more energy than does the same amount of seeds.

The argument relies on which one of the following questionable assumptions?

(A) Birds of different species do not generally have the same overall energy requirements as each other.

(B) The nectar-eating bird does not sometimes also eat seeds.

(C) The time it takes for the nectar-eating bird to eat a given amount of nectar is not longer than the time it takes the seed-eating bird to eat the same amount of seeds.

(D) The seed-eating bird does not have a lower body temperature than that of the nectar-eating bird.

(E) The overall energy requirements of a given bird do not depend on factors such as the size of the bird, its nest-building habits, and the climate of the region in which it lives.

PrepTest112 Sec4 Q19

Step 3:	Step 4:

Expert Analysis

Here's how an LSAT expert approached the question you just completed.

Step 2: *Conclusion*: Between birds with equal energy requirements, seed-eaters spend more time eating than nectar-eaters *because* *Evidence*: A given amount of seeds provides less energy than the same amount of nectar.	**Step 1:** This is a Flaw question, but the correct answer will state the author's "questionable assumption" rather than giving an abstract description of the reasoning error.

30. Birds need so much food energy to maintain their body temperatures that some of them spend most of their time eating. But a comparison of a bird of a seed-eating species to a bird of a nectar-eating species that has the same overall energy requirement would surely show that the seed-eating bird spends more time eating than does the nectar-eating bird, since a given amount of nectar provides more energy than does the same amount of seeds.

The argument relies on which one of the following questionable assumptions?

(A) Birds of different species do not generally have the same overall energy requirements as each other.

(B) The nectar-eating bird does not sometimes also eat seeds.

(C) The time it takes for the nectar-eating bird to eat a given amount of nectar is not longer than the time it takes the seed-eating bird to eat the same amount of seeds.

(D) The seed-eating bird does not have a lower body temperature than that of the nectar-eating bird.

(E) The overall energy requirements of a given bird do not depend on factors such as the size of the bird, its nest-building habits, and the climate of the region in which it lives.

PrepTest112 Sec4 Q19

Step 3: The author draws a conclusion about time spent eating from evidence about the amount eaten, so the assumption is that it takes the same amount of time to eat equal portions of seeds and nectar. There is no evidence to suggest that's the case, and if it isn't true, this argument falls apart.	**Step 4:** (C) accurately states the author's unsupported assumption.

Wrong answers: (A) is an Irrelevant Comparison; the author explicitly qualifies the conclusion as being limited to birds with "the same overall energy requirement[s]." (B) distorts the argument which is comparing seed-eaters to nectar-eaters and does not address species who might eat both. (D) is an Irrelevant Comparison; presumably, lower body temperature would mean lower energy requirements, however the author restricts the argument to birds with comparable energy needs. (E) Outside the Scope; the factors that contribute to the birds' energy requirements are irrelevant to the speed at which they consume nutrients.

Hint: This is a very challenging question, with dense language in the stimulus and answer choices. The flaw, however, is quite common.

Step 2:	Step 1:

31. Some statisticians claim that the surest way to increase the overall correctness of the total set of one's beliefs is: never change that set, except by rejecting a belief when given adequate evidence against it. However, if this were the only rule one followed, then whenever one were presented with any kind of evidence, one would have to either reject some of one's beliefs or else leave one's beliefs unchanged. But then, over time, one could only have fewer and fewer beliefs. Since we need many beliefs in order to survive, the statisticians' claim must be mistaken.

The argument is most vulnerable to criticism on the grounds that it

(A) presumes, without providing any justification, that the surest way of increasing the overall correctness of the total set of one's beliefs must not hinder one's ability to survive

(B) neglects the possibility that even while following the statisticians' rule, one might also accept new beliefs when presented with some kinds of evidence

(C) overlooks the possibility that some large sets of beliefs are more correct overall than are some small sets of beliefs

(D) takes for granted that one should accept some beliefs related to survival even when given adequate evidence against them

(E) takes for granted that the beliefs we need in order to have many beliefs must all be correct beliefs

PrepTest111 Sec1 Q23

Step 3:	Step 4:

Expert Analysis

Here's how an LSAT expert approached the question you just completed.

Step 2: *Conclusion:* The statisticians' claim* is wrong *because* *Evidence:* (1) The statisticians' claim would leave us with fewer and fewer beliefs, and (2) we need many beliefs to survive. *The best way to ensure your beliefs are correct: never change beliefs except to discard disproven ones.	**Step 1:** "[V]ulnerable to criticism . . ." signals a Flaw question; the correct answer describes the argument's faulty logic.

31. Some statisticians claim that the surest way to increase the overall correctness of the total set of one's beliefs is: never change that set, except by rejecting a belief when given adequate evidence against it. However, if this were the only rule one followed, then whenever one were presented with any kind of evidence, one would have to either reject some of one's beliefs or else leave one's beliefs unchanged. But then, over time, one could only have fewer and fewer beliefs. Since we need many beliefs in order to survive, the statisticians' claim must be mistaken.

The argument is most vulnerable to criticism on the grounds that it

(A) presumes, without providing any justification, that the surest way of increasing the overall correctness of the total set of one's beliefs must not hinder one's ability to survive

(B) neglects the possibility that even while following the statisticians' rule, one might also accept new beliefs when presented with some kinds of evidence

(C) overlooks the possibility that some large sets of beliefs are more correct overall than are some small sets of beliefs

(D) takes for granted that one should accept some beliefs related to survival even when given adequate evidence against them

(E) takes for granted that the beliefs we need in order to have many beliefs must all be correct beliefs

PrepTest111 Sec1 Q23

Step 3: First, remember that your task is to describe the author's reasoning error, so stay focused on the argument. The conclusion is that the statisticians are wrong. Why? Because their claim isn't workable. But does that matter? If one claims that the best way to prevent all car accidents is to have no cars, that's right, even if it will never happen because we need vehicles to survive. You're mistaken to say that claim is wrong.

Step 4: (A) exposes the flaw in the argument: It attempts a practical critique of an abstract claim. The statisticians don't argue that people should (or even *could*) actually follow their plan, just that it is the best way to ensure the overall correctness of one's belief set.

Wrong answers: (B) 180. The author does not neglect this; indeed, the foundation of the argument is that one cannot add new beliefs while following the statistician's rule and that is why we'll inevitably have fewer and fewer. (C) Irrelevant comparison. The author's objection is based on the belief that a large number of beliefs is necessary for survival, and not on a comparison of overall correctness percentages. (D) This may be the author's belief, but it is not a flaw in the argument, which says that the problem with the statistician's claim is that it will lead to having too few beliefs. (E) distorts the author's point, which is not that we would be left with too few correct beliefs, but rather too few beliefs, period.

Hint: Keep your eyes open for references to causation, even if the argument doesn't use the word "cause."

Step 2:	Step 1:

32. Physician: Heart disease generally affects men at an earlier age than it does women, who tend to experience heart disease after menopause. Both sexes have the hormones estrogen and testosterone, but when they are relatively young, men have ten times as much testosterone as women, and women abruptly lose estrogen after menopause. We can conclude, then, that testosterone tends to promote, and estrogen tends to inhibit, heart disease.

The physician's argument is questionable because it presumes which one of the following without providing sufficient justification?

(A) Hormones are the primary factors that account for the differences in age-related heart disease risks between women and men.

(B) Estrogen and testosterone are the only hormones that promote or inhibit heart disease.

(C) Men with high testosterone levels have a greater risk for heart disease than do postmenopausal women.

(D) Because hormone levels are correlated with heart disease they influence heart disease.

(E) Hormone levels do not vary from person to person, especially among those of the same age and gender.

PrepTest111 Sec3 Q25

Step 3:	Step 4:

Expert Analysis

Here's how an LSAT expert approached the question you just completed.

Step 2: *Conclusion*: Testosterone promotes heart disease; estrogen prevents heart disease *because* *Evidence*: (1) On average, men experience heart disease earlier than women, who tend to get it after menopause. (2) Young men have 10x the testosterone of women, and (3) women lose estrogen after menopause.	**Step 1:** This Flaw question stem tells you that the correct answer will paraphrase the author's unwarranted assumption.

32. Physician: Heart disease generally affects men at an earlier age than it does women, who tend to experience heart disease after menopause. Both sexes have the hormones estrogen and testosterone, but when they are relatively young, men have ten times as much testosterone as women, and women abruptly lose estrogen after menopause. We can conclude, then, that testosterone tends to promote, and estrogen tends to inhibit, heart disease.

The physician's argument is questionable because it presumes which one of the following without providing sufficient justification?

(A) Hormones are the primary factors that account for the differences in age-related heart disease risks between women and men.

(B) Estrogen and testosterone are the only hormones that promote or inhibit heart disease.

(C) Men with high testosterone levels have a greater risk for heart disease than do postmenopausal women.

(D) Because hormone levels are correlated with heart disease they influence heart disease.

(E) Hormone levels do not vary from person to person, especially among those of the same age and gender.

PrepTest111 Sec3 Q25

Step 3: This is a classic correlation-versus-causation error. The evidence demonstrates a rough correlation among heart disease and the two hormones, while the conclusion claims the hormones respectively "promote" and "inhibit" heart disease.	**Step 4:** (D) accurately states the author's causation-versus-correlation error and is correct.

Wrong answers: (A) Distortion. The author does not claim that the hormones are the "primary factors." (B) Distortion. The author does claim that these hormones are *exclusively* responsible. (C) Irrelevant Comparison. The author doesn't get into relative risk between the younger male and older female groups. (E) Extreme. The author doesn't make any such strong claims about differences among individuals.

Congratulations on working through the important Flaw question type! You'll see examples of many of the common LSAT flaws in the Perform quiz that follows.

Chapter Perform Quiz

Perform   This Perform quiz has 12 Flaw questions. They are presented without any notes, hints, or prompts for a more test-like experience while you work. Try to get as many correct answers as possible in 9 minutes. When you finish, check your performance against the Answer Key and Evaluate Your Performance for tips on how best to improve. Then, come back to complete any questions you skipped or guessed on and finish up by reviewing all the questions with the expert analyses in your online companion.

33. Restaurant manager: In response to requests from our patrons for vegetarian main dishes, we recently introduced three: an eggplant and zucchini casserole with tomatoes, brown rice with mushrooms, and potatoes baked with cheese. The first two are frequently ordered, but no one orders the potato dish, although it costs less than the other two. Clearly, then, our patrons prefer not to eat potatoes.

Which one of the following is an error of reasoning in the restaurant manager's argument?

(A) concluding that two things that occur at the same time have a common cause

(B) drawing a conclusion that is inconsistent with one premise of the argument

(C) ignoring possible differences between what people say they want and what they actually choose

(D) attempting to prove a claim on the basis of evidence that a number of people hold that claim to be true

(E) treating one of several plausible explanations of a phenomenon as the only possible explanation

PrepTest110 Sec2 Q3

34. Commissioner: Budget forecasters project a revenue shortfall of a billion dollars in the coming fiscal year. Since there is no feasible way to increase the available funds, our only choice is to decrease expenditures. The plan before you outlines feasible cuts that would yield savings of a billion dollars over the coming fiscal year. We will be able to solve the problem we face, therefore, only if we adopt this plan.

The reasoning in the commissioner's argument is flawed because this argument

(A) relies on information that is far from certain

(B) confuses being an adequate solution with being a required solution

(C) inappropriately relies on the opinions of experts

(D) inappropriately employs language that is vague

(E) takes for granted that there is no way to increase available funds

PrepTest112 Sec4 Q6

35. Proponent: Irradiation of food by gamma rays would keep it from spoiling before it reaches the consumer in food stores. The process leaves no radiation behind, and vitamin losses are comparable to those that occur in cooking, so there is no reason to reject irradiation on the grounds of nutrition or safety. Indeed, it kills harmful Salmonella bacteria, which in contaminated poultry have caused serious illness to consumers.

    Opponent: The irradiation process has no effect on the bacteria that cause botulism, a very serious form of food poisoning, while those that cause bad odors that would warn consumers of botulism are killed. Moreover, Salmonella and the bacteria that cause botulism can easily be killed in poultry by using a safe chemical dip.

Which one of the following could the opponent properly cite as indicating a flaw in the proponent's reasoning concerning vitamin losses?

(A) After irradiation, food might still spoil if kept in storage for a long time after being purchased by the consumer.

(B) Irradiated food would still need cooking, or, if eaten raw, it would not have the vitamin advantage of raw food.

(C) Vitamin loss is a separate issue from safety.

(D) Vitamins can be ingested in pill form as well as in foods.

(E) That food does not spoil before it can be offered to the consumer is primarily a benefit to the seller, not to the consumer.

PrepTest111 Sec1 Q6

36. It is widely believed that by age 80, perception and memory are each significantly reduced from their functioning levels at age 30. However, a recent study showed no difference in the abilities of 80-year-olds and 30-year-olds to play a card game devised to test perception and memory. Therefore, the belief that perception and memory are significantly reduced by age 80 is false.

The reasoning above is most vulnerable to criticism on the grounds that it fails to consider the possibility that

(A) the study's card game does not test cognitive abilities other than perception and memory

(B) card games are among the most difficult cognitive tasks one can attempt to perform

(C) perception and memory are interrelated in ways of which we are not currently aware

(D) the belief that 80-year-olds' perception and memory are reduced results from prejudice against senior citizens

(E) playing the study's card game perfectly requires fairly low levels of perception and memory

PrepTest111 Sec4 Q8

37. A university study reported that between 1975 and 1983 the length of the average workweek in a certain country increased significantly. A governmental study, on the other hand, shows a significant decline in the length of the average workweek for the same period. Examination of the studies shows, however, that they used different methods of investigation; thus there is no need to look further for an explanation of the difference in the studies' results.

The argument's reasoning is flawed because the argument fails to

(A) distinguish between a study produced for the purposes of the operation of government and a study produced as part of university research

(B) distinguish between a method of investigation and the purpose of an investigation

(C) recognize that only one of the studies has been properly conducted

(D) recognize that two different methods of investigation can yield identical results

(E) recognize that varying economic conditions result in the average workweek changing in length

PrepTest110 Sec2 Q9

38. Some psychologists claim that, in theory, the best way to understand another person would be through deep empathy, whereby one would gain a direct and complete grasp of that person's motivations. But suppose they are right; then there would be no way at all to achieve understanding, since it is psychologically impossible to gain a direct and complete grasp of another person's motivations. But obviously one can understand other people; thus these psychologists are wrong.

The argument is most vulnerable to the criticism that it

(A) fails to adequately define the key phrase "deep empathy"

(B) assumes something that it later denies, resulting in a contradiction

(C) confuses a theoretically best way of accomplishing something with the only way of accomplishing it

(D) accepts a claim on mere authority, without requiring sufficient justification

(E) fails to consider that other psychologists may disagree with the psychologists cited

PrepTest110 Sec2 Q11

39. The consumer price index is a measure that detects monthly changes in the retail prices of goods and services. The payment of some government retirement benefits is based on the consumer price index so that those benefits reflect the change in the cost of living as the index changes. However, the consumer price index does not consider technological innovations that may drastically reduce the cost of producing some goods. Therefore, the value of government benefits is sometimes greater than is warranted by the true change in costs.

The reasoning in the argument is most vulnerable to the criticism that the argument

(A) fails to consider the possibility that there are years in which there is no change in the consumer price index

(B) fails to make explicit which goods and services are included in the consumer price index

(C) presumes, without providing warrant, that retirement benefits are not generally used to purchase unusual goods

(D) uncritically draws an inference from what has been true in the past to what will be true in the future

(E) makes an irrelevant shift from discussing retail prices to discussing production costs

PrepTest112 Sec1 Q12

40. President of the Regional Chamber of Commerce: We are all aware of the painful fact that almost no new businesses have moved into our region or started up here over the last ten years. But the Planning Board is obviously guilty of a gross exaggeration in its recent estimate that businesses are leaving the region at the rate of about four a week. After all, there were never more than about one thousand businesses in the region, so if they were really leaving at such a rate, they would all have been gone long ago.

The argument is most vulnerable to criticism on the ground that it

(A) focuses on what is going out of a system while ignoring the issue of what is coming into the system

(B) confuses a claim about a rate of change within a system with a claim about the absolute size of the system

(C) argues against a position simply by showing that the position serves the interest of the Planning Board

(D) treats a claim about what is currently the case as if it were a claim about what has been the case for an extended period

(E) attacks what was offered as an estimate on the ground that it is not precise

PrepTest111 Sec3 Q13

41. Mayor: The law prohibiting pedestrians from crossing against red lights serves no useful purpose. After all, in order to serve a useful purpose, a law must deter the kind of behavior it prohibits. But pedestrians who invariably violate this law are clearly not dissuaded by it; and those who comply with the law do not need it, since they would never cross against red lights even if there were no law prohibiting pedestrians from crossing against red lights.

The mayor's argument is flawed because it

(A) takes for granted that most automobile drivers will obey the law that prohibits them from driving through red lights

(B) uses the word "law" in one sense in the premises and in another sense in the conclusion

(C) ignores the possibility that a law might not serve a useful purpose even if it does deter the kind of behavior it prohibits

(D) fails to consider whether the law ever dissuades people who sometimes but not always cross against red lights

(E) provides no evidence that crossing against red lights is more dangerous than crossing on green lights

PrepTest111 Sec4 Q13

42. Philosopher: Scientists talk about the pursuit of truth, but, like most people, they are self-interested. Accordingly, the professional activities of most scientists are directed toward personal career enhancement, and only incidentally toward the pursuit of truth. Hence, the activities of the scientific community are largely directed toward enhancing the status of that community as a whole, and only incidentally toward the pursuit of truth.

The reasoning in the philosopher's argument is flawed because the argument

(A) improperly infers that each and every scientist has a certain characteristic from the premise that most scientists have that characteristic

(B) improperly draws an inference about the scientific community as a whole from a premise about individual scientists

(C) presumes, without giving justification, that the aim of personal career enhancement never advances the pursuit of truth

(D) illicitly takes advantage of an ambiguity in the meaning of "self-interested"

(E) improperly draws an inference about a cause from premises about its effects

PrepTest111 Sec4 Q18

43. A recent study of 6,403 people showed that those treated with the drug pravastatin, one of the effects of which is to reduce cholesterol, had about one-third fewer nonfatal heart attacks and one-third fewer deaths from coronary disease than did those not taking the drug. This result is consistent with other studies, which show that those who have heart disease often have higher than average cholesterol levels. This shows that lowering cholesterol levels reduces the risk of heart disease.

The argument's reasoning is flawed because the argument

(A) neglects the possibility that pravastatin may have severe side effects

(B) fails to consider that pravastatin may reduce the risk of heart disease but not as a consequence of its lowering cholesterol levels

(C) relies on past findings, rather than drawing its principal conclusion from the data found in the specific study cited

(D) draws a conclusion regarding the effects of lowering cholesterol levels on heart disease, when in fact the conclusion should focus on the relation between pravastatin and cholesterol levels

(E) fails to consider what percentage of the general population might be taking pravastatin

PrepTest111 Sec4 Q24

44. People ought to take into account a discipline's blemished origins when assessing the scientific value of that discipline. Take, for example, chemistry. It must be considered that many of its landmark results were obtained by alchemists—a group whose superstitions and appeals to magic dominated the early development of chemical theory.

The reasoning above is most susceptible to criticism because the author

(A) fails to establish that disciplines with unblemished origins are scientifically valuable

(B) fails to consider how chemistry's current theories and practices differ from those of the alchemists mentioned

(C) uses an example to contradict the principle under consideration

(D) does not prove that most disciplines that are not scientifically valuable have origins that are in some way suspect

(E) uses the word "discipline" in two different senses

PrepTest111 Sec3 Q26

Answer Key

33. E; 34. B; 35. B; 36. E; 37. D; 38. C; 39. E; 40. D; 41. D; 42. B; 43. B; 44. B

Evaluate Your Performance

To assess your strengths and opportunities from this Perform quiz, go to the corresponding chapter in your online companion. There you'll find recommendations based on your performance along with complete worked-example explanations (written by a Kaplan LSAT expert) for each of the questions in this Perform quiz.

CHAPTER 11

Strengthen/Weaken Questions

Strengthen/Weaken Question Basics

The third major Assumption Family question type is Strengthen/Weaken questions. These are very practical questions. Indeed, they are the kinds of questions lawyers might ask because the correct answer provides a piece of *evidence* that would help convince someone that an argument is more or less likely to be true. That's exactly what lawyers hope the evidence they introduce in court will do.

Prepare

LEARNING OBJECTIVE

In this section, you'll learn to:

- Identify and answer Strengthen/Weaken questions.

Expect to see around ten Strengthen/Weaken questions on a given LSAT administration. That's worth around 12% of your LSAT score, making these the single most common Logical Reasoning question type. Practice Strengthen/Weaken questions throughout your LSAT prep.

You can identify Strengthen/Weaken questions from question stems such as these:

Which one of the following, if true, most strengthens the argument?

PrepTest112 Sec4 Q20

Which one of the following, if added as a premise to the argument, most helps to justify its conclusion?

PrepTest112 Sec4 Q15

Which one of the following statements, if true, most weakens the critic's argument?

PrepTest110 Sec3 Q20

Which one of the following, if true, most undermines the journal's argument?

PrepTest111 Sec1 Q13

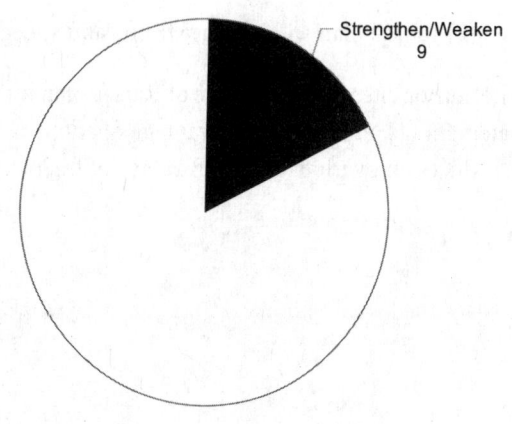

Approximate Number of Strengthen/Weaken Questions per LSAT

Strengthen/Weaken
9

Source: All officially released LSAT exams, 2016-2020

K 385

> **STRENGTHEN/WEAKEN QUESTIONS AT A GLANCE**
>
> **Task:** Provide a fact that would make the conclusion more (Strengthen) or less (Weaken) likely to follow from the evidence.
>
> **Strategy:** Analyze the argument, determine the author's assumption, and then choose the answer containing a fact that supports or undermines the author's reasoning.
>
> **Frequency:** LSAT tests released from 2016 through 2020 had an average of 4.4 Strengthen/Weaken questions per section. During this same period, the numbers of Strengthen and Weaken questions were evenly balanced. Both subtypes accounted for 46 percent of the questions in this category, while Evaluate questions accounted for only 8 percent (well under one per section, on average).

First and foremost, when approaching Strengthen/Weaken questions, remember that they are Assumption Family questions. Untangle the stimulus by analyzing the argument; identify and paraphrase the conclusion and evidence, and anticipate arguments in the familiar patterns you've seen already in Assumption and Flaw questions. After identifying the argument's assumption, ask yourself what kinds of facts would make the assumption more or less likely to be true. As you evaluate the answer choices, keep in mind that strengtheners do not have to prove the conclusion, but just make it more likely to be correct. Likewise, weakeners don't have to disprove the argument, but just make the conclusion less likely to follow from the evidence provided.

Strengthening or Weakening Overlooked Possibilities

Overlooked Possibilities arguments are more common than Mismatched Concepts in Strengthen/Weaken questions (and especially so in Weaken questions). The characteristically overbroad conclusions in Overlooked Possibilities arguments lend themselves easily to Strengthen/Weaken questions. Consider the following argument:

> The health of the city's economy is threatened by traffic congestion in the city's financial district. Rafiq's infrastructure plan will have traffic flowing smoothly again in and around the financial district. Therefore, the city should adopt Rafiq's plan.

Here are two facts. Which strengthens and which weakens the argument?

> (1) Rafiq's plan will not divert funds from any of the city's health and welfare programs.
>
> (2) Rafiq's plan will increase traffic and speed limits near schools and residential areas.

[The author cites one advantage of Rafiq's plan and recommends on that basis that the city adopt the plan. Statement (1) adds another advantage of adopting the plan and, thus, strengthens the argument. Statement (2) introduces an overlooked disadvantage of the plan, thereby weakening the argument.]

Strengthening or Weakening Mismatched Concepts

Mismatched Concepts are less common than Overlooked Possibilities (again, especially in Weaken questions). When you do encounter a Mismatched Concepts argument here, look for the fact that supports or undermines the assumed connection. Consider the following argument:

The team captain's primary goal is to enhance team morale and enthusiasm. Thus, one of the captain's responsibilities is the continual development and training of less skilled players.

Here are two facts. Which strengthens and which weakens the argument?

(1) The ability and performance of all players affects a team's morale and enthusiasm.

(2) A team's morale and enthusiasm typically follow from the example set by the team's most skilled players.

[In this argument, the author concludes that a team captain should be *responsible for the development* of less skilled players because a team captain's *goal is morale and enthusiasm*. Statement (1) strengthens the argument by bridging the evidence and conclusion. Statement (2) weakens the argument by asserting that morale and enthusiasm spring from the example of the best players, not improving the weaker ones.]

Now, try a Weaken question on your own to get familiar with this question type. When you're finished, compare your work to that of the LSAT expert in the worked example on the next page.

Step 2:	Step 1:

1. High school students who feel that they are not succeeding in school often drop out before graduating and go to work. Last year, however, the city's high school dropout rate was significantly lower than the previous year's rate. This is encouraging evidence that the program instituted two years ago to improve the morale of high school students has begun to take effect to reduce dropouts.

Which one of the following, if true about the last year, most seriously weakens the argument?

(A) There was a recession that caused a high level of unemployment in the city.

(B) The morale of students who dropped out of high school had been low even before they reached high school.

(C) As in the preceding year, more high school students remained in school than dropped out.

(D) High schools in the city established placement offices to assist their graduates in obtaining employment.

(E) The antidropout program was primarily aimed at improving students' morale in those high schools with the highest dropout rates.

PrepTest112 Sec4 Q11

Step 3:	Step 4:

Expert Analysis

Here's an example of an LSAT expert's work on the question you just saw.

Step 2: *Conclusion*: The high school dropout reduction program is working *because* *Evidence*: The dropout rate (students leaving high school to go to work) was significantly lower last year.	**Step 1:** A standard Weaken question stem: the correct answer will make the conclusion less likely to follow from the evidence.

1. High school students who feel that they are not succeeding in school often drop out before graduating and go to work. Last year, however, the city's high school dropout rate was significantly lower than the previous year's rate. This is encouraging evidence that the program instituted two years ago to improve the morale of high school students has begun to take effect to reduce dropouts.

    Which one of the following, if true about the last year, most seriously weakens the argument?

    (A) There was a recession that caused a high level of unemployment in the city.

    (B) The morale of students who dropped out of high school had been low even before they reached high school.

    (C) As in the preceding year, more high school students remained in school than dropped out.

    (D) High schools in the city established placement offices to assist their graduates in obtaining employment.

    (E) The antidropout program was primarily aimed at improving students' morale in those high schools with the highest dropout rates.

    PrepTest112 Sec4 Q11

Step 3: This is an archetypal Overlooked Possibilities argument. The author concludes that a possible cause (the dropout-reduction program) is *the* cause. The evidence is that the effect the program was intended to have is occurring. To weaken the argument, find an answer that gives a different reason (something other than the program) why this effect may be happening.	**Step 4:** (A) weakens the argument by providing a different reason students may be staying in school. Failing students may be staying in school not because of the program but because they see there are no jobs to go to.

Wrong answers: (B) Outside the Scope. The origin of students' perception of failure is irrelevant to the author's claim that the program is working now. (C) Outside the Scope. The author doesn't claim that a majority of students are or were dropping out, just that the dropout rate has declined. (D) Outside the Scope. We don't have enough information to assess this office's effect on the situation: e.g., Is this for placement after graduation? Does the office help students find part-time jobs they can hold while remaining in school? (E) Irrelevant. The program's methodology is not in question.

Now, try out a Strengthen question as well. Some test takers are initially more comfortable with Weakeners, others with Strengtheners, but everyone who practices and reviews can improve on both. When you're finished here, compare your work to the expert worked example on the next page to see the Kaplan method and strategies in action.

Step 2:	Step 1:

2. Consumer advocate: The introduction of a new drug into the marketplace should be contingent upon our having a good understanding of its social impact. However, the social impact of the newly marketed antihistamine is far from clear. It is obvious, then, that there should be a general reduction in the pace of bringing to the marketplace new drugs that are now being tested.

Which one of the following, if true, most strengthens the argument?

(A) The social impact of the new antihistamine is much better understood than that of most new drugs being tested.

(B) The social impact of some of the new drugs being tested is poorly understood.

(C) The economic success of some drugs is inversely proportional to how well we understand their social impact.

(D) The new antihistamine is chemically similar to some of the new drugs being tested.

(E) The new antihistamine should be on the market only if most new drugs being tested should be on the market also.

PrepTest112 Sec4 Q20

Step 3:	Step 4:

Expert Analysis

Here's an example of an LSAT expert's work on the question you just saw.

Step 2: *Conclusion*: In general, we should slow the pace at which new drugs, now being tested, are brought to market *because*

Evidence: (1) New drugs should not be brought to market before their social impacts are clear, and (2) the social impact of the new antihistamine is not clear.

Step 1: A straightforward Strengthen question: the correct answer is a fact that will make the conclusion more likely to follow from the evidence.

2. Consumer advocate: The introduction of a new drug into the marketplace should be contingent upon our having a good understanding of its social impact. However, the social impact of the newly marketed antihistamine is far from clear. It is obvious, then, that there should be a general reduction in the pace of bringing to the marketplace new drugs that are now being tested.

Which one of the following, if true, most strengthens the argument?

(A) The social impact of the new antihistamine is much better understood than that of most new drugs being tested.

(B) The social impact of some of the new drugs being tested is poorly understood.

(C) The economic success of some drugs is inversely proportional to how well we understand their social impact.

(D) The new antihistamine is chemically similar to some of the new drugs being tested.

(E) The new antihistamine should be on the market only if most new drugs being tested should be on the market also.

PrepTest112 Sec4 Q20

Step 3: The argument draws a conclusion about new drugs in general on the basis of evidence about a particular antihistamine. The author must assume that the other new drugs have potential social impacts comparable to the new antihistamine.

Step 4: (A) does the prediction one better by saying that the potential impacts of the other new drugs are *even less* well understood than those of the new antihistamine. Accepting the author's premise that new drugs should be delayed until their social impacts are known, this choice makes the conclusion's call for a *general* slowdown much stronger.

Wrong answers: (B) doesn't strengthen the conclusion's call for a *general* slowdown even if it would call for a slowdown of *some* drugs that are poorly understood. (C) might be of interest to drug companies looking to cash in, but it doesn't impact the author's reasoning which is based on safety concerns. (D) might support a slowdown on these particular ("chemically similar") drugs, but it doesn't strengthen the author's call for a "general reduction in pace." (E) gets the argument's reasoning backward; the author uses the poorly understood antihistamine as evidence for a general slowdown in approvals, while this choice suggests that approval of a majority of pending drugs would justify putting the antihistamine on the market.

> ## LSAT STRATEGY
>
> Some facts to remember about Strengthen and Weaken questions:
>
> - A correct answer does not have to prove or disprove the conclusion; it just has to make the conclusion more or less likely to follow from the evidence.
> - Overlooked Possibilities is the most common argument type, especially in Weaken questions.
> - To strengthen an argument containing Overlooked Possibilities, choose the answer that rules out a possible objection; to weaken such an argument, look for a fact that introduces an overlooked objection.
> - To strengthen an argument containing Mismatched Concepts, choose the answer that helps to affirm the author's assumption; to weaken such an argument, look for a fact that undermines the assumption.

There are a couple of subtypes you may see for Strengthen/Weaken questions. Both have been rare on recently released tests, and both apply the same analysis and strategies you'll use to make short work of standard Strengthen and Weaken questions. Before heading to full-question practice, take a minute to get introduced to Strengthen/Weaken **except** questions and Evaluate questions.

Less Common Strengthen/Weaken Questions

Strengthen/Weaken EXCEPT Questions

These questions are quite rare. The key to answering these questions is to characterize the one right and four wrong answers before evaluating the choices.

> Each of the following, if true, weakens the
> politician's argument **except:**
>
> *PrepTest111 Sec4 Q17*

> Each of the following, if true, would strengthen
> the statistician's argument **except:**
>
> *PrepTest111 Sec1 Q15*

> ## LSAT STRATEGY
>
> Some facts to remember about Strengthen and Weaken EXCEPT questions:
>
> - Always slow down and characterize the one right and four wrong answer choices.
> - The correct answer in a Strengthen EXCEPT question will either weaken the argument or have no impact.
> - The correct answer in a Weaken EXCEPT question will either strengthen the argument or have no impact.

Evaluate Questions

Occasionally, the LSAT asks a question about a fact's relevance to the argument. Think of these as Strengthen-or-Weaken questions, because the disposition of the correct answer will impact the argument either positively or negatively. All four wrong answers will cite issues *irrelevant* to the argument.

> The answer to which one of the following questions would most help in evaluating the columnist's argument?
>
> *PrepTest112 Sec1 Q24*

LSAT STRATEGY

Some facts to remember about Evaluate questions:

- These questions are similar to Strengthen and Weaken questions.
- Untangle the stimulus; then find the assumption.
- The correct answer will often present a question, any answer to which has a positive or a negative impact on the argument. In other words, the correct answer asks the question you'd want to know the answer to in order to *evaluate* the argument.

Try out a Weaken **except** question on your own. When you're finished, compare your work to that of an LSAT expert in the worked example on the next page.

Step 2:	Step 1:

3. Politician: All nations that place a high tax on income produce thereby a negative incentive for technological innovation, and all nations in which technological innovation is hampered inevitably fall behind in the international arms race. Those nations that, through historical accident or the foolishness of their political leadership, wind up in a strategically disadvantageous position are destined to lose their voice in world affairs. So if a nation wants to maintain its value system and way of life, it must not allow its highest tax bracket to exceed 30 percent of income.

Each of the following, if true, weakens the politician's argument **except:**

(A) The top level of taxation must reach 45 percent before taxation begins to deter inventors and industrialists from introducing new technologies and industries.

(B) Making a great deal of money is an insignificant factor in driving technological innovation.

(C) Falling behind in the international arms race does not necessarily lead to a strategically less advantageous position.

(D) Those nations that lose influence in the world community do not necessarily suffer from a threat to their value system or way of life.

(E) Allowing one's country to lose its technological edge, especially as concerns weaponry, would be foolish rather than merely a historical accident.

PrepTest111 Sec4 Q17

Step 3:	Step 4:

Expert Analysis

Here's an LSAT expert strategic approach to the Weaken **except** question you just tried out.

Step 2: *Conclusion*: If a nation wants to keep values and way of life, it must keep taxes at 30% or less *because* *Evidence*: (1) If high income tax → negative tech innovation incentive, and (2) If negative tech innovation → lag in international arms race. (3) If at a strategic disadvantage → lose voice in world affairs.	**Step 1:** Four answer choices will weaken the argument; the correct choice will either strengthen it or have no impact.

3. Politician: All nations that place a high tax on income produce thereby a negative incentive for technological innovation, and all nations in which technological innovation is hampered inevitably fall behind in the international arms race. Those nations that, through historical accident or the foolishness of their political leadership, wind up in a strategically disadvantageous position are destined to lose their voice in world affairs. So if a nation wants to maintain its value system and way of life, it must not allow its highest tax bracket to exceed 30 percent of income.

Each of the following, if true, weakens the politician's argument **except:**

(A) The top level of taxation must reach 45 percent before taxation begins to deter inventors and industrialists from introducing new technologies and industries.

(B) Making a great deal of money is an insignificant factor in driving technological innovation.

(C) Falling behind in the international arms race does not necessarily lead to a strategically less advantageous position.

(D) Those nations that lose influence in the world community do not necessarily suffer from a threat to their value system or way of life.

(E) Allowing one's country to lose its technological edge, especially as concerns weaponry, would be foolish rather than merely a historical accident.

PrepTest111 Sec4 Q17

Step 3: This argument is a long chain of conditional statements with some gaps along the way. The author must assume that taxes higher than 30% dissuade technological innovation, that lagging in the arms race leads to a strategic disadvantage, *and* that losing its voice in world affairs will cost a nation its values and way of life. The four wrong answers will attack these links in the chain.	**Step 4:** (E) is irrelevant to the argument's chain of logic, and thus, neither weakens nor strengthens the argument. The author sees the same impact on any nation at a strategic disadvantage, whether it was the result of foolishness or accident.

Wrong answers: (A) weakens the argument by rebutting the assumption that any income tax greater than 30% hampers technological innovation. (B) weakens the argument's general presumption that technological innovation requires a profit motive. (C) weakens the argument by undermining the assumption that a country's strategic advantage requires leadership in the arms race. (D) weakens the argument by denying the assumption that a nation must sustain international influence to preserve its values and way of life.

Next up, try out an Evaluate question for good measure.

Here's an Evaluate question for you to complete. This argument might look familiar; you saw it way back at the start of Part III, when you were first learning to identify an argument's assumption. When you're finished, check your work against the expert example on the next page.

Step 2:	Step 1:

4. Columnist: George Orwell's book *1984* has exercised much influence on a great number of this newspaper's readers. One thousand readers were surveyed and asked to name the one book that had the most influence on their lives. The book chosen most often was the Bible; *1984* was second.

The answer to which one of the following questions would most help in evaluating the columnist's argument?

(A) How many books had each person surveyed read?

(B) How many people chose books other than *1984*?

(C) How many people read the columnist's newspaper?

(D) How many books by George Orwell other than *1984* were chosen?

(E) How many of those surveyed had actually read the books they chose?

PrepTest112 Sec1 Q24

Step 3:	Step 4:

Expert Analysis

See how a top scorer approached the Evaluate question you just tried out.

Step 2: *Conclusion*: 1984 (the book) has influenced a great number of this paper's readers *because*

Evidence: 1984 came in second (behind the Bible) in a survey of 1,000 readers who were asked to name the book most influential in their lives.

Step 1: This is an Evaluate question, a variant on Strengthen/Weaken questions in which the correct answer is a question relevant to the argument in the stimulus.

4.   Columnist: George Orwell's book *1984* has exercised much influence on a great number of this newspaper's readers. One thousand readers were surveyed and asked to name the one book that had the most influence on their lives. The book chosen most often was the Bible; *1984* was second.

The answer to which one of the following questions would most help in evaluating the columnist's argument?

(A) How many books had each person surveyed read?

(B) How many people chose books other than *1984*?

(C) How many people read the columnist's newspaper?

(D) How many books by George Orwell other than *1984* were chosen?

(E) How many of those surveyed had actually read the books they chose?

PrepTest112 Sec1 Q24

Step 3: The argument here has a variation on the percent-versus-number flaw, but in this case it's a rank-versus-number flaw. The columnist assumes the second-place finisher must have gotten a large number of votes. That could be true, but what if first place got 950 votes, *1984* in second place got, let's say, four, and the rest were scattered among a couple dozen other books. The relevant question is how many people actually picked *1984*.

Step 4: (B) would give you the information you need; if you know how many people picked books other than *1984*, you can subtract that number from 1,000 to find the number of votes for *1984*. Then, you'd be able to determine if the columnist's conclusion has merit.

Wrong answers: (A) This is irrelevant to the question of how many people chose *1984* as most influential. (C) This question could be relevant to the conclusion, but only in conjunction with the numbers from the survey, and only under the assumption that, for some reason, the survey results might not be representative of the paper's readership. (D) The number of other books chosen will not establish the number of readers who picked 1984; you'd need the sum of the votes those other books got, and that's what the correct answer (B) asks for. (E) This is a thought-provoking question, but one irrelevant to determining the survey numbers.

Congratulations on learning about Strengthen and Weaken questions. This is a very important category for the simple reason that it is so commonly tested. Mastery of these question types can make a huge difference to your LSAT performance, and for that reason, there is a relatively long Practice set in this chapter, and a longer-than-usual Perform quiz at the end, too. Do your best!

Practice Try each of the following Strengthen/Weaken questions. Don't worry too much about your timing here. Complete all four steps of the Logical Reasoning Method for each question, jotting down your notes whenever it is helpful to do so. After each question, review your work with the expert analysis that follows.

Hint: If an author claims that there is *no* difference between two things, ask if they've really ruled out all the possible differences.

Step 2:	Step 1:

5. Nutritionist: Recently a craze has developed for home juicers, $300 machines that separate the pulp of fruits and vegetables from the juice they contain. Outrageous claims are being made about the benefits of these devices: drinking the juice they produce is said to help one lose weight or acquire a clear complexion, to aid digestion, and even to prevent cancer. But there is no indication that juice separated from the pulp of the fruit or vegetable has any properties that it does not have when unseparated. Save your money. If you want carrot juice, eat a carrot.

Which one of the following, if true, most calls into question the nutritionist's argument?

(A) Most people find it much easier to consume a given quantity of nutrients in liquid form than to eat solid foods containing the same quantity of the same nutrients.

(B) Drinking juice from home juicers is less healthy than is eating fruits and vegetables because such juice does not contain the fiber that is eaten if one consumes the entire fruit or vegetable.

(C) To most people who would be tempted to buy a home juicer, $300 would not be a major expense.

(D) The nutritionist was a member of a panel that extensively evaluated early prototypes of home juicers.

(E) Vitamin pills that supposedly contain nutrients available elsewhere only in fruits and vegetables often contain a form of those compounds that cannot be as easily metabolized as the varieties found in fruits and vegetables.

PrepTest112 Sec1 Q2

Step 3:	Step 4:

Expert Analysis

Review an example of an LSAT expert's work on the question you just completed.

Step 2: *Conclusion*: Juicers are a waste of money *because* *Evidence*: Juice has no special health properties you wouldn't get from just eating the fruit or vegetable it comes from.	**Step 1:** "[C]alls into question . . ." signals a Weaken question; the correct answer is a fact that will make the conclusion less likely to follow from the evidence.

5. Nutritionist: Recently a craze has developed for home juicers, $300 machines that separate the pulp of fruits and vegetables from the juice they contain. Outrageous claims are being made about the benefits of these devices: drinking the juice they produce is said to help one lose weight or acquire a clear complexion, to aid digestion, and even to prevent cancer. But there is no indication that juice separated from the pulp of the fruit or vegetable has any properties that it does not have when unseparated. Save your money. If you want carrot juice, eat a carrot.

Which one of the following, if true, most calls into question the nutritionist's argument?

(A) Most people find it much easier to consume a given quantity of nutrients in liquid form than to eat solid foods containing the same quantity of the same nutrients.

(B) Drinking juice from home juicers is less healthy than is eating fruits and vegetables because such juice does not contain the fiber that is eaten if one consumes the entire fruit or vegetable.

(C) To most people who would be tempted to buy a home juicer, $300 would not be a major expense.

(D) The nutritionist was a member of a panel that extensively evaluated early prototypes of home juicers.

(E) Vitamin pills that supposedly contain nutrients available elsewhere only in fruits and vegetables often contain a form of those compounds that cannot be as easily metabolized as the varieties found in fruits and vegetables.

PrepTest112 Sec1 Q2

Step 3: The nutritionist concludes that juicers have no value for one reason: the juice they produce is not nutritionally different from the fruit it comes from. But, what if juice has other advantages? This is a classic Overlooked Alternatives argument. Weaken it by finding an advantage or benefit of juice the nutritionist failed to see.	**Step 4:** (A) does the job; even if the juice provides no unique nutrition, it is easier to consume, so maybe the juicer is worth it after all.

Wrong answers: (B) 180. This choice strengthens the nutritionist's argument by providing another disadvantage of juice. (C) Outside the Scope. The fact that likely consumers could easily afford the juicer doesn't affect the nutritionist's argument that the juicer is without value. (D) Outside the Scope/180. This choice offers no advantages of juice over whole fruits and vegetables, and, if anything, makes the nutritionist even more convincing as a person informed about juicers. (E) Outside the Scope. This choice offers no advantages to juice over whole fruits and vegetables, so it cannot weaken the argument.

Hint: Take note of the author's method of argument; it provides a clue about how to strengthen the argument.

Step 2:	Step 1:

6. Opponents of peat harvesting in this country argue that it would alter the ecological balance of our peat-rich wetlands and that, as a direct consequence of this, much of the country's water supply would be threatened with contamination. But this cannot be true, for in Ireland, where peat has been harvested for centuries, the water supply is not contaminated. We can safely proceed with the harvesting of peat.

Which one of the following, if true, most strengthens the argument?

(A) Over hundreds of years, the ecological balance of all areas changes slowly but significantly, sometimes to the advantage of certain flora and fauna.

(B) The original ecology of the peat-harvesting areas of Ireland was virtually identical to that of the undisturbed wetlands of this country.

(C) The activities of other industries in coming years are likely to have adverse effects on the water supply of this country.

(D) The peat resources of this country are far larger than those of some countries that successfully harvest peat.

(E) The peat-harvesting industry of Ireland has been able to supply most of that country's fuel for generations.

PrepTest111 Sec3 Q3

Step 3:	Step 4:

Expert Analysis

Review an example of an LSAT expert's work on the question you just completed.

Step 2: *Conclusion*: Peat farming does not alter the ecological balance of our wetlands or threaten to contaminate the water supply *because* *Evidence*: Ireland has harvested peat for centuries and its water supply is not contaminated.	**Step 1:** This is a straightforward Strengthen question stem; the correct answer will make the conclusion more likely to follow from the evidence.

6.   Opponents of peat harvesting in this country argue that it would alter the ecological balance of our peat-rich wetlands and that, as a direct consequence of this, much of the country's water supply would be threatened with contamination. But this cannot be true, for in Ireland, where peat has been harvested for centuries, the water supply is not contaminated. We can safely proceed with the harvesting of peat.

Which one of the following, if true, most strengthens the argument?

(A) Over hundreds of years, the ecological balance of all areas changes slowly but significantly, sometimes to the advantage of certain flora and fauna.

(B) The original ecology of the peat-harvesting areas of Ireland was virtually identical to that of the undisturbed wetlands of this country.

(C) The activities of other industries in coming years are likely to have adverse effects on the water supply of this country.

(D) The peat resources of this country are far larger than those of some countries that successfully harvest peat.

(E) The peat-harvesting industry of Ireland has been able to supply most of that country's fuel for generations.

PrepTest111 Sec3 Q3

Step 3: Arguing by analogy, the author concludes that their country can safely harvest peat from its wetlands because Ireland has safely harvested peat for centuries. The author must assume that Ireland's ecosystem is sufficiently similar to their country's to justify making this conclusion. Any answer choice that confirms the similarities or rules out a relevant difference between the author's country and Ireland will strengthen the argument.	**Step 4:** (B) directly confirms the similarity between the ecosystem from which peat is harvested in Ireland and that of the author's country thereby strengthening the argument.

Wrong answers: (A) Outside the Scope. Knowing that all ecosystems change over time neither helps nor hurts the author's contention that it is safe to harvest peat from their country's wetlands. (C) Outside the Scope. This question asks for an answer that strengthens the author's conclusion that it is safe to harvest peat in their country's wetlands, not for general information about threats to the water supply. (D) Irrelevant Comparison. Without knowing whether Ireland is one of the countries mentioned, it is unclear if this statement helps or hurts the argument. (E) While this is good news for Ireland, it doesn't provide any information to suggest that Ireland's peat-rich areas are similar to those in the author's country.

Hint: What is the difference in scope between the two pieces of evidence?

Step 2:	Step 1:

7. Standard archaeological techniques make it possible to determine the age of anything containing vegetable matter, but only if the object is free of minerals containing carbon. Prehistoric artists painted on limestone with pigments composed of vegetable matter, but it is impossible to collect samples of this prehistoric paint without removing limestone, a mineral containing carbon, with the paint. Therefore, it is not possible to determine the age of prehistoric paintings on limestone using standard archaeological techniques.

Which one of the following, if true, most seriously weakens the argument?

(A) There exist several different techniques for collecting samples of prehistoric pigments on limestone.

(B) Laboratory procedures exist that can remove all the limestone from a sample of prehistoric paint on limestone.

(C) The age of the limestone itself can be determined from samples that contain no vegetable-based paint.

(D) Prehistoric artists did not use anything other than vegetable matter to make their paints.

(E) The proportion of carbon to other elements in limestone is the same in all samples of limestone.

PrepTest110 Sec3 Q6

Step 3:	Step 4:

Expert Analysis

Review an example of an LSAT expert's work on the question you just completed.

Step 2: *Conclusion*: Standard archaeological techniques cannot establish the age of prehistoric paintings *because*

Evidence: (1) Samples of prehistoric paintings cannot be collected without including carbon-containing limestone, and (2) standard archaeological techniques can date the prehistoric paint but only if there is no carbon included.

Step 1: A straightforward Weaken question stem: the correct answer presents a fact making it less likely that the conclusion follows from the evidence.

7. Standard archaeological techniques make it possible to determine the age of anything containing vegetable matter, but only if the object is free of minerals containing carbon. Prehistoric artists painted on limestone with pigments composed of vegetable matter, but it is impossible to collect samples of this prehistoric paint without removing limestone, a mineral containing carbon, with the paint. Therefore, it is not possible to determine the age of prehistoric paintings on limestone using standard archaeological techniques.

Which one of the following, if true, most seriously weakens the argument?

(A) There exist several different techniques for collecting samples of prehistoric pigments on limestone.

(B) Laboratory procedures exist that can remove all the limestone from a sample of prehistoric paint on limestone.

(C) The age of the limestone itself can be determined from samples that contain no vegetable-based paint.

(D) Prehistoric artists did not use anything other than vegetable matter to make their paints.

(E) The proportion of carbon to other elements in limestone is the same in all samples of limestone.

PrepTest110 Sec3 Q6

Step 3: The author makes it clear that the paint samples (which are vegetable matter) could be dated if there were no carbon contamination, but that the paint can't be collected without including some carbon. To weaken this argument, the correct answer will have to suggest another way to get a carbon-free paint sample.

Step 4: (B) does the trick. If the carbon can be removed from the sample after collection, then standard archaeological techniques can be used to date the paint.

Wrong answers: (A) However many techniques there are, the argument makes it clear that the paint sample cannot be gathered without getting some limestone mixed in. (C) The age of the limestone (presumably millions of years old) doesn't help; we want to know when the paint was applied to it. (D) 180. The fact that there are no other types of paint strengthens the argument; it's all or nothing with the vegetable-based paints. (E) Unfortunately, the presence of carbon (however much there is) means vegetable matter cannot be dated using standard archaeological techniques, so this choice neither weakens nor strengthens the argument.

Hint: How many potential harms has the author ruled out?

Step 2:	Step 1:

8. Lobsters and other crustaceans eaten by humans are more likely to contract gill diseases when sewage contaminates their water. Under a recent proposal, millions of gallons of local sewage each day would be rerouted many kilometers offshore. Although this would substantially reduce the amount of sewage in the harbor where lobsters are caught, the proposal is pointless, because hardly any lobsters live long enough to be harmed by those diseases.

Which one of the following, if true, most seriously weakens the argument?

(A) Contaminants in the harbor other than sewage are equally harmful to lobsters.

(B) Lobsters, like other crustaceans, live longer in the open ocean than in industrial harbors.

(C) Lobsters breed as readily in sewage-contaminated water as in unpolluted water.

(D) Gill diseases cannot be detected by examining the surface of the lobster.

(E) Humans often become ill as a result of eating lobsters with gill diseases.

PrepTest111 Sec1 Q8

Step 3:	Step 4:

Expert Analysis

Review an example of an LSAT expert's work on the question you just completed.

Step 2: *Conclusion*: The proposal to reroute sewage away from the harbor where lobsters are caught is pointless *because* *Evidence*: Even though sewage causes gill disease in lobsters, lobsters rarely live long enough to be harmed by it.	**Step 1:** A straightforward Weaken question stem: the correct answer will make the conclusion less likely to follow from the evidence.

8. Lobsters and other crustaceans eaten by humans are more likely to contract gill diseases when sewage contaminates their water. Under a recent proposal, millions of gallons of local sewage each day would be rerouted many kilometers offshore. Although this would substantially reduce the amount of sewage in the harbor where lobsters are caught, the proposal is pointless, because hardly any lobsters live long enough to be harmed by those diseases.

Which one of the following, if true, most seriously weakens the argument?

(A) Contaminants in the harbor other than sewage are equally harmful to lobsters.

(B) Lobsters, like other crustaceans, live longer in the open ocean than in industrial harbors.

(C) Lobsters breed as readily in sewage-contaminated water as in unpolluted water.

(D) Gill diseases cannot be detected by examining the surface of the lobster.

(E) Humans often become ill as a result of eating lobsters with gill diseases.

PrepTest111 Sec1 Q8

Step 3: This is a classic Overlooked Possibilities argument. The author concludes that a proposal is pointless on the basis of one reason not to worry. Such arguments can always be weakened by an answer choice that cites another reason to be worried. So, predict that the correct answer will cite a problem other than the one the author rules out (lobsters being harmed by gill disease).	**Step 4:** (E) provides a harm that the proposal will help to solve—people getting sick from eating the diseased lobsters—even if the lobsters don't live long enough to be harmed.

Wrong answers: (A) This is unfortunate, but irrelevant to the argument at hand. (B) Irrelevant Comparison. The proposal is aimed at cleaning up the harbor waters, and there is not enough information here to know if the rerouted sewage poses any threat to the open-ocean lobsters. (C) Irrelevant Comparison. The proposal is aimed at reducing the number of lobsters with gill disease, not at increasing their reproduction. (D) Outside the Scope. How gill disease is diagnosed has no effect on the argument.

Hint: When you see a Strengthen/Weaken question with a dialog stimulus, pay attention to whose argument will be weakened and whose will be strengthened by the correct answer.

Step 2:	Step 1:

9. Parent P: Children will need computer skills to deal with tomorrow's world. Computers should be introduced in kindergarten, and computer languages should be required in high school.

    Parent Q: That would be pointless. Technology advances so rapidly that the computers used by today's kindergartners and the computer languages taught in today's high schools would become obsolete by the time these children are adults.

Which one of the following, if true, is the strongest logical counter parent P can make to parent Q's objection?

(A) When technology is advancing rapidly, regular training is necessary to keep one's skills at a level proficient enough to deal with the society in which one lives.

(B) Throughout history people have adapted to change, and there is no reason to believe that today's children are not equally capable of adapting to technology as it advances.

(C) In the process of learning to work with any computer or computer language, children increase their ability to interact with computer technology.

(D) Automotive technology is continually advancing too, but that does not result in one's having to relearn to drive cars as the new advances are incorporated into new automobiles.

(E) Once people have graduated from high school, they have less time to learn about computers and technology than they had during their schooling years.

PrepTest111 Sec1 Q4

Step 3:	Step 4:

Expert Analysis

Review an example of an LSAT expert's work on the question you just completed.

Step 2: P—*Conclusion*: Computers should be introduced in kindergarten and computer languages should be required in high school *because*

Evidence: Children will need computer skills in the future.

Q—*Conclusion*: P's recommendation is pointless *because*

Evidence: Tech changes so fast that what kids learn today will be obsolete by the time they're adults.

Step 1: This is a true Strengthen/Weaken question with a dialog stimulus; the correct answer here will weaken Q's response, thus strengthening P's argument.

9.   Parent P: Children will need computer skills to deal with tomorrow's world. Computers should be introduced in kindergarten, and computer languages should be required in high school.

  Parent Q: That would be pointless. Technology advances so rapidly that the computers used by today's kindergartners and the computer languages taught in today's high schools would become obsolete by the time these children are adults.

Which one of the following, if true, is the strongest logical counter parent P can make to parent Q's objection?

(A) When technology is advancing rapidly, regular training is necessary to keep one's skills at a level proficient enough to deal with the society in which one lives.

(B) Throughout history people have adapted to change, and there is no reason to believe that today's children are not equally capable of adapting to technology as it advances.

(C) In the process of learning to work with any computer or computer language, children increase their ability to interact with computer technology.

(D) Automotive technology is continually advancing too, but that does not result in one's having to relearn to drive cars as the new advances are incorporated into new automobiles.

(E) Once people have graduated from high school, they have less time to learn about computers and technology than they had during their schooling years.

PrepTest111 Sec1 Q4

Step 3: The correct answer will need to supply a reason P's recommendation is valuable even if the computers and languages kids learn today are obsolete by the time they're adults.

Step 4: (C) provides a strong counter to Q's response. If the learning they do makes them more proficient at interacting with computer technology generally, then the children will benefit even if the specific machines and languages used now are obsolete by the time they're adults.

Wrong answers: (A) suggests that ongoing learning will be required whether P's recommendation is followed or not. (B) is just a general observation; it doesn't help or hurt either parent's argument. (D) Knowing how to drive a car is not a good analogy for learning computer languages, which is more like learning to engineer or program cars. (E) This fact doesn't counter Q's contention that such training will be obsolete by the time students learning it are adults.

Hint: Even when an author presents some evidence, you can strengthen the argument by providing more.

Step 2:	Step 1:

10. The television show *Henry* was not widely watched until it was scheduled for Tuesday evenings immediately after *That's Life*, the most popular show on television. During the year after the move, *Henry* was consistently one of the ten most-watched shows on television. Since *Henry*'s recent move to Wednesday evenings, however, it has been watched by far fewer people. We must conclude that *Henry* was widely watched before the move to Wednesday evenings because it followed *That's Life* and not because people especially liked it.

Which one of the following, if true, most strengthens the argument?

(A) *Henry* has been on the air for three years, but *That's Life* has been on the air for only two years.

(B) The show that replaced *Henry* on Tuesdays has persistently had a low number of viewers in the Tuesday time slot.

(C) The show that now follows *That's Life* on Tuesdays has double the number of viewers it had before being moved.

(D) After its recent move to Wednesday, *Henry* was aired at the same time as the second most popular show on television.

(E) *That's Life* was not widely watched during the first year it was aired.

PrepTest112 Sec4 Q12

Step 3:	Step 4:

Expert Analysis

Review an example of an LSAT expert's work on the question you just completed.

Step 2: *Conclusion*: People watched *Henry* because it was on after *That's Life* (*TL*), and not because they liked *Henry because*

Evidence: A viewership timeline (1) Before *Henry* followed *TL*: low, (2) While following *TL*: high, (3) After moving away from *TL*: low, again.

Step 1: A straightforward Strengthen question stem: the correct answer makes the conclusion more likely to follow from the evidence.

10. The television show *Henry* was not widely watched until it was scheduled for Tuesday evenings immediately after *That's Life*, the most popular show on television. During the year after the move, *Henry* was consistently one of the ten most-watched shows on television. Since *Henry*'s recent move to Wednesday evenings, however, it has been watched by far fewer people. We must conclude that *Henry* was widely watched before the move to Wednesday evenings because it followed *That's Life* and not because people especially liked it.

Which one of the following, if true, most strengthens the argument?

(A) *Henry* has been on the air for three years, but *That's Life* has been on the air for only two years.

(B) The show that replaced *Henry* on Tuesdays has persistently had a low number of viewers in the Tuesday time slot.

(C) The show that now follows *That's Life* on Tuesdays has double the number of viewers it had before being moved.

(D) After its recent move to Wednesday, *Henry* was aired at the same time as the second most popular show on television.

(E) *That's Life* was not widely watched during the first year it was aired.

PrepTest112 Sec4 Q12

Step 3: The author presents a fairly convincing correlation as is, but the task is to find yet another reason to believe *Henry*'s popularity was due to its following *That's Life* in the Tuesday-night schedule. The correct answer will supply another fact supporting this assumption.

Step 4: (C) If another show also saw a substantial boost from following *That's Life* in the schedule, the author's assumption that the same situation benefitted *Henry* is more likely to be correct.

Wrong answers: (A) is irrelevant; *Henry* wasn't popular until it followed *That's Life*, regardless of how long the latter has been on the air. (B) 180. This fact suggests that the time slot following *That's Life* does not inherently boost viewership. (D) 180. If competition with a popular show on another network is a factor, that weakens the author's claim that *Henry*'s reduced viewership is because people just don't like *Henry* that much. (E) Outside the Scope. The trajectory of *That's Life*'s popularity is irrelevant to the author's explanation; the stimulus makes it clear that when *Henry* was following it, *That's Life* was TV's most popular show. **Caution**: Never assess two answer choices together. In this question, trying to rationalize the statements in choices (A) and (E) simultaneously with the statements in the stimulus will just lead to confusion. Evaluate choices one at a time, and only against the stimulus or your Step 3 prediction, never against each other.

Hint: If you find out your first source for some information is not credible, does that mean the information was wrong?

Step 2:	Step 1:

11. Journal: In several psychological studies, subjects were given statements to read that caused them to form new beliefs. Later, the subjects were told that the original statements were false. The studies report, however, that most subjects persevered in their newly acquired beliefs, even after being told that the original statements were false. This strongly suggests that humans continue to hold onto acquired beliefs even in the absence of any credible evidence to support them.

Which one of the following, if true, most undermines the journal's argument?

(A) Regardless of the truth of what the subjects were later told, the beliefs based on the original statements were, for the most part, correct.

(B) It is unrealistic to expect people to keep track of the original basis of their beliefs, and to revise a belief when its original basis is undercut.

(C) The statements originally given to the subjects would be highly misleading even if true.

(D) Most of the subjects had acquired confirmation of their newly acquired beliefs by the time they were told that the original statements were false.

(E) Most of the subjects were initially skeptical of the statements originally given to them.

PrepTest111 Sec1 Q13

Step 3:	Step 4:

Expert Analysis

Review an example of an LSAT expert's work on the question you just completed.

Step 2: *Conclusion*: Humans hold onto acquired beliefs even without credible support *because*   *Evidence*: Subjects who acquired new beliefs from statements in a psychological study retained those beliefs after being told the statements were false.

Step 1: "[M]ost undermines" signals a Weaken question; the correct answer will make the journal's conclusion less likely to follow from its evidence.

11. Journal: In several psychological studies, subjects were given statements to read that caused them to form new beliefs. Later, the subjects were told that the original statements were false. The studies report, however, that most subjects persevered in their newly acquired beliefs, even after being told that the original statements were false. This strongly suggests that humans continue to hold onto acquired beliefs even in the absence of any credible evidence to support them.

Which one of the following, if true, most undermines the journal's argument?

(A) Regardless of the truth of what the subjects were later told, the beliefs based on the original statements were, for the most part, correct.

(B) It is unrealistic to expect people to keep track of the original basis of their beliefs, and to revise a belief when its original basis is undercut.

(C) The statements originally given to the subjects would be highly misleading even if true.

(D) Most of the subjects had acquired confirmation of their newly acquired beliefs by the time they were told that the original statements were false.

(E) Most of the subjects were initially skeptical of the statements originally given to them.

PrepTest111 Sec1 Q13

Step 3: The author concludes that humans retain acquired beliefs "even in the absence of any credible information." The evidence, however, only says that the subjects were later told that the statements that originally prompted the new beliefs were false, not that the *beliefs* were false or that there is no other support for those beliefs. The journal's argument, it seems, assumes that the only support these subjects had for their beliefs were the original, ostensible false statements. An answer choice identifying other credible reasons for these beliefs will weaken the journal's conclusion.

Step 4: (D) weakens the argument by stating that the subjects who retained their beliefs did, in fact, have evidence for them before being told that the original statements from the experiment were false.

Wrong answers: (A) The accuracy of the beliefs is Outside the Scope; this argument is about retaining beliefs (true or not) without evidence for them. (B) 180. This choice supports the journal's conclusion by explaining why the subjects may hold onto their beliefs even after learning that the triggering statements are false. (C) is irrelevant as the journal's argument hinges on the fact that the subjects were told the statements are false, not on any supposition that the content of the statements is misleading. (E) 180. If anything, this choice would strengthen the journal's conclusion that people hold onto acquired beliefs in the absence of support.

Hint: Don't rush through Steps 2 and 3; being able to state the argument's assumption is very helpful when evaluating Strengthen question answer choices.

Step 2:	Step 1:

12. Some people claim that every human discovery or invention is an instance of self-expression. But what they seem to ignore is that, trivially, anything we do is self-expressive. So, until they can give us a more interesting interpretation of their claim, we are not obliged to take their claim seriously.

Which one of the following, if true, provides the most support for the reasoning above?

(A) All claims that are trivial are uninteresting.

(B) Most people do not take trivial claims seriously.

(C) No claims that are trivial are worthy of serious consideration.

(D) Every claim is open to both interesting and uninteresting interpretations.

(E) Every interpretation is either trivial or uninteresting.

PrepTest110 Sec2 Q14

Step 3:	Step 4:

Expert Analysis

Review an example of an LSAT expert's work on the question you just completed.

Step 2: *Conclusion*: We do not have to take seriously the claim that every human discovery or invention is an example of self-expression *because*

Evidence: Trivially speaking, anything humans do is self-expression.

Step 1: A Strengthen question: the correct answer will make the conclusion more likely to follow from the evidence.

12. Some people claim that every human discovery or invention is an instance of self-expression. But what they seem to ignore is that, trivially, anything we do is self-expressive. So, until they can give us a more interesting interpretation of their claim, we are not obliged to take their claim seriously.

Which one of the following, if true, provides the most support for the reasoning above?

(A) All claims that are trivial are uninteresting.

(B) Most people do not take trivial claims seriously.

(C) No claims that are trivial are worthy of serious consideration.

(D) Every claim is open to both interesting and uninteresting interpretations.

(E) Every interpretation is either trivial or uninteresting.

PrepTest110 Sec2 Q14

Step 3: The author concludes that we are not obliged to consider a particular claim because the claim is trivial (of little value or importance) because it is already obvious. The correct answer will support the idea that trivial claims need not be taken seriously.

Step 4: (C) states the author's assumption as a principle or general rule which, if valid, strengthens the argument.

Wrong answers: (A) This choice doesn't link trivial claims to claims we are not obliged to take seriously. (B) Outside the Scope. Whether the majority act in accordance with the author's conclusion is irrelevant to the author's reasoning. (D) Extreme. Perhaps only some statements can be interpreted both ways; this would not affect the argument. (E) Extreme. The author thinks the claim at issue in the argument is both trivial and uninteresting; perhaps there are others that they would consider nontrivial and interesting.

Hint: The correct answer to a Strengthen **except** question could weaken the argument, but it doesn't have to. What other characteristic could it have?

Step 2:	Step 1:

13. Statistician: A financial magazine claimed that its survey of its subscribers showed that North Americans are more concerned about their personal finances than about politics. One question was: "Which do you think about more: politics or the joy of earning money?" This question is clearly biased. Also, the readers of the magazine are a self-selecting sample. Thus, there is reason to be skeptical about the conclusion drawn in the magazine's survey.

Each of the following, if true, would strengthen the statistician's argument **except**:

(A) The credibility of the magazine has been called into question on a number of occasions.

(B) The conclusions drawn in most magazine surveys have eventually been disproved.

(C) Other surveys suggest that North Americans are just as concerned about politics as they are about finances.

(D) There is reason to be skeptical about the results of surveys that are biased and unrepresentative.

(E) Other surveys suggest that North Americans are concerned not only with politics and finances, but also with social issues.

PrepTest111 Sec1 Q15

Step 3:	Step 4:

Expert Analysis

Review an example of an LSAT expert's work on the question you just completed.

Step 2: *Conclusion:* The financial magazine's conclusion that North Americans are more concerned about their personal finances than they are about politics is questionable *because*

Evidence: (1) The magazine's survey asked a biased question, and (2) the magazine's readers may not be a representative sample.

Step 1: This is a Strengthen EXCEPT question; the correct answer will weaken the argument or do nothing, while it is the four wrong answers that will strengthen the argument.

13. Statistician: A financial magazine claimed that its survey of its subscribers showed that North Americans are more concerned about their personal finances than about politics. One question was: "Which do you think about more: politics or the joy of earning money?" This question is clearly biased. Also, the readers of the magazine are a self-selecting sample. Thus, there is reason to be skeptical about the conclusion drawn in the magazine's survey.

Each of the following, if true, would strengthen the statistician's argument EXCEPT:

(A) The credibility of the magazine has been called into question on a number of occasions.

(B) The conclusions drawn in most magazine surveys have eventually been disproved.

(C) Other surveys suggest that North Americans are just as concerned about politics as they are about finances.

(D) There is reason to be skeptical about the results of surveys that are biased and unrepresentative.

(E) Other surveys suggest that North Americans are concerned not only with politics and finances, but also with social issues.

PrepTest111 Sec1 Q15

Step 3: The statistician assumes that biased questions and unrepresentative samples call survey results into question. The four wrong answers will strengthen that position. The correct answer will either give a reason to trust the magazine's conclusion or simply be Outside the Scope.

Step 4: (E) is Outside the Scope—the introduction of a third concern and the lack of a ranking between politics and finance do not affect the statistician's argument. Because this choice *does not* strengthen the argument, it is correct.

Wrong answers: (A) strengthens the statistician's argument by offering an additional reason to be skeptical of the magazine's credibility. (B) strengthens the statistician's argument by offering a reason to be skeptical of magazine surveys generally. (C) strengthens the statistician's argument by citing other surveys that produced different results. (D) strengthens the argument by directly confirming the validity of the statistician's stated concerns.

Hint: How do you weaken a claim that a conclusion is based on an unrepresentative sample? (Demonstrate that it *is* representative.)

Step 2:	Step 1:

14. Dietary researcher: A recent study reports that laboratory animals that were fed reduced-calorie diets lived longer than laboratory animals whose caloric intake was not reduced. In response, some doctors are advocating reduced-calorie diets, in the belief that North Americans' life spans can thereby be extended. However, this conclusion is not supported. Laboratory animals tend to eat much more than animals in their natural habitats, which leads to their having a shorter life expectancy. Restricting their diets merely brings their caloric intake back to natural, optimal levels and reinstates their normal life spans.

Which one of the following, if true, would most weaken the dietary researcher's argument?

(A) North Americans, on average, consume a higher number of calories than the optimal number of calories for a human diet.

(B) North Americans with high-fat, low-calorie diets generally have a shorter life expectancy than North Americans with low-fat, low-calorie diets.

(C) Not all scientific results that have important implications for human health are based on studies of laboratory animals.

(D) Some North Americans who follow reduced-calorie diets are long-lived.

(E) There is a strong correlation between diet and longevity in some species of animals.

PrepTest110 Sec2 Q17

Step 3:	Step 4:

Expert Analysis

Review an example of an LSAT expert's work on the question you just completed.

Step 2: *Conclusion*: Doctors' recommendations for humans to eat reduced-calorie diets to extend their life spans is unsupported *because* *Evidence*: The laboratory research on which it is based merely restored its animal subjects to their natural calorie intake. (Lab animals tend to eat more calories than they would in the wild.)	**Step 1:** A standard Weaken question stem: the correct answer is a fact making the conclusion less likely to follow from the evidence.

14. Dietary researcher: A recent study reports that laboratory animals that were fed reduced-calorie diets lived longer than laboratory animals whose caloric intake was not reduced. In response, some doctors are advocating reduced-calorie diets, in the belief that North Americans' life spans can thereby be extended. However, this conclusion is not supported. Laboratory animals tend to eat much more than animals in their natural habitats, which leads to their having a shorter life expectancy. Restricting their diets merely brings their caloric intake back to natural, optimal levels and reinstates their normal life spans.

Which one of the following, if true, would most weaken the dietary researcher's argument?

(A) North Americans, on average, consume a higher number of calories than the optimal number of calories for a human diet.

(B) North Americans with high-fat, low-calorie diets generally have a shorter life expectancy than North Americans with low-fat, low-calorie diets.

(C) Not all scientific results that have important implications for human health are based on studies of laboratory animals.

(D) Some North Americans who follow reduced-calorie diets are long-lived.

(E) There is a strong correlation between diet and longevity in some species of animals.

PrepTest110 Sec2 Q17

Step 3: The argument concludes that the doctors' recommendation (lower-calorie diets) is unfounded because it is based on skewed research on laboratory animals. To weaken this argument the correct answer will offer a fact that shows the doctors' advice is nonetheless good for humans. The stimulus offers a clue: lab animals eat more calories than they would in the wild. What if humans eat more calories than they should?	**Step 4:** (A) weakens the argument by showing that humans are actually in the same situation as the laboratory animals, eating more calories than is optimal. Thus, reduced-calorie diets would put humans back in sync with their "optimal levels" just as similar diets do for the lab animals.

Wrong answers: (B) 180. If true, this statement strengthens the argument. (C) Outside the Scope. Where else useful scientific results come from has no effect on the validity of this argument. (D) This might strengthen the argument, but without more information (What percentage? Did they reduce their calorie intake from a higher-calorie diet? Etc.), this vague assertion has no effect. (E) Without information about humans, this statement neither strengthens nor weakens the argument.

Hint: You don't have to be a subject matter expert to evaluate arguments on the LSAT; the correct answer undermines the author's reasoning.

Step 2:	Step 1:

15. Archaeologist: A skeleton of a North American mastodon that became extinct at the peak of the Ice Age was recently discovered. It contains a human-made projectile dissimilar to any found in that part of Eurasia closest to North America. Thus, since Eurasians did not settle in North America until shortly before the peak of the Ice Age, the first Eurasian settlers in North America probably came from a more distant part of Eurasia.

Which one of the following, if true, most seriously weakens the archaeologist's argument?

(A) The projectile found in the mastodon does not resemble any that were used in Eurasia before or during the Ice Age.

(B) The people who occupied the Eurasian area closest to North America remained nomadic throughout the Ice Age.

(C) The skeleton of a bear from the same place and time as the mastodon skeleton contains a similar projectile.

(D) Other North American artifacts from the peak of the Ice Age are similar to ones from the same time found in more distant parts of Eurasia.

(E) Climatic conditions in North America just before the Ice Age were more conducive to human habitation than were those in the part of Eurasia closest to North America at that time.

PrepTest111 Sec4 Q20

Step 3:	Step 4:

Expert Analysis

Review an example of an LSAT expert's work on the question you just completed.

Step 2: *Conclusion*: The earliest Eurasian settlers in North America came from more distant parts of Eurasia *because*

Evidence: (1) A North American projectile found in an animal skeleton from the peak of the Ice Age did not resemble projectiles from the parts of Eurasia close to North America, and (2) Eurasians first settled in North America around the peak of the Ice Age.

Step 1: A straightforward Weaken question stem; the correct answer will make the conclusion less likely to follow from the evidence.

15. Archaeologist: A skeleton of a North American mastodon that became extinct at the peak of the Ice Age was recently discovered. It contains a human-made projectile dissimilar to any found in that part of Eurasia closest to North America. Thus, since Eurasians did not settle in North America until shortly before the peak of the Ice Age, the first Eurasian settlers in North America probably came from a more distant part of Eurasia.

Which one of the following, if true, most seriously weakens the archaeologist's argument?

(A) The projectile found in the mastodon does not resemble any that were used in Eurasia before or during the Ice Age.

(B) The people who occupied the Eurasian area closest to North America remained nomadic throughout the Ice Age.

(C) The skeleton of a bear from the same place and time as the mastodon skeleton contains a similar projectile.

(D) Other North American artifacts from the peak of the Ice Age are similar to ones from the same time found in more distant parts of Eurasia.

(E) Climatic conditions in North America just before the Ice Age were more conducive to human habitation than were those in the part of Eurasia closest to North America at that time.

PrepTest111 Sec4 Q20

Step 3: The argument assumes that the projectile found in the mastodon sheds light on the part of Eurasia the earliest Eurasian settlers in North America came from. "It's not like anything nearby, so they came from further away." But, the evidence says only that the projectile was "human-made." The author overlooks the possibility that the projectile may not provide evidence for their conclusion, and may not even be from Eurasia.

Step 4: (A) provides a fact that makes the projectile irrelevant to the author's conclusion; since it doesn't resemble any Eurasian projectiles, it doesn't support the author's conclusion that the earliest arrivals came from more distant parts of Eurasia.

Wrong answers: (B) Outside the Scope. Whether settled or nomadic, the projectile doesn't make them more or less likely to be the earliest settlers in North America. (C) is irrelevant; if the two projectiles are similar, then neither resembles any Eurasian projectiles. (D) 180. This evidence strengthens the argument's conclusion, albeit not on the basis of this particular projectile find. (E) Outside the Scope. This fact leaves open the possibility that North America was an even more desirable destination for those from more distant parts of Eurasia.

Hint: Just because an argument's evidence is reasonable doesn't mean it is complete.

Step 2:	Step 1:

16. Thirty years ago, the percentage of their income that single persons spent on food was twice what it is today. Given that incomes have risen over the past thirty years, we can conclude that incomes have risen at a greater rate than the price of food in that period.

Which one of the following, if assumed, helps most to justify the conclusion drawn above?

(A) The amount of food eaten per capita today is identical to the amount of food eaten per capita thirty years ago.

(B) In general, single persons today eat healthier foods and eat less than their counterparts of thirty years ago.

(C) Single persons today, on average, purchase the same kinds of food items in the same quantities as they did thirty years ago.

(D) The prices of nonfood items single persons purchase have risen faster than the price of food over the past thirty years.

(E) Unlike single persons, families today spend about the same percentage of their income on food as they did thirty years ago.

PrepTest110 Sec3 Q21

Step 3:	Step 4:

Expert Analysis

Review an example of an LSAT expert's work on the question you just completed.

Step 2: *Conclusion*: Income has risen faster than the price of food has in the past 30 years *because* *Evidence*: 30 years ago, single people spent double the portion of their paychecks on food than they do now.	**Step 1:** An assumption question asking for the choice that "helps most to justify the conclusion" is just a Strengthen question in disguise. Look for the choice that makes the conclusion more likely to follow from the evidence.

16. Thirty years ago, the percentage of their income that single persons spent on food was twice what it is today. Given that incomes have risen over the past thirty years, we can conclude that incomes have risen at a greater rate than the price of food in that period.

Which one of the following, if assumed, helps most to justify the conclusion drawn above?

(A) The amount of food eaten per capita today is identical to the amount of food eaten per capita thirty years ago.

(B) In general, single persons today eat healthier foods and eat less than their counterparts of thirty years ago.

(C) Single persons today, on average, purchase the same kinds of food items in the same quantities as they did thirty years ago.

(D) The prices of nonfood items single persons purchase have risen faster than the price of food over the past thirty years.

(E) Unlike single persons, families today spend about the same percentage of their income on food as they did thirty years ago.

PrepTest110 Sec3 Q21

Step 3: The argument provides reasonable but incomplete evidence for the conclusion. The correct answer will rule out one or more overlooked possibilities.	**Step 4:** (C) helps the argument by ruling out the possibility that people 30 years ago were buying more expensive types of food than people today. If they were, it stands to reason that they would spend a higher portion of their paychecks on food even if income growth hadn't outpaced food prices during that time period.

Wrong answers: (A) If this choice were about the amount of food purchased, it could help the argument, but the amount *eaten* muddies the water. (B) It sounds like today's singles have the right idea, but without knowing the amount of food they purchase or knowing whether healthier foods are cheaper or more expensive, this choice cannot strengthen the argument. (D) The relative price of nonfood items is Outside the Scope. (E) The information about families is Outside the Scope, and is bound to be inapplicable without information about relative family size.

Hint: Evaluate the answer choices strictly; do they really support the prediction in the argument's conclusion based on the argument's evidence?

Step 2:	Step 1:

17. The new agriculture bill will almost surely fail to pass. The leaders of all major parties have stated that they oppose it.

Which one of the following, if true, adds the most support for the prediction that the agriculture bill will fail to pass?

(A) Most bills that have not been supported by even one leader of a major party have not been passed into law.

(B) Most bills that have not been passed into law were not supported by even one member of a major party.

(C) If the leaders of all major parties endorse the new agriculture bill, it will pass into law.

(D) Most bills that have been passed into law were not unanimously supported by the leaders of all major parties.

(E) Most bills that have been passed into law were supported by at least one leader of a major party.

PrepTest111 Sec3 Q21

Step 3:	Step 4:

Expert Analysis

Review an example of an LSAT expert's work on the question you just completed.

Step 2: *Conclusion*: The new agriculture bill will fail *because* *Evidence*: All major parties' leaders have stated their opposition to the bill.	**Step 1:** A standard Strengthen question: the correct answer will provide a fact that makes the conclusion more likely to follow from the evidence. Note: the stem tells you the conclusion is a prediction.

17. The new agriculture bill will almost surely fail to pass. The leaders of all major parties have stated that they oppose it.

Which one of the following, if true, adds the most support for the prediction that the agriculture bill will fail to pass?

(A) Most bills that have not been supported by even one leader of a major party have not been passed into law.

(B) Most bills that have not been passed into law were not supported by even one member of a major party.

(C) If the leaders of all major parties endorse the new agriculture bill, it will pass into law.

(D) Most bills that have been passed into law were not unanimously supported by the leaders of all major parties.

(E) Most bills that have been passed into law were supported by at least one leader of a major party.

PrepTest111 Sec3 Q21

Step 3: The conclusion is a prediction that the bill will not pass based on evidence that the major parties' leaders have voiced their opposition. The author assumes that when the leaders of all major parties voice opposition to a bill, the bill will fail. The correct answer will supply a fact that supports that assumption.	**Step 4:** (A) fits the situation in the argument and supports the author's assumption. If the majority of bills lacking the support of all ("not even one") major party leaders have not passed, it is more likely that this one won't pass either.

Wrong answers: (B) Extreme. The argument in this question has evidence about party leaders, not all party *members*. (C) Outside the Scope. This condition—the *support* of all major party leaders—does not fit the situation in this argument. (D) Outside the Scope. Knowing that bills *pass* without unanimous support does not strengthen a prediction of failure for a bill lacking all support. (E) is subtly Outside the Scope. Knowing that most bills that *pass* have support from at least one major party leader does not provide information about what happens to most bills lacking the support of all major party leaders.

Hint: Some dated subject matter, but evergreen logical reasoning in the arguments.

Step 2:	Step 1:

18. Tony: A new kind of videocassette has just been developed. It lasts for only half as many viewings as the old kind does but costs a third as much. Therefore, video rental stores would find it significantly more economical to purchase and stock movies recorded on the new kind of videocassette than on the old kind.

Anna: But the videocassette itself only accounts for 5 percent of the price a video rental store pays to buy a copy of a movie on video; most of the price consists of royalties the store pays to the studio that produced the movie. So the price that video rental stores pay per copy would decrease by considerably less than 5 percent, and royalties would have to be paid on additional copies.

Which one of the following, if true, would contribute most to a defense of Tony's position against Anna's reply?

(A) The price that video rental stores pay for movies recorded on videocassettes is considerably less than the retail price of those movies.

(B) A significant proportion of the movies on videocassette purchased by video rental stores are bought as replacements for worn-out copies of movies the stores already have in stock.

(C) The royalty fee included in the price that video rental stores pay for movies on the new kind of videocassette will be half that included in the price of movies on the old kind.

(D) Given a choice, customers are more likely to buy a movie on videocassette than to rent it if the rental fee is more than half of the purchase price.

(E) Many of the movies rented from video rental stores, particularly children's movies, average several viewings per rental fee.

PrepTest111 Sec3 Q24

Step 3:	Step 4:

Expert Analysis

Review an example of an LSAT expert's work on the question you just completed.

Step 2: Tony—Conclusion: Video rental stores will find the new tape more economical *because* *Evidence*: The new tape costs 33% of the old tape's cost but lasts 50% as long as the old tape. Anna—Most of the cost associated with videotapes is in royalties, and the tape cost is just 5%. The stores won't save much on the tapes and will have to pay royalties for the new copies.	**Step 1:** This is a Strengthen question with a dialog stimulus; the correct answer will make the first speaker's argument more likely to be true. Expect the correct answer to directly address the second speaker's attack on the first speaker's argument.

18. Tony: A new kind of videocassette has just been developed. It lasts for only half as many viewings as the old kind does but costs a third as much. Therefore, video rental stores would find it significantly more economical to purchase and stock movies recorded on the new kind of videocassette than on the old kind.

    Anna: But the videocassette itself only accounts for 5 percent of the price a video rental store pays to buy a copy of a movie on video; most of the price consists of royalties the store pays to the studio that produced the movie. So the price that video rental stores pay per copy would decrease by considerably less than 5 percent, and royalties would have to be paid on additional copies.

Which one of the following, if true, would contribute most to a defense of Tony's position against Anna's reply?

(A) The price that video rental stores pay for movies recorded on videocassettes is considerably less than the retail price of those movies.

(B) A significant proportion of the movies on videocassette purchased by video rental stores are bought as replacements for worn-out copies of movies the stores already have in stock.

(C) The royalty fee included in the price that video rental stores pay for movies on the new kind of videocassette will be half that included in the price of movies on the old kind.

(D) Given a choice, customers are more likely to buy a movie on videocassette than to rent it if the rental fee is more than half of the purchase price.

(E) Many of the movies rented from video rental stores, particularly children's movies, average several viewings per rental fee.

PrepTest111 Sec3 Q24

Step 3: To strengthen Tony's argument, the correct answer will need to provide a way that the new tapes can offset the additional royalties spent on new copies because the new tapes last only half as long as the old ones.	**Step 4:** (C) is the only answer choice that addresses the royalties issue raised in Anna's reply. It strengthens Tony's argument by showing that royalty costs will be a wash: the tapes last 50% as long and the royalty fees are 50% less.

Wrong answers: (A) Outside the Scope. The argument is about the economic advantage for tape rentals, not retail sales. (B) Outside the Scope. The reasons for purchasing new tapes is irrelevant to both speakers' arguments. (D) Irrelevant Comparison. How consumers arrive at their purchase-versus-rent decision does not impact either argument in the dialog. (E) Outside the Scope. Nothing in this answer choice suggests a difference in this behavior between the old and new types of tape.

Hint: The subject matter of this argument is dated now—"Voice mail" used to be two words?!?!—but overlooked possibilities arguments are forever.

Step 2:	Step 1:

19. Telephone companies are promoting "voice mail" as an alternative to the answering machine. By recording messages from callers when a subscriber does not have access to his or her telephone, voice mail provides a service similar to that of an answering machine. The companies promoting this service argue that it will soon make answering machines obsolete, since it is much more convenient, more flexible, and less expensive than an answering machine.

Which one of the following, if true, most calls into question the argument made by the companies promoting voice mail?

(A) Unlike calls made to owners of answering machines, all telephone calls made to voice-mail subscribers are completed, even if the line called is in use at the time of the call.

(B) The surge in sales of answering machines occurred shortly after they were first introduced to the electronics market.

(C) Once a telephone customer decides to subscribe to voice mail, that customer can cancel the service at any time.

(D) Answering machines enable the customer to hear who is calling before the customer decides whether to answer the telephone, a service voice mail does not provide.

(E) The number of messages a telephone answering machine can record is limited by the length of the magnetic tape on which calls are recorded.

PrepTest112 Sec4 Q24

Step 3:	Step 4:

Expert Analysis

Review an example of an LSAT expert's work on the question you just completed.

Step 2: *Conclusion*: "Voice mail" will make answering machines obsolete *because* *Evidence*: "Voice mail" is more convenient, flexible, and economical than answering machines.	**Step 1:** "[C]alls into question" indicates a Weaken question; note that the argument is made by "companies promoting" something, so expect the evidence to be one-sided.

19. Telephone companies are promoting "voice mail" as an alternative to the answering machine. By recording messages from callers when a subscriber does not have access to his or her telephone, voice mail provides a service similar to that of an answering machine. The companies promoting this service argue that it will soon make answering machines obsolete, since it is much more convenient, more flexible, and less expensive than an answering machine.

Which one of the following, if true, most calls into question the argument made by the companies promoting voice mail?

(A) Unlike calls made to owners of answering machines, all telephone calls made to voice-mail subscribers are completed, even if the line called is in use at the time of the call.

(B) The surge in sales of answering machines occurred shortly after they were first introduced to the electronics market.

(C) Once a telephone customer decides to subscribe to voice mail, that customer can cancel the service at any time.

(D) Answering machines enable the customer to hear who is calling before the customer decides whether to answer the telephone, a service voice mail does not provide.

(E) The number of messages a telephone answering machine can record is limited by the length of the magnetic tape on which calls are recorded.

PrepTest112 Sec4 Q24

Step 3: Like any advertising copy, the message here is one-sided: our product will win because of all its positive attributes. To weaken the argument, then, the correct answer merely needs to cite a negative attribute or disadvantage to voicemail.	**Step 4:** (D) gives a disadvantage of voicemail compared to answering machines, thereby weakening the argument. (Historically, of course, caller ID cleared up the problem and we haven't seen answering machines for a couple decades now.)

Wrong answers: (A) 180. This cites yet another advantage of voicemail, thereby strengthening the conclusion. (B) Outside the Scope. Knowing when answering machines were at peak popularity does not weaken the conclusion that voice mail will prevail now. (C) 180. This rules out a potential concern over voicemail (getting locked into a contract), so it strengthens the argument. (E) 180. This cites a disadvantage of answering machines, thereby strengthening this pro-voicemail argument.

Hint: Make sure you understand the basis of the author's comparison in arguments like this one.

Step 2:	Step 1:

20. Although wood-burning stoves are more efficient than open fireplaces, they are also more dangerous. The smoke that wood-burning stoves release up the chimney is cooler than the smoke from an open flame. Thus it travels more slowly and deposits more creosote, a flammable substance that can clog a chimney—or worse, ignite inside it.

Which one of the following, if true, most seriously weakens the argument?

(A) The most efficient wood-burning stoves produce less creosote than do many open fireplaces.

(B) The amount of creosote produced depends not only on the type of flame but on how often the stove or fireplace is used.

(C) Open fireplaces pose more risk of severe accidents inside the home than do wood-burning stoves.

(D) Open fireplaces also produce a large amount of creosote residue.

(E) Homeowners in warm climates rarely use fireplaces or wood-burning stoves.

PrepTest110 Sec2 Q25

Step 3:	Step 4:

Expert Analysis

Review an example of an LSAT expert's work on the question you just completed.

Step 2: Conclusion: Wood-burning stoves are more dangerous than fireplaces *because* *Evidence*: (1) The smoke in the chimney of a wood-burning stove is cooler than that from a fireplace, and (2) cooler smoke leaves more flammable creosote in the chimney.	**Step 1:** This is a standard Weaken question stem; the correct answer will offer a fact making the conclusion less likely to follow from the evidence.

20. Although wood-burning stoves are more efficient than open fireplaces, they are also more dangerous. The smoke that wood-burning stoves release up the chimney is cooler than the smoke from an open flame. Thus it travels more slowly and deposits more creosote, a flammable substance that can clog a chimney—or worse ignite inside it.

Which one of the following, if true, most seriously weakens the argument?

(A) The most efficient wood-burning stoves produce less creosote than do many open fireplaces.

(B) The amount of creosote produced depends not only on the type of flame but on how often the stove or fireplace is used.

(C) Open fireplaces pose more risk of severe accidents inside the home than do wood-burning stoves.

(D) Open fireplaces also produce a large amount of creosote residue.

(E) Homeowners in warm climates rarely use fireplaces or wood-burning stoves.

PrepTest110 Sec2 Q25

Step 3: The author concludes that wood-burning stoves are more dangerous than fireplaces for one reason: cooler, slower-moving smoke leaves more flammable creosote in the chimneys of wood-burning stoves. The author must think this is the only factor, or at least the most important factor, in comparing the safety of wood-burning stoves to that of fireplaces. You can weaken the argument by showing other ways in which fireplaces are more dangerous than (or wood-burning stoves safer than) their counterparts.	**Step 4:** (C) weakens the argument by stating a comparative *disadvantage* in the safety of fireplaces compared to that of wood-burning stoves.

Wrong answers: (A) There are two problems with this choice: (1) we don't know how common these high-end stoves are, and (2) even if they produce less creosote, they may still *deposit* more of it in the chimney due to their relatively cool smoke. (B) This choice doesn't distinguish between stoves and fireplaces, so it cannot help or hurt the comparative argument. (D) distorts the argument, which focuses not on the production of creosote, but on how much creosote is *deposited* in the chimney by the stove's relatively cooler, slower-moving smoke. (E) does not distinguish between stoves and fireplaces so it cannot weaken the argument about their comparative safety.

Congratulations! You've learned and practiced a lot about the most common Logical Reasoning question type: Strengthen/Weaken questions. When you're ready, assess your skills with the Perform quiz.

Chapter Perform Quiz

Perform This Perform quiz has 12 Strengthen/Weaken questions. They are presented without any notes, hints, or prompts for a more test-like experience while you work. Try to get as many correct answers as possible in 20 minutes. When you finish, check your performance against the Answer Key and Evaluate Your Performance for tips on how best to improve. Then, come back to complete any questions you skipped or guessed on and finish up by reviewing all of the questions with the expert analyses in your online companion.

21. More and more computer programs that provide solutions to mathematical problems in engineering are being produced, and it is thus increasingly unnecessary for practicing engineers to have a thorough understanding of fundamental mathematical principles. Consequently, in training engineers who will work in industry, less emphasis should be placed on mathematical principles, so that space in the engineering curriculum will be available for other important subjects.

Which one of the following, if true, most seriously weakens the argument given for the recommendation above?

(A) The effective use of computer programs that provide solutions to mathematical problems in engineering requires an understanding of mathematical principles.

(B) Many of the computer programs that provide solutions to mathematical problems in engineering are already in routine use.

(C) Development of composites and other such new materials has meant that the curriculum for engineers who will work in industry must allow time for teaching the properties of these materials.

(D) Most of the computer programs that provide solutions to mathematical problems in engineering can be run on the types of computers available to most engineering firms.

(E) The engineering curriculum already requires that engineering students be familiar with and able to use a variety of computer programs.

PrepTest111 Sec3 Q1

22. For the next year, the Chefs' Union has requested a 10 percent salary increase for each of its members, whereas the Hotel Managers' Union has requested only an 8 percent salary increase for each of its members. These facts demonstrate that the average dollar amount of the raises that the Chefs' Union has requested for next year is greater than that of the raises requested by the Hotel Managers' Union.

Which one of the following, if true, most strengthens the argument?

(A) The Chefs' Union has many more members than does the Hotel Managers' Union.

(B) The Chefs' Union is a more powerful union than is the Hotel Managers' Union and is therefore more likely to obtain the salary increases it requests.

(C) The current salaries of the members of the Chefs' Union are, on average, higher than the current salaries of the members of the Hotel Managers' Union.

(D) The average dollar amount of the raises that the members of the Chefs' Union received last year was equal to the average dollar amount of the raises that the members of the Hotel Managers' Union received.

(E) The members of the Chefs' Union received salary increases of 10 percent in each of the last two years, while the members of the Hotel Managers' Union received salary increases of only 8 percent in each of the last two years.

PrepTest111 Sec3 Q4

23. It has been claimed that television networks should provide equal time for the presentation of opposing views whenever a television program concerns scientific issues—such as those raised by the claims of environmentalists—about which people disagree. However, although an obligation to provide equal time does arise in the case of any program concerning social issues, it does so because social issues almost always have important political implications and seldom can definitely be settled on the basis of available evidence. If a program concerns scientific issues, that program gives rise to no such equal time obligation.

Which one of the following, if true, most seriously weakens the argument?

(A) No scientific issues raised by the claims of environmentalists have important political implications.

(B) There are often more than two opposing views on an issue that cannot be definitely settled on the basis of available evidence.

(C) Some social issues could be definitely settled on the basis of evidence if the opposing sides would give all the available evidence a fair hearing.

(D) Many scientific issues have important political implications and cannot be definitely settled on the basis of the available evidence.

(E) Some television networks refuse to broadcast programs on issues that have important political implications and that cannot be definitely settled by the available evidence.

PrepTest112 Sec1 Q8

24. Opponent of offshore oil drilling: The projected benefits of drilling new oil wells in certain areas in the outer continental shelf are not worth the risk of environmental disaster. The oil already being extracted from these areas currently provides only 4 percent of our country's daily oil requirement, and the new wells would only add one-half of 1 percent.

Proponent of offshore oil drilling: Don't be ridiculous! You might just as well argue that new farms should not be allowed, since no new farm could supply the total food needs of our country for more than a few minutes.

Which one of the following, if true, most weakens the drilling proponent's reply?

(A) New farms do not involve a risk analogous to that run by new offshore oil drilling.

(B) Many of the largest oil deposits are located under land that is unsuitable for farming.

(C) Unlike oil, common agricultural products fulfill nutritional needs rather than fuel requirements.

(D) Legislation governing new oil drilling has been much more thoroughly articulated than has that governing new farms.

(E) The country under discussion imports a higher proportion of the farm products it needs than it does of the oil it needs.

PrepTest111 Sec3 Q8

25. A recent study suggests that Alzheimer's disease, which attacks the human brain, may be caused by a virus. In the study, blood from 11 volunteers, each of whom had the disease, was injected into rats. The rats eventually exhibited symptoms of another degenerative neurological disorder, Creutzfeldt-Jakob disease, which is caused by a virus. This led the scientist who conducted the study to conclude that Alzheimer's disease might be caused by a virus.

Which one of the following statements, if true, would most strengthen the scientist's hypothesis that Alzheimer's disease is caused by a virus?

(A) Alzheimer's disease in rats is not caused by a virus.

(B) Creutzfeldt-Jakob disease affects only motor nerves in rats' limbs, not their brains.

(C) The virus that causes Creutzfeldt-Jakob disease in rats has no effect on humans.

(D) The symptoms known, respectively, as Creutzfeldt-Jakob disease and Alzheimer's disease are different manifestations of the same disease.

(E) Blood from rats with Creutzfeldt-Jakob disease produced no symptoms of the disease when injected into other experimental rats.

PrepTest111 Sec4 Q10

26. The five senses have traditionally been viewed as distinct yet complementary. Each sense is thought to have its own range of stimuli that are incapable of stimulating the other senses. However, recent research has discovered that some people taste a banana and claim that they are tasting blue, or see a color and say that it has a specific smell. This shows that such people, called synesthesiacs, have senses that do not respect the usual boundaries between the five recognized senses.

Which one of the following statements, if true, most seriously weakens the argument?

(A) Synesthesiacs demonstrate a general, systematic impairment in their ability to use and understand words.

(B) Recent evidence strongly suggests that there are other senses besides sight, touch, smell, hearing, and taste.

(C) The particular ways in which sensory experiences overlap in synesthesiacs follow a definite pattern.

(D) The synesthetic phenomenon has been described in the legends of various cultures.

(E) Synesthesiacs can be temporarily rid of their synesthetic experiences by the use of drugs.

PrepTest110 Sec2 Q12

27. It is not good for a university to have class sizes that are very large or very small, or to have professors with teaching loads that are very light or very heavy. After all, crowded classes and overworked faculty cripple the institution's ability to recruit and retain both qualified students and faculty.

Which one of the following, if added as a premise to the argument, most helps to justify its conclusion?

(A) Professors who have very light teaching loads tend to focus their remaining time on research.

(B) Classes that have very low numbers of students tend to have a lot of classroom discussion.

(C) Very small class sizes or very light teaching loads indicate incompetence in classroom instruction.

(D) Very small class sizes or very light teaching loads are common in the worst and the best universities.

(E) Professors with very light teaching loads have no more office hours for students than professors with normal teaching loads.

PrepTest112 Sec4 Q15

28. Researchers have found that people who drink five or more cups of coffee a day have a risk of heart disease 2.5 times the average after corrections are made for age and smoking habits. Members of the research team say that, on the basis of their findings, they now limit their own daily coffee intake to two cups.

Which one of the following, if true, indicates that the researchers' precaution might NOT have the result of decreasing their risk of heart disease?

(A) The study found that for people who drank three or more cups of coffee daily, the additional risk of heart disease increased with each extra daily cup.

(B) Per capita coffee consumption has been declining over the past 20 years because of the increasing popularity of soft drinks and also because of health worries.

(C) The study did not collect information that would show whether variations in level of coffee consumption are directly related to variations in level of stress, a major causal factor in heart disease.

(D) Subsequent studies have consistently shown that heavy smokers consume coffee at about 3 times the rate of nonsmokers.

(E) Subsequent studies have shown that heavy coffee consumption tends to cause an elevated blood-cholesterol level, an immediate indicator of increased risk of heart disease.

PrepTest112 Sec4 Q17

29. People who have political power tend to see new technologies as a means of extending or protecting their power, whereas they generally see new ethical arguments and ideas as a threat to it. Therefore, technical ingenuity usually brings benefits to those who have this ingenuity, whereas ethical inventiveness brings only pain to those who have this inventiveness.

Which one of the following statements, if true, most strengthens the argument?

(A) Those who offer new ways of justifying current political power often reap the benefits of their own innovations.

(B) Politically powerful people tend to reward those who they believe are useful to them and to punish those who they believe are a threat.

(C) Ethical inventiveness and technical ingenuity are never possessed by the same individuals.

(D) New technologies are often used by people who strive to defeat those who currently have political power.

(E) Many people who possess ethical inventiveness conceal their novel ethical arguments for fear of retribution by the politically powerful.

PrepTest112 Sec4 Q18

30. Critic: Political utility determines the popularity of a metaphor. In authoritarian societies, the metaphor of society as a human body governed by a head is pervasive. Therefore, the society-as-body metaphor, with its connection between society's proper functioning and governance by a head, promotes greater acceptance of authoritarian repression than do other metaphors, such as likening society to a family.

Which one of the following statements, if true, most weakens the critic's argument?

(A) In authoritarian societies, the metaphor of society as a family is just as pervasive as the society-as-body metaphor.

(B) Every society tries to justify the legitimacy of its government through the use of metaphor.

(C) The metaphor of society as a human body is sometimes used in nonauthoritarian societies.

(D) Authoritarian leaders are always searching for new metaphors for society in their effort to maintain their power.

(E) The metaphor of society as a human body governed by a head is rarely used in liberal democracies

PrepTest110 Sec3 Q20

31. Ringtail opossums are an Australian wildlife species that is potentially endangered. A number of ringtail opossums that had been orphaned and subsequently raised in captivity were monitored after being returned to the wild. Seventy-five percent of those opossums were killed by foxes, a species not native to Australia. Conservationists concluded that the native ringtail opossum population was endangered not by a scarcity of food, as had been previously thought, but by non-native predator species against which the opossum had not developed natural defenses.

Which one of the following, if true, most strongly supports the conservationists' argument?

(A) There are fewer non-native predator species that prey on the ringtail opossum than there are native species that prey on the ringtail opossum.

(B) Foxes, which were introduced into Australia over 200 years ago, adapted to the Australian climate less successfully than did some other foreign species.

(C) The ringtail opossums that were raised in captivity were fed a diet similar to that which ringtail opossums typically eat in the wild.

(D) Few of the species that compete with the ringtail opossum for food sources are native to Australia.

(E) Ringtail opossums that grow to adulthood in the wild defend themselves against foxes no more successfully than do ringtail opossums raised in captivity.

PrepTest110 Sec3 Q24

32. A 1991 calculation was made to determine what, if any, additional healthcare costs beyond the ordinary are borne by society at large for people who live a sedentary life. The figure reached was a lifetime average of $1,650. Thus people's voluntary choice not to exercise places a significant burden on society.

Which one of the following, if true and not taken into account by the calculation, most seriously weakens the argument?

(A) Many people whose employment requires physical exertion do not choose to engage in regular physical exercise when they are not at work.

(B) Exercise is a topic that is often omitted from discussion between doctor and patient during a patient's visit.

(C) Physical conditions that eventually require medical or nursing home care often first predispose a person to adopt a sedentary lifestyle.

(D) Individuals vary widely in the amount and kind of exercise they choose, when they do exercise regularly.

(E) A regular program of moderate exercise tends to increase circulation, induce a feeling of well-being and energy, and decrease excess weight.

PrepTest112 Sec1 Q25

Answer Key

21. A; 22. C; 23. D; 24. A; 25. D; 26. A; 27. C; 28. C; 29. B; 30. A; 31. E; 32. C

Evaluate Your Performance

To assess your strengths and opportunities from this Perform quiz, go to the corresponding chapter in your online companion. There you'll find recommendations based on your performance along with complete worked-example explanations (written by a Kaplan LSAT expert) for each of the questions in this Perform quiz.

CHAPTER 12

Assumption-Family Principle Questions

Principle questions mimic other question types, including Assumption and Strengthen questions from the Assumption Family. These will be covered in this section. In the next chapter, you'll see Principle questions that test Parallel Reasoning, and in Chapter 14, those that test Inference question skills.

LEARNING OBJECTIVES

In this chapter, you'll learn to:

- Recognize Principle question stems, and distinguish Assumption-Family Principle questions from other Inference-based Principle questions.
- Identify and answer Principle-Strengthen questions.
- Identify and answer Principle-Assumption questions.

On a typical LSAT, expect to see four or five Principle questions. That's approximately 6% of your overall LSAT score. Three or four of these will almost always be Assumption-Family Principle questions that test the same skills as Strengthen and Assumption questions. The other one (or, rarely, two) Principle questions will be Principle-Inference questions. You'll cover those in Part IV of the book along with Inference questions.

Approximate Number of Principle Questions per LSAT

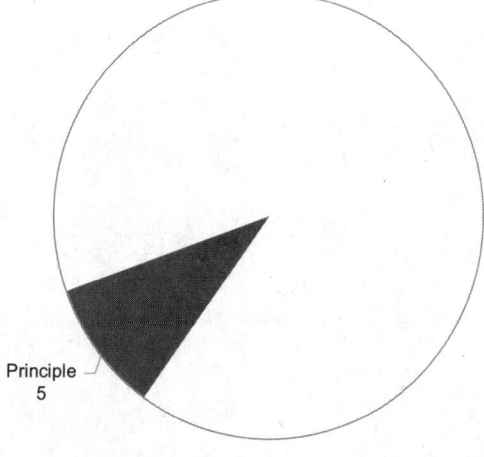

Principle
5

Source: All officially released LSAT exams, 2016-2020

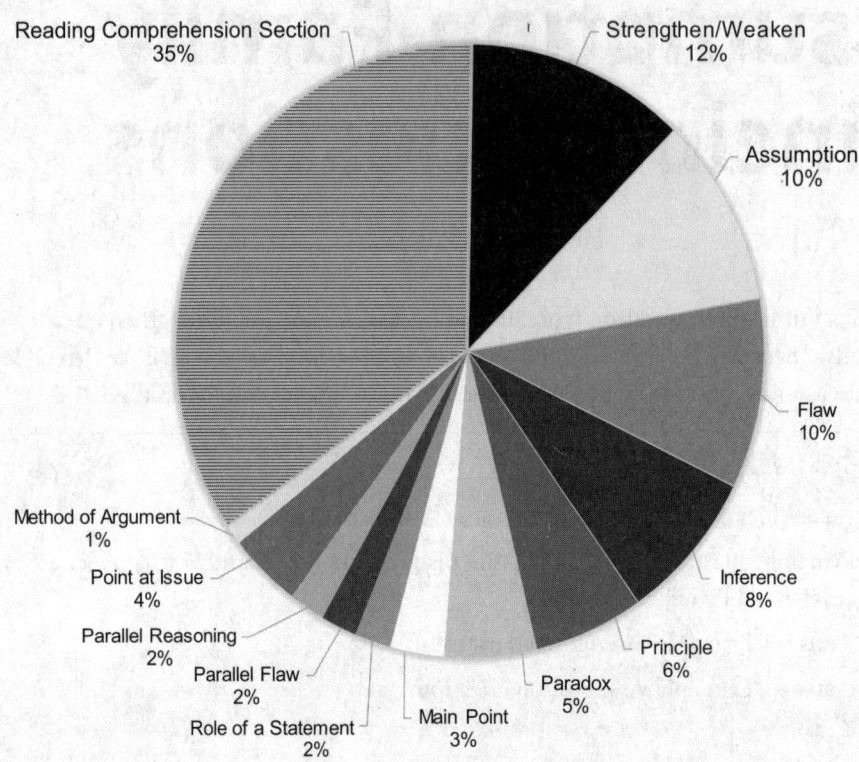

Percentage of All Questions per LSAT by Logical Reasoning Question Type

Reading Comprehension Section 35%

Strengthen/Weaken 12%

Assumption 10%

Flaw 10%

Inference 8%

Principle 6%

Paradox 5%

Main Point 3%

Role of a Statement 2%

Parallel Flaw 2%

Parallel Reasoning 2%

Point at Issue 4%

Method of Argument 1%

Source: All officially released LSAT exams, 2016-2020

You've already learned the core reasoning skills rewarded in Assumption-Family Principle questions— they're the same ones tested in Strengthen and Assumption questions—but distinguishing among the various types of Principle questions can be a bit tricky at first. So, before getting into question analysis and practice, spend a little time getting familiar with the variety of Principle question stems. Knowing your task is, after all, Step 1 of the Logical Reasoning method.

Identify Principle Question Subtypes

LEARNING OBJECTIVE

In this section, you'll learn to:

- Recognize Principle question stems, and distinguish Assumption-Family Principle questions from other Inference-based Principle questions.

On the LSAT, think of a *principle* as you would a law, a general rule applicable to all relevant cases. A question that asks you to either identify or apply a general rule is a Principle question. These question stems typically use the word *principle*, but occasionally, they may use words like *proposition* or *policy* instead. Be on the lookout for tasks such as "most closely conforms to," "best illustrates," "helps to justify," and "underlies the argument."

> Which one of the following principles, if valid, most helps to justify the reasoning above?
>
> *PrepTest112 Sec1 Q15*

> Which one of the following principles underlies the arbitrator's argument?
>
> *PrepTest107 Sec1 Q19*

> The parent's experience with the child most closely conforms to which one of the following generalizations?
>
> *PrepTest111 Sec3 Q5*

> Which one of the following judgments most closely conforms to the principle cited above?
>
> *PrepTest104 Sec4 Q3*

Distinguishing Types of Principle Questions

Principle-Strengthen: In the first example above, your task is to identify the principle that will help justify the argument. This is just like a Strengthen question except that the correct answer will be a broad, general statement instead of a specific fact.

Principle-Assumption: In the second example above, your task is to identify the principle that underlies the argument. And what underlies an argument? That's right, its assumption. Look for the choice that states the argument's assumption in generalized terms.

Principle-Inference (identify): In the third example above, your task is to identify the principle that matches the situation described in the stimulus. Look for the choice that states in broad terms the rule applied in the stimulus. Note: In these questions, the stimulus may not be an argument.

Principle-Inference (apply): In the fourth example above, your task is to find the specific case or example that appropriately applies the broad, general rule stated in the stimulus. Look for the choice that gives a specific case matching the rule. Note: Here, the stimulus will not contain an argument, just a rule.

Practice   Classify the Principle question type in each of the following question stems. Pay attention to whether you're asked to find a specific situation from a general rule or a general rule from a specific situation. When you're finished, compare your work to that of an LSAT expert on the following page.

LSAT Question Stem	My Analysis
1. Which one of the following is a principle underlying the advice given to police officers? *PrepTest107 Sec4 Q17*	
2. Which one of the following principles most strongly supports Professor Wigmore's argument? *PrepTest110 Sec2 Q20*	
3. Which one of the following most accurately expresses the principle illustrated above? *PrepTest110 Sec3 Q1*	
4. Which one of the following principles, if valid, most helps to justify the reasoning above? *PrepTest111 Sec4 Q11*	

Expert Analysis for the Practice exercise may be found on the following page. ▶ ▶ ▶

Expert Analysis

Here's how an LSAT expert analyzed the question stems you just saw.

LSAT Question Stem	Analysis
1. Which one of the following is a principle underlying the advice given to police officers? *PrepTest107 Sec4 Q17*	A "principle underlying" the argument signals a Principle-Assumption question; look for the answer choice that states a general rule matching the argument's specific assumption.
2. Which one of the following principles most strongly supports Professor Wigmore's argument? *PrepTest110 Sec2 Q20*	This is a Principle-Strengthen question. The question stem uses "strongly supports," typical Strengthen question language, but tells you that the correct answer is a *principle* rather than a fact. Look for the answer choice stating a broad rule that helps justify the argument's conclusion based on its evidence.
3. Which one of the following most accurately expresses the principle illustrated above? *PrepTest110 Sec3 Q1*	This is a Principle-Inference question. The stimulus ("above") will present a case or example that *illustrates* a principle which is then *expressed* in the correct answer.
4. Which one of the following principles, if valid, most helps to justify the reasoning above? *PrepTest111 Sec4 Q11*	The phrase "helps to justify" identifies this as a Principle-Strengthen question. Look for the choice that provides a broad-based principle that helps establish the argument's conclusion based on its evidence.

TEST DAY TIP

Principle-Strengthen are about three times more common than any of the other Principle question subtypes. Using Strengthen question tactics and strategies helps you become faster and more accurate on these questions, too.

ASSUMPTION-FAMILY PRINCIPLE QUESTIONS AT A GLANCE

Task: Identify whether the question is asking for the principle that acts as the argument's assumption ("underlies the argument") or as a strengthener ("most justifies").

Strategy: Use the same skills you would to answer an Assumption or Strengthen question, but phrase your prediction of the correct answer as a broad general rule.

Frequency: On LSAT tests released between 2016 and 2020, there were an average of 2.4 Principle questions per section, of which 1.8 were Assumption-Family Principle questions on average.

Principle-Strengthen Question Basics

LEARNING OBJECTIVE

In this section, you'll learn to:

- Identify and answer Principle-Assumption questions.

Get familiar with Principle-Strengthen questions by trying this one on your own. When you're finished, compare your work with that of an LSAT expert by reviewing the worked example on the next page.

Step 2:	Step 1:

5. In one study, engineering students who prepared for an exam by using toothpicks and string did no worse than similar students who prepared by using an expensive computer with sophisticated graphics. In another study, military personnel who trained on a costly hightech simulator performed no better on a practical exam than did similar personnel who trained using an inexpensive cardboard model. So one should not always purchase technologically advanced educational tools.

Which one of the following principles, if valid, most helps to justify the reasoning above?

(A) One should use different educational tools to teach engineering to civilians than are used to train military personnel.

(B) Hightech solutions to modern problems are ineffective unless implemented by knowledgeable personnel.

(C) Spending large sums of money on educational tools is at least as justified for non-military training as it is for military training.

(D) One should not invest in expensive teaching aids unless there are no other tools that are less expensive and at least as effective.

(E) One should always provide students with a variety of educational materials so that each student can find the materials that best suit that student's learning style.

PrepTest112 Sec1 Q15

Step 3:	Step 4:

Expert Analysis

Take a look at how an LSAT expert applied the steps of the Logical Reasoning Method to this Principle-Strengthen question.

Step 2: *Conclusion*: Don't always buy high-tech educational tools *because* *Evidence*: in two cases, students who prepared using low-tech tools did just as well as those who used expensive, high-tech tools.	**Step 1:** This is a straightforward Principle-Strengthen question; the correct answer will cite a broad-based rule in line with the argument's assumption.

5. In one study, engineering students who prepared for an exam by using toothpicks and string did no worse than similar students who prepared by using an expensive computer with sophisticated graphics. In another study, military personnel who trained on a costly hightech simulator performed no better on a practical exam than did similar personnel who trained using an inexpensive cardboard model. So one should not always purchase technologically advanced educational tools.

Which one of the following principles, if valid, most helps to justify the reasoning above?

(A) One should use different educational tools to teach engineering to civilians than are used to train military personnel.

(B) Hightech solutions to modern problems are ineffective unless implemented by knowledgeable personnel.

(C) Spending large sums of money on educational tools is at least as justified for non-military training as it is for military training.

(D) One should not invest in expensive teaching aids unless there are no other tools that are less expensive and at least as effective.

(E) One should always provide students with a variety of educational materials so that each student can find the materials that best suit that student's learning style.

PrepTest112 Sec1 Q15

Step 3: The students in each study performed equally well whether they used low- or high-tech learning tools. So, why is the author against high-tech solutions? Because, according to the evidence, they are expensive. The correct answer will say something along the lines of: don't spend extra money if the cheaper solution works just as well.	**Step 4:** (D) matches the argument's assumption and is correct.

Wrong answers: (A) Irrelevant comparison. The stimulus came to a similar conclusion in both the engineering and military training situations. (B) Outside the Scope. The stimulus does not touch on the requirements for effective implementation of training solutions. (C) Irrelevant comparison. The stimulus does not compare or contrast the two training contexts; it cites both as relevant to the larger point that high-tech tools shouldn't always be sought. (E) sounds well intentioned, but it does not fit the argument in the stimulus.

Well done. Before moving to the practice set, get familiar with another Assumption-Family Principle question variant.

Principle-Assumption Question Basics

LEARNING OBJECTIVE

In this section, you'll learn to:

• Identify and answer Principle-Assumption questions.

Get familiar with this rare Assumption Family question type by trying a Principle-Assumption question on your own. When you're finished, compare your work to that of an LSAT expert with the worked example on the following page.

Step 2:	**Step 1:**

6. Arbitrator: The shipping manager admits that he decided to close the old facility on October 14 and to schedule the new facility's opening for October 17, the following Monday. But he also claims that he is not responsible for the business that was lost due to the new facility's failing to open as scheduled. He blames the contractor for not finishing on time, but he too, is to blame, for he was aware of the contractor's typical delays and should have planned for this contingency.

Which one of the following principles underlies the arbitrator's argument?

(A) A manager should take foreseeable problems into account when making decisions.

(B) A manager should be able to depend on contractors to do their jobs promptly.

(C) A manager should see to it that contractors do their jobs promptly.

(D) A manager should be held responsible for mistakes made by those whom the manager directly supervises.

(E) A manager, and only a manager, should be held responsible for a project's failure.

PrepTest107 Sec1 Q19

Step 3:	**Step 4:**

Expert Analysis

Take a look at how an LSAT expert applied the Logical Reasoning Method to the Principle-Assumption question you just tried.

Step 2: *Conclusion*: The shipping manager shares the blame (with the contractor) for losses that happened because the new facility was not open on time *because*

Evidence: He should have planned for routine delays of which he was cognizant.

Step 1: The phrase "underlies the … argument" identifies this as a Principle-Assumption question; the correct answer will be a broad rule that matches the argument's specific assumption.

6. Arbitrator: The shipping manager admits that he decided to close the old facility on October 14 and to schedule the new facility's opening for October 17, the following Monday. But he also claims that he is not responsible for the business that was lost due to the new facility's failing to open as scheduled. He blames the contractor for not finishing on time, but he too, is to blame, for he was aware of the contractor's typical delays and should have planned for this contingency.

Which one of the following principles underlies the arbitrator's argument?

(A) A manager should take foreseeable problems into account when making decisions.

(B) A manager should be able to depend on contractors to do their jobs promptly.

(C) A manager should see to it that contractors do their jobs promptly.

(D) A manager should be held responsible for mistakes made by those whom the manager directly supervises.

(E) A manager, and only a manager, should be held responsible for a project's failure.

PrepTest107 Sec1 Q19

Step 3: Note that the arbitrator does not exonerate the contractor but says the manager is "also to blame" because the contractor's delays were typical, and thus, should have been anticipated. The correct answer will say something along the lines of "managers share blame when they can anticipate typical delays and don't take action."

Step 4: (A) matches the specific prediction in the argument (and the prediction in Step 3) and is correct.

Wrong answers: (B) distorts the argument; the arbitrator doesn't let the contractor completely off the hook, but attributes some of the fault to the manager who should have expected the contractor's *typical* delays. (C) Outside the Scope. The argument doesn't suggest that the shipping manager was responsible for the contractor's performance. (D) Outside the Scope. Nothing in the argument suggests that the contractor reported to the shipping manager. (E) distorts the arbitrator's conclusion, which is that the manager *shares* blame with the contractor.

Now, try some individual Assumption-Family Principle questions in the following Practice set. Each question has a hint. Keep it in mind as you work through the steps of the Logical Reasoning Method on each question.

Practice Try each of the following Principle-Strengthen questions. Don't worry too much about your timing here. Complete all four steps of the Logical Reasoning Method for each question, jotting down your notes whenever it is helpful to do so. After each question, review your work with the Expert Analysis that follows.

Hint: Try to boil the argument down to its simplest distinctions: what is the difference in scope between the theories in the evidence and in the conclusion?

Step 2:	Step 1:

7. One approach to the question of which objects discussed by a science are real is to designate as real all and only those entities posited by the most explanatorily powerful theory of the science. But since most scientific theories contain entities posited solely on theoretical grounds, this approach is flawed.

Which one of the following principles, if valid, most helps to justify the reasoning above?

(A) Any object that is posited by a scientific theory and that enhances the explanatory power of that theory should be designated as real.

(B) Objects posited for theoretical reasons only should never be designated as real.

(C) A scientific theory should not posit any entity that does not enhance the explanatory power of the theory.

(D) A scientific theory should sometimes posit entities on grounds other than theoretical ones.

(E) Only objects posited by explanatorily powerful theories should be designated as real.

PrepTest111 Sec4 Q11

Step 3:	Step 4:

Expert Analysis

Here's how an LSAT expert worked through the question you just completed.

Step 2: *Conclusion*: It is flawed to think the "real" entities in a given science are all of the ones postulated by that discipline's most powerful explanatory theory, *because* *Evidence*: Most theories have wholly theoretical entities.	**Step 1:** This is a standard Principle-Strengthen question stem; the correct answer supplies a broad rule supporting the argument's assumption.

7. One approach to the question of which objects discussed by a science are real is to designate as real all and only those entities posited by the most explanatorily powerful theory of the science. But since most scientific theories contain entities posited solely on theoretical grounds, this approach is flawed.

Which one of the following principles, if valid, most helps to justify the reasoning above?

(A) Any object that is posited by a scientific theory and that enhances the explanatory power of that theory should be designated as real.

(B) Objects posited for theoretical reasons only should never be designated as real.

(C) A scientific theory should not posit any entity that does not enhance the explanatory power of the theory.

(D) A scientific theory should sometimes posit entities on grounds other than theoretical ones.

(E) Only objects posited by explanatorily powerful theories should be designated as real.

PrepTest111 Sec4 Q11

Step 3: To paraphrase this dense stimulus in simple terms, the author's point is that there's nothing so special about the most powerful theory that its theoretical entities should be designated as more "real" than any other theory's postulated entities are. The correct answer will supply a rule that supports this contention.	**Step 4:** (B) is correct; it nails down the argument with a blanket rule: don't designate any purely theoretical entities as real.

Wrong answers: (A) distorts the argument by introducing a new criterion—*enhancing* a theory's explanatory power—that is not discussed in the stimulus. (C) distorts the argument by introducing a new criterion—*enhancing* a theory's explanatory power—that is not discussed in the stimulus. (D) Outside the Scope. The author's concern is which posited entities should be designated as real, not why theories posit entities in the first place. (E) 180. This is precisely the position of the "one approach" the argument rejects.

Hint: Argument analysis is the foundation of all Assumption Family questions; what are distinct terms in the conclusion and evidence here?

Step 2:	Step 1:

8. Studies of the reliability of eyewitness identifications show little correlation between the accuracy of a witness's account and the confidence the witness has in the account. Certain factors can increase or undermine witness's confidence without altering the accuracy of the identification. Therefore, police officers are advised to disallow suspect lineups in which witnesses can hear one another identifying suspects.

Which one of the following is a principle underlying the advice given to police officers?

(A) The confidence people have in what they remember having seen is affected by their awareness of what other people claim to have seen.

(B) Unless an eyewitness is confronted with more than one suspect at a time, the accuracy of his or her statements cannot be trusted.

(C) If several eyewitnesses all identify the same suspect in a lineup, it is more likely that the suspect committed the crime than if only one eyewitness identifies the suspect.

(D) Police officers are more interested in the confidence witnesses have when testifying than in the accuracy of that testimony.

(E) The accuracy of an eyewitness account is doubtful if the eyewitness contradicts what other eyewitnesses claim to have seen.

PrepTest107 Sec4 Q17

Step 3:	Step 4:

Expert Analysis

Compare your work to that of an LSAT expert on the question you just completed.

Hint: Argument analysis is the foundation of all Assumption Family questions; what are distinct terms in the conclusion and evidence here?

Step 2: *Conclusion*: The police should not use line-ups in which witnesses can hear other witnesses identify suspects *because*

Evidence: There are factors that strengthen or weaken a witness's confidence in their identification (even though those factors don't change the witness's accuracy).

Step 1: When you're asked for an "underlying" principle—signaling a Principle-Assumption question—look for the choice with a broad rule that matches the argument's specific assumption.

8. Studies of the reliability of eyewitness identifications show little correlation between the accuracy of a witness's account and the confidence the witness has in the account. Certain factors can increase or undermine a witness's confidence without altering the accuracy of the identification. Therefore, police officers are advised to disallow suspect lineups in which witnesses can hear one another identifying suspects.

Which one of the following is a principle underlying the advice given to police officers?

(A) The confidence people have in what they remember having seen is affected by their awareness of what other people claim to have seen.

(B) Unless an eyewitness is confronted with more than one suspect at a time, the accuracy of his or her statements cannot be trusted.

(C) If several eyewitnesses all identify the same suspect in a lineup, it is more likely that the suspect committed the crime than if only one eyewitness identifies the suspect.

(D) Police officers are more interested in the confidence witnesses have when testifying than in the accuracy of that testimony.

(E) The accuracy of an eyewitness account is doubtful if the eyewitness contradicts what other eyewitnesses claim to have seen.

PrepTest107 Sec4 Q17

Step 3: To bridge the mismatched concepts here, the author must assume that hearing other witnesses identify suspects is one of the factors that can alter a witness's confidence in their own identification of a suspect.

Step 4: (A) matches the assumption in the stimulus argument precisely, and is correct.

Wrong answers: (B) Outside the Scope. The issue in the stimulus argument is about overhearing other witnesses, not about the number of suspects in the lineup. (C) Outside the Scope. This argument is not about the accuracy of the identification, but about the witness's confidence in it. (D) Irrelevant comparison. Nothing in the argument attempts to compare or rank the importance of accuracy versus confidence; presumably, both are important. (E) Outside the Scope. The stimulus argument is about witnesses' confidence, not their accuracy, in making identifications.

Hint: Just like those in standard Strengthen questions, the correct answer in Principle-Strengthen makes the argument's conclusion more likely to follow from its evidence; i.e., the correct answer strengthens the assumption.

Step 2:	Step 1:

9. Professor Chan: The literature department's undergraduate courses should cover only true literary works, and not such frivolous material as advertisements.

Professor Wigmore: Advertisements might or might not be true literary works but they do have a powerfully detrimental effect on society—largely because people cannot discern their real messages. The literature department's courses give students the critical skills to analyze and understand texts. Therefore, it is the literature department's responsibility to include the study of advertisements in its undergraduate courses.

Which one of the following principles most strongly supports Professor Wigmore's argument?

(A) Advertisements ought to be framed in such a way that their real messages are immediately clear.

(B) Any text that is subtly constructed and capable of affecting people's thought and action ought to be considered a form of literature.

(C) All undergraduate students ought to take at least one course that focuses on the development of critical skills.

(D) The literature department's courses ought to enable students to analyze and understand any text that could have a harmful effect on society.

(E) Any professor teaching an undergraduate course in the literature department ought to be free to choose the material to be covered in that course.

PrepTest110 Sec2 Q20

Step 3:	Step 4:

Expert Analysis

Here's how an LSAT expert worked through the question you just completed.

Step 2: Chan—Lit department courses should cover only real literature not frivolous things like advertisements. Wigmore—*Conclusion*: The Lit department has a responsibility to include advertisements in its courses *because* *Evidence*: Misunderstood advertisements are dangerous to society, and it is the Lit department's job to give students the skills to analyze texts.	**Step 1:** This is a Principle-Strengthen question with a dialog stimulus; the correct answer strengthens the second speaker's conclusion.

9.   Professor Chan: The literature department's undergraduate courses should cover only true literary works, and not such frivolous material as advertisements.

Professor Wigmore: Advertisements might or might not be true literary works but they do have a powerfully detrimental effect on society—largely because people cannot discern their real messages. The literature department's courses give students the critical skills to analyze and understand texts. Therefore, it is the literature department's responsibility to include the study of advertisements in its undergraduate courses.

Which one of the following principles most strongly supports Professor Wigmore's argument?

(A) Advertisements ought to be framed in such a way that their real messages are immediately clear.

(B) Any text that is subtly constructed and capable of affecting people's thought and action ought to be considered a form of literature.

(C) All undergraduate students ought to take at least one course that focuses on the development of critical skills.

(D) The literature department's courses ought to enable students to analyze and understand any text that could have a harmful effect on society.

(E) Any professor teaching an undergraduate course in the literature department ought to be free to choose the material to be covered in that course.

PrepTest110 Sec2 Q20

Step 3: Wigmore concludes that the Lit department has an obligation to include advertisements in its courses. The evidence is that part of the Lit department's job is to give students the tools to analyze texts, and that should include advertisements (even if they aren't "literature") because, if poorly understood, they are dangerous to society. Wigmore assumes the department's obligations cover the analysis of texts beyond Chan's "true literary works."

Step 4: (D) matches the reasoning of Wigmore's argument piece-by-piece—supporting his rationale (if misunderstood, advertisements can be dangerous to society) and conclusion (thus, the Lit Department should cover advertisements)—and is correct.

Wrong answers: (A) Outside the Scope. Wigmore's argument is about what the Lit department should cover, not what advertisers should produce. (B) distorts Wigmore's argument, which holds that the Lit department should cover advertisements *even if they aren't* true literature. (C) is too broad to support Wigmore's specific argument, which is aimed at what the Lit department is justified in teaching, not broadly at what *all* students should take. (E) does match Wigmore's rationale, which is based on the kind of material the department should cover, not on the discretion of individual professors.

Nice work! Now, assess your Principle-Strengthen question skills with the following Perform quiz.

Chapter Perform Quiz

Perform   This Perform quiz has 4 Principle-Strengthen questions. They are presented without any notes, hints, or prompts for a more test-like experience while you work. Try to get as many correct answers as possible in 5 minutes. When you finish, check your performance against the Answer Key and Evaluate Your Performance for tips on how best to improve. Then, come back to complete any questions you skipped or guessed on and finish up by reviewing all of the questions with the expert analyses in your online companion.

10. Lecturer: Given our current state of knowledge and technology, we can say that the generalization that the entropy of a closed system cannot decrease for any spontaneous process has not been falsified by any of our tests of that generalization. So we conclude it to be true universally. Yet, it must be admitted that this generalization has not been conclusively verified, in the sense that it has not been tested in every corner of the universe, under every feasible condition. Nevertheless, this generalization is correctly regarded as a scientific law; indeed, it is referred to as the Second Law of Thermodynamics.

Which one of the following principles, if valid, most justifies the lecturer's classification of the generalization described above?

(A) Whatever is a scientific law has not been falsified.

(B) If a generalization is confirmed only under a few circumstances, it should not be considered a scientific law.

(C) Whatever is true universally will eventually be confirmed to the extent current science allows.

(D) If a generalization is confirmed to the extent current science allows, then it is considered a scientific law.

(E) Whatever is regarded as a scientific law will eventually be conclusively verified.

PrepTest111 Sec1 Q2

11. Ethicist: In a recent judicial decision, a contractor was ordered to make restitution to a company because of a bungled construction job, even though the company had signed a written agreement prior to entering into the contract that the contractor would not be financially liable should the task not be adequately performed. Thus, it was morally wrong for the company to change its mind and seek restitution.

Which one of the following principles, if valid, most helps to justify the ethicist's reasoning?

(A) It is morally wrong for one party not to abide by its part of an agreement only if the other party abides by its part of the agreement.

(B) It is morally wrong to seek a penalty for an action for which the agent is unable to make restitution.

(C) It is morally wrong for one person to seek to penalize another person for an action that the first person induced the other person to perform.

(D) It is morally wrong to ignore the terms of an agreement that was freely undertaken only if there is clear evidence that the agreement was legally permissible.

(E) It is morally wrong to seek compensation for an action performed in the context of a promise to forgo such compensation.

PrepTest110 Sec3 Q16

12. On the surface, Melville's Billy Budd is a simple story with a simple theme. However, if one views the novel as a religious allegory, then it assumes a richness and profundity that place it among the great novels of the nineteenth century. However, the central question remains: Did Melville intend an allegorical reading? Since there is no textual or historical evidence that he did, we should be content with reading Billy Budd as a simple tragedy.

Which one of the following most accurately expresses the principle underlying the argument?

(A) Given a choice between an allegorical and a nonallegorical reading of a novel, one should choose the latter.

(B) The only relevant evidence in deciding in which genre to place a novel is the author's stated intention.

(C) In deciding between rival readings of a novel, one should choose the one that is most favorable to the work.

(D) Without relevant evidence as to a novel's intended reading, one should avoid viewing the work allegorically.

(E) The only relevant evidence in deciding the appropriate interpretation of a text is the text itself.

PrepTest113 Sec3 Q22

13. When investigators discovered that the director of a local charity had repeatedly overstated the number of people his charity had helped, the director accepted responsibility for the deception. However, the investigators claimed that journalists were as much to blame as the director was for inflating the charity's reputation, since they had naïvely accepted what the director told them, and simply reported as fact the numbers he gave them.

Which one of the following principles, if valid, most helps to justify the investigators' claim?

(A) Anyone who works for a charitable organization is obliged to be completely honest about the activities of that organization.

(B) Anyone who knowingly aids a liar by trying to conceal the truth from others is also a liar.

(C) Anyone who presents as factual a story that turns out to be untrue without first attempting to verify that story is no less responsible for the consequences of that story than anyone else is.

(D) Anyone who lies in order to advance his or her own career is more deserving of blame than someone who lies in order to promote a good cause.

(E) Anyone who accepts responsibility for a wrongful act that he or she committed is less deserving of blame than someone who tries to conceal his or her own wrongdoing.

PrepTest112 Sec4 Q23

Answer Key

10. D; 11. E; 12. D; 13. C

Evaluate Your Performance

To assess your strengths and opportunities from this Perform quiz, go to the corresponding chapter in your online companion. There you'll find recommendations based on your performance along with complete worked-example explanations (written by a Kaplan LSAT expert) for each of the questions in this Perform quiz.

CHAPTER 13

Parallel Flaw and Parallel Principle Questions

There are two more Assumption Family question types, both of the parallel-arguments variety. Parallel Flaw questions present a flawed argument in the stimulus and ask you to find an answer choice with an argument that demonstrates the same flaw. Similarly, Parallel Principle questions give you a stimulus argument illustrating an underlying principle and ask for a choice based on the same principle.

LEARNING OBJECTIVES

In this chapter, you'll learn to:

- Identify and answer Parallel Flaw questions.
- Identify and answer Parallel Principle questions.

There is almost always one Parallel Flaw question per Logical Reasoning section, meaning you'll see two scored Parallel Flaw questions per text. That's worth around 2.5% of your LSAT score. Parallel Principle questions are so uncommon that it is unlikely that you'll encounter one on your exam; to see more than one Parallel Principle question in a single LSAT is passingly rare.

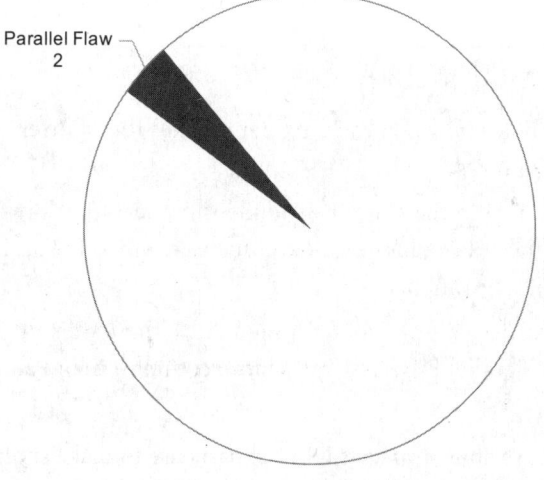

Approximate Number of Parallel Flaw Questions per LSAT

Parallel Flaw
2

Source: All officially released LSAT exams, 2016-2020

Like the Parallel Reasoning questions you learned about in Part II of this book, some Parallel Flaw questions can be quite long, so pay attention in the following pages to strategies for handling these questions efficiently and with confidence. Parallel Principle questions, when they appear, are usually on the shorter side, and if you remember to zero in on the underlying rule illustrated by the assumption, these questions should not present a big timing challenge.

Parallel Flaw Questions

There is one way in which Parallel Flaw questions are more straightforward than Parallel Reasoning questions; that is because, in Parallel Flaw questions, you already know from the question stem that the argument will be flawed.

Prepare

LEARNING OBJECTIVE

In this section, you'll learn to:

- Identify and answer Parallel Flaw questions.

You can identify Parallel Flaw questions from question stems like these.

> The flawed reasoning in the argument above
> most closely parallels that in which one of the
> following?
>
> _PrepTest111 Sec1 Q24_

> Which one of the following contains
> questionable reasoning most similar to that
> in the argument above?
>
> _PrepTest112 Sec4 Q25_

PARALLEL FLAW QUESTIONS AT A GLANCE

Task: Identify the answer choice in which the argument makes the same error(s) in reasoning that the argument in the stimulus commits.

Strategy: Analyze the argument in the stimulus and identify the author's reasoning error(s). Evaluate the answer choices to find the one containing an argument in which the author commits the same error(s) as did the author of the stimulus.

Frequency: On LSAT tests released from 2016 through 2020, there were an average of 1.0 Parallel Flaw questions per section. Parallel Flaw is slightly more common than Parallel Reasoning.

The following page outlines the various strategies LSAT experts use to make short work of Parallel Flaw questions.

Compare Flaws. After all the work you did earlier in the section on Flaw questions, this tactic should feel familiar. Analyze the argument in the stimulus and describe the error in reasoning. Evaluate the answer choices by looking for the only one that contains exactly the same flaw.

TEST DAY TIP

A Parallel Flaw argument may commit more than one reasoning error. If that's the case, then the argument in the correct answer will commit all of the same flaws.

Compare Conclusions. This is the same technique used in Parallel Reasoning questions. Keep in mind that qualifying or softening a conclusion often makes an Overlooked Possibilities argument's reasoning sound. That is, softening the conclusion removes the flaw.

Compare Formal Logic. Just as in Parallel Reasoning, when a Parallel Flaw argument is easily diagrammed in Formal Logic shorthand, comparing the argument structures can be even more efficient than describing the conclusion. Consider this argument:

> Whenever Craig goes shopping, Anne goes shopping too. Craig isn't shopping today, so Anne must not be shopping either.

Here are two more arguments. Which one is flawed in exactly the same way as the one in the example?

(1) The zookeeper must not be feeding the penguins. This is obvious from the fact that he is not feeding the seals. Whenever the zookeeper feeds the seals, he also feeds the penguins.

(2) Joan is not taking calculus this semester. Joan will take only classes also taken by Barbara, and Barbara is not taking calculus this semester.

Some LSAT experts sketch out the formal logic in shorthand, lining up the parts of the argument to see which answer choice matches the stimulus.

(stimulus)	(1)	(2)
[Ev1] *If C → A*	[Ev1] *If feed S → feed P*	[Ev1] *If J → B*
[Ev2] *NOT C today*	[Ev2] *NOT feed S*	[Ev2] *NOT B*
[Concl] *NOT A today*	[Concl] *NOT feed P*	[Concl] *NOT J*
Flaw: negating terms without reversing them	Flaw: negating terms without reversing them	No flaw; the second piece of evidence and the conclusion form the correct contrapositive

This makes it easy to see that choice (1) contains the parallel flaw. When you use this technique, you'll want to sketch out the logic in the stimulus argument, but you may not need to sketch it out for every answer choice. Still, this is a good reminder of why it is valuable to practice jotting down formal logic shorthand in case you want to quickly use it on test day.

TEST DAY TIP

If an answer choice contains an argument with sound reasoning, it cannot be the correct answer to a Parallel Flaw question.

Now, try a Parallel Flaw question on your own. Use any or all of the available strategies. When you're finished, review your work with the expert worked example that follows.

Step 2:	Step 1:

1. Many people are alarmed about the population explosion. They fail to appreciate that the present rise in population has in fact been followed by equally potent economic growth. Because of this connection between an increase in population and an increase in economic activity, population control measures should not be taken.

The questionable pattern of reasoning in the argument above is most similar to that in which one of the following?

(A) Subscribers to newsmagazines are concerned that increased postage costs will be passed on to them in the form of higher subscription rates. But that is a price they have to pay for having the magazines delivered. No group of users of the postal system should be subsidized at the expense of others.

(B) Most of the salespeople are concerned with complaints about the sales manager's aggressive behavior. They need to consider that sales are currently increasing. Due to this success, no action should be taken to address the manager's behavior.

(C) Parents are concerned about their children spending too much time watching television. Those parents should consider television time as time they could spend with their children. Let the children watch television, but watch it with them.

(D) Nutritionists warn people not to eat unhealthy foods. Those foods have been in people's diets for years. Before cutting all those foods out of diets it would be wise to remember that people enjoy culinary variety.

(E) Some consumers become concerned when the price of a product increases for several years in a row, thinking that the price will continue to increase. But these consumers are mistaken since a long-term trend of price increases indicates that the price will probably decline in the future.

PrepTest111 Sec4 Q6

Step 3:	Step 4:

Expert Analysis

Here's how an LSAT expert approached the Parallel Flaw question you just tried. Note the expert's willingness to use multiple strategies for maximum efficiency in evaluating the answer choices.

Step 2: *Conclusion*: Population control measures should not be taken *because* *Evidence*: increased population correlates to increased economic activity.	**Step 1:** The phrases "questionable pattern of reasoning" and "most similar to" indicate a Parallel Flaw question; the correct answer illustrates the same flaw illustrated in the stimulus.

1. Many people are alarmed about the population explosion. They fail to appreciate that the present rise in population has in fact been followed by equally potent economic growth. Because of this connection between an increase in population and an increase in economic activity, population control measures should not be taken.

The questionable pattern of reasoning in the argument above is most similar to that in which one of the following?

(A) Subscribers to newsmagazines are concerned that increased postage costs will be passed on to them in the form of higher subscription rates. But that is a price they have to pay for having the magazines delivered. No group of users of the postal system should be subsidized at the expense of others.

(B) Most of the salespeople are concerned with complaints about the sales manager's aggressive behavior. They need to consider that sales are currently increasing. Due to this success, no action should be taken to address the manager's behavior.

(C) Parents are concerned about their children spending too much time watching television. Those parents should consider television time as time they could spend with their children. Let the children watch television, but watch it with them.

(D) Nutritionists warn people not to eat unhealthy foods. Those foods have been in people's diets for years. Before cutting all those foods out of diets it would be wise to remember that people enjoy culinary variety.

(E) Some consumers become concerned when the price of a product increases for several years in a row, thinking that the price will continue to increase. But these consumers are mistaken since a long-term trend of price increases indicates that the price will probably decline in the future.

PrepTest111 Sec4 Q6

Step 3: Here's a classic Overlooked Possibilities argument: We should not try to prevent a thing (population growth) from happening because that thing correlates to one advantage (stimulates economic activity). The correct answer will apply the same faulty logic to a different subject. With such long answer choices, however, you may want to evaluate conclusions first, eliminating any choice that does not recommend against preventing something.	**Step 4:** (B) matches the stimulus in every respect, right down to the background information that people are concerned about the thing the author recommends against changing.

Wrong answers: (A) The conclusion is an assertion of fact—"that is the price they have to pay"—not a negative recommendation, and the evidence is an appeal to fairness—"no group . . . should be subsidized at the expense of others"—not a correlated advantage. (C) This argument does not demonstrate a reasoning error; you can disagree with it, but basically, its conclusion is an *affirmative* recommendation that just says, "Look at things a different way." (D) There's not much of a match here at all: the conclusion is different (a warning rather than a recommendation) and the evidence does not show a correlation to any advantage. (E) The conclusion here—a negative assertion of fact ("consumers are mistaken")—does not match that in the stimulus—a negative recommendation ("measures should not be taken").

Good job. Before moving on to additional Parallel Flaw practice, take a few minutes to get familiar with Parallel Principle questions.

Parallel Principle Questions

Parallel Principle questions ask you to identify the principle underlying the argument in the stimulus, and then, find the answer in which the argument has a similar principle underlying it. Much like Parallel Reasoning, the answer choices are likely to contain subject matter different than that in the stimulus argument.

Prepare

LEARNING OBJECTIVE

In this section, you'll learn to:

- Identify and answer Parallel Principle questions.

You can identify Parallel Principle questions from question stems like these.

> Which one of the following conforms most
> closely to the principle illustrated above?
>
> *PrepTest111 Sec1 Q7*

> Which one of the following illustrates a
> principle most similar to that illustrated by
> the passage?
>
> *PrepTest112 Sec1 Q17*

PARALLEL PRINCIPLE QUESTIONS AT A GLANCE

Task: Identify the principle underlying the argument in the stimulus and use that principle to distinguish the one answer containing an argument with a similar principle underlying it.

Strategy: Analyze the stimulus argument and identify the principle underlying its assumption. Evaluate the choices by spotting the one with a principle paralleling that of the argument in the stimulus.

Frequency: Parallel Principle questions are extremely rare. On LSAT tests released between 2016 and 2020, there were just four in total (an average of less than one per year).

The expert approach to Parallel Principle questions is simpler and more direct than those for Parallel Reasoning and Parallel Flaw questions. Parallel Principle questions rarely, if ever, have a long stimulus or long answer choices (so there's not much utility in comparing conclusions), and they hardly ever feature formal logic (so no need for sketching out conditional statements). Just paraphrase the principle underlying the stimulus and use that as your prediction for the correct answer.

Try a Parallel Principle question on your own to get the feel of these rare questions. When you're finished, compare your work to that of an LSAT expert with the worked example on the next page.

Step 2:	Step 1:

2. The best way to write a good detective story is to work backward from the crime. The writer should first decide what the crime is and who the perpetrator is, and then come up with the circumstances and clues based on those decisions.

Which one of the following illustrates a principle most similar to that illustrated by the passage?

(A) When planning a trip, some people first decide where they want to go and then plan accordingly, but, for most of us, much financial planning must be done before we can choose where we are going.

(B) In planting a vegetable garden, you should prepare the soil first, and then decide what kinds of vegetables to plant.

(C) Good architects do not extemporaneously construct their plans in the course of an afternoon; an architectural design cannot be divorced from the method of constructing the building.

(D) In solving mathematical problems, the best method is to try out as many strategies as possible in the time allotted. This is particularly effective if the number of possible strategies is fairly small.

(E) To make a great tennis shot, you should visualize where you want the shot to go. Then you can determine the position you need to be in to execute the shot properly.

PrepTest112 Sec1 Q17

Step 3:	Step 4:

Expert Analysis

Here's how an LSAT expert approached the Parallel Principle question you just tried out.

Step 2: The first sentence effectively states the principle which is fleshed out by the rest of the stimulus: The *best way* to write a good mystery is to work backward from the crime so you can get the right setup.	**Step 1:** When both the stimulus and the correct answer provide examples illustrating the same broad-based rule, you have a Parallel Principle question.

2. The best way to write a good detective story is to work backward from the crime. The writer should first decide what the crime is and who the perpetrator is, and then come up with the circumstances and clues based on those decisions.

Which one of the following illustrates a principle most similar to that illustrated by the passage?

(A) When planning a trip, some people first decide where they want to go and then plan accordingly, but, for most of us, much financial planning must be done before we can choose where we are going.

(B) In planting a vegetable garden, you should prepare the soil first, and then decide what kinds of vegetables to plant.

(C) Good architects do not extemporaneously construct their plans in the course of an afternoon; an architectural design cannot be divorced from the method of constructing the building.

(D) In solving mathematical problems, the best method is to try out as many strategies as possible in the time allotted. This is particularly effective if the number of possible strategies is fairly small.

(E) To make a great tennis shot, you should visualize where you want the shot to go. Then you can determine the position you need to be in to execute the shot properly.

PrepTest112 Sec1 Q17

Step 3: The correct answer will illustrate the same principle—the best approach is to work backward from the desired end point to establish the foundation—in a different context.	**Step 4:** (E) is correct; it illustrates the same principle as that illustrated in the stimulus: the best approach to something is to work backward from an end result to get the right setup.

Wrong answers: (A) distorts the principle by introducing qualifiers such as *some* and *most of us*; moreover, it is not stating a judgment about the *best way* to do something. (B) 180. This choice recommends doing the setup work first, as opposed to visualizing the end point first. (C) does not match the stimulus; first, it does not opine on the *best way* to do something, and second, it says nothing about deciding the end point first and then working backwards. (D) does not match the stimulus; while it is a recommendation for the best way to do something, it does not suggest visualizing an endpoint and working backward from there.

Nice work. You'll see another Parallel Principle question in the Practice set that follows. Give it your best effort.

Practice Try each of the following Parallel Flaw and Parallel Principle questions. Don't worry too much about your timing here. Complete all four steps of the Logical Reasoning Method for each question, jotting down your notes whenever it is helpful to do so. After each question, review your work with the expert analysis that follows.

Hint: How can you use the conditional statements in the stimulus to evaluate the answer choices?

Step 2:	Step 1:

3. Societies in which value is measured primarily in financial terms invariably fragment into isolated social units. But since money is not the main measure of value in nonindustrial societies, they must tend in contrast to be socially unified.

The flawed reasoning in which one of the following is most similar to that in the argument above?

(A) Animals of different genera cannot interbreed. But that does not prove that jackals and wolves cannot interbreed, for they belong to the same genus.

(B) Ecosystems close to the equator usually have more species than those closer to the poles. Thus, the Sahara Desert must contain more species than Siberia does, since the latter is farther from the equator.

(C) Insects pass through several stages of maturation: egg, larva, pupa, and adult. Since insects are arthropods, all arthropods probably undergo similar maturation processes.

(D) Poets frequently convey their thoughts via nonliteral uses of language such as metaphors and analogies. But journalists are not poets, so surely journalists always use language literally.

(E) Technologically sophisticated machines often cause us more trouble than simpler devices serving the same function. Since computers are more technologically sophisticated than pencils, they must tend to be more troublesome.

PrepTest110 Sec3 Q23

Step 3:	Step 4:

Expert Analysis

Here's how an LSAT expert approached the Parallel Flaw question you just saw.

Step 2: *Conclusion:* Nonindustrial societies must be socially unified *because* *Evidence:* (1) Societies that measure value in financial terms are fragmented, and (2) nonindustrial societies do not measure value in financial terms.	**Step 1:** This is a standard Parallel Flaw question stem; the correct answer contains an argument with the same reasoning error as the argument in the stimulus.

3. Societies in which value is measured primarily in financial terms invariably fragment into isolated social units. But since money is not the main measure of value in nonindustrial societies, they must tend in contrast to be socially unified.

The flawed reasoning in which one of the following is most similar to that in the argument above?

(A) Animals of different genera cannot inter-breed. But that does not prove that jackals and wolves cannot interbreed, for they belong to the same genus.

(B) Ecosystems close to the equator usually have more species than those closer to the poles. Thus, the Sahara Desert must contain more species than Siberia does, since the latter is farther from the equator.

(C) Insects pass through several stages of maturation: egg, larva, pupa, and adult. Since insects are arthropods, all arthropods probably undergo similar maturation processes.

(D) Poets frequently convey their thoughts via nonliteral uses of language such as metaphors and analogies. But journalists are not poets, so surely journalists always use language literally.

(E) Technologically sophisticated machines often cause us more trouble than simpler devices serving the same function. Since computers are more technologically sophisticated than pencils, they must tend to be more troublesome.

PrepTest110 Sec3 Q23

Step 3: Translate and align the formal logic to reveal the flaw. Note: The shorthand uses "MVFT" for "measures value in financial terms."

[Ev1] If Soc MVFT → fragmented

[Ev2] If Non-Ind Soc → NOT MVFT

[Concl] If Non-Ind Soc → NOT fragmented

The conclusion treats the two evidentiary statements as if they combine, but they don't. The result of the second one is negative and the trigger of the first is positive. To think they combine is to confuse sufficiency for necessity. The correct answer will line up with exactly the same mistake.

Step 4: (D) makes the same mistake in formal logic. If you diagram the argument in this choice, it comes out as follows:

[Ev1] If poet → nonliteral language

[Ev2] If journalist → NOT poet

[Concl] If journalist → NOT nonliteral language

This demonstrates the parallel flaw. Note:

"literal" = "NOT nonliteral" in the conclusion.

Wrong answers: (A) There is no flaw here. The evidence states that jackals and wolves are not different genera, so the rule that animals of different genera cannot interbreed does not apply to them. (B) This choice has a different flaw than that in the stimulus; the flaw here is drawing a definitive conclusion ("must contain more") from probabilistic evidence ("usually have more"). (C) The flaw in this choice is assuming, without evidence, that insects are representative of all arthropods. (E) There are two problems here, but neither matches the stimulus argument's confusion of sufficient and necessary. The flaws in this choice are (1) assuming that computers and pencils serve the same function, and (2) that conflating "*often* cause us more trouble" with "*must* tend to be more troublesome."

Hint: What does the phrase *due to* tell you about the principle underlying this short stimulus?

Step 2:	Step 1:

4. Due to wider commercial availability of audio recordings of authors reading their own books, sales of printed books have dropped significantly.

Which one of the following conforms most closely to the principle illustrated above?

(A) Because of the rising cost of farm labor, farmers began to make more extensive use of machines.

(B) Because of the wide variety of new computer games on the market, sales of high-quality computer video screens have improved.

(C) Because a new brand of soft drink entered the market, consumers reduced their consumption of an established brand of soft drink.

(D) Because a child was forbidden to play until homework was completed, that child did much less daydreaming and focused on homework.

(E) Because neither of the two leading word processing programs has all of the features consumers want, neither has been able to dominate the market.

PrepTest111 Sec1 Q7

Step 3:	Step 4:

Expert Analysis

Here's how an LSAT expert approached the Parallel Principle question you just saw.

Step 2: This case attributes a drop in sales of printed books to increased availability of authors reading their own works as audiobooks.	**Step 1:** This is a Parallel Principle question; the case in the stimulus illustrates a general rule and the correct answer illustrates the same rule in a different context.

4. Due to wider commercial availability of audio recordings of authors reading their own books, sales of printed books have dropped significantly.

Which one of the following conforms most closely to the principle illustrated above?

(A) Because of the rising cost of farm labor, farmers began to make more extensive use of machines.

(B) Because of the wide variety of new computer games on the market, sales of high-quality computer video screens have improved.

(C) Because a new brand of soft drink entered the market, consumers reduced their consumption of an established brand of soft drink.

(D) Because a child was forbidden to play until homework was completed, that child did much less daydreaming and focused on homework.

(E) Because neither of the two leading word processing programs has all of the features consumers want, neither has been able to dominate the market.

PrepTest111 Sec1 Q7

Step 3: The correct answer will match the case illustrated by the stimulus: a decline in the popularity of an existing form of a product due to the availability of a new form of the product.	**Step 4:** (C) provides the matching case—an existing form of a product declines because of the availability of a new form of the product—and is correct.

Wrong answers: (A) does not match the stimulus; the change described here is triggered by rising prices, not the availability of a new form of an existing product. (B) does not match the stimulus; this example is not about the replacement of an existing product, but rather, its improvement. (D) Is not even similar to the stimulus; this is about a person changing their behavior to achieve a desired result based on delayed gratification. (E) does not match the stimulus; this is about a stalemate between two products, not a new one replacing an existing one.

Hint: How does the change in scope between evidence and conclusion help you know what to look for as you evaluate the answer choices?

Step 2:	Step 1:

5. In every case of political unrest in a certain country, the police have discovered that some unknown person or persons organized and fomented that unrest. Clearly, therefore, behind all the cases of political unrest in that country there has been a single mastermind who organized and fomented them all.

The flawed reasoning in the argument above most closely parallels that in which one of the following?

(A) Every Chicago driver has a number on his or her license, so the number on some Chicago driver's license is the exact average of the numbers on all Chicago drivers' licenses.

(B) Every telephone number in North America has an area code, so there must be at least as many area codes as telephone numbers in North America.

(C) Every citizen of Edmonton has a social insurance number, so there must be one number that is the social insurance number for all citizens of Edmonton.

(D) Every loss of a single hair is insignificant, so no one who has a full head of hair at twenty ever becomes bald.

(E) Every moment in Vladimir's life is followed by a later moment in Vladimir's life, so Vladimir's life will never end.

PrepTest111 Sec1 Q24

Step 3:	Step 4:

Expert Analysis

Here's how an LSAT expert approached the Parallel Flaw question you just saw.

Step 2: *Conclusion*: A single person is behind all cases of political unrest in the country *because* *Evidence*: A person or persons are behind all cases of political unrest in the country.	**Step 1:** A typical Parallel Flaw question stem: the correct answer commits the same reasoning error that the argument in the stimulus commits.

5. In every case of political unrest in a certain country, the police have discovered that some unknown person or persons organized and fomented that unrest. Clearly, therefore, behind all the cases of political unrest in that country there has been a single mastermind who organized and fomented them all.

The flawed reasoning in the argument above most closely parallels that in which one of the following?

(A) Every Chicago driver has a number on his or her license, so the number on some Chicago driver's license is the exact average of the numbers on all Chicago drivers' licenses.

(B) Every telephone number in North America has an area code, so there must be at least as many area codes as telephone numbers in North America.

(C) Every citizen of Edmonton has a social insurance number, so there must be one number that is the social insurance number for all citizens of Edmonton.

(D) Every loss of a single hair is insignificant, so no one who has a full head of hair at twenty ever becomes bald.

(E) Every moment in Vladimir's life is followed by a later moment in Vladimir's life, so Vladimir's life will never end.

PrepTest111 Sec1 Q24

Step 3: Here, the conditional logic ("every case" and "all the cases") is a bit of a red herring. The flaw is simply taking the fact that every case of political unrest has someone (or some *ones*) behind it to mean that there is a *single mastermind* behind them all. The correct answer will mirror this confusion between "everyone one of a certain thing" and "there is exactly one of this certain thing that everyone has."	**Step 4:** (C) matches the flaw in the stimulus and is correct.

Wrong answers: (A) goes off track by concluding that one example of a certain thing (the driver's license number) is the average of all such examples; the correct match would have been to conclude that there is exactly one number on every Chicago driver's license. (B) distorts the argument by concluding that there are as many of one thing as there are of another; the matching conclusion would have been "there is exactly one area code had by all telephone numbers." (D) This argument ends with a negative prediction; that doesn't match the conclusion in the stimulus. (E) This argument ends with a negative prediction; that doesn't match the conclusion in the stimulus.

Hint: This is a lengthy question. What strategy helps you get through the answer choices quickly?

Step 2:	Step 1:

6. The judgment that an artist is great always rests on assessments of the work the artist has produced. A series of great works is the only indicator of greatness. Therefore, to say that an artist is great is just to summarize the quality of his or her known works, and the artist's greatness can provide no basis for predicting the quality of the artist's unknown or future works.

Which one of the following contains questionable reasoning most similar to that in the argument above?

(A) The only way of knowing whether someone has a cold is to observe symptoms. Thus, when a person is said to have a cold, this means only that he or she has displayed the symptoms of a cold, and no prediction about the patient's future symptoms is justified.

(B) Although colds are very common, there are some people who never or only very rarely catch colds. Clearly these people must be in some way physiologically different from people who catch colds frequently.

(C) Someone who has a cold is infected by a cold virus. No one can be infected by the same cold virus twice, but there are indefinitely many different cold viruses. Therefore, it is not possible to predict from a person's history of infection how susceptible he or she will be in the future.

(D) The viruses that cause colds are not all the same, and they differ in their effects. Therefore, although it may be certain that a person has a cold, it is impossible to predict how the cold will progress.

(E) Unless a person displays cold symptoms, it cannot properly be said that the person has a cold. But each of the symptoms of a cold is also the symptom of some other disease. Therefore, one can never be certain that a person has a cold.

PrepTest112 Sec4 Q25

Step 3:	**Step 4:**

Expert Analysis

Here's how an LSAT expert approached the Parallel Flaw question you just saw.

Step 2: *Conclusion*: An artist's greatness does not predict the quality of the artist's unknown or future works *because* *Evidence*: The only evidence of an artist's "greatness" is a series of great works, so [subsidiary conclusion] calling an artist great is a summary of the artist's *known* works.	**Step 1:** A Parallel Flaw question: the correct answer will commit the same reasoning error as that in the stimulus.

6. The judgment that an artist is great always rests on assessments of the work the artist has produced. A series of great works is the only indicator of greatness. Therefore, to say that an artist is great is just to summarize the quality of his or her known works, and the artist's greatness can provide no basis for predicting the quality of the artist's unknown or future works.

Which one of the following contains questionable reasoning most similar to that in the argument above?

(A) The only way of knowing whether someone has a cold is to observe symptoms. Thus, when a person is said to have a cold, this means only that he or she has displayed the symptoms of a cold, and no prediction about the patient's future symptoms is justified.

(B) Although colds are very common, there are some people who never or only very rarely catch colds. Clearly these people must be in some way physiologically different from people who catch colds frequently.

(C) Someone who has a cold is infected by a cold virus. No one can be infected by the same cold virus twice, but there are indefinitely many different cold viruses. Therefore, it is not possible to predict from a person's history of infection how susceptible he or she will be in the future.

(D) The viruses that cause colds are not all the same, and they differ in their effects. Therefore, although it may be certain that a person has a cold, it is impossible to predict how the cold will progress.

(E) Unless a person displays cold symptoms, it cannot properly be said that the person has a cold. But each of the symptoms of a cold is also the symptom of some other disease. Therefore, one can never be certain that a person has a cold.

PrepTest112 Sec4 Q25

Step 3: With long answer choices, one strategy is to evaluate conclusions first. Here, you're looking for a strong negative prediction about the subject's observable output (i.e., the artist's works). After eliminating any choices with non-matching conclusions, compare the evidence, which has a subsidiary conclusion.

Step 4: (A) is correct. The conclusion is about the observable output (can't predict future symptoms), and it matches the stimulus (can't predict future works). Likewise, the evidence (saying someone has a cold is just summarizing their symptoms) matches the stimulus (saying an artist is great is just summarizing their works).

Wrong answers: (B) The conclusion here is an assertion of fact, not a prediction; and there is no subsidiary conclusion in the evidence. (C) This one goes off base by not being about the observables, i.e., the symptoms and works. (D) The conclusion is a negative prediction, but neither it nor the evidence is about the observable output, i.e., the artist's works or the cold sufferer's symptoms. (E) The conclusion here is a negative assertion of fact, not a prediction.

Now that you've had some practice with individual questions, assess your Parallel Flaw skills with the following Perform quiz. Note: Because they are so rare, no Parallel Principle questions are included in the assessment.

Chapter Perform Quiz

Perform This Perform quiz has 3 Parallel Flaw questions. They are presented without any notes, hints, or prompts for a more test-like experience while you work. Try to get as many correct answers as possible in 5 minutes. When you finish, check your performance against the Answer Key and Evaluate Your Performance for tips on how best to improve. Then, come back to complete any questions you skipped or guessed on and finish up by reviewing all the questions with the expert analyses in your online companion.

7. The student body at this university takes courses in a wide range of disciplines. Miriam is a student at this university, so she takes courses in a wide range of disciplines.

Which one of the following arguments exhibits flawed reasoning most similar to that exhibited by the argument above?

(A) The students at this school take mathematics. Miguel is a student at this school, so he takes mathematics.

(B) The editorial board of this law journal has written on many legal issues. Louise is on the editorial board, so she has written on many legal issues.

(C) The component parts of bulldozers are heavy. This machine is a bulldozer, so it is heavy.

(D) All older automobiles need frequent oil changes. This car is new, so its oil need not be changed as frequently.

(E) The individual cells of the brain are incapable of thinking. Therefore, the brain as a whole is incapable of thinking.

PrepTest111 Sec3 Q6

8. Kostman's original painting of Rosati was not a very accurate portrait. Therefore, your reproduction of Kostman's painting of Rosati will not be a very accurate reproduction of the painting.

Which one of the following is most similar in its flawed reasoning to the flawed reasoning in the argument above?

(A) George's speech was filled with half-truths and misquotes. So the tape recording made of it cannot be of good sound quality.

(B) An artist who paints a picture of an ugly scene must necessarily paint an ugly picture, unless the picture is a distorted representation of the scene.

(C) If a child's eyes resemble her mother's, then if the mother's eyes are brown the child's eyes also must be brown.

(D) Jo imitated Layne. But Jo is different from Layne, so Jo could not have imitated Layne very well.

(E) Harold's second novel is similar to his first. Therefore, his second novel must be enthralling, because his first novel won a prestigious literary prize.

PrepTest112 Sec1 Q21

9.   Lawyer: The defendant wanted to clear the snow off his car and in doing so knocked snow on the sidewalk. This same snow melted and refroze, forming ice on which the plaintiff fell, breaking her hip. We argue that the defendant maliciously harmed the plaintiff, because malice is intention to cause harm and the defendant intentionally removed the snow from his car and put it on the sidewalk, which, unbeknownst to the defendant at the time, would subsequently cause the injury suffered by the plaintiff.

The flawed reasoning in which one of the following is most similar to that in the lawyer's argument?

(A) Alice asked her sister to lie in court. Unbeknownst to Alice's sister, lying in court is against the law. So what Alice asked her sister to do was illegal.

(B) Bruce wanted to eat the mincemeat pie. Unbeknownst to Bruce, the mincemeat pie was poisonous. So Bruce wanted to eat poison.

(C) Cheryl denigrated the wine. Cheryl's sister had picked out the wine. So though she may not have realized it, Cheryl indirectly denigrated her sister.

(D) Deon had lunch with Ms. Osgood. Unbeknownst to Deon, Ms. Osgood is generally thought to be an industrial spy. So Deon had lunch with an industrial spy.

(E) Edwina bought a car from Mr. Yancy, then resold it. Unbeknownst to Edwina, Mr. Yancy had stolen the car. So Edwina sold a stolen car.

PrepTest110 Sec2 Q24

Answer Key

7. B; 8. A; 9. B

Evaluate Your Performance

To assess your strengths and opportunities from this Perform quiz, go to the corresponding chapter in your online companion. There you'll find recommendations based on your performance along with complete worked-example explanations (written by a Kaplan LSAT expert) for each of the questions in this Perform quiz.

PART FOUR

Non-Argument Questions

CHAPTER 14

Inference Questions

The Non-Argument Family

Not all questions in the Logical Reasoning section involve analyzing or evaluating arguments. A significant number of questions test your ability to make deductions. Kaplan refers to these as Inference questions, with an inference—in LSAT terms—being a valid deduction from a set of statements or a brief narrative. Inference questions give you a set of facts or assertions and ask for a statement supported by them or, in some cases, for a statement that must be true based on them. A handful of Inference questions involve general principles. Sometimes these Principle-Inference questions state a general principle and then ask for a specific case that correctly applies it; at other times, they describe a specific case and ask you to infer the principle upon which it was decided. Another Non-argument question type—Paradox questions—gives you two seemingly inconsistent statements and asks for a fact that would help explain or reconcile the apparent discrepancy.

The typical recent LSAT has featured six or seven Inference questions, one or maybe two Principle-Inference questions, and three or four Paradox questions, for an average of 11 Non-Argument questions overall. That comes out to right around 14% of all points available on a given LSAT administration. So, while not as significant as the Assumption Family, the Non-Argument Family can still provide a large boost to your LSAT score.

Approximate Number of Questions per LSAT by Logical Reasoning Question Family

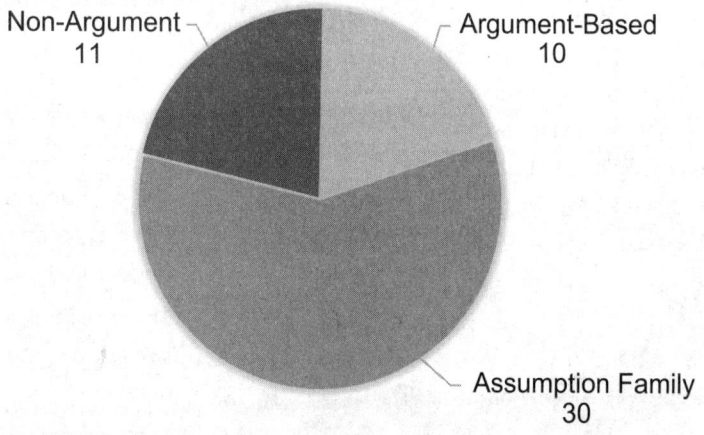

Source: All officially released LSAT exams, 2016-2020

Percentage of All Questions Per LSAT by Logical Reasoning Question Family

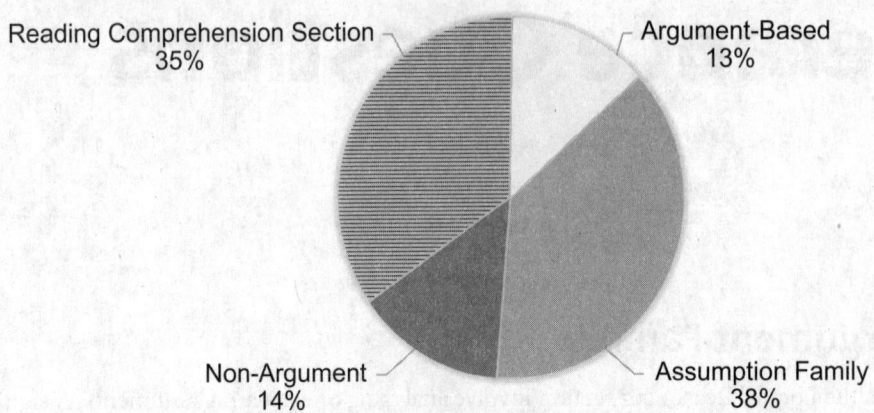

Reading Comprehension Section
35%

Argument-Based
13%

Non-Argument
14%

Assumption Family
38%

Source: All officially released LSAT exams, 2016-2020

These questions are not based on arguments; there's no need for you to determine conclusion and evidence here or to try to figure out what an author is assuming. Rather, these questions all reward you for seeing the implications of facts and assertions. In the Non-Argument Family, you're interested in what follows from the statements in the stimulus, not in what you could add to the stimulus to make it stronger, weaker, or more complete.

The best way to see the fundamental difference between Argument-Based or Assumption Family questions and the Non-Argument questions you'll cover in this part of the book is to set questions of each type side by side.

Strengthen Question

20. Consumer advocate: The introduction of a new drug into the marketplace should be contingent upon our having a good understanding of its social impact. However, the social impact of the newly marketed antihistamine is far from clear. It is obvious, then, that there should be a general reduction in the pace of bringing to the marketplace new drugs that are now being tested.

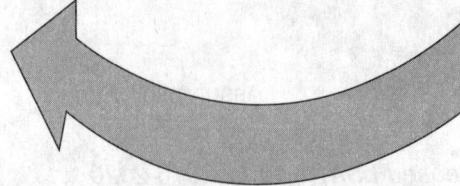

Which one of the following, if true, most strengthens the argument?

(A) The social impact of the new antihistamine is much better understood than that of most new drugs being tested.

(B) The social impact of some of the new drugs being tested is poorly understood.

(C) The economic success of some drugs is inversely proportional to how well we understand their social impact.

(D) The new antihistamine is chemically similar to some of the new drugs being tested.

(E) The new antihistamine should be on the market only if most new drugs being tested should be on the market also.

PrepTest112 Sec4 Q20

Inference Question

Light is registered in the retina when photons hit molecules of the pigment rhodopsin and change the molecules' shape. Even when they have not been struck by photons of light, rhodopsin molecules sometimes change shape because of normal molecular motion, thereby introducing error into the visual system. The amount of this molecular motion is directly proportional to the temperature of the retina.

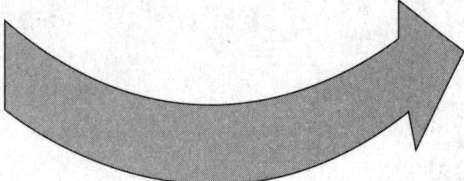

Which one of the following conclusions is most strongly supported by the information above?

(A) The temperature of an animal's retina depends on the amount of light the retina is absorbing.

(B) The visual systems of animals whose body temperature matches that of their surroundings are more error-prone in hot surroundings than in cold ones.

(C) As the temperature of the retina rises, rhodopsin molecules react more slowly to being struck by photons.

(D) Rhodopsin molecules are more sensitive to photons in animals whose retinas have large surface areas than in animals whose retinas have small surface areas.

(E) Molecules of rhodopsin are the only pigment molecules that occur naturally in the retina.

PrepTest110 Sec3 Q19

Notice that in the Non-Argument Inference question above, the statements in the stimulus lead to the correct answer. In the Assumption-Family Strengthen question on the preceding page, however, the correct answer supports or supplements the argument in the stimulus. This pattern holds true for all questions in these families.

Inference Question Basics

Inference questions present a stimulus containing a number of related statements and assertions, or a short narrative. You are then asked to find an answer choice that must, could, or cannot be true based on those statements.

LEARNING OBJECTIVES

In this section, you'll learn to:

- Distinguish among "strongly supported" Inference questions, "must be true" Inference questions, and Inference **except** questions.
- Make valid deductions from Inference question stimuli in a number of ways.
- Identify and answer "strongly supported" Inference questions.
- Identify and answer "must be true" Inference questions.
- Identify and answer Inference **except** questions.
- Identify and answer Principle-Inference questions.

On test day, you will be asked to correctly answer approximately six or seven Inference questions. That's approximately 11% of all Logical Reasoning questions, or roughly 8% of all the questions on a given LSAT. This is a high-yield question type, and is even more important because you will use your Inference question skills to answer one or two Principle-Inference questions per test as well. You'll see examples of those questions later in the chapter.

Approximate Number of Inference Questions per LSAT

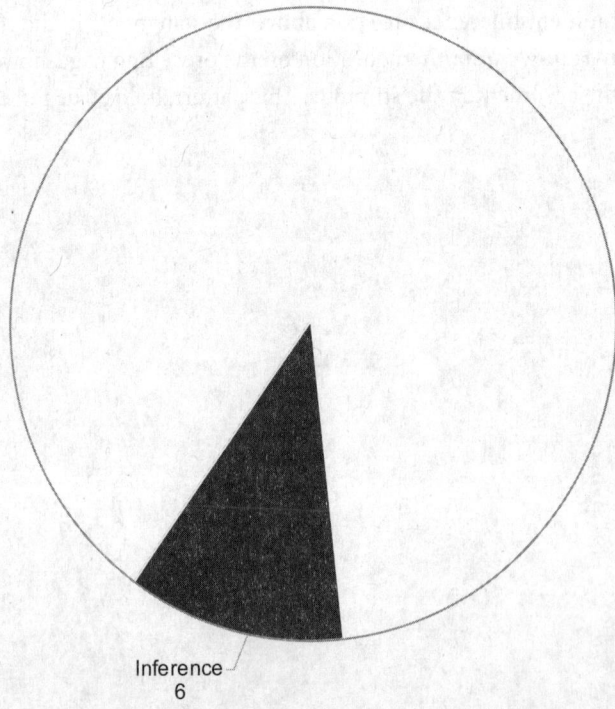

Inference
6

Source: All officially released LSAT exams, 2016-2020

INFERENCE QUESTIONS AT A GLANCE

Task: Identify the choice that must, could, or cannot be true based on a set of statements.

Strategy: Catalog the statements in the stimulus: Identify the most concrete statement; combine related statements; note relationships indicated by keywords; and/or use Formal Logic to evaluate the answer choices.

Frequency: LSAT tests released from 2016 to 2020 had an average of 3.2 Inference questions per section. Incidentally, on most tests, the Inference questions are split just about 50-50 between those calling for the answer most strongly supported by the stimulus and those calling for a correct answer that must be true based on the stimulus. In addition, you are likely to see one or two Principle-Inference questions per LSAT.

Distinguish Among Inference Question Subtypes

Prepare

LEARNING OBJECTIVE

In this section, you'll learn to:

- Distinguish among "strongly supported" Inference questions, "must be true" Inference questions, and Inference **except** questions.

You can identify Inference questions from stems like these.

> Which one of the following is most strongly
> supported by the information above?
>
> *PrepTest112 Sec4 Q22*

> The information above most strongly supports
> which one of the following?
>
> *PrepTest112 Sec1 Q4*

> If the statements above are true, which one of the
> following must also be true?
>
> *PrepTest112 Sec1 Q11*

> Which one of the following can be properly inferred
> from the information above?
>
> *PrepTest112 Sec1 Q14*

> If the statements above are true, then each of the
> following statements could also be true **except:**
>
> *PrepTest110 Sec3 Q22*

> The statements above provide some support for
> each of the following **except:**
>
> *PrepTest111 Sec4 Q1*

Split up those question stems by twos. The first two stems indicate "strongly supported" Inference questions. In them, the correct answer is the one that receives support from the stimulus. The four incorrect answers do not receive support from the stimulus; they are likely to be outside the scope, present irrelevant comparisons, be too extreme to be supported, or be 180s (at odds with the statements in the stimulus). Note: In "strongly supported" Inference questions, the stimulus does not have to *prove* the correct answer (although occasionally, it might).

The next two stems indicate "must be true" Inference questions. Here, the correct answer is established by the stimulus. If the stimulus is true, the correct answer unequivocally follows from them. The four wrong answers *could be false*. These questions often contain Formal Logic which allows for precise deductions.

The last two stems are examples of Inference **except** questions. In these question types, take a moment in Step 1 of the Logical Reasoning Method to be sure you can accurately characterize the one correct and four incorrect answers. In the examples above, for instance, "each of the following . . . could also be true **except**" means that the correct answer *must be false*, while "some support for each of the following **except**" indicates only that the correct answer does not receive support; it could be false or simply out of scope.

Practice Evaluate the following Inference question stems. Characterize the correct and incorrect answer choices: *must be true, could be false, receives support*, etc.

Question Stem	My Analysis
1. If all of the statements above are true, then which one of the following must be true?	**1 Right:** **4 Wrong:**
2. Which one of the following can be properly inferred from the information above?	**1 Right:** **4 Wrong:**
3. Which one of the following is most strongly supported by the information above?	**1 Right:** **4 Wrong:**
4. Which one of the following statements would most reasonably complete the argument?	**1 Right:** **4 Wrong:**
5. If all of the statements above are true, which one of the following CANNOT be true?	**1 Right:** **4 Wrong:**
6. The statements above, if true, provide support for each of the following **except:**	**1 Right:** **4 Wrong:**
7. If the statements above are true, then each of the following could also be true **except:**	**1 Right:** **4 Wrong:**
8. The facts above, if true, provide the strongest evidence against which one of the following?	**1 Right:** **4 Wrong:**

Expert Analysis

Here's how an LSAT expert would characterize the correct and incorrect answers in those Inference question stems.

Question Stem	Analysis
1. If all of the statements above are true, then which one of the following must be true?	**1 Right:** Must be true **4 Wrong:** Could be false
2. Which one of the following can be properly inferred from the information above?	**1 Right:** Must be true **4 Wrong:** Could be false
3. Which one of the following is most strongly supported by the information above?	**1 Right:** Is supported by the stimulus **4 Wrong:** Is not supported by the stimulus
4. Which one of the following statements would most reasonably complete the argument?	**1 Right:** Represents the conclusion that follows closely from the stimulus's evidence **4 Wrong:** Is not a direct conclusion from the stimulus's evidence
5. If all of the statements above are true, which one of the following CANNOT be true?	**1 Right:** Must be false **4 Wrong:** Could be true
6. The statements above, if true, provide support for each of the following EXCEPT:	**1 Right:** Is NOT supported by the stimulus **4 Wrong:** Is supported by the stimulus
7. If the statements above are true, then each of the following could also be true EXCEPT:	**1 Right:** Must be false **4 Wrong:** Could be true
8. The facts above, if true, provide the strongest evidence against which one of the following?	**1 Right:** Is *weakened* by the stimulus **4 Wrong:** Is not weakened by the stimulus (could be strengthened by the stimulus or outside the scope)

Once you know what an Inference question is asking for, Step 2 of the Logical Reasoning Method is to untangle the stimulus. Because Inference questions seldom contain arguments, you won't be looking for conclusions and evidence. In the next section of this chapter, you'll see how LSAT experts strategically read Inference stimuli and then arrange (or "catalog") the statements for quick, accurate analysis of the answer choices.

Make Valid Deductions in Inference Questions

Prepare

LEARNING OBJECTIVE

In this section, you'll learn to:

- Make valid deductions from Inference question stimuli in a number of ways.

Without an argument in the stimulus to analyze, untrained test takers may have difficulty knowing where to focus their attention in Inference stimuli. LSAT experts, on the other hand, know the keys to untangling them.

LSAT STRATEGY

Some facts to remember about LSAT inferences:

- An inference follows only from the facts given. No outside knowledge is required.
- An inference need not be mind-blowing. Sometimes it will be simple, even obvious.
- An inference may come from a single statement, or it may require combining statements.
- It may not be necessary to take into account all the facts given in the stimulus.

Approach Inference questions with rigor and discipline. Answer the question directly from the statements. Make sure you consider what the statements do and do not mean. Consider the following:

> Most members of my sorority are in-state students, and most members of my sorority enjoy playing volleyball.

> Which of the following statements is a valid inference based on those statements?

> (1) Most members of my sorority are in-state students who enjoy playing volleyball.

> (2) At least one member of my sorority is an in-state student who enjoys playing volleyball.

If you said (2), then you're correct. Statement (1) could be true, but it is not supported by the original statement, which doesn't give you enough information to conclude that most of the sorority's members have both characteristics. Statement (2), on the other hand is firmly established by the original statement because if the majority of members are in-state *and* the majority enjoy volleyball, then both statements must be true of at least one member.

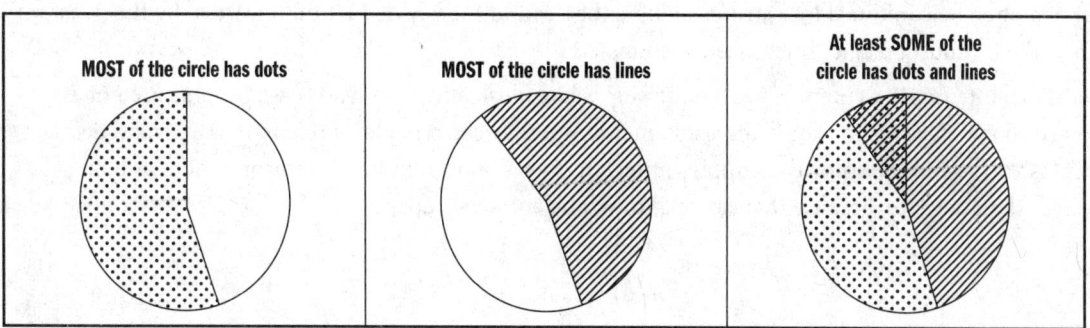

In Inference questions, it is essential that you avoid adding statements based on outside knowledge or on your own assumptions. What is your first reaction to the following statements?

> Company Z is planning its annual team-building and motivational meeting. To determine the location for this year's meeting, the planning committee surveyed the members of the company's two largest divisions—Sales and Service—asking if they preferred to meet in Orlando or Las Vegas. The committee was surprised by the results. The members of the Sales team overwhelmingly preferred Las Vegas.
>
> What can you deduce about the preferences of the Service team employees?

It is natural, upon reading that short narrative, to assume that members of the Service team overwhelmingly preferred Orlando, isn't it? Your brain is attracted to the symmetry that would bring to the results. But the correct answer to that question is "Nothing. The Service team's results are not mentioned."

As LSAT test takers in general, and especially when it comes to Inference questions, it is important to realize when statements are unsupported. If this were the stimulus to an Inference question calling for an answer supported by the statements above, then one (or more) of the *wrong* answers would almost certainly contain a statement about the Service team's preferences. In fact, about the only thing you can infer from that short narrative is that the planning committee expected that the Sales team would prefer to meet in Las Vegas.

Summarize the Stimulus and Catalog the Statements

Expert test takers read Inference question stimuli strategically, first by summarizing the purpose of the statements; e.g., *a study and its results, two assertions and an implication of one of them; statements about two groups of people*, etc. On test day, you won't need to write down this summary, but do so in practice to reinforce the habit of getting an overview of the stimulus content.

Next, the LSAT expert takes a moment to catalog the relevant statements in the stimulus by noting:

- **Concrete statements:** Strong statements lead to clear deductions. Always take note of unconditional assertions of fact, predictions, or evaluations.

- **Statements that combine:** Inference questions often reward test takers who combine statements to make a valid deduction. Look for sentences that share a subject or a predicate, and consider what you learn when they are combined.

- **Opinion and Point of View:** Evaluative words (e.g., *unfortunately, brilliant, inconclusive*, etc.) and contrast signals (e.g., *but, yet, despite, although*, etc.) are important clues to how the author or speaker understands the relationship among the statements in the stimulus. Be on the lookout for these words and use them to summarize the stimulus and make deductions.

- **Formal Logic:** If-then statements always contain at least one deduction: their contrapositive. Moreover, they can often be combined into strings of logic that lead to the key deduction rewarded by the question (especially in "must be true" Inference questions).

- **Qualified statements**: Sentences containing words like *most, often, many, several*, or *some* are not as strong as concrete assertions or if-then statements, but they can still play a role in making valid deductions (as you saw in the sorority example earlier). It is also important not to interpret them as being stronger than they are, because that can lead to wrong answers traps.

LSAT STRATEGY

Levels of Certainty

Here are the types of statements you'll encounter in Inference stimuli, arranged from most concrete to least:

- **Unqualified Assertions** (e.g., *Bruno is an employee* or *It will rain on Tuesday*)

- **Conditional Statements/Formal Logic** (e.g., *If the company hopes to meet its budget, then it must cut travel costs* or *MacIlleny will lose the election unless the county sees record voter turnout*)

- **Statements with "most" or "a majority"**—This means more than half but could include all (e.g., *Most employees of Company Y have worked in the industry for more than a decade* or *A majority of those polled reported at least one service interruption during the past year*).

- **Statements with "some" or "few"**—This means anywhere from one to all, just not zero (e.g., *Some accountants are lawyers*).

Practice Now, try untangling the stimuli from some official LSAT Inference questions. Read the hints and answer the questions in the "My Analysis" column. When you're finished, compare your work to that of an LSAT expert on the pages following this exercise. Note: You'll see the full questions associated with these stimuli in the Practice sections for the various Inference question subtypes—"strongly supported," "must be true," and Inference **except**—later in the chapter.

Concrete Statements

LSAT Stimulus	My Analysis
9. Twelve healthy volunteers with the Apo-A-IV-1 gene and twelve healthy volunteers who instead have the Apo-A-IV-2 gene each consumed a standard diet supplemented daily by a high-cholesterol food. A high level of cholesterol in the blood is associated with an increased risk of heart disease. After three weeks, the blood cholesterol levels of the subjects in the second group were unchanged, whereas the blood cholesterol levels of those with the Apo-A-IV-1 gene rose 20 percent.	**The stimulus describes a study's methodology and results. Where is the strongest statement likely to be? What can you deduce from it?**
PrepTest112 Sec4 Q10	

Combine Statements

LSAT Stimulus	My Analysis
10. Critic: Emily Dickinson's poetry demonstrates that meaning cannot reside entirely within a poem itself, but is always the unique result of an interaction between a reader's system of beliefs and the poem; and, of course, any two readers from different cultures or eras have radically different systems of beliefs. *PrepTest112 Sec4 Q7*	Which statements in this stimulus when combined lead to a valid deduction? What is it?

Opinion and Point of View Word

LSAT Stimulus	My Analysis
11. Zachary: The term "fresco" refers to paint that has been applied to wet plaster. Once dried, a fresco indelibly preserves the paint that a painter has applied in this way. Unfortunately, additions known to have been made by later painters have obscured the original fresco work done by Michelangelo in the Sistine Chapel. Therefore, in order to restore Michelangelo's Sistine Chapel paintings to the appearance that Michelangelo intended them to have, everything except the original fresco work must be stripped away. Stephen: But it was extremely common for painters of Michelangelo's era to add painted details to their own fresco work after the frescos had dried. *PrepTest111 Sec4 Q26*	Dialog stimuli are rare in Inference questions, but this one is illustrative. What does the second speaker signal about his statement's relationship to the first speaker? What can you deduce if the second speaker is correct?

Formal Logic

LSAT Stimulus	My Analysis
12. If Slater wins the election, McGuinness will be appointed head of the planning commission. But Yerxes is more qualified to head it since she is an architect who has been on the planning commission for fifteen years. Unless the polls are grossly inaccurate, Slater will win. *PrepTest112 Sec1 Q14*	**Which statements here contain conditional (If-then) statements? Can they be combined to reach a valid deduction?**

Uncertain Statements

LSAT Stimulus	My Analysis
13. Though many insects die soon after reproducing for the first time, some may live for years after the survival of the next generation has been secured. Among the latter are some insects that work for the benefit of the ecosystem—for example, bees. *PrepTest110 Sec3 Q13*	**How are the two "some" statements related here? Can you use them to make a valid deduction? How strong should that deduction be?**

Expert Analysis

Here's how an LSAT expert would analyze those Inference question stimuli.

Concrete Statements

LSAT Stimulus	Analysis
9. Twelve healthy volunteers with the Apo-A-IV-1 gene and twelve healthy volunteers who instead have the Apo-A-IV-2 gene each consumed a standard diet supplemented daily by a high-cholesterol food. A high level of cholesterol in the blood is associated with an increased risk of heart disease. After three weeks, the blood cholesterol levels of the subjects in the second group were unchanged, whereas the blood cholesterol levels of those with the Apo-A-IV-1 gene rose 20 percent. *PrepTest112 Sec4 Q10*	**The stimulus describes a study's methodology and results. Where is the strongest statement likely to be? What can you deduce from it?** *The study's results will contain the strongest statement(s) and are most likely to lead to additional deductions.* *Here, it is clear from the results that something in the Apo-A-IV-2 gene must prevent or reduce blood cholesterol.*

Combine Statements

LSAT Stimulus	My Analysis
10. Critic: Emily Dickinson's poetry demonstrates that meaning cannot reside entirely within a poem itself, but is always the unique result of an interaction between a reader's system of beliefs and the poem; and, of course, any two readers from different cultures or eras have radically different systems of beliefs. *PrepTest112 Sec4 Q7*	**Which statements in this stimulus when combined lead to a valid deduction? What is it?** *Here, the strongest statements are signaled by "always" and "of course."* *Combining those statements leads to the deduction that readers from different cultures or from different eras will have different interpretations of the same poem.*

Opinion and Point of View Word

LSAT Stimulus	My Analysis
11. Zachary: The term "fresco" refers to paint that has been applied to wet plaster. Once dried, a fresco indelibly preserves the paint that a painter has applied in this way. Unfortunately, additions known to have been made by later painters have obscured the original fresco work done by Michelangelo in the Sistine Chapel. Therefore, in order to restore Michelangelo's Sistine Chapel paintings to the appearance that Michelangelo intended them to have, everything except the original fresco work must be stripped away. Stephen: But it was extremely common for painters of Michelangelo's era to add painted details to their own fresco work after the frescos had dried. *PrepTest111 Sec4 Q26*	**Dialog stimuli are rare in Inference questions, but this one is illustrative. What does the second speaker signal about his statement's relationship to the first speaker? What can you deduce if the second speaker is correct?** *The second speaker, Stephen, begins their response with a contrast signal, "but." Combine Stephen's response with the last thing Zachary said. If Stephen is correct, you can deduce that stripping away everything except the original fresco work might not restore the Sistine Chapel to Michelangelo's intended appearance.*

Formal Logic

LSAT Stimulus	My Analysis
12. If Slater wins the election, McGuinness will be appointed head of the planning commission. But Yerxes is more qualified to head it since she is an architect who has been on the planning commission for fifteen years. Unless the polls are grossly inaccurate, Slater will win. *PrepTest112 Sec1 Q14*	**Which statements here contain conditional (If-then) statements? Can they be combined to reach a valid deduction?** *The first and third sentences are If-then statements. Translated into Formal Logic shorthand, they read:* If S wins → McG app'd head of planning If polls accurate → S wins *They combine to produce:* If polls accurate → McG app'd head of planning

Uncertain Statements

LSAT Stimulus	My Analysis
13. Though many insects die soon after reproducing for the first time, some may live for years after the survival of the next generation has been secured. Among the latter are some insects that work for the benefit of the ecosystem—for example, bees. *PrepTest110 Sec3 Q13*	**How are the two "some" statements related here? Can you use them to make a valid deduction? How strong should that deduction be?** *Here, the two "some" statements are nested, the second applying to a subset of the first. From them, you can deduce: Some bees (or "at least one kind of bee") stay alive after reproducing. Be on the lookout for wrong answers that refer to all or most bees, or that say things like "bees are the insects most likely to continue living after reproduction."*

Now that you've learned what Inference questions are asking for and seen the ways that LSAT experts untangle their stimuli, it's time to get some practice with the various Inference question subtypes. Along the way, you'll learn the most important strategies associated with each one.

"Strongly Supported" Inference Questions

LEARNING OBJECTIVE

In this section, you'll learn to:

- Identify and answer "strongly supported" Inference questions.

Here again are examples of typical "strongly supported" Inference question stems.

> Which one of the following is most strongly
> supported by the information above?
>
> *PrepTest112 Sec4 Q22*

> The information above most strongly supports
> which one of the following?
>
> *PrepTest112 Sec1 Q4*

Correct answers in "strongly supported" reward you for staying in scope and avoiding extreme language. As you work through the practice questions in this section, note how often the correct answer employs language such as "some," "in part," "at least one," "may," or "possible." Correct answers in these questions are supported, not necessarily proven, by the statements in the stimulus.

It is rare to see formal logic in "strongly supported" Inference questions, and you may find it difficult to formulate a clear-cut prediction for what the correct answer will say. That's alright. When the stimulus contains a strong sentence or statements that combine to produce a deduction, use them to help you evaluate the choices, but don't re-read the stimulus multiple times looking for a magic phrase. When you don't see the stimulus "pointing" at a specific deduction, simply characterize the stimulus—e.g., *a medical study and its result, a new procedure and its pros and cons, a contrast*, etc.—and evaluate the answers. Eliminate those that are too extreme, venture outside the scope, offer irrelevant comparisons, or contradict something in the stimulus.

And remember that the correct answer to "strongly supported" Inference questions are rarely mind blowing. If you evaluate an answer choice and think, "Well, that's *obvious* from what the stimulus says," it is probably correct.

Now, try a "strongly supported" Inference question on your own. Take your time and work through all four steps of the Logical Reasoning Method. When you're finished, review an LSAT expert's work on the next page.

Step 2:	Step 1:

14. Zoos have served both as educational resources and as entertainment. Unfortunately, removing animals from their natural habitats to stock the earliest zoos reduced certain species' populations, endangering their survival. Today most zoo animals are obtained from captive breeding programs, and many zoos now maintain breeding stocks for continued propagation of various species. This makes possible efforts to reestablish endangered species in the wild.

Which one of the following statements is most strongly supported by the information above?

(A) Zoos have played an essential role in educating the public about endangered species.

(B) Some specimens of endangered species are born and bred in zoos.

(C) No zoos exploit wild animals or endanger the survival of species.

(D) Nearly all of the animals in zoos today were born in captivity.

(E) The main purpose of zoos has shifted from entertainment to education.

PrepTest111 Sec3 Q16

Step 3:	Step 4:

Expert Analysis

Here's an example of that question as worked through by an LSAT expert.

Step 2: A short narrative about unfortunately past practices of zoos and the course correction they've made: Early zoos endangered species by removing them from their natural habitats, but now, zoos breed animals to maintain various species, and this helps reestablish them in the wild.	**Step 1:** This is a typical "strongly supported" Inference question; the statements in the stimulus make the correct answer more likely to be true.

14. Zoos have served both as educational resources and as entertainment. Unfortunately, removing animals from their natural habitats to stock the earliest zoos reduced certain species' populations, endangering their survival. Today most zoo animals are obtained from captive breeding programs, and many zoos now maintain breeding stocks for continued propagation of various species. This makes possible efforts to reestablish endangered species in the wild.

Which one of the following statements is most strongly supported by the information above?

(A) Zoos have played an essential role in educating the public about endangered species.

(B) Some specimens of endangered species are born and bred in zoos.

(C) No zoos exploit wild animals or endanger the survival of species.

(D) Nearly all of the animals in zoos today were born in captivity.

(E) The main purpose of zoos has shifted from entertainment to education.

PrepTest111 Sec3 Q16

Step 3: The correct answer will get support from this narrative. As you evaluate the choices, eliminate any that are too extreme, outside the scope, or in conflict with the stimulus.	**Step 4:** (B) is a classic "strongly supported" answer choice that avoids extreme language and simply paraphrases part of the stimulus, in this case, its final sentence and a half.

Wrong answers: (A) Outside the Scope/Extreme. This choice is not supported by the stimulus, which says only that zoos are educational resources. The stimulus does not specify the subject of that education, and certainly does not state or suggest that zoos are *essential* to public education. (C) Extreme. The stimulus says that *most* zoo animals are now obtained from breeding programs, and that *many* zoos help maintain various species, but this does rule out some continued bad actors. (D) Extreme. The stimulus says *most* zoo animals now come from breeding programs; that stops short of saying *nearly all* zoo animals are born this way. (E) Irrelevant comparison. The stimulus states that zoos have both of these roles, but does not say one or the other is the *main purpose*.

With that example and everything you've learned so far about "strongly supported" Inference questions in mind, it's time for some practice questions.

Practice Try each of the following "strongly supported" Inference questions. Some may contain arguments you analyzed earlier in the chapter. Don't worry too much about your timing here. Complete all four steps of the Logical Reasoning Method for each question, jotting down your notes whenever it is helpful to do so. After each question, review your work with the expert analysis that follows.

Hint: In "strongly supported" Inference questions, your instinct should be to avoid extreme wording.

Step 2:	Step 1:

15. In speech, when words or sentences are ambiguous, gesture and tone of voice are used to indicate the intended meaning. Writers, of course, cannot use gesture or tone of voice and must rely instead on style; the reader detects the writer's intention from the arrangement of words and sentences.

Which one of the following statements is most strongly supported by the information above?

(A) The primary function of style in writing is to augment the literal meanings of the words and sentences used.

(B) The intended meaning of a piece of writing is indicated in part by the writer's arrangement of words and sentences.

(C) It is easier for a listener to detect the tone of a speaker than for a reader to detect the style of a writer.

(D) A writer's intention will always be interpreted differently by different readers.

(E) The writer's arrangement of words and sentences completely determines the aesthetic value of his or her writing.

PrepTest111 Sec4 Q3

Step 3:	Step 4:

Expert Analysis

Step 2: A contrast is set up: When speaking, we can get the meaning of ambiguous language from gesture and tone. Writers, however, must use style, i.e., the arrangement of words and sentences.

Step 1: A standard "strongly supported" Inference question stem: the correct answer is the only one that receives support from the stimulus.

15. In speech, when words or sentences are ambiguous, gesture and tone of voice are used to indicate the intended meaning. Writers, of course, cannot use gesture or tone of voice and must rely instead on style; the reader detects the writer's intention from the arrangement of words and sentences.

Which one of the following statements is most strongly supported by the information above?

(A) The primary function of style in writing is to augment the literal meanings of the words and sentences used.

(B) The intended meaning of a piece of writing is indicated in part by the writer's arrangement of words and sentences.

(C) It is easier for a listener to detect the tone of a speaker than for a reader to detect the style of a writer.

(D) A writer's intention will always be interpreted differently by different readers.

(E) The writer's arrangement of words and sentences completely determines the aesthetic value of his or her writing.

PrepTest111 Sec4 Q3

Step 3: The correct answer will be consistent with the statements in the stimulus. If the scenario laid out here doesn't point to a specific implication, evaluate the choices by looking for the one that is consistent with the stimulus, and eliminating any that are too extreme, outside the scope, or in conflict with the stimulus.

Step 4: (B) is consistent with the second half of the contrast laid out in the stimulus, and is thus correct. Note that the choice avoids extreme language, an important characteristic of the correct choice in "strongly supported" Inference questions.

Wrong answers: (A) Extreme. The stimulus states that style is used by writers to help readers interpret ambiguous language, but it neither states nor implies that this is style's *primary* purpose. (C) Irrelevant comparison. The stimulus doesn't consider which of the ways to interpret ambiguous language is easier or harder. (D) Outside the Scope. The stimulus doesn't state or imply that "style" leads to dissimilar interpretations on the part of readers. (E) Extreme. The phrase "completely determines" pushes this choice beyond what the stimulus can support.

Hint: You saw this question's stimulus earlier. Which statement in the stimulus is most likely to lead to a strong deduction?

Step 2:	Step 1:

16. Twelve healthy volunteers with the Apo-A-IV-1 gene and twelve healthy volunteers who instead have the Apo-A-IV-2 gene each consumed a standard diet supplemented daily by a high-cholesterol food. A high level of cholesterol in the blood is associated with an increased risk of heart disease. After three weeks, the blood cholesterol levels of the subjects in the second group were unchanged, whereas the blood cholesterol levels of those with the Apo-A-IV-1 gene rose 20 percent.

Which one of the following is most strongly supported by the information above?

(A) Approximately half the population carries a gene that lowers cholesterol levels.

(B) Most of those at risk of heart disease may be able to reduce their risk by adopting a low-cholesterol diet.

(C) The bodies of those who have the Apo-A-IV-2 gene excrete cholesterol when blood cholesterol reaches a certain level.

(D) The presence of the Apo-A-IV-1 gene seems to indicate that a person has a lower risk of heart disease.

(E) The presence of the Apo-A-IV-2 gene may inhibit the elevation of blood cholesterol.

PrepTest112 Sec4 Q10

Step 3:	Step 4:

Expert Analysis

Step 2: A study's methodology and results are presented, along with an assertion:

[method] Two groups—one with gene 1 and one with gene 2—consumed identical diets with a high cholesterol food added.

[result] After three weeks, the gene 1 group's blood cholesterol was up 20%, but the gene 2 group's blood cholesterol was unchanged.

[assertion] High blood cholesterol is correlated with heart disease.

Step 1: This is a standard "strongly supported" Inference question; the correct answer gets support from the stimulus.

16. Twelve healthy volunteers with the Apo-A-IV-1 gene and twelve healthy volunteers who instead have the Apo-A-IV-2 gene each consumed a standard diet supplemented daily by a high-cholesterol food. A high level of cholesterol in the blood is associated with an increased risk of heart disease. After three weeks, the blood cholesterol levels of the subjects in the second group were unchanged, whereas the blood cholesterol levels of those with the Apo-A-IV-1 gene rose 20 percent.

Which one of the following is most strongly supported by the information above?

(A) Approximately half the population carries a gene that lowers cholesterol levels.

(B) Most of those at risk of heart disease may be able to reduce their risk by adopting a low-cholesterol diet.

(C) The bodies of those who have the Apo-A-IV-2 gene excrete cholesterol when blood cholesterol reaches a certain level.

(D) The presence of the Apo-A-IV-1 gene seems to indicate that a person has a lower risk of heart disease.

(E) The presence of the Apo-A-IV-2 gene may inhibit the elevation of blood cholesterol.

PrepTest112 Sec4 Q10

Step 3: The study suggests that something about gene 2 prevents an increase in blood cholesterol, and thus, might reduce the risk of heart disease. Look for a choice that rewards that deduction, and eliminate choices that are too extreme, outside the scope, or in conflict with the stimulus.

Step 4: (E) is correct; it follows from the description of the study and avoids language too extreme to be supported by the stimulus.

Wrong answers: (A) Distortion. The study was designed with two equal groups, but the stimulus doesn't say that is proportional to the genes' distribution in the general population. (B) Extreme. The stimulus cites a correlation between high cholesterol and heart disease, but does not suggest that this is responsible for *most* heart disease. (C) Outside the Scope. The study suggests that gene 2 reduces blood cholesterol in some way, but the stimulus is silent as to *how* it does so. (D) 180. The group with gene 1 had higher blood cholesterol, which suggests they may be at greater risk for heart disease.

Hint: Do you feel like this stimulus is leading to an overall takeaway or conclusion? Does that support one of the answer choices?

Step 2:	Step 1:

17. Gene splicing can give rise to new varieties of farm animals that have only a partially understood genetic makeup. In addition to introducing the genes for whichever trait is desired, the technique can introduce genes governing the production of toxins or carcinogens, and these latter undesirable traits might not be easily discoverable.

The statements above, if true, most strongly support which one of the following?

(A) All toxin production is genetically controlled.

(B) Gene splicing to produce new varieties of farm animals should be used cautiously.

(C) Gene splicing is not effective as a way of producing new varieties of farm animals.

(D) Most new varieties of farm animals produced by gene splicing will develop cancer.

(E) Gene splicing will advance to the point where unforeseen consequences are no longer a problem.

PrepTest111 Sec1 Q12

Step 3:	Step 4:

Expert Analysis

Step 2: The first statement outlines a scientific procedure: gene splicing can produce new varieties of farm animals.

The second statement provides pros and cons: gene splicing can select for desired traits *but* can also introduce toxins and carcinogens (that may be hard to discover).

Step 1: A standard Inference question stem: the correct answer will be the only one to receive support from the statements in the stimulus.

17. Gene splicing can give rise to new varieties of farm animals that have only a partially understood genetic makeup. In addition to introducing the genes for whichever trait is desired, the technique can introduce genes governing the production of toxins or carcinogens, and these latter undesirable traits might not be easily discoverable.

The statements above, if true, most strongly support which one of the following?

(A) All toxin production is genetically controlled.

(B) Gene splicing to produce new varieties of farm animals should be used cautiously.

(C) Gene splicing is not effective as a way of producing new varieties of farm animals.

(D) Most new varieties of farm animals produced by gene splicing will develop cancer.

(E) Gene splicing will advance to the point where unforeseen consequences are no longer a problem.

PrepTest111 Sec1 Q12

Step 3: Inference question stimuli sometimes lead you right up to a conclusion, but don't state it. Here, the implication is that the production of gene-spliced varieties should be monitored and that we shouldn't rush into their production or consumption. Look for a choice in line with this inference.

Step 4: (B) is the natural implication of the statements in the stimulus and is correct. Note that this choice is not too extreme; it does not, for example, say something like "gene splicing must be halted."

Wrong answers: (A) Extreme. The stimulus states one way in which toxins may be produced, but does not rule out other ways. (C) 180. The stimulus states directly that gene splicing can produce new varieties of farm animals. (D) Extreme/Outside the Scope. Nothing in the stimulus supports an inference about *most* gene-spliced varieties; moreover, it is unclear whether potential carcinogens would affect the animals or humans consuming the animals' products. (E) Outside the Scope. The stimulus deals only with the current state of gene splicing; it does not make or support any predictions for the future.

Hint: Are there statements in the stimulus that combine to produce a deduction?

Step 2:	Step 1:

18. Light is registered in the retina when photons hit molecules of the pigment rhodopsin and change the molecules' shape. Even when they have not been struck by photons of light, rhodopsin molecules sometimes change shape because of normal molecular motion, thereby introducing error into the visual system. The amount of this molecular motion is directly proportional to the temperature of the retina.

Which one of the following conclusions is most strongly supported by the information above?

(A) The temperature of an animal's retina depends on the amount of light the retina is absorbing.

(B) The visual systems of animals whose body temperature matches that of their surroundings are more error-prone in hot surroundings than in cold ones.

(C) As the temperature of the retina rises, rhodopsin molecules react more slowly to being struck by photons.

(D) Rhodopsin molecules are more sensitive to photons in animals whose retinas have large surface areas than in animals whose retinas have small surface areas.

(E) Molecules of rhodopsin are the only pigment molecules that occur naturally in the retina.

PrepTest110 Sec3 Q19

Step 3:	Step 4:

Expert Analysis

Step 2: Three statements:

(1) A reaction: Retinas register light when photons hit rhodopsin molecules and change their shape.

(2) An anomaly: rhodopsin molecules sometimes change shape due to normal motion (and the eye makes an error).

(3) A rule: the warmer the retina, the more normal molecular motion.

Step 1: A classic "strongly supports" Inference question stem: the correct answer will be the only one that receives support from the stimulus.

18. Light is registered in the retina when photons hit molecules of the pigment rhodopsin and change the molecules' shape. Even when they have not been struck by photons of light, rhodopsin molecules sometimes change shape because of normal molecular motion, thereby introducing error into the visual system. The amount of this molecular motion is directly proportional to the temperature of the retina.

Which one of the following conclusions is most strongly supported by the information above?

(A) The temperature of an animal's retina depends on the amount of light the retina is absorbing.

(B) The visual systems of animals whose body temperature matches that of their surroundings are more error-prone in hot surroundings than in cold ones.

(C) As the temperature of the retina rises, rhodopsin molecules react more slowly to being struck by photons.

(D) Rhodopsin molecules are more sensitive to photons in animals whose retinas have large surface areas than in animals whose retinas have small surface areas.

(E) Molecules of rhodopsin are the only pigment molecules that occur naturally in the retina.

PrepTest110 Sec3 Q19

Step 3: Combining the second and third statements gives the deduction: the warmer the retina, the more erroneous registrations of light. Look for a choice that rewards that deduction, and eliminate choices that are too extreme, outside the scope, or in conflict with the stimulus.

Step 4: (B) is correct; it rewards the deduction derived from combining the stimulus' second and third sentences: as the retina warms, the number of erroneous registrations of light increases.

Wrong answers: (A) Outside the Scope. The stimulus does not state or imply that light heats the retina. (C) is unsupported; the stimulus states that as the retina warms, normal molecular motion increases, but it does not state or imply that the response to photons is slowed. (D) Irrelevant comparison. The stimulus says nothing about the size of retinal surface areas. (E) Outside the Scope. The stimulus is silent on the number of types of pigment molecules in the retina.

Hint: You saw this rare dialog stimulus earlier. Pay attention to the wording of the question stem and the point of view of Stephen's response.

Step 2:	Step 1:

19. Zachary: The term "fresco" refers to paint that has been applied to wet plaster. Once dried, a fresco indelibly preserves the paint that a painter has applied in this way. Unfortunately, additions known to have been made by later painters have obscured the original fresco work done by Michelangelo in the Sistine Chapel. Therefore, in order to restore Michelangelo's Sistine Chapel paintings to the appearance that Michelangelo intended them to have, everything except the original fresco work must be stripped away.

  Stephen: But it was extremely common for painters of Michelangelo's era to add painted details to their own fresco work after the frescos had dried.

Stephen's response to Zachary, if true, most strongly supports which one of the following?

(A) It is impossible to distinguish the later painted additions made to Michelangelo's Sistine Chapel paintings from the original fresco work.

(B) Stripping away everything except Michelangelo's original fresco work from the Sistine Chapel paintings would be unlikely to restore them to the appearance Michelangelo intended them to have.

(C) The painted details that painters of Michelangelo's era added to their own fresco work were not an integral part of the completed paintings' overall design.

(D) None of the painters of Michelangelo's era who made additions to the Sistine Chapel paintings was an important artist in his or her own right.

(E) Michelangelo was rarely satisfied with the appearance of his finished works.

PrepTest111 Sec4 Q26

Step 3:	Step 4:

Expert Analysis

Step 2: Zachary: *Conclusion*—To see Michelangelo's intention for the Sistine Chapel, we must strip away everything except the original fresco *because* *Evidence*—We know later artists painted on top of Michelangelo's Sistine Chapel frescoes. Stephen: *But*, at Michelangelo's time, artists might paint over their own frescoes, too.	**Step 1:** A rare Inference question with a dialog stimulus; here, the correct answer will receive support from Stephen's addition to Zachary's argument.

19. Zachary: The term "fresco" refers to paint that has been applied to wet plaster. Once dried, a fresco indelibly preserves the paint that a painter has applied in this way. Unfortunately, additions known to have been made by later painters have obscured the original fresco work done by Michelangelo in the Sistine Chapel. Therefore, in order to restore Michelangelo's Sistine Chapel paintings to the appearance that Michelangelo intended them to have, everything except the original fresco work must be stripped away.

    Stephen: But it was extremely common for painters of Michelangelo's era to add painted details to their own fresco work after the frescos had dried.

Stephen's response to Zachary, if true, most strongly supports which one of the following?

(A) It is impossible to distinguish the later painted additions made to Michelangelo's Sistine Chapel paintings from the original fresco work.

(B) Stripping away everything except Michelangelo's original fresco work from the Sistine Chapel paintings would be unlikely to restore them to the appearance Michelangelo intended them to have.

(C) The painted details that painters of Michelangelo's era added to their own fresco work were not an integral part of the completed paintings' overall design.

(D) None of the painters of Michelangelo's era who made additions to the Sistine Chapel paintings was an important artist in his or her own right.

(E) Michelangelo was rarely satisfied with the appearance of his finished works.

PrepTest111 Sec4 Q26

Step 3: Stephen's addition has a clear implication: If you strip back to just the frescoes, you might lose Michelangelo's *intentional* additions. Look for an answer choice in line with this reasoning.	**Step 4:** (B) provides the logical extrapolation of Zachary's and Stephen's combined remarks, and is correct.

Wrong answers: (A) 180. This statement is impossible to square with Zachary's premise that later additions "have obscured" the original, and his recommendation to strip away the later painting wouldn't make sense. (C) 180. If this were true, Stephen would not have started his response with "*[b]ut*," because he would have seen no dilemma arising from stripping the work all the way back to the original frescoes. (D) Outside the Scope. The speakers aren't debating the artistic value of the additions; Zachary contends that stripping away the additions is necessary to reveal Michelangelo's *intended* appearance for the chapel, and it is this contention that Stephen disputes. (E) Outside the Scope. Neither speaker addresses the statement in the choice.

On most tests, "strongly supported" Inference questions are roughly as common as the next subtype, the "must be true" Inference question.

"Must Be True" Inference Questions

LEARNING OBJECTIVE

In this section, you'll learn to:

- Identify and answer "must be true" Inference questions.

Here again are some typical examples of "must be true" question stems.

> If the statements above are true, which one of the
> following must also be true?
>
> *PrepTest112 Sec1 Q11*

> Which one of the following can be properly inferred
> from the information above?
>
> *PrepTest112 Sec1 Q14*

In this Inference question subtype, the correct answer is *established* by the stimulus text. If the statements in the stimulus are true, then the correct answer must be true as well. Hence, the name. Practically speaking, this means that the stimulus statements are generally stronger, and the correct answers generally more easily predicted than those in "strongly supported" Inference questions are.

Formal logic is very common in "must be true" Inference questions, both in stimuli and in the answer choices. This is so true that you'll have a short Formal Logic Workshop before the main set of Practice questions for this section.

In all "must be true" Inference questions, wrong answers to be on the lookout for include 180s (statements that contradict something stated in the stimulus) and Distortions (choices that, while not in direct conflict with the stimulus, mangle or confuse stimulus statements in an inaccurate manner). A classic Distortion wrong answer associated with Formal Logic is one that confuses necessity for sufficiency, or vice versa, in other words, one that reverses an If-then statement without negating its terms, or negates its terms without reversing their order.

Consider this example:

All imported items on our website come with free shipping. (*If II* $\rightarrow$ *FS*)

If that statement is true, which one of the following must also be true?

1. Any item that comes with free shipping is imported. (*If FS* $\rightarrow$ *II*)
2. Any item that does not come with free shipping is not imported. (*If ~FS* $\rightarrow$ *~II*)
3. Any item that is not imported does not come with free shipping. (*If ~II* $\rightarrow$ *~FS*)

Only choice (2) follows logically from the original statement. It is the contrapositive of the original statement. Choices (1) and (3) are Distortion wrong answers. Choice (1) reverses the original statement's terms without negating them (it treats the necessary term as if it were sufficient), and choice (3) negates the original statement's terms without reversing them (it treats the sufficient term as if it were necessary).

Now, try to complete a "strongly supported" Inference question featuring a stimulus you saw earlier in the chapter on your own. Take your time and work through all four steps of the Logical Reasoning Method even if you remember the stimulus. When you're finished, review an LSAT expert's work on the next page.

Step 2:	Step 1:

20. Though many insects die soon after reproducing for the first time, some may live for years after the survival of the next generation has been secured. Among the latter are some insects that work for the benefit of the ecosystem—for example, bees.

Which one of the following can be properly inferred from the information above?

(A) Survival of the species, rather than of the individual, is the goal of most insect populations.

(B) Insects that do not play a vital role in the ecosystem are more likely to die after reproducing for the first time.

(C) Most bees live well beyond the onset of the generation that follows them.

(D) Those bees that reproduce do not always die soon after reproducing for the first time.

(E) Most insects are hatched self-sufficient and do not need to be cared for by adult insects.

PrepTest110 Sec3 Q13

Step 3:	Step 4:

Expert Analysis

Here's how an LSAT expert worked through that question.

Step 2: Two "some" statements: (1) some insects live well after the next generation's survival is ensured, and (2) among these are some species (e.g., bees) that benefit the ecosystem.	**Step 1:** This is a Standard "must be" Inference question; the correct answer follows unequivocally from the stimulus.

20. Though many insects die soon after reproducing for the first time, some may live for years after the survival of the next generation has been secured. Among the latter are some insects that work for the benefit of the ecosystem—for example, bees.

Which one of the following can be properly inferred from the information above?

(A) Survival of the species, rather than of the individual, is the goal of most insect populations.

(B) Insects that do not play a vital role in the ecosystem are more likely to die after reproducing for the first time.

(C) Most bees live well beyond the onset of the generation that follows them.

(D) Those bees that reproduce do not always die soon after reproducing for the first time.

(E) Most insects are hatched self-sufficient and do not need to be cared for by adult insects.

PrepTest110 Sec3 Q13

Step 3: The two statements are already combined: the group in the second is a subset of that in the first. Use them to evaluate the statements eliminating answers that are too extreme, outside the scope, or in conflict with the stimulus.	**Step 4:** (D) is correct. If some insect species live past their first reproduction, and if some of those are bees, then it is certain that bees do not always die after their first reproduction.

Wrong answers: (A) Outside the Scope. The stimulus does not get into insect species' *goals*. (B) Outside the Scope. The stimulus says nothing about the *likelihood* that insect species survive past their first reproduction, only that *some* do, and of those, *some* benefit the environment. (C) Extreme. The stimulus doesn't support any conclusions about *most* insect species; it says only that *some* species outlive their first reproduction, and of those, *some* benefit the environment. (E) Outside the Scope. The stimulus is wholly silent on the care and raising of young insects.

On the next page, try one more "must be true" Inference question and then compare your work to the expert analysis. After that, you'll have a short Formal Logic Workshop that includes full-question practice with a few more "must be true" Inference questions.

Practice Try the following "strongly supported" Inference question. Don't worry too much about your timing here. Complete all four steps of the Logical Reasoning Method for each question, jotting down your notes whenever it is helpful to do so. After you're finished, review your work with the expert analysis that follows.

Hint: Read strategically. What is the purpose of the scientist's last sentence?

Step 2:	Step 1:

21. Scientist: Some critics of public funding for this research project have maintained that only if it can be indicated how the public will benefit from the project is continued public funding for it justified. If the critics were right about this, then there would not be the tremendous public support for the project that even its critics acknowledge.

If the scientist's claims are true, which one of the following must also be true?

(A) The benefits derived from the research project are irrelevant to whether or not its funding is justified.

(B) Continued public funding for the research project is justified.

(C) Public support for the research project is the surest indication of whether or not it is justified.

(D) There is tremendous public support for the research project because it can be indicated how the public will benefit from the project.

(E) That a public benefit can be indicated is not a requirement for the justification of the research project's continued public funding.

PrepTest111 Sec3 Q20

Step 3:	Step 4:

Expert Analysis

Here's how an LSAT expert completed the question you just saw.

Step 2: The scientist responds to critics of public funding for a research project. Critics' claim: Justification of continued public funding *requires* a demonstration of future public benefit. Scientist's response: The project has enormous support from the public, so the critics are incorrect.	**Step 1:** A standard "must be true" Inference question stem: the correct answers validity will be established by the stimulus.

21. Scientist: Some critics of public funding for this research project have maintained that only if it can be indicated how the public will benefit from the project is continued public funding for it justified. If the critics were right about this, then there would not be the tremendous public support for the project that even its critics acknowledge.

If the scientist's claims are true, which one of the following must also be true?

(A) The benefits derived from the research project are irrelevant to whether or not its funding is justified.

(B) Continued public funding for the research project is justified.

(C) Public support for the research project is the surest indication of whether or not it is justified.

(D) There is tremendous public support for the research project because it can be indicated how the public will benefit from the project.

(E) That a public benefit can be indicated is not a requirement for the justification of the research project's continued public funding.

PrepTest111 Sec3 Q20

Step 3: The scientist's response is oblique, but essentially contends that the project's "tremendous public support" means that a demonstration of public benefits is *not needed* to justify its continued public funding. Look for the choice that articulates this implication of the scientist's response.	**Step 4:** (E) is correct; this choice makes explicit the scientist's implication: proof of public benefit is not needed to justify the project's continued public funding.

Wrong answers: (A) Extreme. Saying that public benefits are *irrelevant* overstates the scientist's point, which is that continued public funding should not require an indication of how the public will benefit. (B) Extreme. The scientist's point is that the critics' requirement (demonstrate the benefits) is not needed to justify continued public spending. (C) Extreme. The scientist does claim that public support is the ultimate justification for a project, just that it is strong enough in this case that public funding shouldn't be contingent on a demonstration of benefits. (D) Distortion. This choice draws a link where none is necessarily implied in the scientist's statements. The tremendous public support may be because the project is really cool or because it is championed by a beloved celebrity, and not because the public expects a benefit from it. Who knows? The scientist's point is that such support overrides the need to demonstrate public benefits to justify continued public spending for the project.

Formal Logic Workshop 3

Prepare   In "must be true" Inference questions, your complete Formal Logic toolkit is put to the test. You must recognize conditional statements, accurately translate them into If-then terms, and accurately spot links between statements that lead to chains of logic (and, thus, further deductions). You'll also be rewarded for being able to confidently use the contrapositives of statements in two ways: first, contrapositives help you identify links between conditional statements, and second, correct answers in "must be true" Inference questions are often written in the contrapositive form of the deduction you've made.

To get ready for some full-question practice, analyze the following stimuli from "must be true" Inference questions testing Formal Logic. You'll recognize one of them from earlier in the chapter, but the other two you haven't seen before.

For each of the following stimuli, (1) identify the statements containing Formal Logic, (2) translate each of these into If-then terms, (3) link statements to make additional deductions, and (4) express these deductions in their contrapositive forms as well.

LSAT Stimulus	My Analysis
22. If Slater wins the election, McGuinness will be appointed head of the planning commission. But Yerxes is more qualified to head it since she is an architect who has been on the planning commission for fifteen years. Unless the polls are grossly inaccurate, Slater will win.	
PrepTest112 Sec1 Q14	
23. If there are any inspired performances in the concert, the audience will be treated to a good show. But there will not be a good show unless there are sophisticated listeners in the audience, and to be a sophisticated listener one must understand one's musical roots.	
PrepTest111 Sec3 Q18	
24. Any sale item that is purchased can be returned for store credit but not for a refund of the purchase price. Every home appliance and every piece of gardening equipment is on sale along with selected construction tools.	
PrepTest112 Sec1 Q11	

Expert Analysis

Here's how an LSAT expert analyzed the stimuli you just saw.

LSAT Stimulus	Analysis
22. If Slater wins the election, McGuinness will be appointed head of the planning commission. But Yerxes is more qualified to head it since she is an architect who has been on the planning commission for fifteen years. Unless the polls are grossly inaccurate, Slater will win. *PrepTest112 Sec1 Q14*	The first and third sentences are conditional, formal logic statements. *If S wins → McG appointed PC head* *If polls accurate → S wins.* Deduction: *If polls accurate → McG appointed PC head* Contrapositive: *If McG NOT appointed PC head → polls NOT accurate.*
23. If there are any inspired performances in the concert, the audience will be treated to a good show. But there will not be a good show unless there are sophisticated listeners in the audience, and to be a sophisticated listener one must understand one's musical roots. *PrepTest111 Sec3 Q18*	The first sentence is a conditional, formal logic statement, and the second sentence contains two more conditional, formal logic statements. *If inspired performances → good show* *If good show → some sophisticated listeners* *If sophist'd listener → understand musical roots* Deduction: All three statements form a logic chain. *If inspired performances → good show → some sophisticated listeners → understand musical roots* Contrapositive: *If NOT understand musical roots → NO sophisticated listeners → NOT good show → NO inspired performances*

LSAT Stimulus	Analysis
24. Any sale item that is purchased can be returned for store credit but not for a refund of the purchase price. Every home appliance and every piece of gardening equipment is on sale along with selected construction tools. *PrepTest112 Sec1 Q11*	The first sentence and the first part of the second sentence are complex conditional, formal logic statements: *If home appliance → on sale* *If gardening equipment → on sale* *If on sale → return for store credit* *If on sale → no refund* Deduction:

	If home appliance OR gardening equipment	→	can return for credit AND NO refund

Contrapositive:

	If CANNOT return or credit OR can get refund	→	NOT home appliance AND NOT gardening equipment

---

TEST DAY TIP

LSAT experts vary in how much Formal Logic they write out on their scratch paper. In practice, get used to jotting down translations and contrapositives so that you'll be ready to do so when it is helpful on test day.

Now, put those Formal Logic skills to work with the full questions from which those stimuli were drawn. Remember to be on the lookout for wrong answer choices that distort the deductions you've been able to make.

Practice   Try each of the following "must be true" Inference questions containing the stimuli you just analyzed. Don't worry too much about your timing here. Complete all four steps of the Logical Reasoning Method for each question, jotting down your notes whenever it is helpful to do so. After each question, review your work with the expert analysis that follows.

Hint: How can you combine the Formal Logic deduction with the other statement in this stimulus?

Step 2:	Step 1:

25. If Slater wins the election, McGuinness will be appointed head of the planning commission. But Yerxes is more qualified to head it since she is an architect who has been on the planning commission for fifteen years. Unless the polls are grossly inaccurate, Slater will win.

Which one of the following can be properly inferred from the information above?

(A) If the polls are grossly inaccurate, someone more qualified than McGuinness will be appointed head of the planning commission.

(B) McGuinness will be appointed head of the planning commission only if the polls are a good indication of how the election will turn out.

(C) Either Slater will win the election or Yerxes will be appointed head of the planning commission.

(D) McGuinness is not an architect and has not been on the planning commission for fifteen years or more.

(E) If the polls are a good indication of how the election will turn out, someone less qualified than Yerxes will be appointed head of the planning commission.

PrepTest112 Sec1 Q14

Step 3:	Step 4:

Expert Analysis

Here's how an LSAT expert worked through the question you just tried.

Step 2: Two conditional statements and an assertion: (1) If S wins the election, then McG will head up the planning commission. (2) Unless polls are grossly wrong, S wins. (3) Y, an architect with 15 years planning experience, is more qualified than McG to head up the planning commission.	**Step 1:** The phrase "properly inferred" connotes a classic "must be true" Inference question; the correct answer is established by the statements in the stimulus.

25. If Slater wins the election, McGuinness will be appointed head of the planning commission. But Yerxes is more qualified to head it since she is an architect who has been on the planning commission for fifteen years. Unless the polls are grossly inaccurate, Slater will win.

Which one of the following can be properly inferred from the information above?

(A) If the polls are grossly inaccurate, someone more qualified than McGuinness will be appointed head of the planning commission.

(B) McGuinness will be appointed head of the planning commission only if the polls are a good indication of how the election will turn out.

(C) Either Slater will win the election or Yerxes will be appointed head of the planning commission.

(D) McGuinness is not an architect and has not been on the planning commission for fifteen years or more.

(E) If the polls are a good indication of how the election will turn out, someone less qualified than Yerxes will be appointed head of the planning commission.

PrepTest112 Sec1 Q14

Step 3: Simplify and combine the statements. Remember that "unless" means *if not*, so if the polls are *not* grossly inaccurate means the polls are pretty accurate. Thus, the reasoning goes: *If polls are accurate* $\rightarrow$ *S wins* $\rightarrow$ *McG (who is not as well qualified as Y) appointed to head the planning commission.* Use that deduction to evaluate the choices.	**Step 4:** (E) accurately extrapolates the full implications of the statements in the stimulus, and is correct.

Wrong answers: (A) Distortion. If someone other than Slater wins, you have no idea who will be appointed to head up the planning commission. (B) Distortion. Another election winner might appoint McGuiness; the stimulus is silent on this prospect. (C) Distortion. The stimulus speaks only to Yerxes qualifications, but gives no indication that any candidate would appoint Yerxes. (D) Distortion. For sure, McGuiness has not done both of the things that, taken together, make Yerxes better qualified to head the commission, but it is possible that McGuiness has done one (or the other) of them.

Hint: What Formal Logic errors are committed in this question's wrong answer choices? Can you spot them?

Step 2:	Step 1:

26. If there are any inspired performances in the concert, the audience will be treated to a good show. But there will not be a good show unless there are sophisticated listeners in the audience, and to be a sophisticated listener one must understand one's musical roots.

If all of the statements above are true, which one of the following must also be true?

(A) If there are no sophisticated listeners in the audience, then there will be no inspired musical performances in the concert.

(B) No people who understand their musical roots will be in the audience if the audience will not be treated to a good show.

(C) If there will be people in the audience who understand their musical roots, then at least one musical performance in the concert will be inspired.

(D) The audience will be treated to a good show unless there are people in the audience who do not understand their musical roots.

(E) If there are sophisticated listeners in the audience, then there will be inspired musical performances in the concert.

PrepTest111 Sec3 Q18

Step 3:	Step 4:

Expert Analysis

Here's how an LSAT expert worked through the question you just tried.

Step 2: Three conditional statements:

(1) If inspired performances → good show

(2) No good show unless some sophisticated listeners

(3) A sophisticated listener needs to understand their musical roots.

Step 1: A strongly worded "must be true" Inference question; the stimulus will unequivocally establish the validity of the correct answer.

26. If there are any inspired performances in the concert, the audience will be treated to a good show. But there will not be a good show unless there are sophisticated listeners in the audience, and to be a sophisticated listener one must understand one's musical roots.

If all of the statements above are true, which one of the following must also be true?

(A) If there are no sophisticated listeners in the audience, then there will be no inspired musical performances in the concert.

(B) No people who understand their musical roots will be in the audience if the audience will not be treated to a good show.

(C) If there will be people in the audience who understand their musical roots, then at least one musical performance in the concert will be inspired.

(D) The audience will be treated to a good show unless there are people in the audience who do not understand their musical roots.

(E) If there are sophisticated listeners in the audience, then there will be inspired musical performances in the concert.

PrepTest111 Sec3 Q18

Step 3: Translate the statements into If-then form to see their relationship:

If inspired performances → good show

If good show → some sophisticated listeners

If sophist'd listener → understand musical roots

All of the statements link up, which means the contrapositives do too:

If not understand musical roots → no sophisticated listeners → not good show → no inspired performances

The correct answer will be an accurate deduction from some or all of this chain and is likely to be phrased in the contrapositive.

Step 4: (A) is a valid deduction from the chain of formal logic statements and is phrased in the language of the contrapositive. The logic tells you that sophisticated listeners are necessary for a good show, and that a good show is necessary for inspired performances. Thus, if there are no sophisticated listeners, then there will be no inspired performances.

Wrong answers: (B) Distortion. The stimulus establishes a good show as *sufficient* to know that listeners who understand their musical roots were present, but this choice treats it as *necessary*. (C) Distortion. The stimulus establishes the presence of listeners who understand their musical roots as *necessary* for inspired performances, but this choice treats it as *sufficient*. (D) This choice distorts the stimulus in multiple ways; for example, it confuses the presence of listeners who understand their musical roots (necessary for a good show) with the presence of people who *do not* understand their musical roots (which does not trigger any deductions in the stimulus). (E) Distortion. This choice reverses the terms in the logic without negating them; in other words, it treats a *necessary* term (the presence of sophisticated listeners) as if it were *sufficient*.

Hint: In the stimulus, you learn the rules for the return of items that are on sale. What do you know about items that are not on sale?

Step 2:	Step 1:

27. Any sale item that is purchased can be returned for store credit but not for a refund of the purchase price. Every home appliance and every piece of gardening equipment is on sale along with selected construction tools.

If the statements above are true, which one of the following must also be true?

(A) Any item that is not a home appliance or a piece of gardening equipment is returnable for a refund.

(B) Any item that is not on sale cannot be returned for store credit.

(C) Some construction tools are not returnable for store credit.

(D) No piece of gardening equipment is returnable for a refund.

(E) None of the things that are returnable for a refund are construction tools.

PrepTest112 Sec1 Q11

Step 3:	Step 4:

Expert Analysis

Here's how an LSAT expert worked through the question you just tried.

Step 2: Two complex conditional statements, and one less specific statement:

(1) If an item is on sale, then it can be returned for credit but not for a refund.

(2) If an item is a home appliance or a piece of gardening equipment, then it is on sale.

(3) Some construction tools are on sale.

Step 1: This is a standard "must be true" Inference question; treat the stimulus as factual, and find the one answer that must follow from it.

27. Any sale item that is purchased can be returned for store credit but not for a refund of the purchase price. Every home appliance and every piece of gardening equipment is on sale along with selected construction tools.

If the statements above are true, which one of the following must also be true?

(A) Any item that is not a home appliance or a piece of gardening equipment is returnable for a refund.

(B) Any item that is not on sale cannot be returned for store credit.

(C) Some construction tools are not returnable for store credit.

(D) No piece of gardening equipment is returnable for a refund.

(E) None of the things that are returnable for a refund are construction tools.

PrepTest112 Sec1 Q11

Step 3: Break the complex statements into two statements each, and arrange them for clarity:

If home appliance → on sale

If gardening equipment → on sale

Some construction tools on sale

If on sale → return for store credit

If on sale → no refund

Combine the statements to deduce that one cannot get a refund for any home appliances or gardening equipment. One may be able to get a refund on a construction tool if it is not on sale. Use the deductions to find the one must-be-true answer choice.

Step 4: (D) is unequivocally established by combining the statements in the stimulus, and is thus correct.

Wrong answers: (A) 180. For sure, some construction tools (those that are on sale) cannot be returned for a refund; there may be other kinds of items on sale, too, of course. (B) Distortion. The stimulus contains no information about items that are not on sale; the rules for their return are unknown. (C) Distortion. It is possible that all construction tools may be returned for store credit; those that are on sale can definitely be returned for credit, and the stimulus provides no information about those that aren't on sale. (E) Distortion. The stimulus says only that "selected construction tools" are on sale (and, thus, refunds aren't available for those), but some, then, might not be on sale, and you don't know the rules for the return of those.

Inference Except Questions

> **LEARNING OBJECTIVE**
>
> In this section, you'll learn to:
>
> • Identify and answer Inference **except** questions.

Here again are some examples of typical Inference **except** question stems.

> If the statements above are true, then each of the
> following statements could also be true **except:**
>
> *PrepTest110 Sec3 Q22*

> The statements above provide some support for
> each of the following **except:**
>
> *PrepTest111 Sec4 Q1*

The official LSAT always bolds the word—e.g., **except**, **least**, etc.—indicating the negative qualification that distinguishes this Inference question subtype. You'll see them displayed that way in this book to help you react quickly and confidently any time you spot one. That said, this Inference question subtype is rare, and there's a good chance you won't see one on test day, so don't spend too much energy hunting down extra examples of these to practice.

When you do encounter these questions, take Step 1 of the Logical Reasoning Method very seriously. Characterize the one correct and four incorrect answer choices. Just as there are "must be true" and "strongly supported" Inference questions, there are "must be false" and "lacks support" Inference **except** questions.

> When the correct answer "must be false," it contradicts the stimulus, and the four wrong answers "could be true," meaning that they may be in line with the stimulus, or simply outside the scope.

> When the correct answer merely "lacks support" from the stimulus, it could be outside the scope or at odds with the stimulus, while the four wrong answers will receive support from the stimulus. The wrong answers here will look like correct answers for "strongly supported" Inference questions.

After Step 1, approach these questions just like you do the more common Inference question varieties. Practice a couple of examples to get the hang of characterizing the answer choices, and if you still find them confusing, go back to the question stem exercise near the start of this chapter.

Now, try to complete an Inference **except** question featuring a stimulus you saw earlier in the chapter on your own. Take your time and work through all four steps of the Logical Reasoning Method even if you remember the stimulus. When you're finished, review an LSAT expert's work on the next page.

Step 2:

Step 1:

28. Critic: Emily Dickinson's poetry demonstrates that meaning cannot reside entirely within a poem itself, but is always the unique result of an interaction between a reader's system of beliefs and the poem; and, of course, any two readers from different cultures or eras have radically different systems of beliefs.

If the critic's statements are true, each of the following could be true **except:**

(A) A reader's interpretation of a poem by Dickinson is affected by someone else's interpretation of it.

(B) A modern reader and a nineteenth-century reader interpret one of Shakespeare's sonnets in the same way.

(C) A reader's interpretation of a poem evolves over time.

(D) Two readers from the same era arrive at different interpretations of the same poem.

(E) A reader's enjoyment of a poem is enhanced by knowing the poet's interpretation of it.

PrepTest112 Sec4 Q7

Step 3:

Step 4:

Expert Analysis

Here's an example of that question as worked through by an LSAT expert.

Step 2: Two assertions:

(1) The meaning of poetry always comes from the interaction between the reader's system of beliefs and the poem (ex. Dickinson).

(2) Readers from different cultures or time periods always have different systems of beliefs.

Step 1: In this Inference **except** question the correct answer *must be false* based on the stimulus.

28. Critic: Emily Dickinson's poetry demonstrates that meaning cannot reside entirely within a poem itself, but is always the unique result of an interaction between a reader's system of beliefs and the poem; and, of course, any two readers from different cultures or eras have radically different systems of beliefs.

If the critic's statements are true, each of the following could be true **except:**

(A) A reader's interpretation of a poem by Dickinson is affected by someone else's interpretation of it.

(B) A modern reader and a nineteenth-century reader interpret one of Shakespeare's sonnets in the same way.

(C) A reader's interpretation of a poem evolves over time.

(D) Two readers from the same era arrive at different interpretations of the same poem.

(E) A reader's enjoyment of a poem is enhanced by knowing the poet's interpretation of it.

PrepTest112 Sec4 Q7

Step 3: Combine the two statements to deduce that readers from different time periods or from different cultures will find different meanings from the same poem. The correct answer will be false based on this deduction. The wrong answers will either agree with the deduction or fall outside the scope of the stimulus.

Step 4: (B) is correct; this statement is diametrically opposed to the deduction that readers from different eras will find different meanings in the same poems.

Wrong answers: (A) This statement does not conflict with the stimulus or its implications; therefore, it is incorrect in this *must be false* Inference question. (C) The stimulus does not state or imply that a reader must maintain just one interpretation over time, so this answer does not conflict with the stimulus and is incorrect for this *must be false* Inference question. (D) The stimulus does not state or imply that readers from the same era must find identical meanings in a poem; this answer does not conflict with the stimulus and is thus incorrect in this *must be false* Inference question. (E) The stimulus says nothing about a reader's enjoyment, so this choice does not conflict with the stimulus and is thus incorrect for a *must be false* Inference question.

Now, practice with a couple Inference **except** questions you're seeing for the first time. Compare your work with that of the LSAT expert after each item.

Practice Try the following Inference **except** questions. Don't worry too much about your timing here. Complete all four steps of the Logical Reasoning Method for each question, jotting down your notes whenever it is helpful to do so. After you're finished, review your work with the expert analysis that follows.

Hint: What are the characteristics of the one correct and four incorrect answer choices here?

Step 2:	Step 1:

29. Viruses can have beneficial effects. For example, some kill more-complex microorganisms, some of which are deadly to humans. But viruses have such simple structures that replacing just a few of a beneficial virus's several million atoms can make it deadly to humans. Clearly, since alterations of greater complexity than this are commonly produced by random mutations, any virus could easily become dangerous to humans.

If the statements above are true, then each of the following statements could also be true **except:**

(A) Random mutation makes some deadly viruses beneficial to humans.

(B) Some organisms of greater complexity than viruses are no more likely than viruses to undergo significant alterations through random mutation.

(C) Some microorganisms that are more complex than viruses are beneficial to humans.

(D) Some viruses that fail to kill other viruses that are deadly to humans are nevertheless beneficial to humans.

(E) No virus that is deadly to organisms of greater complexity than itself is beneficial to humans.

PrepTest110 Sec3 Q22

Step 3:	Step 4:

Expert Analysis

Here's how an LSAT expert completed the question you just tried.

Step 2: Two contrasting assertions (one with an example) and a conclusion extrapolated from them: (1) Viruses can be beneficial (ex. killing more-complex microorganisms), *but* (2) changing just a few atoms in a virus can make it deadly. (3) *So*, any virus can become dangerous because random mutation can change a few atoms in viruses.	**Step 1:** A "must be false" Inference question: the correct answer here is impossible based on the stimulus.

29. Viruses can have beneficial effects. For example, some kill more-complex microorganisms, some of which are deadly to humans. But viruses have such simple structures that replacing just a few of a beneficial virus's several million atoms can make it deadly to humans. Clearly, since alterations of greater complexity than this are commonly produced by random mutations, any virus could easily become dangerous to humans.

If the statements above are true, then each of the following statements could also be true **except:**

(A) Random mutation makes some deadly viruses beneficial to humans.

(B) Some organisms of greater complexity than viruses are no more likely than viruses to undergo significant alterations through random mutation.

(C) Some microorganisms that are more complex than viruses are beneficial to humans.

(D) Some viruses that fail to kill other viruses that are deadly to humans are nevertheless beneficial to humans.

(E) No virus that is deadly to organisms of greater complexity than itself is beneficial to humans.

PrepTest110 Sec3 Q22

Step 3: Some Inference question stimuli contain arguments, but your task is not to analyze them as you would in Assumption Family questions. Instead, use the statements to evaluate the choices. Remember that here the stem calls for the one choice that *must be false*.	**Step 4:** (E) is correct in this "must be false" question because it directly contradicts the example used to support the stimulus's first statement: one way in which viruses can benefit humans is by killing more-complex microorganisms.

Wrong answers: (A) This is possible; the stimulus says beneficial viruses can turn bad, so why not vice versa? (B) This is possible. The only thing the stimulus says about organisms more complex than viruses is that viruses can sometimes kill them; it is silent on the likelihood of their mutation. (C) This is possible; the stimulus mentions more-complex microorganisms that are harmful to humans, but does not rule out the existence of beneficial ones, too. (D) This is possible; the stimulus cited viruses that kill more-complex microorganisms as one example of beneficial viruses, but did rule out other possible benefits.

Hint: How can you use the paradox presented in the stimulus to help you evaluate the answer choices?

<table>
<tr><td>**Step 2:**</td><td>**Step 1:**</td></tr>
</table>

30. Multiple sclerosis is an autoimmune disease: white blood cells attack the myelin sheath that protects nerve fibers in the spinal cord and brain. Medical science now has a drug that can be used to successfully treat multiple sclerosis, but the path that led medical researchers to this drug was hardly straightforward. Initially, some scientists believed attacks characteristic of multiple sclerosis might be triggered by chronic viral infections. So in 1984 they began testing gamma interferon, one of the body's own antiviral weapons. To their horror, all the multiple sclerosis patients tested became dramatically worse. The false step proved to be instructive however.

Which one of the following is **least** compatible with the results of the gamma interferon experiment?

(A) Gamma interferon stops white blood cells from producing myelin-destroying compounds.

(B) Administering gamma interferon to those without multiple sclerosis causes an increase in the number of white blood cells.

(C) Medical researchers have discovered that the gamma interferon level in the cerebrospinal fluid skyrockets just before and during multiple sclerosis attacks.

(D) It has now been established that most multiple sclerosis sufferers do not have chronic viral infections.

(E) The drug now used to treat multiple sclerosis is known to inhibit the activity of gamma interferon.

PrepTest111 Sec4 Q22

<table>
<tr><td>**Step 3:**</td><td>**Step 4:**</td></tr>
</table>

Expert Analysis

Here's how an LSAT expert completed the question you just tried.

Step 2: Background: MS is caused by white blood cells attacking the myelin sheath, and there's now a successful treatment. In the past, scientists thought MS might be viral, so they tried gamma interferon, a naturally occurring antiviral. The result of the gamma interferon experiment was that patients got worse.	**Step 1:** A rare Inference question stem; here, the four wrong answers are compatible with the results described in the stimulus, while the correct answer is not.

30. Multiple sclerosis is an autoimmune disease: white blood cells attack the myelin sheath that protects nerve fibers in the spinal cord and brain. Medical science now has a drug that can be used to successfully treat multiple sclerosis, but the path that led medical researchers to this drug was hardly straightforward. Initially, some scientists believed attacks characteristic of multiple sclerosis might be triggered by chronic viral infections. So in 1984 they began testing gamma interferon, one of the body's own antiviral weapons. To their horror, all the multiple sclerosis patients tested became dramatically worse. The false step proved to be instructive however.

Which one of the following is **least** compatible with the results of the gamma interferon experiment?

(A) Gamma interferon stops white blood cells from producing myelin-destroying compounds.

(B) Administering gamma interferon to those without multiple sclerosis causes an increase in the number of white blood cells.

(C) Medical researchers have discovered that the gamma interferon level in the cerebrospinal fluid skyrockets just before and during multiple sclerosis attacks.

(D) It has now been established that most multiple sclerosis sufferers do not have chronic viral infections.

(E) The drug now used to treat multiple sclerosis is known to inhibit the activity of gamma interferon.

PrepTest111 Sec4 Q22

Step 3: This stimulus is similar to those in Paradox questions. Why would gamma interferon, an antiviral, make MS patients worse? The wrong answers will all explain some way in which gamma interferon promoted white blood cells to harm the myelin sheath.	**Step 4:** (A) is a 180, and is therefore correct in this "**least** compatible" Inference question. If gamma interferon prevented white blood cells from harming the myelin sheath, MS patients would have gotten better, not worse, when taking it.

Wrong answers: (B) This choice provides a reason MS patients would have gotten worse when taking gamma interferon; thus, it is incorrect in this "**least** compatible" Inference question. (C) This choice correlates gamma interferon with severe MS symptoms and is thus incorrect for this "**least** compatible" Inference question. (D) This is consistent with the result that gamma interferon, an antiviral, did not help MS patients; thus, it is incorrect in this "**least** compatible" Inference question. (E) It makes sense that the successful MS treatment would counteract a substance that worsened MS patients' symptoms; thus, this choice is incorrect in a "**least** compatible" Inference question.

In the next section of this chapter, you'll cover the last Inference-question variant, the rare Principle-Inference subtype.

Principle-Inference Questions

LEARNING OBJECTIVE

In this section, you'll learn to:

* Identify and answer Principle-Inference questions.

You can identify Principle-Inference questions from stems like these.

> Which one of the following most accurately expresses
> the principle illustrated above?
>
> *PrepTest110 Sec3 Q1*

> The parent's experience with the child most closely
> conforms to which one of the following generalizations?
>
> *PrepTest111 Sec3 Q5*

> Each of the following principles is logically consistent
> with the columnist's conclusion **except:**
>
> *PrepTest111 Sec3 Q19*

Most Principle questions—those you learned about in Chapter 11—mimic the skills associated with Assumption, Strengthen, and Parallel Reasoning questions. Occasionally, however, Principle questions test Inference question skills. These Principle questions ask you either to identify a general rule from a specific case (the first question stem above) or to spot a specific case that follows from a general rule (the second question stem above). Very rarely, the test will ask you to identify a principle that conflicts with a specific case (the third question stem above).

INFERENCE-BASED PRINCIPLE QUESTIONS AT A GLANCE

Task: Identify the principle illustrated by the specific case in the stimulus, or apply the principle stated in the stimulus to the specific case in the correct answer.

Strategy: In Identify the Principle questions, use the narrow example or case in the stimulus to find the matching broad principle or rule in the correct answer. In Apply the Principle questions, use the broad principle or rule in the stimulus to find a specific matching example or case in the correct answer.

Frequency: LSAT tests released from 2016 to 2020 had an average of 2.4 Principle questions per section. On average, just 0.6 were Inference-Based Principle questions, less than one per section.

Now, complete a Principle-Inference question on your own. Here, the broad principle in the correct answer will match the case described in the stimulus. Take your time and work through all four steps of the Logical Reasoning Method even if you remember the stimulus. When you're finished, review an LSAT expert's work on the next page.

Step 2:

Step 1:

31. Parent: I had tried without success to get my young child to brush her teeth. I had hoped that she would imitate me, or that she would be persuaded by reason to brush her teeth. Then, I made a point of brushing her teeth for her immediately before reading her a story before her naps and at night. After several weeks, when I would pick up a storybook at these times, she began automatically to retrieve her toothbrush and brush her teeth herself.

The parent's experience with the child most closely conforms to which one of the following generalizations?

(A) Children are most effectively taught to do something by someone's setting an example.

(B) Children more readily adopt a behavior through habit and repetition than through other means.

(C) Children are too young to understand rational arguments for adopting a behavior.

(D) Children often imitate the behavior of others rather than listening to reason.

(E) Children ordinarily act contrary to their parents' expectations in order to get more attention.

PrepTest111 Sec3 Q5

Step 3:

Step 4:

Expert Analysis

Here's a worked example of the question you just saw showing an LSAT expert's approach to each step.

Step 2: A parent relates how they got a child to brush her teeth: Setting an example and persuasion did not work. Brushing the child's teeth right before each story-time did, however, as the child would brush her own teeth when the parent got a storybook.

Step 1: This is a Principle-Inference question in which the correct answer provides a principle that fits the specific case outlined in the stimulus.

31. Parent: I had tried without success to get my young child to brush her teeth. I had hoped that she would imitate me, or that she would be persuaded by reason to brush her teeth. Then, I made a point of brushing her teeth for her immediately before reading her a story before her naps and at night. After several weeks, when I would pick up a storybook at these times, she began automatically to retrieve her toothbrush and brush her teeth herself.

The parent's experience with the child most closely conforms to which one of the following generalizations?

(A) Children are most effectively taught to do something by someone's setting an example.

(B) Children more readily adopt a behavior through habit and repetition than through other means.

(C) Children are too young to understand rational arguments for adopting a behavior.

(D) Children often imitate the behavior of others rather than listening to reason.

(E) Children ordinarily act contrary to their parents' expectations in order to get more attention.

PrepTest111 Sec3 Q5

Step 3: The correct answer will offer a general rule that fits this parent's case. Look for a choice along these lines: Repeatedly doing something at the same time can be effective in getting a child to adopt the behavior even when imitation and persuasion don't work.

Step 4: (B) matches the parent's effective method—instilling habit and repetition—and is correct.

Wrong answers: (A) 180. The parent's example—"I had hoped that she would imitate me"— did not work. (C) This distorts the argument, which says that persuasion did not work, but doesn't state or imply that this is because the child is too young to understand the reasoning. (D) Irrelevant comparison. In this parent's case, neither imitation nor reasoning worked. (E) Outside the Scope. The argument does not address any psychological explanations for the child's initial failure to brush her teeth.

Practice Try the following Principle-Inference questions. Don't worry too much about your timing here. Complete all four steps of the Logical Reasoning Method for each question, jotting down your notes whenever it is helpful to do so. After you're finished, review your work with the expert analysis that follows.

Hint: In this question, is the principle in the stimulus or in the answer choices?

Step 2:	Step 1:

32. If a doctor gives a patient only a few options for lifestyle modification, the patient is more likely to adhere to the doctor's advice than if the doctor gives the patient many options.

Which one of the following most accurately expresses the principle illustrated above?

(A) People are especially likely to ignore the advice they get from doctors if they are confused about that advice.

(B) People dislike calculating the best of a variety of choices unless they can see a clear difference among the benefits that would result from each choice.

(C) The tendency people have to alter their behavior varies inversely with the number of alternatives available to them for behavior modification.

(D) Most people are unlikely to follow their doctor's advice unless they can vividly imagine the consequences of not following the advice.

(E) In getting good results, the clarity with which a doctor instructs a patient is of equal importance to the accuracy of the doctor's diagnosis on which that instruction is based.

PrepTest110 Sec3 Q1

Step 3:	Step 4:

Expert Analysis

Here's how an LSAT expert completed the question you just tried.

Step 2: A single rule: Patients are more likely to follow doctor's advice (for lifestyle modification) if given fewer options.	**Step 1:** This is a Principle-Inference question asking you to apply the principle in the stimulus to the example in the correct answer.

32. If a doctor gives a patient only a few options for lifestyle modification, the patient is more likely to adhere to the doctor's advice than if the doctor gives the patient many options.

Which one of the following most accurately expresses the principle illustrated above?

(A) People are especially likely to ignore the advice they get from doctors if they are confused about that advice.

(B) People dislike calculating the best of a variety of choices unless they can see a clear difference among the benefits that would result from each choice.

(C) The tendency people have to alter their behavior varies inversely with the number of alternatives available to them for behavior modification.

(D) Most people are unlikely to follow their doctor's advice unless they can vividly imagine the consequences of not following the advice.

(E) In getting good results, the clarity with which a doctor instructs a patient is of equal importance to the accuracy of the doctor's diagnosis on which that instruction is based.

PrepTest110 Sec3 Q1

Step 3: Apply the principle to evaluate each choice. The correct answer will follow from the idea that the more options a doctor gives, the less likely a patient is to follow any of them.	**Step 4:** (C) is a direct paraphrase of the principle in the stimulus and is correct.

Wrong answers: (A) Distortion. This choice requires an additional step—more options make a doctor's advice confusing—that is not stated in the stimulus. (B) Outside the Scope. This choice requires several assumptions not supported by the stimulus, for example, that more options make it harder to distinguish among benefits, and that patients' aversion to calculating benefits makes them less likely to follow a doctor's advice. (D) Distortion. This choice suggests that what's important is how well the doctor can describe the negative consequences of ignoring the advice. (E) Outside the Scope. This states a different rule of thumb for doctor's giving advice, but does not follow from the principle in the stimulus.

Hint: Be sure you've accurately characterized the correct answer before evaluating the answer choices.

Step 2:	Step 1:

33. Columnist: A recent study suggests that living with a parrot increases one's risk of lung cancer. But no one thinks the government should impose financial impediments on the owning of parrots because of this apparent danger. So by the same token, the government should not levy analogous special taxes on hunting gear, snow skis, recreational parachutes, or motorcycles.

Each of the following principles is logically consistent with the columnist's conclusion **except:**

(A) The government should fund education by taxing nonessential sports equipment and recreational gear.

(B) The government should not tax those who avoid dangerous activities and adopt healthy lifestyles.

(C) The government should create financial disincentives to deter participation in activities it deems dangerous.

(D) The government should not create financial disincentives for people to race cars or climb mountains, even though these are dangerous activities.

(E) The government would be justified in levying taxes to provide food and shelter for those who cannot afford to pay for them.

PrepTest111 Sec3 Q19

Step 3:	Step 4:

Expert Analysis

Here's how an LSAT expert completed the question you just tried.

Step 2: Start with the conclusion: The government should not impose "danger" taxes on equipment associated with potentially dangerous recreational activities. The reasoning: Owning a parrot increases the risk of lung cancer, but no one thinks parrot ownership should be taxed for this reason.	**Step 1:** In this rare Principle-Inference **except** question, the correct answer states a principle that is *not* consistent with the columnist's conclusion. This is similar to a "must be false" Inference **except** question.

33. Columnist: A recent study suggests that living with a parrot increases one's risk of lung cancer. But no one thinks the government should impose financial impediments on the owning of parrots because of this apparent danger. So by the same token, the government should not levy analogous special taxes on hunting gear, snow skis, recreational parachutes, or motorcycles.

Each of the following principles is logically consistent with the columnist's conclusion **except:**

(A) The government should fund education by taxing nonessential sports equipment and recreational gear.

(B) The government should not tax those who avoid dangerous activities and adopt healthy lifestyles.

(C) The government should create financial disincentives to deter participation in activities it deems dangerous.

(D) The government should not create financial disincentives for people to race cars or climb mountains, even though these are dangerous activities.

(E) The government would be justified in levying taxes to provide food and shelter for those who cannot afford to pay for them.

PrepTest111 Sec3 Q19

Step 3: The correct answer is the only one stating a principle inconsistent with the columnist's main point. The four wrong answers will state principles that do not conflict with the columnist's takeaway; that means they may agree with the columnist or simply be outside the argument's scope.	**Step 4:** (C) directly conflicts with the columnist's conclusion and is therefore the correct answer to this Principle **except** question.

Wrong answers: (A) As long as the taxes are not "special taxes" "imposed because of th[e] apparent danger" of the equipment, this does not run afoul of the columnist's conclusion. (B) The columnist says nothing about who the government should exempt from taxation, so this choice is not inconsistent with the columnist's conclusion. (D) This is a close one, but the columnist's conclusion says the government should not impose special taxes on *equipment*, not that it should avoid disincentivizing certain *activities*. (E) The columnist's argument does not touch on the goals that justify taxation in general, so this choice doesn't present any conflict with the argument's conclusion.

Congratulations on working through the important Inference question type with its several unique variants! You'll see examples of all the Inference subtypes in the Perform quiz that follows.

Chapter Perform Quiz

Perform This Perform quiz has 11 Inference questions. They are presented without any notes, hints, or prompts for a more test-like experience while you work. Try to get as many correct answers as possible in 15 minutes. When you finish, check your performance against the Answer Key and Evaluate Your Performance for tips on how best to improve. Then, come back to complete any questions you skipped or guessed on and finish up by reviewing all of the questions with the expert analyses in your online companion.

34. The graphical illustrations mathematics teachers use enable students to learn geometry more easily by providing them with an intuitive understanding of geometric concepts, which makes it easier to acquire the ability to manipulate symbols for the purpose of calculation. Illustrating algebraic concepts graphically would be equally effective pedagogically, even though the deepest mathematical understanding is abstract, not imagistic.

The statements above provide some support for each of the following **except:**

(A) Pictorial understanding is not the final stage of mathematical understanding.

(B) People who are very good at manipulating symbols do not necessarily have any mathematical understanding.

(C) Illustrating geometric concepts graphically is an effective teaching method.

(D) Acquiring the ability to manipulate symbols is part of the process of learning geometry.

(E) There are strategies that can be effectively employed in the teaching both of algebra and of geometry.

PrepTest111 Sec4 Q1

35. For newborns of age four to six weeks whose mothers have been the primary caregivers, the following is true: When the newborns are crying due to hunger or other similar discomfort, merely hearing the mother's voice will lead to a temporary halt in crying, while the voices of others do not have this effect.

Which one of the following is most reasonably supported by the information above?

(A) Babies more easily learn to recognize the voices of their mothers than the voices of other people.

(B) A mother's voice is the first thing a baby learns to recognize.

(C) Babies associate the voice of the primary caregiver with release from discomfort.

(D) Often only a primary caregiver can provide comfort to a newborn.

(E) Discomfort in newborns is best relieved by hearing the mother's voice.

PrepTest110 Sec2 Q4

36. A certain gene can be stimulated by chemicals in cigarette smoke, causing lung cells to metabolize the chemicals in a way that makes the cells cancerous. Yet smokers in whom this gene is not stimulated have as high a risk of developing lung cancer from smoking as other smokers do.

If the statements above are true, it can be concluded on the basis of them that

(A) stimulation of the gene by chemicals in cigarette smoke is not the only factor affecting the risk for smokers of developing lung cancer

(B) nonsmokers have as high a risk of developing lung cancer as do smokers in whom the gene has not been stimulated

(C) smokers in whom the gene has been stimulated are more likely to develop lung cancer than are other smokers

(D) the gene is more likely to be stimulated by chemicals in cigarette smoke than by other chemicals

(E) smokers are less likely to develop lung cancer if they do not have the gene

PrepTest112 Sec4 Q4

37. Most antidepressant drugs cause weight gain. While dieting can help reduce the amount of weight gained while taking such antidepressants, some weight gain is unlikely to be preventable.

The information above most strongly supports which one of the following?

(A) A physician should not prescribe any antidepressant drug for a patient if that patient is overweight.

(B) People who are trying to lose weight should not ask their doctors for an antidepressant drug.

(C) At least some patients taking antidepressant drugs gain weight as a result of taking them.

(D) The weight gain experienced by patients taking antidepressant drugs should be attributed to lack of dieting.

(E) All patients taking antidepressant drugs should diet to maintain their weight.

PrepTest112 Sec1 Q4

38. Company policy: An employee of our company must be impartial, particularly when dealing with family members. This obligation extends to all aspects of the job, including hiring and firing practices and the quality of service the employee provides customers.

Which one of the following employee behaviors most clearly violates the company policy cited above?

(A) refusing to hire any of one's five siblings, even though they are each more qualified than any other applicant

(B) receiving over a hundred complaints about the service one's office provides and sending a complimentary product to all those who complain, including one's mother

(C) never firing a family member, even though three of one's siblings work under one's supervision and authority

(D) repeatedly refusing to advance an employee, claiming that he has sometimes skipped work and that his work has been sloppy, even though no such instances have occurred for over two years

(E) promoting a family member over another employee in the company

PrepTest112 Sec1 Q5

39. A number of measures indicate the viability of a nation's economy. The level and rate of growth of aggregate output are the most significant indicators, but unemployment and inflation rates are also important. Further, Switzerland, Austria, Israel, Ireland, Denmark, and Finland all have viable economics, but none has a very large population. Switzerland and Austria each have populations of about seven million; the other populations are at least one-fourth smaller.

Which one of the following is most strongly supported by the information above?

(A) A nation's economic viability is independent of the size of its population.

(B) Having a population larger than seven million ensures that a nation will be economically viable.

(C) Economic viability does not require a population of at least seven million.

(D) A nation's population is the most significant contributor to the level and rate of growth of aggregate output.

(E) A nation's population affects the level and rate of growth of aggregate output more than it affects unemployment and inflation rates.

PrepTest112 Sec1 Q16

40. People should avoid taking the antacid calcium carbonate in doses larger than half a gram, for despite its capacity to neutralize stomach acids, calcium carbonate can increase the calcium level in the blood and thus impair kidney function. Moreover, just half a gram of it can stimulate the production of gastrin, a stomach hormone that triggers acid secretion.

Which one of the following is most strongly supported by the information above?

(A) Cessation of gastrin production is a more effective method of controlling excess stomach acid than is direct neutralization of stomach acid.

(B) People who avoid taking more than half a gram of calcium carbonate are less likely than average to suffer from impaired kidney function.

(C) Doses of calcium carbonate smaller than half a gram can reduce stomach acid more effectively than much larger doses do.

(D) Half a gram of calcium carbonate can causally contribute to both the secretion and the neutralization of stomach acids.

(E) Impaired kidney function may increase the level of calcium in the blood.

PrepTest110 Sec2 Q19

41. Lathyrism, a debilitating neurological disorder caused by the consumption of the legume Lathyrus sativus, is widespread among the domestic animals of some countries. Attempts to use rats to study lathyrism have generally failed. Rats that ingested Lathyrus sativus did not produce the symptoms associated with the disorder.

Which one of the following is most strongly supported by the information above?

(A) The physiology of rats is radically different from that of domestic animals.

(B) The rats did not consume as much Lathyrus sativus as did the domestic animals that contracted lathyrism.

(C) Not all animal species are equally susceptible to lathyrism.

(D) Most of the animals that can contract lathyrism are domestic.

(E) Laboratory conditions are not conducive to the development of lathyrism.

PrepTest111 Sec1 Q19

42. All social systems are based upon a division of economic roles. The values of a social system are embodied in the prestige accorded persons who fill various economic roles. It is therefore unsurprising that, for any social system, the introduction of labor-saving technology that makes certain economic roles obsolete will tend to undermine the values in that social system.

Which one of the following can most reasonably be concluded on the basis of the information above?

(A) Social systems will have unchanging values if they are shielded from technological advancement.

(B) No type of technology will fail to undermine the values in a social system.

(C) A social system whose values are not susceptible to change would not be one in which technology can eliminate economic roles.

(D) A technologically advanced society will place little value on the prestige associated with an economic role.

(E) A technological innovation that is implemented in a social system foreign to the one in which it was developed will tend to undermine the foreign social system.

PrepTest111 Sec4 Q21

43. In a recent study, a group of subjects had their normal daily caloric intake increased by 25 percent. This increase was entirely in the form of alcohol. Another group of similar subjects had alcohol replace nonalcoholic sources of 25 percent of their normal daily caloric intake. All subjects gained body fat over the course of the study, and the amount of body fat gained was the same for both groups.

Which one of the following is most strongly supported by the information above?

(A) Alcohol is metabolized more quickly by the body than are other foods or drinks.

(B) In the general population, alcohol is the primary cause of gains in body fat.

(C) An increased amount of body fat does not necessarily imply a weight gain.

(D) Body fat gain is not dependent solely on the number of calories one consumes.

(E) The proportion of calories from alcohol in a diet is more significant for body fat gain than are the total calories from alcohol.

PrepTest112 Sec4 Q22

44. To be horrific, a monster must be threatening. Whether or not it presents psychological, moral or social dangers, or triggers enduring infantile fears, if a monster is physically dangerous then it is threatening. In fact, even a physically benign monster is horrific if it inspires revulsion.

Which one of the following logically follows from the statements above?

(A) Any horror-story monster that is threatening is also horrific.

(B) A monster that is psychologically dangerous, but that does not inspire revulsion, is not horrific.

(C) If a monster triggers infantile fears but is not physically dangerous, then it is not horrific.

(D) If a monster is both horrific and psychologically threatening, then it does not inspire revulsion.

(E) All monsters that are not physically dangerous, but that are psychologically dangerous and inspire revulsion, are threatening.

PrepTest110 Sec2 Q23

Answer Key

34. B; 35. C; 36. A; 37. C; 38. A; 39. C; 40. D; 41. C; 42. C; 43. D; 44. E

Evaluate Your Performance

To assess your strengths and opportunities from this Perform quiz, go to the corresponding chapter in your online companion. There you'll find recommendations based on your performance along with complete worked-example explanations (written by a Kaplan LSAT expert) for each of the questions in this Perform quiz.

CHAPTER 15

Paradox Questions

Paradox Question Basics

Prepare Paradox questions present two facts that appear to be in conflict, and then ask you to select the answer that provides information that, if true, helps to explain the confusing situation or resolve the seeming contradiction.

LEARNING OBJECTIVE

In this section, you'll learn to:

- Identify and answer Paradox questions.

Typically, there are around four Paradox questions on the typical LSAT test. These questions account for roughly 5% of your LSAT score.

You can identify Paradox questions from question stems like these. The verbs resolve, reconcile, and explain almost always indicate Paradox questions.

Which one of the following, if true, most helps to resolve the apparent discrepancy in the information above?

PrepTest111 Sec1 Q21

Which one of the following, if true, does the most to reconcile the apparent conflict in the moral system described above?

PrepTest110 Sec2 Q7

Which one of the following, if true, best helps to explain why the sale of the company's cologne dropped that year?

PrepTest111 Sec1 Q25

Each of the following, if true, would help resolve the apparent discrepancy described above **except:**

PrepTest111 Sec3 Q12

Approximate Number of Paradox Questions per LSAT

Paradox
4

Source: All officially released LSAT exams, 2016-2020

Key to your success with Paradox questions is the ability to quickly and accurately spot the seeming contradiction in the stimulus, and then anticipate the sort(s) of fact that will show why the statements that appeared to be at odds are actually consistent with one another.

PARADOX QUESTIONS AT A GLANCE

Task: Select the one answer containing a fact that would help explain or resolve an apparent discrepancy.

Strategy: Identify the apparent contradiction or inexplicable situation in the stimulus. Make a general prediction of the type of fact needed to resolve the paradox. Use your paraphrase of the paradox and your broad prediction to evaluate the answer choices.

Frequency: On LSAT tests released from 2016 through 2020, there were an average of 1.9 Paradox questions per section.

To get a feel for these skills, try a Paradox question on your own. Take your time and work through all four steps of the Logical Reasoning Method. When you're finished, review an LSAT expert's work on the next page.

Step 2:	Step 1:

1. A company that produces men's cologne had been advertising the product in general-circulation magazines for several years. Then one year the company decided to advertise its cologne exclusively in those sports magazines with a predominantly male readership. That year the company sold fewer bottles of cologne than it had in any of the three immediately preceding years.

Which one of the following, if true, best helps to explain why the sale of the company's cologne dropped that year?

(A) Television advertising reaches more people than does magazine advertising, but the company never advertised its cologne on television because of the high cost.

(B) The general-circulation magazines in which the company had placed its advertisements experienced a large rise in circulation recently.

(C) Most men do not wear cologne on a regular basis.

(D) Women often buy cologne as gifts for male friends or relatives.

(E) Successful advertisements for men's cologne often feature well-known athletes.

PrepTest111 Sec1 Q25

Step 3:	Step 4:

Expert Analysis

Study the strategies an LSAT expert used to tackle the question you just saw.

Step 2: One year, a company advertised its men's cologne in sports magazine with mostly male readership instead of general-circulation magazines as it had before

but

that year, the company's sales of men's cologne dropped.

Step 1: A Paradox question stem: the correct answer will help to resolve an apparent contradiction, here, one related to the company's sales figures.

1. A company that produces men's cologne had been advertising the product in general-circulation magazines for several years. Then one year the company decided to advertise its cologne exclusively in those sports magazines with a predominantly male readership. That year the company sold fewer bottles of cologne than it had in any of the three immediately preceding years.

Which one of the following, if true, best helps to explain why the sale of the company's cologne dropped that year?

(A) Television advertising reaches more people than does magazine advertising, but the company never advertised its cologne on television because of the high cost.

(B) The general-circulation magazines in which the company had placed its advertisements experienced a large rise in circulation recently.

(C) Most men do not wear cologne on a regular basis.

(D) Women often buy cologne as gifts for male friends or relatives.

(E) Successful advertisements for men's cologne often feature well-known athletes.

PrepTest111 Sec1 Q25

Step 3: The correct answer will help explain why the men's cologne sold better when advertised to a general readership than when advertised in sports magazines with mostly male readers. The four wrong answers will leave the paradox unresolved or make it even more confusing.

Step 4: (D) provides a reason that advertising to the general public would boost sales of the company's men's cologne, and is correct.

Wrong answers: (A) Outside the Scope. If the company never used television advertising, this choice cannot explain the result of a change in the company's magazine advertising. (B) Outside the Scope. This suggests that the potential value of general-circulation advertising is now even greater, but does not help explain why sports-magazine advertising was a failure. (C) Outside the Scope. Adding this fact to the stimulus does not help explain the decline in sales based on the change in advertising. (E) Outside the Scope/180. The stimulus doesn't mention any changes in the content of the company's ads, but if the ads in the sports magazines featured famous athletes, this fact might make the paradox even more confusing.

Take note of how the LSAT expert paused long enough in Step 2 to make sure they understood and could articulate the nature of the paradox or the confusing facts outlined in the stimulus. Next up, try an exercise that will help you sharpen your analytical skills for untangling Paradox question stimuli.

Use Keywords to Spot the Apparent Contradiction

Most Paradox question stimuli contain contrast keywords such as *however*, *despite*, *although*, *but*, *yet*, or *on the other hand* that signal the two facts that seem to be in conflict. In the stimuli that follows, identify and paraphrase the apparent discrepancy or anomaly, and then anticipate the kind of fact that would help provide a resolution for each one.

LSAT Stimulus	My Analysis
2. A patient complained of feeling constantly fatigued. It was determined that the patient averaged only four to six hours of sleep per night, and this was determined to contribute to the patient's condition. However, the patient was not advised to sleep more. *PrepTest111 Sec1 Q21*	**Contrast keyword:** **The paradox:** **What could resolve the paradox?:**
3. A certain moral system holds that performing good actions is praiseworthy only when one overcomes a powerful temptation in order to perform them. Yet this same moral system also holds that performing good actions out of habit is sometimes praiseworthy. *PrepTest110 Sec2 Q7*	**Contrast keyword:** **The paradox:** **What could resolve the paradox?:**

LSAT Stimulus	My Analysis
4. Last year a large firm set a goal of decreasing its workforce by 25 percent. Three divisions, totaling 25 percent of its workforce at that time, were to be eliminated and no new people hired. These divisions have since been eliminated and no new people have joined the firm, but its workforce has decreased by only 15 percent. *PrepTest111 Sec4 Q4*	**Contrast keyword:** **The paradox:** **What could resolve the paradox?:**
5. In a poll of eligible voters conducted on the eve of a mayoral election, more of those polled stated that they favored Panitch than stated that they favored any other candidate. Despite this result, another candidate, Yeung, defeated Panitch by a comfortable margin. *PrepTest112 Sec4 Q5*	**Contrast keyword:** **The paradox:** **What could resolve the paradox?:**

Expert Analysis

What could resolve the paradox? Here's how an LSAT expert analyzed the stimuli you just saw.

LSAT Stimulus	Analysis
2. A patient complained of feeling constantly fatigued. It was determined that the patient averaged only four to six hours of sleep per night, and this was determined to contribute to the patient's condition. However, the patient was not advised to sleep more. *PrepTest111 Sec1 Q21*	**Contrast keyword:** *However* **The paradox:** The apparent contradiction: A patient's fatigue was caused in part by not sleeping enough *but* the patient was not told to get more sleep. **What could resolve the paradox?:** To explain this confusing situation, you need a fact that helps explain why a patient who is diagnosed as needing more sleep would not be *told* to get more sleep.
3. A certain moral system holds that performing good actions is praiseworthy only when one overcomes a powerful temptation in order to perform them. Yet this same moral system also holds that performing good actions out of habit is sometimes praiseworthy. *PrepTest110 Sec2 Q7*	**Contrast keyword:** *Yet* **The paradox:** One tenet of a moral system says that good actions deserve praise only if a person overcame temptation to do the action *but* another tenet of the system says that sometimes a good action performed by habit is praiseworthy. **What could resolve the paradox?:** Here, resolving the paradox requires a fact that helps explain how an action performed out of habit can also be one that requires you to overcome temptation.

LSAT Stimulus	My Analysis
4. Last year a large firm set a goal of decreasing its workforce by 25 percent. Three divisions, totaling 25 percent of its workforce at that time, were to be eliminated and no new people hired. These divisions have since been eliminated and no new people have joined the firm, but its workforce has decreased by only 15 percent. *PrepTest111 Sec4 Q4*	**Contrast keyword:** *but* **The paradox:** [planned reduction] A company closed three divisions (which represented 25% of its workforce last year) and made no new hires *but* [actual reduction] the company's workforce has decreased by only 15%. **What could resolve the paradox?:** To resolve the apparent discrepancy, you'll need a fact that helps explain why the company's workforce did not decline by 25%. So, look for something that tells you how it is that the other 10% from the shuttered divisions are still with the company.
5. In a poll of eligible voters conducted on the eve of a mayoral election, more of those polled stated that they favored Panitch than stated that they favored any other candidate. Despite this result, another candidate, Yeung, defeated Panitch by a comfortable margin. *PrepTest112 Sec4 Q5*	**Contrast keyword:** *Despite* **The paradox:** In an election eve poll, Panitch was favored by more voters than any other candidate was *but* on election day, Yeung beat Panitch handily. **What could resolve the paradox?:** Explaining the outcome requires a fact that reveals why the poll was so far off. From your knowledge of Flaw questions, you can predict what some of these might be: changed circumstances, unrepresentative sample, etc.

Good work. You'll revisit these stimuli in the context of their full questions in the Practice set for this chapter. Before turning to that, take a moment to get familiar with the fairly common Paradox **except** subtype.

Paradox Except Questions

While still a minority of Paradox questions, the Paradox **except** variety is regularly featured. It's not uncommon to see one Paradox **except** question among the four (or so) Paradox questions on a typical LSAT. Almost always, the question stem asks for a correct answer that does not help to resolve or explain the apparent discrepancy in the stimulus. And that means that each of the four *wrong* answers will help. The correct answer will either be outside the scope, or it will make the situation even more confusing or paradoxical. Untangle the stimulus the same way you would on any Paradox question, but remember that when you find a fact that helps resolve the paradox, it is *incorrect* for this question.

Try a Paradox **except** question on your own. When you're finished, compare your work to that of an LSAT expert on the next page.

Step 2:	Step 1:

6. To acquire a better understanding of the structure and development of the human personality, some psychologists study the personalities of animals.

Each of the following, if true, contributes to an explanation of the practice mentioned above **except:**

(A) The actions of humans and animals are believed to be motivated by similar instincts, but these instincts are easier to discern in animals.

(B) The law forbids certain experiments on humans but permits them on animals.

(C) It is generally less expensive to perform experiments on animals than it is to perform them on humans.

(D) Proper understanding of human personality is thought to provide a model for better understanding the personality of animals.

(E) Field observations of the behavior of young animals often inspire insightful hypotheses about human personality development.

PrepTest110 Sec3 Q2

Step 3:	Step 4:

Expert Analysis

Study this worked example to see expert strategies applied to a Paradox **except** question.

Step 2: Some psychologists' goal is to understand human personality structure and development *but* they study animal personalities.	**Step 1:** In this Paradox **except** question, the four wrong answers will help to resolve an apparent contradiction, but the correct answer will not.

6. To acquire a better understanding of the structure and development of the human personality, some psychologists study the personalities of animals.	Each of the following, if true, contributes to an explanation of the practice mentioned above **except:** (A) The actions of humans and animals are believed to be motivated by similar instincts, but these instincts are easier to discern in animals. (B) The law forbids certain experiments on humans but permits them on animals. (C) It is generally less expensive to perform experiments on animals than it is to perform them on humans. (D) Proper understanding of human personality is thought to provide a model for better understanding the personality of animals. (E) Field observations of the behavior of young animals often inspire insightful hypotheses about human personality development. *PrepTest110 Sec3 Q2*

Step 3: Four answers will provide facts that show why it might make sense for psychologists trying to understand human personalities to study those of animals. The correct answer will not help to explain this approach, meaning that it will either be outside the scope or will make the study of animal personalities seem inappropriate or unhelpful for the psychologists' goals.	**Step 4:** (D) gets the relationship backwards, and is thus correct. This choice suggests that those seeking to understand animal personalities would benefit from studying humans.

Wrong answers: (A) gives a practical reason for the psychologists' choice to study animals; thus, this choice is incorrect in this Paradox **except** question. (B) gives a legal reason for the psychologists' choice to study animals; thus, this choice is incorrect in this Paradox **except** question. (C) gives an economic reason for psychologists to conduct the animal research; thus, this choice is incorrect in this Paradox **except** question. (E) provides a successful example of the psychologists' approach in action; thus, this choice is incorrect in this Paradox **except** question.

You'll try your hand at more Paradox **except** questions in the Practice set that follows and in the Perform quiz at the end of the chapter.

Practice Try each of the following Paradox questions. Some contain arguments you analyzed earlier in the chapter. Don't worry too much about your timing here. Complete all four steps of the Logical Reasoning Method for each question, jotting down your notes whenever it is helpful to do so. After each question, review your work with the expert analysis that follows.

Step 2:	Step 1:

7. A certain moral system holds that performing good actions is praiseworthy only when one overcomes a powerful temptation in order to perform them. Yet this same moral system also holds that performing good actions out of habit is sometimes praiseworthy.

Which one of the following, if true, does the most to reconcile the apparent conflict in the moral system described above?

(A) People who perform good actions out of habit have often acquired this habit after years of having resisted temptation.

(B) Most people face strong moral temptation from time to time but few people have to endure it regularly.

(C) People virtually always perform actions they think are good, regardless of what other people may think.

(D) Since it is difficult to tell what is going on in another person's mind, it is often hard to know exactly how strongly a person is tempted.

(E) It is far more common for people to perform good actions out of habit than for them to do so against strong temptation.

PrepTest110 Sec2 Q7

Step 3:	Step 4:

Expert Analysis

Here's how an LSAT expert approached the question you just tried.

Step 2: One tenet of a moral system says that good actions deserve praise only if a person overcame temptation to do the action *but* another tenet of the system says that sometimes a good action performed by habit is praiseworthy.	**Step 1:** "[R]econcile the apparent conflict" indicates a Paradox question; the correct answer will help explain the seeming discrepancy.

7. A certain moral system holds that performing good actions is praiseworthy only when one overcomes a powerful temptation in order to perform them. Yet this same moral system also holds that performing good actions out of habit is sometimes praiseworthy.

Which one of the following, if true, does the most to reconcile the apparent conflict in the moral system described above?

(A) People who perform good actions out of habit have often acquired this habit after years of having resisted temptation.

(B) Most people face strong moral temptation from time to time but few people have to endure it regularly.

(C) People virtually always perform actions they think are good, regardless of what other people may think.

(D) Since it is difficult to tell what is going on in another person's mind, it is often hard to know exactly how strongly a person is tempted.

(E) It is far more common for people to perform good actions out of habit than for them to do so against strong temptation.

PrepTest110 Sec2 Q7

Step 3: The correct answer will help explain how an action performed out of habit can also be one that requires you to overcome temptation.	**Step 4:** (A) zeroes right in on the connection that needs to be made to resolve the apparent discrepancy, and is correct.

Wrong answers: (B) Irrelevant comparison. There's nothing in the stimulus about the portion of the population who may be doing such praiseworthy actions. (C) Outside the Scope. As described in the stimulus, the moral system doesn't say anything about a person's *intention* to do good or other people's *perception* of your actions. (D) Outside the Scope. Nothing in the stimulus suggests that other people need to know or confirm that an actor overcame temptation. (E) Irrelevant comparison. Information about the frequency or infrequency of actions does not help resolve the paradox described in the stimulus.

Step 2:

Step 1:

8. In a poll of eligible voters conducted on the eve of a mayoral election, more of those polled stated that they favored Panitch than stated that they favored any other candidate. Despite this result, another candidate, Yeung, defeated Panitch by a comfortable margin.

Each of the following, if true, contributes to a resolution of the discrepancy described above **except:**

(A) Of Yeung's supporters, a smaller percentage were eligible to vote than the percentage of Panitch's supporters who were eligible to vote.

(B) A third candidate, Mulhern, conducted a press conference on the morning of the election and withdrew from the race.

(C) The poll's questions were designed by staff members of Panitch's campaign.

(D) Of the poll respondents supporting Yeung, 70 percent described the election as "important" or "very important," while 30 percent of respondents supporting Panitch did the same.

(E) The poll, conducted on a Monday, surveyed persons in the downtown area, and the percentage of Yeung's supporters who work downtown is lower than that of Panitch's supporters.

PrepTest112 Sec4 Q5

Step 3:

Step 4:

Expert Analysis

Here's how an LSAT expert approached the question you just tried.

Step 2: In an election eve poll, Panitch was favored by more voters than any other candidate was *but* on election day, Yeung beat Panitch handily.	**Step 1:** In this Paradox **except** question, each of the four wrong answers helps explain the paradox, but the correct answer does not.

8. In a poll of eligible voters conducted on the eve of a mayoral election, more of those polled stated that they favored Panitch than stated that they favored any other candidate. Despite this result, another candidate, Yeung, defeated Panitch by a comfortable margin.

Each of the following, if true, contributes to a resolution of the discrepancy described above **except:**

(A) Of Yeung's supporters, a smaller percentage were eligible to vote than the percentage of Panitch's supporters who were eligible to vote.

(B) A third candidate, Mulhern, conducted a press conference on the morning of the election and withdrew from the race.

(C) The poll's questions were designed by staff members of Panitch's campaign.

(D) Of the poll respondents supporting Yeung, 70 percent described the election as "important" or "very important," while 30 percent of respondents supporting Panitch did the same.

(E) The poll, conducted on a Monday, surveyed persons in the downtown area, and the percentage of Yeung's supporters who work downtown is lower than that of Panitch's supporters.

PrepTest112 Sec4 Q5

Step 3: The four wrong answers will explain why the poll was favorable for Panitch even though he lost to Yeung the next day. (From your knowledge of Flaw questions, you can predict what some of these might be: changed circumstances, unrepresentative sample, etc.) The correct answer will either fall outside the scope or will make the paradox even more confusing.	**Step 4:** (A) makes the paradox even more confusing because the survey polled eligible voters, and that's the group that would have to have heavily favored Yeung in the election. That makes (A) the correct answer for this Paradox **except** question.

Wrong answers: (B) If many of Mulhern's voters switched to Yeung after the announcement, this choice provides a changed circumstance that helps explain the paradox, making this a wrong answer for a Paradox **except** question. (C) provides a reason the poll's results may have been skewed, making this a wrong answer for a Paradox **except** question. (D) supplies a reason to think voter turnout for Yeung may have been significantly higher than that for Panitch, making this a wrong answer for a Paradox **except** question. (E) This is a classic unrepresentative sample flaw, making this a wrong answer for a Paradox **except** question.

Step 2:

Step 1:

9. Last year a large firm set a goal of decreasing its workforce by 25 percent. Three divisions, totaling 25 percent of its workforce at that time, were to be eliminated and no new people hired. These divisions have since been eliminated and no new people have joined the firm, but its workforce has decreased by only 15 percent.

Which one of the following, if true, contributes most to an explanation of the difference in the planned versus the actual reduction in the workforce?

(A) The three divisions that were eliminated were well run and had the potential to earn profits.

(B) Normal attrition in the retained divisions continued to reduce staff because no new people were added to the firm.

(C) Some of the employees in the eliminated divisions were eligible for early retirement and chose that option.

(D) As the divisions were being eliminated some of their employees were assigned to other divisions.

(E) Employees in the retained divisions were forced to work faster to offset the loss of the eliminated divisions.

PrepTest111 Sec4 Q4

Step 3:

Step 4:

Expert Analysis

Here's how an LSAT expert approached the question you just tried.

Step 2: [planned reduction] A company closed three divisions (which represented 25% of its workforce last year) and made no new hires

but

[actual reduction] the company's workforce has decreased by only 15%.

Step 1: This standard Paradox question stem even outlines the subject of the apparent discrepancy; use that as you untangle the stimulus.

9.   Last year a large firm set a goal of decreasing its workforce by 25 percent. Three divisions, totaling 25 percent of its workforce at that time, were to be eliminated and no new people hired. These divisions have since been eliminated and no new people have joined the firm, but its workforce has decreased by only 15 percent.

Which one of the following, if true, contributes most to an explanation of the difference in the planned versus the actual reduction in the workforce?

(A) The three divisions that were eliminated were well run and had the potential to earn profits.

(B) Normal attrition in the retained divisions continued to reduce staff because no new people were added to the firm.

(C) Some of the employees in the eliminated divisions were eligible for early retirement and chose that option.

(D) As the divisions were being eliminated some of their employees were assigned to other divisions.

(E) Employees in the retained divisions were forced to work faster to offset the loss of the eliminated divisions.

PrepTest111 Sec4 Q4

Step 3: The correct answer will help to explain why the company's workforce did not decline by 25%. So, look for an answer that tells you how the other 10% from the shuttered divisions are still with the company. The four incorrect answers will be outside the scope, or will be 180s that make the paradox even more confusing.

Step 4: (D) helps explain how 10% of the workforce that had worked in the eliminated divisions remains with the company now, and is thus correct.

Wrong answers: (A) Outside the Scope. Knowing the business potential of the shuttered divisions does nothing to explain how some of their employees are still on the payroll. (B) 180. If there are fewer employees in the remaining divisions, it would seem that the workforce reduction should have been even greater than 25%, not less. (C) Irrelevant comparison. It should make no difference in the workforce reduction numbers whether those who left were laid off or retired; the paradox is how some 10% of the company's workforce remains on the payroll. (E) Outside the Scope. The *number* of remaining employees, not their workload, is the subject that the correct answer must address.

Step 2:	Step 1:

10. Raisins are made by drying grapes in the sun. Although some of the sugar in the grapes is caramelized in the process, nothing is added. Moreover, the only thing removed from the grapes is the water that evaporates during the drying, and water contains no calories or nutrients. The fact that raisins contain more iron per calorie than grapes do is thus puzzling.

Which one of the following, if true, most helps to explain why raisins contain more iron per calorie than do grapes?

(A) Since grapes are bigger than raisins, it takes several bunches of grapes to provide the same amount of iron as a handful of raisins does.

(B) Caramelized sugar cannot be digested, so its calories do not count toward the calorie content of raisins.

(C) The body can absorb iron and other nutrients more quickly from grapes than from raisins because of the relatively high water content of grapes.

(D) Raisins, but not grapes, are available year round, so many people get a greater share of their yearly iron intake from raisins than from grapes.

(E) Raisins are often eaten in combination with other iron containing foods, while grapes are usually eaten by themselves.

PrepTest112 Sec1 Q9

Step 3:	Step 4:

Expert Analysis

Here's how an LSAT expert approached the question you just tried.

Step 2: Raisins contain more iron per calorie than grapes *but* Nothing is added and no calories or nutrients removed in the grape-to-raisin process, which caramelizes the sugar in the grapes.	**Step 1:** The phrase "helps to explain" identifies this as a Paradox question; the correct answer will provide a fact that explains the apparent discrepancy in the stimulus.

10. Raisins are made by drying grapes in the sun. Although some of the sugar in the grapes is caramelized in the process, nothing is added. Moreover, the only thing removed from the grapes is the water that evaporates during the drying, and water contains no calories or nutrients. The fact that raisins contain more iron per calorie than grapes do is thus puzzling.

Which one of the following, if true, most helps to explain why raisins contain more iron per calorie than do grapes?

(A) Since grapes are bigger than raisins, it takes several bunches of grapes to provide the same amount of iron as a handful of raisins does.

(B) Caramelized sugar cannot be digested, so its calories do not count toward the calorie content of raisins.

(C) The body can absorb iron and other nutrients more quickly from grapes than from raisins because of the relatively high water content of grapes.

(D) Raisins, but not grapes, are available year round, so many people get a greater share of their yearly iron intake from raisins than from grapes.

(E) Raisins are often eaten in combination with other iron containing foods, while grapes are usually eaten by themselves.

PrepTest112 Sec1 Q9

Step 3: For raisins to have more iron per calorie, either iron is added or calories removed during the caramelizing process. Look for an answer choice that explains how this happens.	**Step 4:** (B) provides an explanation for the paradox: in the caramelizing process, calories from sugar are rendered indigestible, so they aren't counted in the calculation.

Wrong answers: (A) Outside the Scope. The paradox isn't about iron per volume, but rather iron per calorie. (C) Outside the Scope. The paradox isn't about relative speed of nutrient absorption, but rather about iron content per calorie. (D) Outside the Scope. The paradox isn't about which food contributes more nutrients to consumers' annual diet; it is about iron content per calorie. (E) Outside the Scope. The paradox is about the relative iron content per calorie between grapes and raisins; this choice is about iron consumption, and it brings in iron from other food sources.

Step 2:

Step 1:

11. It is clear that humans during the Upper Paleolithic period used lamps for light in caves. Though lamps can be dated to the entire Upper Paleolithic, the distribution of known lamps from the period is skewed, with the greatest number being associated with the late Upper Paleolithic period, when the Magdalenian culture was dominant.

Each of the following, if true, contributes to an explanation of the skewed distribution of lamps **except:**

(A) Artifacts from early in the Upper Paleolithic period are harder to identify than those that originated later in the period.

(B) More archaeological sites have been discovered from the Magdalenian culture than from earlier cultures.

(C) More efficient lampmaking techniques were developed by the Magdalenian culture than by earlier cultures.

(D) Fire pits were much more common in caves early in the Upper Paleolithic period than they were later in that period.

(E) More kinds of lamps were produced by the Magdalenian culture than by earlier cultures.

PrepTest112 Sec1 Q23

Step 3:

Step 4:

Expert Analysis

Here's how an LSAT expert approached the question you just tried.

Step 2: Humans used lamps throughout the Upper Paleolithic [U.P.] era *but* the distribution of lamps (that we know about) is skewed to the late U.P. (the time of the Magdalenian culture).	**Step 1:** In this Paradox **except** question, the correct answer is the only one that will not help to resolve the apparent discrepancy in the stimulus.

11. It is clear that humans during the Upper Paleolithic period used lamps for light in caves. Though lamps can be dated to the entire Upper Paleolithic, the distribution of known lamps from the period is skewed, with the greatest number being associated with the late Upper Paleolithic period, when the Magdalenian culture was dominant.

Each of the following, if true, contributes to an explanation of the skewed distribution of lamps **except:**

(A) Artifacts from early in the Upper Paleolithic period are harder to identify than those that originated later in the period.

(B) More archaeological sites have been discovered from the Magdalenian culture than from earlier cultures.

(C) More efficient lampmaking techniques were developed by the Magdalenian culture than by earlier cultures.

(D) Fire pits were much more common in caves early in the Upper Paleolithic period than they were later in that period.

(E) More kinds of lamps were produced by the Magdalenian culture than by earlier cultures.

PrepTest112 Sec1 Q23

Step 3: The four wrong answers will provide facts that help explain why we have identified more lamps from the late U.P. even though humans used them throughout the U.P. era. The correct answer will not help explain this, meaning it will be outside the scope or will make the paradox even more confusing.	**Step 4:** (E) This choice would explain why archaeologists find more types of lamps from the late U.P. era, but not why they've found more lamps, period. It does not help to resolve the skewed data, and is therefore, the correct answer to this Paradox **except** question.

Wrong answers: (A) suggests there may be artifacts from earlier parts of the U.P. era that we have failed to identify as lamps; that would help explain why we know of more lamps from the late U.P., and so, it is incorrect. (B) simply suggests that we've found more late U.P. lamps because we've found more late U.P. sites; this would help resolve the paradox, and so, it is incorrect. (C) If late U.P. humans had more efficient techniques, it would explain why they perhaps made more lamps; that in turn, would help explain why more late U.P. lamps have been found, making this a wrong answer. (D) If earlier U.P. humans used fire pits for light, perhaps they made or used fewer lamps; this helps explain the paradox, and is, therefore, an incorrect answer.

Step 2:	Step 1:

12. A patient complained of feeling constantly fatigued. It was determined that the patient averaged only four to six hours of sleep per night, and this was determined to contribute to the patient's condition. However, the patient was not advised to sleep more.

Which one of the following, if true, most helps to resolve the apparent discrepancy in the information above?

(A) The shorter one's sleep time, the easier it is to awaken from sleeping.

(B) The first two hours of sleep do the most to alleviate fatigue.

(C) Some people require less sleep than the eight hours required by the average person.

(D) Most people who suffer from nightmares experience them in the last hour of sleep before waking.

(E) Worry about satisfying the need for sufficient sleep can make it more difficult to sleep.

PrepTest111 Sec1 Q21

Step 3:	Step 4:

Expert Analysis

Here's how an LSAT expert approached the question you just tried.

Step 2: The apparent contradiction: A patient's fatigue was caused in part by not sleeping enough *but* the patient was not told to get more sleep.	**Step 1:** The phrase "apparent discrepancy" indicates a Paradox question; look for the one choice that explains how the statements in the stimulus are actually consistent.

12. A patient complained of feeling constantly fatigued. It was determined that the patient averaged only four to six hours of sleep per night, and this was determined to contribute to the patient's condition. However, the patient was not advised to sleep more.

Which one of the following, if true, most helps to resolve the apparent discrepancy in the information above?

(A) The shorter one's sleep time, the easier it is to awaken from sleeping.

(B) The first two hours of sleep do the most to alleviate fatigue.

(C) Some people require less sleep than the eight hours required by the average person.

(D) Most people who suffer from nightmares experience them in the last hour of sleep before waking.

(E) Worry about satisfying the need for sufficient sleep can make it more difficult to sleep.

PrepTest111 Sec1 Q21

Step 3: The correct answer will help explain why a patient that needs more sleep was not told to get more sleep. If a clear or natural explanation to the paradox doesn't occur to you, use your understanding of the seeming contradiction to evaluate the choices, eliminating any that do not contribute to a resolution of the statements.	**Step 4:** (E) helps resolve the paradox by providing a reason not to *tell* the patient to get more sleep; telling them so might actually make it harder to sleep.

Wrong answers: (A) Outside the Scope. Nothing in the stimulus suggests that the patient has trouble waking or needs to be easily woken. (B) 180. If this is true, the situation gets even more confusing, as the stimulus clearly states that the patient's four-to-six hours of sleep per night is contributing to their fatigue. (C) Irrelevant Comparison. The stimulus states that *this* patient needs more than the four-to-six hours of sleep they're currently getting, so this general statement doesn't help resolve the paradox. (D) Outside the Scope. Nothing in the stimulus suggests that nightmares are an issue in this patient's case.

Congratulations on completing the learning and practice portions of this chapter on Paradox questions. When you're ready, try the Perform quiz that follows to assess your skills on this new question type.

Chapter Perform Quiz

Perform This Perform quiz has 5 Paradox questions. They are presented without any notes, hints, or prompts for a more test-like experience while you work. Try to get as many correct answers as possible in 9 minutes. When you finish, check your performance against the Answer Key and Evaluate Your Performance for tips on how best to improve. Then, come back to complete any questions you skipped or guessed on and finish up by reviewing all of the questions with the expert analyses in your online companion.

13. Many elementary schools have recently offered computer-assisted educational programs. Students' reactions after several years have been decidedly mixed. Whereas students have found computers very useful in studying arithmetic, they have found them of little help in studying science, and of no help at all with their reading and writing skills.

Which one of the following, if true, most helps to explain the students' mixed reactions?

(A) Students in these schools began reading and doing arithmetic before learning to use computers.

(B) Of the disciplines and skills mentioned, the exactness of arithmetic makes it most suitable to computer-assisted education.

(C) Many elementary school teachers are reluctant to use computer technology in their classrooms.

(D) Young students are more likely to maintain interest in training programs that use the newest computers and video graphics than in those that do not.

(E) The elementary schools have offered more computer-assisted programs in reading and writing than in arithmetic and science.

PrepTest110 Sec2 Q5

14. Although marathons are 26.2 miles (42.2 kilometers) long and take even world-class marathoners over 2 hours to run, athletes who train by running 90 minutes a day fare better in marathons than do those who train by running 120 minutes or more a day.

Each of the following, if true, contributes to an explanation of the difference in marathon performances described above **except:**

(A) The longer period of time that one runs daily, the greater the chances of suffering adverse health effects due to air pollution.

(B) The longer the period of time that one runs daily, the easier it is to adjust to different race lengths.

(C) The longer the run, the more frequent is the occurrence of joint injuries that significantly interfere with overall training.

(D) Runners who train over 90 minutes per day grow bored with running and become less motivated.

(E) Runners who train over 90 minutes per day deplete certain biochemical energy reserves, leaving them less energy for marathons.

PrepTest111 Sec1 Q10

15. Despite the fact that antilock brakes are designed to make driving safer, research suggests that people who drive cars equipped with antilock brakes have more accidents than those who drive cars not equipped with antilock brakes.

Each of the following, if true, would help resolve the apparent discrepancy described above **except:**

(A) Most cars equipped with antilock brakes are, on average, driven more carelessly than cars not equipped with antilock brakes.

(B) Antilock brakes malfunction more often than regular brakes.

(C) Antilock brakes require expensive specialized maintenance to be even as effective as unmaintained regular brakes.

(D) Most people who drive cars equipped with antilock brakes do not know how to use those brakes properly.

(E) Antilock brakes were designed for safety in congested urban driving, but accidents of the most serious nature take place on highways.

PrepTest111 Sec3 Q12

16. When astronomers observed the comet Schwassman-Wachmann 3 becoming 1,000 times brighter in September 1995, they correctly hypothesized that its increased brightness was a result of the comet's breaking up—when comets break up, they emit large amounts of gas and dust, becoming visibly brighter as a result. However, their observations did not reveal comet Schwassman-Wachmann 3 actually breaking into pieces until November 1995, even though telescopes were trained on it throughout the entire period.

Which one of the following, if true, most helps to resolve the apparent conflict in the statements above?

(A) Comets often do not emit gas and dust until several weeks after they have begun to break up.

(B) The reason comets become brighter when they break up is that the gas and dust that they emit refract light.

(C) Gas and dust can be released by cracks in a comet even if the comet is not broken all the way through.

(D) The amount of gas and dust emitted steadily increased during the period from September through November.

(E) The comet passed close to the sun during this period and the gravitational strain caused it to break up.

PrepTest112 Sec1 Q13

17. Most doctors recommend that pregnant women eat a nutritious diet to promote the health of their babies. However, most babies who are born to women who ate nutritious diets while pregnant still develop at least one medical problem in their first year.

Which one of the following, if true, does most to resolve the apparent discrepancy in the information above?

(A) Women who regularly eat a nutritious diet while pregnant tend to eat a nutritious diet while breast-feeding.

(B) Most of the babies born to women who did not eat nutritious diets while pregnant develop no serious medical problems later in childhood.

(C) Babies of women who did not eat nutritious diets while pregnant tend to have more medical problems in their first year than do other babies.

(D) Medical problems that develop in the first year of life tend to be more serious than those that develop later in childhood.

(E) Many of the physicians who initially recommended that pregnant women consume nutritious diets have only recently reaffirmed their recommendation.

PrepTest111 Sec4 Q12

Answer Key

13. B; 14. B; 15. E; 16. C; 17. C

Evaluate Your Performance

To assess your strengths and opportunities from this Perform quiz, go to the corresponding chapter in your online companion. There you'll find recommendations based on your performance along with complete worked-example explanations (written by a Kaplan LSAT expert) for each of the questions in this Perform quiz.

PART FIVE

Countdown to Test Day

CHAPTER 16

Logical Reasoning Section Management

Here in Part V of this book, you'll learn about how to get ready for your official LSAT administration.

Chapter 16: Test Day provides strategies and tips for making the most out of the days leading up to your test and tells you what to expect on the day of your actual LSAT. It includes a Spotlight feature on Unusual Question Stems, a source of anxiety for some test takers who worry that they'll encounter something totally unexpected. An expert member of Kaplan's LSAT Channel faculty will show you how to find familiar patterns in these seemingly odd questions and turn them to your advantage.

Chapter 17: Logical Reasoning Section Management zeroes in the best ways to improve timing and efficiency in the Logical Reasoning sections. Chapter 17 consists primarily of a Spotlight feature dedicated to Logical Reasoning Section Management. Your Kaplan instructor will tell you where in the section to expect the easiest questions, how to find the "danger zone," and go over best practices for strategic skipping and guessing on the hardest questions. There are also instructions for how to take a full Practice section in your online resources, and how to review it with complete analysis and explanations, including *video explanations* for every question.

You're getting near the end of this book, so finish up strong!

Logical Reasoning Section Timing: The Basics

Every LSAT teacher and coach wishes they had a dime for every student who has said, "If I just had more time, I know I could get almost everything right on this test." It's a natural feeling because timing is such a big part of the LSAT. It is very important to remember that every test taker feels the pressure of the clock. The best LSAT test takers, however, respond not by wishing they had more time, but by saying, "We all have the same amount of time; I'm going to use it more effectively!"

The Spotlight that accompanies this chapter—and especially its video lesson—will give you the LSAT expert's strategies and tips for using your 35 minutes to maximize your score. Read through the short Spotlight text and then give the Kaplan instructor your full attention. You'll have a chance to put your newfound Logical Reasoning section management skills to the test right away. In the online companion for this book, there is a complete released Logical Reasoning section that you can take.

Taking the Timing Section

In the online companion for this book, find the assignment labeled Logical Reasoning Section Practice. There, you'll be able to launch a full Logical Reasoning section from PrepTest 112. You'll take it in Kaplan's digital testing environment. As you work, remember to use the Kaplan Logical Reasoning Method you've been learning throughout this book, but also remember to use the new section management skills you just learned in the Spotlight.

Self Proctor

Complete the section under timed, test-like conditions. Give yourself 35 minutes, and finish in one uninterrupted sitting.

Scoring

After you finish the section, you'll see the percent of questions you got correct and an item-review list that will show which questions you got right, which you got wrong, and what the correct answer was for each item.

Review

Each item in the review screen will link to written explanations, and just below the tab from which you launched your practice section, you'll see a tab titled Video Explanations: Logical Reasoning Section Practice from which you can launch short videos (one for each question) in which a Kaplan instructor goes over the best approaches and strategies.

Good luck!

CHANNEL SPOTLIGHT

Logical Reasoning—Managing the Section

By Kaplan LSAT Channel Faculty

 Watch the video lesson for this Spotlight in your online Study Plan.

Throughout the LSAT, there is always a tension between speed and accuracy. The Logical Reasoning sections are no exception. With 25 questions to read, analyze, and evaluate in just 35 minutes, you have, on average, only about 1 minute 20 seconds per question. Given those tight constraints, every test taker feels some degree of time pressure. Great test takers, however, maximize their scores in Logical Reasoning not only by mastering the question types and their associated skills, but also by managing the section to prioritize easier and more familiar questions. Top scorers train themselves to avoid "ego battles" with individual questions and to make the best decisions about where to spend their valuable time in the section.

In the video lesson that accompanies this Spotlight, you'll learn how LSAT experts use the format of the Logical Reasoning section to their advantage. Some of the concepts you'll see here—such as triage and strategic skipping and guessing—are similar to those LSAT experts use in the Reading Comprehension section. Because of the structural differences between the Reading Comprehension and Logical Reasoning sections, however, it is important for you to learn how to deploy these strategies effectively in Logical Reasoning. To do that, you need a little background on how the testmaker arranges the questions within the Logical Reasoning section.

The Danger Zone

Kaplan collects and analyzes performance data on every LSAT released by LSAC. When several tests' worth of performance results for Logical Reasoning are aggregated, an important pattern emerges in the Logical Reasoning section.

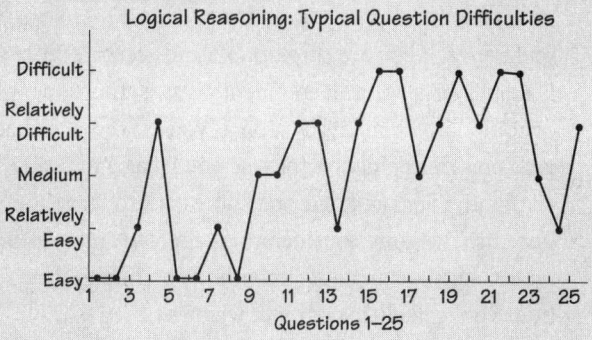

Logical Reasoning: Typical Question Difficulties

On every LSAT, some of the test's easiest—and hardest—questions are found in the Logical Reasoning section. While it is generally fair to say that the questions increase in difficulty as you progress through a section, the data reveal a more nuanced arrangement. In many sections, a single difficult question is placed among the first eight or so questions. Likewise, one or two easier questions routinely appear among the section's final four or five questions. The most important revelation, however, is that, in most Logical Reasoning sections, there is a concentration of high-difficulty questions that runs roughly from Question 15 to Question 21. At Kaplan, we refer to that band of the section as the Danger Zone. It is here that test takers are most likely to get questions incorrect, and it is here that they are most likely to lose control of time management.

In the Spotlight video, the LSAT expert will provide additional insight into the Danger Zone, and the patterns of questions typically found there. For now, keep the definition of the Danger Zone in mind as you learn the fundamentals of Logical Reasoning section management.

Triage in Logical Reasoning

Triage is a process used to determine priorities for action. In the Reading Comprehension section, you triage (at least initially) among whole passages. In other words, you are choosing to prioritize or deprioritize blocks of five to eight questions at a time. That approach won't work in Logical Reasoning where every question is independent and comes with its own stimulus. Trying to prioritize among 25 questions (or even among five to ten of them) before starting to answer any of them would be a waste of time. In the Logical Reasoning section, your best approach is to work question by question, but with the skill and familiarity to quickly and confidently identify the ones you may want to skip initially, flag, and come back to.

To triage effectively in Logical Reasoning, you will need to know your personal strengths and weaknesses. At least some of your prioritization will be based on preference. If you are comfortable and accurate with Formal Logic, you can confidently attack questions with conditional statements as soon as you see them. If that is an area of trepidation for you, you'll flag a question containing Formal Logic and come back to it as time permits. The same considerations apply to any question type. Capitalize on your strengths by getting to the questions you're likely to get right, whatever they may be.

Beyond playing to your individual strengths as a test taker, it's valuable to remember the Danger Zone pattern discussed above. You can confidently assume that *most* of the early questions will be straightforward, but you should also expect to find a relatively hard question in the mix. When you encounter that first difficult and time-consuming question, don't let it stop your momentum. If you spend two or three minutes on a single question at this point, you are already throwing off your timing for the whole section. Likewise, make sure you give yourself a chance to answer

the questions at the end of the section; at least one or two of them is likely to be easier than what has come before. Most importantly, remember where the Danger Zone is found, typically Questions 15–21. Some test takers find it advantageous to work through the first fourteen questions in an LR section, and then skip to the end and work backward to Question 15. If that approach seems like it might be helpful to you, try it out the next time you practice a full, timed Logical Reasoning section.

Strategic Skipping and Guessing in Logical Reasoning

In Logical Reasoning, where you must evaluate each question individually, triage and strategic skipping go hand in hand. Just keep this principle in mind: Strategic skipping and guessing means skipping and guessing when it is in *your interest* do so. To put it another way, don't get into an "ego battle" with any Logical Reasoning question. Every question on the LSAT is worth the same value. There is no bonus for answering hard questions. One of the quickest ways to lose control of time management in Logical Reasoning is to overinvest in a single question, and one of the main reasons test takers do that is because they feel they must solve *that question*. The result is that these test takers wind up skipping and guessing out of frustration, or after investing two minutes or more in a difficult question.

It is far better to make the decision to skip a question quickly and confidently. Remember, you are only skipping the question temporarily. When you do this, use the flag tool to mark the question so that you can come back to it after you've racked up all the easier and faster points available to you. When you get low on time, you can always click to bubble in a guess for any question you've skipped, and you can do so proudly, with the knowledge that you've guessed only on a question that would have been difficult to get anyway. Don't forget to select an answer for every question (even if it is just a guess) as there is no wrong-answer penalty on the LSAT.

Practicing Logical Reasoning Section Management and Assessing Your Skills

To get the feel for the section-management strategies you'll learn in this Spotlight video lesson, you'll need to put them into practice on real Logical Reasoning sections. The LSAT expert will give you good techniques and exercises that will help you evaluate your timed performance and find the areas in which you can improve. If you are using LSAC Prep-Tests as part of your preparation, set aside *at least* two or three tests to use for "timing" practice. You need not do the entire test in one sitting, but you will need to clear 35 minutes from your schedule for uninterrupted timed section practice. Follow the best practices from this Spotlight and the accompanying video lesson, and evaluate your section management along with your performance on individual questions. Like any other section on the LSAT, Logical Reasoning requires a combination of mastery and timing skills. Review your section performance thoroughly, studying the questions you got right as well as those you got wrong.

There is one complete Logical Reasoning section in the online companion for this book. Find it under the heading Logical Reasoning Section Practice. It comes with complete analysis and explanations, including video explanations for each question.

But, you'll want to more—much more—practice than that. A subscription to LSAC's LawHub Advantage gives you access to 58 full-length PrepTests; that's more than 125 Logical Reasoning sections. Pair that with a subscription to Kaplan's LSAT Link or Link+ to get complete analysis and explanations for every question in every one of those officially released LawHub Prep-Tests. Visit **www.kaptest.com/lsat/courses/lsat-self-study** today.

Complete answers and explanations are provided in the LSAT Channel Spotlight video "Logical Reasoning—Managing the Section" in your online Study Plan.

CHAPTER 17

Test Day

Planning for Your Test Administration

Is it starting to feel like your whole life is a buildup to the LSAT? You've known about it for years, worried about it for months, and now spent weeks (at least) in solid preparation for it. As the test gets closer, you may find your anxiety building. Don't worry; after the preparation you've done, you're in good shape for the test. The key to calming any pre-test jitters is to be prepared for the road to test day and beyond.

Test Modality

The first question is where you'll be testing. LSAC has been offering the LSAT as a remotely proctored, take-at-home test since 2021. That is the most popular testing modality, and likely the one you'll be using. Here's the page for more information about remote testing: **www.lsac.org/lsat/about/remote-modality**. Starting in 2023, however, LSAC began providing an in-person testing option that allows students to take their test at a Prometric testing center. For more information about this option, visit **www.lsac.org/lsat/about/test-center-modality**. Whichever modality you choose, your LSAT will be identical to that of all other test takers in your administration; the timing, length, sections, and indeed, questions are the same regardless of where you take your LSAT.

Score Preview

Another decision you need to make when planning your official LSAT is whether to register for LSAC's Score Preview option. Score Preview allows you to see your LSAT score before deciding whether to cancel your score on a given administration. With Score Preview, you have six days after scores are released to choose to keep your score (in which case it is released to all schools to which you apply) or to cancel (in which case, your record will indicate a canceled test, but no score will be reported). Schools will not know whether you chose to cancel after seeing your score. At the time of this writing, the cost of score preview is $45 if you purchase prior to the test dates of your administration, and $75 if you choose to purchase within the specified period after your test (approximately 10 days, and definitely before scores from your test administration are released). For more information, visit **www.lsac.org/lsat/lsat-scoring/lsat-score-preview**.

A word of caution: While the Score Preview option has many benefits, don't be cavalier about it. A test canceled under Score Preview still counts as an administered LSAT on your record. You are allowed to take the LSAT only five times during the current rolling five-year reporting period and only seven times in your lifetime, so don't just "wing it" because you purchased Score Preview and wind up throwing away one of your allotted administrations.

K **603**

Schedule your test well in advance. The registration deadlines are posted here **www.lsac.org/LSATdates**. With your test date in place, you can plan your study schedule (remember, there are helpful tips and tools for that in your online companion for this book) and set your sights on success.

The Week Before the Test

Your goal during the week before the LSAT is to set yourself up for success on test day. Up until this point, you have been working to build your LSAT potential, but test day is about achievement.

LSAT STRATEGY

Things to Do Leading Up to Test Day:

- Get your body on schedule for the time of your test, and do LSAT questions at that same time of day.
- Eat, sleep, and exercise.
- Prepare your testing area, and test your equipment.
- Make sure roommates or family know your test date and time to ensure a distraction-free environment.
- Check **www.lsac.org** for the most recent test day guidelines.
- Decide whether to take the test or withdraw.

Prepping yourself for success begins with taking care of your basic needs: food, sleep, and exercise. It's easy to get caught up in the stress of balancing your life with LSAT practice, but if taking an extra hour to study every night leaves you sleep deprived and exhausted on test day, it's hurting you more than helping. Figure out what time you need to go to sleep the night before the exam, and make sure you're in bed at that time *every night* the week before the exam, especially if you're a night owl who gets a second wind late in the evening. If possible, start doing some LSAT work—even if it's only a few problems—at the same time that you will be taking your test. Finally, if you are someone who regularly engages in physical activity, this is *not* the week to stop. Physical activity helps lower stress and increases production of dopamine and norepinephrine, two neurotransmitters that improve memory, attention, and mood!

During this week, you should also decide on and set up the room and desk you'll use to take the test, especially if that space is different from the room or desk you normally use to study. Take a practice test (or at least a timed section) with this configuration to ensure that it is as quiet and comfortable as you imagine. If you live with roommates or family members, let them know about your testing schedule to ensure they'll be able to give you the privacy and quiet you'll need during your LSAT. Taking those steps now will pay off by preventing unexpected situations when it matters most.

LSAC REQUIREMENTS

Acceptable Identification: www.lsac.org/lsat/taking-lsat/identification-accepted-lsat-admission

LSAC photo requirements: www.lsac.org/jd/lsat/day-of-test/photo-requirements

Also, at least a week prior to your test, make sure to double-check your registration against the government-issued ID you'll be showing to the proctor on camera. Be sure that the names match and that the ID isn't expired! (As of the time this book went to press, LSAC accepts photo IDs that expired *within 90 days of the test date*, but check the LSAC website for the latest information.) If the names don't match, contact LSAC *immediately* so you can remedy the situation. If that isn't fixed by test day, you may not be allowed to take the exam. You will also need a passport-style photograph to upload to your LSAC account. The deadline to upload the photo is approximately one month before test day. Confirm your photo upload deadline by checking the LSAC website. LSAC is strict about the photo requirements, so Kaplan recommends that you have your photos taken professionally at a place that specializes in passport photos.

PLAN YOUR REMAINING STUDY TIME

- Balance stress management and study.

- Study areas of greatest strength, not only areas of greatest opportunity.

- The majority of your work should be under timed conditions—either full-length LSATs or Timing practice on full sections.

- Be sure you are familiar with the digital test interface (by practicing with tests in LSAC's LawHub).

- Still review the Answers and Explanations for every practice problem (using Kaplan's LSAT Link or Link+).

- Remember that you are going to law school!

The kind of practice that you do the week before the exam is important. Resist the temptation to focus on your weaknesses, and instead focus primarily on shoring up your strengths. The reality is that you are more likely to grab a few points in your strengths at the last minute than you are in the areas you struggle with the most. Of course, work on all sections of the LSAT during this time.

Keep in mind that the LSAT is a test of timing and endurance. In the days leading up to the test, most of your work should be under timed conditions, and you should try to fit in a complete test or two if you have the time in your schedule. Having said that, do not fall into the trap of doing nothing but full-length tests right before the LSAT. Just as world-class athletes don't engage in exhausting practice sessions right before a match or race, you need to balance practice and fatigue. Watch your stress levels, too: Taking too many exams can lead to a stress spiral that is hard to climb out of.

Finally, the week before the exam is the time to decide whether you are ready to take your test. As of this writing, LSAC's policy allows you to withdraw your registration all the way up until 11:59 p.m. Eastern time on the night before your exam without it showing up on your record. There is no right or wrong answer to the question of whether you are ready to take your exam, but if you are having any doubts, ask yourself two questions:

- What is the lowest score I would be okay with an admissions officer seeing?

- Am I scoring at least that high now?

You can choose your goals in life, but you can't always choose your timelines. If the answer to the second question is a resounding no, then it may be in your best interest to change your test date. Though there is a modest benefit to applying early, submitting a score that is well below a school's median is more likely to result in a faster rejection than a surprise admission. Don't expect any miracles on test day. It's possible that your score will suddenly jump up to an all-time high on the day of the exam, but it isn't likely. More to the point, it's risky.

The Day Before the Test

The day before the test is as important as the six days before it. The first instinct of most test takers is to cram as much as possible in hopes of grabbing a few last-second points. But the LSAT isn't a test that can be crammed for. You should think of test day as game day. Make sure you can reach your potential when it counts. Relax the day before the test to hit your peak performance when it matters most.

LSAT STRATEGY

The day before the test:

- Relax! Read a book, watch a movie, take a walk, or go shopping.

- Don't take any full-length tests, and preferably don't study at all.

- Gather the things you'll want during the test—your government-issued ID (required), five sheets of blank scratch paper, a few sharp pencils, tissues, etc.

- Eat a healthy meal for dinner and get plenty of sleep.

The advice in that LSAT Strategy callout is hard to follow, but trust Kaplan's decades of experience with tens of thousands of students. Make the day before the test a wonderful, relaxing day. There's a good chance that during the last few weeks or months, the stress of balancing LSAT prep with the rest of your busy life has meant you've had less time to yourself or with your family and loved ones. Spend a day with your significant other or kids. Go to the spa or spend the day watching a movie marathon. Whatever you do, make sure the day is as restful and relaxing as possible. Put your LSAT materials away and leave them there because, while you aren't going to cram your way to a good score, you may cram your way to a bad one. Think of how you normally feel when you get a score on something that is less than you hoped for. Now imagine how it would feel the day before the exam and what that kind of anxiety could do to you. The benefits to studying the day before are almost nonexistent, but the risks are sky-high.

Don't forget to cap off the day with a healthy dinner and a good night's sleep. It's not going to be easy to fall asleep the night before the test, so make sure you are in bed on time. Resist the urge to stare at a television or computer screen: They tend to make it even harder to sleep. For what it's worth, however, the most important night's sleep isn't the night before the test; it's two nights before the test. For various reasons, the effects of sleep deprivation tend to skip a day, so getting a great night's sleep two nights before the exam will help make sure that you are well rested the day of the test!

The Morning of the Test

Use test day morning to relax, focus, and gather your confidence before the test. Get up early to give yourself some time to wake up, have breakfast, and prepare your testing space. If you have an afternoon testing time, plan your morning accordingly. A relaxed morning is a much better start than a frantic, stressful one. Make sure breakfast has a good balance of protein and carbohydrates. You'll need the energy later!

Dress comfortably in a way you don't mind being seen on camera. The proctors will take your picture and a picture of your photo ID and will be watching you throughout the exam. Remember too that you may not wear a hat or a hood (unless it is subject to a religious exemption) or sunglasses, and you may not have a purse, bag, briefcase, or backpack in the room with you during your LSAT.

LSAT STRATEGY

On the morning of the test:

- Get up early enough that you don't have any rush to get ready before your testing time.
- Eat a healthy breakfast.
- Dress comfortably for your space and remember that you will be on camera throughout the test.
- Clear any forbidden objects from your testing area.

LSAC strictly forbids several other kinds of items from being on the desk or in the room where you are testing. The proctor will have you point your camera around the room to ensure forbidden items are not present. The full rules for the test are given in LSAC's candidate agreement: **ww.lsac.org/about/lsac-policies/lsaccandidate-agreement**. Read it carefully prior to test day.

LSAT FACTS

The following items are prohibited:

- Cell phones
- Electronic devices of any kind, including tablets, digital watches, exercise devices, and timers
- Headphones or earbuds (plain foam ear plugs are permitted with your proctor's approval)
- Backpacks, bags, or purses
- Mechanical pencils
- Papers or books (other than five sheets of plain scratch paper)
- Hats and hoods (other than religious items)

Note: The strategies outlined here and on the following page refer to the remotely proctored ("test-at-home") experience. If you are taking the LSAT in a testing center, please see **www.lsac.org/lsat/about/test-center-modality**.

During Check-In and the Test

Without a doubt, the best part of the "take-at-home" LSAT experience is the fact that there is no need to travel to a testing site, worry about parking, wait to check in, and watch as other nervous test takers (Prometric sites administer a wide variety of tests) go through the same thing. Still, there are several requirements you must meet for your testing space and equipment. You can find the complete LSAC test day checklist for remote test takers here: **www.lsac.org/lsat/taking-lsat/remote-checklist**.

LSAC requires you to open your proctoring application 30 minutes before the start of your test. You can join the session for your test a few minutes early, but if you're more than 10 minutes early, you'll see a wait screen until the proctor joins and activates your session. To start your LSAT, you will log in to your proctoring software (LSAC provides instructions for making an account) and click "Start Session." Follow the setup process—there's a tech check, photo-ID verification, and installation of a test-recovery app—and then you'll meet a proctor who will direct you to LSAC's LawHub (you'll already be familiar with it from ample practice), where you'll launch your LSAT.

You'll need your LSAC username and password to log in, so make sure you remember them. The proctor will have you read the rules out loud and check a box to indicate your agreement. At this point, the proctor will enter a password that activates a start button on your screen.

Click that, and your LSAT test will begin.

LSAT FACTS

Pre-test procedures:

- Log in to your proctoring software (LSAC will provide instructions for making an account) at least 30 minutes prior to your testing time.
- Follow the setup process—you'll need a Prometric username and password, then there's a tech check followed by photo ID verification, and then you can click on the launch test button.
- That will direct you to LSAC's LawHub, where you'll use your LSAC username and password to log in.
- You'll need to read and agree to a certifying statement, and then you can . . .
- Click BEGIN to start your official LSAT.

Once the test begins let all your practice and preparation take over. Identify the questions and use the Kaplan methods, strategies, and tactics you've learned for each section and question type. Use the expert section-management techniques from your LSAT Channel Spotlight sessions, and rock your LSAT test day.

After the first two sections, you'll have a 10-minute break. Follow the proctor's permission before moving around or leaving the room. You cannot use any electronic device during the intermission, and you may not use the computer you are testing on for any other purpose.

The testing process will begin again after a full 10 minutes has elapsed. There's another check-in process with the proctor, and once that's completed, you can resume the test with Section 3. Again, let all of your preparation take over. If you've trained and practiced like a Kaplan LSAT expert, there won't be any surprises on the test, and you'll be confident you're ready for these last two sections.

After the fourth section of the test is complete, you'll rip up your scratch paper, and hit a SUBMIT button to make it official. Take a moment to relax and breathe. Congratulations! You have finished the scored sections of the LSAT. The only section that now remains is LSAT Argumentative Writing, which you will take at some point relatively soon after your test. Though the Argumentative Writing task can be a nice addition to your application, it is nowhere near as important as what you'll have just accomplished.

LSAT STRATEGY

During the test:

- Let all your training and preparation take over.

- Identify the questions, and use the Kaplan methods, strategies, and tactics you've learned for each section and question type.

- Use the section management techniques you've learned from Kaplan LSAT experts.

- Answer every question.

- Relax during the break.

- Don't worry about how you're scoring. Don't try to figure out which section is the experimental one. Focus only on what's in front of you.

After the test, your focus will likely shift to the Law School application process: writing a winning Personal Statement, soliciting excellent Letters of Recommendation, pulling together your undergraduate transcripts, a resume, and more. Kaplan can be a valuable partner on this stage of your law school journey as well. To find out more about how working with a Kaplan's admissions consultant can help your applications stand out, **www.kaptest.com/lsat/practice/law-school-admissions-consulting** or call 1-800-KAPTEST.

Unusual Question Stems

By Kaplan LSAT Channel Faculty

 Watch the video lesson for this Spotlight in your online Study Plan.

Why is it, even when we know we've prepared well, that we can still get anxious about a big test or game or life event? It is, of course, because these things are important. It means a lot to us that they go perfectly, or as close to it as we can get. Channel that motivation the right way, and it can inspire us to do more practice, review more tests, and push ourselves to even greater score improvement. But, when we sometimes let it get the best of us, caring so much can manifest itself as test anxiety. And one of the surest signs of test anxiety is when we find ourselves worrying that we'll run into something unexpected.

Now, any Kaplan veteran LSAT instructor—together we've worked with many tens of thousands of LSAT test takers—will tell you that if you've seriously worked your way through a book like this one, if you have taken and reviewed practice tests, and if you've really committed yourself to the LSAT prep process, there will be nothing on your LSAT that you haven't seen (and analyzed . . . and answered) before. This Spotlight gives us one more chance to prove it.

You know that voice in your head that says, "But what if, WHAT IF on my test, there's a question type I've never seen before?!?!" Call up that anxious part of yourself and have them spend a few minutes with a Kaplan LSAT expert who will demonstrate that even

those occasional weirdly-worded, hard-to-categorize questions are filled with familiar LSAT patterns, and that you have the strategies to answer them. Remind that anxious part of yourself, too, that all of the test takers out there who haven't matched your level of prep will also see the weird question, but for them, it will just be weird.

In the video, your Kaplan instructor will use the following question as examples of how LSAT experts respond when they see an unusual Logical Reasoning question.

A running track with a hard surface makes for greater running speed than a soft one, at least under dry conditions, because even though step length is shorter on a hard surface, the time the runner's foot remains in contact with the running surface is less with a hard surface.

Which one of the following, if true, is evidence that the explanation given above is only a partial one?

(A) Dry running conditions can be guaranteed for indoor track races only.

(B) In general, taller runners have greater average step length than shorter runners do.

(C) Hard tracks enhance a runner's speed by making it easier for the runner to maintain a posture that minimizes wind resistance.

(D) The tracks at which the world's fastest running times have been recorded are located well above sea level, where the air is relatively thin.

(E) To remain in top condition, a soft track surface requires different maintenance procedures than does a hard one.

PrepTest111 Sec3 Q9

12. Politician: My opponents argue that the future of our city depends on compromise—that unless the city's leaders put aside their differences and work together toward common goals, the city will suffer. However, the founders of this city based the city's charter on definite principles, and anyone who compromises those principles betrays the city founders' goals. What my opponents are advocating, therefore, is nothing less than betraying the goals of the city's founders.

Critic: I'm afraid your argument is flawed. Unless you're assuming that the differences among the city's leaders are differences of principle, your argument depends on a misleading use of the term _____.

Which one of the following provides the most logical completion of the critic's statement?

(A) betray

(B) common

(C) compromise

(D) principles

(E) opponents

PrepTest110 Sec3 Q12

57. Jordan: If a business invests the money necessary to implement ecologically sound practices, its market share will decrease. But if it doesn't implement these practices, it pollutes the environment and wastes resources.

Terry: But if consumers demand environmental responsibility of all businesses, no particular business will be especially hurt.

In which one of the following exchanges is the logical relationship between Jordan's and Terry's statements most similar to the logical relationship between their statements above?

(A) Jordan: Either it will rain and our plans for a picnic will be thwarted or it won't rain and the garden will go yet another day without much-needed watering.

Terry: But if it doesn't rain, we can buy a hose and water the garden with the hose.

(B) Jordan: Each person can have either an enjoyable life or a long life, for one must eat vegetables and exercise continuously to stay healthy.

Terry: That's not true: there are many happy health-conscious people.

(C) Jordan: If taxes are raised, many social problems could be solved, but if they're lowered, the economy will grow again. So we can't have both social reform and a growing economy.

Terry: But if taxes remain at their current level, neither social problems nor the economy will get worse.

(D) Jordan: If we remodel the kitchen, the house will be more valuable, but even if we do, there's no guarantee that we'll actually get more for the house when we sell it.

Terry: But if we don't remodel the kitchen, we might get even less for the house than we paid for it.

(E) Jordan: If the dam's spillway is opened, the river might flood the eastern part of town, but if the spillway is not opened, the dam might burst.

Terry: There's no real danger of the dam's bursting, but if we get more heavy rain, opening the spillway is the most prudent policy.

PrepTest110 Sec3 Q25

Complete answers and explanations are provided in the LSAT Channel Spotlight video "Unusual Question Stems" in your online Study Plan.

Appendices

Logical Reasoning Patterns and Strategies

Logical Reasoning

Logical Reasoning Method

> **THE KAPLAN LOGICAL REASONING METHOD**
>
> **STEP 1** Identify the Question Type
>
> **STEP 2** Untangle the Stimulus
>
> **STEP 3** Predict the Correct Answer
>
> **STEP 4** Evaluate the Answer Choices

Evidence and Conclusion

Keywords

Conclusion:		Evidence:
Therefore	Obviously	Because
Thus	Hence	Since
It is clear	As a result	For
It follows that	This proves that	From the fact that
That is why	Studies suggest	After all
So	This shows	It is clear from
Consequently	Clearly	

Conclusion Types

CONCLUSION TYPES

In an LSAT argument, the conclusion almost always matches one or more of these six types:

- Value Judgment (an evaluative statement; e.g., Action X is unethical or Y's recital was poorly sung)
- If/Then (a conditional prediction, recommendation, or assertion; e.g., If X is true, then so is Y or If you are an M, you should do N)
- Prediction (X *will* or *will not* happen in the future)
- Comparison (X is taller/shorter/more common/less common/etc. *than* Y)
- Assertion of Fact (X is true or X is false)
- Recommendation (we *should* or *should not* do X)

Common Argument Structures

Remember that while the specifics change from question to question, there are certain argument structures that appear repeatedly on the LSAT. When you recognize one of these, you'll have a ready-made prediction as to the assumption, strengtheners, and weakeners. You'll also have insight into the author's flaw: the failure to consider the possible ways of weakening the argument.

C: Conclusion
E: Evidence
A: Assumption
S: Strengthener
W: Weakener

Mismatched Concepts

In arguments with Mismatched Concepts, the conclusion typically contains a new concept or term that was not mentioned in the evidence. When the concept only appears in the conclusion, without the author providing evidence about it, the author must be making an assumption about that term. The assumption will link that unique conclusion term (that doesn't appear in the evidence) to a unique evidence term (that doesn't appear in the conclusion). Just recognizing the Mismatched Concepts can often be enough to get you to the right answer. However, there are four standard relationships that can be applied to the unique terms. Learning these relationships can both help you to learn to recognize the Mismatched Concepts to begin with and add efficiency to your assessment of the answer choices.

MISMATCHED CONCEPTS RELATIONSHIPS

The most commonly assumed relationships between Mismatched Concepts are:

- The terms or concepts are alike/equivalent.
- The terms or concepts are mutually exclusive.
- One term or concept is needed for the other.
- One term or concept represents the other.

I) Equivalent ("similar")—Author shifts topics or terminology in moving from evidence to conclusion so that it is apparent that the author considers the evidence term and the conclusion term to be alike, or at least similar in some way.

C: Solar energy (**X**) is the wave of the future.

E: More and more people will demand cleaner fuels (**Y**).

A: *Solar energy* (**X**) equates with *cleaner fuels* (**Y**). (**X is similar to/equated with Y**)

W: A reason solar energy is not clean, e.g., mining the rare metals used in the panels is environmentally damaging or some overlooked alternative, e.g., wind is cleaner and cheaper. (**Attack the connection between X and Y; a potential difference**)

S: Reasons that firm up the connection (that solar energy really is clean) or eliminate a weaken possibility, e.g., doubts about the feasibility of solar energy are unfounded. (**Firm up the connection between X and Y; undermine potential differences**)

II) Mutually Exclusive ("different")—Just like the previous example, except that it is apparent that the author considers the unique evidence term and unique conclusion term to be different. Either the evidence or the conclusion will be phrased negatively ("not") while the other will be phrased positively. So, if the author believes that evidence of X results in a conclusion of *Not Y* (or vice versa), the author assumes that X and Y are different or incompatible.

C: Solar energy (**X**) is the wave of the future.

E: World governments are restricting sources of "greenhouse gases." (**No Y**)

A: *Solar energy* is **not** a *source of greenhouse gases.* (**X and Y are different/incompatible**)

W: A reason solar energy could be a source of greenhouse gases, e.g., mining, manufacture and shipping of panels currently uses substantial amounts of fossil fuels. (**A way that X and Y could be similar/compatible or undermine a purported difference**)

S: A reason supporting that solar energy does not directly or indirectly produce significant greenhouse gases (**Further support for the difference/incompatibility of X and Y**)

III) Requirement ("needs")—Evidence of the absence of one thing being used to support a conclusion that something else is precluded indicates that the author assumes the first thing is a requirement for the other. Evidence of *No X* supporting a conclusion of *No Y* assumes that *Y* requires *X*.

C: Most people cannot switch to solar energy. (**No X**)

E: Most people cannot make an upfront investment of over $10,000. (**No Y**)

A: Switching to solar energy requires an upfront investment of over $10,000. (**If no Y then no X; X needs Y**)

W: A reason that an upfront investment is not needed, e.g., solar companies will provide leases with no upfront costs. (**A reason to believe that Y is not a requirement for X**)

S: A reason supporting that $10,000 upfront is typically required, e.g., solar companies will only provide leases with no upfront costs to homeowners with top 10% credit scores. (**Support that Y is a requirement for X**)

IV) Representative ("reps")—Evidence of a subset or smaller group used to make a conclusion about a larger group assumes that the subset is representative of the larger.

C: Renewable energy can cost effectively meet the world's energy needs. (**Broad conclusion group/situation**)

E: Studies show that solar power could feasibly meet all power needs in Arizona. (**Specific evidence group/situation**)

A: Solar power in Arizona is representative of the potential of renewable energy worldwide. (**The specific evidence group/situation applies broadly to conclusion group/situation**)

W: A reason that Arizona is not representative of the entire world, e.g., 360 days of intense sunshine with a relatively low population concentrated in two urban areas (**A characteristic or bias inherent in the evidence group/situation that undermines applying it to the broader conclusion group/situation**)

S: A reason that supports applying the Arizona results to the rest of the world, e.g., other studies indicate that political and public support for infrastructure investment is the key factor and levels of support in Arizona are similar or lower than most other areas of the world. (**A reason to believe that the evidence group/situation does represent the conclusion group situation or undermining a potential difference**)

Overlooked Possibilities

OVERLOOKED POSSIBILITIES PATTERNS

Overlooked Possibilities arguments tend to fit one of the following patterns:

- Arrives at a claim of causation based on evidence of correlation
- Does not consider potential advantages or disadvantages when offering a recommendation
- Makes a prediction by assuming that circumstances will or will not change
- Assumes that something will occur simply because it could occur
- Confuses sufficient and necessary terms
- Fails to consider other explanations, reasons, or outcomes based on the evidence

I) **Causation—**

   a. **Correlation to Causation ("Causal Classic")**—if the author jumps from evidence of a correlation to a conclusion claiming causation, the author overlooks the three **ARC** possibilities: an **A**lternative cause; **R**everse causation; or **C**oincidence.

C: The stabilization of the economy has largely been a result of the stabilization of the housing market. (**A claim of causation—recognized by phrases such as "result of"; "produced"; "led to"; "because of"; "due to"**)

E: The stabilization of the economy has coincided with the stabilization of the housing market. (**Evidence of a correlation—recognized by phrases such as "coincided with"; "simultaneously"; "subsequent to"; or any suggestion that two things or occurrences are related in time or location**)

A: There's *not* one of the standard alternatives to a claim of causation, e.g., 1) the resurgence in consumer spending was *not* the primary reason for the stabilization of the economy, 2) the stabilization of the economy was *not* itself the cause of the stabilization of the housing market, or 3) it was *not* just a coincidence that both trends occurred at relatively the same time. (**Not one of the ARC alternatives to a claim of causation: Not an Alternative cause; Not Reverse causation; Not Coincidence**)

W: Any of the ARC alternatives to a claim of causation, e.g., 1) a resurgence in consumer spending *was* the primary reason for the stabilization of the economy, 2) rather than a result, the stabilization of the economy *was* the cause of the stabilization of the housing market, or 3) evidence that the housing market and the overall economy do not typically affect each other. (**One of ARC: Alternative cause; Reverse causation; Coincidence/Not connected**) Note: you would not weaken such a claim of causation by suggesting that either the housing market or the economy has not actually stabilized; accept the evidence as true.

S: Elimination of any of the ARC alternatives, e.g., there has *not* been a resurgence in consumer spending, or a broad indication that all else is equal/nothing else could be involved. **(Elimination of any ARC possibilities; in terms of elimination of Alternative causes, the Strengthen answer may undermine a specific alternative cause or more broadly indicate that all else is equal, such as in a two-group study, in which a factor found in one group is claimed to be the cause of a result specific to that group, a strengthen answer choice would indicate that the two groups are otherwise identical in all other respects)**

       b.   **Causal Explanation of Observed Phenomenon ("Funky Phenom")**—in these causal arguments, rather than identifying a specific correlation between two phenomena in the evidence and jumping to a claim that one causes the other, the author's evidence simply consists of an observation of an interesting phenomenon—often somewhat paradoxical—and the conclusion proposes an explanation for its cause. Rather than the 3 ARC alternatives in classic causation, usually only alternative causes (i.e., alternative explanations) are relevant.

C: The sociologist claims that the third graders are displaying an innate sense of egalitarianism. **(A causal explanation of the interesting, often paradoxical, phenomenon noted in the evidence)**

E: A sociologist observes that third grade students wearing mid-tier priced sneakers generally have more friends that those wearing higher priced sneakers. **(Simply the mention of an interesting phenomenon; note in this pattern the evidence does not answer the "why?" of the conclusion; it might seem like background or initially like a conclusion. Recognize this type of evidence by a phrase such as "researchers have observed" that indicates some scientist or academic is pointing out something they noticed that they find interesting; the role of a scientist then becomes to hypothesize some causal explanation, which is the conclusion in this pattern)**

A: There is no other explanation for the popularity of third graders wearing mid-tier sneakers besides an innate egalitarianism. **(No other explanation/alternative cause)**

W: Any alternative explanation, e.g., the most popular mid-tier priced sneaker is endorsed by the latest pop sensation and *all the cool kids wear them*. **(An alternative explanation)**

S: Any support for the author's explanation (often in this pattern there isn't any initial evidence supporting the author's explanation of the phenomenon besides its mere existence), e.g., other studies have noted a trend for greater egalitarianism in people under the age of 10, or any evidence that undermines any alternative explanation, e.g., there did not appear to be anything else special or unique about the mid-tier sneakers besides their moderate price. **(Support for author's explanation or reason undermining any potential alternative explanations)**

II) Recommendations—The author suggests for or against a course of action based on a single benefit or downside, respectively. Any recommendation should be based on a balancing of pros and cons, and assumes that one outweighs the other. LSAT authors will typically only mention what supports their recommendation, without consideration of the other side.

C: "You really should hit up this pizza joint." **(A recommendation for or against a course of action)**

E: "The beer selection is the bomb." **(A positive or negative aspect)**

A: No other factors would undermine the recommendation. **(Pros outweigh the cons, if any; vice versa)**

W: "Yeah, but the pizza itself is dry and chewy." **(A downside; or a positive if recommendation was against)**

S: "But it's a buck a slice and $3 pitchers, and after a few cold ones the pizza tastes pretty . . . alright."

       (Another upside or elimination of a downside or the reverse if initially a recommendation against)

III) Predictions—A conclusion that is future looking/predictive typically relies on evidence of past trends. This assumes that there will not be a change in circumstances.

C: "My team is going to win on Sunday." (**A prediction of a future event**)

E: "The last six times we played your team, we won each by an average of 12 points." (**Past trends; existing circumstances**)

A: No change in circumstances would affect the likelihood of the predicted result. (**The past is predictive of the future; circumstances won't change**)

W: "Sorry, but didn't you hear that your star quarterback somehow managed to break his jaw in practice and is out for six weeks?" (**A change in circumstances**)

S: "Actually, our defense is generally credited with our team's success in those games and all our defensive stars are healthy and ready to play." (**An indication of consistency/no change in circumstances**)

IV) Level of Certainty—(could vs will; belief vs fact)—Another Overlooked Possibilities pattern is an author jumping from indefinite evidence (something *could* happen; people *believe* something; etc.) to a very definite conclusion (it *will* happen; it factually *is* the case).

C: Next year will show the strongest economic growth of the last 50 years. (**A definite statement of fact**)

E: According to a survey, a majority of economists believe that there is the potential for a 6% growth in GDP. (**A possibility or belief**)

A: The potential believed in by most economists will come to be. (**The possibility or belief will bear out**)

W: Historically, economist predictions have not accurately foreseen the next year's level of GDP growth. (**An indication that the possibility or belief will not bear out**)

S: A World Bank report extensively detailed factors supporting the potential for such levels of GDP growth. (**A further indication that the possibility or belief will bear out**)

V) Sufficiency/Necessity—The author provides evidence that one thing is sufficient to lead to a result, but then reaches a conclusion that indicates it is necessary for the result to occur. (Less commonly, an author will provide evidence of a necessary condition and then conclude that it is sufficient to guarantee a result).

C: It is almost certain that the soccer field will not be re-sodded. (**No X**)

E: 1) The school board will re-sod the soccer field if the PTA bake sale raises $1000; 2) it is highly unlikely the bake sale will raise that much. (**Y → X; No Y**)

A: The only way to re-sod the soccer field is with PTA bake sale money. (**X → Y; something that is sufficient to cause a result is the only thing that could cause that result; ignores that there could be other ways for the result to occur**)

W: In past years, in which the PTA bake sale failed to raise the funds, the local car dealership that sponsors the team paid to re-sod the field. (**X does not require Y; even though Y will trigger X, X could occur in the absence of Y**)

S: This year, no other potential sources of funds will be available due to extensive budget cuts. (**X really does require Y**)

VI) "No other . . . " (factors, reasons, outcomes, explanations)—Somewhat of an Overlooked Possibilities catch-all category, an author of an LSAT argument may simply ignore or fail to consider other factors, options, outcomes, explanations, possibilities, reasons, etc. A handy way to phrase the assumption to an Overlooked Possibilities argument is to start with "No other _____" and fill in the blank as appropriate: "No other factor"; "No other explanation"; "No other option." Generally, recognize an Overlooked Possibilities argument from a conclusion that seems to follow from the evidence but is worded more forcefully or absolutely than such evidence really supports. Some of the previous specific Overlooked Possibilities patterns could fall under this umbrella description, and you've seen the "no other _____" phrasing above already.

C: "I'll bet you anything that Andrew wore his blue Italian designer suit to his Supreme Court argument today." (**An absolutely worded, forceful conclusion that seems to admit of only one possibility**)

E: "He told me that he wore his gray French designer suit to the appellate argument in the case and he never wears the same suit to both." (**Evidence that is not quite as restrictive as the author's conclusion suggests**)

A: Andrew has no other suits. ("**No other _____**": **no other factor; no other option; no other explanation, etc.**)

W: "I'll take that bet; he bought a great pin-striped suit in India just last week." (**Some other _____: option, factor, explanation, reason, etc.**)

S: "Actually, I spilled red wine on that suit when we went to the opera on Saturday." (**Direct support for the initial conclusion or elimination of a weaken possibility**)

Formal Logic in Mismatched Concepts

Many of the arguments containing Mismatched Concepts are, or could easily be, expressed in conditional Formal Logic statements. It might sound awkward to say:

> If a work is a photograph, then it expresses the artist's worldview. Therefore, if a work is a photograph, it is an interpretation of reality. *Paraphrase of PrepTest61 Sec2 Q13*

Nevertheless, the reasoning in the argument, and thus, the author's assumption, is exactly the same.

The advantage of recognizing Formal Logic in Assumption Family questions is that it highlights the Mismatched Concepts very clearly.

	Sample Argument			**Analysis**
Evidence	If photograph	→	**express artist's worldview**	If A → **B**
Conclusion	If photograph	→	**interpretation of reality**	If A → **C**

This provides a neat visual depiction of the argument that makes the author's assumption clear.

	Sample Argument			**Analysis**
Evidence	If photograph	→	**express artist's worldview**	If A → **B**
Assumption	**If express artist's worldview**	→	**interpretation of reality**	**If B → C**
Conclusion	If photograph	→	**interpretation of reality**	If A → **C**

TEST DAY TIP

LSAT experts differ on how much of the Formal Logic they actually write out on test day: Some jot down shorthand nearly every time they encounter Formal Logic while others do it only in the most complex arguments. Practice both approaches to find which works better for you. You may find that being more explicit with Formal Logic initially helps you spot patterns that you'll better analyze in your head later on.

Making It More Difficult: Adding an Extra Concept in the Evidence

Many LSAT arguments with Mismatched Concepts feature two evidentiary statements that can be combined to help you determine the author's assumption. Consider this argument:

> Every member of my research team is an honors student, and every honors student has completed the Great Ideas course. Thus, every member of my research team has read Plato's *Symposium*.

When you combine the two statements in the evidence, this argument takes exactly the same form as the argument about photographs.

	Sample Argument			Analysis
Evidence 1	If research team	→	*honors*	If A → X
Evidence 2	If honors	→	*Great Ideas course*	If X → B
Evidence [combined]	If research team	→	**Great Ideas course**	If A → **B**
Assumption	**If Great Ideas course**	→	**read Plato's *Symposium***	**If B → C**
Conclusion	If research team	→	**read Plato's *Symposium***	If A → **C**

Whenever you see two statements in the evidence of an argument containing Mismatched Concepts, consider whether you can combine them into a single, relevant piece of evidence.

Same Necessary Term

So far, the examples you've seen have had the mismatched terms in the necessary (or "then") clause of the Formal Logic statements. Occasionally, you'll see LSAT examples in which the mismatched terms are in the sufficient (or "If") clause. For example:

> Those who are nostalgic for the 1960s love the theater's new musical. So, Ella is going to love the new musical.

	Sample Argument			Analysis
Evidence	If **nostalgic for the 1960s**	→	love the new musical	If **A** → B
Assumption	**If Ella**	→	**nostalgic for the 1960s**	**If C → A**
Conclusion	If **Ella**	→	love the new musical	If **C** → B

Mismatched Concepts in the Evidence—Rare

Very rarely, the LSAT will feature an argument with Mismatched Concepts in which the "gap" is between two pieces of evidence rather than between the evidence and the conclusion. Here's an example:

> On extremely cold days, people are more physically uncomfortable. Moreover, people who are less aware of danger are more likely to jaywalk. From this it can be concluded that on extremely cold days, people are more likely to jaywalk.

	Sample Argument			Analysis
Evidence 1	If extremely cold day	→	**more physically uncomfortable**	If A → **B**
Assumption	**If more physically uncomfortable**	→	**unaware of danger**	**If B → C**
Evidence 2	If **unaware of danger**	→	more likely to jaywalk	If **C** → D
Conclusion	If extremely cold day	→	more likely to jaywalk	If A → D

Negation

Be careful negating terms when using the Denial Test. The negation of "hot" isn't "cold," it's "not hot."

All ↔ not all

None ↔ some

More ↔ less than or equal

Fewer ↔ more than or equal

Must be ↔ need not be

Can be ↔ cannot be

Quantities in Logical Reasoning

Out of a group of 100, here's what each of the following numerical terms means. Be careful; logical meaning on the LSAT is not the same as the way we often use numerical terms in everyday life; notice that most of the terms below just mean "more than zero." In Logical Reasoning questions, it is often helpful to focus on the minimum quantity possible.

None	0
Some	1–100
Few	1–100
Many	1–100
Most	51–100
All	100

Flawed Arguments

- Failure to Consider Alternative Possibilities/ Overlooked Explanations
- Correlation versus Causation
- Necessity versus Sufficiency
- Scope Shift—general mismatched concepts between evidence and conclusion
- Representativeness—the study/survey does not involve a large enough quantity or variety of subjects/respondents
- Equivocation—a term is used inconsistently
- Part versus Whole
- Circular Reasoning—the conclusion relies on the evidence and vice versa

- Evidence Contradicts Conclusion
- Number versus Percent
- Belief/Opinion versus Fact
- *Ad Hominem* Attack—the author attacks the argument-maker, rather than the argument
- Absence of Evidence is Evidence of Absence
- Inappropriate Reliance on Authority
- Possibility versus Certainty
- Group versus Member

Difficult Questions

How does the Testmaker make a Logical Reasoning question harder?

- Formal Logic in the stimulus
- A long, complex stimulus, or one involving numbers (remember, the LSAT doesn't require you to do math!)
- A convoluted question stem
- Answer choices that are subtly flawed and appear right before the correct answer choice
- Answer choices that are difficult to comprehend (the more confusing it is, the more likely the answer choice is a distracter)
- Answer choices that are extremely similar, and thus harder to differentiate from each other
- General or abstract answer choices (remember to look for one that matches piece by piece with your specific prediction)
- Changing the terminology in the answer choice from what's written verbatim in the stimulus

Logical Reasoning Wrong Answer Types

LOGICAL REASONING: WRONG ANSWER TYPES

- **Outside the Scope**—a choice containing a statement that is too broad, too narrow, or beyond the purview of the stimulus

- **Irrelevant Comparison**—a choice that compares two items or attributes in a way not germane to the author's argument or statements

- **Extreme**—a choice containing language too emphatic to be supported by the stimulus; extreme choices are often (though not always) characterized by words such as *all, never, every,* or *none*

- **Distortion**—a choice that mentions details from the stimulus but mangles or misstates what the author says or implies about those details

- **180**—a choice that directly contradicts what the correct answer must say (for example, a choice that strengthens the argument in a Weaken question)

- **Faulty Use of Detail**—a choice that accurately states something from the stimulus but in a manner that answers the question incorrectly; this type is rarely used in Logical Reasoning

---

When Certain Wrong Answer Types Apply:

Extreme

Extreme language is a major problem for most questions throughout LR and RC. The only question types for which extreme language is not a problem are Sufficient Assumption, Strengthen, Weaken, and Principle (Strengthen). Remember that extreme language is usually a very bad thing for a Necessary Assumption question. It is only Sufficient Assumptions for which too extreme is unlikely to be a problem. In fact, for a Sufficient Assumption question you actually must have an absolute forceful answer to prove the conclusion true.

Out of Scope

Out of scope is always a problem, but especially for Assumption (both Necessary and Sufficient Assumptions) and Inference questions. For Strengthen, Weaken, and Paradox questions, be hesitant to get rid of something because it sounds new; the new explanation or factor or alternative possibility is often what will weaken an argument or resolve the paradox. Also, if the answer says "not" and is excluding something that the author didn't think about, that answer is not bringing in out of scope information. So, if the argument does not talk at all about rainbows, and answer C that says "rainbows are NOT found in the area" it is not bringing in out of scope information, and it may be correct. If this is a Necessary Assumption question, the easy test is to use the Denial Test by taking out the word "not" and seeing whether the denied answer makes the argument fall apart.

APPENDIX B

Formal Logic

Keywords

Sufficient:	Necessity:	Mutually Exclusive:
If	Then	No
All	Requires	Incapable
Any	Guarantees	Impossible
Every	Must	Cannot
Each	Necessary	None
When	Bound to lead to	Neither . . . nor
Whenever	Are destined to	Never
Wherever	Only (if)	
The only	Results in	
	Produces	
	Sure to	
	Always	
	Unless	
	Depends on	
	Without	

Translating Conditional Statements into If-Then Format

Formal Logic Statement	Analysis		
If A, then B	If A	→	B
All C are D	If C	→	D
Every E is F	If E	→	F
If G, then not H	If G	→	~H
No I are J	If I	→	~J
Only K are L	If L	→	K
M only if N	If M	→	N
The only O are P	If O	→	P
No Q unless R	If Q	→	R
S unless T	If ~S	→	T
No U without V	If U	→	V
Without W, no X	If X	→	W
Y if, but only if, Z	If Y	→	Z
	If Z	→	Y
AA if, and only if, BB	If AA	→	BB
	If BB	→	AA
If CC, then neither DD nor EE	If CC	→	~DD AND ~EE
FF if GG	If GG	→	FF
HH is always II	If HH	→	II

Contrapositives

FORMING THE CONTRAPOSITIVE

- Reverse the sufficient and necessary terms.
- Negate each term.
- Change and to or and change or to and (whenever applicable).

Formal Logic Statement			Contrapositive		
If A	→	B OR C	If ~B AND ~C	→	~A
If D	→	E AND F	If ~E OR ~F	→	~D
If G OR H	→	J	If ~J	→	~G AND ~H
If K AND L	→	M	If ~M	→	~K OR ~L
If N AND O	→	P AND R	If ~P OR ~R	→	~N OR ~O
If S OR T	→	U AND V	If ~U OR ~V	→	~S AND ~T
If W AND X	→	Y OR Z	If ~Y AND ~Z	→	~W OR ~X
If AA OR BB	→	CC OR DD	If ~CC AND ~DD	→	~AA AND ~BB

A Note about Cause-and-Effect Relationships

Cause and effect are important concepts in the law and affect the outcome of many legal cases. Thus, the reasoning underlying cause and effect is tested regularly on the LSAT. The reasoning errors of confusing correlation for causation, or of assuming that some result has only one cause when, in fact, there are multiple factors at work, are often found in the arguments of Logical Reasoning questions.

Some conditional Formal Logic statements reflect a cause-and-effect relationship, but not all. And not all cause-and-effect statements can be expressed in "If . . . then" terms. It is important not to confuse the two. Here's a handy way to categorize the relationships between causal statements and conditional statements.

Statements in Which the Cause Is Sufficient, but Not Necessary, for the Result

In this type of statement, the result is guaranteed any and every time that the cause occurs. For example: *If you drop this television from the top of the building, then it will smash.*

But the television could get smashed in other ways, too, right? So while dropping it off of the building is sufficient to smash the TV, it is not necessary. If someone told you their TV got smashed, you wouldn't know for certain that it had been dropped from a great height.

Statements in Which the Cause Is Necessary, but Not Sufficient, for the Result

In this type of statement, the trigger could not happen without the result. You may know, for example, that certain types of ulcers are caused by exposure to the bacteria *Helicobacter pylori*. Thus, we could say: *If a person develops a duodenal ulcer, he has been infected by* H. pylori.

But not everyone who is exposed to the bacteria develops ulcers. Other factors are at work as well. The ulcer is sufficient evidence of exposure to the bacteria, but not the other way around.

Statements in Which the Cause Is Both Necessary and Sufficient for the Result

In this type of statement, the result occurs if, and only if, the cause is present. For example: *Water will freeze into ice if, and only if, it is kept below 32° Fahrenheit.*

Water will always freeze when it is below 32° Fahrenheit, and only under that condition.

Statements That Reflect Causation but Are Not Conditional Statements

Some statements reflect causality but are not strong enough or certain enough to be written in "If . . . then" form. For example: *Texting while driving may cause you to get into an accident.*

The word *may* makes this statement too uncertain to translate into conditional Formal Logic terms. In a particular case, we may know that texting while driving was the direct cause of an accident, but we cannot say: *If a person texts while driving, then he will get into an accident.* Nor can we say: *If a person got into an accident, then he was texting while driving.* The best we could say here is: *Texting while driving increases your chances of getting into an accident.*

Logical Reasoning Question Database

Below you see the first page of Kaplan's Logical Reasoning Question Database showing the question type and difficulty of every question currently available in the officially released PrepTests on LSAC's LawHub. The full Database of more than 3,900 Logical Reasoning questions can be found in this book's online companion.

PrepTest #	Section #	Q#	Question Type	Question Subtype	except/ least/ cannot	Star Rating
101	2	1	Flaw			2
101	2	2	Inference	Strongly Supports		1
101	2	3	Method of Argument			1
101	2	4	Strengthen/Weaken	Strengthen	EXCEPT	2
101	2	5	Parallel Flaw			1
101	2	6	Flaw			2
101	2	7	Strengthen/Weaken	Weaken	EXCEPT	1
101	2	8	Flaw			1
101	2	9	Principle	Identify/Strengthen		1
101	2	10	Role of a Statement			1
101	2	11	Inference	Must Be True		1
101	2	12	Main Point			2
101	2	13	Parallel Reasoning			2
101	2	14	Point at Issue			4
101	2	15	Main Point			1
101	2	16	Strengthen/Weaken	Evaluate the Argument		2
101	2	17	Assumption	Necessary		1
101	2	18	Paradox			4
101	2	19	Strengthen/Weaken	Weaken	EXCEPT	3
101	2	20	Strengthen/Weaken	Weaken	EXCEPT	3
101	2	21	Assumption	Sufficient		3
101	2	22	Principle	Identify/Assumption		4
101	2	23	Flaw			3